Madame

nous est tant ... que bonnement

scaurions dire ne exprimer ... grant plaisir jo

consolation que nous en avons / et especialement de veir b

noble ~~personne~~ presence / ce que avons le ...

tant par les grans ...

sa grace la attu...

...ntiellee amytye ...

...re noz bons ...

...nd ... la gl... ... ce tout sera par ...

...randement augmentee quasi par

...re affection que leur portons

In primis ...

angelis quod tantum ... per ... solis [illegible]

et humanissimis ... rebus amplissimis ... et quod ... et ap...

... [illegible] ... fidei ... [illegible]

... [illegible] ... [illegible]

sue magestati et ... [illegible]

ad ... et complacenciam suam et quod post ... [illegible]

... [illegible]

... [illegible] ... anglie ...

... [illegible] ...

et quod ... [illegible]

... [illegible] ... studebit ...

# LETTERS AND PAPERS

ILLUSTRATIVE OF THE

# REIGNS OF RICHARD III. AND HENRY VII.

# LETTERS AND PAPERS

ILLUSTRATIVE OF

# THE REIGNS

OF

# RICHARD III. AND HENRY VII.

EDITED

BY

JAMES GAIRDNER.

PUBLISHED BY THE AUTHORITY OF THE LORDS COMMISSIONERS OF HER MAJESTY'S TREASURY, UNDER THE DIRECTION OF THE MASTER OF THE ROLLS.

VOL. I.

LONDON:
LONGMAN, GREEN, LONGMAN, AND ROBERTS.

1861.

Printed by
Eyre and Spottiswoode, Her Majesty's Printers,
For Her Majesty's Stationery Office.

## TABLE OF CONTENTS.

# PREFACE.

# PREFACE.

IN the Preface to a former Volume of this Series, the Editor had occasion to speak of the extreme paucity and meagreness of contemporary narratives of the reign of Henry VII. The information derived from these amounts to little more than a mere outline of events, and requires in a peculiar degree the collateral light of documents. It appeared, therefore, to be an object of some importance to collect in one publication whatever fragments of unedited correspondence the period might be found to yield.

Special importance of documents where other historical materials are scanty.

Such materials are for the most part unknown, and where known are not easily consulted. Important original letters have lain buried among the confused and long neglected stores of the Chapter House at Westminster; others, no less important, have been turned into mere shreds and fragments, if not totally destroyed, by the disastrous fire in the Cottonian Library; others have been, too evidently, separated at times from the collections to which they originally belonged, to enrich private libraries and, in the course of time, to be sold at auctions as curious autographs. There is no clue to their lurking places, even where they are most accessible. In the best known collection of all, that of Sir Robert Cotton, things are heaped together with little or no arrangement, and many important papers, imperfectly or inaccurately catalogued, are certain to escape the diligence of the most studious inquirer.

Difficulty of knowing and consulting them.

Their places of deposit.

Documents, such as we should call State papers, were in early times preserved in the treasury of the Exchequer. Of those which were once kept there a large number of the most interesting are now in the Cottonian library. But the great bulk is still in the original collection, till lately kept in the Chapter House at Westminster, and now in the General Repository of the Public Records. The principal contents of this volume relating to the reign of Henry VII., are derived from these two sources.

For the age preceding Henry VII. this country does not afford any great store of similar materials; but there is a very valuable register of the correspondence of Richard III., from which hitherto only extracts and single letters have been printed. By transcribing this so far as it has not been published, we have been able to bring together papers both of Richard III. and Henry VII., in which it will be seen that the historic interest of the two reigns is inseparable. For though the battle of Bosworth, which placed Henry on the throne, is one of the most marked eras in English history, the events which immediately led to it, and have a most important bearing on the whole of Henry's reign, date from the death of Edward IV.

Insecurity of the throne shown by letters of the period.

The chief point illustrated by the papers here collected,—the great fact that pervades nearly every one of them, is the insecurity of the throne, both in Richard's time and in Henry's. This may perhaps be attributed to the circumstance that neither of these sovereigns had a legitimate right; but in truth it was hard to tell in that age wherein legitimate right consisted. According to the view which posterity has sanctioned, such right did not belong originally to the house of Lancaster, and if it had accrued to them by long possession, it was finally lost by weakness and misgovernment. It might be thought to have rested with the house of York, but it was forfeited by internal dissension, cruelty, and usurpation. Much certainly was done to establish it by the union of the two dynasties, but for some time that union was precarious, and not altogether free from objection. Divine right had not yet been invented to tell men where allegiance was due. It could not have been recognized in such an age.

Different principles which regulated the succession in different ages.

In truth, this celebrated doctrine has scarcely had justice done to its historical significance. Its extravagance has been made the theme of well merited satire by many great writers, and it is now so generally viewed as an exploded absurdity that it may seem strange to speak of it as an abiding constitutional truth. Yet such it undoubtedly is, and the principle, though no longer spoken of by name, is practically operative still. By a modified theory of divine right the king never dies, nor requires his Parliament to ratify his title. It was otherwise in early times. Before the 17th century we look in vain for anything like that clear recognition of a definite hereditary principle which governs the succession in our own days. Under the old Saxon and Norman kings, when the throne fell vacant, the power of nominating a successor was exercised by the witan or lords of the council. But the English respect for birth, proceeding from a strong belief in the virtue of blood and lineage, which practically limited the elective principle, operated gradually to weaken and annul it. In the days of the later Plantagenets the crown was clearly looked upon as an inheritance, but the question from whom it was derived occasioned civil war. Under the Tudors it was anxiously sought to establish a clear principle, but in vain; the many marriages of Henry VIII. served only to complicate the difficulty which, it seems, they were intended to remove. A Protestant faction attempted to prevent the succession of Mary; the Jesuits thought the title of Elizabeth indefensible. Some conceived that Mary queen of Scots was the rightful queen of England. Some expected on the death of Elizabeth a bloody competition for the crown.[1] Conspiracies to dethrone that queen produced a strong popular reaction, and a sanctity was ascribed to royalty which it had never known before. The rights of the crown must be above all question, whether of pope or parliament. James I. succeeded accordingly by divine right alone; there was no other principle on which his claim could be vindicated. His succession was in distinct opposition to more than one Act of Parliament,[2] but there

---

[1] In 1594, nine years before James's Accession, Parsons the Jesuit published "A Conference "about the next succession to the "Crown of Ingland." In this work he entered very minutely into the history of the succession, and pointed out the claims which might be advanced on the death of Elizabeth by many different families descended from Edward III., claims which there was some danger might even be disputed with bloodshed. Owing to various acts of bastardy, attainders, and other statutes, the question of law was extremely perplexing. Parsons himself, after reviewing the arguments for and against each possible competitor, comes to no definite conclusion. When the question came to be decided the practical good sense of the nation at once adopted a principle which cleared it of all legal subtleties.

[2] In fact, the legislation upon the subject had overshot the mark, and tended rather to increase than to diminish uncertainty. On the fall of Anne Boleyn, a flaw was discovered in her marriage with Henry VIII., so that Elizabeth was declared illegitimate, as Mary had been before. Parliament, therefore, in 1536, limited the succession to such legitimate issue as the king should have by Jane Seymour or any other; and in default of such issue gave Henry himself power to dispose of the crown by will (Stat. 28 Hen. VIII., c. 7.) A few years later, when it appeared evident that Henry would leave no legitimate issue except Edward, he obtained the concurrence of parliament (Stat. 35 Hen. VIII., c. 1), to an arrangement that if Edward should die without issue, Mary should succeed, and if she died without issue, Elizabeth. And in the contingency which actually happened of Elizabeth also dying without issue, it was again enacted that the descent should be as Henry should think fit to order in his will. It was a strong proof of confidence in the king, but a bad precedent, especially as it encouraged Edward VI. to think he, too, might will away the crown, even without an Act of Parliament, which was the occasion of very sad events. However, by the Statute Henry's will was law, and Henry willed that on his son and his two daughters all dying without issue, the crown should go to the descendants of his younger

could be no doubt it was for the peace of England. Happy would it have been for this country if the new doctrine could have been at once accepted in the same moderate form in which it is accepted now. We need not recall further how sadly it was mistaken,—how civil war again broke loose,—how royalty erred and suffered, and a new dynastic rivalry was created. Thank God, all these controversies have long been ended, and are not be revived.

The politic rule of the Tudors generally, and of Henry VII. in particular, did much to secure for England the blessings of domestic peace In the latter part of Henry's reign we find men debating the chances of the succession in a manner which shows that even then the true principle of descent had not been sufficiently determined. "It is not long sithens," said Sir Hugh Conway, "his highness was sick, and lay then "in his manor of Wanstead. It happened the same "time me to be amongst many great personages, the "which fell into communication of the king's grace, "and of the world that should be after him if his "grace happened to depart. Then, he said, that some "of them spoke of my lord of Buckingham, saying "that he was a noble man and would be a royal "ruler. Other there were that spake, he said, in like "wise of your traitor Edmund De la Pole, but none of "them, he said, that spake of my lord prince."[1] It would appear that those personal qualities which com-

Doubts regarding it in Henry VII.'s time.

sister Mary, passing over those of his elder sister Margaret Queen of Scots, from whom James I. was descended. This arrangement was confirmed by another act on the succession of Elizabeth (Stat. 1., Eliz. c. 3), and unquestionably during the greater part of Elizabeth's reign there was no desire for a Stewart's succession. It might have been questioned, also, whether James was not excluded by the Statute 17 Eliz. c. 1., which enacted that any attempt against the Queen in behalf of one who might have a prospective title to the Crown, barred the pretender's claim for ever after.

[1] Page 233.

mand the respect of the multitude might tempt any nobleman of the blood royal to aspire to the crown. The father of the duke of Buckingham above mentioned did so and suffered for it in the reign of Richard III.;[1] he himself did so and suffered for it in the reign of Henry VIII.; and the great dramatist who has made every one familiar with the story of his arrest and execution, paints also the sympathy of the populace with his fallen greatness, and makes the king himself bear witness to his personal accomplishments.[2]

Harl. MS. 433.

The register of Richard III.'s correspondence, of which mention has been made above, is contained in MS. 433 of the Harleian Collection in the British Museum. The volume appears to have been a docket book kept by Russell, bishop of Lincoln, of all the letters and documents that passed through his hands in his official capacity as Chancellor during the reigns of Edward V. and Richard III. It may be considered as divided into two sections. The larger consists of copies or minutes of formal documents, such as the grants and warrants which passed the Great Seal, the Privy Seal, or the king's Signet; the other is a letter book, containing copies of the correspondence of Richard with foreign sovereigns, instructions to ambassadors, proclamations, and other papers relating to affairs of state. It is from this latter portion only that our gleanings have been made.

The historical importance of such a MS. requires no comment. The volume is well known and has been often referred to by historical writers, though few of the entries have hitherto been printed entire. It is said to have belonged to the great lord Burleigh; at a later period it was the property of Strype. It is

---

[1] By his own confession to Morton, though his subsequent rebellion was ostensibly in favour of Richmond, he at first entertained a hope of obtaining the crown himself. I have no doubt his rebellion was animated by that hope only.

[2] Shakespeare's Henry VIII., Act I., Scene II.

described by Wanley in the Harleian Catalogue at much greater length than any other MS. of the collection. Several of the letters it contains will be found in Rymer; some in Ellis, and other more recent publications. Mr. Nichols has edited for the Camden Society such of its contents as belong to the Reign of Edward V. But many of the most important papers of Richard the Third's time have not been printed till now, some having apparently escaped notice altogether. The interest of No. xii. especially is so peculiar that there can be no doubt the French hand in which it is written has been the only cause why it has not been quoted.

None of the entries in the second or letter-book part of the volume belong to the reign of Edward V. The earliest in the first part is dated 5th of May 1483, the day after that young king's arrival in London. About that time or shortly after, Russell was appointed Chancellor. For nine years previously he had been keeper of the Privy Seal, and he is mentioned in More's History of Richard III. as "a wise man and "a good, and of much experience, and one of the "best learned men, undoubtedly, that England had in "his time." It is important in many respects that the character of Richard's chancellor is vouched for on such good authority.

Funeral of Edward IV.

Our volume commences with an account, derived from a MS. in the Herald's College, of the funeral rites of Edward the Fourth. It is characteristic of the olden time that pageants were so minutely and carefully recorded, while events of such awful moment as the *coup d'état* of the 13th of June, when the Protector suddenly ordered Hastings to the block, the executions of Rivers, Vaughan, and Grey, the usurpation of Richard III., and the death of his nephews, are so slightly noticed in contemporary letters and narratives, that doubts have been raised as to every circumstance connected with them. Yet we cannot consider this due so much to any general indifference to crime, as to the high importance then attached to whatever was visible and tangible. Pageants were not only regarded with an interest as mere shows for which the world has now grown too old, but were in themselves affairs of state of some importance. It must also be considered that the act of writing was not then so natural and spontaneous as it is with us. Private letters in the fifteenth century were almost always of a business character, and when the minds of men were strongly excited their hands were accustomed to wield heavier weapons than goose quills.[1] A pageant on the other hand, was essentially a peaceful exhibition. It was arranged beforehand to the smallest detail,—it could be observed minutely and chronicled with accuracy.

In this case we have a complete muster roll of the lords and gentlemen of rank who were in London at the time of Edward the Fourth's death. The principal actors in the events which followed were all absent,—Glocester, Buckingham, Rivers, and the young king himself; but there was a large attendance both of the old and new nobility. The blood relations of Edward's queen—the marquis of Dorset, Sir Richard and Sir Edward Woodville, met in peace over the grave of Edward with Hastings, Stanley, and the Earl of Lincoln. In less than four weeks the marquis and the Woodvilles were declared enemies of the Government, and ships were fitted out to take Sir Edward at sea.[2]

---

[1] Thus Simon Stalworthe in one of his short letters to Sir William Stonor (Excerpta Historica, p. 16) mentions the general distrust that prevailed after the execution of Hastings, and says that a large body of men from the North was expected in London, adds that he "is "so sick" (apparently from mere agitation) "he can hardly hold a "pen." Under the pressure of danger men now write letters of considerable length, as was shown by the correspondence during the Crimean war.

[2] Nichols' Grants of Edward V., pp. 2, 3.

Another contemporary account of this funeral is to be found in the MS. journals of Roger Machado, also in the Herald's College (Arundel MS. 51.) It is written in French, is imperfect at the beginning, and not so minute in its details, but so far as it goes, agrees pretty closely with that which we have printed. The conclusion of the ceremony, which the latter omits to relate, is worthy of notice.

"After the said noble king was thus placed in the ground the great officers of his noble house, to wit, the great steward, the chamberlain, the treasurer of his noble household, the controller, threw all their staves into the grave of the king in token of being men without a master, and out of their offices. And in like manner all the heralds threw their coats of arms, which belonged to the king, into the said grave; and immediately there were rendered to the said heralds other coats of arms of the kings of England, which they put on. And after the said coats of arms were given them they all cried "Le roy est vif! Le roy est vif! "Le roy est vif!" Praying to God; and saying Pater noster, and Ave Maria, for the defunct."

Circumstances connected with the accession of Richard III.

Of the three short months of violence and terror which compose the reign of Edward the Fifth, our letters and papers give us no further intelligence. All such materials connected with that period have been already printed either in Drake's Eboracum, Davis' York Records, the Paston Letters, or Mr. Nichols' Grants of Edward V. Mr. Nichols' Historical Introduction contains some important remarks in correction of Lingard and Sharon Turner, which show how difficult it is to avoid rash assumptions in dealing with this obscure portion of our history. It is my desire in these pages to avoid as far as possible, making statements, the truth of which is open to controversy, but one important fact relating to the accession of Richard III. appears to me to have been misunderstood even by Mr. Nichols. It is known that writs were sent out on the 13th of May for a Parliament to meet on the 25th of June. On the 21st of June, however, a writ of *supersedeas* was received in the City of York to prevent its assembling; and Mr. Nichols considers that the Parliament did not actually meet, a fact which he says is further declared in the act of settlement of the first year of Richard III. Now the words of that Act do indeed declare that there was no true and legal parliament, but they appear no less distinctly to show that there was the semblance of such a thing. In plain ordinary language the parliament really did meet, but the meeting was an informal one, and what was done was of doubtful validity until confirmed by a parliament regularly assembled. Parliament did meet, and the petition to Richard to assume the Crown was presented by a deputation of the lords and commons of England, accompanied by another from the City of London, on the very day[1] that had been originally appointed for its meeting. The previous issuing of the *supersedeas* to some of the boroughs may, perhaps, account for the informality. That act may, as likely as not, have been the work of Richard's enemies; the portion of the council which met at the Tower, while Richard and his friends held meetings at Crosby's Place.

---

[1] Sir Thomas More's History of Richard III. (which, there is reason to believe, is a translation of a work of Morton), though it speaks slightingly of the whole affair, fixes the date exactly. Dr. Shaw's celebrated sermon at Paul's Cross was on Sunday the 22d June. Buckingham's speech at the Guildhall, according to More, was on the Tuesday following (i.e., the 24th) Then he tells us. "on "the morrow after (the 25th) the "mayor with all the aldermen and "chief commoners of the ciry in "their best manner apparelled, "assembling themselves together, "resorted unto Baynard's Castle "where the Protector lay. To "which place repaired also the "duke of Buckingham with divers "noblemen with him besides many "knights and other gentlemen," &c. This 25th of June, as we have said, was the very day originally appointed for parliament to meet. "The next day," we then read, "the Protector with a great "train went to Westminster Hall," &c. It is true that Richard himself, in his instructions to Lord Mountjoy hereafter mentioned, speaks as if the petition was not presented to him till the 26th, the same day that he took his seat on the throne in Westminster Hall, and commenced to reign as king. But here, I have little doubt that More is more accurate.

This much at least is certain that a speech was prepared for the opening of that Parliament by the Lord Chancellor, which has been printed by Mr. Nichols. The Chancellor expected that the young king was to meet his Parliament in person, and according to custom he grounded his oration upon a text of Scripture. The words occurred in the service of the Nativity of St. John the Baptist, which was the day before the speech was to be delivered; *Audite, insulæ, et attendite, populi de longe; Dominus ab utero vocavit me*[1] (Isaiah xlix. 1.) The isles, he said, were the lords Spiritual and Temporal, the people from afar were the Commons. God had called the king to rule over them in his tender age. The simile was dwelt upon after the fashion of the times, and apparently with a pointed personal allusion. Islands, although surrounded with water, were themselves firm ground; there was more surety and firmness in them "than in the sea or any great *Rivers.*" The unstable water which surrounded them was the lower people, as St. John said in the Apocalypse (xvii. 15), "The waters which thou sawest are peoples "and nations." There were many important things in which the king required the advice of Parliament to assist his inexperience. His father in his latter days had felt much anxiety on account of the bad faith frequently exhibited by his allies. But it was of chief importance that the authority of the Protector should be confirmed until the king attained his majority; "among all the causes of the assembling of the Par-"liament in this time of the year, this is the greatest "and most necessary first to be affirmed."[2]

---

[1] "I have taken a trimembered text, such as I found in the divine service of yesterday's feast, the which to my purpose 'implieth the present estate of our nobles, our commons and of our glorious prince and King, Edward V. here present." Nichols' Grants of Edward V. p. xxxix.

[2] Ib. p. xlix.

This speech, most probably, was not delivered. When Parliament met it agreed to strengthen Richard's authority, not by confirming him as Protector, but by placing him upon the throne.

Let us here say what can be said, not to palliate the conduct of Richard III., but to make it intelligible, as far as our knowledge and judgment will permit. In the broad view of history which necessarily presents itself to most minds, the murder of his nephews must appear virtually to have been a part of the act of usurpation. In point of time it followed very close, and the natural inference seems to be that it was deliberately planned to give security to a throne so wrongfully acquired. It is not necessary, however, to entertain quite so dark a view. Detestable as the act must be under any aspect, we had rather not regard it as having been cogitated and considered for several weeks before. If it was, it certainly was the reverse of politic, for there can hardly be a doubt that whatever disaffection was previously felt to Richard's cause, gained strength from the moral indignation which that act aroused. However we may be accustomed to regard the celebrated scene in the Guidhall, he was certainly at first supported by more than a few hired retainers of Buckingham; and we may be tolerably certain that the mere change of sovereigns was not at that time so repugnant to the feelings of Englishmen, as it afterwards appeared when the sequel was divulged. Whether Richard's plea was true that his brother's children were by law illegitimate, is a question which need not be here discussed; but there had been enough of evil in the minority to reconcile most men to its termination. The state of anarchy had been simply intolerable; London had been kept in a continual ferment with plots and counterplots; and it is certain the spirit of faction was not wholly on Richard's side.

Richard's message to the garrison of Calais.

Two days after his accession Richard sent an important message to Calais by Lord Mountjoy. The garrison there had, on receiving the news of Edward the Fourth's death, taken an oath of fealty to his son, declaring that they would keep the town, castle, and marches for king Edward the Fifth, and not suffer any one to enter with an armed force except the king himself or lord Hastings his lieutenant. Shortly afterwards, perhaps after the execution of Hastings, which took place on the 13th of June, lord Dynham wrote from Calais to the duke of Glocester as Protector, desiring an answer to certain questions and petitions from the inhabitants, of which the first related to this oath. In answer Mountjoy, who was soon afterwards appointed lieutenant of Guines, was instructed to say that as the oath had been taken in ignorance of "the very sure " and true title which our sovereign lord that now is " hath and had the same time to the crown of Eng-" land," every true Englishman was bound to disregard it and tender his fealty to the real king, "whose " sure and true title," say the instructions, "is evi-" dently showed in a bill of petition which the lords " spiritual and temporal and the commons of this land " solemnly porrected unto the king's highness at Lon-" don, the 26th day of June. Whereupon the kings " said highness, notably assisted by well near all the " lords, spiritual and temporal, of this realm went the " same day unto his palace of Westminster, and there in " such royal [estate] honourably apparelled, within the " great hall there, took possession and declared his mind " that the same day he would begin to reign upon his " people; and from thence rode solemnly to the cathedral " church of London, and was received there with pro-" cession, with great congratulation and acclamation of " all the people in every place and by the way that " the king was in that day." The estimate which a king like Richard the Third chooses to give of his own popularity is of course open to suspicion, but the above extract manifestly contains some facts which could not have been misstated.

His relations with foreign powers:—Spain.

We see most of Richard, however, in his relations with foreign powers. A friendly message was received from Spain, desiring alliance with England against France, and the ambassador gave a singular explanation of the causes which had led queen Isabella before to favour France against England. Edward the Fourth had committed a most unkingly act in making a real love match, and Isabella "was turned in her heart from "England for his refusing of her and taking to his "wife, a widow of England; for the which cause, also, "was mortal war betwixt him and the earl of War-"wick, the which took ever her part to the time of "his death." Edward IV., however, was now dead; Lewis XI. had broken four principal articles of his treaty with her, and would not allow her to marry her son to the heiress of Navarre. She was, therefore, anxious to renew a good understanding with England. Her ambassador was received by Richard with great magnificence at Warwick. According to Rous, who lived in the neighbourhood, and probably was present on the occasion, he also brought a proposal for the marriage of Richard's only son with one of the daughters of Ferdinand and Isabella. To this we know not what reply was made. To the other overture, Richard returned a cordial answer, and proposed to renew a league made with Henry IV. of Castile. But he seems to have had no wish to provoke hostilities with France, and made no reply to that part of her proposal.

Britanny was at this time offering an asylum to his most dangerous enemies. In July Richard sent thither Dr. Hutton to propose a diet for putting an end to private acts of hostility which had taken place between the subjects of England and the duchy. The death of Edward IV. had been supposed to put an end to existing treaties, and the commerce between the two countries had suffered in consequence. While anxious that things should be put on an amicable footing it is evident that Richard had little confidence in the duke. He proposed that the diet should be in England and nowhere else; and he instructed Hutton to "feel and "understand the mind and disposition of the duke "anempst Sir Edward Woodville and his retinue, "practising by all means to him possible to ensearch "and know if there be intended any enterprise out "of land upon any part of this realm." At the same time he expressed his willingness to satisfy all just claims of the duke's subjects, and promised that an agreement made by the late king for compensation to some Breton merchants should be carried out whenever Edward's will was administered.

In August, just two months after Richard's accession, the duke despatched George de Mainbier to England in answer to this overture, promising to send ambassadors about the feast of All Saints, after the meeting of the estates of the duchy, to treat on the subject of Hutton's charge. The duke complained much of the depredations of the English, and was anxious to show that for his part he had risked the enmity of France out of friendship to Richard. Henry, earl of Richmond, was then an exile in the duke's dominions. Though afterwards King of England, his claim by mere lineal descent was never of the strongest, and but for the great crime of Richard III. it would not have been even plausible. But, such as they were, even his pretensions might have disquieted the late minority, as they did with better reason the reign of Richard himself. Since the death of Edward IV. Lewis XI. had made repeated applications to the duke to deliver him into his hands, and finding that his demands were not listened to threatened war. Of course this gave the duke a strong claim to the support of England. Richard was entreated to consider "the great "power of men of war, artillery, and finances which the "said king of France has, and the nearness of the said

" kingdom to the duchy of Britanny, the two lands " joining together without having between them brook " or river which might hinder the said King of France " from entering the said duchy of Britanny with all " his power." The duke asked for 4,000 English archers to be maintained six months at the expense of England, and followed by others if necessary, for whom he would pay himself. Richard sent aid, but not immediately, nor to the full extent of his demands. On the 26th of June next year, he commissioned lord Grey of Powis to go to Britanny with 1,000 archers, which was probably all the force he could with prudence spare.

He might, indeed, have found two very fair excuses for refusing the desired assistance altogether. Lewis XI., of whom the duke stood in awe, was actually dead at the date of Mainbier's instructions; and, what still more completely altered the case, the earl of Richmond in less than two months sailed for Britanny to invade England, aided by money from the duke. Such were the obligations of Richard III. to Britanny.

France. As for France, the few short letters that had passed been Richard and Lewis XI. in the brief interval between the accession of the one and the death of the other scarcely enable us to judge what might have been the relations between the two countries had Lewis lived a little longer. When he died he left his son Charles VIII. a minor under the care of his sister, Madame de Beaujeu. France was in one respect happier than England had been after the death of Edward IV., for Charles was in his 14th year and might soon be declared out of his minority, while the prospect of a long minority in England, attended with constant intrigues and conspiracies for power, had in all probability done much to favour the usurpation of Richard III. But even in France the manifest lineal right did not silence the pretensions of rival claimants to the throne. Two princes of the blood Royal, the duke of Orleans, afterwards Lewis XII., and the duke of Bourbon, came forward to dispute the crown. It was objected to Charles that he was not only a boy, but that his complexion was that of a physically weak boy. As for his sister, the law did not suffer a woman to reign, and it seemed unreasonable that she should bear the rule.[1]

The question was referred to the Estates General, which met at Tours in January. The session was opened by the chancellor, Guillaume de Rochefort, in a speech in which he pointedly referred to the parallel case of England, and urged them to take warning by what had happened there only a few months previously. France, he remaked, with a strange forgetfulness of his country's history, had never been unfaithful to her king, but England had openly sanctioned usurpation. "See," he said, "what has taken place in that "country since the death of King Edward. Consider "his children, already tall and brave, butchered with "impunity, and the crown transferred to the assassin "by the favor of the people."[2] The estates came to the determination that Charles, having attained the age of 14, should be considered out of his minority; that the lady of Beaujeu, however, should still have the care of his person, and that all acts of state should be administered by a council of 12 persons. It was a clumsy compromise and proved a failure. The Council of twelve became mere ciphers, and the lady of Beaujeu usurped all authority. The consequence was that the country was soon involved in civil war.

---

[1] Mezeray.

[2] "Regardez, je vous prie, les "évenements qui apres la mort du "roi Edouard, sont arrivés dans "ce pays. Contemplez ses enfans, "déja grands et braves, massacrés impunément. et la couronne transportée à l'assassin par "la faveur des peuples."--*Journal des Etats Generaux de France tenus a Tours en* 1483-4, *p.* 39. It is important to remark that this was said in January 1484. The usurpation of Richard was in the preceding June, and the murder of his nephews is believed to have been in August.

We have no correspondence between Richard III. and France after the death of Lewis XI. We only know that his rival Henry, on the failure of his first expedition to England, which was intended to act in concert with Buckingham, returned to Britanny, and when he was about to be delivered up by Britanny, found a refuge in France under the protection of Madame de Beaujeu. Here he matured his plans in safety. Even Calais was not in complete subjection to Richard III. The imprisoned earl of Oxford prevailed upon James Blount, captain of Hammes, to let him have his liberty, and both repaired to Richmond in France. The castle of Hammes itself held for a time against king Richard.[1]

Contrast between the reigns of Richard III. and Henry VII.

A comparison of the reigns of Richard III. and Henry VII. cannot fail to show us how much the destinies of a nation may be influenced for good or evil by the personal character of its sovereign. Their position upon the throne, their relations to their subjects, and to foreign powers, were not materially different. They might both be considered as usurpers; both had to meet rebellions in their own dominions; both had rivals abroad supported by foreign princes. But Richard was the last of a family of soldiers; Henry the beginner of a dynasty of statesmen. The morality of statesmenship in that day was not high, but it was better than the cruelty of brute force and violence, and it secured for itself that supremacy which force and violence had been unable to attain. There was a recklessness in the personal character of the princes of the House of York that might have sufficed to ruin their cause, apart from their internal divisions, injustice, and ferocity. The Tudor throne had to be

[1] A short MS. Chronicle in Trinity College, Dublin (E. 1. 26), mentions that "the sege of Ham-"mys by king Richard the iijde. "was the xv. daie of Decembur, "A°. Domini M¹. iiijc. lxxxiiij." Hall mentions the circumstance, but does not give the date.

supported by the most cautious diplomacy, and by a strict regard for law. For law, generally speaking, as the instrument of justice, but in some cases, undoubtedly, as a means of oppression. The very fact that it was so perverted is a proof of Henry's greatness. That a king, whose title was one of the most ambiguous ever seen in England, who was frequently troubled with rebellion, and placed on the throne by a successful rebellion himself, should have succeeded in making the authority of law so strong as not only to enable him to put down his enemies, but to become in his hands an engine of extortion, is evidence of Henry's ability as a statesman quite as great as the respect entertained for him by foreign sovereigns.

Peaceful policy of Henry VII.

Henry's foreign policy was always in favour of peace. No one knew better than he the expediency of non-interference in the affairs of other kingdoms, and the advantage of husbanding the resources of a wasted country. Though the designs of France against Brittany aroused a strong feeling in England both in favour of an old ally and against an ancient enemy, all the national eagerness for war could not impel him to prosecute it in earnest. He did indeed raise benevolences, cross the sea, and make a short campaign, but he returned without striking a blow. Having secured payment from France for the expenses of the expedition, and an annual sum which might be looked upon as tribute, he withdrew his forces and left Brittany to its fate. The old pretensions of our kings to France had never been given up; another king would have attempted to show that the English were still masters there; but Henry knew that it was impracticable, and cared more for policy than glory.

His French campaign

His mode of dealing with Scotland.

His conduct towards Scotland was a still more remarkable instance, not only in itself but in its consequences. In France he preserved a friend, while forced to put on the guise of enmity; in Scotland he conciliated an enemy and laid the foundation of an ultimate union. He was not less aware than his predecessors of the necessity of having some control over the Northern kingdom, but he adopted a different method to secure it. Instead of raising up a spirit of opposition by the old assertion of feudal sovereignty, he at first made friends within the kingdom itself to keep the king in check. He bound the Earl of Angus by indenture, under certain circumstances, to make war on James the Fourth—that powerful Earl of Angus who had acquired the surname of Bell-the-Cat, by taking the lead among the Scotch nobles in opposition to James III.[1] He engaged at the same time the attainted lord Bothwell and Sir Thomas Todd to seize the person of the King of Scots and his brother and carry them to England. Lord Bothwell was a useful instrument; though he did not effect that object, he was of great service some years later, when James undertook an invasion in favour of Perkin Warbeck. By him Henry secured the assistance of James's own brother, the Duke of Ross, and of other Scottish nobles, to throw every obstacle in the way of the expedition. By him he was informed minutely of all the preparations that had been made,—of the Scotch king's pecuniary necessities,—of the number of guns in Edinburgh Castle,—of the place where the Scottish forces were to muster, and the fact that they had but four or five days' provisions,—of the facility with which their retreat might be cut off, and of the excellent opportunity that existed for burning all the navy and seaport towns of Scotland. But Henry was kinder to Scotland than some of her own sons.

Fox's negotiations.

A few months after the invasion, while Warbeck was yet in Scotland, occurred the most formidable of all the rebellions that troubled Henry's reign. By some

[1] According to Douglas' Peerage of Scotland, (I. 131), he was made high Chancellor of Scotland in 1493, which was two years after his covenant with Henry VII. One year before it he had a licence from Henry to come to England on pilgrimage. Scotch Roll, 5 Henry VII.

mismanagement, the Cornish malcontents were allowed to make their way unopposed to within view of London. They were defeated at Blackheath on the 22nd of June, 1497. Warned by the danger which had thus been averted, Henry, a fortnight afterwards, drew up instructions for Fox to treat for peace with James. The document is an interesting specimen of his wary policy. Terms had already been offered by the Earl of Angus and Lord Hume on the part of Scotland. Henry could not afford to throw away the chance thus offered, but disguised his own anxieties. He selected Fox, probably his ablest minister, to negotiate, and provided him with two separate sets of instructions. The first declared that the offers of Angus and Hume were unsatisfactory, and that peace could not possibly be made without further concessions. Every effort was to be used to induce James to consent to one of two alternatives. In the first place, what Henry would have preferred to everything else, Fox was to insist on the delivery of Perkin Warbeck, on whose account the late invasion of England had been undertaken; "the which deliverance," the king added, "we "desire not for any estimation that we take of him, "but because our said cousin received him within his "land, and favourably hath entreated him and divers "others of our rebels during the peace concluded be- "twixt us both; and over that, having him in his "company, entered in puissance within our land, the "which was the cause and ground of the breach of "the said peace. And less, therefore, may we not do "with our honor than to have the deliverance of him, "though the deliverance or having of him is of no "price nor value." Anticipating opposition here, however, Henry offered, as an alternative, to make peace on the following conditions: first, that James should send an embassy to England; second, that he should come himself to a personal interview there with Henry; third, that he should be bound under ecclesiastical censures to the observance of the treaty; and, fourth, that he should make compensation for injuries done in the war, giving hostages for the fulfilment of these conditions. Beyond this, it was to appear that Fox had no further commission; and he had it in his discretion to show his instructions to the Scotch commissioners to give them that impression. The fact was, however, that he was empowered to go much further, and if peace could not be made with the conditions desired by Henry, he was directed by the other set of instructions to accept the offers of Angus and Hume without modification.

Warbeck actually left Scotland the day after the date of Fox's instructions,[1] so that the question of delivering him up could no longer be entertained. A truce was shortly afterwards concluded, which a few years later was superseded by a permanent peace; and in 1503 James was married to the Princess Margaret. Exactly a hundred years later their descendant James the Sixth of Scotland mounted the English throne. When another hundred years had passed, and four years more, not only the crowns of England and Scotland, but the kingdoms themselves were united.

Ireland.

Ireland, too, under Henry VII., almost belongs to the Department of Foreign Affairs. It is, indeed, under English rule, for the governing race acknowledge their allegiance; but it cannot, from the nature of things, be very much under English control. What was remarked by the late Lord Macaulay of India was necessarily true at that time of a country much nearer home. Ireland could only be governed in Ireland in spite of all the efforts made to govern it in England. English laws, English dress, English customs, might be imposed by authority; Kildare might be displaced by Poynings as Lord Deputy, and every act of the Irish legislature might be dictated by the English

[1] Tytler's Scotland, IV. 330.

council; but the practical business of government could only be carried on upon the spot. The breadth of St. George's Channel lay between the deputy and his responsibility.

Ireland had all along been more favourable to the House of York than to the Lancastrian line. The Duke of York, father of Edward the Fourth, had large possessions there, and, when sent thither to put down a rebellion in the reign of Henry the Sixth, used his personal influence with such good effect, that he and his family were ever afterwards held in high respect. Even under Edward the Fourth, however, the authority of the crown had once been most outrageously set at nought. The Earl of Kildare had summoned a parliament in defiance of an explicit prohibition from the king, and that parliament had passed acts and levied a subsidy. His son, the eighth earl, succeeded him as Lord Deputy in the later years of Edward IV., and was continued in it by Richard III. A Kildare was not to be removed by a king newly seated on an uneasy throne; but from the very first Henry saw the importance of obtaining some feeble security for his faithfulness. John Estrete was sent to Ireland, almost at the very commencement of this reign,[1] to tell him in answer to a request he had put in to have the deputyship confirmed to him for a term of nine or ten years, that the king was desirous to consult him personally upon the affairs of the country. The king was aware what good service he had rendered to Edward the Fourth, especially after he had been with him in England, and considering his long experience, thought no man more competent to advise him. He

[1] That his instructions, printed at page 91, were not given him by Richard III. as supposed in the Catalogue of the Cottonian MSS., is I think sufficiently shown by their general nature, which is much more in accordance with the politic character of Henry than that of Richard.

therefore desired, not for the first time, that Kildare should repair to his presence before a certain day, promising on his so doing, not only to confirm him in the lieutenancy. but to make him a grant in tail of the manor of Leixlip and the keeping of Wicklow castle. Besides these conditions, the earl had been so bold as to demand written assurances under the seals of the king and some of the nobles for his security while in England. This was declared to be inconsistent with the king's honour, and Kildare was informed that he must content himself with an ordinary protection under the sign manual. The story, whether true or not, of his burning Cashel cathedral, and pleading, when called to answer before the council, that he had only done it because the archbishop was inside, gives us a notion of utter irresponsibility, which is borne out by the most authentic documents. On another occasion when Henry summoned him to England, he took no notice of the letter for ten months, and at last sent an excuse backed by the lords of the Irish parliament, stating that his presence was so essential to the peace of the country that he could not be spared.[1]

Spain.

Of all Henry's foreign alliances the most important was with Spain. He appears from the first to have looked upon it as a country destined to be great, and he was not mistaken. Spain had already somewhat recovered from severe internal struggles, such as had lately desolated England; and the consolidation of power at which Henry aimed had been in part effected by Ferdinand and Isabella. Out of the four Christian kingdoms in the Peninsula, the two most powerful were united by their marriage, and there appeared some hope at length of driving out the Moors. Scarce

[1] See Appendix A. p. 377. A suspicion that might arise as to the date of the lords' letter (4 June), or of the king's letter therein mentioned (28 July) being a clerical error, is completely removed by Kildare's letter which follows.

had Henry been three years upon the throne when he began to negotiate for the marriage of his son Arthur with Catherine of Arragon. Though planned when they were both infants, unlike the generality of such projects it took effect when they came of age. It took effect because England and Spain had both grown stronger in the interval. Granada had surrendered to the victorious arms of Ferdinand, and the last embers of discord had been crushed out in England, not without cruelty and injustice, in the execution of the son of Clarence.[1]

For more than a century after the alliance or the enmity of Spain was the leading feature in the foreign politics of England.

The Spanish correspondence in this volume belongs chiefly to the period just before Catherine's arrival in England. It is full of the expression of Henry's desire for the marriage, and his impatience to see it accomplished. That period was the turning point in his reign, when he got out of troubled waters into comparative rest and tranquillity. He was now too strong to be disquieted by impostors employed to work out the designs of others. He was strong with foreign powers, and not less so in the good will of his subjects. The shows and "goodly disguisings" which welcomed Cathe-

[1] Hall says in relation to this,—"The fame after his death sprung "that Ferdinand king of Spain "would never make full conclu-"sion of the matrimony to be had "between prince Arthur and the "lady Catherine his daughter, nor "send her into England, as long "as this earl lived; for he im-"agined that as long as any earl "of Warwick lived, that England "should never be cleansed or "purged of civil war and privy "sedition." Lord Bacon also mentions a tradition that a long time afterwards when Catherine of Arragon was first informed of Henry VIII.'s intention to procure a divorce from her, she used some words to the effect "that she had "not offended; but it was a judg-"ment of God, for that her for-"mer marriage was made in blood, "meaning that of the earl of "Warwick." The importance attached by Ferdinand to the execution of Clarence is confirmed by the first paragraph of De Puebla's letter printed at page 113.

rine to England reflected truly the happiness of a contented people.

The satisfaction which this great alliance gave the king himself may be judged from the anxiety with which he had so long looked forward to it. Its accomplishment was in every way a joy and triumph. Parental pride and political ambition were equally gratified; and a pleasing dream might be indulged of a future line of kings descended from a prince named Arthur, peacefully inheriting the claims both of York and Lancaster. Alas! that dream was soon to be dispelled. In proportion as the hope was great, was the disappointment bitter; nor are we without warrant in asserting that Henry's feelings were better than those of a mere politician. An unknown but contemporary writer has left us this touching record of the manner in which he and his queen received the heavy blow.

Death of Prince Arthur.

"In the year of our Lord God 1502, the second day of April, in the castle of Ludlow, deceased Prince Arthur, first begotten son of Our Sovereign Lord King Henry the Seventh, and in the 17th year of his reign. Immediately after his death Sir Richard Poole, his chamberlain, with other of his council, wrote and sent letters to the king and council at Greenwich, where his grace and the queen then was, and certified him of the prince's departure. The which council discreetly sent for the king's ghostly father, a friar Observant, to whom they showed these most sorrowful and heavy tidings, and desired him in his best manner to show it to the king. He in the morning of the Tuesday following, somewhat before the time accustomed, knocked at the king's chamber-door; and when the king understood it was his confessor, he commanded to let him in. The confessor then commanded all those present to avoid, and after due salutation began to say, *Si bona de manu Dei suscipimus, mala autem quare non sustineamus?* and so showed his grace, that his dearest son was departed to God. When his grace understood that sorrowful heavy tidings, he sent for the queen, saying that he and his queen would take the painful sorrows together. And after that she was come and saw the king her lord, and that natural and painful sorrow, as I have heard say, she with full great and constant comfortable words besought his grace, that he would, first after God, remember the weal of his own noble person, the comfort of his realm and of her. She then said that my lady, his mother, had never no more children but him only, and that God, by his grace, had ever preserved him, and brought him where that he was. Over that, how that God had left him yet a fair prince, two fair princesses; and that God is where he was, and we are both young enough; and that the prudence and wisdom of his grace sprung over all Christendom, so that it should please him to take this accordingly thereunto. Then the king thanked her of her good comfort. After that she was departed and come to her own chamber, natural and motherly remembrance of that great loss smote her so sorrowfully to the heart that those that were about her were fain to send for the king to comfort her. Then his grace of true, gentle, and faithful love, in good haste came and relieved her, and showed her how wise council she had given him before; and he for his part would thank God for his son, and would she do in likewise."[1]

At this time, though there were no more disturbances from impostors, attempts in favour of the House of York were not altogether at an end. The story of the earl of Suffolk has hitherto been very imperfectly told, and cannot be fully read without the aid of papers which are here for the first time published We will therefore relate it, as it appears in these documents and in other sources, as briefly as possible.

When Richard III. lost his only son in March, 1484, he declared his nephew, the earl of Lincoln, son of John, duke of Suffolk, his successor in the kingdom. He at the same time arranged a marriage for Anne De la Pole, a daughter of the same house, with the duke of Rothesay, heir apparent of the Scottish throne But these projects for the elevation of the family vanished on Richard's death, and the disappointment was not unfelt by the younger members. Suffolk himself, not being of the blood royal, did not provoke the jealousy of Henry VII, but was a loyal subject all his days. He was appointed to bear the new king's sceptre at the coronation, and treated with every mark of confi-

The Suffolk family.

[1] Leland's Collectanea, v. 373-4.

dence. Even his sons for a time retained their allegiance, and when in the spring of 1486, lord Lovel took up arms against Henry, the earl of Lincoln repaired to the king at York. Next year, however, Lincoln revolted, and it became at once apparent that he had not altogether abandoned his prospects in regard to the succession. He was present at "a great council" summoned by Henry at Sheen in the beginning of the year to meet an embassy which had arrived from France. Immediately after, he secretly left the country, and joined lord Lovel and the other adherents of the House of York in Flanders. Simnel was then in Ireland, enacting the character of the earl of Warwick, and laying claim to the crown as the son of Clarence. Lincoln had seen the earl of Warwick at Sheen just before his departure, but he did not scruple to declare Simnel to be the real earl pursuing his just right. He joined the mock king in Ireland, accompanied him into England, and perished at the battle of Stoke, fighting in the cause of one whom he knew very well to be an impostor. An act of attainder, of course, passed against him, so that his lands could not descend to his younger brothers; and his father died in 1491, of grief, it is said, for the ruin of his family.

Edmund de la Pole.

His brother Edmund, however, did not allow his hopes to be dashed by adverse fortune, an impoverished patrimony or a family disgrace. He is described as a man of violent temper, rash, and headstrong. His letters certainly give us the impression of a rude and careless writer. Their spelling is anomalous and unintelligible far beyond the ordinary even of illiterate men in those days, and the handwriting is sprawling and irregular to match. It is true that the earliest notice found of him, when he was a student at Oxford, speaks of his "penetrating, eloquent, and brilliant genius;"[1]

[1] Napier's Historical Notes of the Parishes of Swyncombe and Ewelme, p. 162.

but it must be understood that this was in a letter addressed by the university to his uncle king Edward the Fourth. On his father's death he succeeded to the dukedom of Suffolk; but the family estate being reduced by his brother's attainder, he made a compromise with the king to content himself with the dignity of an earl on the restoration of a portion of the confiscated lands. He continued in favour for some years. In 1494 he took a leading part in the tournament at the creation of prince Henry as duke of York, and gained one of the prizes for the second day's achievements. Next year he received the king under his own roof at Ewelme. Soon after he was made a knight of the garter, and on St. George's day, in 1499, he was present at a chapter of that order.[1] It must have been very shortly after this that he first manifested disaffection.

All that has hitherto been known of the story of his revolt is derived from Polydore Virgil and his translator Hall. Though in some respects inaccurate, we cannot relate the leading facts of it better than in the words of the latter. His revolt as related by Hall.

"A few months before the marriage of Prince Arthur, Edmund Pole, earl of Suffolk, son to John duke of Suffolk and lady Elizabeth, sister to king Edward the Fourth, being stout and bold of courage, and of wit rash and heady, was indicted of homicide and murder, for slaying of a mean person in his rage and fury. And although the king pardoned him whom he might justly have condemned for that offence, yet, because he was brought to the King's Bench bar and arraigned (which fact he reputed to be a great maim and blemish to his honor), took it seriously, and shortly after for his displeasure fled to Flanders, without any licence or safe conduct given him of the king, to the lady Margaret, his aunt on the mother's side. Nevertheless, whether he was stirred by his privy friends or moved by the king, or whether he, trusting on his unviolated truth, feared no danger nor penalty, he returned again, and excused himself so to the king that he

[1] Napier's Swyncombe and Ewelme, p. 168.

was thought to be guiltless and inculpable of any crime that could be objected to him, and therefore he was permitted to go frankly at his liberty and pleasure.

"But when this marriage of prince Arthur was kept at London with great pomp and solemnity, and that all the nobility were set on pleasure and solace, and that the king himself was principally given to joy and rejoicing, this Edmund, either for that he had been at great and excessive charges at the same triumph and solemnity, and by reason thereof sore charged with debt,—either solicited, allured, and provoked by that old venomous serpent the duchess of Burgoyn, ever being the sower of sedition and beginner of rebellion against the king of England,—or else stimulate and pricked with envy, which could not patiently with open eyes see and behold king Henry, being of the adverse line to his lineage, so long to reign in wealth and felicity,—in conclusion, with his brother Richard, fled again into Flanders. This sad chance, I think, happened among the great joys and solaces of king Henry, lest that he might not by overmuch forget himself; which displeasure at another time before to have chanced it is manifest and well known to you.

"When the king understood certainly that this earl was departed and returned again, he was not a little vexed and unquieted, mistrusting that some new tumultuous business should be begun again, and chiefly therefore blamed himself of foolish folly that he had given him his pardon for his offence lately committed; although it was manifest enough that he did it for this purpose, that he might dissemble and wink at the matter so long until such time he had some sure token and perfect knowledge of his conjuration, the which he perceived now to be surely attempted and begun. As soon as Edmund De la Pole Earl of Suffolk was fled again into Flanders, Sir Robert Curzon, whom the king had promoted to the honour of knighthood and made captain of Hammes castle, a valiant and circumspect man, dissimulating himself to be one of that conspiracy, went into Flanders, doubtless to espy what was done there by the Lady Margaret against King Henry. This opinion was settled in every man's head at the first broaching of the matter, and so yet continueth, grounding upon this principle that he, neither vexed nor molested with any point of displeasure or injury by his prince or any other, fled to the king's enemies; and after all things were known, opened, pacified, and suppressed, he willingly returned, and was received into high favour with the king his master and sovereign lord. Howbeit the king, like a wily fox, knowing the faithful intent of this Sir Robert, and intending to put him out of all jealousy and suspicion with the Lady Margaret and Edmund De la Pole, caused the said earl and the said Sir Robert Curzon and five persons more to be accursed at Paul's Cross, the first Sunday of November, as enemies and rebels to him and his realm. But, howsoever it chanced, whether it were for the easing of his heart or from some privy policy, the king after the marriage of his son Prince Arthur was so vigilant, so circumspect, and so intentive that he espied and tried out such as he knew partly to be the inventors of mischief against him, and partly to bear no goodwill or sincere affection towards his person, that he could readily name and rehearse their names and surnames; whereof a great part were within a few days apprehended and taken. And among them Lord William Courtney, son to Edward Earl of Devonshire (a man of great nobility, estimation, and virtue, which married Lady Catherine, daughter to King Edward), Lord William, brother to Edmund Earl of Suffolk, Sir James Tyrell, Sir John Wyndham. Both these Williams before rehearsed, were rather taken of suspicion and jealousy because they were near of blood to the conjurators, than for any proved offence or crime. . . . . . . . And Sir James Tyrell and John Wyndham, because they were traitors and so attainted, the 6th day of May they were on Tower Hill beheaded. But when the Earl of Suffolk heard that some of his friends were put to execution and some other committed to perpetual prison and captivity, he was in a great agony and fear of himself; and so, being clearly desperate to have any fortunate success in his pretensed enterprise, wandered about all Germany and France for aid and succour, proving if he could find any aid or succour at their hands. But when he perceived no steadfast ground to catch anchor upon (to the intent that in conclusion he might understand that a shameful death due to a man for his offences and crimes cannot by man's help or man's reason be either eschewed or diverted from him) he submitted himself under the obeisance and defence of Philip, Archduke of Austria and Burgoyn and Earl of Flanders. But Richard, his brother, being an expert and politic man, so craftily conveyed and wisely ordered himself in this stormy tempest, that he was not entrapped either with net or snare."

Corrections to be made in Hall's account.

This account is in the main corroborated by the papers relating to Suffolk here published, and may be presumed to be correct wherever we have no better information. The chronology, however, is a little erroneous. The indictment of homicide appears to have been, not a few months, but three years before Arthur's marriage; for it was found by Mr. Napier among the records of the Queen's Bench in Michaelmas term 14 Henry VII. (1498). Lingard also surmised from the act of attainder that the date of his first flight must have been as early as the 1st of July, 1499, from which day the forfeiture was to take effect retrospectively, and this conjecture is confirmed by article xvii., which shows that when Sir Richard Guildford and Richard Hatton were despatched on a mission to the archduke in September of that year they received instructions to use every effort to persuade Suffolk to return. He appears to have been, not at the court of Margaret of Burgundy, but at Calais, or perhaps more strictly speaking at Guisnes, with Sir James Tyrell, who was executed three years afterwards as one of his adherents. At this time Henry conceived no mischief was done past mending. Suffolk had not openly renounced his allegiance, and if he could be induced voluntarily to return, the matter would attract no further observation. If not, he was to be formally summoned on his allegiance by the authorities at Calais. He did return voluntarily. He was received again into favour, and treated so entirely as one on whom no suspicion rested, that in the next year, 1500, he followed the king over to Calais.[1]

In the year after, he was again a fugitive. This second flight occurred at the date to which the first is attributed, that is to say, shortly before Arthur's marriage. It certainly was not caused by the expenses he had incurred at that celebration, for he was then in Germany. Our papers now afford much more full information than Hall and Polydore; and it appears that in this case the Macchiavellian character of Henry's policy has been somewhat over-estimated. Curzon was not sent after Suffolk, but went before him. So early as the 29th of August, 1499, he obtained licence

[1] Chronicle of Calais, p. 3.

from the king to quit his post as captain of Hammes castle to fight in the cause of the church against the infidels.[1] In this service he succeeded in gaining the high esteem of Maximilian, who created him a baron of the empire.[2]

Talking of the affairs of England with the emperor, Curzon was encouraged to speak of the "murders and tyrannies" of Henry, and the design of Edmund De la Pole to recover what he called his right. Maximilian at once declared his sympathy with De la Pole. He told Curzon that if so prominent a member of the House of York would come and trust himself to his protection, he would assist him to obtain the crown of England; and declared that he would not desert him, though the enterprise should cost him as much as a year's value of all his dominions. It was on being informed of this that Suffolk left England a second time, in the month of August 1501.[3] He at once repaired to the Tyrol, where the emperor then was, rehearsed certain injuries that he alleged Henry had done to him, and said that it had been the king's intention to murder him and his brother. Maximilian welcomed the fugitive as his kinsman, and showed him every attention, but at first declined to assist him on the ground of the existing amity between England

---

[1] Rymer, xii. 729.

[2] Gough's Camden, ii. 306. It is also said that he was made a baron of England by Henry VIII., but perhaps the truth is only that he was licensed to bear his foreign title. He is not noticed by any of the Peerage historians.

[3] "In this year in the month of "August departed secretly out of "the land the Earl of Suffolk, and "so sailed into France, accom- "panied him with Sir Robert "Curzon, knight, before season in "like manner departed. For the "which the king charged all offi- "cers, as searchers and other, to "make due search, every man in "his country to see that none "other in like manner departed "his land without his licence." MS. Cott., Vitellius A. xvi., f. 183. The statement that the earl sailed to France probably means no more than that he went beyond sea: otherwise it was written in ignorance.

and his son the Archduke. When, however, Suffolk was going to have retired and sought his fortune elsewhere, the emperor pressed him to remain till he had more fully deliberated how he could assist him. He, accordingly, did remain at Imst the space of six weeks, and was then offered the aid of from 3,000 to 5,000 soldiers for one, two, or three months. A formal agreement was then drawn up between him and the imperial treasurer; and leaving his steward Killingworth at the court, he went to Aix-la-Chapelle with letters of recommendation from the emperor to help him to obtain that assistance which Aix was best able to afford.

Suffolk's disappointment.

His expectations were doomed to be wholly disappointed. From a mutilated and very illegible MS. we can just make out that the emperor's promises were from time to time evaded by different excuses. In the spring of 1502, the plan was that Suffolk should embark from Denmark.[1] When this failed, the emperor proposed to make terms between him and Henry VII.; then threw out a hint that he might obtain assistance from France; and then found out and was forced to acknowledge that Henry would listen to no proposition in his favour.[2] Still he went on advising the earl to have patience, and that he would yet assist him; and still, when the time came, he was unable to redeem his promise. Suffolk was most bitterly disappointed; he felt that he had been betrayed. In private letters to Killingworth he complained of the emperor's dissimulation, and bid him tell his Majesty plainly that he had left his country on the promise of imperial aid, and by so doing had forfeited as much property as would have supported an invading army of 10,000 men. Meanwhile his friends in England were being apprehended and exe-

[1] Page 138.

[2] Pages 140, 141.

cuted, and he himself was not secure against being delivered by treachery into Henry's hands.[1]

Arrest of Sir James Tyrell.

The arrest of Sir James Tyrell was well calculated to alarm him. Sir James had been induced to leave Guisnes castle where he was besieged by the whole army of Calais, on the promise of the Lord Privy Seal that he should go and come in security, and when he came on board ship, Sir Thomas Lovel bid him send a token to his son whom he had left in charge there, to deliver up the castle; threatening, if he did not comply, to throw him overboard. The token was sent, the castle surrendered, and both Tyrell and his son were thrown into the Tower.[2] The father alone suffered the extreme penalty of the law.[3]

On the 20th of June the same year, a treaty was made at Antwerp between Henry VII. and Maximilian by which the emperor was bound not to receive within his dominions any English rebels, or allow others to give them the slightest assistance, even if they should be of the rank of dukes,[4] as De la Pole pretended still to be. This treaty was confirmed by Henry on the 14th of August. It was what Henry had determined to obtain from the moment he

---

[1] Pages 179, 180.

[2] Page 181.

[3] In the reign of Henry VIII., in reference to another case of a boy being implicated in the treason of his father, Sir Brian Tuke wrote to Wolsey to intercede in these words: "Like it your grace, I am neither "moved of affection, meed or other "partial cause, as I take God to record, for I never knew nor saw "the parties, nor have to do with "any their friends, alliance, or acquaintance; but whether it be of "fatherly compassion, for I have "children of mine own, and one "much of that age, *vel nescio quo* "*spiritu ductus*, the remembrance of "this innocent hath caused me that "in my bed this night I could not "forbear to water my plants, having "in fresh remembrance what I knew "in King Henry the Seventh's "days was considered and alledged "touching the difference between "the King's laws and an instinct "and law that is in nature; when "Sir James Tyrell and Sir John "Wyndham were put to death, and "their sons upon that consideration "pardoned." State Papers, iv. 487, 8.

[4] "Etiamsi ducali aut alia dignitate quacumque præfulgeant." Rymer, xiii. 23.

heard that De la Pole had gone to the emperor. A month after his flight[1] Sir Charles Somerset and William Warham received power to treat with Maximilian; but it was not without months of delay and considerable haggling about the terms, that the treaty was thus concluded. Maximilian had so far pledged himself, in words at least, to De la Pole, that he could not immediately consent to order him out of his dominions, and he alleged that rebels could not be banished from the free towns of Germany without the consent of the electors. At last, however, the terms were agreed to, and Maximilian ratified the treaty at Augsburg, on the 28th of July. On the same 28th of July (the coincidence was not accidental) he signed an acquittance for 10,000*l.* received from Henry for prosecuting the war against the Turks.

The Turks. Only in the preceding year the pope himself had sought Henry's aid against the Turks in vain. Such aid did not appear uncalled for: the Turks were the dread of Christendom, and were no imaginary danger. If any thing could have made the nations of Europe combine for a common object it was the fear of them. For a century they had been steadily extending their conquests, and more particularly since the fall of Constantinople. They were by this time masters of about the same territory as at present, with the addition of Greece. In the course of the next 30 years they captured Rhodes and nearly dismembered Hungary. Their fleets scoured the Mediterranean. It was not certain that they might not ravage Italy, and even make the pope fly from Rome. From time to time attempts were made to combine against them the arms of Christian nations but without result. Christian princes were seldom at peace among themselves, and when they were, they did not trust each other. The pope at this time was

[1] On the 28th Sept. 1501. Rymer, xiii. 18.

the notorious Alexander VI., and however willing he might be to collect money for a crusade it was pretty certain he would not devote it to such an object. When he applied to Henry VII. for this purpose Henry mocked him with an answer worthy of Roman diplomacy itself, except that it was more honest in the transparency of its real meaning. He would be very sorry, he said, if the Turk came into Italy or disturbed the peace of Christendom; but for his own part, thank God! he was at peace with all Christian princes. It was very laudable in the pope to propose to go in person against the infidels with the help of France and Spain; Henry was sorry he was too far off to give assistance. It was quite right that Germans, Hungarians, Bohemians, and Poles should do their best, as they knew the mode of warfare of the Turks; but Henry's council were of opinion that England could do little good. The voyage between this country and Italy generally took the Venetian galleys seven months, and preparations could not be made for months to come.[1] Such were the excuses offered to the pope. It cannot be supposed that Henry had much greater confidence in Maximilian; but the 10,000*l.* he gave him were doubtless well laid out. It was very well known that the emperor was always in want of money, and that money was omnipotent with him. The 10,000*l.* was but the price of the treaty which was to deprive De la Pole of the power of doing harm.

Ferdinand's ambassador in Germany promises to secure Edmund De la Pole.

Henry had now reigned about seventeen years, and it was not for the interest of himself and his subjects only that he should remain in undisturbed possession of the throne. The alliance by which he had so greatly strengthened himself made it also a matter of interest to Ferdinand and Isabella, that nothing should be allowed

[1] Ellis' Letters, First Series, i. 49.

to interrupt the natural course of the succession. They accordingly wrote to their ambassador in Germany, Don Juan Manuel, to urge the emperor to expel De la Pole from his dominions, telling him that they considered it a thing that directly concerned themselves. Don Juan obeyed his instructions, and afterwards wrote to Spain, that he had made the matter safe. De la Pole was to be delivered to the ambassador by a certain day, and Ferdinand made arrangements for consigning him to the custody of his general Gonsalo Fernandes at Naples, until it was known what Henry wished to be done with him. The scheme, however, did not take effect, De la Pole made his escape from Germany, and Ferdinand was greatly displeased with his ambassador.[1]

France also was willing to serve Henry in this matter. Lewis XII. made a spontaneous offer to procure, by a bribe to certain friends in Germany, the delivery of De la Pole into Henry's hands. Matthew Baker was instructed to reply that the king did not hold De la Pole of any consequence, but would wish to have him "pour l'ounneur quil en peult advenir," and accordingly would be glad if his good brother would get him and as many of his followers as possible taken and handed over to him. For this he would not grudge 10,000 or 12,000 crowns of gold. It appears that at this time, June 1502, De la Pole, despairing of assistance from Maximilian, was going to seek it from the Count Palatine.[2]

De la Pole enters Gueldres.

About Easter, in the year 1504, the exile obtained permission from the Duke of Gueldres to enter his territory. His object, as he afterwards states in a letter to his brother, was to visit George duke of Saxony, at that time governor of Friesland, from whom he intended to ask aid to pay his debts. He was so

[1] Memorials of Henry VII., pp. 268 and 412.

[2] Lettres de Rois, &c. de France et d'Angleterre, ii. 514 sq.

hard beset by creditors, that he had been obliged to leave his brother Richard at Aix as a hostage. But instead of attaining this object he was made prisoner by the duke of Gueldres; and before getting finally released from his power, his debts, we may presume, were considerably augmented. Among his papers is a draft agreement in the handwriting of Killingworth (Art. XXXVIII.), by which the duke consents to set him at liberty on payment of 2,000 florins for the expenses he had incurred in Gueldres. It is evident this proposition was made, not by the duke but to him, and represents the terms that De la Pole was willing to submit to.

Little as this looks like over-friendly treatment, at first he appears to have been too well received, and James IV. of Scotland, whose own contingent interest in the English succession was endangered, thought it necessary, notwithstanding his old and cordial alliance with Gueldres, to write his mind to the duke in the following fashion:—

"First of all, you cursorily allude to what our servant Patrick Halyburton formerly demanded of you touching Edmund De la Pole, late earl of Suffolk, and you refer to copies of letters on this subject. This brevity is agreeable, that a tedious repetition may be avoided. You need not have excused the humbleness of the secretary, for the time required that a wary and reserved messenger should be sent . . . . . . Secondly, you relate your vigilance about the affair entrusted to you, for which we return you our best thanks. But you imply that the opportunity for accomplishing the thing well is over, this Edmund having gone over some time ago to the king of the Romans. We leave this for the present. Thirdly, about Easter, in the year 1504, you write that there came to you a servant of De la Pole, desiring that his lord might be permitted to reside in your dominions; which in your fourth article you plainly acknowledge that you readily granted, so that at this moment he freely inhabits your country. *Letter of James IV. to the duke of Gueldres.*

Herein, beloved kinsman, I may with the more freedom accuse you of violating your engagements; for you formerly promised

Letter of James IV. to the duke of Gueldres.

us in your letters that you would absolutely deny him your dominions, make proclamation every where against him, and severely punish any contravention of it. You allege as your reason for doing so, that having taken counsel, you expected it would be of great use to you with our father the king of England, to admit him within your bounds, so that a condition of peace might be procured by your mediation, for which he promised you full power and authority. What our opinion is understand in a few words. It is useless excusing yourself to men of experience with a feigned pretext of mediation; you make but a lame defence of your innocence. Nothing could justify you in departing from your promise for the sake of a perfidious man without consulting me to whom you had bound yourself, especially when De la Pole's inconstancy was already more than sufficiently known to you; to whom formerly, though a fugitive suppliant rebel, when he returned to England the king most mercifully forgave all his revolt. Therefore I tell you this as a thing most sure and certain. The king's prudence deigns not now either to recall De la Pole from his error, or to listen to any composition; that rebels by the infliction of the due punishment of treason may lay aside contumacy and impiety. He considers, besides, that it is neither compatible with kingly honour, nor is any prince accustomed to make peace with a subject. A king is merciful to a subject when he is worthy of pardon. So that either you have been inconsiderate, or, what I fain would rather believe, his coming to you was without permission, nor was any assurance given him that it should be with impunity, but by accident he has escaped your vigilance; and on this I congratulate you, and give you thanks.

You add, fifthly, that by the agency of De la Pole, in Gelderland, an armed band of about 6,000 foot has often met in your country under leaders, but for what object was unknown. You say that it was suspected they would turn their arms against England, and that you gave orders to the authorities at all your ports to prevent this, and that no fleet should be allowed to sail, warning De la Pole, at the same time that he should not fraudulently use the impunity extended to him in your dominions against the law of nations, nor attempt anything hostile against England, which would offend the bond of our relationship; and that satisfied with this, he desisted. In so far as you were serviceable in this matter, cousin, I owe you much; but you would have done better to have passed over the circumstance in silence, and not allowed a vain hope to carry you through tortuous ways. It is quite absurd in you to pretend, nor does it appear probable to us, that a needy man whom you supply with food keeps a thousand armed men in his pay. One of two things, I think you are attempting, either that the king of England through vain fear shall conciliate De la Pole, or that he shall expect to see him restored by your arms. It is nonsense talking of fear in a king hitherto unconquered, whose friendship the greatest princes eagerly embrace, and who by his bravery has repeatedly overcome, with great slaughter, strong bands of enemies; and as to restoring De la Pole in England, if you or the greatest prince of all Europe entertained such a notion, and if De la Pole had conspired to bring in a rebel, the enterprise might lead to greater difficulties, and be remembered for ages. Beware. This Edmund will deceive you by too much promising of friends; he, who lately, after actually returning, and being fully restored to his friends by the king, fled from his country and supporters in poverty and dearth of friends. I wish, therefore, you had refrained from empty threats, and talking of his boasted power.

In connection with this you say, in the sixth place, that from the needy poverty of De la Pole, you have sustained no small charges ever since he came to you, and that you will not be able to bear them longer, for the heavy expenses of war. Pray excuse me, illustrious cousin, if I deal not gently with you now. You treat kindly a rebel of England, an exile from the greater part of Christendom, to the disgust of your friends, and to the complication even of your own affairs, at a time when you ought to be conciliating princes rather than exasperating them. Is this what has come of our supplications? Is our bond of consanguinity at an end? Have your promises come to this? Over-trustful that I was! I represented you to my most illustrious father the king of England, as a well meaning and friendly prince: you openly declare yourself his enemy, and the sole refuge of his rebels. And for these egregious merits, forsooth, you demand, in the seventh place, that we should come to your succour against the great and powerful kings of the Romans and Castile, who for our sake ordered this Edmund, whom you cherish, away from their persons and their kingdoms. See, then, how you are your own enemy, how incompatible are the things you demand with what you do, and how justly they are refused to you; unless we were to be guilty of enmity against friends, ingratitude to those who deserve well of us, and perfidy towards allies. Which things, in as much as they are unworthy of kings, in so much are they adverse to your demands being complied with, and if they be true, alienate us from you entirely. Nor do we like to irritate against you the mind of our most excellent father with your useless figments, lest from your vain letters his wisdom think little of you, or from being a troublesome person should think you the more so, because you do not stand to your promises; because you thoughtlessly, and on frivolous grounds evade fulfilment of your pledges; because you boast the pretended power of De la Pole; who, if you permitted it, would by this time have wandered over the world in disguise, or have fallen long ago into the power of the king.

Do not think that we have written to you too harshly; it concerns the surest interest of our most illustrious father, our most serene brother, our most gentle wife. . . . . Whom if you love me, you will not regard otherwise . . . . But the unhappy De la Pole is an obstacle to our desires; so long as he is secure, you will never be conscious of our wealth, or of that of friends. Your hateful guest denies you arms, men, and money. Therefore, duke and kinsman, as soon as you can, get rid of this unhappy wretch, and strive yet to reconcile yourself to our most benevolent father, by the same way by which you have offended him, you may study to conciliate him. Send away that perfidious man who has made new attempts in your dominions without your orders, since he neither satisfies you nor his creditors, nor is bound by the law of nations; and if you abide honourably by your promise, we will strive to replace our mutual good will, and to moderate the violence offered to you."[1]

De la Pole is delivered up to Philip, king of Castile.

It was not an enviable lot, however, to be in the hands of the duke of Gueldres. Suffolk was confined in the town of Wageningen. He attempted to escape towards Thiel, but had not proceeded a mile before he was recaptured and brought back. He had still some hope of regaining his liberty through the medium of Philip, king of Castile, between whom and the duke of Gueldres arrangements were then making for a peace, but he had great misgivings. "The duke of Gueldres' "servants said plainly he would not come to the king

[1] Epistolæ Regum Scotorum, vol. i. pp. 11, sq. In January 1507, when De la Pole was safe in the Tower, and when Henry VII. was inclined to favor the Burgundians in their war with Gueldres, James threatened England with war if he should attack the duchy. Ib, p. 40.

"as long as the king of Romans is there, with great "words."[1] De la Pole, therefore, wrote urgently to Killingworth to see Philip at Brussels, and intreat him to get him "out of that man's hand." "And say "these words," he adds, "If I were in the furthest "end of the world I would be at his commandment "to fulfil his pleasure and commandment as any ser-"vant of his house."[2] On the 28th of July 1505, his wishes were partly accomplished. The peace was made, and the duke of Gueldres delivered him up along with the city of Hattem into the hands of the king of Castile. But only a few days later, his servant, the bastard of Oyskerk, writes to Killingworth that Philip had delivered him again into the hands of the duke to occupy his old quarters at Wageningen. This, however, appears to have been but an interim arrangement. De la Pole's chaplain and other servants could have access to speak with him, and he himself desired them not to be dissatisfied on his account.

About this time, probably, was written the paper which forms our No. XXXVI. It is a corrected draft in the handwriting of Killingworth, of a letter intended to be addressed to his master. It conveys excuses from some person unnamed, mentioned only as "your "friend," for not having communicated with De la Pole earlier, as he had hoped to send him news from England. This friend I take to have been one Paul Zachtlevent, who is mentioned by his Christian name in the latter part of the letter, a merchant of Amsterdam, born in Pomerania, who had given him pecuniary assistance. He sends De la Pole four ells of satin by a servant of his own rather than by De la Pole's chaplain, Sir Walter, who might have been stopped. "And "he bade me write to you," says Killingworth, "that

[1] Edmund De la Pole to Don Peter, Ellis' Letters, Third Series, i. 131.

[2] Page 253.

"touching you he heareth nothing but good." Nevertheless, as the writer was going to have hinted, he was not altogether satisfied about De la Pole's prospects; but on second thoughts the expression of suspicion was struck out of the letter. One thing, however, there was no concealing: it was all Killingworth could do to get him to furnish a gown for De la Pole and a gown and bonnet for Sir George Nevill. Concerning some further advances he had been asked to make for De la Pole's servants, and for payment of a debt to "the host in Zwolle," he hesitated to give an answer. We next come to a singular passage. Whether "Mr. Paul," who is now mentioned by name, be the friend above alluded to is not absolutely certain; but there can be no doubt he is the Paul Zachtlevent mentioned in another letter. This Paul, it appears, had lent money to Perkin Warbeck, whom he calls the duke of York; and in order to obtain repayment, he was reduced to two very unpromising alternatives. The first was to send in his claim to Henry VII., threatening, if the king did not discharge it, to give his utmost support to De la Pole; the second was, to obtain a certificate signed by De la Pole, that Perkin Warbeck was the true duke of York, on which he believed that the king of Denmark and the duke of Pomerania would grant him letters of marque against the English merchants.

A creditor of Perkin Warbeck.

The stipulation for De la Pole's ransom already mentioned is dated 24th of September 1505. He retired again into Philip's territory, and the next notice is a letter written by himself from Namur on the 17th of November.[1] It was but a change of keepers, for here too, he was in prison, the rigor of his confinement only mitigated by promises from Philip, to which, in

[1] Page 270.

his despair, he attached an unreal value.[1] Philip was then preparing to embark for his new kingdom of Castile, and De la Pole seems to have been anxious before he left to obtain some pecuniary relief for himself and his brother. He endeavoured to make friends with some of Philip's council. His old creditors at Aix were advised to wait upon the King of Castile. They returned empty-handed and again dunned his brother for their money. They threatened to proclaim Edmund to the world as a perjured promise-breaker, and gave significant hints to Richard that if he could not satisfy their claims they would sell him to King Henry. For the possession of his person, alive or dead, Henry was ready to pay them all that they demanded; and Richard feared to be seen in the streets of Aix, lest he should be seized and delivered up to some emissary of England. His brother sent Oyskerk and Killingworth to Philip to obtain a remedy; but several weeks passed away, and Richard was still in the same precarious situation. On the 4th of January following he wrote to his brother:—

Danger of Richard De la Pole at Aix.

"I have received your letter by Sir Thomas, the morrow after New Year's Day, by the which I have no comfort. And here I lie in great pain and poverty for your grace, and no manner of comfort I have of your grace or none other; nor none is coming, as far as I can see. Wherefore I pray God to send me out of this world. Sir, as for the matter that I sent you word of, ye sent me word ye could not do nothing therein because ye were in the King of Castile's hands; and the same answer I have made, and as soon as I have any word of it, I shall inform your grace thereof. Sir, I have put away all my folks, and the bringer hereof can show you what danger I am in. Sir, by my truth, ye deal very hardly with me, I being your brother, in many things. I know not what the meaning is, as God knoweth."[2]

---

[1] Page 276.

[2] Ellis' Letters, Third Series, i. 129, 130.

These are sad and painful words enough, but Edmund's fate was still more unhappy. The time was now at hand when the protection he had received from Philip was to be withdrawn, and himself delivered to his mortal enemy. Philip set sail in the beginning of January, and was driven by stress of weather to land in England. Henry took advantage of the accident to show him a little kingly hospitality, invest him with the garter, and obtain from him some concessions, of which one was the delivery of Edmund De la Pole. Unconscious of what awaited him, the prisoner at Namur meanwhile proposed making overtures to Henry for a reconciliation. Misfortune had not taught him humility. His commission to Killingworth and Griffith to treat on this subject, is worded in the style of a sovereign prince, and the object of it is stated to be to appease "the troubles that are in the "realm of England by reason that it standeth betwixt "the King of England and me as it doth." The terms on which he would condescend to receive the king's pardon were inconceivably extravagant. The earldom of Suffolk to which the king had limited him in the days of his loyalty was not enough for him now; he demanded the dukedom. The dukedom itself was not enough for him without the restoration of certain lands which Edward IV. had compelled his father to release to the college of Windsor. As it was possible Philip might wish to keep him in captivity, Henry himself was to use efforts for his liberation, and to respect the rights of his widow and daughter if he should die in prison. William De la Pole and his other adherents in England were to be set free. On these conditions he would consent to be the king's true subject.

Edmund De la Pole proposes to bargain for the king's pardon.

He is delivered up to Henry VII

While De la Pole was thus, within the walls of a prison at Namur, offering conditions of reconciliation to Henry, Philip in whose power he was, having been driven to land at Weymouth, was on this way to visit Henry at Windsor. The tempest which had cast him on the shores of England was one which the Londoners must have long remembered. The brazen eagle on the spire of St. Paul's cathedral was blown down, and in its fall battered to the ground the sign of the Black Eagle tavern in Cheapside. As the Emperor bore an eagle in his arms the omen was believed to point at him. It was considered to be accomplished in the ill fortune of his son who was thus assailed by tempest in going to his own kingdom, and who did not live long after he had arrived there. A close resemblance was not sought for between the portent and the event; but Edmund De la Pole was not unlike the meaner eagle brought down by the misfortune of the other. Being in England, Philip yielded to the personal influence of Henry, concessions which he would not have made elsewhere. He signed the commercial treaty long held in detestation by the Flemings as the *intercursus malus*, and shortly after consented to the extradition of De la Pole. A contemporary narrative of Philip's reception in England says that he offered this last without solicitation;[1] but it is much more likely, as stated by Hall and Polydore, that he consented only when he found no excuses would be accepted, and on a promise given by Henry that De la Pole's life should be spared.[2] That promise was not violated during the life of Philip or

[1] Memorials of Henry VII., p.302.

[2] Adrian de Croy writes to Maximilian 23rd March 1505-6 :— "Dautrepart, Sire, ledit Seigneur "roy votre filz s'est tellement "trouvé pressé du roy d'Angleterre "qu'il lui a convenu mectre en ses "mains monseigneur de Suffolc, "moyennant son appoinctement, "contenant entre autre choses aboli- "cion et pardon de tout ce qu'il puet "avoir mespris et offencé envers "ledit Seigneur roy d'Angleterre, "lequel a aussi promis et donné "son scelle de bien traictier icellui "seigneur de Suffolk toute sa "vie." Chmel's Urkunden zur Geschichte Maximilians I., p. 229.

during that of Henry himself; but an ugly tradition is preserved by lord Herbert of Cherbury, that Henry, before he left the world, recommended his son to do that which he had promised not to do himself. However this may be, the truth is that in the year 1513, when England was at war with France, and Richard De la Pole took service under the French king against his country, Edmund was sent to the block, apparently without having committed any new offence of his own.

**Killingworth's letters to Maximilian in his behalf.**

Thus the adventures of Edmund De la Pole came to an end: in March he was delivered up and lodged in the Tower. We hear no more of him in these papers except that his faithful Killingworth still continued to do for him what yet remained in his power, still hoping, from the promises of the emperor, that some arrangement might be made with Henry for his liberation. To this end he writes to Maximilian in very miserable Latin:—"As to my fidelity to the said lord "duke, I remit myself to your sacred Majesty, because I "have proved it well to the knowledge of your sacred Majesty for six whole years, and now I am in the "seventh year; and under correction of your Majesty, "that is sufficient trial for a man; and I have served "my said lord duke for 20 years, which is not a "small period. And for the service of my said lord "duke I have left my wife, friends, and goods, which, "though it be an unnatural thing, grieves me little, "but the evil fortune of my said lord duke grieves "me very much."[1]

Richard De la Pole was more fortunate, because more politic, than his brother. We cannot trace his history minutely, but it appears that the year after Edmund's being delivered up, he took refuge in Hungary. On the 18th April, 1507, he writes from Buda to Erard

[1] Page 312.

De la Marck, bishop of Liege, to thank him for some measures he was taking in behalf of his brother.[1] A few years later we find him, as already mentioned, in the service of France. He was looked upon as one of the most distinguished of the French captains, and fell, with the flower of their army, at the battle of Pavia, where Francis I. was taken prisoner, in 1525.

The papers from which most of the above information is derived are a portion of the correspondence of Suffolk and his steward Killingworth, which appears to have found its way into the hands of Henry the Seventh. Some of them perhaps may have been seized when Suffolk himself was sent prisoner to England in 1506; but I am more inclined to think that the whole correspondence was seized at a later period. They are almost all letters addressed to Killingworth or copies in his hand; and the later letters of Killingworth to the emperor are drafts in his hand also.

**The Low Countries after the death of Philip.**

One subject now mainly occupies the short remainder of the reign. The relations, commercial and political, between England and the Low Countries, have at this time a peculiar interest. The death of Philip in 1506 left those provinces defenceless against France, and threw the government of Castile again into the hands of Ferdinand. Philip's eldest son, afterwards Charles V., was then only six years old, and it was necessary for the States to appoint a regent; his widow Joanna was queen of Castile in her own right, but, owing to her unhappy mental debility, unfitted to reign. During the life of Philip, France and Arragon had combined to disturb his government in both parts of his dominions; on his death Castile became an easy prey to Ferdinand, and the Low Countries, which were perpetually suffering from French interference, expected renewed aggressions. Charles of Gueldres and Robert De la

[1] Ellis' Letters, Third Ser., i. 141.

Marck made inroads and ravaged them with the connivance of Lewis XII. Henry VII. was looked to for his support, both by Philip and Maximilian; but though he sent Francis Marsin to dissuade Lewis from countenancing Gueldres,[1] he had recommended to Philip that the disputes should be arranged by the arbitration of himself and Lewis.[2] In his view the true policy was to conciliate France, and he had good cause to interest himself in the government of the Low Countries. A marriage was at that time arranged between him and Margaret of Savoy, Philip's sister, who on her brother's death was appointed regent of the Netherlands. Her father, Maximilian, thought highly of the match and recommended it to her by several arguments. She herself made objections, but it does not appear that the project was ever abandoned on the part of England; for only half a year before Henry's death no less a person than Thomas Wolsey was sent over to the Netherlands to promote it.

Wolsey's negotiations.

There is a marvellous story told by Cavendish of Wolsey's being employed by Henry VII. on a mission to the emperor, which he accomplished with such expedition as to return to the court at Richmond on the third night after his despatch How far this may be an exaggeration, we cannot say; but Bernard André notes in his Annals of Henry VII., that on the 8th August 1508, a messenger returned from Calais with remarkable celerity.[3] There are, among the Cottonian MSS, a number of papers in Wolsey's own hand, relating to a mission of his on the matter above referred to. Unfortunately they are so burnt about the margins that, between the difficulty of the handwriting and the mutilation, it is impossible to extract any meaning from a mere perusal of the MSS. themselves. A record, how-

---

[1] Lettres de Louis XII., t. i. 78

[2] Page 298.

[3] Memorials of Henry VII., p. 127.

ever, of negotiations by Wolsey at this early period, appeared to me too interesting to be given up without some effort to make it intelligible. I transcribed it line for line, leaving blanks where the original was mutilated or presented doubtful readings. By comparison of one paper with another I found much that was lost was capable of being supplied. At last I was able to ascertain that the whole budget belonged to the months of October and November 1508, and had reference to the conferences then held preparatory to the treaty of Cambray.[1]

In the beginning of that year[2] was sent over to England in embassy from Margaret of Savoy, George de Theimseke, provost of Cassel, whom Sir Thomas More a few years later met at Bruges, and mentions in his Utopia as a man of great eloquence, learning, and experience in affairs. His letters to Margaret printed in this volume show that he was urgent to procure the armed interposition of England against France and Gueldres; but he could not prevail. He found Henry and his council were determined not to go to war; he told Margaret they must depend upon themselves alone, and suggested that he could probably do her better service at home than attempting to make friends of the friends of fortune. In point of fact, Henry wished them to make peace with France, and thought this course would be politic for themselves. He told the provost that France was far too strong to be successfully resisted, and that if he could advise the emperor he would show him a thing which would be

[1] Lord Bacon, who mentions this mission of Wolsey, probably saw these papers, for many of the facts in his history of Henry VII. are derived from the MSS. in his friend, Sir Robert Cotton's library. It is to be regretted he did not give them more attention, as they were then unmutilated. In a marginal note of that age they are erroneously dated 1504.

[2] He arrived in London on the 3rd of February 1508.—Bern. André, Memorials of Henry VII., p. 108.

much more to his advantage. He could tell him how, as guardian of his grandson Charles, he might obtain the entire administration of Castile, where Ferdinand's authority was regarded as a usurpation; but he declined to tell the means to any but the emperor himself. Those means, however, appeared a little later, when Edmund Wingfield, the English Ambassador, advised Margaret to endeavour, during the conferences at Cambray, to loosen the bond between Lewis XII. and the king of Arragon which, so long as it existed, preserved the latter in the government of Castile. If this policy had taken effect and Henry had lived a little longer, there can be no doubt it would have given him a footing in Spain; for, as Bacon truly says, " as for Maximilian, upon twenty respects, he could " not have been the man."

It was at this time Wolsey was sent over to the Low Countries. His instructions were to communicate with a person who is always mentioned in the despatches by the name of A., concerning whom we discover that he was an ecclesiastic, had considerable influence with the emperor, and held benefices in England. These facts enable us to identify him pretty safely with the bishop of Gurk, who was one of the emperor's council, and to whom Henry had granted the archdeaconry of Surrey. Gurk was going to take part in the conferences of Cambray, where many things were to be determined affecting not only France and the empire, but the whole of Europe. Henry hoped, through his means, to obtain the government of the Low Countries, and promised, in the event of his success, to give him the principal control there. To cement the political alliance Henry proposed to give his daughter Mary to the young archduke Charles, and to marry her aunt the regent himself. If Gurk could bring these two marriages to take effect, the king would give him new benefices in England to the value of 1,000 nobles a year. The papers relating to these negotiations will be found in Appendix B. (No. VI.)

This was not the first mission in which Wolsey had been engaged by Henry VII. Though the fact appears to be unknown, he was sent to James IV. of Scotland in the spring of the same year in which he was sent to Gurk. The object was to keep James true to his alliance with England, for Scotland at that time showed a considerable disposition to be troublesome. Contrary to the treaties, ambassadors passed and repassed through England, without demanding Henry's safe conduct, to Gueldres and other countries which England had no reason to regard with favour. The Earl of Arran and his brother, Sir Patrick Hamilton, had thus passed through to France. On their return, Henry ordered them to be detained in London, under such very lenient custody that they were banqueted by the lord mayor and one of the sheriffs. Sir Patrick Hamilton himself wrote to Margaret that the earl had been well treated, but he reported the contrary to James, and James would listen to no explanations. A despatch written by Wolsey, from Scotland, upon this subject, has already been printed by Pinkerton,[1] but is erroneously attributed by him to Dr. West, the historian, not being aware that the MS. from which he printed was in Wolsey's handwriting.

I have found other evidence of this mission of Wolsey's in a panegyric afterwards written upon the cardinal when he was in the height of his greatness. A MS. poem[2] which describes his rise in the style of a prophecy contains these lines:—

" Illum purpuream princeps cum accerset ad aulam
Septimus Henricus, sæcli laus prima futuri,
Præficietque sui rebus majoribus orbis;

[1] Hist. of Scotland, ii. 445.

[2] Royal MS. 12 A. lxii., Brit. Mus.

Usque adeo ut quondam transmiserit inclyta ad agri
Regna Caledonii legatum, fœdera sanctæ
Confirmaturum pacis, quo rex Iăcobus
Tempore fulva manu gestabit sceptra potenti."

In commenting upon the historical materials for this reign it may seem an omission to pass over in silence the extortions of Empson and Dudley, and the misguided statesmanship whose paramount object was to make the crown rich and powerful. About this well known blot in Henry's reign our letters and papers are silent, but the evidences of it may be found among the records of the Exchequer. The abuse is also, with others of which we have seen some specimens, very pointedly alluded to by More in his Utopia:[1]—

"But what (said he) if I should sort with another kind of ministers, whose chief contrivances and consultations were, by what art treasure might be heaped up? Where one proposes . . . . . . . . Another proposes a pretence of war that so money may be raised in order to the carrying it on, and that a peace might be concluded as soon as that was done; and this was to be made up with such appearances of religion as might work on the people, and make them impute it to the piety of their prince, and to his tenderness of the lives of his subjects. A third offers some old musty laws that have been antiquated by a long disuse, and which, as they had been forgotten by all the subjects, so they had been also broken by them; and that the levying of the penalties of those laws, as it would bring in a vast treasure, so there would be a very good pretence for it, since it would look like the executing of law and the doing of justice."

[1] The value of this notable work, in connection with Tudor history, has never been sufficiently recognized. The character there given of Cardinal Morton (the only portrait we possess of Henry's great minister), and the discussions on the principal evils of the time and the means to mend them, not to mention the illustration afforded by the very plan and subject of the work, of the influence of a newly discovered world upon men's thoughts and imagination, render the Utopia really one of the most important historical monuments of this dark period.

It is time now to leave these letters and papers to tell their own tale. Those in the present volume are necessarily an imperfect collection; but they will be found to contain most important documents in the British Museum and other public repositories in this country, which had not before been edited. Others of no less interest will be given in a second volume. The collection of materials so dispersed, has been a work of difficulty, and the search for them has not always been satisfactory. In some cases papers, known once to have existed, are not now to be found.[1] Sometimes two portions of the same MS. were found apart from each other—even in different volumes. Imperfect, however, as this attempt may be, the editor cannot but hope that his labours will have done something to redeem from neglect and confusion original sources of information touching an important period of English history.

I must not omit to state that I am indebted to Sir Charles Young, Garter King of Arms, for calling my attention to the description of Edward the Fourth's funeral, which forms the first article in this volume.

---

[1] In a catalogue of documents in the State Paper Office, compiled in the 17th century (Addit. MS. 11, 593, Brit. Mus.) are notices of some letters not known to be now extant. Among others the following:—

"A letter of Mr. Svile (*sic*, for Stile), the king's Ambassador with the king of Arragon touching the king's marriage with the lady Katherine, his brother's widow, Anno 1505." (N.B. This description is evidently from an endorsement of Henry VIII.'s time.)

"A letter of Perkin Warbeck, in the name of Richard, one of the sons of the Duke of Clarence, directed to the Earl of Desmond in Ireland, to come into Scotland to his assistance" (also mentioned by Ware).

"A letter from Mr. Molesworth, the king's agent at Rome, to king Henry VII."

## CHRONOLOGICAL TABLE OF CONTENTS,

### WITH NOTICES OF SOME ORIGINAL LETTERS PRINTED IN OTHER PUBLICATIONS.

Page

A.D. 1483.

26 Aug. XII. From the duke of Britanny. Instructions to George de Mainbier, to show the king of England, that the duke will send an ambassador about All Saints' day, after the meeting of the Estates of Britanny; that depredations are committed at sea on his subjects by the English; that Lewis XI. threatens him with war if he do not give up to him the earl of Richmond; and that the duke requires the aid of a body of English archers . . . . . 37

[Aug.] *Ellis' Letters, Second Ser.* I. 156.—Lord Dynham to the lord Chancellor. Death of Lewis XI. Campaign of the archduke Maximilian in the Netherlands, — surrender of Utrecht. The king should have a fleet between Dover and Calais, &c. [MS. Harl. 433, f. 233 b.]

XIII. Government of Ireland. Instructions to William Lacy sent to Ireland. Edward the king's son to be lieutenant of Ireland, and Kildare his deputy . . . . . 43

XIV. Custody of Guisnes Castle. Instructions to lord Dynham and others. Sir Ralph Hastings to deliver to them the town and castle of Guisnes. Mountjoy to have the keeping of it . . 46

XV. Answer to the message of Isabella of Castile. Instructions to Bernard De la Forssa. England proposes a renewal of the league made between Edward IV. and Henry IV. of Castile . . 48

16 Aug. XVI. James III. to Richard III. Proposing to send an embassy to treat of peace . . 51

16 Sept. XVII. Richard III. to James III. Offering a safe conduct for his ambassadors . . . 53

9 Sept. *Rymer*, XII. 200. Richard III. to Isabella of Spain. Sends Bern. de la Forssa to her upon the business for which she sent Sasiola. [MS. Harl. 433, f. 246 b.]

9 Sept. *Rymer*, XII. 201. Same to Peter de Mendoza, cardinal of Toledo, on the same subject,—and a similar letter to the bishop of Palencia. [MS. Harl. 433, f. 246.]

10 Sept. *Rymer*, XII. 201. Same to Count Haro (whose name Rymer has omitted to print), on the same subject.—And a similar letter to the Count Leryn. [*ib.*]

A.D. 1483. Page

12 Sept. *Rymer*, XII. 202. Same to Ferdinand of Spain. On the same subject. [MS. Harl. 433, f. 245 b.]

12 Sept. *Rymer*, XII. 202. Same to Isabella. On the same subject. [*ib.*]

6 Nov. *Ellis, Third Ser.* I. 109. James III. to Richard III. In answer to XVII. Sends the names of the lords whom he wishes to send in embassy; and proposes an abstinence of war till the 15th of March. [MS. 433, f. 248 b.]

12 Oct. *Ellis, Second Ser.* I. 159. Richard III. to the bishop of Lincoln. Requiring him to send or bring the Great Seal. [Rec. Off.]

2 Dec. *Ellis, Third Ser.* I. 111. Richard III. to James III. Sends the safe conduct. The abstinence must be deferred until the coming of the embassy. [Harl, 433, f. 248 b.]

22 Nov. XVIII. The duke of Britanny's warrant to

A.D. 1484. advance money to the earl of Richmond . . 54

18 Jan. *Rymer*, XII. 210. Letter of the Emperor Frederick III. in favour of Nicholas de Poplâir. [MS. Harl. 433, f. 255.]

10 Feb. *Ib.* 211. Richard III. to John Maximilian Sforza duke of Milan, in favour of Gulielmus and Nicholaus de Ariotis, who wish to return to Milan, their brother Germanus being dead. [*Ib.* f. 249.]

*Ib.* 212. Same to Ludovico Maria Sforza duke of Bari. On the same subject. [*Ib.* 250.]

29 Feb. *Ib.* 214. Same to the Pope. Sends Thomas [Langton] bishop of St. David's to inform him touching his elevation to the throne. Recommends John Sherwood to be bishop of Durham. [*Ib.* 250 b.]

2 Mar. *Ib.* 216. Richard III. to the Pope. Requesting him to make Sherwood a Cardinal. [*Ib.* f. 254.]

2 Mar. *Ib.* 217. Same to the Cardinals. On the same matter. [*Ib.* f. 254 b.]

9 Mar. *Ib.* 220. Same to the Pope. Credentials for Langton, bishop of St. David's, the archdeacon of Richmond (Sherwood) and John Dunmow, Canon of Windsor. [*Ib.* f. 252 b.]

A.D. 1484. Page

10 Mar. *Rymer*, XII. 220. Same to Cardinal St. George. Thanks for his letters of congratulation on his accession, &c. [*Ib.* f. 251.]

10 Mar. *Ib.* 221. Same to Cardinal St. Mark. Thanks for the favour he bears to Sherwood as expressed in his letters of the 20th Jan. [*Ib.*]

10 Mar. [1484?] *Halliwell's Letters*, I. 153. Circular of Richard III. to the bishops for the suppression of immorality. [*Ib.* f. 281.]

11 Mar. *Rymer*, XII. 221. Richard III. to Charles VIII. Credence for the bishop of St. David's. [*Ib.* f. 251 b.]

31 Mar. *Ib.* 244. Same to the Pope. The bishop of Durham has to protect the realm against the Scots. In one castle 100 soldiers must be kept even in peace. The king begs therefore that he may be released from payment of a portion of the first fruits. [*Ib.* f. 252 b.]

31 Mar. *Ib.* 225. Same to the Cardinal. To the same effect. [*Ib.* f. 253.]

13 April. XIX. Instructions to Northumberland herald to arrange an abstinence of war between England and Scotland . . . . . . 55

July. XX. Regulations for the Council of the North, under the earl of Lincoln as president, for preserving impartiality, &c. The council to sit at York at least once a quarter, and take cognisance of all offences against the peace . . . . 56

21 July. XXI. James III. to Richard III. Naming his ambassadors, who are to be at Nottingham on the 7th Sept. . . . . . 59

7 Aug. XXII. Richard III. to James III. Sending a safe conduct for the embassy . . . . 61

9-14 Sept. XXIII. Reception of the Scotch Ambassadors at Nottingham . . . . . . 63

Sept. XXIV. Message to the earl of Desmond. Instructions to the bishop of Enachden to tell him how his father's services to the king's father, Richard duke of York, are appreciated, &c. 67

XXV. Message to the earl of Kildare and other lords. Instructions to the bishop of Enachden to tell Kildare how O'Neil and O'Donnell shall be dealt with touching the earldom of Ulster. Desmond to wear English clothing, &c. . 71

A.D. 1484. Page

Oct. XXVI. Instructions to Sir Marmaduke Constable, steward of the honour of Tutbury. Measures against retaining, giving liveries, extortion of bailiffs, subletting the king's lands, &c. . 79

XXVII. "A remembrance made" for the more speedy collection of the revenue and better administration of Crown lands . . . 81

5 Dec. *Halliwell's Letters*, I. 151 (Translation). Richard III. to Leonard de Prato. Permitting him to come to England for the visitation of the Order of St. John. [Harl. 433, f. 272 b.]

Dec. XXVIII. Preparations for defence. Instructions to commissioners appointed in every county to muster and review men for the king's service . 85

7 Dec. [Not printed. See 23 June 1485.] Proclamation against the earl of Richmond's adherents. [Harl. 433, f. 273 b.]

8 Dec. XXIX. Richard III. to the dean and chapter of Salisbury. Recommending them to elect Langton bishop of St. David's as their bishop . 87

1485. 22 June. *Halsted's Richard III.*, vol. ii. p. 560. Instructions to commissioners of array in every shire. [Harl. 433, f. 220.]

22 June. *Ib.* p. 562. Letters to sheriffs to reside at their shire towns. [Ib. f. 220 b.]

23 June. *Ib.* p. 563; and *Fenn's Letters*, II. 318. Renewal of the proclamation of 7 Dec. preceding. [Imperfect in MS. Harl. 433. f. 220 b.]

## Henry VII.

1486? I. Instructions to John Estrete, sent to the earl of Kildare to require his presence in England, the king desiring to have his advice upon the government of Ireland . . . . 91

1486. (circa) App. B. No. I. Heads of an oration to be made by the English ambassador at Rome to the pope and cardinals . . . . 421

1487? 13 May. *Halliwell's Letters*, I. 171. Henry VII. to the earl of Ormond on the landing of the rebels in Ireland. [Titus, B. xi. f. 24.]

A.D. 1497. Page

12 Sept. *Ellis, First Ser.* I. 32. Henry VII. to Sir Gilbert Talbot. Perkin has landed in Cornwall. Orders Sir Gilbert to be at Woodstock without delay "with six score tall "men on horseback."

17 Sept. VIII. Sir Henry Wentworth to Sir William Calverley. News of Warbeck's landing in Cornwall . . . . . . . 112

18 Sept. *Ellis, First Ser.* I. 36. The earl of Devonshire to Henry VII. Account of the siege of Exeter by Warbeck.

20 Sept. *Ellis, First Ser.* I. 34. Henry VII. to the bishop of Bath and Wells. The siege of Exeter.

17 Oct. *Halliwell's Letters*, I. 175. Henry VII. to the city of Waterford. Of Warbeck's attempt on Exeter, &c. [Lamb. MS. 632, f. 251 b.]

23 Oct. *Archæol.* XXVII. 209. Henry VII. to De Puebla. [Egerton 616.]

3 Dec. *Wood's Royal and Illust. Ladies*, I. 114. Eliz. queen of Henry VII. to Isabella of Spain.

1498. App. B. No. III. Norroy's mission to James IV. 424

1499. App. B. No. IV. Despatches of Warham and Hatton relative to the commerce with the Netherlands . . . . . . . 425

15 June. IX. The cardinal of Sienna to Henry VII. On the promotion of Thomas Jane to the bishopric of Norwich. Rhodes threatened by the Turk, &c. . . . . . . . 112

15 June. X. Henry VII. to Ferdinand and Isabella. Thanking them for comprising England in their treaty with France . . . . . 110*

1 Aug. XI. Elizabeth queen of Henry VII. to Ferdinand II. of Spain. Recommending Henry Still, who desires to serve him against the Infidels . 111*

Sept. XVII. Private instructions to Sir Richard Guildford and Richard Hatton, to urge Edmund De la Pole to return to England . . 129

[Date?] App. B. No. V. Instructions to Richmond king of arms sent to Maximilian and Philip . . 425

1500. 11 Jan. XII. De Puebla to Ferdinand and Isabella. The tranquillity of England established; the Scotch marriage; the expected arrival of Catherine, &c. . . . . . . 113

# NOTE.

## DE PUEBLA'S CIPHER, pp. 114, 115.

By the kindness of Mr. Bergenroth at Simancas I am enabled to present the reader with a key to the words in cipher in De Puebla's despatch of the 11 Jan. 1500.

Page.
114. dcclxxv., an error for dccclxxv., *vuestras altezas*,—your highnesses.
115. mccxviij°., *la fija del Rey de los Romanos*,—(Margaret) daughter of the King of the Romans.
,, dccccxxj., *el Rey de Escocia*,—the King of Scotland.
,, mdxxxix., Milan.
,, dcc°lxxx°j., *el Rey de Francia*,—the King of France.

# CORRIGENDA.

Page 9, l. 14, alter [3] to [1] in reference to foot note.
72, l. 4, *dele* "said" repeated.
92, l 15, *for* "this" *read* "his."
95, l. 9, *dele* comma after "potificalesve."
118, l 11 of text and l. 12 of translation, *for* "Pantales" *read* "Pantaleon."
124, l 15, *for* "sul" *read* "sus."
136, marginal note, *for* "500" *read* "5000."
229, last line of text, *dele* hyphen.
230, l. 6, *for* "Reuntu" *read* "Renntn."
327, l. 2 from bottom of text and of translation, *for* "Baenst" *read* "Baeust."

# LETTERS AND PAPERS

ILLUSTRATIVE OF THE

# REIGNS OF RICHARD III. AND HENRY VII.

# LETTERS, ETC.

## I.

### Funeral of Edward the Fourth.

[MS. I. 7. f. 7. College of Arms.]

Here foloith the Ordenaunces which shalbe done in the observaunce at the deth and buryall of a annoynted king.

When that a king annoynted ys deceassed, after his body spurged, it most be washed and clensed by a bishop for his holy annoyntment. Then the body most be bamed, if it may be goton, and wraped in lawne or reynes, then hosen shertes and a pair of shone of redde lether, and do over hym his surcote of clothe, his cappe of estat over his hede, and then laie hym on a faire burde covered with clothe of gold, his one hand upon his bely, and a septur in the other hand, and on his face a kerchief, and so shewid to his nobles by the space of ij. days and more if the weder will it suffre. And when he may not goodly lenger endure, take hym away, and bowell hym and then eftsones bame hym, wrappe hym in raynes well trameled in cordis of silke, then in tartryne trameled, and then in velvet, and then in clothe of gold well trameled; then lede hym and coffre hym, and in his lede with hym a plait of his still, name and date of our, &c. And if ye care hym, make a ymage like hym, clothed in a surcote with mantill of estat, the laices goodly lyeng on his bely, his septur in his hand, and his crown on his hede, and so carry him in a chair opon, A.D. 1483. April.

A.D. 1483. April. with lightes, baners, accompanyed with lordys and estates as the counsaill can best devyse, havyng the horse of that chair traped with dyvers trapers, or els with blacke trapers with scochons richely beten, and his officers of armes abowt hym in his cottes of armes. And then a lord or a knyght with a courser traped of his armes upon hym, his salet or basnet on his hede crowned, a shilde and a spere tyll he come to his place of his entring. And at the masse the same to be offered by noble princes.

But when that noble king, Edward the iiij., was deceased at Westminster in his palais, which was the x[1] day of Aprell, the xxiij yere of his reigne, first the corps was laide upon a burde, all naked saving he was covered from the navyll to the kneys, and so laie x. or xij ours that all the lordys bothe spirituall and temporall, then being in London or nere ther abowt, and the maier of London with his brether sawe hym so lying. And then he was sered, and so brought into the chapell on the morne after, wher were songon thre solempne masses; the first of Our Lady, the ij[de] of the Trenitie, the thrid of requiem (the which was songon by the bishop of Chechestre). And at after none ther were songon diriges and commendacions. And after that he had the holl sawter said by his chapell; and at nyght well wached with nobles and other his servauntes, whose names appere in the wache roll, from the first nyght unto the tyme his [body[2]] was buryed. And at the masse of requiem the lord Dacre, the quenes chaumberlain, offred for the quene; and the lordys temporall offred daily at the same masse, but the lordys spirituall offred not to the bishop but to the high auter, and other the kinges servantes offred also. This order was kept in the palais

[1] Edward died on the 9th. The writer appears to have made an error of one day throughout in his computation of the days of the month.

[2] Om. in MS.

viij dais, saving after the first day ther was but one solempne masse wich alwais was songon by a bishop. A.D. 1483. April.

And on the Wednesday the xvij[1] day of the moneth aforesaid, the corps was conveyed into the abbey, borne by divers knyghtes and esquiers at were for his bodye; that is to saie, Sir Edward Standley, Sir John Savage, Sir Thomas Worthley, Sir Thomas Mullineux, Wellys,[2] John Cheyny, maister of the kinges horse, Water Hongerford, Guy of Wolston, John Sabacotes, Thomas Tyrell, John Riseley, Thomas Dacre, John Noreys, Boys de Brytaill, Christofer Colyns, having upon the corps a riche and a large clothe of gold with a crosse of white clothe of gold above, above that a riche canape of clothe imperiall frynged with gold and blewe silk, borne by Sir Thomas Seintleger, Sir William A Parre, comptroller, Sir John Assheley, and Sir William Stoner, knightes; and at every corner abaner, the first of the Trenite, the which was borne by Sir Henry Ferris, the seconde of Our Lady, borne by Sir Jamys Radcliff, the thrid of Saint George, borne by Sir George Browne, the iiij of Saint Edward borne by Sir Gilbert Debynham. And the lord Haward[3] bare the kinges baner next before the corps amonges the officers of armes, wher was ordened a worthy herse, like as it apperteneth, having before hym a great procession, and the archibishop of Yorke,[4] chancelor of England, the bishop of London,[5] the bishop of Chestre,[6] the bishop of Bathe,[7] the bishop of Chechestre,[8] the bishop of Norwiche,[9] the bishop of Durham,[10] the bishop of Lyncolne,[11] the

---

[1] 16th. The 17th was a Thursday.

[2] Christian name omitted.

[3] John Howard, afterwards created duke of Norfolk by Richard III. on his accession.

[4] Thomas Scott or Rotherham.

[5] Thomas Kemp.

[6] That is to say, of Coventry and Lichfield, Chester not being at that time a see. His name was John Halse or Hales.

[7] Robert Stillington.

[8] Edward Story.

[9] James Goldwell.

[10] William Dudley.

[11] John Russell, afterwards chancellor.

A.D. 1483. April. bishop of Ely,[1] the bishop of Rochestre,[2] the abbot of Awendon, the abbot of Barmsey. Thise lordys foloed the corps and abowt the corps, being then ther the erle of Lincolne,[3] the marques Dorset,[4] the erle of Huntyndon,[5] the vicecounte Barkley,[6] the lord Standeley,[7] stward, &c., the lord Hastinges and the kinges chamberlain, the lord Dacre the queenes chaumberlain, the lord Dudley, the lord of Burgenye, the lord Audeley, the lord Ferrys,[8] the lord Lysley,[9] the lord Morley, Sir Richard Wodvile, Sir Edward Wodvile, the lord Cobham, the lord Wellys, Sir John Bourser, Sir Thomas Bourser and Sir Thomas Bowser, of Barneys; which lordys were [in][10] the herse that service, and on the morne also the service at Westmestre, was done by the archbishop of Yorke. And at the masse the abbot of Barmsey was dekon. And in that herse abowt the corps and the clothe of gold above said there was a personage like to the symilitude of the king in habet royall crowned with the crown oon his hede, holding in the one hand a septur, and in the other hand a ball of silver and gilt with a crosse pate. And after that the lordys that were within the herse and bishops had offred, the maier of London [11] offred, next after hym the chief juges and other juges, and knyghtes of the kinges howse with the barons of the eschequier and aldermen of London, as the nyght weyned too. And when the masse was done, and all other solempnitie,

[1] John Morton, afterwards Cardinal Morton.

[2] Edmund Audley.

[3] John Dela Pole, son of John duke of Suffolk by Elizabeth sister of Edward IV.

[4] Thomas Grey, stepson of Edward IV.

[5] William Herbert, created by Edward IV.

[6] William de Berkeley, created by Edward IV.; afterwards created earl of Nottingham by Richard III.

[7] Thomas Stanley, created by Henry VII. earl of Derby.

[8] Walter Devereux, lord Ferrers of Chartley.

[9] Edward Grey, second son of Edward lord Grey of Groby. He was created a viscount by Richard III., on his accession.

[10] Om. in MS.

[11] Edmund Shaw, goldsmith.

and the lordys were redy for to ryde, ther was ordened a royall chair covered with blacke velvet, having above that a blacke clothe of gold, with a white crosse of gold, under that a blacke magestie, clothe of sarsenet drawen with vj coursers traped with blacke velvet, with certein scochons beton upon sarcenet with fyne[1] upon the fore horse, and the thil horse sat ij chariot men, and on the iiij other horse sat iiij horsemen. On either syde of the forsaid draught went dyvers knyghtes and esquiers for the body and other, summe leyng ther handes to the draught and somme leding the horse in tyme thei passed the townes. And the lord Haward, the kinges banerer, rode next befor the forhorse, bering the kinges baner upon a courser traped with blacke velvet with dyvers scochons of the kinges armes, with his morning hode upon his hede. A.D. 1483. April.

When the corps, with the personage as above, with procession of bishoppes *in pontificalibus* and the iiij order of freris, was conveyd to the chair, and in order as above, to Charing, wher the bishoppes sensed the chair, and the lordys toke ther horses and so proceded to Syon that nyght, wher at the chirche dore the bishoppes sensed the corps, and the corps and the personage was borne as before into the quere, and ther the bishop of Durham dyd the service; and on the moro in like order as above he was conveyed to the chair, and from thens to Wyndesor, wher, at Eton, the bishop of Lincolne and the bishop of Ely, with the colege, met and sensed the corps; and so proceded to the castell by the way at the brigge, and met the procession of Wyndesor at the castell gate. Tharchibishop of Yorke and the bishop of Wynchestre sensed the corps, being ther with the bishop of Norwiche, the bishop of Duresme, the bishop of Rochestre, with the chanons of the colege and the kinges chapell, and so proceded to the new chirche.

---

[1] Sic in MS.

A.D. 1483. April. wher in the quere was ordened a mervelus well wrought herse, and furthwith dirige, and in the evening thei of the colage said the holl sawter. And ther was a great wache that nyght by great lordys, knyghtes, esquiers for the body, gentilmen usshers and other whose names ensue, &c. First, within the horse,[1] the lord of Burgeyne, the lord Audeley, the lord Morley, the lord Lysley, the lord Haward, the lord Wellis, the lord Lawar, the lord FitzHugh, the lord Cobbam, Sir John of Arundell, Sir Thomas Bourser of Barneyse, knyghtes; without the herse, Sir Thomas Seintleger, Sir Gilbert Debeham, Sir Herry Ferris, Sir John Savage, Sir Edward Standeley, Sir Thomas Wortley, Sir Thomas Mullineux, Sir William Parker, Sir William Stoner; esquiers for the body, John Cheyne, maister of the horse, William Barkley, William Odall, Robert Poyntz, John Riseley, Lois de Brytails, Antone Malyverer, John Sabacotes; gentilmen usshers, William Colyngborne, Edward Hargill, Bassett,[2] Nicholas Cromer, William Mydilton, Christofer Colyns, William Clifford; officers of armes, Garter[3] and Norrey[4] kinges of armes, Glocestre, Ruigecrosse, Gynys, Harington pursyvauntes; esquiers of howsehold, Thomas Mortymer, Dymmok,[2] Redmell Delamere, Edmond Gorgis; yemen usshers, William Rider, Roger Chelsall, George Cheyne, James Pemberton, with dyvers and many yemen of the crowne and of the chaumber and howsehold which held torchies.

And on the moro after the commendacions began the masse of Our Lady songon by the bishop of Duresme; at which masse Sir Thomas Bourser offred the masse peny because their was no greater estat present, and after hym all other as were in the herse. After that masse was done began the masse of the Trenitie songon

[1] Sic in MS.
[2] Christian name omitted.
[3] John Wrythe.
[4] John Moore.

by the bishop of Lincolne; at which masse therl of Huntyndon offred the masse peny, and after hym other lordys and nobles as above. At the begyning of the masse of requiem, which was songon by the archbishop of Yorke, the officers of armes went to the vestry, wher thei receyved a riche embrothered cote of armes, which Garter king of armes held with a great reverence as he cowd with that at the hed of the herse tyll the offring tyme. At which tyme, after therl of Lyncolne had offred the masse penny, presented it to the marques Dorset and to therl of Huntyngdon, they offred it, and the said Garter receyved it again of the archbishop, and held it still at the high auter ende tyll the masse was done. Likewise in forme Clarencieux[5] and Norrey[2] kinges of armes received the shilde, and at offering tyme presented it to the lord Maltravers and to the vicecounte Barkley. But ther was a question whether the sonne and heier of an erle should go above a vicounte. And Marche and Yreland king of armes received a riche sword which had byn send from the Pope, and in likeforme behaved themself and presented to Sir John and Sir Thomas Bourser the kinges auntes sonnes. Also Chestre[3] and Leicestre[4] herauldys receyved a basnet of a riche crown of gold, and presented it to the lord Hastinges. And Glocestre[5] and Buckingham[6] herauldes, with Ruigecrosse, Roseblache, Calais, Guynes, Barwike, and Harington, pursyvauntes, went [with][7] the knyghtes and esquiers for the body to the chirche dore for to receyve of Sir John Cheyny, maister of the horse, the man of armes, which was Sir William APar re, armed at all peces saving he was bareheded, having an axe in his hand, the pomell doneward, and

A.D. 1483. April.

[1] Thomas Holme, afterwards Sir Thomas Holme.
[2] John Moore.
[3] Thomas Whiting.
[4] Probably Roger Machado, who is mentioned by this name in Richard III.'s time.
[5] Ric. Champney ?
[6] Unknown.
[7] Om. in MS.

A.D. 1483. April.

thus companyed to the queie dore, wher he dyd alight. And the decon toke the horse which was traped with a riche traper of the kinges armes, wher the lord Audeley and the lord Ferrys receyved the man of armes, and with the forsaid company of knyghtes and esquiers, herauldys and pursyvauntes, accompanyed him to his offring: which done, every lord in mornyng habet offred for hymself, and after that dyverse other noble knyghtes officers, &c. Incontynent that done, the lordes offred certein clothes of gold to the corps, everyche after his degre or estat, that ys to saye, therl of Lincolne iiij by cause he was the kinges nevewe and sonne and heir of the duke of Suffolk, the marques of Dorset iiij, the erle of Huntyngdon iij, the lord Maltravers ij, by that he was sonne and heier to the erle of Arundelle, the vicounte Barkley ij; and every baron and other knyghtes morners by cause of nyghnes of blode. I cannot order how they offred, by cause the prese of the people was soo great bytwene them and me, but the lowest in estat or degre to the corps begane first. The names of the barons and knyghtes aforesaid; the lord Standeley, the lord Hastinges, the lord Audeley, the lord Burgeyne, the lord Dudley, the lord Ferris, the lord Fitz Hewe, the lord Delawar, the lord Morley, the lord Lysley, the lord Cobham, the lord Haward, the lord Wellys, the lord Mountjoye, Sir John of Arundell, Sir John[1] * * *

---

[1] Here the account is abruptly discontinued.

## II.

[Harl. 433, f. 238.]

### Copies of Instruccions furst after the begynnyng of the Reigne of King Richard the Thrid, etc.

Thies be the articles of instruccions geven to the lord Montjoie, maister Johne Cooke, archidekyn of Lincolne, and Sir Thomas Thwaytes, knightes, answering to the lettre of the lord Dynham, late direct unto the kinges grace as then Protector of England, which lettre resteth in iiij principalle poyntes. A.D. 1483. 28 June.

The first article remembred the othe which they of Calais perteynyng to any of the thre jurisdiccions ther incontynent upon knawlage of the deth of king Edward the iiij^th, whome God assoille, commen unto them, made holy togedyr upon a booke to be true unto king Edward the v^th, his son, as their liege lord, and to kepe the towne, castelle, and marchies of Calais truly to him, and to suffre no man with power to entre into the same, except the kinges persone or the lord Hastinges, then being the kinges lieutenant, and not without due payment to be made to the souldiors and other officers of alle that to theim shalbe founde due for the sure keping of the said towne and marches. The oath of allegiance to Edward V.

As to that article. It shalle move beside that how be it suche othe of ligeance was made sone upon the dethe of the said king Edward the iiij^th to his sone, not onely at Calais but also in diverse places in England by many gret astates and personages, being than ignorant of the verraye sure and true title which oure soverayn lord that now is, king Richard the iij^de, hath and had the same tyme to the coroune of England; That othe not withstanding now every good true Englissheman is bounde upon knowlage had of the not to be considered binding,

A.D. 1483. 28 June.

said verray true title to depart from the first othe so ignorantly gyven to him to whom it apperteyned not, and therupon to make his outhe of newe and owe his service and fidelite to him that good lawe, reason, and the concorde assent of the lordes and comons of the royaume have ordeigned to reigne upon the people, which is oure said soverayn lord king Richard the iij[de], brother to the said king Edward the iiij[th], late decessed, whome God pardone; whose sure and true title is evidently shewed and declared in a bill of peticion which the lordes spirituelx and temporelx and the commons of this land solemplye porrected unto the kinges highnes at London, the xxvj[ti] day of Juyn. Whereupon the kinges said highnes, notably assisted by welle nere alle the lordes spirituelle and temporelle of this royaume, went the same day unto his palais of Westminster, and ther in suche roialle honorable appareilled within the gret halle ther, toke possession and declared his mynde that the same day he wold begyn to reigne upon his people; and from thens rode solemply to the cathedralle cherche of London, and was resseyved ther with procession with grete congratulacion and acclamacion of alle the people in every place and by the weye that the king was in that day. The copy of the whiche bille the king will to be sent unto Calais, and ther to be redd and understanded, togeder with thise presentes. Desiring right effectuously alle maner persones of the said thre jurisdiccions what astate, degre, or condicion that they be of, and also them of Guysnes and Hammes, to make their feithes and othes to him as to thair soverayn lorde, like as the lordes spirituelx and temporelx, and many other noble men in gret nombre being in England, frely and of goode herte have done for their partes. And that the said towne of Calais, alle castelles and forteresses being within the said marches they wille saufly kepe unto the behoove of oure said soverayn lord king Richard the

the lords having found Richard III. the true heir to the throne.

iij[de], and them not to deliver to any persone but by his commaundement onely. A.D. 1483. 28 June.

The second article comprised in the lettre of the said lord Dynham concerned a peticion made by him in the names of him selff and other which do thair daly servises at Calais, that they might not be hurted by any act to be made in the parliament which they thought then shold have holde, or in any other wise, uppon any grauntes of offices, fermes, landes, fees, or privileges to them made, as wele within England as within the said towne and marches, but that they might enyoie alle suche possessions and grauntes as they had at the tyme of the decesse of the said king Edward the iiij[th], and that wayes may be founde that good assured payment may be had and contynued for the ordinarie nombre of the souldiors of the said towne and marches as it hath bene hiderto. How grantees and office-holders are effected by the demise of the crown

To that it may be said that the king wolle make to be serched in his recordes and elleswhere the trouth may be best knawen, what direccions have be taken in like case of change by the kinges that have [been][1] before, latting the same lord Dynham and alle they of his company to wit, that his grace wolle considre the gode and feithfulle services that they have done ther, and see that every persone be allowed and rewarded according to his merites, in as good maner and forme as any suche like persones have be seeyn to by any of the kinges noble auncestres in yeres past, his prerogatif and dignite roialle alweys saved. to be inquired into.

The iij[de] article remembreth the crewe of souldiors which be now bothe at Calais, Guysnes, and Hammes, and how they have hiderto be paied monethly; and how dangerous it were for the suerte of the towne, if the said crewe shuld either faille in their nombre, or in the maner of their said payment, &c. Pay of the garrisons.

---

[1] Om. MS.

A.D. 1483. 28 June.

Therto the king wolle it be said, that his highnes considereth wele the weight of that article, and that therto he trusteth ther shalbe no lak in him as touching thentreting togeder of the said crewe, and the monethly payment of their wages. For his grace maketh daily provision therfore, like as within short tyme they shalbe therof largely acertayned. And than his entent is that none of the said souldiors, either of the crewe or of the ordenarye shalbe discharged or put out of wages without true contentacion and payment of the same.

Compensation for lands flooded by order of Edward IV. for the defence of Calais.

As for the iiij^th and last articlue, wherin the said lord Dynham besecheth the kinges grace to have consideracion to the gret losses that diverse persones ther have susteyned by latting in of the salt water, and therby drownyng of much land to them belonging, lyeng nigh the towne of Calais, which drownyng was made by the commaundement of the king that dede is for the suerte of the said towne, and desiring therfore, that the said persones may have somme resonable recompense for their said hurtes, either there or elleswhere.

The king thinketh that desire resonable, and is content that the said lord Dynham sue for alle and everiche of the said persones so hurted, shewyng the certaynte of every mannys hurt in that behalve, wherin his highnes wolle provide suche convenient recompense as of reason they shalbe content with.

Officers to serve at Calais.

Memorandum, that the kinges highnes is pleased that his commissioners now sent to Calais deliver the said towne, with the hool gouvernaunce of the same, to the lord Dynham, as to the kinges depute there, he so to contynue during the kinges pleasure.

Item, that Sir Humfrey Talbot, marsshalle, John Foskewe, maister porter, Adryan Whitell, countroller, and Sir Richard Tunstalle, depute of the castelle, and

Sir John Dunn, depute of the toure of Risbank, contynue in their offices during the kinges pleasure. A.D. 1483. 28 June.

Item, that they put Sir Thomas Thwaytes in thoffice of tresorership of Calais, and discharge William Slyfeld of the same office

Item, that William Roosse, vitailler of Calais, contynue in his office.

Item, that Sir John Blunte, knighte, lord Mountjoie, be put in possession of lieutenantcy of Guysnes, and Sir Rauff Hastinges discharged of the same.

Item, that Jamys Blunt contynue lieutenant of the castelle of Hames.

Item, that the said commissioners take a vewe of the nombre of the crewe, and also to take a vewe of the artillerie and habilimentes of werre of Calaise, Guysnes, and Hammes, and to bring writing therof to the king.

Item, to appoynte with Sir Rauff Hastinges, on the kinges behalve; that he shalle peasibly have, occupie, and enyoie alle such offices, landes, possessions, and other goodes meveable, as he hath in those parties there; and also to treate and appoynte with him for alle suche stuff and habiliments of werre as he hathe ordeyned for the defence of the castelle of Guysnes.

By the King.

Trusty, etc. And wolle and desire you that ye yeve full feith and credence to our trusty servantes Robert Bradboury, Robert Allerton, Hugh Bago, and Thrustayn Hatefelde, in suche thinges and newes as we have commaunded thaym to shewe unto you on oure behalve; which by you herd we pray you to disclose to suche of oure subgettes as be under your rule in our castelle ther, as by your wisdome shalbe thought most according. And of their disposicions, which we trust verraily wolbe with oure pleasure, we desire you furthwith in alle hast possible to accertayn oure righte trusty and welbeloved the lord Mountjoie, Sir Thomas

A.D. 1483. 28 June. Thwaytes, and maister John Cooke, oure commissioners at Dover; whome we have carged there to abide your answere, and that had, to addresse them over unto you, fully instructed of our ferther mynde and pleasure in every thing concernyng the same. Faille ye not the premisses, as ye woll do us specialle pleasure. Yoven under oure signet at our cite of London, the xxviij[ti] day of Juyn.

To Sir Rauff Hastinges, knight,
lieutenant of our castelle of Guysnes.

---

III.

[MS. Harl., 433, f., 239 b.]

COPIE OF PROCLAMACIONS MADE AFORE THE CORONACION RICARDI III[ci].

July. For preservation of the peace. RICHARD, by the grace of God, king of England and of France and lord of Ireland, straitly chargeth and commandeth, undre peyn of deth, that noo manere of personne, of what estate, degre or condicion soever he bee, for old or new quarel, rancor, or malice, make any chalenge or affray, nor robbe or dispoille any personne, nor breke any saintuaries, wherthurgh his peax shalbee broken, or any sedicion or distourbance of his said peax shall happenne, within this his citie of London or any place therunto adjoynyng. And in caas peradventure that any mysrewled or mysadvised personne attempte to do the contrary, our said souverain lord chargeth that noon othre personne for familiarite, affeccion, or othre cause, yeve help or assistence to the personne soo offending, bot that every personne, being present at the place and tyme of suche offense doon, put hym in his uttermost devoir that the personne soo offending bee broughte and delivered to the maire of the said citie of London for his franchise, or to the stieward of the kinges houshold within the precincte of the yerde, as the caas shal require, by thaym suerly to bee kept unto the tyme the kinges highnesse, certified of the manere of thoffense, shewe unto thaym his mynde and pleasure what forthre shalbee doon in that behalve. A.D. 1483. July.

And also our said soverain lord, considring how it is unto hym and this his land both honourable and proffitable that straungers and aliens, being at this tyme within the said citie and places therunto adjoynyng, upon the trust of amitie, confederacions, or treuxes, bee peasibly and laufully entreated, chargeth therfor and commaundeth under peyn of deth that noo manere persone make any quarel or unlawfully doo any bodily harme or hurt to any of the said estraungers or aliens, nor robbe or dispoille any of thaym in thair goodes or catailles in any wise. Aliens to be treated amicably

And over this, our said souverain lord straitly chargeth and commaundeth, that no manere of man, upon peyn of emprisonment at his pleasure, take any manere of loging within the citie of London or suburbes of the same, or other places nygh adjoynyng, bot by thappointement and assignation of suche herbigeour or herbigeours as by the kinges highnesse shalbee appointed. Lodgings to be allotted by the king's harbingers

And to thentent that peax and tranquillite amonges his people may bee rathre kept and had, and thoccasion of breche of the same duely remoeved, our said souverain lord straitly chargeth and commaundeth that every man bee in his loging by x. of the clok in the nyght, and that noo personne othre than such that his highnesse hath licenced or shal licence within the franchise of the said citie or in places therunto nygh adjoynyng, bere any manere of wepon such as has been underwriten; that is to say, glayves, billes, long debeofes, long or short swerdes and buklers, under peyn of forfaitur and losyng of the same and emprisonment of hym or thaym that soo offendeth, to endure at the kinges pleasure. No man to be abroad after 10 at night.

A.D. 1483. July.

## IV.

## Negotiation for the Restitution of French Prizes.

[MS. Harl. 433. f. 240.]

Instruccions geven to Thomas Grafton, merchaunt of the staple, and to William Laverok, sent by the king to Boloigne to have communicacion with the lord Cordes or his deputees or deputee for disaresting and restitucion of two shippes perteynyng to the lord Cordes within the haven of Sandewiche, and other in the West Contre pertenyng to other Frenshemen, if they be asked of the partie, and of many other shippes and goodes pertenyng to divers Englisshemen arrested in the parties of Fraunce on the other partie.

First, the shall see and understande what power any suche deputees or deputee of the said lord Cordes will shewe; and therupon, if any suche be had sufficient forto trete and appoynt in this mater, they shalle, by vertue of the kinges comission to them delivered entre communicacion therupon, which may be suche as foloweth. That is to say, that how be it upon a spoille of an Englisship afore Boloigne doon by Frenshemen to the gret hurt and prejudice of certain Englisshe merchauntes, the said two shippes were put under arrest at Sandewich at the sute and instaunce of the same merchauntes (for the which the restitucion of the same shippes was delayed at the tyme that the servantes of the said lord Cordes demaunded it in England of the King that is decessed, whome God pardone): yit so it was that the same King afore his dethe was in full purpos and mynde to have entended the said restitucion demaunded, so that his subgettes, their shippes and goodes for that cause arrested in Fraunce might be also delivered and

Restitution of two French ships arrested intended by Edward IV.

restored, and therfore willed that my lord Dynham shuld assaie some practik therin and fele the mynde of the said lord Cordes, like as the king is enformed that he hath done, and brought it to this poynt, that it pleased the said lord Cordes to write unto him his lettres of the date of the xxvij[ti] day of May at Hesdin. By the which it appereth that upon the sending of eny persones of this partie to Boloigne ayenst any certain day to be appoincted to speke of the meanes of the said restitucion to be made, the said lord Cordes therof before advertised woll send his commissioners thider ayenst the same day to procede summarily in the same mater, like as in the said lettres, wherof ther is a copie redy to be shewed, more plainly it is expressed. And forasmoche as the said lord Cordes asketh in his said lettres not onely restitucion of his shippes but also satisfaccion of his damages and interesse, &c., they shall fele to what summe the said damages and interesses woll amounte, and insist for the moderacion thereof asmoche as they can. And when they have brought it as lawe as they may, shewing and allegging the gret damages and interesse whiche Englisshemen have borne and sustened by prinse and arrestes committed by the Frensshe partie ayenst them, shall assent that the said ij shippes with asmoche appareill as was in theim at the tyme of the arrest (and, where any therof is lost, other as good to be purveied therfore), shalbe restored by a certayn day to be appoincted, suche as within the which the said shippes may be wele rigged; provided and assented by the said lord Cordes or his deputees, how and by what day the persones, shippes and goodes of the realme of England taken and arrested in the realme of Fraunce shalbe delivered. In practesing wherof they shall, by as good discrecion as they can, insiste to have good suertee for the same deliveraunce, and within how many dayes after the restitucion the

A.D. 1483. July.

Commissioners empowered to treat with those of the Sieur Des Querdes.

A.D. 1483. July.

said ij shippes pertenyng to the said lord Cordes, the said generall restitucion for Frensshe partie shalbe made. And therupon, if it be asked, the said ij shippes of Fraunce arrested in the west contre shalbe promised and assured to be delivered. And as for other prises and takinges uppon the see of either partie, of England and of Fraunce, they shall speke that ther may be a diete appoincted betwene bothe kinges for reformacion of alle attemptates, to be entended at more leyser, that the truex that yet endureth may be wele observed herafter. In alle which matiers, they shalle do pass, write and sealle, with the said lord Cordes or his deputees under suche forme and maner as they can best fynde them agreable unto according to thentent before specified. And if nede be, they shalle apoincte an other diete for thexecucion of the premisses or any part therof, certefying from tyme to tyme with alle diligence the kinges counsaill of suche defficultes and novelties as they shall happe to finde in any of the premisses.

Letter of the Sieur Des Querdes.

MONSIEUR DE DYNHAM, je me recommande a vous. Jay receu voz lettres ou mescripvez la response dunes lettres que pieça vous ay escript par Calais, affin dappaiser les questions et arrests par moy faiz sur les subgetz du roy Dangleterre. Et ensuivant ce que je vous ay escript, quant nos navires, dommages, et interestz me seront rendouz je serray prest de faire lever la main

---

TRANSLATION.

MY LORD DYNHAM, I commend myself to you. I have received your letters in which you write to me, in answer to a letter which I long ago wrote to you by Calais [pursuivant] in order to set at rest the disputes and arrests made by me upon the subjects of the king of England. And, in accordance with what I wrote to you, when our ships, losses, and injuries are restored to me, I shall be ready to remove my hand from

de tous les arrestz que a ceste cause jay fait faire; et veul bien commetere aucun a Boullongne pour avoir adviz et communicacion avecques ceulx que y vouldrez envoyer, affin de regarder les moyens comment ceste restitucion de mesdicts navires se devra faire, et aussi la main levee desdicts arrestz. Et quant vous vouldrez aller sommerement en ceste matiere, vous ne trouverez de ma part point de delaye en ce qui serra appointe parles deputez de vostre part et de la menne. Et pourrez prendre jour pour faire trouver vos gens audict Boulone, et le faire savoir a mon lieutenant audict lieu pour men advertier, et les mens se y trouveront. Esperant que ceste chose puisse prendre briefve fyne. Et a tant, Monsieur de Dynham, je prye nostre Seigneur quil vous ait en Sa saincte garde. Escript a Hesdin le xxvij^e jour de May. A.D. 1483. July.

(Ainsi signe) Le bien vostre,

PHE. DE C.

A Mons. de Dynham,
Lieutenant de Calays.

---

all the arrests that I have caused to be made on this account; and I will commission some one at Boulogne to have advice and communication with those whom you propose to send thither, in order to consider the means how this restitution of my said ships is to be made, and also the release of the said arrests. And if you would proceed promptly in this matter, you shall not find any delay on my part in that which shall be arranged by the deputies of your side and my own. You may choose a day for your people to be at Boulogne aforesaid, and intimate it to my lieutenant at the said place, that he may let me know, and my people shall be there. Hoping that this affair may speedily be brought to a conclusion. And so, my lord Dynham, I pray our Lord to have you in His holy keeping. Written at Hesdin, the 27th day of May.

Wholly yours,

(Signed) PH[ILIPP]E DE C[ORDES.]

To Lord Dynham,
Lieutenant of Calais.

A.D. 1483. July.

V.

OVERTURE TO BRITANNY FOR MUTUAL REDRESS.

[MS. Harl. 433. f. 241.]

INSTRUCCIONS geven to doctor Thomas Huton upon the lettre of credence which he shall deliver to the duc of Britaine on the behalve of the kinges highnes.

FIRST, after recomendacions and reverences according, he shall shewe unto the said duc or to his counsaill the good wille and purpos that the king and the nobles of this lande have and bere unto the duc and his subgettes, according to suche convencions as have be made betwene the king our late soverayn lord decessed and the said duc.

Item, that how be it upon the hasty departyng of the said king out of this worlde diverse folkes of simple disposicion, peraventure supposing that the peas had be expired by the deth of the said king, felle to prinses and takinges upon the see, the oo partie ayenst the oder, to the gret trouble and hinderaunce of thentercours and fete of merchandises exercised by the subgettes of both the sides. Yet it is thought that by meane of a diete to be sette betwene bothe princes a full reformacion of alle attemptates may wele be had; wherunto the king and the counsaille of England wilbe wele disposed, so that the duc wille for his part be of the same disposicion. And as touching certain persones of Britan which have made long sute in England, and yet be not recompensed according to suche direccions as the king decessed toke with them in his lyff, he may say that their recompense must growe of the goodes and tresoure

Diet proposed.

belonging to the said king decessed, whereof as yet no man hath takyn adminystracion. And assone as administracion shalbe committed to suche persones as wolle take the charge upon them, the dukes said subgettes shalbe paied and contented with the first creditoures. A.D. 1483. July.

Item, in communicacion to be ferther had upon the premisses, and namely touching the said diete, he shall move, speke and accorde upon a certain tyme and place, when and where the commissaries and compleynauntes of bothe parties may assemble, so that a sufficiaunt and resonable warnyng therupon be had afore, provided that the place be in England and no where elles.

Item, he shall fele and understand the mynde and disposicion of the duc anempst Sir Edward Wodevile and his reteignue, practizing by all meanes to him possible to enserche and knowe if ther be entended eny enterprise out of land upon any part of this realme, certifieng with all diligence all the newes and disposicion ther from tyme to tyme.

---

## VI.

### Relations with Spain.

[MS. Harl. 433, f. 241.]

Instruccions geven by the king to Barnard de la Forssa to be shewed and opened to the kinges cousyns, the king and quene of Castelle.

First, after the presentacion of the kinges lettres to his said cousyns with recomendacions in suche case acoustumed, he shall shewe and remembre the said king of the tendre love, trust, and effeccion that the king

A.D. 1483. July.

oure brother now deceased (whome God pardon) had and bare towardes his said cousyns, latting them wit that his highnes is and evere entendeth to be of like disposicion towardes them in alle thinges that he may conveniently doo to their honnor and pleasure. And in likewise by alle meanes convenient the said Barnard shalle shewe that the king trusteth that his said cousyns wolbe of like benevolence and disposicion towardes him.

Diet agreed to by Edward IV., and Ferdinand and Isabella.

And where in the yere last passed the kinges said brother sent his ambassiate to his said cousyns for diverse maters then not fully concluded, and amonges other for thentreteignyng of the peas, ligue, and amyte passed and concluded betwixt his highnes and Henry late king of Castelle, against which many attemptates have be and daily be committed; whereof, if due reformacion were not had, the said peax, ligue, and amite cowd not long contynue: it was therfore appoynted and concluded with his said cousyns to have had a diette in Spayn at Midsomer then next following, or afor, to the which the kinges said brother was fully agreed.

But for asmoche as it pleased Almighti God to call him out of this miserable worlde unto his mercy afore the tyme appoynted for the said diette; after whose decesse no gret maters might conveniently be appointed afore the king coronacion and ordering of his realme:

The said Barnard shall, for that and other causes suche as shalle best serve after his discrecion, excuse the tarying of comyssioners that shuld have come to that diette, and, by the auctorite and power to the said Barnard comitted by the kinges comission, agree and appoynte[1] with the kinges said cousyns or their commissioners to a new day of meting for reformacion of the said attemptates, suche as shall pleas the kinges cousyns aforesaid.

A new day to be named.

[1] *appoynted*, MS.

And that the said Barnard after thappoyntmentes of a day of meeting soo agreed, in alle goodly hast acertain the king and his counsell of the same, to thentent that commissioners may be sent thider sufficiently instructe and auctorized for due reformacion of the said attemptates to be had and made of their partie. A.D. 1483. July.

---

## VII.

### Lewis XI. to Richard III.

[MS. Harl. 433, f. 236 b.]

Monsieur mon cousin,—Jay veu les lettres que mavez escriptez par vostre herault Blanc Sanglier, et vous mercye des nouvelles que mavais fait savoir. Et se je vous puis fair quelque service je le feray de tresbon cueur, car je vueil been avoir vostre amytie. E a Dieu, monsieur mon cousin. Escript aux Montilz lez Tours, le xxi$^{me}$ jour de Juillet.

Loys.

Villechartre.

---

#### Translation.

My lord and cousin,—I have seen the letters that you have written to me by your herald Blanc Sanglier, and thank you for the news of which you have apprised me. And if I can do you any service I will do it with very good will, for I desire to have your friendship. And farewell, my lord and cousin. Written at Montilz lez Tours, the 21st day of July.

Lewis.

Villechartre.

---

A.D. 1483. 30 July.

## VIII.

### Philip of Austria to Richard III.

[MS. Harl., 433 f. 236 b.]

Demanding redress for acts of piracy and murder.

Treshault et trespuissant prince, treshonnoure sieur et cousin, je me recommande a vous, tant comme je puis. Et vous plaise savoir, treshault et trespuissant prince, treshonnoure sieur et cousin, que pluseurs plaintes et doleances mont este faictes par mes subges de cestui mon pays et conte de Flandres dez prinses qui journellement se font sur mer par lez subges de vostre royaume, en quoy pluseurs de mesdits subgets, tant de mez villes de Neuport, Ostende, Dunkerke et autres ont este tresgrandement et excessivement interessez et adommagies, en tant que par ceulx de vostre dit royaume, qui se tiennent atout pluseurs navires sur mer, ilz ont este prins et destroussez; et leurs biens, marchandises, et navires vendus et butinez en icellui vostre royaume comme biens dennemis. Et que plus

---

Translation.

Most high and mighty prince, most honored lord and cousin, I commend me to you as much as I may. And please it you to know, most high and mighty prince, most honored lord and cousin, that many complaints and grievances have been made to me by my subjects of this my country and earldom of Flanders of the seizures daily made at sea by the subjects of your kingdom, wherein several of my said subjects, as well of my towns of Neuport, Ostende, Dunkirk, as others, have been very greatly and excessively wronged and injured, in as much as they have been taken and plundered by those of your realm, who keep always several vessels at sea; and their goods, merchandise, and ships, sold and plundered in that your realm, as goods of enemies. And, what is more, several of my said subjects

est, les pluseurs de mesdits subges ont este gettez outre bort et inhumainement mis a mort. Lesquelz exploiz, qui sont exploiz de guerre et dennemis, ont desja este contynuez par trois moys et plus, en venant parce directement contre lentrecours dela marchandise qui est entre vostre royaume et les subges[1] dicellui dunepart, et mez pays, seigneuries, et subges dautre. Duquel entrecours ceulx de vostredit royaume ont joy et joyssent soubz moy et sont en tous leurs negoces et affaires traicties en toute raison et justice. Neantmoins mesdits subges ainsi adommagies et interessez, quelque poursuite quilz ont faicte devers vous, nont[2] peu avoir ne obtenir restitucion diceulx leurs damages et biens ainsi a eulx prins. Et, que plus est, iceulx adommagies et autres mes subges qui frequentent la mer en la pescherie dez harencs et autrement marchandament mont raporte que lez navires de guerre de vostredit royaume estans en mer se A.D. 1483. 30 July.

---

have been thrown overboard and cruelly put to death. Which acts, being acts of war and of enemies, have already been continued for three months and more, in direct contravention of the treaty of merchandise which exists between your realm and subjects on the one side, and my countries, lordships, and subjects on the other; of which treaty, those of your said realm enjoy the benefit under me and are treated in all their affairs according to reason and justice. Nevertheless, my subjects thus wronged and injured, whatever suit they have made towards you, have not been able to obtain restitution of those their damages and goods thus taken. And, moreover, those thus injured and others my subjects who frequent the sea in the herring fishery and other mercantile traffic, have reported to me that the vessels of war of your said realm, being on the sea, vaunt that they

---

[1] *et les subges* repeated in MS. | [2] *nont* repeated in MS.

A.D. 1483. 30 July.

vantent de continuer de plus en plus sur eulx lesdits exploiz de guerre, et en tout cas lez traictier comme ennemis; en me requerant sur letout lez pourveoir au bien et a la seurte deulx et tellement quilz puissent paisiblement frequenter et hanter la mer. Et pource, treshault et trespuissant prince, treshonnoure sieur et cousin, comme de ma part jay entretenu et fait entretenir ledit entrecours dela marchandise envers ceulx de vostredit royaume et que entre vous et moy na aucune cause ne occasion de guerre, mais toute amitie et bonne intelligence de mon coste, rescrips pardevers vous par ladvis deceulx de mon sang et dez autres de mon grant conseil ordonnez lez moy. Et vous prie et requiers tant acertes et effectueusement comme faire puis, que en entretenant ledit entrecours dela marchandise qui sera le commun bien de vostredit royaume et de mesdits pays, vous vueillies faire cesser et deporter lez gens de guerre de cellui vostre royaume estans sur mer de plus faire aucuns exploiz de guerre sur mez subges de mondit pays de Flandres, ains

will continue more and more against them the said deeds of war, and in all cases treat them as enemies; requiring me, all things considered, to provide for their good and safety so that they may peaceably frequent the sea. Wherefore, most high and mighty prince, most honored lord and cousin, as on my part I have kept, and caused to be kept, the said treaty of merchandise towards those of your said kingdom, and as between you and me there is no cause or occasion of war, but all amity and good understanding on my side, I write to you by the advice of those of my kin and the others of my great council appointed to be about me, and pray and request you as truly and affectionately as I can, that in keeping the said treaty of merchandise, which will be for the common weal of your said realm and of my said countries, you will stop, and cause to be removed the men of war of your said realm being on the sea from further doing any deeds of war against my subjects of my said country of Flanders,

lez souffrir et parmectre paisiblement hanter et frequenter la mer en leurs negoces et marchandises et aussi en vostredit royaume sans lez prendre ne leur faire aucun desplaisir en corps ne en biens, toutainsi que jay fait, et que vouldriez que je feisse doresenavant a voz subges hantans et frequentans mondit pays de Flandres ; et avecque ce faire rendre et restituer a iceulx mez subges adommagies leurs biens, navires, et marchandises qui leur ont este prins et destroussez sur mer par ceulx de vostredit royaume, comme raison est, et que selon le dit entrecours faire se doit, et tellement que de raison ilz aient cause de eulx tenir contens. Et pourtant que ceste matiere est fort a cueur a mesdits subges jenvoye devers vous Replemonde porteur de cestes, mon officier darmes, pour vous soliciter et me reporter vostre response; vous priant et requerant, comme dessus, vouloir faire ce que dit est. En quoy faisant me ferez chose tresagreable. Et sil y a chose que pour vous faire puisse, A.D. 1483. 30 July.

and allow them peaceably to frequent the sea in their business and merchandise, and likewise in your said realm, without taking them or doing them any injury in body or goods, even as I have done, and as you would wish that I should do henceforward to your subjects frequenting my said country of Flanders; and, moreover, cause to be restored to those my subjects aggrieved their goods, ships, and merchandise which have been taken and plundered from them on the sea by those of your said realm, as reason is and according to the treaty should be done, and so as of reason they have cause to be satisfied. And because this matter much concerns my said subjects I send towards you Replemonde, bearer of these, my officer of arms, to solicit you and bring me back your answer; praying and requesting you, as above, that you will do what is aforesaid, wherein you will do me a singular pleasure. And if there be anything which I can do for

A.D. 1483. 30 July. en le me signifiant je lacompliray de bon cueur, aydant nostre Seigneur, qui vous, treshault et trespuissant prince, treshonnoure sieur et cousin, vous ait en Sa garde.

Escript en ma ville de Gand, le penultime jour de Juillet, lan iiij^xx et troys.

Vostre cousin,

PHILIPPE DOSTRICE, duc de Bourgogne, de Brabant, de Lembourg, et de Luxembourg, conte de Flandres, de Haynnau, de Hollande, de Zellande, et de Namur.

DE BEER.

A treshault et trespuissant prince, treshonnoure sieur et cousin, le roy Dangleterre.

---

you, on your signifying it to me, I will perform it with good will, with the help of our Lord, whom I pray, most high and mighty prince, &c., to have you in His keeping.

Written in my town of Ghent, the penult day of July, the year '83.

Your cousin,

PHILIP OF AUSTRIA, duke of Burgundy, Brabant, Lembourg and Luxembourg, count of Flanders, Hainault, Holland, Zealand, and Namur.

DE BEER.

To the most high and mighty prince, most honored lord and cousin, the king of England.

## IX.

A.D. 1483. 8 Aug.

### MESSAGE OF QUEEN ISABELLA OF CASTILE.

[MS. Harl. 433, f. 235.]

EA quæ ego, Graufidius de Sasiola, indignus atque humilis orator serenissimæ atque potentissime dominæ reginæ Ispaniarum, supremæ dominæ meæ, virtute credentiarum serenitatis suæ dixi, affirmavi, et promisi illustrissimo atque potentissimo principi Angliæ, etc., regi, coram dominis de consilio suo, in die, mense, et anno infrascriptis, in villa de Warrewic, sunt quæ sequuntur.

Desires peace with England,

In primis enim dixi quod intentio, voluntas, et propositum deliberatum dictæ serenissimæ dominæ reginæ, supremæ dominæ meæ, est habere bonam et firmam pacem cum dicto illustrissimo rege Angliæ, et cum subditis terris et dominiis suis et integraliter cum toto regno suo.

Et subsequenter, est de mente et intentione dictæ supremæ dominæ meæ reginæ denuo facere, inire, et firmare cum dicto domino rege bonas et firmas ligas, confœderationes, et alligantias, ut sint initi, alligati, et confœderati firma liga confœderationeque optima adinvicem se coadunanda tanquam boni et fideles cognati et confœderati.

and is ready to give assistance against Lewis XI.

Et subsequenter, virtute dictarum credentiarum ex parte dictæ serenissimæ dominæ reginæ, supremæ dominæ meæ, dixi et promisi, quod si dictus dominus rex Angliæ velit movere guerram contra regem Lodowicum Franciæ ad recuperandas terras, dominia, et possessiones suas quæ sunt de pertinentibus coronæ Angliæ, quod dicta domina regina dabit dicto domino regi, gentibus et capitaneis suis, omnes portus suos maritimos liberos et

A.D. 1483. 8 August. securos, et victualia et arma necessaria in bono foro et pretio, et per mare naves suas armatas pro justis stipendiis.

Item, per terram, si opus fuerit, milites et equestres, viros fortes optimeque munitos, et pedestres, ejusdem generis viros, in copia numeroque competentibus ad justa stipendia dicti domini regis. Quæ omnia dicit dicta domina regina tam pro se quam pro illustrissimo atque potentissimo principe domino suo Ispaniarum rege. Quæ omnia dicta, acta, et promissa fuerunt per me dictum oratorem octava die mensis Augusti, anno Domini m.cccclxxxiij°.

Cause of her alienation from Edward IV.

Besides thise instrucciones geven in writing by this orator he shewed to the kinges grace, by mouth, that the quene of Castelle was turned in hur hart fro England in tyme past for the unkyndeness the which she toke against the king last decessed, whom God pardon, for his refusing of her and taking to his wiff a wedowe of England; for the which cause also was mortalle werre betwixt him and the erle of Warrewyk, the which toke ever hur part to the tyme of his deth. And therfore she moved for thise cause against hur natur, the which was ever to love and favor England, as he said; she toke the Frenche kinges part, and made liges and confideracions with him.

Now the king is dede that shewed hur this unkyndenesse; and, as he said, the Frenche king hath broken four principall articles appointed, concluded, and sealed betwixt him and the king of Castelle and hur. Wherfore, she now retournyng to hur naturall kinde and disposicion, desireth suche thinges to be appointed and concluded betwixt thise two reyalmes, England and Spayne, as ye may understande by thise instruccions of hur said oratour.

An nother cause which moved her to depart fro the king Luys, was that she had a graunt of the quene of Naver[1] to have hur doughter and heir[2], for the prince of Castell,[3] hur son, if the consent of king Loys might therin have ben had. And forsomoche, as he by no maner meane wold be therunto agreable she taketh a gret displeasure with him, and desireth by alle meanes to hur possible to make thise alliaunces and confederacions with the kinges good grace, as be shewed in thise instruccions. A.D. 1483, 8 August.

She hath in hur possession, as hur said oratour saith, the towne of Pampillion, and a m^l^. speres therin; and the nobles and citees of Naver have answerd plainly unto hur, that if the quene of Naver wold be disposed, as she is not, to mary hur said doughter at the wille and pleasure of king Loys, they will deliver unto hur alle the strang townes and castelles of the said kingdom of Naver. She lieth with a gret part of the nobles of Spayne, a litille from Victoria, not two dayes jorney from Naver.

The nombre of speres and horsmen the which the king shalle have of Spayne shalbe at his pleasure, x.m^l^. speres if he will, or moo, and xxx.m^l^. fotemen. Thus the said oratour saith by mouth, and offreth him selff also to write the same like as he hathe done as afore.

---

[1] Madeleine, widow of Gaston de Foix, prince de Viane, and from 1479 to 1483, regent in behalf of her son Francis Phœbus, who died in the beginning of the latter year.

[2] Catherine, sister of Francis mentioned in the preceding note, and by his death queen of Navarre in 1483.

[3] John, prince of Castile, ob. 1497.

A.D. 1483.
18 August.

X.

RICHARD III. TO LEWIS XI.

[MS. Harl. 433. f. 237.]

Desiring to know what protection will be given to English merchants in France.

MONSIEUR, mon cousin, jay veu lez lettres que mavez envoiees par Boukingham leherault, par lesquelles jentens que voulez bien avoir mon amitie, dont je suis bien content, en bonne forme et maniere; car je nentens point rompre telles treves comme cydevant estoient conclutes entre feu de tresnoble memoire le roy mon frere trespasse et vous, pour le terme dicelles. Toutesfois lez marchans de cestui mon royaume Dangleterre, voyans lez grandes occasions a eulx donnees par vos subges en prenant les navires et marchandises et autrement, doubtent grandement de eulx aventurer daller a Bourdeaulx et ailleurs en vostre obeissance, jusques ace quilz puissent estre asseurez depar vous depovoir seurement et sauvement exercer le fait de leursdits marchandises en tous lez lieux de

---

TRANSLATION.

MY lord, my cousin, I have seen the letters you have sent me by Buckingham herald, whereby I understand that you wish to have my amity, of which I am very glad, in good form and manner; for I do not mean to break such truces as have hitherto been concluded between the late king of most noble memory, my brother deceased, and you, for the term of the same. Nevertheless, the merchants of this my kingdom of England, seeing the great occasions given them by your subjects by taking vessels and merchandise and otherwise, doubt greatly to adventure themselves to go to Bordeaux and elsewhere in your obeisance, until they may be assured on your part that they may surely and safely exercise the feat of their said merchandise in all the places of your said obeisance,

vostredit obeissance, accordant audroit desdites treves. A.D. 1483.
Sur quoy, affin que mesdits subges et marchans ne 18 August.
soient deceubz soubz umbre dicelle, je vous prie que par mon serviteur ce porteur, lun des chevaucheurs de mon escuierie, me vueillies faire savoir par escript vostre plaine entencion, ensemble se chose desirez que pour vous puisse, pour lacomplir de bon cueur. Et adieu soiez, monsieur mon cousin.

Escript en mon chasteau de Lexcestre, le xviij[e] jour daoust.

---

according to the right of the said truces. Upon which matter, in order that my said subjects and merchants be not deceived under the shadow of the same, I pray you that by my servant, this bearer, one of the grooms of my stable, you will let me know by writing your full intention, and at the same time if you desire anything that I can do for you, that I may do it with good will. And farewell, my lord my cousin.

Written in my castle of Leicester, the 18th day of August.

---

## XI.

### Richard III. to Lewis XI.

[MS. Harl. 433. f. 237 b.]

Monsieur mon cousin, je me recommande a vous tant comme je puis. Jay rescript a mon serviteur Blanc Sanglier, apresent estant pardevers vous, affin de faire provision daucuns vins du creu de Bourgoingne

Desires a supply of wines of Burgundy.

---

#### Translation.

My lord my cousin, I commend me to you as much as I can. I have written to my servant Blanc Sanglier, now being with you, to make provision of certain wines of the growth of Bur-

A.D. 1483. 20 August. et de la Haulte France pour moy et la royne ma compaigne. Si vous prie pource, monsieur mon cousin, que vueillies donner commandement a voz officiers et subges quilz le seuffrent faire la provision desdits vins et franchement conduire ou faire conduire et passer en cestui mon royaume Dangleterre sans aucun destourbier ou contredit, et vous me ferez en ce ung bien singulier plaisir. Et sil est aucune chose que je puisse faire pour vous, en le me faisant savoir je lacompliray tresvoulentiers, a laide de Dieu, qui, monsieur mon cousin, vous ait en Sa saincte garde.

Escript en mon chasteau de Notingham le xx[e]. jour daoust.

---

gundy and la Haute France, for myself and the queen my consort. I therefore pray you, my lord my cousin, that you will give order to your officers and subjects to suffer him to procure the said wines, and freely conduct them and pass into this my realm of England, without any disturbance or contradiction, and you will do me in this a very singular pleasure. And if there be anything which I can do for you, on your informing me I will accomplish it very willingly with the aid of God, who, my lord my cousin, have you in His holy keeping.

Written in my castle of Nottingham, the 20th day of August.

A.D. 1483.
26 August.

## XII.

### From the Duke of Britanny.

[Harl. 433. f. 247. b.]

Instructions pour Georges de Mainbier presentement envoie par le duc devers le roy Dangleterre dece quil a a dire audit roy.

Premier, apres la presentacion des lettres et recommendacions en la maniere acoustumee, dira audit roy que le duc le remercie tresaffectueusement du bon voelloir et affection quil demonstre avoir a lui, dont il a este acertene, tant par messire Thomas Huton, chaplain et ambassadeur dudit roy que par maistre Francois Dupon, secretaire du duc, nageres retourne devers lui: en le priant de continuer et perseverer. Et certifiera audit roy que le duc na point moins a lui damour et daffection; en quoy il entent de bien en mieulx perseverer.

---

### Translation.

Instructions for George de Mainbier now sent by the duke [of Britanny] towards the king of England, of what he shall say to the said king.

First, after presentation of the letters and recommendations in the usual manner, he shall say to the said king that the duke thanks him most affectionately for the good will and affection which he exhibits towards him, of which he has been assured, both by Mr. Thomas Hutton, chaplain and ambassador of the said king, and by master Francis Dupon, the duke's secretary, lately returned towards him; begging him to continue and persevere. And he shall assure the said king that the duke has not less love and affection for him; in which he intends to persevere from good to better.

A.D. 1483. 26 August.

Item, dira audit roy que le duc le prie lavoir pour excuse de quoy presentement il na envoie devers lui de sez serviteurs pour besoigner et conclure ou fait de la charge baillee audit Huton son ambassadeur, et dont le dit Huton a fait declaracion au duc, sur laquelle le duc lui a fait response telle que ledit roy pourra savoir par sondit ambassadeur. Car le duc, ainsi quil a decoustume chacun an, a fait assigner lez estas de son pays a tenir vers la fin de Septembre prouchain, pour lefait desquelz lui est necessairement requis avoir sez serviteurs avecque lui; mais incontinent aprez lesdits estas finiz, qui dureront lespace de dix ou douze jours, le duc envoiera de sez serviteurs devers lui environ la Toussains, ou plustost sil lui est possible, lesquelz auront puissance de besoignier sur la charge dudit Huton. Et ainsi desire leduc lefaire pour la grant amour et affection quil a audit roy et a son royaume.

The Estates of Britanny to meet in September.

---

Also he shall say to the said king that the duke begs him to hold him excused that he has not at present sent to him any of his servants to treat and conclude of the charge given to the said Hutton his ambassador, and of which the said Hutton has made declaration to the duke, whereupon the duke made him answer such as the said king may know by his said ambassador. For the duke, as he has been accustomed to do every year, has appointed the estates of his country to be held towards the end of September next, for the doing of which it is very necessary to have his servants with him; but immediately after the said estates are ended, which will last the space of ten or twelve days, the duke will send some of his servants to him, about the feast of All Saints, or sooner if it be possible to him, who shall have power to treat upon the charge of the said Hutton. And so the duke desires to do for the great love and affection he bears to the said king and his kingdom.

Semblablement, dira audit roy comme leduc a este adverti que grant nombre de navires dudit royaume Dangleterre se mettent en guerre sur mer, et quilz se sont vantez de prendre et pillier les subgets du duc. Pource dira audit roy que le duc le prie quil face faire deffense a sesdits subgets et autres sur grosses paines de nen riens prendre ne pillier sur lez subgets duduc, et y donner telle provision que telles prinses et roberies cessent pour le temps advenir. Car le duc de sa part veult et entent ainsi le faire. A.D. 1483 25 August.

Pareillement dira audit roy que le roy Loys de France depuis le deces de feu prince de bonne memoire le roy Edward dernier decede, a par plusieurs foiz envoie devers le duc le prier et requerir de lui baillier le sieur de Richemont son cousin. Et a ledit roy Loys fait faire auduc de grans offres; mais le duc ne lui en a donne nul actraict, doubtant que ledit roy Loys en voulsist porter ennuy et dommage Lewis XI. urges him to deliver up the earl of Richmond.

---

Likewise he shall say to the said king how the duke has been advertised that a great number of vessels of the said kingdom of England put themselves in warlike array upon the sea, and have threatened to take and plunder the subjects of the duke. Wherefore he shall say to the said king that the duke requests him to prohibit his said subjects and others under heavy penalties from taking or plundering anything from the subjects of the duke, and to make provision that such seizures and robberies cease for the time to come. For the duke on his part wishes and means so to do.

In the like manner he shall say to the said king, that king Lewis of France, since the decease of the late prince of good memory king Edward last deceased, has several times sent to the duke to pray and request him to deliver to him the lord of Richmond his cousin. And the said king Lewis has made the duke great offers; but the duke has given him no inducement, fearing that the said king Lewis would thereby create annoyance and

A.D. 1483. 26 August.

a aucuns dez amis et bien vueillans duduc. Aloccasion de quoy ledit roy Loys donne grandes menaces auduc de lui faire la guerre, et en sont lez apparaissances grandes.

Maismes remonstrera audit roy lagrant puissance de gens de guerre, artillerie et finances que a le dit roy de France, et la proximite dudit royaume au duche de Bretagne, qui sont joignans ensemble terre a terre, sans y avoir entre deux ruisseau ne riviere qui empesche ne puisse empescher ledit roy de France de faire entree avecque toute sa puissance oudit duche de Bretagne. Et combien que le duc ait bonne et grande puissance de gens de guerre et artillerie, toutesfois il ne lui seroit possible porter longuement le faix de la guerre contre une telle puissance que celle dudit roy Loys sans laide et secours dudit roy Dangleterre et desez autres parens et amis. Parquoy par necessite pourroit le duc estre constrainct a baillier audit roy Loys ledit sieur de Richemont, et faire autres choses

To prevent which, England must aid Britanny against France.

injury to some of the friends and well-willers of the duke. In consequence of which the said king Lewis gives great menaces to the duke of making war upon him, and the appearances of it are great.

Also he shall represent to the said king the great power of men of war, artillery, and finances, which the said king of France has, and the nearness of the said kingdom to the duchy of Britanny, the two lands joining together without having between them brook or river which might hinder the said king of France from entering the said duchy of Britanny with all his power. And although the said duke should have good and abundant strength of men of war and artillery, nevertheless he would not be able long to support the war against such a power as that of the said king Lewis without the aid and succour of the said king of England and of his other cousins and friends. Whereby of necessity the duke might be compelled to deliver to the said king Lewis the said lord of Richmond, and to do other things to which he would be very

qui lui seroit a grant deplaisir pour le dommaige quil congnoist que ledit roy Loys en porteroit et pourroit porter ausdits roy et royaume Dangleterre. A.D. 1483. 26 August.

Pourquoy dira audit roy comme le duc le prie que en entretenant lez amitiez et traicties parcydevant faiz entre ledit feu roy Edward et le duc, il lui plaise secourir le duc alencontre dudit roy Loys, sil encommence la guerre au duc, et lui envoier pour partie de son secours le nombre de iiij.mı archiers Dangleterre, garnis de bons capitaines et dun bon chief, souldoiez pour six moys aux despens dudit roy Dangleterre, et iceulx envoier dedens ung moys aprez la requeste que le duc en fera, ainsi que ledit feu roy Edward avoit promis de faire; et dece baillier son seelle et lenvoier au duc; et aussi envoier auduc, sil le requeroit, oultre ledit nombre de iiij.m[l]. archers, deux ou trois autres mil archers dedens ung autre moys prouchain, garnis de bons capitaines, a la soulde et despens du duc. Et en ce faisant le duc attendra

---

loth for the injury which he knows the said king Lewis would or might inflict upon the said king and kingdom of England.

Wherefore he shall say to the said king how the duke requests him that in maintaining the amities and treaties heretofore made between the said late king Edward and the duke, he will be pleased to succour the duke against the said king Lewis if he commence war against the duke, and send him for part of his succours the number of 4,000 English archers, furnished with good captains and a good chief, and paid for six months at the expense of the said king of England, and to send the same within one month after the duke shall make request for them, as the said late king Edward had promised to do; and to give his seal for this and send it to the duke; and also to send to the duke, if he should require it, besides the said number of 4,000 archers, two or three other thousand archers within another month, furnished with good captains, at the pay and expense of the duke. And so doing the duke

A.D. 1483. 26 August. laventure de la guerre, telle quil plaira a Dieu lui envoier, plustost que baillier en la main dudit roy Loys ledit sieur de Richemont, ne faire chose prejudiciable ausdits roy ne royaume Dangleterre.

Et si ledit roy Dangleterre accorde ledit secours, ledit Georges lui dira que le duc le prie quil lui plaise lui en envoier son seelle et certification par escript par ledit Georges, affin que le duc sen puisse tenir sceur et en asseurer ses subgets, qui sera cause de mouvoir lesdits subgets du duc davoir tousjours de plus en plus ferme amour audit roy et royaume Dangleterre; en lui certifiant que ce faisant il gaignera le duc et le duche pour lui a jamais et les obligera a vouloir et pourchacer a leur pouvoir son bien, sceurte et prosperite en toutes lez facons a eulx possibles.

Ou tout desquelles choses ledit Georges besoingnera en toute diligence sans faire sejour devers ledit roy

---

will await the fortune of war, such as it shall please God to send him, rather than deliver into the hand of the said king Lewis the said lord of Richmond, or do anything prejudicial to the said king or kingdom of England.

And if the said king of England grant the said succours, the said George shall say to him that the duke begs he will be pleased to send his seal and certification of it by the said George in order that the duke may hold himself sure of it, and assure his subjects; which will be a cause to move ' the said subjects of the duke, to have always more and more firm love to the said king and kingdom of England. Certifying him that by so doing he will gain the duke and duchy to himself for ever and oblige them to desire and procure, according to their power, his weal, surety and prosperity by every means to them possible.

In all which things the said George shall acquit himself with all diligence without making longer stay with

fors trois ou quatre jours auplus; et incontinent sen retournera pour advertir le duc du tout. A.D. 1483. 26 August.

Fait et expedie a Nantes le xxvj^e^. jour dAoust, lan mil iiij^c^. iiij^xx^. et trois.

GUEGUEN.

---

the said king, than three or four days at the most; and shall immediately return to apprise the duke of everything.

Done and expedited at Nantes, the 26th day of August, the year 1483.

GUEGUEN.

---

## XIII.

### GOVERNMENT OF IRELAND.

[MS. Harl. 433. f. 242.]

INSTRUCCIONS yeven by the king our soverayn lord to his trusty welbeloved maister William Lacy, sent from his highnes unto his said lande of Irland.

THE said maister William Lacy shal take with him certain the kinges lettres missives under his signet, directe aswell to the counsaille ther in generall as to the particuler persones of the same, and by vertue of thaim he shal shewe and open by wey of credence suche thinges as followen, deviding the maters according to the personages that he shal speke unto.

Item, the said master William shall shewe that the king after the stablisshing of this his realme of England, principally afore othere thinges entendeth for the weele of this lande of Irland to set and advise suche good rule and politique guyding there as any of his noble progenitors have done or entended in tymes past to reduce it.

A.D. 1483. August.

Edward prince of Wales to be lieutenant of Ireland, and Kildare his deputy.

Item, he shal shewe that the king hathe ordeyned for the weele of his lande of Irland the righte highe and mighti prince Edward his first begoten son to be lieutenaunt of his said lande of Irland fro the xix day of July last past during the termes of thre yere next folowing, &c.

Item, he shal shewe that therle of Kildare is ordeyned and made deputie lieutenaunt to Edward his said first begoten sonne during a yere following, to begynne at the last day of August next commyng, and so lenger to contynue at the kinges pleasure, receyvyng for wages and fees rately as it shal be requisite for the same. And the cause is why that the king woll alwey be at his libertee, to thentent the relief of that lande by his inmediat auctorite, whensoever he may have furst leiser therunto.

Item, that in consideracion of the good fame and noble disposicion that Thomas Fitzgerard erle of Kildare is reported to be of, and namely for that he hath endevoired him self by his noble corage wele and feithfully to occupie as lieutenant to Richard late duc of York, the king hath ordeyned the said Thoma Fitzgerard to be deputie of the said mighti prince Edward now lieutenant during the kinges said pleasure.

Item, because the disposition of the said erle of Kildare aught furst to be understande afore any shewe or openyng to be made to other of the counsaille ther, considering that the gret part of al the direccions to be takyn in this behalve, resteth upon his assent in taking upon the said deputacion, therfore the said maister William Lacy shal practise to have speche with him afore any othere.

Item, in delivering the kinges particuler lettres direct to the said erle, and in shewing to him his credence apart, he shal say that the king our soverayn lord hathe the said erle for his gret merits in special favor and tendrenesse, trusting right moche upon his saddenes and trouthe. And for that he hath abled him to be deputie to the said mighti prince his first begoten son, as it shal appere by a commission made to him as deputie. A.D. 1483. August.

Item, the said maister William shal delivere the said erle upon his agrement to take the charge upon him, as well the commission which the king hath made to my lord prince, as that my said lord prince hathe made to him, whiche bothe commissiones the said maister William shal have with him.

Item, upon thacceptacion of the said commissions and office the said maister William shall insist that the said erle come or sende in all possible hast to the king in England to endent with his grace as it shall mowe be best accorded betwene thaim, havyng respecte as well to the ease of this tymes as to othere presidentes passed afore.

Item, the said maister William shall have with him a lettre undre the kinges prive seall concernyng the mynte of Irlande, the whiche lettre is directe unto the lordes of the counsaille there, and he shal ensiste that in al possible hast the content of that lettre be put in execucion.

Item, the said maister William shal shewe that the king wolle that every of the kinges officers shal aswell in his courtes, the chief justices of bothe benches and barons of theschequer as other officers ther, to enyoie theyr offices during the kinges pleasure.

Item, to appoynt officers besides the maister of the mynte, with the advise of the kinges counsaill, as shal finde sufficient suerte for the said office, that is to say, wardeyn and comptroller, &c. of the said mynt.

Item, the said maister William shall have with him a copy of the last indentur, and therupon commune with the said erle by protestacion that nothing shalbe takyn for concluded in that matier without the kinges especiall advise and assent, soo and in

A.D. 1483. August. suche wise that the mater of the said endenture may be wele ripe afore. And as for any certain terme to be assigned therin, the king woll that it be for one yere, to begynne the first day of Octobre next to comme, aud so furthre at the kinges pleasure, the charges and emolymentes to be borne and perceyved rately for suche a tyme above the said yere according to the said indenture.

Item, he shal say to the kinges counsaill there that the kinge woll his sealis of Irland to be renewed, chaunging the graving of the said seales.

Item, to understand the kinges redynes of his lande of Irland.

Item, to shew the kinges counsaille that the king woll the statute of premenire be put in execucion against alle thaim that make labour to have benyfices by provision.

---

## XIV.

### Custody of Guisnes castle.

[MS. Harl. 433. f. 243.]

Instrucciones yeven by the kinges highnes to his fulle trusty counsellors, the lord Dynham, lieutenant of the towne and marches of Caleys; maister John Cooke, archedeacon of Lincoln; Sir Richard Tunstalle, Sir John Scott, and Sir Thomas Thwaytes, knightes, upon certain articles of peticion made by Sir Rauff Hastinges, knight, late lieutenant of the towne and castell of Guysnes.

First, where the said Sir Rauff Hastinges in the first article of his peticions desireth to have the kinges lettres of pardon; and in the secunde article to have the kinges lettres of confirmacion of alle suche landes and offices as he had of the kinges graunt, late deceased, the kinges said commissioners shall have with them his lettres of pardon, and also his lettres of confirmacion of alle suche landes and offices as the said Sir Rauff had of the graunt of king Edward, late decessed, at the tyme of the dethe of the same king; which lettres of pardon and confirmacion the king woll his said commissioners delyver to the said Sir Rauff, he first delyveryng to them to the kinges behoove the kinges towne and castell [of][1] Guysnes. The which towne and castell so by them receyved the king woll they delyver the same to Sir John Blonte, lord Mountjoy, he to have the rewle and keping of the same during the kinges pleasure. A.D. 1483. August.

Lord Mountjoy to have the keeping of Guisnes Castle.

Item, where he desireth in the iij[de] article to have full contentacion of his wages, and of the wages of his felosship, &c., and for all suche reparacions and fortificacions as he hath done upon the said place; the king woll his said commissioners, upon serche by them made what resteth to him and his said felosship due and unpaied, appoynt with him for his and his said fellosshippes contentacion and payment. And in like wise they shall appoynt with him for reparacions and fortificacions by him made necessarie and behovefull to the kinges place there, so that the said Sir Rauff yet hiderton hath not be contented[2] nor allowed for the same.

Item, as touching the iiij[th] article, where he desireth that he may peasibly have and enyoie the wardshippes of the heires of the lord Grey of Wilton, and John Dyne of Northampton, &c., the king woll his said commissioners shall say that the king is right wele content that he have and enjoye all suche barganes as he hath made with his subgettes according to his lawes.

Item, where he desireth to have respite till Michelmisse come xij. moneth of the delyveraunce of the said

[1] Om. in MS.

[2] The final *d* of this word is struck through, but by a later hand.

A.D. 1483. August. place, there to the kinges said commissioners shal saye that the king is no thing content with that desire, as his grace hath shewed his mynde in tymes past fully and fynally determyned in that behalve. But his grace is wele content that his said commissioners finde suche weyes and meanes as the said Sir Rauff shalle move frely without enpechement or trouble remove out of the said place suche goodes and stuff as he hath within the said towne and castell, or other places there. And over that, that the said Sir Rauff be agreed with for alle suche vitailles and stuff as he hath porveyd for the same place, &c.

---

## XV.

### Answer to the Message of Isabella of Castile.

[MS. Harl. 433. f. 244 b.]

Instruccions yeven by the king to Barnard de la Forssa, whome his highnes at this tyme sendeth to his derrest cousyns the king and the quene of Spaigne.

First, after the presenting of the kinges lettres to theim of credence, with suche recommendacions and good wordes as shalbe thought most convenient and acceptable to theim, he shall shewe his credence in maner and forme folowing:

That the king our soverayn lord hath recived a lettre of credence from his derrest cousine the quene of Spaigne by hir orator the bachiler de Sasiola, and by the same hath clerly understande the gret luff and singuler benevolence that hir highnes beres towardes his grace, and therfore thankes her in his hertiest maner, latting her wit that his highnes is of noo lesse good will towardes hir housband and hir, but woll in all convenient wises be as glad to do that, that may be to the honour and wele of theim and their realmes as any prince lyvyng. A.D. 1483. August.

And forsomoche as by vertue of credence committed to hir said orator, and by him shewed to the king by mouth and also writing, his grace hath understande his said cousins to be utterly disposed to have with him good and ferme peace, lieges, alliaunces, and confideracions, to thentent that they shuld be joigned, alyed, and confederate in perfite liege and confideracion as good and feithfulle cousins and cofiderates:

The said Barnard shall in that behalve say that the king therfore thankes his said cousins in his hertiest maner, and is therof as desirus as they be, and wolle to the perfeccion therof intende by alle weyes and meanes convenient and resonable. And how that incontinent upon the said credence so opened the king, seing that the said orator whiche had no specialle commission in writing, nor instruccions so large as shuld be requisite to the making of so grete a ligue, made to be serched up the ligue that was last taken betwene the late king Edward, his brother, and king Henry of Castille, late brother of the said quene, whome God pardone. Wherby it was thought unto him and his counsaille that the beginnyng of the best intelligence betwene both parties shuld be grounded upon the articles of the said ligue, considering that by long and ripe advise and deliberacion the articles of the said ligue were practized and concluded.

England proposes a renewal of the league made between Edward IV. and Henry IV. of Castile.

And over this the said Barnard shalle shewe that the king our soverayn lord, not willing any long tracte of tyme or other impediment of so goodly and behovefull entent shuld be on his partie, and specially when he is so instanced by the said orator to sende thider in all goodly hast for full expedicion of the same, his highnes hath at this tyme sent thider the said Bernard to common of the best and spediest wayes.

A.D. 1483. August.

In which communicacion the said Barnard shalle by alle meanes of policie dryve theim to conforme[1] the olde ligue without making of a newe; to the whiche if they can be founde by his wisdome agreable, than he shall mow desire to have suche forme of commission made by the kinges cousyns ther to suche as shalle please them to deliver to him their part of the ligue sealed as he hath to deliver the kynges parte also sealed, keping him close alwey from knowleging that that he hath any suche commission or ligue sealed unto suche tyme as he utterly understande their myndes of suche commission and delivere to be made by theim.

And in case they wolle in no wise agree to make any suche confirmacion of the ligue now made, but utterly insiste to make a new, either like or more large with some new articles, then he shall labor by his wisdome the wayes that suche orators may be sent with him into England, as may have of the kinges cousins their fulle auctorite and power to common, appoincte and conclude, as by theim the said mater may take good affecte[2] and conclusion.

Morover the king is content that whethir the ligue shalbe desired to be alle new made, or any addicions to be had to the olde, the said Barnard speke frely with theim of suche new articles as they desire, and that he common and debate upon theim in suche wise as by his discrecion shalbe thought best for the king and his land, advoiding as moche as he can any gret and certaine charges that the king might be put unto; provided alwey that by any thing so to be spoken, commoned, or treated the king be not bounden above the olde articles, but be at his hole libertie in alle suche new maters unto the commyng

[1] Sic in MS.

[2] *and conclude,—effecte*] repeated in MS.

of thenbassate of Castille into England, and till they and the kinges commissaries have throughly passed in all poyntes. A.D. 1483. August.

Item, where the said Bernard hathe an other commission to treate and appointe upon attemptates aswele with the governors of the provinces as with the counsaille of the king and quene, and to appoincte a diete for the same; the king wolle that he doo and procede in thoos maters according to the said commission, and to suche instruccions as he had delivered unto him therupon afore.

---

## XVI.

### James III. to Richard III.

[MS. Harl. 433, f. 246 b.]

By the King of Scottes.

Right excellent, hie and mighti prince and right trusty and welbeloved cousing,—We commende us unto you in the most hertlie wise. And how beit that oft tyme afore certain rupcioun, breke and distrublaunce has bene betwixt the realmes of Ingland and Scotland be the werkyngis and menys of evil disposed persones, incontrarie our mynde and entencion, as God knowes; Nevertheless we remayne in the said propose afore like as we wraite to the right noble prince your brother, quham God assoilze, to observe and kepe luff, pece, concorde and amyte with alle Cristyne princes, and above others with our nichebouris and realmes next approchand to the bordures of our realme of Scotland, for the good of peax, and till enchew the effusioun of Cristyn blode. Now at this tyme has sende to you our lovit serviture Dingvale persewand with thir oure lettres, that we may be certifiit of your noble mynde

Proposing eight months' abstinence of war, with a view to a permanent peace,

A.D. 1488. 16 August.

twiching the good of peas in tyme commyng to be observed and kept betwixt your realme of Ingland and oures of Scotland. And gif it bei sene expedient and proffitable unto you that ane abstinence of werre war taken be sey and lande for the space of aught monethis for the fyne and entent that the gret commissioners of both the realmes might mete at convenient and custumable place on ne bordures for the propose above expremit. Or gif it were thought more expedient for the gude of the said mater that certaine lordes of our realme in our legacion come within your realme of England, and till appointe, aggre, and concorde upon the goode of peax (they havyng conduyt of your highnes for thaim, their famuliaris and servituris to the noumyr of lxxx of persones or within, quahis names our said serviture shall shewe you gevin to him in writ), the abstynence of werre enduring in the meane tyme. Praying your sercnite that ye will certifie us of your good mynde and disposicion in alle hast in the premisses by your writing with our said serviture or any other of youres, As we trust in your right excellent cousinage, the quylk God kepe. Written under our signet at Edingburgh, the xvj day of August.

Or, to send an embassy.

To, &c., the King of Ingland.

## XVII.

### Richard III. to James III.

[MS. Harl. 433, f. 247.]

By the King of England.

A.D. 1483. 16 Sept. Offering a safe-conduct if he will send ambassadors.

Right high and mighti prince, right trusty and welbeloved cousin, we commaunde us unto you. And where as by your lettres brought unto us by your pursevaunt Dyngvale, as amongst other largely shewed that for occasion in tyme past thenterupcion, breche, and disturbaunce of peas betwixt both realmes, hath growen thrugh the meanes of evyll disposed persones contrarie to your mynde and entencioun, and that ye remayne in good purpoos to thobservaunce of love, peas, and concorde of the same royalmes to be had, and for that entent have sent, at this tyme, unto us your said pursuyvant to understande our goode mynde in that behalve, meovyng us for that cause that certaine your legates mought come unto us enstructed with your mynde in that partie; cousyn, we acertaine you our mynde and disposicion is and ever shalbe confirmable to the will and pleasur of God our aller Creatour in all resounable and convenient peax, without fenyng, that shuld be desired of us by any nacion. And if that your desire and pleasure be to sende hider suche personnages to treate for thaccomplisshing therof, we, havyng knowlage fro you of their names, shall yeve unto theim oure sure saufconduyt for ane resonable nombre and season. And God kepe you, right high and mighti prince, our right trusty and welbeloved cousyn. Yeven the xvj[th] day of September.

To, &c., the King of Scottes.

## XVIII.

### The Duke of Britanny's Warrant to advance money to the Earl of Richmond.

[From the orig., MS. Cott. Julius, B. vi. 95, on parchment.]

A.D. 1483. 22 Nov. Francoys, par la grace de Dieu, duc de Bretaigne, conte de Montfort, de Richemont, dEstampes, et de Vertus, a noz bien amez et feaulx conseillers, les gens de noz comptes, salut. Nous vous mandons et commandons expressement que allouez et passez, en clere mise et descharge, anostre bien ame et feal Gilles Thomas, tresorier de nostre espergne, a ses comptes, quant mestier en aura, la somme de dix mil escuz dor, quil a baillee des deniers de nostredite espergne, de nostre expres commandement et ordonnance, par maniere de prest, a nostre treschier et tresame cousin le sire de Richemont, sans aucune difficulte y faire, raportant seulement ces presentes aveeques relacion de nostredit cousin de les avoir receuz, comme dit est, car tel est nostre plaisir; nonobstant quelzconques

---

Translation.

Francis, by the grace of God, duke of Britanny, earl of Montfort, of Richmond, of Estampes, and of Vertus, to our well-beloved and faithful counsellors, the auditors of our accounts, greeting. We command you expressly that you allow and pass in full payment and discharge, to our well-beloved and faithful Giles Thomas, treasurer of our exchequer, in his accounts, if he shall require it, the sum of ten thousand crowns of gold, which he has delivered of the monies of our said exchequer, by our express commandment and order, in the way of loan, to our most dear and well-beloved cousin the lord of Richmond, without making any difficulty therein, bringing back only these presents with our said cousin's acknowledgment of having received them, as is

mandemens, ordonnances, deffenses, restrinctions, ou autres choses a ce contraires. Donne en nostre ville de Nantes, le xxijme jour de Novembre, lan mil cccc. quatrevings et troys. A.D. 1483. 22 Nov.

(L.S.) FRANCOYS.

Par le duc de son commandement,

Gueguen.

---

said, for such is our pleasure: notwithstanding whatsoever commands, orders, prohibitions, restrictions, or other things to the contrary. Given in our town of Nantes, the 22nd day of November, in the year 1483.

FRANCIS.

By the duke's command,

Gueguen.

---

## XIX.

[MS. Harl. 433, f. 238.]

INSTRUCCIONS geven to Northumbreland herauld by the kinges grace at Notingham, the xiijth day of Aprill, to be by him executed. A.D. 1484. 13 April.

FURST, the king wol that the said Northumbreland make his tarying and abode at Berwik from the tyme of his commyng thider unto the xv. day of May next commyng, to thentent that the Scottisshe ambassiadours within that day may certefie him of suche thinges as they have promysed the kynges grace to doo before that day.

Item, the king wol that if the said Northumbreland by the said enbassators be certefyed there that theire prince is agreed and concluded to have an abstynence of werre, bothe by see and land, to endure to Cristemasse or Alhalowentyde at the lest, than the said Northumbreland to common and cause a certein day

To arrange an abstinence of war between England and Scotland.

A.D. 1484. 13 April.

to be appointed, that aswele the same abstynence may within and upon the borduris of Scotland as upon the bordures of England, Berwike, and Donnebarre be proclaymed, and, the said abstynence concluded to see be proclaymed in alle places afore expressed and elleswhere on the bordures of England accustumed the same day.

Item, the king wol that if there be desired a saufconduyt for the said ambassiatours or any moo joyned with theim to come into this royaume for the good of peas to be laboured to his grace, than the same Northumbreland to delyver to suche as from the Scottes king cometh the saufconduyt to him delyvered in that behalf.

Item, that in the said abstynence that hit be ordeyned that no grownde on the West bordures called Batabelle Grounde be othrewise occupyed than hit is at this day by any partie, &c.

---

## XX.

### Regulations for the Council of the North.

[MS. Harl. 433. f. 264 b.]

A.D. 1484, July.

Thise Articles folowing be ordeyned and stablisshed by the kinges grace, to be used and executed by my lord of Lincolne,[1] and the lordes and other of his counselle in the North Parties for his sueretie and welthe of thenhabitantes of the same.

Imparti-ality to be observed.

Furst, the king wolle that none lord ne other persone appoynted to be of his counselle, for favor, affeccion, hate, malice, or mede, do ne speke in the counselle

---

[1] John De la Pole, earl of Lincoln, the king's nephew.

otherwise then the kinges lawes and good conscience shalle require, but be indifferent and no wise parcell, as ferr as his wit and reason woll geve him, in all maner maters that shalbe mynestred afore theym. A.D. 1484. July.

Item, that if there be any mater in the said counselle moved which toucheth any lord or other persone of the said counselle, than the same lord or persone in no wise to syt or remayn in the said counselle during the tyme of thexamynacion and ordering of the said mater enlesse he be called, and that he obeie and be ordured therin by the remenant of the said counsell.

Item, that no maner mater of gret weght or substaunce be ordered or determyned within the said counselle enlesse that two of thise, that is to say

* * * * * * *[1]

with our said nepveu be at the same, and they to be commissioners of our peax thoroughout these parties.

Item, that the said counselle be, hooly if it may be, onys in the quarter of the yere at the leste, at York, to here, examyne and ordre alle billes of compleyntes and other there before theym to be shewed, and oftyner if the case require. The Council to sit at York, at least once in a quarter of a year.

Item, that the said counselle have auctorite and power to ordre and direct alle riottes, forcible entres, distresse takinges, variaunces, debates and other mysbehavors ayenst our lawes and peas committed and done in the said parties. And if any suche be that they in no wise can thoroughly ordre, than to referre it unto us, and therof certifie us in alle goodly hast therafter.

Item, the said counselle in no wise determyn mater of land without thassent of the parties.

Item, that our said counselle for great riottes done and committed in the gret lordships or otherwise by

[1] Blank in MS.

A.D. 1484. July. any persone, committe the said persone to warde to oon of our castelles nere where the said riott is committed. For we wolle that alle our castelles be our gaole; and if noo suche castelle be nere, than the next common gaole.

Item, we wolle that our said counselle incontynent after that they have knowlage of any assembles or gaderinges made contrarie oure lawes and peas, provide to resiste, withstande, and ponysshe the same in the begynnyng according to their demerites, without ferther deferring or putting it in respecte.

Item, that alle lettres and writinges by our said counselle to be made for the due executing of the premisses be made in our name, and the same to be endoced with the hande of our nepveu of Lincolne undre nethe by thise wordes *Per Consilium Regis.*

Item, that oon suffisaunt persone be appoynted to make out the said lettres and writinges and the same put in regestre from tyme to tyme, and in the same our said nepveu and suche with him of our said counselle then being present, setto their handes and a seale to be provided fre for the sealing of the said lettres and writinges.

Item, we wolle and streitly charge alle and singuler our officers, true liegemen and subgiettes in thise North Parties to be at alle tymes obeieng to the commaundementes of our said counselle in our name and duely to execute the same as they and every of theym wolle eschue our gret displeasure and indignacion.

Memorandum, that the kinges grace afore his departing do name the lordes and other that shalbe of his counselle in these parties to assiste and attende in that behalve upon his nepveu of Lincolne.

Item, memorandum that the king name certen lierned men to be attending here, so that oon alweys at the lest be present, and at the meting at York to be alle there. A.D. 1484. July.

Item, that the king graunt a commission to my lord of Lincolne and other of the counselle according to theffect of the premisses.

---

## XXI.

### James III. to Richard III.[1]

[MS. Harl. 433. f. 263 b.]

Right excellent, hie, and michti Prince, and right traist and welbelovit cousing, we commende us unto you in the maist hertly wise. Signifying unto your cousinage that we are nowe advertisit by the relacion of our traist and welbelovit cousing and counsaillor Robert lord Lile, our lovit squier Duncane of Dundas, and also by the feithfulle repoort of your familier squier Edward Gower shewen to certain lordes of our counsaille and by thaim to us, that your cousinage is wele appliit and inclynit to the gud of trewes [and][2] abstinence of werre betuix you and us, our realmes and lieges, and also that luf, amytie, and specialle alliauncez of mariage was avisit, appointit, and concludit betwix your blode and oures; whereunto we ar in likewise inclinit. And according to your empleasire and to shew in that parte oure gud mynde to the commone gude of treux and abstinence of were, We have fynijt and ordand our traist and welbelovit cousinges and counsalors Coline erle of Ergile, lord Cambell Lorne our chaunceler, a reverend fader in God William bisshop of Abberdene, Robert lord Lile, Lau-

A.D. 1484. 21 July.

Naming his ambassadors.

---

[1] Headed in the original MS. "The king of Scottes lettre sent to the "king."

[2] Om. in MS.

A.D. 1484. 21 July. rence lord Oliphant, Johnne of Drummond of Stobhalle and maister Archibald of Quhitelawe, archidene of Lothiane our secretare, with fulle powair and commission to comme within your royaume unto you to your towne of Notingham the vij day of Septembre next to comme, to avise, common, and conclude upon trewes and abstinence of weir to be observit and kepeit betuix your lieges and oures. And also upon luf, friendship, aliaunces, and mariage to be had betuix your maist noble blude and oures, like as we were present in propre persone to the ferme observacion and stabiliment of the said trewx. And like as ye have geven in charge to your squier forsaid that abstinence of weir be had betuix the realmes be see and land, and commaundit your wardeins, lieutenantes, admiralles, and capitaines of weir, that none hosting, riding, truble, nor noo manere of weir be made by any Englisshemen agains us, our realme or lieges, and that reformacion salbe made of alle attemptates that shal happen to be doon or commyttit be see or by land unto the agayncummyng of our ambaxiators of England, and viij dayes efter their cummyng within our royaume, we have in likewise commaundit oure wardains, lieutenantes, admiralles, and capitaignes of werre that nane hosting, riding, truble, nor no manere of weir, be maid by any our lieges agains your royaume or lieges, and that reformacion salbe made of alle attemptates that sall happen to be done or committit by see or by land, unto the againe cummyng of our ambaxiators of England, and viij dayes after thair cummyng within our royaume according to your worship and oures. And to the eise of your lieges and oures that shalle happen in the meane tyme to susteyne dampnage or scathe in their persones or goodes; and that your saufconduyt in the meantyme may be sent to the persones aboue expremit to the nombre of a c. of hors or within, to come to your toune above expremit. Richt excellent hie and michty prince and traist cousing, the Blessit Trinitie have you in keping. Writen undre our signet at Edingburghe, the xxj day of July, A.D. 1484. 21 July.

JAMES.

## XXII.

### RICHARD III. TO JAMES III.[1]

[MS. Harl. 433. f. 264.]

RIGHT high and mighty prince, right trusty and welbeloved cousin, we commaunde us unto you in the moost herty wise. And where it hath pleased your cousinage to addresse unto us nowe of late your honorable lettres by our trusty servant and squier Edward Gower, signifiing by the same howe that upon the retornyng of your trusty and welbeloved cousin and counsaillor Robert lord Lile from us into your royaume agayne, and by his relacion and otheis ye have ben advertised of our mynde as touching the good of peas and abstinence of werre betwene bothe royaumes. Whereunto we shewed us wele applied and inclyned in suche manere as we largely commoned with the same lord Lile and yave in charge to our said servant topen unto your said highnesse or to suche lordes of your counsaille as it wold please you to depute and assigne to here the same. And that thereupon your said cousinage likewise inclyned, and according to our pleasire hathe lymited and ordeigned certaine grete lordes and othre of your counsaille with ful powair and commission to comme into our towne of Notingham the vij day of Septembre next to comme, to advyse, common, and conclude upon treux and absty-

A.D. 1484. 7 Aug. Sending a safeconduct for the above ambassadors.

[1] In the MS. this letter immediately follows the preceding, and is headed "The kinges lettres of an-"swere unto the same."

A.D. 1484. 7 Aug. nence of werre to be observed and kept betwix your lieges and oures; and also upon love and frendship aliaunces and mariages to be had in your blode and oures, like as in your said lettres it is conteigned more at large. Right highe and mighty prince, righte trusty and welbeloved cousin, we late your cousinage wite that this your loving and toward disposicion is to us right agreable, trusting that by the mean of this your ambassade instructed in al the forsaid maters as plenerly as the caas shal require, and to doo therein as largely in al pointes as ye were present in propre persone, according to that that is expressed in your said lettres, suche good weyes shalbe taken betwix bothe royaumes whereby effusion of Christen blood may be eschewed, love and tendrenesse growe daily and encreace, aswele betwix you and us as the inhabitauntes of bothe royaumes, whiche we take God in witnesse we as hertly have entended with good condicions, and soo shal hereafter, as any prince lyving cann or may. And to thentent no thing faille necessary or behoveful to the spedy execucion of the premisses, nor of your partie ne of oures, we have passed our lettres patentes of saufconduyt undre our gret seale for the sure commyng, abiding, and retornyng of your said ambassade, and the same lettres sent by this berer according to your desire and pleasure. Right high and mighty prince, right trusty and welbeloved cosyn, the blessed Trinite have you in his keping. Yeven undre our signet at our palois of Westminster, the vijth day of August.

RICARDUS REX.

## XXIII.

### Reception of the Scotch Ambassadors.

[This article is derived from two leaves which, although contained in the Cottonian Volume Caligula B.v., originally belonged to a MS. now in Vespasian C.xvi. At the end of folio 79 of the latter volume is an incomplete sentence, which will be found continued at f. 147 of Calig. B.v. The portion in Vespasian C.xvi. is the speech of Archibald Whitelaw, which it is scarcely necessary to print, as Bucke has given some extracts (Kennet's Complete Hist., I. 572), that pretty tolerably indicate its general character. The only fact of interest that it contains is a statement that the speaker had been sent ambassador by James II., about 25 years before, to the king's father (Richard Duke of York), in Ireland, and concluded a treaty with him]. A.D. 1484 Sept.

ix^no^ die Septembris apud castrum de Notyngham.

It ys advysed certeyn lordys that ys to wyte the byshopp of Synt Asse,[1] therle of Notyngham, lord * * * * * * * * * *[2] Maister Thomas Utton, doctor of canon, and other knyghtes whele yncompanied to mete with the lordys and other commyng out of Scotland yn ambassad un to the kynges hyghnes, and they to convey the seyd ambassadors un to ther logyng yn the towne of Notyngham, etc.

xj^mo^ die Septembris.

Thus day at aftyr none thembassadors cam yn to Nothyngham acompanid with suche lordys and other as ys a fore sayd, etc.

---

[1] Richard Redman.

[2] A line and a half blank in MS.

A.D 1484.
Sept.

xiij^mo die Septembris apud castrum Nothyngham, anno regni regis Ricardi Tertii secundo.

| | | |
|---|---|---|
| Lincolniensis Cancellarius. | Archiepiscopus Ebor. REX. | Dux Norffolckiæ. |
| Gunthorp, c.p.s. | Thambassadors of Scotland, that ys to say, | Comes Northumbriæ. |
| Wygorniensis. | Coly, erle of Erguile, Chauncellor of Scot- | |
| Assavensis. | land, the bysshopp of Aberdeyn, lord Lyle, | Comes Salopiæ. |
| | lord Olivant, lord Drummond of Stobhall, | |
| | maister Archibald Qwitlawe, archidiacon | Comes Nothyngham. |
| | of Loudon, secretary, Lyon kinge of armys, | |
| | and Dunkan of Dundas, cam yn to the | |
| Mr Barow, clericus rotu- | kynges presence by fore hygh messe of | Stanley. |
| lorum. | thys same day, the kyng beyng in hys gret | Scropp Hupsale. |
| | chaumbre undyr hys clothe of ryall astate, | |
| Decanus Ebor. | beyng then and there a waytying up on | Fytz Hugh. |
| Mr. Lee. | hys seyd hyghnes, by syde the lordys and | Hastyng. |
| Mr. T. Hutton. | other of hys counsell, many nobyll knyghtes | Dudley. |
| | and squyers, as wele for hys body as other | Straunge. |
| | of hys most royall howsold; and ther | |
| | the forsayd mayster Archibald, one of the | |
| | seyd ambassadors purposyd a oracyon yn | |
| | furme and maner as here after folowyth. | Sir Richard Ratclyff. |

A.D. 1484. Sept.

Sir Thomas Borough.
Sir Robert Percy.
Sir * *[1] Constable.
Sir Rychard Croftys.
Sir Jamys Tyrell.
Sir Gerney Clefton.

And after the seyd oracion was finished the seyd Mr. Archibald delyvered to the kynges grace a commissyon under the Gret Seall of Scotland for the abstines of were by twyen England and Scotland, and a nother commissyon undyr the seyd Gret Seall of Scotland for maryage by twyene the prince of Scottis and one of the kynges blood. The tenors of bothe commissyons folowyth here after as more largely yt schall a pere yn the end therof, by indentors to be made up on the same; whych commissyons the kyng delyvered un to my lor chaunceller, whych so don he purposed an answer by wey of oracyon yn laude and preeyse of the seyd Mr. Archebald, the tenor whereof folowyth next after the seyd oracyon.

[1] Blank in MS.

A.D. 1484. Sept. xiiij^mo^. die Septembris apud castrum Nothyngham.

Thyes be the names of the lordys whome the kynges hyghnes hath ordeyned and mad to be hys commissarys ther to appoynt, accord, and conclude with the forseyd orators of Scotland, that ys to sey, the erle of Arguile, the bysshopp of Aberdyen, and other, etc., for the peace to be made of bothe reamys. The tenor of her commissyon here after mor at large yt schall appere by indentors yn thend of the same.

John, bysshopp of Lincoln, chaunceller.
Richard, bysshopp of Seint Assaph.
John, duc of Norffolk.
Henry, erle of Northumbyrland.
Mr. John Gunithrop, c. p. s.
Sir Thomas Stanley lord Stanley.
Sir [George Stanley][1] lord Straunge.
Sir [John Grey][1] lord Powes.
Sir Herry lord Fyghugh.
Sir Humfrey lord Dacres.
Sir Thomas Barow, mayster of the Rolles.
Sir Thomas Bryan, cheffe juge of the Comyn Place.
Sir Rychard Ratclyff.
William Catesby.
Rychard Salkeld.

Item, the namys of the lordys that schall commyn for the maryage.—

Thomas, archybysshop of York.
John, bysshop of Lyncoln, canc' of England.
John, duc of Norffolk:—
John, erle of Nothyngham.
John, bysshopp of Worcester.
John Sutton lord Dudley.
[Thomas][1] lord Scroop Upsale.

---

[1] Blank in MS

Sir Wylliam Husey, knyghte, cheffe justices of y^e kynges benge. A.D. 1484. Sept.

Sir Rychard Ratclyff.

William Catesby.

The tenor of ther commissyon more at large yt schall appere here after by indentors.

Hæc indentura facta inter nos Thomam, Dei gratia Eboracensem archyepiscopum Angliæ primatem et Apostolicæ Sedis legatum, Johannem Lincolniensem cancellarium Angliæ, et Johannem Wigorniensem, episcopos; Johannem ducem Norffolckiæ comitem marescalli, marescallum et admirallum Angliæ, dominum de Moubray de Segrave et Howard, Willielmum comitem Nothynghamiæ dominum Barkeley, Johannem Sutton dominum Dudley, Johannem dominum Scroop de Massam, milites; Willielmum Husey capitalem justiciarium domini regis ad placita coram ipso rege tenenda, militem, Ricardum Radclyff ordinis garterii, militem,[1] et Willielmum Catesby armigerum pro corpore excellentissimi[2] . . . .

---

## XXIV.

### Message to the Earl of Desmond.

[MS. Harl. 433, f. 265 b.]

Instruccions geven by the kinges grace to his counsellor the bisshop of Enachden,[3] to be shewed in his behalf to his cousyn therle of Dessemond, and other nobles and gentiles of his land of Irland.

Furst, where the said bisshop hath enfourmed his said grace of the good toward disposicion and herty Services done by Desmond's

---

[1] *inclitem*, MS.

[2] Here the MS. breaks off abruptly.

[3] His name was Thomas Baret. See Patent 24 Feb., 2 Ric. III., p. 2, No. 133, Calendar of Patent Rolls, printed in Report ix. of the Deputy Keeper of the Public Records, App. ii. p. 120.

A.D. 1484. Sept.

father to the king's father, Richard duke of York.

desire that the said erle hathe for to doo him pleasur and service to his power, as feithfully and humbly as any other of the kinges subgiettes; the said bisshop shalle on the kinges behalve thanke him, shewing that aswele for the noblesse of bloode, as remembryng the manyfold notable service and kyndnesse by therles fadre unto the famous prince the duc of York the kinges fader at diverse seasons of grete necessite in thoos parties to his gret jeopardies and charges doon, causeth the kinges grace to accepte and reteigne him in the tendre favor of the same, trusting of his contynuaunce.

The earl shall be free to prosecute those who procured his father's death.

Also, he shalle shewe that albe it the fadre of the said erle, the king than being of yong age, was extorciously slayne and murdred by colour of the lawes within Irland by certain persones than havyng the governaunce and rule there, ayenst alle manhode, reason, and good conscience; yet, notwithstanding that the semblable chaunce was and hapned sithen within this royaume of Eingland, as wele of his brother the duc of Clarence as other his nigh kynnesmen and gret frendes, the kinges grace alweys contynueth and hathe inward compassion of the dethe of his said fadre, and is content that his said cousyn now erle by alle ordinate meanes and due course of the lawes, when it shalle lust him at any tyme herafter to sue or attempt for the punysshement therof.

Oath of allegiance to be taken by him.

Also, the kinges grace wolle that the said bisshop have auctorite for to take in the kinges name of the said erle his othe of ligeaunce as other lordes have doon here within this his royaume after the fourme here ensuyng:—"I, A. erle of Dessemond, become true and feithfulle liegeman unto my soverayn lord Richard the iij^de., by the grace of God, king of England, and of Fraunce, and lord of Irland, and to his heires kinges of England, and to him and theim my feith and trouth shalle bere during my lif naturalle, and with him and in his cause and quarelle at alle tymes, shalle take his partie and be redy to leve and dye ayenst alle erthly creatures, and utterly endevor me to the resistence and suppressing of his ennemyes, rebelles and traitors if [I][1] shalle any knowe to the uttermost of my power, and nothing concele that in any wise may be hurting to his noble and roialle persone. Soo helpe me God and thise Holy Evangelyes." A.D. 1484. Sept.

Also, the said bisshop shalle shewe unto the said erle the kinges gret pleasur touching his dealing or entring into any mariage with any blood without thadvise and knowlage of his grace, considred that the same with alle celerite entendeth forto ordeigne and provide in that behalve for his said cousyn in suche wise and of suche noble blode as shalle redounde to his weele and honnor, and of alle his frendes and kynnesmen, trusting that the said erle wolle remembre the same and utterly applie him therunto. The king will provide a marriage for him.

Also, the said bisshop upon perfite understanding that the said erle shalbe of hoole entencion, and promise to his powair to perfourme the premisses, and over that utterly to dispose for many consideracions concernyng the kinges highe pleasur and entent, for to renounce the wering and usage of the Irisshe arraye, and from thensfurthe to geve and applie him self to use the maner of thapparelle for his persone after the Englisshe guyse; and after the fasshon that the kinges grace sendeth unto him by the said bisshop, aswele of gownes, doublettes, hosen and bonettes, and soo folowingly in tyme commyng as the caas or chaunge of the said fasshion shalle require, that than the said bisshop shalle deliver unto his said cousyn in most convenient place and honnorable presence the kinges lyvree, that is to wite, a coler of gold of his devise, and other apparelle forsaid for his persone. He is to give up the Irish habit.

[1] Om. in MS.

A.D. 1484. Sept. Also, above alle other thinges he shalle shewe the said erle that the kinges grace in noo wise wolle oure hooly modre the Churche to be wronged, deroged, or prejudiced neither in liberties, fraunchies, grauntes, custumes, or any other spirituell emolumentes belonging to the same, but that his said cousyn shalle mayntene, assiste, and support it in every behalve, as justice and righte requiereth; and over that to see that no maner robberys, spoliacions, oppressions or extorcions be suffred to be committed amongst any of the kinges subgiettes of thoos parties, of what astate, degree, or condicion soever they be, and in caas any happen to be, to see theim so offending utterly to be punyssed according with the kinges lawes. And that the said erle shalle by alle weys and meanes of pollycie see and provide that by the passage of the commune highe wayes there the kinges subgiettes may be assured to goo and passe without robbing and unlawfulle letting; so that the said erle, according to the kinges gret trust, and also to his graciouse demeanyng here in this royme of England may appere and be named a veray justicer, aswele for his propre honnor and wele as for the comon wele of those parties, &c.

## XXV.

### Message to the Earl of Kildare, &c.

[MS. Harl. 433, f. 266 b.]

Credence given by the kinges grace to his counsaillor the bisshop of Enachden to be shewed on the kinges behalve to Therle of Kildare. A.D. 1484. 22 Sept.

Furst, he shalle shew unto the said erle that the specialle and singuler cause of his message at this tyme is to endevor him to accomplisshe the kinges gret desire forto enduce by alle meanes possible suche persones as deteigne and kepe from his grace his right and enheritaunce of his erldom of Wolstre, and that it may be ordeyned and brought to the kinges handes and possession, as it hathe been in late dayes of his progenitors. Wherin the king said grace thinketh and perfitely understandeth that no man can do more than his said cousyn, seeng and considred that the gret Onealle that hath maried the said erles sustre hathe and occupieth most part therof; whome the kinges grace for the cause of that mariage and the love of his said cousyn, wolle be the rather applied to accept into his favor, as his brother late king of England before had his fader, and gave unto him his lyvree.

How O'Neill and O'Donnell shall be dealt with touching the earldom of Ulster.

Moreovere, if Odomnaylle, by the meanes that the kinges grace hath committed, and shewed unto the said bisshop, wolle come in, and either to be his liegeman or true peax man, that his said cousyn of Kildare shalbe content so to receive and entre[1] him, as the said bisshop shalle advise him more at large

[1] Sic, for *entreat?*

A.D. 1484. 22 Sept. by mouthe, or at the leest that his said cousyn, setting apart almaner parcialite, affeccion, or favor, shalle take partie, fortefie and support thoos of them havyng of the said said lyvelode, by whoos meanes, strenghte, and commyng in the said erldome may sonnest be had and reduced to the kinges handes and possession.[1]

Also, over this, he shalle shewe to the said erle that the kinges wille and pleasur is that he for his part, the Plonkettes, or any other lord or noble man of that land, bordurer or other, shalle in alle wise conforme and applie him to alle suche good weyes, meanes, and advertesementes touching the goode effecte, and wele of the premisses as by the said bisshop shalbe devised in any wise.

Passport for the bishop.

RICHARD, &c. To alle maires, shireffes, bailliefes, constables, and alle maner otheir our officers, liegemen, and subgiettes, aswele within this our royaume as oure land of Irland, whom unto thise presentes shalbe shewed, greting. Forsomoche as we sende at this tyme into our said land the reverende fadre in God, oure fulle welbeloved counsellor the bisshop of Enachden into those parties for certain gret maters concernyng our pleasur, and the prosperous wele of our said land; we, therfore, desire and nathelesse commaunde you that in his passage and repassage by you ye goodly and curtesly, accept and entreate him and his servantes in every behalve, and with the more tendre benivolence at oure instaunce, as ye desire to please us. Yeven, &c. at Westminster, the xxij$^{ti}$ day of September, A$^{o}$ ij$^{do}$.

---

[1] In the blank space at the end of this paragraph the words "A$^{r}$ 3$^{e}$" occur in the same hand as the text.

*Parcelles of the clothing to be delivered by the said bisshop to the said erle.*[1] A.D. 1484. September.

FURST, a long gowne of cloth of gold lyned with sattan or damaske.

Item, a long gowne of velvet lyned with sattayn or damask.

Item, two dublettes, oon of velvet and an other of cremysen saten.

Item, thre shertes and kyrcheffes for thre stomakers.

Item, thre pair of hosen; oon of scarlet, an other violet, and the third blake.

Item, thre bonettes, two hattes, and two tippetes of velvet.

Item, the said bisshop hath a lettre direct to Piers Curtesse, keper of the gret warderop for the deliver of the said stuff.

Item, a nother lettre direct to Mr. William Dawbeney, clerk of the kinges juelles, to deliver unto the said bisshop for the said erle of Dissemond, a coler of gold of xx^ti oz., xxx^ti li.

*To therl of Desmond.*

Desiring him to wear English clothing.

RIGHT trusty and right welbiloved cousin, we grete you hertily wele. Lating you wite that nat oonly the zelous desir and herty affeccion that ye bere unto us according to the duetie of your ligeance, rapported on your behalve by the reverend fader in God, our ful trusti counseillor the bisshop of Enachden, bringer of these, bot also the reteignyng in our mynde of the manifold benivolent services and kindenesse by our cousin your fader in sundrie wise to the famous prince of noble memorie our fader, whom God rest, in

[1] Desmond, not Kildare, this schedule manifestly referring to the letter which follows.

A.D. 1484. September. seasons of great necessite, and after that to our brother, late king, doon and shewed, causen us to have and accepte you into our singler favor and grace. And forasmoch as it hathe pleased God to sende now the rule of this your reame, to have you the more tenderly recommended in the same as our said counseillor hath more plainly to shewe unto you aswele therin as our entent and pleasure for to have you to use the manere of our English habite and clothing; for the which cause we sende you by hym a coller of gold of our liveree and divise with othre apparaill for your persoune of Thenglish fassion, which we wol ye shal receyve of hym in our name as we have advised; trusting that at somme convenient season herafter we shal have you to comme over unto us hider, and bee more expert, both in the maner and condicions of us and othre honorable and goodly behavynges of our subgettes here, as by instruccions we have informed hym therin more at large. And as touching your demeanyng in mariage, that for special causes greatly resteth in our mynde and pleasure, we have in likewise shewed unto hym the same by our said instruccions, to whom in declaring therof, and of everi othre thing concernyng the premisses, we desire you to yeve unto hym ful feith and credence, and with al effect applie and endevoir you to thexecucion and performyng of the same, as our great trust is in you. Yeven, &c. the xxix. day of Septembre.

*To Therle of Kildare.*

The earl of Lincoln appointed lieutenant of Ireland. RIGHT trusti, &c. Certifieng you that as touching the lieutenantship of our land of Irland, we have ordeigned and appointed our entierly biloved nepveu Therl of Lincolne to that office; and have advised and willed him that ye shalbe his deputie in the same, wherunto he is agreable, as your servant besides this can accertaigne you more at large; in the which we pray you to doo and continue as ye have doon for the good and wele of our said land. And over this where as we sende at this tyme unto thoes parties the reverend fader in God our ful trusti counseillor the bisshop of Enachden, bringer of these, for certain materes greatly concernyng our pleasure, which by our commandement he hath to shewe unto you, we desire you therin to yeve unto hym ful feith and credence, and with al diligence to the performyng of the same, what great pleasure in soo doing ye shal ministre unto us oure said counsaillor shal in like wise on our behalve enforme you. Yeven, &c. the xxij. day of Septembre. A.D. 1484. September.

*To the Lord Barrey of Monyster.*

Right trusti, &c. And where as we bee informed by the reverend fader in God, our ful trusti counseillor the bisshop of Enachden, how that in dayes heretofore in parte aswele thorough your awne negligence for lak of due sute and labor, as otherwise, ye have ben injured and wronged of certain lyvelode and landes, that ye clayme of enheritaunce, lieing in Wales; we assure you that if ye by your self, or any other persone for you, shalle lust to make diligence for your recovere therof, after the processe and due ordure of our lawes we shalle shew you therin any thing that may apperteyne, asferforth as your said right, and our lawes shalle require in any wise. And over that for the true hert and feith that by our said counsellor we understande ye bere unto us according to the dutie of your liegeaunce be unto you and alle your kynnesmen verray good and graciouse soverayn lord in any other cause or mater, as we have commaunded him to shewe unto you in our behalve; to whome herin ye wille geve playne credence, as our trust is in you. Yoven, &c. the xx^td^ day of Septembre.

Touching lands withheld from him in Wales.

A.D. 1484. September.

*To John Power and Piers Power, and aither of them.*

Acknowledging their services against the king's enemies, and urging them to unity.

RIGHTE trusty and welbeloved we grete you wele. Latting you wite that we have understande by the credable reaporte of reverende fadre in God the bisshop of Enachden of youre fast and good demeanyng, and specially in repressing and subduyng of our ennemyes in thoose parties, according to the duetie of your liegeaunce. For the which and your perfite contynuaunce in the same we shalbe verrey good and graciouse soverayn lord unto you and alle your kynnesmen. Desiring you both and aither of you to see that ye and they deale of oon accorde and unite, advoiding alle variaunces and stryves amonges you, as ye and they desire to please us. And our said counsellor hath in our name to shew unto you more at large concernyng the same, to whome therin ye will geve pleyne credence, as our trust is in you. Yeven, &c. the xxij[ti] day of Septembre.

*To &c.*[1]

Thanking him for his fidelity to the king and his father.

RIGHT trusty and welbeloved, we grete you wele. And have understanden to oure fulle good pleasur by the reaport of the reverende fader in God, oure fulle trusty counsellor, the bisshop of Enachden, this berer, that ye be descended of the auncien blood and lynage of our auncestres of Wolster, and also the good feithfulle hert and obeissaunce that ye bere unto us according to the duetie of your liegeaunce. Reteynyng also in mynde the noble service that ye and your kynnesmen in dayes past have doon unto the famouse prince of noble memorie, our fader (whom Jesu rest), and other our progenitors. For the which we can you specialle thankes, desiring you in our herty wise fermely to contynue the same towardes us, and that

[1] Sic in MS.

ye of that blood amongest you applie and dispose you to be of oon demeanyng and unite for the wele of your self and of the contre there, exhorting other lordes and gentilles, as ferforth as ye may to doo the same, as our trust is in you. Latting you wite that we more at large have enstructed our said counsellor with our ferther mynde and pleasur in our name to shew unto you; wherein ye will geve unto him plaine credence, and in alle wise conforme you to thutter accomplisshing therof. For the whiche soo doyng we assure you to bee good and gracious soverayn lord unto you and alle your kynnesmen in any your causes herafter. Yoven under our signet at Westminster, the xxj. day of Septembre. A.D. 1484. September.

Item, two other lettres of the same reteignew.

*To Sir Alexander Plunkett.*

Trusty and welbeloved we grete you wele. And late you wite we have understande by the credable reaport of the reverend, &c., the bisshop of Enachden of your fast and good demeanyng, and specially in repressing and subduyng of our ennemyes in those parties, according to the duetie of your liegeaunce, for the whiche and your perfite contynuaunce in the same we shalbe verray good and graciouse soverayn lord unto you and alle your kynnesmen, as our said counsellor hath in our name to shewe unto you more at large concernyng the same; to whome therin ye will geve pleyne credence, as our trust is in you. Yoven, &c., the xx[ti] day of September. Commending his fidelity in warring against the Irish.

A like lettre to Sir Rowland Eustace, tresourer of Irland.

A like lettre to Sir Olivere Plonkett.

A like lettre to the Baron of Delevyn,

A like lettre to the Viscount of Gormeston.

A.D. 1484. September.

*To the Lord Barry et Monystre.*

To the same effect.

RIGHT trusty and welbeloved, we grete you wele, Latting you wite we be enformed by the reverende fader, &c., the bisshop of Enachden, that ye be enhabited in thextreme parties upon our ennemyes of the wilde Iresshe, and according to your liegeaunce daily kepe werre with them in the defense of your self and other our subgiettes there to your gret troubles, hurtes and charges. For the which we can you gret thankes, desiring you so perfilty to contynue, whiche we shalle not unremembre, but for the same be unto you and alle your kynnesmen good and graciouse soverayn lord in alle your causes herafter, as our said counsellor hath by our commaundement to shew unto you more at large; to whome therin ye will geve fulle feith and credence. Yoven, &c. the xxij day of September.

A like lettre to the lord Staundon of Connaghte.

A like lettre to the lord Nangle of Connaghte.

A like lettre to the lord Excestre of Connaghte.

A like lettre to the lord Roche.

A like lettre to the lord Byrmyngeham of Connaghte.

A like lettre to the lord Barryet of Connaght.

And a nother lettre not directed.

## XXVI.

A.D. 1484. October.

[MS. Harl. 433, f. 270.]

INSTRUCCIONS yeven by the king unto Sir Marmaduc Constable, knighte, steward of thonnor of Tutbury.

FURST, that the said sir Marmaduc shalle take the othe of alle thinhabitauntes within the said honnor that they shalbe true and feithfulle liegemen unto the king, and not to be reteigned to any lord or other, but immediatly to the kinges grace. Against retaining

Also, the said sir Marmaduc shalle see that no lyveres ne conysaunce be geven within the said honnor contrarie to the lawe and to the statutes therof made. and giving liveries,

Also, where heretofore diverse extorcions and oppressions have ben doon by the countie baillieffes, upon trust that they shuld contynue and not to be removed from their offices, the king wolle that fromhensfurth the said sir Marmaduc put able and wele disposed persones in the said bailliefwykes, suche as been sufficient to answere the king of his duetie; and they to be chaunged from yere to yere, and that a proclamacion to be made at every gret court that if any persone wolle come and compleyn of any of the said baillieffes that they shalbe herd, and due reformacion and punysshement be had according to the kinges lawes and their demerites. extortion of bailiffs,

Also where as there be certen fermeholdes laten to diverse persones which occupie but litille, or summe part therof to their owne propre use and make leesses of the residue over unto other suche as be not the kinges tenantes, the king willing his tenantes to be preferred to suche fermholdes and to be fermours immediatly to his grace, wolle that the said sir Marmaduc discharge alle fermors of alle such parcelles soo subletting the king's lands,

A.D. 1484. October.

sette over by lesses unto other and to late the same fermes amonges the kinges tenantes to suche as be able to do the king service and to answere him of his ferme.

and waste of the king's woods.

Also the king wolle that the said sir Marmaduc wele and diligently survie alle his wooddes within the said honnor, and to see that noo waast be made in theim, ne that no brusing be made in them in the wynter season but suche as shalbe necessarie, and to the leest hurt to the kinges woodd.

Also the said sir Marmaduc to see that there be noo wood fallen within the said honnor for paleyng but such as is moost mete and convenient for the same, and the coppies of the said pailling wood with the brewsing that is metely for thexpenses of the kinges houshold or his reparacions be kept therfore, the residue to be praysed and sold to the kinges most advauntages.

Also the kinge wolle that noo lyverey trees be geven within his parkes and woodes but oonly under his speciall warrant or suche as have it by specialle graunt of olde tymes past.

Means to secure efficient officers.

Also, where as the king hath enlarged the fees of his parkers, to thentent they shuld be attending daily on their offices when they awaite not on his grace, and in their absence make sufficient deputies suche as wilbe of good demenaunce to the kinges wod and game, the king wolle that if any suche depute be founden not suffisaunt ne of good demeanaunce then the said sir Marmaduc to discharge him and to certifie the kinges grace, that a suffisaunt deputie may be put in his rowme; and also that no parker have of duetie in any of the kinges parkes over ij kyen and two horsses.

Also the king wolle that tharbage of alle his parkes be latten or approwed to the kinges moost advantages, savyng suffisaunt pasture for the dere, and the kynges fermes not dymynysshed; forseen alway that the parkers of the same be neither fermors nor approwers of the said herbage. A.D. 1484. October.

Also that the lieutenant, the boweberer and receivors of wardes be suche persones as be of good demeanaunce ayenst the kinges wood and game and sworne to the same; and that they and every of theym wele and duely oversee the game and woddes in the parkes and waardes of the said honnor according to their offices as they have bene accustomed afore tyme.

Also the said sir Marmaduc to put into thoffice of bailliefwykes that be accomptauntes, good and suffisaunt persones and suche as be able to doo the king service and to content the king of suche as they shalbe charged withalle upon their accomptes.

---

## XXVIJ.

[MS. Harl. 433, f. 271.]

A REMEMBRAUNCE made, aswele for hasty levy of the Kynges revenues growing of alle his possessions and hereditamentes, as for the profitable astate and governaunce of the same possessions.

FURST, that alle the kinges officers of his court of eschequier use and execute hasty processe ayenst almaner persones accomptable, and other being the kinges dettors, as the caas shalle require; and also to here and determyne accomptes of the same, and thissues, proffuytes, and revenues commyng therof to be levied and paied into the kinges receipt without delaye.

Also that no persone accomptable, ne other persone being in dette to the king, have any respet, stalment, or favor in the said court, whereby the kinges dueties may be delayed over the space of iiij monethes next after the tyme that any suche persone owith to yelde his accompt, or owith to pay his debt, whatsoever it

A.D. 1484. be. For it hath bene said that many diverse officers accomptable have bene respected of their accomptes from yere to yere, and also of their paymentes by space of many yeres, to the kinges gret hurt, in tymes passed.

Also that no officers havyng office in the said court of theschequier have or occupie any office in the receipt.

Also it is thoughte that the auditors of the said eschequier shuld yerely make a boke of alle the revenues, issues, and proffuytes growing of alle shireffes, eschetors, collectors of custumes and subsides, tresourer of Calais and Guysnes collectors of dismes, baillieffes of cities, burghes, and portes, and of alle other maner officers accomptable of the said eschequier, with the reprises and deduccions therof, and the same boke to declare afore suche persones as the kinges good grace shalle like to assigne to here and to see it; whereupon his grace may yerely se the prouffites of the said court.

Also that the tresourer of England for the tyme being yerely shuld make a declaracion of alle suche money as is received or assigned within his office, be it in the receipt or be it otherwise, for that yere afore the said yeres.

Also that the said court of eschequier be clerely dismyssed and discharged with any medling with any forayn lyvelode in taking of accomptes, as Wales, duchies of Cornewaille, York, Norffolk, Erldoms of Chestre, Marche, Warrewick, Sarum, and of alle othre landes being in the kinges handes be reason of forfaictor; whiche is thought most behovefulle and profitable to be assigned to othre foreyn auditours for diverse causes ensueing, etc.; that is to sey:—

First, for more hasty levie of money. Also for more ease and lesse coste of the officers of suche lyvelode

Also for cause that the lordshippes may be yerely surveied by the stiwardes, auditors, and receivours in the tyme of accomptes of officers of the same for reparacions, wodesales, and for othre direccions to be had amonge the tenantes, with many mo causes necessarye, etc. A.D. 1484.

And where that many lordshippes, manours, londes, and tenementes perteynyng to the crowne bene committed to diverse persones for fermes in certeyn, by the whiche the kinges woddes and his courtes, with othre casueltics, bene wasted and lost to his gret hurt, and gret allouances had for raparacions of his castelles and manors, and they not forthy repaired, as it is said; and also the said lordshippes ofte tyme set within the value; it is thoughte that a foreyn auditor shuld be assigned for alle lordshippes, manors, landes, and tenementes belonging to the crowne, and a receivor for the same yerely to ride, surveie, receyve, and remembre in every behalf that myghte be most for the kinges profite, and therof yerely to make report of the astate and condicion of the same; by the which the kinges grace shuld knowe alle the lordshippes that perteyneth to his crowne, whiche as nowe be unknowyn, as it is said, etc.

Also, it is thoughte that suche certayn auditors as ben of gode, true, and sadde disposicion and discrecion, shuld be assigned to here and determyne thaccomptes of alle the kinges foreyn livelode as is above discharged fro theschequier, and to have so many auditours and no mo but as may conveniently and diligently determyn the said livelode betwixt Michelmas and Candelmes, with sadde and discrete examinacion of alle defaultes and hurtes of alle officers accomptable severaly in their offices executing, wherein thawditors of theschequier can never have so evydent knowlege for reformacion of the same.

Also, that the receivours of gode and true disposicion and also of havour of richesse be assigned to the said

A.D. 1484. lyvelode; and they to se for reparacions of castelles, manors, milnes, parkes and othre, and in the cirquyte of their receipt they to sethe wele of every lordshippe.

Also, it is thoughte that alle auditours afore said, aswele of theschequier as of foreyn livelode, shuld yerely make declaracion of alle suche livelod as they have in charge, afore suche persones as the kinges grace wol therto assigne at London, alway betwixt Candelmes and Palmesonday, so that his grace may be asserteyned yerely of the hole revenues of alle his livelode, and what therof is paid and what is owing, and is whos defaute.

Also, where that lordes, knightes, and esquiers, many of them not lettered, bene made stewardes of the kinges livelod in diverse countres, thay taking gret fynes and rewardes of the kinges tenantes to ther propre use, to the kinges hurt and poveresshinge of his said tenantes, and also wanting cunnyng and discrecion to ordre and directe the said lyvelode lawfully, with many moo inconvenientes. Therfor it is thoughte that lerned men in the lawe where most profitable to be stiwardes of the said livelod for many causes concernyng the kinges profite and the wele of his tenantes.

Also, it is thoughte that alle londes being in the kinges handes by reason of wardeshipp of lordes sonez or othre noble men shuld not be let to ferme hold for a certeyn, but that the same landes shuld remayne in the kinges handes during the nonnage and that auditours of the same londes shuld yerely determyne thaccomptes therof and to make declaracion as is above said, for the more profite to the king, &c.

Also, for temporalties of bisshopriches, abbayes, and priories in likewise, &c.

Also, it is thoughte that alle the forsaid auditours every yere at the fest of Michelmes next after the declaracion made of alle foreyn lyvelod by for the said persones by the king so assigned, shuld delivere or doo to be delivered the bookes of accomptes of the same into the kinges eschequier afore the barons ther after the first yere of the premisses, ther to remayne of recorde, so that the bookes of accomptes of the later yere be alway in the handes of the said auditours for their presidence, the duchie of Lancastre, the lordshippes of Glamorgan and Bergevenny alwey except, &c. A.D. 1484.

---

## XXVIII.

### Preparations for Defence.

[MS. Harl. 433, f. 274.]

Instruccions geven by the kinges grace to the commissioners appointed in every shire of this his royaume. December.

Furst, that they on the kinges behalf thanke the people for theire true and lovying disposicions shewed to his highnesse the last yere for the suertie and defense of his moost royal persone and of this his royaume ayeinst his rebelles and traytors exhorting theim soo to contynue.

Item, that the said commissioners incontynent after the receipt of theire commissions diligently enquere of alle baillieffes, constables, and other officers of townes, towneships, villages and hundredes within the procincte of theire commission, the nombre of persones suffisauntly horsed, harneysed, and arrayed as by every of theim severelly were graunted to doo the kinges grace service before the olde commissioners whansoever his highnesse shuld commaunde theim, for certaine dayes in theire said grauntes expressed, for the resisting and subduyng of his enemyes, rebelles, and traytours; and of the same persones and theire array to take a good vieu and see that they be hable men

A.D. 1484. December. and wele horsed and herneysed, and noo rascal, and to endevoire theim to encrease the nombre by theire wisedoms and policies if they can.

Item, that they also diligently enquere of al suche money for the wages of the said persones as in every place hath ben gadred and leveyed, and to whoos handes and keping the same was delyvered, and wheder it soo resteth or not; and thereupon to ordre and see that the same money be alwayes redy in the constable or baillieffes handes or othre by theire discrecions, to be delyvered to the said persones without any manere delay when they shalbe commaunded to doo the king service; and in likewise to ordre and see in every place where no suche money have be gadered and leveyed, that it forthwith be leveyed and delyvred to the handes of the constable, baillieffes, or othre; there to remayn and surely to be kept for the wages of the personages soo by theim graunted to doo his grace service.

Item, in caas that any parte of the same money heretofore leveyed be by any persone taken out of the keping of any of the said constables, baillieffes, or othre ayeinst theire willes or othrewise, that than the said commissioners not oonly see the same restored to the said constables, but also the soo taker to be commytted to warde and punysshed after theire discrecions.

Item, that the said commissioners at the vieu of the said persones, yeve theim strait commaundementes to attende upon suche capitaynes as the kinges grace shal appoint theim to attende upon, and on noon othre, as they wol advoyde the kinges highe displeasire at theire utterest perilles.

Item, that the said commissioners on the kinges behalf yeve straitly in commaundement to all knightes, squiers, gentilmen, and othre, being hable men of theire bodyes, to doo the kinges grace service to prepare and arredy theimself in theire persons soo to doo when they shalbe thereunto warned and commaunded without any excuse, as they wil advoyde the kinges highe displeasire at theire perilles. A.D. 1484. December.

Item, that the said commissioners in al goodly hast certefie by writing to the kinges grace theire ordering of the premisses in every behalf, with the names of the persones soo by theim seen and vieued.

Item, to shewe to alle lordes, noblemen, captaynes, and othre that the kinges noble pleasire and commaundement is, that they truely and honorably, almanere quarelles, grugges, rancors, and unkyndenesse layed aparte, attende and execute the kinges commaundement, and everyche be loving and assisting to othre in the kinges quarelles and cause, shewing theim plainly that whosoever attempt or presume the contrary, the kinges grace wol soo punysshe theim that al alle othre shal take example by theim, &c.

---

## XXIX.

[MS. Harl. 433. f. 273.]

RICARDUS REX.[1]

By the king.

TRUSTY and welbeloved, we grete you wele. And forasmoche as by calling from this uncertaine and transitory lif of your late bisshop, ye stande destitute and desolate of a pastoralle hede and spirituelle governor; for the whiche, by auctoritie of oure licence royal, ye must hastely procede to theliting of a newe pastor and bisshop: We, havyng tendre regarde aswele unto the laudable merites, highe vertues, and profounde

---

[1] Added in another hand of the period "littera bona."

A.D. 1484. 8 Dec. cunnyng, that the righte reverend fader in God, our righte trusty and righte welbeloved counsaillor, the bisshop of St. David,[1] is notarily knowen to be of, as unto othre his notable desertes, contynued trouthe, and feithful services to us in sundry wises doon to our singler pleasire, desire and hertly pray you that in your said eleccion ye wol have him to the said preemynence and pastoralle dignitie before alle othre especially recommended and preferred. Wherein we doubte not ye shal not oonly provyde righte sadly for the wele of the said cure, and for the honnor of our cathedralle churche there to the pleasire of God, but also cause us to departe with you the more largely the favor of our good grace in suche thinges as may be for the universal wele of you and of our said churche in tyme to come. Yeven undre our signet at oure palois of Westminster the viijth day of Decembre.

To our trusty and welbeloved the dean and chapitre of oure cathedral churche of Sarum.

---

[1] Thomas Langton.

# HENRY VII.

# HENRY VII.

## I.

[MS. Cott., Titus B. xi. f. 23.]

INSTRUCCIONS yeven by the kinges grace unto h counseillour and servant John Estrete to be shewed to Therl of Kildare, etc. A.D. 1486?

FURST, as touching the article of the peticions of the said erl for to have his office of deputie lieutenant of that land for the terme of ix. or x. years, the said John Estrete shall say that to thentent the kinges grace may tho better counseill, conclude and devise for the bringing of his land of Irland into pleyn obeissaunce and suche estate, welth and prouffitte as it hath be in tyme passed, he desireth in that partie to here thadvise of the said erl, considering that for the long rule that he hath borne there, ther can no man therin better counsaill his grace than he.

The king, desiring Kildare's advice upon the govern-ment of Ireland.

Item, his grace hath ben wele advertised that the said erl in his said office served king Edward the iiij[th] nobely, trewely, and hardely, and moche better after the tyme he had been with him in this his royalme.

Item, his grace trusteth that upon mutuall sight and communicacion had betwixt his grace and his said cousin, his grace shall the rather be enclined to take his said cousin into his nigh favor and grace, and his said cousin on his partie shall moche the better be couraged, moved and sturred trewely and fastely to serve his grace, and therupon in his owne

A.D.1486? persone conclude, not oonly for himself, but also for his childern, bredern, kynne and alies according to the secrete credence whiche the said John Estrete on the behalve of the said [erl shewe]d u[nto the kin]ges grace. For whiche causes and the perfite performacion of the same the king willeth and desireth his said cousin . . . . . her . . . sses and excuses aparte, and be with him personelly in this his royalme before the furst day of August next commyng, whersoev[er] his grace shall than be. And for the suretie of his persone and of alle suche as shall comme in his company for the tyme of his or their commyng, abiding, and retornyng, the king marveilleth that he can desire any promises, seales, or writinges of any of his lordes more than of this grace oonly, considering not oonly that suche a suretie can not stand with the kinges honour, but also that neither the said erl ne any other hath seen that his grace hath broken promyse or assurance by him made unto any persone. Wherfor his grace sendeth by the said John Estrete unto the said erl his lettres of proteccion and tuicion undre his signet and signemanuell, whiche he wol as duely kepe and see kept as if they were passed undre the seales of alle the lordes of his land.

requires his presence in England before the 1st of August.

Item, the said John Estrete shall say that upon the said erles commyng and being with the king by the said day, the king shall as benignely, tendrely and largely take him into the favor of his grace as ever did King Edward the iiij[th], and in so ample wise departe with him as shalbe to thencrése of his honor, prouffite and preferring, and at the same tyme enlarge his graunte of his said office of deputie lieutenant of that his land for ix. or x. yeres according to his desire.

[Item,] to the second article of the said erles peticions concernyng thassignacion of m[l]. li. for his wages in the said office, the said [John E]strete s[hall say] that the kinges pleasir is that the said erl, at his forsaid commyng unto his grace, bring with him in writing the certainte of the kinges revenues of that his land of Irland, with the charges going oute of the same, whiche seen shall mowe appere what remayneth clierly unto his grace, and if the same wol answere the said m$^{l}$. li. the king is content at his commyng unto his grace to make him a graunte therof for his wages. And in caas the said revenues comme not clerely to somoche, his grace wol than at the commyng of the said erl soo covenant and indent with him for the certainte of his wages and contentacion of the same as of reason he shal have cause to hold him content and pleased. A.D.1486?

Item, where the said erl desireth to have of the kinges graunte to him and his heires masles the manoir of Lexlep and the koping of the castell of Wekenlowe, the said John shall say that upon the said erles commyng unto his grace, the king is content and wol make him a sufficient graunte therof according to his desir.

Item, finally, the said John shall shewe unto the said erl that there is noo thing doon by the said erl in tyme . . . d ne sur . . . . r reporte of him made unto the king ne favour, affeccion or ennemyte of any persone of [w]hat condicion so ever he be, that shall torne his grace from the said erl, but that upon his commyng unto his presence he shalbe as good and gracious lord unto him as is above rehersed, and more largely if the said erl can it reasonably desire. In witnesse wherof, his grace hath with his signemanuell signed thies instruccions and caused his signet to be put unto the same.

(*Endorsed.*) Instruccions unto John Estrete into Irland.

II.

HENRY VII. TO THE POPE.

[From the Vatican Transcripts in the Brit. Museum, MS. Addit. 15,385. f. 315. Headed "Ex Autogr. libro Memorabilium Pii II.," pag. 101. t° Arm M., caps. III.]

*Sanctissimo clementissimoque Domino nostro Papæ.*

A.D. 1487. 5 July.

BEATISSIME pater, post humillimam commendationem et devotissima pedum oscula beatorum. Cum divina clementia certissima nobis et manifestissima signa nuper dederit, quibus solvendi potestatem atque ligandi tam vestræ Sanctitati ejus vices gerenti quam prædecessoribus successoribusve suis traditam, ratam omnino, stabilem, perpetuam atque irrevocabilem esse perpetuoque fore ostendit, non possumus certe quin vestram Sanctitatem ad sui et sacrosanctæ istius Sedis Apostolicæ consolationem non mediocremque lætitiam certiorem reddamus, et tanti nostri gaudii participem faciamus. Rem itaque uti se habet ordine perscribemus. Cum in hostes rebellesque nostros paulo antea exercitum duxissemus, atque his admodum propinqui essemus facti, ut sæpe ex fraudulenta hominum natura fieri solet, adversa et prorsus erronea et conficta de nobis et nostro exercitu fama Londonias et apud Westmonasterium fuerat perlata, sicuti et in plures alias regni partes licenter evagaverat. Ferebatur enim tam nos in fugam versos quam universum nostrum exercitum dissipatum. Ea igitur re audita, nonnulli ex his qui ob sua patrata vel in nos vel in alios scelera, privilegiis Westmonasterii et immunitatibus gaudere [speraverant],[1] arbitrantes sibi ea tempestate omnia esse permissa, potissimum quod, nefario quovis scelere perpetrato, liberam ad ipsum eundem privilegiatum locum se habere semper putent

When the king went against the rebels rumors were spread that his army had been routed.

[1] Om. in MS.

A.D. 1487. 5 July.

redeundi facultatem, sicuti aliis nostris literis ad vestram Sanctitatem pro reformandis hujusmodi enormitatibus latius scripsimus, arma sumentes ut eorum domos quos nobiscum esse cognoscerent ad bella[1] profectos spoliarent et in scelus quodque prorumperent, continuo in unum sunt congregati. Ex horum numero quidam Johannes Swit, homo magis temerarius quam audax, sociis omnibus silentibus, "Et quid," inquit, "ad censuras ecclesiasticas, pontificalesve, potestates? "Videtisne hujusmodi interdicta nullius omnino esse "momenti, posteaquam ante oculos habetis eos ipsos "qui ea pro se impetrarunt esse profligatos, et in capita "eorum omne anathema esse conversum?" Hæc ubi pronuntiavit, illico in terram mortuus cecidit, ejusque facies et corpus totum ipsa caligine nigrius confestim apparuit; paulo vero postea cadaver ipsum tantum ex se fœtorem emisit ut ad id accedere nemo prorsus posset. Hæc res sic gesta est, Beatissime Pater, nec nisi ita certo esse sciremus ad vestram Sanctitatem scripsissemus. Agimus profecto gratias Omnipotenti Deo quas possumus uberiores, qui pro sua ineffabili misericordia tantum in regno nostro de fide Christiana miraculum ostenderit. Agimus quoque et vestræ Sanctitati amplissimas, quoniam ad jacenda pacis in hoc regno nostro fundamenta suos nobis favores gratiose sit impartita. Sed de hac re hactenus.

Appalling fate of a despiser of papal interdicts.

Cum nonnulli ex prælatis Hiberniæ, archiepiscopus scilicet Dublinensis,[2] archiepiscopus Armachanensis[3] et episcopi Medensis[4] et Darensis,[5] tam in nostri dominii quam censurarum ecclesiasticarum contemptum, rebellibus hostibusque nostris opem et juvamen impenderint, ac spurium quemdam puerum,[6] quem victoria potiti in

Requests that the Irish bishopsw ho favored Lambert Simnel may be excommunicated.

[1] *bellos*, MS.
[2] Walter Fitz Simons.
[3] Octavian de Palatio. See Appendix A.
[4] John Pain.
[5] Donald O'Fallon, bp. of Derry.
[6] Lambert Simnel.

A.D. 1487. 5 July. manibus nostris habemus, ad rebellium ipsorum et hostium nostrorum confingentium puerum ipsum ducis quondam Clarentiæ filium esse, in regem Angliæ coronarunt, ad grave nostrum et totius regni nostri præjudicium, vestram Sanctitatem humillime imploramus ut præfatos prælatos in censuras incursos ecclesiasticas postulare velit, atque in eos de jure procedere. Faciet equidem hac vice vestra Sanctitas justissimi inprimis prontissimique pontificis officium, et a lege Dei deviantes in rectam viam et semitas salutis reducet, rem præterea supra quam dici possit efficiet et nobis gratissmam; aliis denique ne hujusmodi imposterum facinora aggrediantur certissima relinquet documenta. Id ut agat vestra Sanctitas etiam atque etiam ex animo rogamus. Ex regia nostra juxta Castellum Kenelworth die quinto Julii, 1487.

Ejusdem Sanctitatis vestræ,
Devotissimus atque obsequentissimus filius,
Dei gratia Rex Angliæ et Franciæ ac
Dominus Hiberniæ,
HENRICUS.[1]

Literæ suprascriptæ restitutæ fuerunt D. Secretario.

---

[1] *Hulricus* in the transcript.

## III.

### HENRY VII. TO THE SPANISH CAPTAINS IN BRITANNY.

[MS. Egerton 616, f. 2.]

A.D. 1490. 15 Aug.

HENRICUS Dei gratia Rex Angliæ et Franciæ ac dominus Hiberniæ, magnificis atque eximiis dominis F. R., oratori, et comiti de Salinas, ac Petro Carillo, serenissimorum principum regis ac reginæ Castellæ, Legionis, Aragonii ac Siciliæ, etc. capitaneo, et ducibus exercitus, salutem et prospera votorum incrementa. Accepimus literas vestras decimo septimo die Julii scriptas quibus vestram credenciam in magnificos oratores serenissimorum principum vestrorum hic existentes factam intelleximus. Ipsos igitur dominos oratores audivimus. Hi namque pro parte vestra nobis exposuerunt cum sit quod vestri supremi in mandatis vobis dedissent ut cum primum Britanniam intrassetis, cum armatis nostris quos illic] habemus velletis vos conjungere, et vos tamen, ob certas quasdam causas eorundem principum vestrorum jussis in hunc usque diem non paruissetis, præfatos vestros supremos id factum molesto animo ferre, atque etiam vos timere ne et nos quoque ex eadem re gravem aliquam cepissemus displicentiam; causasque vestras cur non fueritis cum nostris juncti iidem oratores nobis ostenderunt. Equidem, magnifici viri, licet inter nos et serenissimos vestros principes conventum esset ut cum armatis nostris istic existentibus quam primum vos adjungeretis, tanta tamen est nostra erga serenissimos vestros supremos affectio et præcipua amoris mutui vicissitudo ut rem ipsam modeste feramus, nec persuadeamus aliquam idcirco esse nobis illatam injuriam. Diximus itaque præfatis dominis oratoribus ut ad serenissimos vestros principes scriberent et pro vestra excusatione ostenderent nos nullam exinde cepisse displicentiam. Putamus eos illico scripturos et desiderio vestro esse satis-

Holds them excused for delaying to join the English forces in Britanny.

A.D. 1490. 15 Aug.

facturos, quod si opus fuerit ut nos quoque ad suas sublimitates pro eadem causa scribamus id faciemus perlibenter. Interea tamen vestras nobilitates rogamus ut pro illa cordiali atque intima amicitia et conjunctione quam cum supremis vestris habemus, ita vos gerere velitis ut tam vestrorum principum obedientissimi quam et nostri amantissimi facile possitis ab omnibus judicari. Erit autem id nobis vehementissime gratum. Ex regia nostra de Eltam, die xv Augusti m.cccc.lxxxx°.

HENRICUS REX.[1]

*Addressed:* Magnificis atque eximiis dominis Francisoo de Rojas, oratori, ac comiti de Salinas, capitaneo generali, et Petro Carillo, serenissimorum regis et reginæ Hyspaniæ deputatis in Britannia missis, amicis nostris carissimis.

*Endorsed.* Littera Regis Angliæ;—*also,* Del Rey de Inglaterra al conde de Salinas y a Rojas, etc.;—*in a third place,* Littera Regis Angliæ ad comitem de Salinas, etc.

---

## IV.

### HENRY VII. TO THE BISHOP OF DURHAM.[2]

[MS. Cott., Titus F. iii. f. 91.]

BY THE KING.

H. R.

A.D. 1491. 5 Feb.

The king will respect the

RIGHT reverend fader in God, right trusty and right welbeloved, we grete you wel. And have seyn youre writing of the date of the xxvj. day of January, wherby and other wayes we understande wel that Sir

[1] Below the signature is written in a modern hand "Del Rey Henrico de Inglaterra del su mano;" but the signature is in the same hand as the letter itself, which, though undoubtedly contemporary, is not Henry's. The letter is therefore only a copy, though folded and addressed like an original.

[2] John Sherwood.

Robert Chambrelayne and diverse personnes with hym in company be taken at Hertilpole, within the precinct of the fraunchise of Saint Cuthebert belonging to you and to youre chirche of Duresme. Wherin ye beseche us humbly that we wol not doo breke, nor interupte the said franchises. We late you wite that for thonnor of God and of that glorioux Confessor Saint Cuthebert, we be and shalbe as good and favorable souverain lord unto you and to thoes franchises and libertees as any oure noble progenitors hathe been in tyme passed, and shal moche rather assist and defende theym then in any wise suffre theym to be interupted or defeicted. Desiring and hertily praying you that oure trusty and welbeloved servaunt Sir Edward Pykering, knight for oure body, may bring the said Sir Robert and thoes other oure rebelles and traitours to our presence. And if youre shirief of the bisshopriche have the conveyance according to your said fraunchise, both of our said servant and of our rebelles and traitors asfer as the bondes streicheth of youre said libertiees, for the better saufgard of the same, we shalbe therwith content and plaised. And astouching the goodes taken with our said rebelles, we be content also ye have theym, if that your said fraunchises so require: how be it the lord Clifford maketh clayme unto theym by raison of certain his libertees that he pretendeth to have in the lordship of Hert and Hertilpole forsaid. And inasmoche as for divers grete considerations it behoveth us to understande what writinges and othre goodes our said rebelles had with theym, we eftsonnes praye you that by billes endented betwene you and your officers on the oon part and our said knight on the other, we may be certefyed purticulierly and by parcelles of all [su]che writinges and goodes as shalbe founde in their caskettes, males, tronkkes, or in othre their cariages. Assuring you that our mynde ys not therby nor othrewise to breke or interupt your said fraunchises, but rathre

A.D. 1491. 5 Feb. franchise of St. Cuthbert in the matter of Sir Robert Chamberlain's arrest.

A.D. 1491. 5 Feb. to . . . . .[1] and defende theym as above. Yeven under our signet at our paloys of Westminster, the v[th] day of Februarij.

*Addressed:* To the Right Reverend Fa[der in God, our] right welbeloved the bi[shop of Duresme].

---

## V.

### Petrus Carmelianus to Ferdinand and Isabella of Spain.

[Holograph, MS. Egerton 616. f. 4.]

A.D. 1496. 2 July. Serenissimi atque invictissimi principes et domini, domini mei observandissimi. Post humillimam ac devotissimam commendationem. Quantopere sim ego, fuerimque semper, ac perpetuo sim futurus vestris majestatibus affectus, nulla certe lingua, nullove sermone aut epistola referre possem. Quoniam vero dominus doctor de Puebla, vestrarum majestatum orator insignis, hujus mei animi et sinceræ mentis plane conscius est, non me extendam ulterius ad servitutis meæ quam gero erga vestras serenitates sinceritatem ostendendam, quandoquidem ab ipso domino oratore, viro curiosissimo, et omnium quos unquam norim aut viderim diligentissimo, non dubitem easdem vestras majestates certiores antehac sæpe esse factas. Satis sit me esse ac semper fore vestris celsitudinibus tanta fide et devotione obstrictum, ut addi prorsus possit nihil, nec aliud quicquam gratius mihi obtingere posse quam, post illud quod serenissimo domino meo regi debeo

---

[1] Lost by the mutilation of the MS.

servitium, de vestris majestatibus benemereri valeam. Habeo gratias sempiternas vestris sublimitatibus pro literis suis gratiosissimis superioribus annis ad me datis, atque illas humiliter obsecro ut mihi ignoscere velint quod nihil ante hunc diem ad easdem scripserim; hocque meum tam diuturnum silentium in meliorem partem accipiant, nec meæ negligentiæ aut oblivioni quovismodo, sed temporum qualitati hanc tantam meam taciturnitatem ascribant. Cæterum, serenissimi principes et domini, domini mei observandissimi, licet satis intelligam vestras serenitates summa prudentia et consilio in suis agendis uti, et ea omnia prospicere quæ sibi commodiora atque honorificentiora esse possint; quoniam, tamen, locorum distantia interdum efficit ut varii varie referant, et veritas rerum quandoque taceatur et occultetur, ego pro illa devotione et fideli mente quam gero erga vestras majestates non postponam demonstrare illis quod sentio quodque certo scio, hoc unum, scilicet, quod fœdus istud affinitatis tamdiu tractatum maxime mihi conducere videtur ut ad effectum deducatur; neque certe me movet amor aut servitus ulla quam exhibeo huic meo serenissimo regi, sed ipsius mei principis virtus inclyta, divinum ingenium et potestas amplissima ad hæc demonstranda me invitant et impellunt. Quam fœcundos autem et uberes fructus hujusmodi vinculum sit pariturum videor ego satis, veluti e sublimi quadam specula, intueri. Consulere autem in tanta re homo ipse imbecilis neque debeo neque possum. Tantum liceat mihi commemorasse quid sentiam; quod si in hoc quoque imprudens aut nimis audax visus fuero, ignoscant, quæso, vestræ majestates desiderio meo atque amori quem gero erga illas, cujus sane tanta est vis et magnitudo, ut fortasse modum excesserit. Superest ut vestræ serenitates felicissime valeant ad vota; et si qua in re studium aut officium meum sibi gratum esse possit, non secus opera

A.D. 1496. 2 July.

Thinks it very desirable that the alliance so long treated for should be concluded.

A.D. 1496. 2 July. mea utantur quam humillimo et fidelissimo quoque suo servulo. Ex Londonia die ij. Julii M°. cccclxxxxvj°.

Vestrarum earundem majestatum,
Humillima creatura,
PETRUS CARMELIANUS BRIXIENSIS,
Serenissimi domini regis Angliæ, etc. secretarius Latinus, etc.

*Addressed:* Serenissimis atque invictissimis principibus et dominis, dominis Ferdinando et Hellisabeth, Dei gratia regi ac reginæ Castellæ, Legionis, Aragonum, Siciliæ, Granatæ, etc., Dominis meis semper observandis.

*Endorsed:* Secretarii regis Angliæ, ii. Julii anno 96.

---

## VI.

### THE CARDINAL OF PERUGIA[1] TO HENRY VII.

[Orig., MS. Cott., Cleop. E. iii. f. 145.]

A.D. 1497. June. Recommending that the vacant see of Worcester be conferred on John de Giglis.

SERENISSIME Rex atque inclyte domine, post commendationes. Scripsi paucis ante diebus ad majestatem vestram regiam quæ nunc non repetam quia puto eas literas una cum iis venturas quibus venerabilem virum dominum Jo. de Giglis vestræ majestatis oratorem iterum ei commendandum uberius duxi. Nam postquam priores erant clausæ intellexi episcopum Wigorniensem vita functum, ejusque ecclesiam regimine pastorali destitutam. Motus itaque benevolentia qua dictum dominum Johannem complector, ob singulares ejus virtutes et propter sinceram fidem quam cognosco illum gerere majestati vestræ, non inconveniens putavi illum

[1] John Lopez, a Spaniard, afterwards abp. of Capua.

commendare ut majestas vestra virum hunc suum fidissimum et integerrimum servitorem ad dictam ecclesiam promoveri faceret: in quo rem quidem dignam se vestra majestas geret, virum de se benemeritum honestando, et Sanctissimo Domino nostro totique huic curiæ gratissimum, ut ex literis Sanctissimi Domini nostri intelliget; mihi vero mirum in modum acceptum, qui cuperem præfatum dominum Johannem pro meritis honestatum videre. Quod si forte majestas vestra aliquam difficultatem faceret, quia timeret ne, si in curia talis ecclesia vacare ex persona ipsius contingeret, alicui provideretur absque voluntate serenitatis vestræ, non est profecto quod timeat in hoc; paucis enim ante annis[1] memini ecclesiam Dunelmensem in curia vacasse, tamen expectata est voluntas majestatis vestræ circiter annum, et ei provisum pro quo majestas vestra supplicavit. Multo magis Sanctissimus Dominus noster expectaret in hoc vestræ Serenitatis voluntatem quum Sanctitatis suæ intuitu et commendatione præfato domino Johanni provideretur. Itaque majestas vestra de hoc satis quieto animo esse potest, quoniam si id eveniret, amici vestri qui norunt morem jam antiquitus observatum non paterentur super eo aliquid innovari. Commendo ergo iterum ex animo ipsum dominum Johannem majestati vestræ, quam Deus felicem conservet. Romæ die . .[2] Junii mcccclxxxxvij.

A.D. 1497. June.

Ejusdem Regiæ Majestatis
Humilis Servitor
Jo. CAR^lis PERUSINUS.

Sacræ Regiæ Majestati Anglorum.

[1] In 1494, when Sherwood bp. of Durham died at Rome. His death happened on the 12th of January, and the temporalities of the see were granted to Richard Fox, on the 8th December following.

[2] Blank in orig.

A.D. 1497. 5 July.

## VII.

### Fox's Instructions to treat with Scotland.

[MS. in Record Office.]

By the King.

Instruccions geven by us to the right reverend father in God the Bisshop of Duresme, keper of [our] pryveseall, for thappesyng of suche questions and debates as resteth bytwixt us and our cosyn the kyng of Scottes.

First, wher dyvers offres wer made by therle of Aunguyssh and the lorde Home in a treatie late had at Jenyn Haugh, it is thought unto us and our counsaill that thos offres in no wise suffiseth to the conservacion of our honour, nor yet for anny convenyent recompence for suche damages as hath ben doon unto us and our subjectes by our seid cousyn. And therfore ye shal demaunde and requyre on our behalve of our seid cousyn to make delyvere unto us of Perkyn Werbek; the which delyveraunce of hym we desire not for anny estimacion that we take of hym, but by cause our seid cousyn reseived hym within his londe and favorably hath entreacted hym and dyvers others of our rebelles duryng the peace concluded by twix us both, and over that, havyng hym in his companygh, entred in puyssaunce within our lande; the whiche was the cause and grounde of the breache of the seid peace. And lesse therfore may we not doo with our honour then to have the delyveraunce of hym, thought the delyveraunce or havyng of hym is of no price nor value. Howe so be it, for the good will and effeccion that we bere unto our seid cousyn we shalbe contented to take such a peace and intelligence with hym as shalbe thought reasonable to ours and his comyssionars, so that he do make de-

To demand the delivery of Perkin Warbeck;

A.D. 1497. 5 July.

lyveraunce unto of us the seid Perkyn, and also do send unto us a solemne ambassate, as was spoken of in the said treacte had at Jenyn Haugh. And wher as it was spoken in the same treacte that our seid cousyn shuld send unto us suche persons in ambassate, and at suche tymes and places as we wold assigne and lymytte; we shalbe contented that he send unto us in ambassate, incontynently and without delay, at suche place within this our realme wher we shalbe atte tyme of their commyng, the reverend father in God the bisshop of Murray, therle of Aunguissh, and the lorde Home his chambrelayn, with suche other as it shal pleace our seid cousyn to sende.

or, if this be refused,

Item, if our seid cousyn wil not be agreable to the delyveraunce of the seid Perkyn unto us, as is before rehersed, the which as we thynke, sith he is not the parson that he surmysed to be when he opteyned his salveconduct of our seid cousyn (as it is wel knowen thurgh all thes parties of the worlde) he myght with his honour and without his damage wel doo, and so sattisfie our mynde for our honour on that behalf; yet we, havyng consideracion to the lovyng mynde of our seid cousyn in the tyme of the rebellion of dyvers of our subjectes, as it is shewed unto us, atte reverence of Almyghty God, and in evytyng theffusion of Christen blode, havyng in our remembraunce the nyghnes of blode by twix us and our seid cousyn, be content to take an other way for the peace by twix us, thowgh non other coude be to us so acceptable nor so wele satisfie our mynde and honour. That is to say, that it may like our seid cousyn furst to sende his solemne ambassate unto us, as is before rehersed; and also the same our cousyn to come in person unto our town of Newe Castell, and further within this our realme; wher we may mete, commen and conclude with hym for thob-

first, an embassy to be sent by James to Henry; and, secondly, a personal interview

A.D. 1497. 5 July. between the two Kings in England.

servyng of the saide peace, and of further intelligence to be taken by twix us and hym, be it by way of aliaunce o[r] other wise; and also for the due ordryng and refourmyng of suche debates and attemptates as shalmow . . . . growe in tyme comyng by twixt our both [subjec]tes, the which can not so brevely and assure[dly be] ordred and concluded by ours and his c[ommissione]rs as sholde mowe be by our selffes beyng [present in] persons. And over that, glad wold we [be to com]me so ferre to see our seid cousyn, [trustyng by the] meane therof that more fast love [and affeccion] thould growe [by twix us, and over that suche] conclusion shulde be taken as shuld be to the pleasour of God, the honour and wele of us both, [our] realmes and subjectes. Accordyng it is to noblesse and also kyndenese that anny too princes so nyghe [of] blode and so nygh inhabited to guyder as our seid cousyn and we be, shuld have by mutuall communicacion a more quayntaunce and a faster benyvolence than is yet by twixt us and our seid cousyn. And for the sure comyng, abydyng and retournyng of the same our cousyn at his pleasour and libertie, ye shal offre on our behalfe suche surety and pleages as shalbe though unto hym, his counseill and to you resonable and behoveful; the which we shal in every thyng do and observe.

If peace be made, the King of Scots to be bound under ecclesiastical censures,

Item, over this it is thought [to us] and our counsail that if we shuld take a peace with our seid cousyn, that he shuldbe bounde to thobservyng of the same and also to thaccomplisshyng and perfourmyng of suche articles as wer communed and treated at Jenyn Haugh, not only by his letter and great seall and solemne othe, but also uppon payn of the censuris of the Holy Cherche and in an obligation of Nisi, to thentent that uppon a light enformacion or suggestion like breche as hath ben of late tyme had shuld not ensue. And we shalbe contented for our parte to be bounde under our lettre and greate seall, and, rather then to faile, to be sworn uppon the Holy Evangelistes for the due observyng on our behalf of the seid peace.[1] A.D. 1497. 5 July.

Hit is not to be mervailed of this our desire though ther be thought therin any inequalite; for the breche of the peace last concluded bytwixt us grewe not, nor yet was doon by us. And also our seid cousyn shuld by force of the seid articles treated at Jenyn Haugh sende unto us his ambassate and revoke the seid salveconduct, and forprice any aide to be gevyn to the seid Perkyn and his adherentes, accordyng to the said communication and treatie, the which resteth only by our seid cousyn to be perfourmed.

Item, moreover it is thought to us and our consail that we may not with our honour take peace with our seid cousyn, as is before rehersed, without that he do make such a convenyent recompence as shalbe thought to the commissioners of us bothe, unto our subiectes for the damages that thei had by the throwyng doon of their castelles and fortilaces atte tyme of his furst beyng within this our lande, havyng then with hym the seid Perkyn and others our rebelles as is before rehersed. and to make compensation for injuries done in the invasion.

Item, over and besides al thes premysses it is behoveful and necessary that in case we shal take peace with our seid cousyn under such modificacions and Hostages required.

[1] *and, rather then to faile . . . peace*]. The second copy of instructions mentioned below, reads as follows:—"and also to be sworn "uppon the Holy Evangelistes for "the due observyng on our behalf "of the seid peace, yf ye can non "otherwise enduce hym. And in "case our seid cousyn wil not "bynde hym self under the censuris "of the Cherch, and in the seid "obligacion of Nisi, yet rather then "to faile, shal we be contented to "take for surety his solemne othe "uppon the Holy Evangelistes with "his lettre and greate seall."

A.D 1497. 5 July.

lymytacions as beth before written, that then uppon the conclusion of the same our seid cousyn shuld fourthwith ley plegges unto us, they to abide aboute us, or in any other place within our obbeisance as shalbe thought good to the comyssioners of bothe parties, men of good estate and condicion, as, two erles or their sonnes and heires, or two barones or their sonnes and heires, thei so to remayne til the seid ambassate come unto us and other thynges concernyng the seid Perkyn Werbek be perfourmed and accomplisshed, as is be fore rehersed. And howe so be it that it is thought unto dyvers discrete and wise men of our consail that consideryng the greate preparacions that we have made, as wel by lande as water, and conveyng of our artillery and vitall, and other preparacions that we have made for the exploite of thes warres in Scottlond to our inestimable charges and costes, we shuld not mowe with our honour so lightly for the perfourmyng and accomplisshyng of the seid premysses, the which ben of smal importance, condescend to a peace with our seid cousyn; yet we atte reverence of our Lorde, and in evytyng of theffusion of Christen blode, and in trust of an assured frendilyhod to be had by twix us bothe, and in especiall consideryng the natural inclynacion, affeccion, and good wil that he, as ye have written, berith and specially bare unto us in the tyme of the forsaid rebellion, be contented, thes premysses by ours and his comyssionars thoroughly assured to be observed and perfourmed as is above rehersed, to take a peace with hym, and theruppon ye to revoke our armee nowe beyng uppon the see. And we shal in like wise restreign our armye by londe and all other hostylite.

Nowe have we shewed unto you our [hole] mynde and pleasure in thes maters. And if the[re] shal growe anny occasion unto . . . . to wri[te . . ] lones

præsidenti summo pontifici et reverendissimis dominis cardinalibus assistentibus, majestatis vestræ literæ quibus ad ecclesiam Noruici inpræsentiarum vacantem reverendum patrem dominum Thomam[1] commendabat, lectæ fuerunt: quæ quidem literæ, cum indignum, ætate scilicet matura, doctrinaque et experientia conspicuum commendarent, non solum s . . placuerunt, sed magnam quoque religionis et prudentiæ laudem recepit vestra majestas, quippe qui nisi dignas et bene meritas personas, omnique commendatione adornatas, ad tantas istic ecclesias promoveri curet. Quæ majestatis vestræ mens utinam cæteris quoque principibus familiarior inesset. Expedita fuit ad vota magno pontificis et sacri collegii assensu promotio ipsa præfati Thomæ ad ecclesiam Noruicensem, sicuti ex literis reverendi domini Wigorniensis[2] oratoris sui lat[ius] confido intellecturam vestram majestatem. Cæterum ut ex iis quæ hic dicuntur aliquid pro officio me[o] vestræ majestati consignificem, etiamsi ipsa plurima ac prope omnia intelligat, hæc non tacebo. Rumore nuper vulgatum est classe illa quam dudum validam paravit et numerosam, Tur[corum] regem Rhodum insulam aggredi statuisse. Utinam mendax sit fama, et vires tan[ti] hostis adversus nos et religionem nostram irritæ sint penitus et vanæ. Hæc cura val[de] solicitat pontificis et sacri collegii mentem. Multa proinde cogitantur, et promoventur q[uæ] adjumento futura sint et saluti illius insulæ et sanctæ fidei nostræ. Milites tamen Rh[o]dienses et magnus indidem magister expeditionem hujusmodi maritimam pridem agnoscentes [ne]quaquam dormierunt. Muniverunt enim se loco, et omni necessario usu armorum, commeatu, [mi]lite, et animo inprimis religioso ac forti, sperantes divini numinis præsidio non solum tue[ri] se egregie adversus feroces hostes, sed victoriam quoque de his Christiano nomini relat . . adeo parati sunt,

A.D. 1499. 15 June. A new bishop of Norwich.

Rhodes threatened by the Turk.

---

[1] Thomas Jane, LL.D. | [2] Silvester de Giglis.

A.D. 1499. 15 June. adeo confidentes. Romanorum deinde regem aiunt cum parte exercit[us] sui in Vallem Telinam quæ Mediolanensi oræ contermina est, descendisse, eo consilio ut in ses[e] Suicenses pluribus viis aggressus citius ad officium et fidem reducat; pressos vero acriter S[uicenses] a rege jam pacem petere: ad quam consequendam Mediolanensis ducis favorem utuntur. Quæ impræsentiarum habui vestræ majestati significanda. Commendo me serenissimæ majestati vestræ, quæ diu felix valeat. Romæ, die xv Junii M. I. D.

Excellentissimæ vestræ majestatis
Humillimus servitor,
F. CARDINALIS SENENSIS.

*Addressed:* Serenissimæ Regiæ Majestati Anglorum.

---

## X.

### HENRY VII. TO FERDINAND AND ISABELLA.

[MS. Egerton 616. No. 8.]

SERENISSIMIS ac potentissimis principibus, dominis FERDINANDO et HELLIZABETH, Dei gratia Regi atque Reginæ Castellæ, Legionis, Aragonum, Siciliæ, Granatæ, etc., consanguineis et germanis nostris carissimis, HENRICUS eadem gratia Rex Angliæ et Franciæ ac dominus Hyberniæ, salutem, et prospera successuum incrementa. Intelleximus ex clarissimo oratore vestro domino doctore de Puebla circa conclusionem vestrarum majestatum cum serenissimo Francorum rege factam, articulum quendam[1] in nostrum favorem per vestras majestates initum; quod sane, si ita res sese habuerit, non potuit nisi ab optimo animo vestrarum majestatum erga nos proficisci, et ingentes gratias de nobis benemereri,

Thanks them for comprising him in their treaty with France.

[1] Corr. from *illum*.

quamquam nostra communis necessitudo, et vinculum quibus invicem astringimur, id genus officii de se postulare videatur. Cæterum ad notitiam nostram pervenit vestras majestates de negotiis nostris et Scoticis sinistre informatas esse, et longe aliter quidem quam veritas habeat. Hinc est quod nos, licet singularis vestra sapientia sit nobis perspecta, persuadeamusque nobis vestras serenitates quæ intelligenda sunt omnia intelligere, præsertim hæc nostra et Scotica, quæ omnibus ferme patent et sunt cognita, habuimus cum præfato domino oratore vestro longam de his rebus collocutionem, qui et ipse ex sese satis hæc omnia intelligit; quem non dubitamus veram vestris majestatibus facturum relationem; quæ felices semper valeant ad vota. Ex castello nostro de Shena, die xv. Junii m°.cccc.lxxxxviiij°. A.D. 1499. 15 June.

HENRICUS R.

*Addressed:* Serenissimis ac potentissimis principibus, dominis Ferdinando et Hellizabeth, Dei gratia Regi atque Reginæ Castellæ, Legionis, Aragonum, Siciliæ, Granatæ, etc., consanguineis et germanis nostris carissimis.

*Endorsed:* A sus al[s]. Del Rey de Inglaterra, xv. de Junio de xcix.

---

## XI.

### ELIZABETH QUEEN OF HENRY VII. TO FERDINAND II.

[MS. Egerton 616. No. 9.]

SERENISSIMO ac potentissimo principi, domino FERDINANDO Dei gratia regi Castellæ, Legionis, Aragonum, Siciliæ, Granatæ, etc., consanguineo ac germano nostro carissimo, HELLIZABETH eadem gratia Regina Angliæ et Franciæ ac domina Hyberniæ, salutem et prosperitatis incrementum. Commendavit serenissimus dominus meus A.D. 1499. 1 Aug. Recommending Henry Still, who desires to serve Ferdinand

A.D. 1499. 1 Aug. against the Infidels.

et maritus vestræ majestati suis literis latorem præsentium Henricum Still, suum fidum ac bonum ser[vitorem, qui] maxime cupit vestræ serenitati contra infideles servitium suum impendere p . . . . . [1]regnum pacatum et tranquillum videt. Is Henricus apprime est nobis notus, et quamvis corpore parvus, inter tamen strenuos et fortes milites bonum nomen tenet, quo fit ut eum nostris favoribus prosequamur, potissimum quod fidus ac diligens semper sit habitus, et adversus Christianæ fidei hostes dimicare intendat. Quare, licet serenissimi nostri consortis commendationem per sese satis esse ducamus, voluimus tamen et nos quoque nostram superaddere. •Rogamus itaque vestram majestatem ex corde ut hominem ipsum nostro etiam intuitu commendatum suscipiat et militiæ suæ ascribat ac favoribus suis prosequatur. In quo vestra majestas nos plurimum sibi devinciet. Non dubitamus equidem ipsum Henricum ita sese habiturum ut et vestræ majestati et nobis gratus et acceptus servitor sit futurus. Reliquum est ut vestra majestas felix sit et longæva; cui communem filiam tam suam quam nostram illustrissimam dominam Katerinam, cujus salutem et incolumitatem semper cupimus, ex corde commendamus. Ex oppido Hamptonæ, die primo Augusti M°cccclxxxxviiij°.

ELYSABETH R.

*Addressed:* Serenissimo ac potentissimo principi domino Ferdinando Dei gratia Regi Castellæ, Legionis, Aragonum, Siciliæ, Granatæ, etc., consanguineo et germano nostro carissimo.

*Endorsed:* Al Rey n. S. Dela Reyna de Inglaterra p° de Agosto de xcviiij.

[1] Paper decayed.

## XII.

### De Puebla to Ferdinand and Isabella.

[MS. Egerton, 616, No. 16.]

A.D. 1500. 11 Jan. The tranquility of England is now thoroughly established.

Muy altos y muy poderosos Principes, Rey y Reyna, Señores.

Despues de por mi besados los reales pies y manos de vuestras altezas, les fago saber que, en dicha de vuestras altezas y de la señora princesa de Gales, esta ya tal este reyno como de quinientos años aca nunca se vido, segund los que mas saben lo dizen y parece por las coronicas; porque sienpre al avia abrojos y espinas de calidad que tenianlos Yngleses causa de no estar asosiego in obediencia a su rey, por aver diversos herederos del reyno, y de tal calidad que la cosa se podia disputar de amas partes. Agora a plazido a Dios que todo se aya purgado y alinpiado justa y devidamente, de manera que una gota de sangre real dudosa no queda a este reyno, sino la verdadera del rey y de la reyna

---

Translation.

Most high and powerful princes, the king and the queen.

After kissing the royal feet and the hands of your highnesses, I cause you to know that by the good fortune of your highnesses and of the lady princess of Wales, this kingdom is at present so situated as has not been seen for the last five hundred years till now, as those say who know best, and as appears by the chronicles; because there were always brambles and thorns of such a kind that the English had occasion not to remain peacefully in obedience to their king, there being divers heirs of the kingdom and of such a quality that the matter could be disputed between the two sides. Now it has pleased God that all should be thoroughly and duly purged and cleansed, so that not a doubtful drop of royal blood remains in this kingdom, except the true blood of the king and queen,

A.D. 1500. 11 Jan.

y para el sello de todo la del señor principe Artur; y porque desto y de la justicia que se fizo de Perquin y del fijo del duque de Clarencia muy largo por diversas vias lo he escripto a vuestras altezas, non les quiero con larga escriptura dar inportunidad.

The Scotch marriage in a fair way to be settled.

El rey de Scocia, sobre su casamiento con la fija del señor rey, parece me que alo que yo tenia por mas dudoso, que era aver de esperar quatro o cinco años de no se casar, a la clara escrivio que era muy contento; no queda diferencia otra sino a la cantidad de la dote, porque dize el rey de Scocia que seria razon que le diesen tanto como dcclxxv. le davan. Este rey dize que le quiere dar dos tanto que el rey Duardo tenia concertado con su padre de le dar, la qual contia no allega a la meytad de lo que el rey de Scocia pide. Y porque me parece que este casamiento viene bien al rey y conozco que vuestras altezas sienpre lo desearon, aprieto quanto puedo, para que la cosa se concluya. Bien creo que el rey de Scocia,

---

and above all, that of the lord prince Arthur. And since of this fact and of the execution which was done on Perkin and on the son of the duke of Clarence, I have written to your highnesses by various ways, I do not wish to trouble you with lengthy writing.

The king of Scotland, it appears, in what I held most doubtful, touching his marriage with the daughter of the king, which was the having to wait and not marry for four or five years, wrote plainly that he was quite satisfied. There is no other point at issue remaining, except as to the amount of the dowry; for the king of Scotland says it would be reasonable that they should give him as much as 775 gave him. This king says that he wishes to give him twice as much as king Edward had agreed with his father to give; which amount does not come up to the half of what the king of Scotland demands. And because it appears to me that this marriage suits the king well, and I know that your highnesses have always desired it, I urge it as much as I can, in order that the matter may come to a conclusion. I well believe that the king of Scot-

segund la gana que muestra, vendria ala razon, y no menos este señor rey, y por dineros pocas vezes se suele desconcertar semejante negocio. Esto me a muy largo comunicado el rey. Crean vuestras altezas que si la venida de mccxviijº., no altera la voluntad de dccccxxj., la cosa es fecha; a especial si vuestras altezas ahincadamente escriviesen al rey de Inglaterra y rey de Escocia.

A.D. 1500. 11 Jan.

En grande cuydado continuo estoy fasta ver aca un criado mio que a vuestras altezas muchos dias ha abie con todo el despacho que me abiaron mandar, en el qual alguna duda tenia sy la cifra tocante al rey de Francia sy venia errada, y parece me que segund lo que don Juan Manuel por su ynstrucion mostro y me dio escripto de su mano y firmado de su nonbre que non fue errada salvo que a quello se fizo y concluyo aca como vuestras altezas me lo abiaron mandar, y caso que despues de aquello algunas cosas ayan sucedido al mundo asi lo de mdxxxix como lomas que cadadia procura dccºlxxxºj., ni por aquello vuestras altezas devrian diferir de me

A despatch in cipher relating to the King of France.

---

land according to the disposition he shows would come to reason, and not less so this king; and seldom is a like negotiation apt to be disturbed by money. This the king has at great length communicated to me. Your highnesses may believe that if the arrival of 1218 do not alter the will of 921, the thing is done; more especially if your highnesses were to write urgently to the king of England and the king of Scotland.

I am in great and constant anxiety until I shall see here one of my servants, whom I many days ago sent to your highnesses with all the dispatch with which you commanded me to send, in which I had some doubt if the cipher relating to the king of France was right. And it appears to me, according to what Don Juan Manuel by his instructions showed and gave me, written by his hand and signed with his name, that there was no mistake, but that that was done and concluded here, as your highnesses had commanded me; and in the event of some things having since happened in the world, as well in reference to 1539 as to the most which 781 every day solicits;

A.D. 1500. 11 Jan.

abiar a quel despacho. Pues deben considerar que aquel venido y la venida de la señora princesa a qui causaran nuevos mundos mucho conformes a la voluntad de vuestras altezas. Esto non lo digo a beneficio de natura sino por que yo y los mas cercanos a este rey esto mesmo dizen, e por las continuas platicas del rey lo mismo se conoce. Asi que a vuestras altezas suplico sin dilacion me manden abiar todo despacho segund que por un memorial que aquel mio llevo avran visto, y a que otro abio, qui a mi parecer la dilacion a semejante negocio non conviene a servicio de vuestras altezas.

The arrival of Catherine of Arragon expected.

Ytem, ya avran memoria vuestras altezas delo que por letras claras, syn yntervenir alguna cifra, me escrivieron cerca de la venida de la señora princesa de Gales diziendo que avia de ser, Dios queriendo, a qui en conpliendo el principe catorze años. Despues de lo qual vino a qui don Juan Manuel, y lo que dixo al rey cerca desto y mostro por ynstruciones de vuestras

---

let not your highnesses on that account postpone sending me that dispatch. Besides, you ought to consider that his coming and the coming of the lady princess to this country will cause a new state of things very agreeable to the will of your highnesses. This I do not say as being naturally so disposed, but because I and those nearest this king say the same thing, and the same is known by the continual sayings of the king. So I entreat your highnesses to send me on without delay every dispatch, as by a memorial which that man of mine carried, you will have seen; and here I send another, because it appears to me that delay in such a transaction does not conduce to the interests of your highnesses.

Also, your highnesses will remember what you wrote to me by clear letters without any cipher in reference to the coming of the lady princess of Wales, saying that she was to be here, God willing, when the prince completed his fourteen years. After which hither came Don Juan Manuel, and what he said to the king in reference to this and showed by instructions from your highnesses was that your highnesses had

altezas fue que vuestras altezas certificavan avia de venir el verano que viene, plaziendo a Dios, y dixo mas que sino lo estorvara la afermedad de vuestra alteza la reyna nuestra señora, que los dias pasados avia tenido que sin esperar esta dilacion de los catorze años del principe fuera ya aca venida la señora princesa, porque este verano, mediante nuestro Señor, vendria a mejor sazon, porque el señor principe avra conplido los xiiij. años; lo qual asi mismo don Juan Manuel me lo dixo y certifico a mi e me lo dio firmado de su nonbre. Per todo lo qual crean vuestras altezas que se adereçan tantos cosas aca para esta venida que non son de creer lo que allo se gasta y continuon, se entiende; y pues asy es suplico a vuestras altezas manden escrevir donde, plaziendo a Dios, a de abarcar la señora princesa, y en que mes, y todo lo mas que a este articulo les parecieren ser su servicio. A.D. 1500. 11 Jan.

Otrosy, ya avran visto vuestras altezas lo que este rey por dobladas letras a escripto, por do avran considerado

---

certified she was to arrive, God willing, in the coming spring; and he said, moreover, if the illness of your highness the queen, our sovereign lady, which you had in past days, did not change the plan, that without waiting for this delay of the fourteen years of the prince the lady princess would already have arrived here, because this spring with the help of our Lord, she would come at a better season, because the prince will have completed his fourteen years; which also Don Juan Manuel told me and assured me of and gave it me signed by his name. By all which your highnesses may be assured that so many things are got ready here for this arrival that it is not to be believed what is spent and will continue to be;—that may be imagined. And since it is so, I entreat your highnesses to write where, God willing, the lady princess is to land, and in what month, and everything else which may seem to you to be for your service in this matter.

Also, your highnesses will already have seen that which this king has written by duplicate letters, by which you will have

A.D. 1500. 11 Jan.

que yo no quise acebtar el obispado ni casamiento, por que me parecio que si tal cosa acebtara cometia especie de prodicion y de mal servidor; y segund a la veresidad en que yo estoy (do gracias a Dios) que tal determinacion fize que tres años a que de un dinero non soy proveydo, de que estoy en mucha afrenta. A causa de un deposito que de mi fue fiado y en guarda puesto, y de otras deudas que me aquexan, umilemente a vuestras altezas suplico y sus reales pies y manos beso, me manden proveer de lo que mes devido por via de aquel que proveyo a don Pedro de Ayala o por via de Pantales y misen[1] Centurio, lo qual recibire en muy señalada merced; y no menos[2] manden responder alo de este mi casamiento, segund que les pareciere mas ser su servicio, que por Dios verdadero, de aquello sere yo mas alegre y contento que de otra cosa alguna.

No tengo de presente que mas escrevir, fasta ver re-

considered that I did not wish to accept the bishopric or the marriage, because it seems to me that if I were to accept any such thing I should commit a kind of treason and act like a bad servant; and according to the truthfulness in which I stand, I give thanks to God that I have so resolved, when for three years now I have not been provided with one fraction of money; on account of which I am in great disgrace. By reason of a deposit made by me and placed in pawn, and of other debts which oppress me, I humbly entreat your highnesses and kiss your royal hands and feet, that you cause me to be provided with what is due to me, by means of him who provided to Don Pedro de Ayala or by way of Pantales and Misen Centurio, which I shall take as a very great mercy; and also cause an answer to be sent as regards this my marriage, according to what shall seem most to be for your service, of which before God truly I shall be more happy and contented than of any other thing.

I have nothing at present more to write, until I shall see

[1] *mfn*, MS.

[2] *no menos*] Reading doubtful, the MS. being worn.

spuesta de tantas como he escripto, o fasta ver aquel mio que tanto a que alla esta; sino que nuestro Señor las vidas y reales estados de vuestras altezas acreciere y prospere con muy mas reynos y señorios y conplimiento de sus deseos en todo. Amen. A.D. 1500. 11 Jan.

De Londre, el xi. de enero de md. años.

Umill siervo de vuestras altezas que sus reales pies y manos beso,

DOTIOR DE PUEBLA.

*Addressed:*—A los muy altos y muy poderosos principes, Rey y Reyna Señores, el Rey y la Reyna nuestros Señores.

*Endorsed:* A sus al. Del dotor de la Puebla, xj. de enero de D.

---

the answer of so many things that I have written about, or until I shall see here that man of mine who has so long been there; unless it be that our Lord may increase the lives and royal estates of your highnesses and bless you with many more kingdoms and dominions, and the accomplishment of your desires in all things.

From London the 11th day of January 1500.

The humble servant of your highnesses who kisses your royal hands and feet,

THE DOCTOR DE PUEBLA.

To the most high and powerful princes,
the king and queen our sovereigns.

---

## XIII.

### HENRY VII. TO FERDINAND AND ISABELLA.

[MS. Egerton, 616, No. 18.]

SERENISSIMIS atque potentissimis principibus dominis FERDINANDO et ELISABETHÆ Dei gratia Regi et Reginæ Castellæ, Legionis, Aragoniæ, Siciliæ, Granatæ, etc., con- A.D. 1500. 20 June.

A.D. 1500. 20 June.

sanguineis et germanis nostris carissimis, HENRICUS eadem gratia Rex Angliæ et Franciæ ac dominus Hiberniæ, salutem et prospera votorum incrementa. Literas vestras clarissimus orator dominus doctor de Puebla nobis tradidit, ex quibus intelleximus gratum fuisse serenitatibus vestris illud matrimonium inter illustrissimos dominos filios utriusque nostros per verba de præsenti contractum, necnon conclusionem mutuæ amicitiæ et confederationis factæ ac initæ inter vestras serenitates et nos. Intelleximus præterea ex relatu ejusdem vestri oratoris majestates vestras decrevisse in fine hujus æstatis illustrissimam dominam Katerinam filiam vestram ac nostram Walliæ principem huc transmittere, ipsumque deliberatum animum vestrum in ea re ex his literis quas ad eundem oratorem dedistis apertius novimus; quæ omnia nobis extitere admodum grata; nec ab re, cum ex tam fausto felicique matrimonio,[1] tamque fido pacis et amicitiæ inter nos firmato fœdere, utrique nostrum, regnis et subditis nostris maximum obventurum bonum non ambigimus. Accepimus insuper ab eodem oratore vestro quasdam serenitatum vestrarum literas pacis et amicitiæ inter majestates vestras et nos initæ et conclusæ confirmatorias, quas quidem vestræ sublimitates pro ejusdem pacis et amicitiæ fortiori stabilimento in formam instrumenti publici redigi manuque et sigillo suis ac aliis firmissimis vinculis roborari fecerunt. Nos quoque pro parte nostra ut eisdem serenitatibus vestris vicissitudinem rependeremus, similes nostras confirmationis literas in præsentia reverendissimi domini Cardinalis Cantuariensis[2] cæterorumque nobilium et magnatum in eisdem nostris literis descriptorum pari firmitate roboratas, eidem oratori vestro dedimus, necnon prædictam amicitiam proclamari mandavimus. Nil aliud jam restat quam ut illustrissima princeps

Is glad they have determined to send Catherine to England at the end of the summer.

---

[1] *matrimō*, MS.

[2] Cardinal Morton.

domina Katerina filia vestra et nostra hujus auspicatæ foederis et amicitiæ inter nos perpetuum futurum pignus ad præstitutum tempus huc transmittatur. Reliquum est ut vestræ sublimitates felicissime faustissimeque semper valeant ad vota. Ex civitate nostra Cantuariæ, vicesimo die mensis Junii, anno Domini Mccccc. A.D. 1500. 20 June.

HENRICUS R.

*Addressed:* Serenissimis atque potentissimis principibus dominis Ferdinando et Elisabeth Dei gratia Regi ac Reginæ Castellæ, Legionis, Aragoniæ, Siciliæ, Granatæ, etc., consanguineis et germanis nostris carissimis.

---

## XIV.

### HENRY VII. TO FERDINAND AND ISABELLA.[1]

[MS. Egerton 616, No. 14.]

SERENISSIMIS ac potentissimis principibus, dominis FERDINANDO et HELLISABETH Dei gratia Regi et Reginæ Castellæ, Legionis, Aragonum, Siciliæ, Granatæ, etc., consanguineis et germanis nostris carissimis, HENRICUS eadem gratia Rex Angliæ et Franciæ ac dominus Hyberniæ, salutem et prospera votorum incrementa. Legimus literas vestrarum majestatum credentiales ex Civilia ultimo Aprilis ad nos datas, quas egregius vir dominus Guttiero Gomez de Fonsalida, commendator de Haro, vester orator, nuper nobis reddidit; cujus credentiam et diligenter et ad longum annotavimus. Ex eo namque primum audivimus, quod vehementer scire A.D. 1500. 24 July.

---

[1] The original of this letter is mutilated; some of the lost words are supplied within brackets.

A.D. 1500. 24 July.

cupiebamus, de bona, scilicet, valetudine, deque felici et prospero statu vestrarum majestatum, simul et de rebellibus Saracenis domitis ac plena victoria et triumpho ex illis reportato; quibus sane omnibus vestris successibus gavisi sumus supra quam dici possit, atque, ut par est, eisdem ex intimo corde gratulamur, quandoquidem vestras omnes secundas res accessionesque et incrementa nobiscum communes reputamus. Deinde exposuit nobis idem orator negotium concernens traductionem illustrissimæ dominæ Chaterinæ communis vestræ ac nostræ filiæ, quam quidem juxta conventa conclusa, et hinc inde inter nos reges determinata, circa finem mensis Septembris proxime instantis indubitanter expectabamus; nec fuit aliquid aliud quod a nobis majore cum desiderio atque ardentiore animi affectu ob singularem quam gerimus in illas affectionem, necnon et desiderium ingens ipsius dominæ videndæ hoc tempore expectaretur. Accepimus itaque ex ipso oratore vestrarum majestatum in declaratione suæ credentiæ nonnulla quibus fieret ut non absque magno incommodo præfata illustrissima domina Catherina infra tempus limitatum traduci ad nos posset; quibus tamen non obstantibus idem orator nomine ac vice vestrarum majestatum obtulit ipsam [dominam . . . . .]o vellemus juxta finem mensis Octobris proxime esse transferendam, demonstravitque idcirco præter nostram omnem spem et expectationem . . . . . . . . rem gratissimam efficeremus si vellemus esse contenti quod ipsius illustrissimæ dominæ Chaterinæ ad nos et ad hoc nostrum regnum traducti[o . . . . .]ram æstatem sit prorogata. Nos vero, licet hujusmodi traductionem summo cum desiderio propediem expectaremus, atque ad [ipsam dominam hon]orifice, ut decet recipiendam non mediocris præparatio esset ubique facta, item et summam illam pecuniarum nobis in dotem prom[issam . . . . . . . .]e ipsius matrimonii nobis solvendam cum ipsa traductione simul in fine dicti mensis Sept[embris expectar]-

Although Henry expected Catherine in England at the end of September,

emus (nam [dilato tempore tr]aductionis sequitur ut ipsa quoque pecuniarum solutio differatur): nihilo tamen minus ob . . . . quam habemus u . . . . vestris . . . . . . majestatibus in quibuscunque valeamus rebus, item et singularem ac paternum nostrum amorem quo ipsam illustrissimam dominam Chaterinam . . . . . pote quod celebrato inter se et illustrissimum principem Arthurum nostrum primogenitum per verba de præsenti matrimonio non aliam eam reputamus quam propriam nostram filiam, nec minore etiam dilectione ipsam prosequamur quam vestræ ipsæ majestates. Nolentes nos ut periculis aliquibus maritimis imminentibus et formidolosis quoquo pacto exponeretur, postpositis omnibus nostris desideriis et complacentiis ac commodis et emolumentis ad nos ratione primæ traductionis spectantibus et pertinentibus, movemur et innitamur ut vestrarum majestatum votis morem geramus. Quocirca ad vestram gratificationem sumus contenti ut præfata illustrissimæ dominæ Chaterinæ ad nos traductio usque ad festum Sancti Johannis Baptistæ[1] proxime futurum sit prorogata; dummodo, tamen, et cum hac conditione et non aliter, quod vestræ majestates in ea forma quam ad illas in scriptis manu nostri secretarii subscriptis cum his mittimus de verbo ad verbum per suas literas suo plumbeo sigillo sigillatas et propriis manibus subscriptas, suis denique corporalibus juramentis præstitis munitas, se nobis obligent, et obligationem ipsam sic roboratam citra festum Natalis Domini proxime futurum, ad nos mitti tradi et deliberari realiter faciant; quoniam si hæc obligatio omitteretur visum est nostris consiliariis quod omnia et singula quæ super dicta traductione fuerant prius inter nos capitulata, conclusa et determinata, prorsus essent extincta et invalida, ipsaque traductio utrinque esset incerta et indeterminata, nosque ideo ob ipsam incertitudinem, ea providere et disponere

A.D. 1500. 24 July.

He is willing to grant a delay till next summer.

[1] 24 June.

A.D. 1500. 24 July.

quæ ad hujusmodi receptionem pertinent, nequaquam possemus. Promittimus autem et per præsentes nos obligamus ubi dictam vestram obligationem nobis realiter tradi et deliberari feceritis nos omnia et singula super dicto contractu matrimoniali antehac inter nos concordata et conclusa, nondum executa, quatenus nos tangunt, firmiter observaturos esse et adimpleturos. Superest ut vestræ majestates felices valeant ad vota. Ex palatio nostro Grenwici die xxiiij Julii M°.ccccc°.

HENRICUS R.

*Addressed:* Serenissimis ac potentissimis principibus dominis Ferdinando et Hellisabeth Dei gratia Regi et Reginæ Castellæ, Legionis, Aragonum, Siciliæ, Granatæ, etc., consanguineis et germanis nostris carissimis.

*Endorsed:* A sul al. Del Rey de Ingleterra xxiii[j] de Julio de D.

---

## XV.

### HENRY VII. TO FERDINAND AND ISABELLA.

[MS. Egerton 616. No. 15.]

A.D. 1500. 18 Dec.

SERENISSIMIS ac potentissimis principibus, dominis FERDINANDO et HELLIZABETH, Dei gratia Regi et Reginæ Castellæ, Legionis, Aragonum, Siciliæ, Granatæ, etc., consanguineis et germanis nostris carissimis, HENRICUS eadem gratia Rex Angliæ et Franciæ ac dominus Hiberniæ, salutem et prospera votorum incrementa. Cum reverendus pater dominus prothonotarius de Ayala nuper nobis ostenderit vestras majestates sibi istuc redeundi potestatem fecisse, putavimus certe quod cum pauco tempore hic penes nos moram traxerit et adventus illustrissimæ dominæ Chaterinæ tantopere instet [quod] non tam cito esset revocandus. Quocirca cum is dominus

Requesting that Ayala may be commanded to remain in England till the arrival of the Princess Catherine.

prothonotarius et nobis et universæ nostræ curiæ plurimum gratus et acceptus sit, nec unquam desistat ea meditari et curare quæ ad nostram et [vestra]rum majestatum dignitatem et honorem pertineant, videtur nobis plurimum conducere ut hic penes nos maneat donec et quousque ipsa [illustrissi]ma domina ad nos venerit, et etiam tanto diutius postea quanto magis vestris majestatibus expediens fuerit visum. Erit nempe (ut . . . opinio) et nobis et ipsi illustrissimæ dominæ non parvum solamen et recreatio, tum o[b] singulare ejus ingenium modestiamque et probitatem, tum etiam ob illius affabilitatem atque hilarem naturam, quibus et nuptias decorare et juveniles principum animos mulcere, alacresque et jucundos retinere possit. Rogamus itaque vestras majestates quatenus eidem domino prothonotario suis literis injungere velint ne a nobis quoquo modo se absentet, quinimmo ipsius illustrissimæ dominæ adventum immoretur, nobisque et illi cum applicuerit, præsertim in nuptiarum solenniis obsequatur, donec aliud a vestris majestatibus mandatum acceperit. In quo sane vehementer nobis gratificabuntur vestræ majestates, quæ diutissime ac felicissime valeant ad vota. Ex oppido nostro Abindoniæ, die xviij°. Decembris m°.cccccº. A.D. 1500 18 Dec.

HENRICUS R.

*Addressed :* Serenissimis ac potentissimis principibus, dominis Ferdinando et Hellisabeth, Dei gratia Regi et Reginæ Castellæ, Legionis, Aragonum, Siciliæ, Granatæ, etc. consanguineis et germanis [nostris] carissimis.

*Endorsed :* A sus al. Del Rey de Ynglaterra xviii° de Des°. de D.

## XVI.

### Henry VII. to Catherine of Arragon.

[From a corrected draft in the King's own hand. MS. Galba B.II., f. 149.]

A.D. 1501. [Oct.] Madame,

. . . . . . . . . . . . . . pardecza en notre roy[aume] nous est tant a . . . . et si tresagreable que bonnement [ne] sçaurions dire ne exprymer le grant plaisir, joye, [et] consolacion que nous en avons, et especialement de voir vostre noble presence,[1] ce que avons souventeffoiz desire et sou[haite,] tant pour les grans graces et vertuz que entendons quil a ple[u a Dieu] *de sa grace a*[2] attribuer a votre personne que aussi p[our la] mutuelle amytye, confederacion et bonne allian[ce qui est] entre noz bons cousins lez roy et royne dEspaig[ne vos p]arens et nous, la quelle a ceste

---

Translation.

Madam,

[Your late arrival] here in our realm is to us so . . . . . . . and so very agreeable, that we cannot well say or express the great pleasure, joy, [and] consolation which we have from it, and especially [in the hope] of seeing your noble presence, which we have often desired, both for the great graces and virtues which we hear it has pleased [God] to give to your person, as also for the mutual amity, confederation, and good alliance between our good cousins the king and queen of Spain [your] parents

---

[1] *personne*, corrected.

[2] The words in italics underlined in orig. and probably meant to be cancelled.

foiz sera par vo[us . . . . e]t grandement augmentee *qu'aussi pour . . . . . . . . tiere affeccion que leur portons.*[1] A.D. 1501. [Oct.]

[Ma]dame, semblablement ce nous a este t[resagreabl]e que vous avez evade et passe lez grans [dangers et per]ilz de la mer, et que estez arryve[2] . . . . . . . . po]rt de salut, vous et vostre belle compaign[ie . . . . . . . nous, et regracions Dieu de tout . . . . . .

[Et] au surplus, Madame, nous vous offr[ons . . . . . et] donnons touz les commodites et a . . . . . . . . . . . s en y a en nostre royaume pour en o . . . . . . . rement a votre bon plaisir et vol . . . . . . gnier.

[Madame,] vous [. . . . . . . . . vous] plaise no[us tenir] et repputer doresena[vant c]ome votre bon et a[ffectionne] pere, aussi familierement que feriez lez roy

---

and us, which at this time will be by you . . . . . and greatly augmented.

Madam, it has likewise been [very satifactory] to us that you have escaped and passed the great [dangers and perils] of the sea, and have arrived [here in a] port of safety, you and your fair company . . . . . us, and we give thanks to God for all . . . . . . ]

And for the rest, madam, we offer . . . . . . and give you all the advantages and . . . . . . . . in our realm, to . . . . of it . . . . at your good will and pleasure . . . . . .

[Madam,] I [beseech you that] it may please you to regard us henceforward as your good and [loving] father, as familiarly as you would do the king and queen your

---

[1] See note 2 in preceding page. | [2] *a bo . . .* scored out.

A.D. 1501. [Oct.] et royne [vos] parens, car de nostre part nous sommez resoluz et del[iberez] de vous traitter recuillir et favoriser comme notre p[ropre et] naturelle fille, et en aucune maniere plus [ou moins cherem]ent que nulz de noz propres et naturelz enfans . . . .

[Ma]dame, il ne mest bonnement possible de vous . . . . en venue, ne de vous recepvoir si bien et favo[rablement que mon] cuer et couraige le desir et que voz vertuz et [ . . . . le merite]nt; mais aumoins, madame, vous plaise [scavoir nostre bon v]ouloir et couraige et de prandre en pa . . . . . .

---

parents, for on our part we are determined to treat, receive, and favour you like our own daughter, and in no wise more [or less dearly] than any of our own children.

Madam, it is hardly possible for me to [meet] you on your arrival, or to receive you so well and favourably [as my] heart and mind desire, and as your virtues and . . . . . merit; but at least, madam, it may please you [to credit my good] will and to take in . . . . . . . .

## XVII.

### Private Instructions touching Edmund De la Pole.[1]

[MS. Cott. Galba B. ii. f. 105.]

* * * * * *

and . . . . . . . . . . . . . . . A.D. 1499
of lawe . . . . . . . . . . . . . Sept.

Furst he shal saye that aftre the said Sir Richard Gilford and maistre Richard Hatton have receyved and seen the Kinges instructions, and theruppon and the contentes of the same communed and wel debated with the said erle of Suffolk, the kinges mynd is that at suche tyme as the caas shal require, and when it shalbe seen moost convenient to them[2] the saide instructions be shewed and redde at length word by word to the said erle, suffring also hymself to rede it if hym liste, and to take it with hym to his lodging and see it at his laiser. And thus they shall doo as of themself and for the favour they specially bere unto hym, and as they soo did without the kinges knowlege.

Guildford and Hatton are to show the instructions they receive to the earl of Suffolk,

And in caas the said erle be content to retorne and comme unto the king undre the oon or the othre of the said condicions or articles conteyned in the said othre instructions, the king wol yet nevertheles that considering the divers great charges that his grace hath committed unto the said comptrollour[3] and doctor to be shewed to his cousin tharcheduc over and above the matiers touching the said erle, and specially forsomoche as the said comptrollour knoweth well that

and to urge him to return to the king;

[1] From a corrected draft, much mutilated. The writing is upon three leaves of paper, of which the second has one side blank, all but a mutilated endorsement, showing that the document must have been originally folded with this leaf outside. Nevertheless the order of the folios appears borne out by internal evidence. The date in the margin is inferred from an entry in Henry VII.'s privy purse expenses. See Excerpta Historica, 123.

[2] *them*] corr. from "the said Sir "Richard." Similar corrections occur throughout.

[3] Sir Richard Guildford was controller of the household.

A.D. 1499. Sept. by Toyson Dorre that was here with the king, his grace wrote to his said cousin that he wolde furthwith sende to hym oon ambassad, and that also the same Toyson Dorre knewe bifore his departing that the said comptrollour shulde be oon of the said ambassad, the said [* f. 105 b. comptrollour* . . . . . . . . . . . . . . . .
. . . . . . . . . . . . . . Tyrell . . . . .
th . . . . . . . . . . . . . . . yng to his grace
And if it . . . . . . . . . erle being determined to come to t . . . . . . difficultie soo to doo, onles he maye have the said comptrollour in his company; the king wol that the said comptrollour endevoire hym for the causes bifore rehersed to contente the said erle to take Sir James Tyrell in his company to the king, and that he hymself maye contynewe furth his journey to tharcheduc; seing as above that the king hathe committed to hym and to maistre Hatton many divers great matiers to be shewed to tharcheduc over and above the matier touching the said erle, and that the king hath written by Toyson Dorre to tharcheduc that he wolde briefly sende unto hym his ambassad. And that also the same Toyson Dorre knewe bifore his departing that the said comptrollour shulde be oon of the said ambassad. And over this the comptrollours name is in the kinges lettres of credence directed to tharcheduc, as well as the name of the said maister Hatton. It standeth also with the kinges great honour, both within his reame and without, that the said erle comme to his grace rathre without the said comptrollour than with him. By thies reasons and suche othre as the said comptrollour shall canne best devise, he shal enduce the said erle to be contented to take in his company to the king the said Sir James and suffre hym departe to the archeduc.

If possible, with Sir James Tyrell.

And if the said erle wol in noowise comme unto the king onlesse he have in his company the said comptrollour, rathre than the matier shulde breke therfor the king is content that he leve his jorney to tharcheduc

If he will not come, except in Guildford's company, the latter

A.D. 1499. Sept. [* f. 106 b.

Shall give up his journey to the archduke.

*. . . . . . . . . . . . . . . . . *tions must ned[es . . . . . . . . . t]hey shal make their*[1] sommonan[ce in the pr]esence of the deputie and counseill of [Calais and of the] maire of the town, the maire or lieutenant of the staple, and suche othre of the most honourable persones of that town as they shal think good.

They shal also bifore the said erle, and in the presence of the said deputie, counseill, mayres and othre, not oonly summarily declare theffect of their othre instructions delivered to theym by the said William Pawne, but also to cause Lathbury, clerk of the cownsell,[2] openly and distinctly to rede theym, and that no man be suffred to departe til this be perfitely doon. And that, the said boke oons redde, they cause the said Lathbury to putte in writing in the ende of the same instructions undre the kings signe manuell in what day, what yere, in what place, and in whoes presences (namyng every of thaym by thair names), the said sommonance was made and boke redde. And that every of the said deputie, counseill, maires or lieutenant, in testimony of the same subscribe with their owne hand their names. And that the said Lathbury doo the same wise.

Item[3]

And if[4] the said Sir Richard perceive that the same erle wol nedes depart and kepe furth his journey without the kinges licence, he shal then,[5] byfor he sommen hym, take hym apart, and as it were of hymselve and

[1] The words in italics scored out in orig.

[2] Corrected from "watche."

[3] Another item of the instructions appears to have been supplied in the left-hand margin opposite this place, but is now entirely lost by the burning of the edge of the MS., unless the fragment noticed at page 132, note [1], be the latter part of it.

[4] *after the said sommonance made to therl of Suffolk.* Struck out.

[5] *he shal then . . . . k[nowledge]* interlined in Fox's hand, and in the margin, instead of the words "the "said Sir Richard shall then," which are struck out.

A.D. 1499. Sept. for the favor he bereth hym, and as it we[r] without the kyngs k[nowledge], shewe to hym that the king wol furthwith advertise every prince standing with him in amytie, aliaunce, and confederacion, that is to saye, the Frenshe king, the kinges of Spayne, Portugal,
[* f. 107. and Scotland,[1] *his grace . . . . . . . . . . . .
. . . . . . . eter soo to doo to thar[cheduc] . . .
. . . . . . s there redy immediatly . . . . [t]he king to make the same advert . . . . . .

He shal also advise the said erle to considre for his owne weal and suretie that this doon he maye make hym wel assured that noon of the said kinges nor princes, nor any othre being in the kynges amitie and confederacion, woll nor maye receyve, favour, socour, or entreteigne, nor suffre hym in any maner of wise to abide or remayne in any place or places of any of their obeissances, but to his uttre clere destruction take and sende hym to the king, for they be bound to the king soo to doo undre their writinges subscribed with their handes, sealed with their seales, and confermed with their othes.

The said Sir Richard shall advise hym sadly to remembre this matier, and therwith rekynne in his mynd what place or prince he hath to goo to for any socour or entreteynement aftre he be thus excluded from France, Spayn, Portugal, Scotland, and tharchedukes lands.

Item,[2]

---

[1] This is the last word of the text on p. 106 b.; but the following words in Ruthall's hand, probably the latter part of the item inserted in the margin, (see note [4] on preceding page), are visible below :—
" . . . . . . the depute the cownsell and the sayd mayrs or leftenant
" . . . . . . s to thentent thay may undyrstand the kyngs gracyous
" . . . . . . sayd erle. And thus to be doon and declaryd as thow;
" . . . . . . fyr and mocion of the sayd depute and cownsell. And
" . . . . . . mawndment or knowlege."

[2] A caret is inserted before the next article, referring to a marginal note now almost entirely lost by the mutilation of the MS.

He muste also remembre that if he be in the company of any prince or any othre persone and make warre against any of the kinges frendes, alies, and confederates, that is to saye the Frenshe king, the kinges of Spayne, Portugal, Naples, or Scotland, or tharcheduc, the duc of Millain, the Venicians or any of the cities of Italy, he shal therby attempte the breche of the kinges peax, his amytie, and confederacion, that he hath with th[e] said kinges, princes, and townes; and in his so doin[g] he shal expressely doo treason against the king* . . . . . . . . . . . . . . [* 107 b. A.D. 1499 Sept.
. . . . . . . . . . . . . . . . . . . . . shewed to therle that he . . . . . . . r entreteigned in France, Spayne, P[ortugal, Scot]land, nor tharchedukes landes, as is als[o] co[n]teyned in the same instructions [and that . . . . . . hym . . . . and fa . . . . . . ].[1] If he than perceyve that the erle (the said sommonance and advertisementes notwithstanding) wol alweys kepe furth his journey, he shal, as of hymself, and as it were for the singlier favour that he bereth to hym, and without any knowlege of the king, saye that albeit the said sommonance for his desertes hath been made to hym, the king is yet nevertheles at his libertie uppon his good abering in his absence to repute hym and take hym and deale with hym as it shal please his grace.

He shal therfor advise hym that during his absence he and his companye behave theym and demeane theym in every place in woord and dede as the kinges true and faithful subgiettes noo thing doing ne saying that myghte sownde to the kinges displesir or dishonour. And he and they soo doing maye fortune at the sute of his frendes, to cause the king in tyme commyng to have pitie, grace, and mercy upon hym, pardonne hym his said disobeissance, and suffre him to retourne and

[1] This very mutilated clause within brackets is added in the margin in Fox's hand.

A.D. 1499. Sept. enjoye that he had when he departed; the whiche othrewise than by his good demeanur and trewe behavyng towardes the king in his absence, he maye never loke to recovere ne comme to agayn.

*Endorsed* (f. 106). . . . . . . . . Maistre Ric. . . . . . . . . . . Archeduc.

---

## XVIII.

### A Statement concerning Edmund De la Pole.

[MS. in Record Office.]

A.D. 1501.

On Maximilian saying he would assist any one of the house of York to regain the crown,

Furst when my lord Corson[1] in his going to Turkey declared to the king[2] the murdres and tyrannyes of H., with the propos of my lord of Suff. ayeinst king H. to recover his right, &c., the kinges majestie aunswerde to my lord Corson, that if his majestie mighte have oon of king Edwardis blode in his handis, he wold helpe him to recover the coroune of England and bee revenged upon H., or elles he wold spende asmuche money as his hole landes were in value for an hole yere.

the earl of Suffolk left England;

Upon this the said duke of Suff. was by the lord Corson acerteyned, and soo departed out of the reame of England. And at the said ducis commyng to Seyntjone,[3] he sent to the kinges majestie his lakkey with his lettres declaring to the king the cause of his commyng, and to knowe his plaisure for his commyng to his presence.

but, on coming to the emperor,

Upon this the said duc camme to the kinges presence at Ympst, declaring playnely to his grace the murdres doon by H., and that H. also entended

---

[1] Sir Robert Curzon, whom Maximilian created a baron of the Empire. See Gough's Camden's Britannia, II., 306.

[2] Maximilian, king of the Romans, commonly called Emperor.

[3] or Seyntrone? Probably St Johann in the Tyrol.

to have murdred him and his brodre, with the wronges H. had doon to him. Wherupon the said duc besought the kinges majestie, insomuche as he was emprower, of his ayde, according to justice to helpe the said duc to his right. A.D. 1501.

The kinges majestie welcommed the said duc, taking him as his kynnesman, and desired him to goo to his logging. And sent to him to his logging his counsaillors doctor Newdek, chaunceller of Austriche, and the quenes chaunceller. Whiche on the kinges behalve shewed to the said duc, that by mean of the pais bytwix H. and my lord archduc, and insomuche also that by the la[kkey] of my lord archduc the kinges majestie had sent to him his seal for tract of pais bytwix his grace and H., his grace mighte not ayde the said duc. Neverthalas, the kinges majestie by his said counsaillors offered to the said duc his saufconduit to abyde within the empier and al other countreys belonging to the kinges patromony and inheritance. was at first denied help;

The said duc with the kinges saufconduit and this aunswer, having the kinges lettres of licence to depart, was contented to have soughte his frendes in other parties, and w[ould] have departed incontinently. And when the duc had thus aunswered, the [ducis] said counsellouers reapported it to the kingis majestie.

And upon that camme the next day again to the said duc the s . . . . . . . with theim and . . . . . . . monsieur le tresorer Bontemps, desiring the said duc [to have] pacience for viij daies, bycause of the businesse his grace then had to doo with [the] cardinal of Roan[1] and other ambassadoures of Fraunce. And that if it wold please the sayd duc soo to doo, the kinges majestie wold studie and divise som waies for the said duc that shuld doo him good.

---

[1] George Amboise.

A.D. 1501. then persuaded to wait at least six weeks; The said duc at the kinges instaunce taried at Ympst by vj wekes, and then camme thider to the said duc the forsaid monsire Tresorer with a lettre from the kinges majestie, to whom the kinges grace desired that the said duc shuld yeve full faith and credence.

The Credence.

and finally promised the aid of 500 soldiers. That the kinges majestie wold helpe the said duc his cousin to his right, insomuche as the tresorer on the kinges behalf offred to the said duc iij. iiij. or v. m[l]. men of warre at his plaisire to serve the said duc for j., ij., or iij. m[onths] . . . . . . . . .
[*p. 2. *they shuld receive any wages of the said duc, and that the said nombre of men shuld bee redy with diligence. Insomuche as Walter Yngar, on of the huisshers of chambre, was then sent to my lord Henry, erl of Ardek, to make redy the said men. The whiche erl had promised the king like nombre of men of warre at the kinges plaisir for iij monethes wheresomever it shuld please the king to sende theym. And if the said erl performed not this matier, the kinges grace wold fynde other remedie for the said nombre of men, and also for shipping, &c. The said iij. monethes ended, the said duc being in his right in England, at his libertie either to contente the waiges thus due, &c., or elles, an other tyme when the kinges majestie shuld have nede, the said duc to ayde his grace with like nombre of men at his charges. And besides this the said duc was moved by Mr. Tresorer in [the] kinges name to bee agreable to certain other thinges, whiche the said duc by his . . . . instructions signed and sealed, performed in every thing as the kinges majestie desired.

The said duc humbly gave thankes, &c., for the kinges offre of ayde and helpe, and concluded with monsire Tresorer to have iiij. m[l]. fotemen, and vj[c].

horsemen. And soo the said duc by thappointement of the king came to Acon, having his lettres of recommendacion to the counsail of the samo towne. A.D. 1501–2. Goes to Aix-la-Chapelle by the emperor's desire.

The said duc leving with the king his steward with thinstructions aforesaid, according to the tresorers desire, to sollicite the said ducis causes, and to conclude in the premisses.

At Brounek[1] the stewerd camme to the kinges presence, and there declared to the king the said credence, [an]d shewed to the king thinstructions aforsaid. With the whiche the king was we[ll c]ontented, and with the said duc, that he upon Bontemps credence had fulfilled the kinges desire, commanding the stewerd to kepe the said instructions, til the commyng of the forsaid Walter Yngar from therl of Ardek.

And then camme the said lord Herry, erl of Ardek, to the king him silf; but the kinges promesse stode voyed, and toke noon effect. The emperor's promise is not fulfilled.

Upon this the steward was sent by the king to the said duc with lettres; to whom the king desired the duc to geve full faith and credence to suche thinges [as the] steward [shewed] to the said duc on the kinges behalf.

The Credence.

[Forasm]uch as the king was then determined to h[av]e goon to . . . . . he for that tyme coulde not performe his [prom]esse made by the . . . . king desired the said duc to bee of good comfort and to . . . . . tyme. And that withoute faille the king wold helpe him oon wa[ye] or other; and if oon waye wold not take another shuld. Insomuche as the king saied, "I see wel this must bee myn owne dede, and I shal pro-[vide] for xxx. m^l^. g'. to bringe this matier to passe." And to thentente the sa[id] duc shuld alwaies be

[1] Brunecken in the Tyrol.

A.D. 1502. sure for shipping the king appointed maistre Basti[am] oon of his chapellains to goo to the king of Denmarc to appointe with him to bee the said ducis frend, and that in noo wise the said king shuld take pais with king H. And his lettres and instructions to the king of Denmarc, maistre Nichola[s] Zigler had in commaundemente to make theym.

The steward being in Ulmes received lettres from the said duc whiche caused him . . . . . again to the king, the sayd maistre Bastiam being ther not goon, and sollicited for . . . . . .

* * * * * *[1]

[* p. 3. * of Denmarc in this weighty matier, and then the king appointed a bisshop in [his] stede.

And when the king had openned his mynd to the bisshop, for his preparacion he desired but viij. daies respect to mak him redy to goo into his countre and to retorne, and in this maner not despached was this bisshop xx daies. And then the king brak to the steward that he must nedes occupie the bisshop to bee a commissioner to goo with the cardynal for to gadre toguid[er the] pardonne money.

Then the king appointed a gentilman Ufford to goo to the king of . . . . Mr. Zigler had made in his lettres and instructions for . . . . And the king was soo good lord to the said duc . . . ma . . upon his suretie and the said dukes moved therl of Ardek . . to the said duc xx.m[l]. guld. to have therfor again xl.m[l]. . . . And that the said erles son shuld have goon with the said duc [into] England. And the kinges majestie caused the tresorer and the steward to commone in this matier with therl of Ardek. Whom by his worde [he] founde soo towardly, that the said xx.m[l]. guld. shuld have been redy [by] Saint Georges Day then next following, and soo this said duc to have [gone] into Denmarc and taken shipping.

---

[1] A line lost by the mutilation of the MS.

Memorandum.—The date of my lordis lettre to the steward that Robert Wellesborne had to king Herry was the xij day of . . . . . . And the . . bytwix the kinges majestie . . . . was taken by the commissioners the xx day of Juyn . . . . . A.D. 1502.

And in the same space the sending into Denmarc, and the xx. m.g. was disappointed. And then the king at Auxborowe showed to the steward tha[t] he wold helpe my lord for all that. And saied there is warre [between] Geldre and Cleve, whiche shuld breke up shortely, and the king . . . . . . . . . wold spede to the duc of Cleve for my lordes helpe at [the com]ing up of the men of warre; and that waye the king sa . . . and . . . wise therof. 20 June. The earl is further disappointed of promised aid.

[The] kinges majestie after being in Ulnes, where the steward . . . . . duc . . . . the king that if he wold not . . . . . . that it might please . . . . . . . . . . his ma[jestie] could not othrewise . . to recompencè to . . . . had by raison of his abiding at the kinges instaunce. And . . . . . . . . . . having the kinges licence and favour was contented to departe and . . . . . . frendes.

Then incontinently by the kinges commandement the treasorer declared [to the] steward the kinges mind for a peace bytwix the said duc and . . . . . . whiche the steward hath in writing to shewe according as the . . . penned it.

iij. myle from Ulmes.

The kinge after, at Yetting castel, openned himself his mind to the steward . . . . . said pais, and desired the steward to have goon and declared the same to his mai[ster] and to have retorned to the king with thaunswer wh . . . to do asmuch as the king determined to . . . .

* * * * * [1]

[1] Probably a line lost.

A.D. 1502. [* p. 4.] *with the steward to the said duc, that they ij. toguider shuld openne the kinges mynd to the said duc for the said pais and bifore the king depached the lakkey to the said duc, certifieng the same duc that within iiij. daies then next after his majestie wold have despached the steward.

Then came my lord Corson to Auxburg to the king to knowe the kinges mynd concerning his promesse aforsaid. The king aunswerd that though he had many thinges to do, yet his grace wold soo doo for the said duc, that he shuld bee contented.

The countie Nasso and Bontemps after by the kinges commaundement delivered [to] my lord Corson and to the stewerd in the presence of thambassador of Spaigue the kinges instructions for tract of pais bytwix my lord and H.

The king him self saied to my lord Corson and to the steward, that al though his grace meved the said duc to this pais, if it pleased the said duc soo to doo at his instaunce, yet for al that the king wold doo for the said duc secretly asmuche as he cowlde. Geving libertie to the same duc at his pleasure to labor to every prince for succor, insomuche as the king was contented that my lord shuld labour to the king of Fraunce, sayeng thise wordes, that, "though his subgettes and myn cannot aggree, yet he and I wolbe frendes shortely. And the king of F. is a man that hath good and wol avaunce money shortely, thinkyng that an othre day my cousin wolbe my good frende and owe me [none] the werse wille."

Maximilian suggests that he should apply to France.

The king said also, that oon of the speciallest causes that he desired the said duc to . . . . was for the sure conveying home of my lord archeduc oute of Spayne into his countrey. Desiring to have the ducs said aunswer by writing. And if the said duc wold conforme him therunto at the kinges desire, his majestie wold performe his sayenges, and also thinstructions aforsaid.

Then aunswered my l. C. and saied to the king,

"If my lord wo[ld consent] to this pais, howe shal he lyve in the mean tyme?" The king [said] to my l[ord] Corson] "Lette me have but my cousin, your maister . . . . . . and my moder, his aunte.[1] We shal soo prov[ide . . . . . . . . . . .] shalhave honnorable entreteignement." A.D. 1502.

. . . . according to the kinges desire and at the ki[nges . . . . . . . . . . . . . . . .
. . . . .] him to this pais, and sent the stewerd to the king with an aunswere . . . . . upon the kinges said instructions. Wherewith the king . . . wel . . . . and promised to the stewerd to have delivered to him furthwith a ml. g. for thentreteignement of the said duc, and appointed v. ml. g. for his dislogge, as R. Ruffyn and Marinyer knowe.

And furthre the king knewe somuche that H. was contented that my lord and my lady his wife shulde bee in the kinges court, and that al suche personnes as were with the said duc that had landes or goodes in England shuld enjoie them and have also recompence of the revenues of the same. And for the conclusion of almaner thinges the king wold then have sent into England diverse honnorable personaiges in ambassade.

*vj Leeges bysydes Auxburgh. [* p. 5.

After this at the towne of Werde the king brake to the steward that he founde king H. variable and that he sigheth[2] wel that king H. mynd was utterly to destroye the said duc and howe that king H. had meved the king to doo thinges whiche shuld bee to the said dukes destruction, wherunto the kinges majestie wold never assent. And therfor the king saied if king Herry contynued in that mynd, his majestie mighte with his honour breke al thinges that were begonne

[1] Margaret of Burgundy. | [2] *sigh*, MS.

A.D. 1503? bytwix him and king H., and helpe the said duc, witho[ut] king H. wold kepe his promesse.

Upon this the king had knoweleege of the comyeng of king H. amba[ssadors] in his commyng to Brabant ward, and then the king shewed to the steward that his grace, the said duc, and king H. ambassadours shuld mete al toguider to commyn and conclude in almaner causes. Insomuche as the king wrote accordingly to t[he] said duc and sent his lettres to Casius for to delivere to the said duc m$^l$. guld.

The king after in Istelgorffe[1] and Weesyll commaunded the steward to goo to Acon to the said duc, there to abide for viij. daies, willing the steward to delivere ag[ain] to his grace the assignement upon Casius for the said m$^l$ guld. And by thende of the said viij. daies, the saied he wold sende to the said duc the said m$^l$ guld. for his entreteignment, and also a saufconduit for the steward that he mighte comme into Braband to sollicite the causes of the said duc; whiche the king performed not. And the king herde the said ducis . . . . . no man thereto aunswere for him, whiche was honnorably nec . . . . . . . .

The s[aid] duc, seing that the king thus dilaied him, sent his pursyvant [ . . . . with] lettres [to th]e king to Andewerpe, beseching his grace for to have knowen his plaisire and [if] the king wold not performe his said promesse, the said duc besoughte the king to geve licence to departe upon such thinges as were conteyned in [the] said ducis lettres.

[The] king then sent to the said duc diverse his lettres desiring him [to have a li]tyll pacience, for within v. or [vj.] daies after he wold sende to the said d[uc certaine] of his counsail to declare to the seid duc the kinges . . . . . . . . . . . . as his grace had openned and declared at large [to the] stew[ard].

[1] Düsseldorf?

. . . . . . . . the moneth of Marche the king sen . . . . . . . . . . . grace had sent his ambassador into England. From [whom] the king had noon answere. But his grace . . . . . . . . . . . . . to sende to the said duc suche aunswere as he shuld bee pleased. A.D. 1503.

---

* . . . . . . . . le Roy des Romaynes et de Ungherie, &c. A.D. 1501. 9 Sept. [* p. 6.

TRESCHIER et tresame cousin,—Nous avons receu voz lettres, ensemble celles que nostre ame et feal chevalier . . . . R. Corson nous ay escript. Par lesquellez avons entendu les causes pour lesquelles estes parti du reame Dangliterre. Et desirez de savoir ou vous nous pourrez veoir et parler anous. Surquoi, treschier et tresame cousin, vous advertisons que avons entencion de demourier encoires par aucunes jours pardeca. [Vous] nous y pourrez trouver. Ce scet nostre Seigneur auquel nous prions quil soit garde de vous. Escript [en] nostre ville Dysbrouch le ix. jour de Septembre, lan xv[c] et ung. Letters from Maximilian to Suffolk.

Per Regem.

MARINIER.

---

TRANSLATION.

The King of the Romans and of Hungary, &c.

MOST dear and well-beloved cousin,—We have received your letters, together with those which our beloved and faithful knight Sir Robert Curson has written to us, whereby we have understood the causes for which you have left the realm of England. And you desire to know where you can see us and speak with us. Wherefore, most dear and well-beloved cousin, we apprise you that it is our intention to remain yet some days here, where you may find us, as knoweth our Lord, whom we pray to be your protector. Written in our town of Innsbruck, the 9th day of September, 1501.

A.D. 1501. 22 Sept. Maximilianus divina favente clementia Romanorum rex semper Augustus.

Letters from Maximilian to Suffolk.

Illustris sincere dilecte,—Audivimus te in Zierl applicuisse. Cum autem hic propter venationis causam sumus te hortamur ut cras de sero huc ad villagium Delfs te transferas. Facies in eo nobis rem pergratam. Datum in Delfs die Mercurii[1] post festum Matthæi Apostoli, anno Domini millesimo quingentesimo primo, regni nostri xvi°.

Ad mandatum domini regis proprium.

23 Sept. Maximilianus[2] ut supra, &c.

Illustris sincere dilecte,—Scripsimus hodie ad te ut cras ad villagium Telphs proficiscereris. Cum autem hoc propter incommoditatem hospitiorum importunum sit, visum est nobis commodius in Pettnau proximo illic loco, quo te præsens noster tabellarius adducet exspectare. Quocirca te hortamur ut sine mora te illuc conferas, ubi quam primum de voluntate nostra te certiorem reddemus. Datum in Telphs nona cal. Octobris,[3] anno ut [supra].

Ad mandatum domini regis proprium.

MARINIER.

Le Roy de Romaynes, &c.

30 Oct. TRESCHIER et tresame cousin,—Combien que essions delibere et estoit nostre desire de voz faire savoir de n[oz] nouvellez, toutesvoyes, obstant les grans et urgent affaires que nous sont survenues depuis nostre departe-

TRANSLATION.

The King of the Romans, &c.

MOST dear and well-beloved cousin,—Although we had determined, and it was our desire to inform you of our news; nevertheless, owing to the great and urgent affairs

[1] 22 Sept.

[2] The original of this letter exists in the Record Office.

[3] 23 Sept., although the date ought to be the same as that of the last letter.

ment de Ympst nous ne lavons peu bonnement faire; mais bien brief nous envoyrons dever vous aucun de nous servitures, et par ycelluy vous signifirons de noz nouvelles. Atant, treschier et tresame cousin, nostre Seigneur soit garde de vous. Escript en nostre ville de Bosseen le penultime jour doctobre, lan xv^c et ung. A.D. 1501. 30 Oct. Letters from Maximilian to Suffolk.

Per regem.

MARINIER.

Le Roy dez Romains et de Hungery. 6 Nov.

TRESCHIER et tresame cousin,—Nous envoyes[1] presentement par dever vous nostre ame et feal conseilleur Jehan Bontemps, seigneur de Salans, pour vous dire et declarier acung choises de nostre parte. Sy vous requirons le vouloir croire pour ceste foys de ce quil vous dire depar nous. Atant, treschier et tresame cousin nostre Seigneur soit garde de vous. Escript a Bosseener le vi. jour de Novembre, lan xv^c et ung.

Per regem.

Ad mandatum domini regis proprium.

---

which have come upon us since our departure from Imst, we have not been well able to do so; but very shortly we will send to you some one of our servants, and by him we will signify to you our news. Thus, most dear and well-beloved cousin, our Lord be your protector. Written in our town of Botzen, the 30th day of October, 1501.

The King of the Romans and of Hungary.

Most dear and well-beloved cousin,—We send to you at present our beloved and faithful counsellor Jean Bontemps, lord of Salans, to say and declare to you certain things on our part. Accordingly we request you to give him credence for this occasion touching what he will say to you on our behalf. Thus, most dear and well-beloved cousin, our Lord be your protector. Written at Botzen, the 6th day of November, 1501.

---

[1] Sic in MS.

A.D. 1502. Memorandum. The lettre in Laten of credence was brenned by my lord that was dated in January, when I was commyng to my lord and retourned bak from Ulmes, was brenned, &c.

20 July.

Le Roy de Romaynes, &c.[1]

TR[ESCHIER et ame cous]in, nous avons receu voz lettres par . . [2] Lagnay porteur de cestes, et entendu ce que nous avez fait dire et declarer par vostre maistre dostell estant dever nous. Surquoy vous advertisons que dedens quatre jours apres le date de cestez renvoyerons dever vous vostre dict maistre dostell, et avec luy ung de noz servitures, par lequel vous ferons faire responce du contynue de vosdites lettres. Atant, treschier et ame cousin, notre Seigneur soit garde de vous. Donne a [3] Yetting, le xx. jour de Jullet, lan xv$^{c}$ deus.

Per regem.

MARINIER.

---

TRANSLATION.

The king of the Romans, &c.

Most dear and well beloved cousin, we have received your letters by . . . Lagnay bearer of these, and understood what you have caused to be said and declared to us by your steward being with us. Whereupon we inform you that within four days after the date of these we will send back to you your said steward, and with him one of our servants, by whom we shall cause answer to be made to you on the contents of your said letters. Thus, most dear and beloved cousin, our Lord be your protector. Given at Yetting, the 20th day of July, 1502.

---

[1] The original of this letter is in the Cottonian Collection, MS. Galba B. IV. f. 132 b., (117 b. of the old foliation), pasted on the back of a letter of later date, with which it has no connexion. The address, is legible through the other letter, "A "nostre treschier et ame cousin, le "duc de Suffock."

[2] The MS. here is illegible, and the original letter is mutilated in the very same place.

[3] *en*, MS., but *a* in orig.

Illustris[1] consanguinee carissime. Cum nuperrime a nobis petieris ut auctoritate nostra tibi indulgere dignaremur quod ubique per totum imperium tibi insidiantes et in te adversa machinantes punire possis; visum fuit id aliquantulum civitatibus imperialibus posse præjudicare. Cumque generale habeas mandatum, ut ubique hujusmodi tuos insidiatores edoceas quod tunc unaquæque civitas ad tui instantiam in eos jus administret. Quapropter tibi scribendum duximus ut in eo contentus esse velis, ne graviora nobis exoriantur incommoda. Datum in oppido nostro Innsprugæ, die xxiiij Februarij, anno Domini M.DII., regnorum nostrorum Romani decimo sexto, Hungariæ [vero duo]decimo. A.D. 1502. 24 Feb. Letters from Maximilian to Suffolk.

Per regem.

Ad mandatum domini regis proprium.

. . . . .

. . . . . . . . . . of Juyl or therin camme Sir Robert Corson. And where a servant of the kinges . . . . . . . . . . and openned the kingis mynd to my lord for a tracte of accorde bytwixt . . . . . . . . . . . . . of his commyng it was known. For Sir Robert wold take upon h . . . . . . . . . . . . . and so he received a mynite of instructions . . . . . . . . . . . . . . . . .
. . . . . to my lorde; and I yode to Frankford for the m[1] . . d. . . . . . . . . . . . . . . . . .
. . . . . namid with his lettres of aunswer touching the said . . . .

Maximilianus divina favente clementia Romanorum rex semper Augustus.

[Illustr]is sincere dilecte, nunciamus dilectioni tuæ oratores serenissimi principis, domini Henrici regis Anglorum Suff (?) . . . . . . . . eos brevi apud nos futuros. Quod cum factum fuerit tractabimus cum

[1] The original of this letter is in the Record Office, and from it some words have been supplied which are illegible in this MS.

A.D. 1502. 21 Dec. eisdem [de] negotiis dilectionis tuæ propter quæ magistrum curiæ tuæ ad nos misisti. Præterea significamus . . . . speramus brevi proficisci versus dilectionem tuam, ubi et simul conveniemus tractaturi latius de omnibus. Quod te latere minime volumus. Datum in oppido Dornstat die xxj[a] Decembris anno xv[c].ij[o].

Per regem.

Ad mandatum domini regis proprium,

COLLAUER DOCTOR.

Memorandum. At this tyme the king wrote [a] lettre in my lordis favour to the bisshop of Lege[1] and to other princes, and the bysshops lettres were delivered to him afore king H. ambassadours.

Item, memorandum touching thambassadours; and therfor the king was not contented and wold not comme by my lord, nor lette me goo with hym into Brabant, but commaunded me to retorne from Geynes in Cleveland to Acon to my lord, and then Don Peter rode in Braband from Andewarp.

Memorandum. So that the king sent a lettre to my lord steward T. that he shuld comeforte my lord, &c., which . . . . . to my lord and lord . . . .

A.D. 1503. 9 Feb. [* p. 7. *TRESCHIER et tresame cousin. Nous avons receu voz lettres escript en nostre ville Dhays le jour et feste de Nostre Dame derrain passe. Lesquelles nous avons venez bien et longue. Surquoy vous advertissons que deans iiij jours nous envoyerons aucun de noz servitures dever vous pour vous advertier de faire response tant sur le continue en vosdictes lettres, que sur ce

TRANSLATION.

MOST dear and well beloved cousin. We have received your letters written in our town of Aix the day and feast of Our Lady last past, which we have regarded well and long. Whereupon we apprise you that within four days we will send to you some of our servants to make answer to you, both upon the

[1] John de Horne.

que avies donne charge a vostre maistre dostell, quest retourne dever vous. Atant, treschier et tresame cousin, nostre Seigneur soit garde de vous. Escript en nostre ville de Anvers le ix[e] jour de Fevrier lan xv[c] et deux. A.D. 1503. 9 Feb. Letters from Maximilian to Suffolk.

Per regem.

Ad mandatum domini regis proprium.

MARINIER.

TRESCHIER[1] et ame cousin, nous avons receu voz lettres par vostre serviteur, porteur de cestes, par lesquelles avons entendu vostre necessitie. Et nous requerez[2] vous aider ainsy que vos dictes lettres le contiennent plusaulong. Surquoy vous advertissons que bien toste envoyerons dever vous et vous advertirons des causes que nous ont fait tant tarder et esperons que en serez[3] bien content. Atant, treschier et ame cousin, notre Seigneur soit garde de vous. Donne en nostre ville Danvers le xix. jour de Mars lan xv[c]. et deux. 19 March.

Per regem.

MARINIER.

---

contents of your said letters and upon that which you gave [in] charge to your steward who is returned towards you. Thus, most dear and well beloved cousin, our Lord be your protector. Written in our town of Antwerp, the 9th day of February, 1502.

MOST dear and beloved cousin, we have received your letters by your servant, bearer of these, whereby we have understood your necessity; and you ask us to aid you, as your said letters contain more at length. Whereupon we intimate to you that we shall forthwith send towards you and inform you of the causes which have made us so long delay; and we hope that you will be satisfied therewith. Thus, most dear, &c. Given in our town of Antwerp, the 19th day of March 1502.

---

[1] The original of this letter exists in the Record Office.

[2] *requirons* in transcript.

[3] *serons* in transcript.

A.D. 1501? Le roy des Romains, nostre seigneur, a fait declarer a messire Robert Corson, en la presence . . . . . . . . . . . Despaigne, les pointz et les articles cy apres declariez . A celle fin que ledict messire Robe[rt] . . . . . . . . . au duc de Suffolk.

Et primers, luy a fait declarier que, actendu que ledict duc de Suffolk est yssu de la con . . . . . . . . . . et dudict roy Despaigne, que sa majestie le vouldroit conseiller et dressier et ses affaires et . . . . a la restituicion de ses biens, rentez et revenues quil ay en reame Dangleterre par condicions honestes, et ainsy en temps deu et possible.

Daultrepart, considere laffinitie que ledict roy Despaigne et monsieur larchiduc ont avec le roy Dangliterre, et les grans affaires que leurs majesties ont a present, semble a roy nostredict seigneur que par amiabletie (?) et par condicions et meanes propries ledict duc de Suffolk doit ace proceder et faire son

---

### Translation.

The king of the Romans, our lord, has caused to be declared to Sir Robert Curson, in the presence [of the ambassadors of the king] of Spain, the points and articles hereafter declared, to this end that the said Sir Robert [may signify them] to the duke of Suffolk.

And first, he had caused to be declared to him that, considering that the said duke of Suffolk is sprung of the [kin of the king of England] and of the said king of Spain, that his majesty would advise and direct him in his affairs . . . . to the restitution of his goods, rents, and revenues which he has in the realm of England by honorable conditions, and also in due season when practicable.

On the other hand, considering the alliance which the said king of Spain and the archduke have at present with the king of England, and the great affairs that their majesties have at present, it appears to the king our said lord that the said duke of Suffolk ought by amicable ways and by proper conditions and means to proceed thereto, and make his treaty thereof,

tracter len, prenant layde et su[ccours] de roy nostre dict seigneur et dudict roy Despaigne; lesquelz pour les causes dessusdictes et saunce aucune doubte . . . . . afaire sondict tractie ason utilitie. Doultre semble au roy nostredict seigneur et audict ambassadeur que lon doit practiquier et solliciter dever le roy dAngliterre quy vueille mettre hors dexil ledict duc, mesme pource quil luy face . . . . et mettre a son franc arbitre sa femme et ses enfans en semble ses nous . . . . . joye de ses rentes et revenues et quil puist tirier ses dictes rentes et revenues hors du . . . . . . . . . . . . . . . . . . . . . . . . . . . . . . . . . . . . . . ction sur . . . . t ainssi l . . gard devroit pur la plusgran[de] suretie et s . . . . . . . . . . . . . . . . . . . . aux gaiges et service dudict roy Despaign[e . . . . . . de . . . z. Et tousjours . . . . du pais du roy des Romaines. Car en se faisant il s . . . . . . a an . . . . . . . de sa par[t . . . . . . ] agreable au Dieu et a lui honorable et ainsi choise aggreable a . . . . . dont il p[eut a]voir aucunes remuneracion deux. Et par ce moyen pource estre . . . . . . . en lon . . . . . . . . .

A.D. 1501?

*Endorsed*: "The matiers as my lord was handelled with the king of Romaynes."

taking the aid and succour of the king our said lord and of the said king of Spain, who for the causes aforesaid, and without any doubt [will assist him] to make his said treaty to his advantage. Besides, it appears to the king our said lord, and to the said ambassador, that direct and indirect application should be made to the king of England, that he would recall the said duke from banishment, even because he would make him . . . . and place at his free disposal his wife and children along with his . . . . . . enjoy his rents and revenues, and that he might draw his said revenues from the . . . . . . . .

[The rest unintelligible.]

## XIX.

[MS. Cott., Galba B. II. f. 52.]

A.D. 1501. H.R. [INSTRUCTIONS given by the] [1] king unto his [right trusty servants, Sir Ch]arles Somerset, knight, his vice[chamberlain] and to Maistre William Warham, maistre of the rolles in the kinges chancellary, for to be shewed to the king of Romayns.

FURST, aftre presentacion of their lettres and due recommendacions they sh[all] saye that the king oure souverain lord hath wel undrestande asw[ell] by the lettres of tharcheduc as also by Mons^r de Sempye and [the] provost of Arres his ambassadours then being in England [with our] [2] said souverain lord that the same archeduc by thordenance of [the king] of Romains had sent oon Maistre Jaques Gowdrant [president of] Burgoigneye to have shewed to our said souverain lord in th[e presence] of the said ambassadours certain credence to hym committe[d by the] said archeduc.

And forasmoche as by the visitacion of God the said Maistre [Jaques] Gowdrant, to the great hevyness and displeasure of our sa[id souverain] lord, saving the will of God, disseced bifore he co[uld come to] his presence, the said ambassadours of tharched[uc, having] the same instruccions that were committed to the said [Maistre

---

[1] The original MS. of this document is so much injured by the fire that many words near the margins are burned away. The true order of the folios has also been disturbed and the greater part of the document dislocated from its true position. The modern foliation of the MS is here given in the margin. In the beginning the bracketed words are supplied from an imperfect modern copy in the same volume made before the fire.

[2] Modern copy also burned.

Jaques], shewed theym aftrewarde to our said souverain lord in [manner following:] A.D. 1501.

That is [to] say, [that the said ki]ng of Romayns considering [like] a verray Catho[lic pri]nce peace and amitie bitwix Cristen princes to be the principal maintenor, defendor and releve [of] the faith of the Churche of Criste, desireth of all his h[eart] love, confederacion, and fraternite of all princes cristened, and amonges othre singlierly with oure said souverain lord, ha[ving][1] in his remembrance the great fraternite and aliaunce [that] hath been bitwix theym in tyme passed, and know[ing] also thentier affection amitie and kyndenes that is [betwixt] oure said souverain lord and the said archeduc his son. [Wherefore] he is contented to have and take aliance, confederacion [amitie] and fraternitee with oure said souverain lord.

The king our souverain lord, seing that the said considera[cion], desire, and contentacion of the said king of Romayns procede[the] not oonly of his great noblesse, wisdom, catholique mynde and godly disposicion for the tuicion and defens of the Churche of Criste, but also of a remembrance of thancie[nt] *fraternite, love, and [*f. 53. [affeccion that in ti]me passed hath be bitwix theym, in his most herty [wise] thanketh the same king of Romayns, assuring him that for the honor of God thexalta[cion] of his Churche and the confusion of the ennemyes of our fai[th] he is for his partie of like desir to have peax with all princes, and specially with hym, remembring that ther hath be not [only] bitwix theym in tyme passed great love, amitie, and ali[ance], but also bitwixt the hool impire and the noble prog[enitors] and antecessours of oure said souverain lord. And over th[is with] moche the bettre will for thentier love and fadrely [affeccion] that he bereth to the said archeduc, whom he tendr[eth no les] than he doeth

[1] Here the copy also is burned.

A.D. 1501.

in maner his propre son the prince of [Wales], and also for the consanguynytee and nyghnes of bl[ood that is] bitwixt the said king of Romains and our said souver[ain lord]. Acertaynyng hym that it shal not faile uppon [the party of] our said souverain lord, but that suche love amy[tee, alliance] [*f. 53 b.] *and confe[deracion shalbe had] and taken bitwix theym as m[ay] be to the hon[or of God] the confort and pleasure of theym, [their] frendes and allyes, and the weal and restfulnesse of the[ir] realmes and subgiettes. And where the said credence shewed by his ordenance to our said souverain lord purpor[teth] that there shalbe noo default in

Maximilian desired to renew the league, according to the overture of lord Bevers, and receive from England 50,000 crowns for an expedition against the Turks;

the said king of Romans, but that the said amitie and confederacion be redintegrate aftre the maner and fourme that the lord Bevers h[ad] in tyme passed made overture of to the same king of Ro[mans] upon the behalve of our said souverain lord. The whiche overture made by the said lord Bevers the same king of Romayns affermeth to be suche as foloweth, that is to say, that for the renovelling of the said amitie our said souverain lord was contente to avance to the said king of Romayns l. m$^{l}$. escuz of goold to furnysshe therwith his entreprises ayenst the Turques.

[*f. 54.

was willing to wear the Garter as formerly, if Henry and the prince of Wales would wear the Toison d'Or;

*It is also sayed in the s[aid credence that] to thentent the same aliaunce and amytee frate[rnal] maye be the moor ferme and stable bitwixt the said kinges, the said king of Roma[ns] is contented aftre the said amitie and aliaunce be passed and renovelled as afore is saide to bere the garter as he hath d[one] in tyme passed, and that tharcheduc shal doo the sa[me]; provided that oure said souverain lord take and bere thordre [of] Thoyson Dorree and cause his son the prince of Wa[les to do] the same.

and hoped Henry would encourage the Crusade,

Moreover the said king of Romayns by the saide cred[ence desireth] that our said souverain lord will suffre the cruciade to [proceed] and take effect, according to thoffre that our said souverain [lord hath] also made to the said king of Romayns to thentent [he may] be the bettre socoured and holpen in his entreprise [against] the Turques. A.D. 1501.

As to this. The said ambassadours shal saye [that our] souverain lord considereth well [that whensoever] *and as often [as any amba]ssadours have passed bitwixt [him] and tharched[uke t]her hath be alwayes incidently sp[eech] and communicacion had bitwixt our said souverain lord and the sa[me] ambassadours for the redintegracion of the said peax, lo[ve], amitee, and confederacion, thoccasion of which [speech] was that where ther was entier love, amytee, kin[deness], and affection bitwixt oure said souverain lord and tha[rcheduke] it was thought evill fitting that ther shulde be any [strange]nesse or unkindenesse bitwixt oure said souverain lord a[nd the] said king of Romains fadre to the said archeduc. But [as touching] any overture for the renovelling of the said amytee m[ade by] the lord Bevers the veray trouth is that our said souverain lord never gave hym commission in that behalve, neithre by mowthe nor yet by writing, nor never was the[re] bitwix our said souverain lord and the said lord Bevers dem[and], offre, and speche of the said somme of money or of any oth[er], nor of any entreprise ayenst the Turques or communicacion of *cruciade, wherof maye [be very clear a]nd evident apperaunce, forsomoche as at the tyme th[at th]e said lord Bevers was in England with oure said souverain lord ther was noo warre, nor yet speche nor likelihode of warre ayenst the said Turques. An[d] if the king shulde undre that maner of forme have graunted any money to any prince it shulde have be thought and spoken [that] he had granted it for a peax, the whiche he never did, nor hi[s] progenitours kinges of England never[1] so

Reply.

[*f. 54 b.

Lord Bevers had no commission on the subject from England.

[*f. 55.

[1] The remainder of the modern copy is lost. The bracketed words after this are supplied from mere conjecture.

A.D. 1501. didde to any prince, [for it] coude not so stande with their honour nor the contentacion of th . . . . .

Neverthelesse good amitie, alliance, and confederacion oo[ns being] had and taken bitwix theym with suche affection folow[ed, that] othre princes myght clerely knowe that ther were good [love and] kindenes bitwixt theym, oure said souverain lord coude be [content] to shewe somoche kindenes on his partie to the said k[ing of] Romayns as to ayde and succour him by some good a[nd honest] meanes for the furnishing of his entreprises ayen[st the Turques,] and rathre to hym than to any othre prince, and sp[ecially for so] good an entent. And in like wise the said a[rchduke and] *oure said so[verain lord could be] righte glad and wel conten[t that the] said ordres of the [Ga]rter and Thoyson Dorree be taken an[d borne] upon bothe parties according to thoverture of the said arch[duke] made by thordenance of the said king of Romayns. And for [the] same oure said souverain lord right hertly thanketh him. And at suche tyme as the said ambassadours shalhave f[ull] communicacion upon the said matiers, and specially upon thami[ty and] tharticles that shalbe couched in the same, they shal [then] forsee that they in noo wise redintegre nor renewe with [the said] king of Romayns the treatie that was last bitwix our s[aid sovereign] lord and hym, forsomoche as it was and is a confeder[ation] and covenant bitwixt theym twayn for warr junctly ma[king] ayenst the Frenshe king, with whom the king hath nowe pe[ace] and amytee for terme of his life; and soo he undrestande[th] that the said king of Romayns and the king of Spayne hat[h], and in like wise tharcheduc and all othre princes.

Henry is willing to give aid against the Turks,

[*f. 55 b.

but not to renew the last treaty, which was against France.

And for their furthre instruccion and informacion for the specia[lties] *of the said amitie they s[hall endeavour] theym to the best of their powayrs to get it passed w . . . . . . es delivered to theym in writing signed

[*f. 101.

with the kinges hand, saving that if they can not have [it] forevermore as it is conteyned in oon of tharticles of the said writing signed with the kinges hand, they shal take it for the lyves of bothe princes and of eithre of theym lenger living a[nd] for oon yere aftre, with a confirmacion of the successour of the [prince] that shal furst deceace as it is purveyed in the treatie of . . . They shal also endevoir theym to have the said amy[tie made] with tharticle of rebelles like as it is ordeyned and mor[e at large] expressed in the furst article concernyng the said r[ebelles, and] the said articles signed with the kinges hand. And [if they can] not obteyne the said article of rebelles aftre the said [manner and] forme, they shal endevoir theym to have the said ar[ticle . . .] aftre the secunde maner and forme as it is expressed [in the] said articles signed with the kinges hand.

A.D. 1501. They shall endeavour to obtain a permanent treaty with an article of rebels.

The said ambassadours shal also surely forsee tha[t in one of] the said ij. articles of rebelles there be a special p[rovision that the] *kinges rebelles . . . . thoes parties aftre and . . . . to the furst ma . . . . hing the said rebelles that nowe be . . . . moore plainly it is expressed amonges the said articles sig[ned] with the kinges hand. And if it can not be soo had, they shal than take it aftre the second forme touching the sa . . . nowe rebelles, as it is also expressed amonges the said a[rticles] signed with the kinges hand.

[*f. 101 b.

They shal also see the banysshement of the said nowe r[ebelles] solempnely doon and proclamed bifore their departin[g from] the king of Romayns. And that thofficer of arm[es who] attendeth upon theym be present to the same. And also cause the said officer of armes behind theym to undrestande [and] see that the said rebelles assuredly departe out of the count[ry] of the said king of Romayns, and that he departe not [but]

They shall see the rebels banished before they leave.

A.D. 1501. he maye bringe the king the verray certaintee of the sam[e]. And if noon of the said articles concernyng the rebelles can [be] obteigned ne noon of the formes [*f. 102. bifore rehersed, the sa[me] ambassadours shal, rathre than they shulde departe without [the] *amytie, passe the said a[mytie with an] article that noo ayde, succor, favo[r], nor relief, neithre in men, money, vitailles, shippes, nor in noon othr[e] maner wise, *publice vel occulte*, be geven to the said rebelles. Albeit they shal saye that oure said souverain lord hath amyte with the Frenshe king, the kinges of Spayne, Portugale, and Scotland, and with tharcheduc with the said articles of reb[elles], and that in tyme passed ther was with a like article for rebe[lles], an amytee concluded bitwix the emperour Sigismund [and the] hool empyre, and the king of England, king Henry t[he Fifth], like as they have therof writing redy to be shewed.

Also, if the said amitie can not be had by noo devoir [with] the confirmacion of the See Apostolique, the said amba[ssadors] shal, rathre then the matier shulde breke for that caus, [leave] without the said confirmacion; and yet to move the said [king of] Romayns to agre to the same confirmacion, they shal [say] that thamytees bitwixt our said souverain lord and t . . . . . . and the king of Scottes and othre princes be con[firmed by the] said See Apo- [*f. 102 b. stolique, and fastly they shal stike . . . . . . *articles of [the said] confirmacion Apostolique as far as the[y] maye conveniently and honestly doo.

They shal also endevoir theym to passe the said amitie with a[n] article that eithre of the princes be bounden to swere, and to see the king of Romayns swere it in his per[sone] or they departe, and that the king swere it in the [presence] of his servant that shal comme for his money. Neverthele[s] if they can not obteyne the said amytie with the said . . . they shal, rathre than faile, passe thamytee without t[he same]. They shal also take with theym oon of the original bu[lles] *contra tumultuantes*, and if they maye finde oportunitee . . mete season, or convenient occasion they shal declare the . . . therof. And also shewe the self bull, if they see that th[ey] maye conveniently soo doo, to the said king of Romayns, and as many othre estates, nobles, and othre, specially prelates of th[e] Churche, as aftre their discrecion they shal thinke good. And specially if thamitie conclude with tharticle of re[belles . . ] *the oon or the othre of the s . . . . es, and elles not. A.D. 1501. [*f. 103.

And in caas the king of Romayns saye that he hath been and is content to have and take the said amitie with oure said souvera[in] lord, soo that he wil avaunce hym the said somme of money, they shal answere hym that the said amytee had and conclu[ded] betwixt theym, the king wolbe content to shewe hym such[e] kindenes as is abovesaid.

The king will advance the money when the treaty is concluded.

And if the said king of Romayns be not contente with t[he said] answer, they shal then saye that our said souverain lor[d perceiveth] wel by thinstruction geven to the said Mr. Jaques t[hat the] said king of Romayns desireth of the king our said souv[erain lord] twoo thinges. The furst is, that the king wolde for his . . . . succour towardes his expedicion ayenst the Turkes avaun[ce to him] the said money, wherby it appereth that he entend[eth to make the] said journey and voyage against the Turkes. Wherin [they shall,] with as good wordes as they can use, geve hym as gr[eat praise] and lawde as they can.

His second desir is that our said souverain lord wil s[uffer the] *cruciate to [have] course within his reame. But wherf[ore] he maketh that desir, they shal saye he hathe not shewe[d nor] oure said souverain lord hathe not yet undrestande. Nevert[heles] they shal saye that astouching the said cruciate, the [pope] [*f. 103 b.

A.D. 1501. hath written to the king for it with right great instaunce . . . . that our said souverain lord suffre thexecucion therof with[in his] reame. But for many causes he hath not yet asse[nted] to the popis desir and if it soo fortune that the ki[ng do] heraftre aggre therto, as they stande in great dou[bt that] he wil doo, they thinke that he wol employe [the money in] that expedicion hymself, and not to suffre themplo[yment] therof by the pope nor noon othre, like as all othr[e princes] doo, for that that is levied by the meanes of the said cru[ciate] within their reames. Albeit they shal saye that the [king], seing the catholique mynd and noble entent of the said king of Romayns ayenst the Turkes, shal peradventure [for] his sake be content aswel to suffre thexecucion of the cruciate within his reame, as also that a good part of t[he] *money that shalbe reyse[d in the] reame by mean of the said cruciate and othrewise be employed ayenst the Turkes by the said king of Romayns. And though the said crucia[te] can not conveniently be put in execucion bifore Lent n[or] the money commyng therof can not be levied within oon yere folowing, nor that the money that shal growe eithre uppo[n] the cruciat, or a disme, subsidie or othrewise, within this re[alme] for thexpedicion ayenst the Turkes, shal not amounte to [a] somme moche above the said x.m[l]. li.; yet, a good a[mity being] furst had bitwixt the king and the king of Romain[s, the said] king shalbe contented to doo hym soo great a plea[sure . . . .] according to his desir to avaunce hym the said [x.m[l]. li.] of the money that shal growe within his reame of t[he said] cruciate, and otherwise, for aide and succor against [the said Turks]. Provided always that the pope, at the sute and re[quest of] the king of Romayns write and sende his breve [to the king,] praying and desiring hym by the same that he [will allow] that the said king of Romains have of the [money that] shalbe levied

Notwithstanding the pope's request, Henry has declined to allow the Crusade money to be collected in England;

[*f. 104.

but might, perhaps, allow it for the sake of Maximilian.

within his reame for thexpedicion [against the] *Turkes, the s[aid sum of x.m$^{l}$. li.] And if the said king of Roma[ins] make doubt or difficultie in the popes agreement to t[he] premisses, or that they fele that he wol be lothe to atte[mpt] the pope in that behalve; They shal then saye th[at to] doo hym the pleasure that the king maye honourabl[y do] in ayding hym towardes his said entreprise ayens[t the] Turkes, he shall peradventure (a good amitie furst [had] betwixt theym) be contente to avaunce hym upon the [money] that shalbe levied within his reame for ayde aye[nst the] Turkes the somme of xx.m$^{l}$. angel nobles. And o . . . . . at his adventure thagrement or disagrement bi[twixt] the pope and hym for that matier. Albe it the sa[id] cruciate can not be executed bifore Lente, nor the [said] money growing therof be levied within oon yere aftr[e,] nor that the money that shal growe eithre upon the cruciate, disme, subsidie, or othrewise within his reame for expedicion ayenst the Turkes shal not amounte to any somme moche above the said x.m$^{l}$ li. A.D. 1501. [*f. 104 b.

*And over this they shal say . . . . . t be not for his sake the king woll not suffre the said money in noo wise to passe his reame nor to be employed neithre by the pope nor by noon othre, but oonly by hymself or his deputees. And if the said king of Romayns saye that he wol sende to the pope to undrestande his will and pleasure in that behalve, they shal than endevoir theym to conclude and passe thamyte, and by vertue of their commission bynde the king to the pay[ment] of x.m$^{l}$. li. if the pope sende hym the said breve and in . . . of the said breve to bind the king in xx.m$^{l}$. angel nobl[es . . . . bringing thamitie with theym, and leving thobligacion . . . . take their leve and comme away, and bringe with theym . . . . a servant of his as he wol depute for the receipt of [the said] money, furnysshed [*f. 96.

A.D. 1501. with suche auctoritees and writinges [as be] specially expressed heraftre.

The said ambassadours shal wisely and discrete[ly endeavour] theymselfes to conclude upon the said x.m$^{l}$. li. in such form] and noon othrewise that the king [*f. 96 b. of Romains . . . . *breve ad . . . . and that the same breve be s[ent] and delivered [to] the king fro the pope aftre the four[me] before reherced, er and bifore the king paye any part [of] the said x.m$^{l}$. li. And also, that thamitie be furst . . concluded betwixt the king and hym aftre the form . . . delivered to theym in writing, signed with the kinges [hand], with tharticle of the rebelles aftre the furst maner, or a[t the] leest aftre the second maner, with a provision that [all the] kinges rebelles now being in thoes parties be immedi[ately] banisshed *sub pœna capitali* aftre oon of the ij. four[mes] bifore rehersed. And in caas they can not ag[re] upon the said x.m$^{l}$. li. with the said condicions concernyng the [said] breve[1] they [shall] then condescende and agree to xx.m$^{l}$. angel nobles without the breve,[2] pr[ovided] that thamitie be also concluded with an article for rebel[les] aftre oon of the said ij. ways and with the same provision [for] the said now rebelles that that is bifore reherced, that is to s[ay] aftre the oon or the othre waye conteyned in the said artic[le] of rebelles.

And, if the said king of Romains be not content [* f. 97. with *neithre of the said w[ays, desiring] theym furthre for the avauncement of the said money, they shal aske howe the king shalbe repayed in caas he wolde lene hym the said mone[y], and what sureties he shalhave for the repayment therof; and if the matier comme to sureties namyng, they shall name Estrelinges, or if they faile, some towne of Flandres,

[1] *Concernyng the [said] breve*. Interlined, apparently in the hand of Wolsey.

[2] Interlined also in Wolsey's hand.

or if it faille tharcheduc, or in default of hym to na[me] hymself to be bounden undre his great seal signed w[ith] his hand. And if he be content to make any of th[ese] sureties they shall then desire to see and undrest[and the] specialtees of the amitie that shal passe bitwix[t them] And if he wolbe content to passe thamitee with th[article] of the rebelles aftre the furst forme therof, and with [the] confirmacion of the pope, and also the banisshem[ent of] the rebelles that nowe be in thoes parties im[mediately] and furthwith, aftre the furst or second way to . . . said rebelles that nowe be, or with tharticle . . . . aftre the said furst forme and with the banis[shement]* of the s[aid rebels] being in thoes parties . . . and immediately after oon of the said ij. formes . . . without the said confirmacion they shal offre by w[ay of] loone xx.m[l]. angel nobles, and not excede that so[mme]. And in caas he wol not accorde hym to the said . . . . with tharticle of the rebelles aftre the said furst f[orme] and that he wol passe it with tharticle concernyng [the] rebelles according to the second forme comprised i[n the] said articles signed with our said souverain lordes han[d . . ] the said confirmacion of the pope, and the banissh[ement] of the said nowe rebelles aftre the furst or secon[d] forme, or with the same article and the said banish[ement] and without the said confirmacion, they shal offr[e . . . ] hym by way of loone xv.m[l]. angel nobles, or if it ca[n] noon othrewise be, xx.m[l]. angel nobles. A.D. 1501. [*f. 97 b.

And in caas he wol not accorde hym to neithre of th[e] said wayes concernyng the said rebelles, that is . *neithre aftre the furs[t nor after the] seconde; And that he wol agree to the thrid way [com]prised amonges the said articles signed with the kinges hand, that is to saye that he shal geve the said rebelles noo ayde, succor nor favor: They shal accorde [*f. 98.

A.D. 1501. theym thereto, and soo passe the said amitie. But they shal noo thing offre, nor geve, nor promyse for this thrid way.

And if he saye that he desireth not the said somme of mo[ney] by way of loone, but by way of a graunt to succour hy[m in] his entreprise ayenst the Turkes, aftre somme hon[est] reasons and difficultees made in that partie t[hey shall] fynally condescende to promyse; furst, the said xv[m.[l] angel] nobles, havyng thamite furst passed. Or if the[y will] not soo agree, than the said xx.m[l]. angel nobles, h[avyng] the said amitie furst passed, with the said article o[f rebelles] aftre the furst or seconde forme, with the banisshe[ment of] rebelles that nowe be in thoes parties inmed[iately and] furthwith aftre oon of their wayes and fou[rmes,
[*f. 98 b. and] *othrew[ise they shall] make noo graunt of any [of the] said sommes of money.

And for the performance herof they shal, according [to] the kinges commission, that they have for that p[urpose] with theyme, bynde the king for the payment of t[he said] somme of money, to be made to any his trusty ser[vantes] to the king for the receipt of the said money . . . bringing with hym and delivering to the king the con[firmation] undre the king of Romayns great seal and signe[d with his] hand, of the treatie that shalbe concluded bitwi[xt the said] commissioners, and bringing also sufficient auctori[ty in] writing in like wise undre the said king of Romai[ns] great seal and signed with his hand to receive the s[aid] money, and also a sufficient quytaunce semblably [undre] his great seal and signed with his hand testefying t[he] payment and receipt of the said money.

And this thus doon and performed upon the behalv[e
[*f. 99. of] *the said king of Ro[mayns, our sai]d souverain lord shal, furthwith and without furthr[e de]lay, cause the said somme of money to be payed to the said servant, be it that he wol have it in the kinges

reame, or by way of eschaunge in any othre convenient place beyond the see within the archedukes obeissaunce where there is any banke. And also at the same tyme deliver to the said servant his confir[macion] of the said treatie undre his great seal signed wi[th] his hand. A.D. 1501.

And if the king of Romains denye and refuse to . . . . the kinges said rebelles nowe being in thoes par[ties], allegging for his excuse that he hath geven the[ym his] savecoduit, the said ambassadours shal saye th[at it] standeth not neithre with honnor of the princes nor g . . . convenience (amytee being bitwixt theym) th[e one of] theym to susteigne the rebelles of the othre; nor [that no] love nor amytie can soo contynewe bitwixt t[heym, for] evil is he worthye to be called my frend that [sustaineth] my mortall ennemye. And therfor if he wo[ld make] *the king [give him] his money he muste of a[ll] reason take suche wayes as the said rebelles be v[oided] his landes and contreys, the whiche they shal s[ay] in their opinion he can noo better do than by . . . of the revocacion of the said saveconduitt, exce[pt that] he hymself or his counseill by their great wis[domes] will devise any othre way. And if he theru[pon] devise any way that maye be sufficient and va . . . for thavoiding of the said rebelles they shal fo[llow] and accepte it. And elles for the revocacion of [the] said saufconduit they shal reasone with hym aft[re the] forme folowing.

The emperor ought not to plead that he has given the rebels a safe conduct, but revoke it.

[*f. 99 b.

Furst, they shal saye that not oonly his predecessour[s] emperours in tyme passed, but also all the hool e[mpire] have had perpetuall amytees with our said souverain lor[des] progenitours kinges of England with semblable provisi[ons] for rebelles, wherof they have autentique writing redy to be shewed, and seing that the king of Ro[mains] may voirably saye that the same amytee in as [much]* as it is perpetuall [ . . . . . . . . a]nd soo at this day standeth in [*f. 100.

A.D. 1501. his ful strength [and] effect, and that in consideracion therof the graunt of the said saveconduitt, insomoche as it is expressly contrary to the said amitee, is voide and oughte not to be availlable to the said rebelles. The said king of Romains maye with all lawe and reason, and of his honnor shulde, and is bounden upon a reasonabl[e] warnyng geven to the said rebelles to departe his landes a[nd] countreys, openly declare the said saveconduitt to have [been] graunted directly ayenst the said amytee, and an[null] and revoke it.

Secondly, they shal saye that the said rebelles [for their] said rebellion against the king be accursed as-we[ll by pope] Innocent that last was, as also by pope Alexan[der that] nowe is. By reason of whiche excommunicacion that [the said] rebelles nowe stande in they shulde have noo recei . . . . biding nor conversacion in the said king of Romayn[es landes] and contreys, nor with, nor amonges his subgiettes, [and] that if the said ambassadours made no sute in . . . . yet, knowlege had of the said excommunicacion, the [*100 b. [said king] of *Roma[yns should not o]nly voide theym in h[is own] persone [but also] cause his subgettes to doo the sa[me.] And seing that the said rebelles stande thus accurs[ed] by the popes bulles, the king of Romayns maye b[e] content that furst the said bulle be openly shewed [to] hym and his counseill and aftreward if he w[old] solempnely publische it as it shal please hym . . . fynably the said saveconduit aftre the premisses d . . . maye and shulde for the same consideracion lau[fully] and honorably be revoked.

By these reasons and suche othre as of their wi[sdoms] they shal finde and devise they shal instante[ly and] stedefastly insiste for the revocacion of the said [safe] conduitt, or at the least that it be voided and an[nulled] by oon mean or by othre.

And if they shal perceyve that the said saveconduit

shal undoubtedly exspire within iij. or vj monethes, or that the king of Romains will in noo wise revoke [it], they shal than offre hym the said sommes of mone[y] aftre the formes and with the condicions bifore reherse[d]. *[An]d that it be paye[d, one half when]soever the said servant furnisshed with the auctoritee[s and w]ritinges bifore said shal comme for it; and the othre half when the said saveconduitt shalbe expired, and they voided. Provided that the said king of Romayns bynde him by the said treatie of thamitee to banisshe theym than, and in the mean tyme yeve theym noo aide succor nor favor etc., as bifore is reherced. A.D. 1501. [*f. 56.

Also, the said ambassadours aftre the said amytee be ha[d and] passed, shal sollicite the king of Romains to write by t . . . to tharcheduc to receive the Garter when the king sh[al send] it to hym, and they to promyse upon the kinges beh[alf] that the prince shal accepte the Thoyson Dorree wh[en the said] archeduc shal sende it to hym.

*Item as touching what . . . ]le hath in ch[arge [to say] to tharch[educ] of mariage bitwixt my lord of Y[ork] the kinges second son and the said archedukes fu[rst] begoten doughtre,[1] if this speche take any eff[ecte] and that tharcheduc answer that he wol g . . . . entende therto or make any othre answer of . . . . of the spede of the matier, the said ambas[sadors] if thamitee conclude with the king of Romay[ns] shal shewe hym suche spede as they ha[d with] tharcheduke touching the said mariage. [*f. 57. Proposed marriage of Henry duke of York and the archduke's daughter.

H. R.

[1] Eleanor, afterwards married to Emmanuel king of Portugal.

## XX.

### Somerset and Warham to Henry VII.

[MS. Cott., Galba B II. 90.]

A.D. 1501. Pleas it your grace to [understond] that, accordyng to suche enstruccions [as your] grace sent unto us by your last lettres, we have enterid communicacion with the [kyng of] Romanys commissioners and shewid to them that their commission was [not] sufficient, and that if we shuld conclude therapon bothe thei and w[e shuld] labor in vayne. Wherunto thei answerid that for asmoche as [there were] communicacions had betwene them and us in tymes past, we . . . . . defaulte in the said commission, thei thought that we fownd . . . . defaulte to none other entent but only to deferre the t[ime, which] we answerid them on our faith and honeste we enten[ded not to do.] That notwithstondyng thei seid they wold not be content . . . . other commission for thei knewe right well as . . . . . shuld send ageyn to the kyng of Romanys he wold ta . . . . . defraude and delaye of tyme; and rather then t[arry] for any other commission then thei have, thei wold . . . . ageyne and entermedill no ferther in the matie[r . . . . . advertise the said kyng of Romanys. Notwithston[ding . . . . contentid with the clause *Omnes et singulos ta . . . . defectus, etc.* to be put in the clause of confirmacion w[hereof we wrote] unto your grace by our last lettres.

After thys the same commissioners shewid unto us [that they would make] noo delay with us and prayed us to doo the same . . . . . amytie that was be[twixt your gr]ace and the archiduke their maister, th[ei] entendid to dele rowndly and playnly

A.D. 1501.

with us, and promysid us on the[ir] othes soo that we wold do in like wise with them to shewe us the resolute mynde of the said kyng, promysing thei wold not stike apon any article that thei thought we of reason ought not to be contentid with. Wherapon we seid we were contentid so to doo, if they wold first disclose their my[nds,] wherunto thei were agreable. And furwith thei declarid as here folowith.

Maximilian will bind himself and the lands of his inheritance, but cannot bind the empire.

Thei seid on their othes that the resolute mynde of the kyng of Romanys was that he was contentid to bynd hym self, his heires and succes[sors,] and also all his subgiettes, and all suche londes as belongid un[to] hym by reason of any enheritaunce, in suche maner and fourme as was conteigned in articles, as we delivered to the said comm[issi]oners to be sent to the kyng of Romanys. And the said kyng knew[e] right well that the kyng of Fraunce ne Spayne, ne yet none other prince otherwise wold be bownde then bynding hym self, [hi]s heires, successors, subgiettes, and alle his enheritable londes; but [as] towching the londes of the empire, whiche he hathe by eleccion [and] not by enheritaunce, withoute the expresse consent of alle the [elize]rs he may in no wise bynde, which elizers he knewe well [wold] never be agreable to bynde the empire to the matier [contei]ned in the seid articles; albeit he was contentid to be [bound] unto your grace in a boke to be made aparte, that he wold not favor, aide, [assist ne suc]cour any that be your rebelles n[ot] being within the empire, nor suche as shall be at any tyme within his lond nor withoute, with any money, shippes, men, armes or victaile, as more playnly is expressid in a [boke of] articles whiche is sent to your grace by this berer, but he [wold not] be agreable to the opyn bannysshement of any your r[ebelles] that be in the londes of the empire nowe, nor of [others] that shall fortune to be your rebelles there at [any time] herafter.

A.D. 1501.

ii. Ferthermore thei shewid unto us that as to[uching tho matter] of confirmacion to be opteigned with censures . . . . of the See Apostolique, the kyng of Romanys w[ould not] therunto agree; for he seith it was never seyn . . . . . submitted his owne persone to be suspendid or . . . . . pope, and withoute the consent if the elizer[s he could not] bynde the londes of the empire to any m[ . . And if] he shuld so do, he shuld not only provoke th . . . . . . . . . . hym, but also alle the hole empire, but . . . . to make any othe to observe alle s[uch . . . . . . ] be concluded betwene your grace . . . . . . . . [1]seying, on their feithes, to be the hole and resolute mynde of th . . . . . . And praied us t[o put ap]arte alle resonynges considering that by the resonyng of us their myndes myght not be removid from the determynate mynde of the said kyng of Romanys, and praied us in like wise to disclose tho determynate mynde of your gra[ce] in this behalfe.

He will not conclude the league unless Heury advance 50,000 crowns for the war against the Turks.

Thei seid also that the kyng of Romanys toke thonkfully [the] offerture of the advauncement of xx$^{ti}$ thowsand angels towardes the warres anempste the Turkes, albeit seyng t[he] ferneis of the journey anempste the same Turkes and the nombre of people that he muste have with hym in his hos[t, he] trustith verily that your grace, being oon of the myghtyest princes [o]f alle the Cristyn faithe, and considering the nyghnes of blodde that is betwene your grace and hym, he doubtid not but your grace wold advaunce unto hym the somme of l. thousand crownes of gold, whiche somme he of longe tyme hathe desired of your gra[ce]. And the same somme so advaunced, the said commissioners seid [th]ei were contentid to conclude amytie as is aforesaid, and elles [no]t in no wise.

[1] Here occurs this marginal note "B. ij$^{dus}$ articulus et ultimus hujus responsi."

[To] this we answerid, considering that the articles whiche [were] delivered to the said commissioners to be sent unto the kyng [of R]omanys were very resonable, and that we thought verily [that] the said kyng of Romanys wold have made no stikyng [therein b]ut passid the same articles in suche maner and fourme [as t]hei were sent unto hym, and that we had so adver[tised] your grace, and accordy[ng thereun]to your grace had sent us your re[solute] mynde; but for asmoche as nowe we understode by their r[eport] that the said kyng wold not passe the said articles in s[uche form] as thei were to hym sent, but that he wold bynde hy[mself] and his londes of his inheritaunce, the whiche londes [are in] ferre contrees to the whiche your subgiettes seldom or [never have] eny resorte, and so that bond shuld be of litill eff[ect. And] where he wold be bownde a parte, for his ow[ne . . . . . ] and wold not bynde the londes of the empire . . . . as for his owne persone, considering the nyghne[s . . . ] also that he is of your order of the garter, h[e . . . ] nor with his honor m[ay in] his owne persone attempte to doo your grace or any of your . . . displeasure. And . . . not be bownde for alle the subgiettis of the emp[ire . . . .] color the said kynges subgiettis of the empire . . . . and socoure your rebelles, as well within the land[es . . . . . ]as withoute. Wherfore we sawe no good . . . . . unto your grace by reason of any of the sa[id . . . .] A.D. 1501.

iii. We[1] shewid ferther unto the said commissio[ners that if] the kyng of Romanys had be contentid to . . . . in like maner as we delivered them to the s . . . . . be sent unto the said [k]yng, [th]en suche a good amytie had and concluded, your grace coulde have

[1] Marginal note, "B. iij[us] articulus et ultimus istius responsi."

A.D. 1501. bene contentid that we shuld, on the behalve of your grace, made offerture of a right goode somme of money to be advaunced to the said kyng for warrys to be made ayenst the infidels; but, for asmoche as he varied from the said articles, we had none expresse instruccions of your myn[de] howe we shuld demeane our selves in this behalve and praie[d] them to have pacience till we had writyn unto your grace to knowe y[our] ferther pleasure in this behalve.

There is no security that the emperor will observe the treaty, unless he is bound under ecclesiastical censures.

[iv.] And where as the said kyng wold in no wise be contentid with the confirmacion of the See Apostolique under the cens[ures] of the churche, we said for asmoche as in tymes past bet[wixt] your grace and the said kyng of Romanys there had ben an amytie concluded, sealid and subscribed with the hand of the said kyng, and that notwithstandyng he observyd not the same; [w]e therfore thought that there coude noo sure amyte contynue [bet]wene your grace and the said kyng withoute the confirmacion [of t]he said See Apostolique. And we said also, that we [saw] no prejudice that shuld comme unto the persone of the [said] kyng in submittyng hym selfe to the censures of said [See] Apostolique, for by Goddis lawe and mannys lawe he was [bound]e to submitte hym selve to the same See Apostolique, a[nd] therunto he shuld be . . . orever he were declarid empero[r.] Wherfore it is to be thought that the said kyng is not myndid to the contynuaunce of any amytie, for [if he] were he wold be agreable to the opteignyng of the [said] confirmacion. But whan he had opteigned of . . . that he wold have, he wold aslitill care for th . . . of this amytie as he hathe for other in tymes past . . . concludid and sealid. Furthermore we shewid to t[he said] commissioners that thei were contentid at our last communica[tion with] them to passe the said article of confirmacion [as we] advertised your grace, wherfore we mervaile that [they] varie from the same.

Wherunto the said commissioners answerid th[at if the kyng] of Romanys wold bynde his londes of enheritau[nce in suche] fourme as his sonne the archeduke was bou . . . . you in any amytie concluded with your Grace, sey[ng . . . . . ] said kynge myght ride in his owne londes belong . . . . . . . enheritaunce from the towne of Brusels in Bra[bant], u[nto the] whiche divers of your merchauntes dayly resort . . . . . . But the londes of the empire he mygh[t [not bind, for] if he shuld it shuld be to his dishonor . . . . . . . . profite. Wherfore he wold not so do f . . . . otherwise promise than he myght . . . . . . . . . . . And as touching the confirmacion of . . . . . . . thei seid in no wise [the kyng m]yght passe it. But thei were right well assured that the said kyng woll aswell kepe suche thinges as shuld be concluded, as though it were confermyd by the said Se[e] Apostolique. For if suche a confirmacion shuld be opteigned, thei thinke there shuld litill effecte folowe of it, in case your grac[e] or elles the said kyng observed it not; for there is no man lyv[ing] that ever hath knowyn eny execucion made anempste any s[ . . . . ] apon the bretche of any amytie by the vertue of the said cla[use] of confirmacion. Wherfore thei thought that the othe of th[e] said kyng shuld cause hym bettir to observe the amytie then shuld the article of confirmacion; for every prince wold think [it] more dishonor to be perjured than he wold for suche a cause strive with the Pope. Thei seid also that thei varied not on [the] article of confirmacion, albeit thei had a communicacion with u[s on] the same confirmacion, yet therapon thei nothing concluded, a[nd] also seying that the said kyng their master, having such resona[ble] groundes as be afore rehersid, was in no wise contentid with the said article of confirmacion. Wherfore thei muste nedes also chaunge their myndes accordyng to the mynde of the said kyng.

A.D. 1501.

Reply of the imperial commissioners.

A.D. 1501. Seying, furthermore, forasmoche as we seid that we had [n]one instruccions from your grace to make offerture of the [ad]vauncing of any somme of money but desired delay to know [your] pleasure in this behalve, thei knewe right well that we [inte]ndid noo thing but to dreve the tyme with them. For [that] we desired a delay for a newe commission to be [obtei]gned of the said kyng, whiche thei denyed. Wherfore thei [seid] we sought a nother occasion of delay in desiring to write [unto] your grace to have newe enstruccions; seying also thei [were] right sory that thei had lost so moche communicacion in idell [worde]s.

To this we answerid . . . . . . . we entendid noo delaies for t[hey] myght right well perceyve that your grace myght in no wise underston[d] what answere the said kyng at this tyme wold send to hys commissioners. And your grace coude not geve us sure and l . . . . instruccions to suche thinges as your grace of a certayntie knewe n[ot of]. After which answere thei were contentid that articles shu[ld be] conceyvid accordyng to this communicacion, and we withoute d[elay should] advertise your grace and knowe your fynall pleasure in all t[hinges]. And we protestyng that, in no wise by an[y thing that] shuld be conteigned in any of the said articles, we ent[ended in] eny wise to bynde your grace, but only to advertise your . . . .

v. Fynally too bokes of articles were by the said comm[issioners] conceyvyd. In the oon boke[1] [the said] kyng is contentid to bynd hym self, his subgiettis [and his] londes to the which he is inheritor. And in the [other he] byndith hym selve as touchyng the em-

[1] *boke.*] The words "which by us was deli[vered unto the] commis- "sioners to be sent to the said kyng of Roma[nys]" here follow, but are struck out.

pire in [such] fourme as more playnly it doith appere in the seid bo[ke and in the] bokes of articles we send your grace at this ty[me by] Berwyke. We endevourid our selfe t . . . . . . boke consernyng the empire an article of . . . . . rebelles that be nowe there, and of all other which may theder resorte, but we coulde m . . . . . . . . . . nothir accordyng to suche articles . . . . . . . . . . . the rebelles . . . . . . . y lord the archiduke, nothir accord[yng] to the article that was concluded with the emperor Sigismond; for thei sey if the said kyng shuld forthwith bannishe your rebelles owte of Acon, yet that bannisshement notwithstond[yng] thei myght there abide, and also in other fraunchesied p[laces]. We desired to have an article for the bannishement of [your] rebelles owte of alle suche places of the empire as were . . . . fraunchesied; and thei seid withoute the consent of th[e] Elizers the said kyng myght not make that graunt, an[d] that we myght well perceyve by the article of rebelles comprised in the amyte concludid with the said Sigesmond, which was not only sealid by the same Sigismond but also confermyd by the said Elizers.

A.D. 1501.

The rebels cannot be banished from franchised places.

Yf your grace can be contentid to accepte the articles which at this tyme we send to your grace in like fourme as thei be conceyvid and none otherwise, yet we knowe by their othes and demoynures that thei in noo wise wolbe contentid with any lesse somme then the somme of l. thousand crownes to be advaunced to thexpedicion of his warres ayenst the Turques. And as touching the place of the paiement of suche money as your grace woll advaunce in this behalve we can nother cause [them] to resceyve it in London, Cales nor Graveling, but with . . . . ht moche payne we have caused them to be contented to [res]ceyve it in suche usuell money as hath course within your [re]alme,

The emperor will not be content with less than 50,000 crowns for the expedition against the Turks.

A.D. 1501. rating every crowne accordyng to his verie value[1] [and the] same to be paied at Seynt Omers.

vj. The said commissi[oners also de]sired us to write to your grace that in case your grace woll advaunce to the said kyng t[he] somme of l. thousand crównes, that it myght please your g[race] to send unto us a copie of suche acquitaunce with the whic[h your] grace wold be contentid at the tyme of the entrechaungy[ng] of bothe your sealis, and the delivere of the said somme, for . . . . shuld conceyve the acquitaunce, at the tyme of the re[ceipt] of the said money your commissioners peradventure shu[ld] think the same acquitaunce sufficient. And soo ther . . . . have matier of delay, of the whiche thei wold b . . . . . .

vij. And as touching the cruciat and dyvers othe[r . . . . . . your grace may perceyve the said kynges mynde in . . . . in Frenche herin enclosid and to us deliverid [by the] said commissioners.

The imperial commissioners intercede for Edmund De la Pole.

[v]iij. The said commissioners desired us to mov[e your grace] to graunt your rebell the late erle of Suffolke . . . . . . bothe for his body and goodes, the whiche if he . . . . . . kyng of Romanys seeing that he hathe amyte . . . . and also that by hys moynes ye be soo gra . . . . . . . hym shall have a resonable occasion to cause [him to] advoide alle the londes of the empire . . . . of hys obeisaunce.

ix.[2] Furthermore the said commissioners moved [us that your grace] shuld take noo displeasure though the sai[d king of] Romanys dyd sett in his howses and by [. . . . such] armes as belongith to the duchie . . . . . . As herunto we answerid that your grace . . . . . . . . that he wa[s . . . . . . . ] of blodde to your grace, and also was a prince of right great

---

[1] *accordyng . . value*] corr. from *to the value of iiijs. sterling.*

[2] Numbered *viij.* in the margin of the MS.

wisdome, wherfore he of hi[s] wisdome wold none otherwise bere the same armes then as he of right ought to doo, and in soo doyng your grace coulde not of reason be displeasid with the setting or bering of the same armes. A.D. 1501.

In our moste humble wise we beseche your grace that in the premisses we may knowe your finalle and resolute pleasure, whiche accordyng to our dueties we shall folowe in every behalve.

---

## XXI.

### Letters of Edmund De la Pole.

[From copies in the Record Office.]

A.D. 1502?

To Sir George Nevill.

Cousin Nevyll, I recommand me to yowe. And it is soo that by this day I truste assuredly that eche thing is at a good point for my departing from hens, and the stewerd[1] is commen hyder with the necessars[2] bifore, and I tarye for noothing but oonly upon the commyng of the Bastard.[3] Wherefor, cousin Nevill, this is my mynd; that maister Wylliam shall goo and speke to the lordes of the thre townes, Zwolle, Campen, and Daventre, after this maner:—That where as I have undrestande by Mr. William, that there was a man of Daventre at the tyme of my departing from Hattam, which camme by the command of the lords of Daventre, to have spoken with me, offering me certain offres, as Mr. William knoweth more at large, I will, furst that Mr. William enquere for the same man and if he be there, and reherse to hym his said message, and lette Mr. William shewe him that he is commen to speke with the lordes of the towne for the same matier. And yf the same man bee not there, lette hym speke in this matter to the lords of the towne, and shewe

About negotiating with the towns of Zwolle, Kampen, and Deventer.

---

[1] Thomas Killingworth.

[2] This word is doubtful, being very badly written.

[3] The Bastard D'Oysekerke.

A.D.1502? to them that I have undrestande of the messaige of the said man, wherupon I sende Mr. William to theym to thentent to knowe more of their mynds touching the same. And yf by any dryfte there comme noon effect thereupon, lette hym doo noo more but handle hym sylf soo that he in any wise, if it bee possyble gette me sure gley of the lordes of Daventre. And thene, gley obteyned, if he can soo dryve, lette the lords of Daventre sende with hym oon to the lords of the other townes, soe it bee by their drife and not by myn. And lette this matier bee handelled as secretly as ye can, and kepe it secretly to you tweyne, as my trust is in you.

---

To Thomas Killingworth.

Thoma, accepi litteras vestras datas xj[a] die Maij, ex quibus intellexi magnam apud nonnullos in hoc sæculo esse dissimulationem; sed de duobus malis minus malum mihi esse eligendum vestris litteris consulitis. Et ideo omnia mea negotia apud R. M. Ro.[1] agenda v. d.[2] committo. Nam video vos omnem diligentiam possibilem meis rebus indies exhibuisse. Video id non oportere facere quod cæteri omnes faciunt, hoc est dissimulatione uti; quod ego pro mea parte faciam, quamquam libenter id facere non cupiam. Ego plane percipio Ro. regem mecum omnia dissimulatione quadam tractare; quare vos volo eadem apud illum dissimulatione uti. Video enim regem cæterosque suos conari me longa mora hic fatigare ut mea bona inutiliter consumam, ut sic paupertate gravatus compellar ad pacem cum H. Angliæ ineundam; quod si ego facere recusarem me vitæ periculo exponerent, quo quidem periculo per media quorundam quos dictus H. pecuniis corrupit omni hora diei maneo. Quare, si dominum regem meas causas indies differre, prout hucusque distulit, intellexerit mentem meam suæ majestati in forma sequenti exponatam.

He must use dissimulation towards Maximilian, as Maximilian does towards his master.

---

[1] *Regiam Majestatem Romanorum.* [2] *vestræ dominationi.*

"Sacratissime rex, per M. Bontemps dominum meum in spe magna posuistis quod si idem dominus meus certis desideriis ex parte vestræ majestatis per dictum Bontemps ei exponendum acquiesceret, quæ quidem desideria ad vestram majestatem per me misit, ei auxilium tam in pecuniis quam hominibus vestra majestas concederet. Et nunquam ab aliquo principe præterquam a vestra majestate auxilium petiit; et vj menses continuis suis expensis in Acon mansit, quo tempore a terra domini archiducis vestri filii in maximum suum præjudicium,[1] nec umquam tam inhumaniter actum est cum aliquo nobili quomodo cum eo actum est. Semper tanquam vester consanguineus expectavit relevamen a vestra majestate, et quamquam alii nonnulli nobiles ei auxilio esse obtulerunt, tamen eorum consilium recusavit, solam suam spem in vestra majestate ponens. Et ex parte domini mei audeo affirmare quod omnia quæ vestræ majestati promittet re ipsa perficiet. Et quia est vobis conjunctus sanguine, solum ad vestram majestatem pro impetrando auxilio venit. Et antequam a regno Angliæ exiret dominus Corson pro parte vestræ majestatis eum certiorem fecit, quod sibi in singulis auxilium daretis; quod ille antequam regnum Angliæ [reliquit][2] amicis suis patefecit, et sub spe habendi auxilii a vestra majestate amici sui consulerunt ei ut ad vestram majestatem veniret; et cum ad vestram majestatem accessisset, Bontemps ex parte vestræ majestatis ei auxilium promisit, et sic amicis suis in Anglia de promisso vestræ majestatis verbum misit. Et quamquam ego palam loquor vestræ majestati rogo parcatis mihi. Et quantum nocet domino meo sua continua mora in Acon vestra majestas facile judicabit, nam ipsis bonis quæ in Flandria et in Anglia amisit et quæ pro se et suis in Acon exposuit, exercitum X.M. virorum potuit in Angliam traducere; præter-

A.D. 1502. 12 May.

and show how injurious to De la Pole is his long tarrying at Aix;

[1] A verb is evidently wanting here. [2] Om. in MS.

A.D. 1502. 12 May.

quam quidam suus amicissimus,[1] qui manerium de Bray juxta Windesoram R. B.[2] militi vendidit, et qui custodiam castri de Porchestre habuit, captus est, et apud Wintoniensem decapitatus; qui cum omnibus bonis quæ in illo castro erant, ad eum veniendo erat; et apud me est unus servitorum suorum Petrus Harter. In Vigilia Ramispalmarum[3] decapitatus est."

and that if the king's second son Henry were to die there would be no doubt of De la Pole's title.

Domina de Ispania reconvaluit. Rogo omnino ut servitorem meum ad me mittatis. Et cum habebitis communicationem cum sacra majestate de meis rebus, dicatis "quod si secundus Henrici filius esset mortuus, nullum esset dubium de titulo domini mei. Et ideo si dominus meus maneret ex ista parte maris usque ad mortem dicti Henrici, qui diu vivere non potest, junior filius suus domino meo in nullo nomine poterit.[4] Et si dominus meus tantam pecuniarum summam in bursa haberet quantam habuit cum primum in has partes applicuit, non diu maneret extra regnum Angliæ." Et si dictus rex de pace ex parte mea cum Henrico facienda vobis aliquod dixerit, patienter eum audietis, et dicatis quod libenter velitis talem esse pacem, sed non audetis[5] alloqui mihi in illa causa, et sic vos plus audietis de eorum mentibus. Sed hoc promitto vobis in mea fide quod nunquam audivi verbum quod Henricus daret mihi meas terras aut pensiones, quod si rex aut alii mihi alloquantur, volo eos audire. Hoc promitto vobis, H. et ego nunquam simul erimus simul[6] in Anglia sine meo vel suo damno; quare velim ne me timeas quicquid de me audieritis, quia sum omni tempore idem homo. Ste. de B. recessit. H. emit eum c. libris, quarum xx. recepit in manibus. Rogo vos ut prudenter videtur ut paretur mihi locus prope mare propter diversas

[1] This was doubtless the "Charles "Ryppon, late of Porchester," mentioned in the act of attainder, 19 Henry VII. See Rolls of Parl. vi. 545.

[2] Probably Sir Reginald Bray.

[3] The eve of Palm Sunday in 1502 was the 19th of March.

[4] Sic.

[5] *audietis*, MS.

[6] Sic.

causas; quantum ad illam materiam de qua E. locutus est ad vos, ut vos alloqueremini regem, rogo quod vos nihil facietis in ea re. Misi ad vos ij[as] litteras cum earum copiis; unam majestati Romanorum, aliam Bontemps. Et infra vj. dies sequentes mittam vobis residuum mentis meæ. A.D. 1502. 12 May.

Et Ja. Ty.[1] pulcris verbis dominus privati sigilli et Dan[2] promittentium ut secure iret et rediret, et datis fidejussoribus, eductus est a castro de Guisnes in quo castro reliquit post se suum filium, et cum primo in mari navem ascenderet, accessit ad eum T. Lo,[3] et præcepit ei ut mitteret signum filio suo quod castrum traderet in manibus dicti Lovel et aliorum; quod si non faceret, doceret eum natare in mari. Et totus exercitus de Calais obsidebat dictum castrum. Et cum dictus Jaco. hoc intelligeret, misit secretum signum filio suo; quod cum filius vidisset reddidit castrum, et tunc dictus Ja. et illius filius positi sunt in Turrim. Et dictum Ja. sui fidejussores salvarunt;[4] sed filius ejus est in periculo. Datum in Acon xij[a] die Maii. Treatment of Sir James Tyrell.

---

MONSIEUR le Tresorer, de bon cueur je me recommende a vous, et vous remercie de ous les plaisirs et peynes lesquelz avez pris tous jours en mees affaires; lesquelz alayde de Dieu je desirvirey ung foys tellement denver vous, que voz serray contente de moy. Et cy jay eut de quoy je vous donne aceste To the Treasurer Bontemps.

TRANSLATION.

MR. TREASURER, I recommend myself cordially to you, and thank you for the pleasure and pains you have always taken in my affairs; which, by the help of God, I shall one day in such manner merit towards you, that you will be satisfied with me. And if I had wherewith, I would give

[1] Sir James Tyrell.
[2] Sic.
[3] Thomas Lovell.
[4] *saluerunt*, MS. Sir James Tyrell, however, was actually executed six days before the date of this letter.

A.D. 1502. 12 May.

heure ; mais jay espoir in brief temps davoir in telle facion qua je porray contente vous et tous mees aultres bonnes amyes. Au surplus, monsieur le Tresorer, je vos prie pour parle au la bonne grace du roy touchant mon caas, le plus favourablement que vous poves comme ma fiance este en vous. Car sur la credence que vous avez monstre a moy a Ymps, depar commandement du roy je pensoy a leheure destre bien pres Dangleterre pour recouvre mon droit. Et oultre je vous face savoir pour certain que le filz du Roy H. lequel avoit espouse la fille du roy Despaigne quil est mort; lequel morit sur le nuyt de paseques flouries.[1] Aultre choise pour le present, cy non que Dieu vous doint bonne vie et longue. Escript au Hayes le xij. jour de May.

Hoped ere this to have been on his way to England to make good his claims.

Le tout vostre,
E. S.

A Monsire le Tresourer Maistre
Jehan Bontemps, Seigneur
de Salans.

---

you at this very hour ; but I have hopes that in short time I shall be so situated as to satisfy you and all my other good friends. Moreover, Mr. Treasurer, I beseech you to speak to the king's good grace touching my case, as favorably as you can, as my trust is in you. Because going upon the letter of credence, which you showed me at Imst, by order of the king, I thought at this hour to have been very near England for the purpose of recovering my right. And besides, I cause you to know for certain, that the son of the king, who had married the daughter of the king of Spain, is dead ; he died on the night of Palm Sunday.[1] No other thing for the present ; except that God give you a good and long life. Written at Aix, the 12th day of May.

Altogether yours,
E. S.

To the Treasurer, Mr. John Bontemps, lord of Salans.

---

[1] This is a mistake. Palm Sunday in 1502 was the 20th of March. Prince Arthur died on the 2nd April.

A.D. 1502. 12 May. To Maximilian.

PLEASE vostre noble grace savoir que jay receu vostre[1] lettres de mon maistre dotell que se tient dever vous, sur le xj. jour de May, escript en vostre ville de Myndelhem le iij. jour dudict moys, par lesquellez je sciet bien que vous estes mon[2] et gracioux seigneur dever moy; pour quoy, sieur, tant humblement comme je puis, je remercye vostre grace, et je mettre tout mon caas en vostre main. Et que vostre grace vueille rementener le loyal cueur et fiance que jay dever vous; car vous estez le prince que jay serche au monde pour avoir ayde et succours et au nul aultre vueille serche. Pour quoy je vous supplie quil vous plaise de vostre grace moy aider; et pur ma part la promesse que jay fait avous par escript, donne en vostre main depar mon maistre dostel, je moy oblige lealment tenir durant ma vie de toute ma puissance. Et que plaise au vostre grace de pense de ma longue demoure perdeca et vieu-

TRANSLATION.

MAY it please your noble grace to know that I received your letters from my steward who is with you, on the 11th day of May, written in your town of Myndelhem, the 3rd day of the said month; by which I well know that you are a gracious master to me, and for which, sire, as humbly as I can, I thank your grace, and will place my whole case into your hands. And may your grace remember the loyal heart and the confidence which I have for you; because you are the prince whom above all in the world I seek to have for an aid and help, and from no one else do I seek it. On account of which I beseech you that it may please you of your goodness to help me; and for my part, the promise which I have made to you in writing, given into your hand by my steward, I do loyally bind myself to keep during my life with all my power. And please it your grace to think of my long residence in this place, and seeing the danger in which my good friends

[1] Sic in MS., *vrẽ*.

[2] Sic.

A.D. 1502. 12 May.

ant le daungier en quoye mees bonnes amies sont et encoures seront tous les jours pluis et pluis en attendant ma venue. Et ainsy jay donne cognoissance a vostre grace pour vrai que le filz du roy H., Arthur, que avoit espouse la fille du roy Despaigne est morte la nuyt de pasques flouries.[1] Et ainsy plaise vostre grace savoir touchant le credence que monsieur le Tresourer maistre J. Bo. moy remonstre depar vous au Ympst, je pense aceste heure destre bien apres Dangliterre, par quoy je pense faire a vostre grace service, devande que leste fuit passe, lequel estoit nul home au monde que desire pluis de vous faire quelque bon service que moy, et cy faire tous jours durant ma vie. Ainsy plaise vostre grace savoir que je suys bien adverty pour vray, que roy H. pourchaisse en tous quartiers et au tous gens que puis rechate pour oor et argent pour moy destroyer; et pourtant, sieur, le pluis longuement que je demoure hors Dangliterre le pluis forte serra roy H. et depure[2] pour

are, and will yet be every day more and more whilst awaiting my arrival. Also I inform your grace, that in truth the son of king Henry, Arthur, who had married the daughter of the king of Spain, died the night of Palm Sunday. And so may it please your grace to know touching the credence which the treasurer, Mr. J. Bontemps, showed me on your part at Imst, I expected at this time to have been very near England, by which I hoped to render your grace a service before the summer were over, as there is no man in the world who desires more to render you some good service than myself, and to do so always during my life. Also may it please your grace to know that I have been truly very well informed that H. king practises in all quarters and with all kinds of people, whom he can corrupt with gold and silver to destroy me; and for all that, sire, the longer I reside out of England the stronger will be king H. and

[1] See page 182, note[1].

[2] *depure*, MS.; apparently for *le pire*.

moy ; pour quoy je vous prie treshumblement que vostre A.D. 1502.
grace ne soit male contente que je escripe avous tant 12 May.
playnement, car il moy touche forte en daunger et necessite ainsy rescripre. Et cy je puis venir moy meismes denver vostre grace, je auserra remontre tous choises a vostre grace pluis et plain de ceste matier et des aultres de lesquelles vostre grace serroit bien contente. Toutesfoys jay rescripe denver mon maistre dostell pluis et playn de ma entencion, et quil vous plaise de vostre grace luy donner credence. Aultre chois, sieur, je ne vous rescripe pour le present, cy non que Dieu vous donne laccomplissement de tous vous haultz et nobles desires. Escript en vostre ville Dhaies le xij. jour de May.

Le tout vostre humble cousin et serviteur,

Ed. Suffolk.

A tres hault, tres puissant, et
tres excellent prince,
le roy des Romaynes.

---

the worse it will be for me; wherefore, I very humbly beseech you, that your grace may not be dissatisfied that I write to you so plainly, because it concerns me much to write thus in danger and necessity. And if I can come myself towards your grace, I will take the liberty to show your grace everything more fully of this matter and of others; of which your grace will be satisfied. Nevertheless, I have written again more fully to my steward of my intention, and may it please you of your grace to give him credence. Other things, sire, I do not for the present write to you, except that God may give you the fulfilment of all your high and noble desires. Written in your town of Aix, the 12th day of May.

Your devoted humble cousin and servant,

Ed. Suffolk.

To the very high, very powerful, and
very excellent prince, the
king of the Romans.

A.D. 1508. Maximilian van Godz gnaden Romysche konyng.[1]

INSTRUCTION was unnser g[etrewer liber Jheronimus] Lay, unnser Jegermaister [in Gheldren bey] Burgermaister und Rat der st[at Aach und sunst] von unsern Wegen handel[l und ausrichten soll].

Aufrungclichen sol er sich zu Inen inn die s[tat Aach fueren] oder sonerr Im solichs nit gelegen sein w[olt, etlich vom Rat] zu Ime gen Mastricht erfordern, und Inen [erstlichen sagen] unnser gnad und alles gut; und darnach an[zaigen, nach dem] der herzog von Suffockh ain zeit lanng bey [Inen In der] Stat Aach gelegen und dar[2] Innen ain Summa [gelts schuldich] sey, Nu mugen sy wissen, das wir und [kunyng Hainnrich] von Engellandt von der Rotten Rosen in k[urz versthiner[3]] zeit ein vertrag mit einander gemacht h[aben. Der] under annderm innhaltet das wir denselhen [herzogen

TRANSLATION.

Maximilian by the Grace of God, King of the Romans.

INSTRUCTION as to what our faithful and beloved Jerome Lay, master of the hunt at Gueldres, shall treat and conclude with the burgomaster and council of the town of Aix, and of other matters in our affairs.

In the first instance, he is to call upon them in the town of Aix, or, in case that should not be convenient to him, to summon some of the members of the council into his presence at Maestricht, and tell them, first, of our grace, &c.; and afterwards inform them, since the duke of Suffolk has staid for some time with them in the town of Aix, and as he owes them a sum of money, they may know now that we and king Henry of England, of the Red Rose, have some short time ago made a contract with one another, which,

[1] The spelling of this document, like that of the preceding letters in the same MS., is very corrupt, and full of gross misreadings, such as *Herhog* for *Herzog*, *gesapt* for *gesagt*, &c. It has been corrected according to the original, which is in the Cottonian collection, MS. Vitellius B.XVIII. f.174, except in the words between brackets, which, in that MS., are burnt away.

[2] Sic, for *da er*.

[3] Sic, for *verstrichener*, orig. burnt.

von] Suffockh in nichte weitter wider den beru[rten kunyng] Hainrichen von Engellandt nit furdern sa[llen.] A.D. 1503.

Und nachdem der gemelt Herzog zu Suffock da[rauf aus unser] Stat Ach verrucken wyl, und unns angezaigt [hat das Er] mit Schulden hinder euch verhest, unnd Ime [nit muglich] sey Euch zu bezalen; wie wol wie Ime [nu dar Innen] hilf zu thun nit schuldig weren, angesebe[n[1] das wie dem] selben herzogen von Suffolk in solicher seiner [sachen zu helffen] nie zugesagt haben, noch auch Ime sunst w[eder mit] sipschaft oder verstenntniss nit verwannt gew[esen, auch noch] nit sein, dan allain das wir Ine in seine[n ellend] mit gnedigen Augen angesehen haben, der Ho[ffnung das] Ime das so er unns angezaigt hat, ergan[gen und wider] faren solt sein;—

So haben wir dannocht Euch zu gut a[uch in Anseh-

---

amongst other things, contains that we are not in any way furthermore to encourage the same duke of Suffolk against the above-mentioned king of England.

And since the aforesaid duke of Suffolk wishes thereupon to quit our town of Aix, and has notified to us that he leaves debts behind him with you, and it is not possible to him to pay you, we (though we are not obliged to give him any help in that matter, considering that we never promised to assist the same duke of Suffolk in such his affairs, nor have ever been connected with him, either through relationship or mutual understanding, nor are so to this present moment, except that we have looked upon him in his misery with merciful eyes, in the hope that what he had notified to us would have taken place), have, nevertheless, for your sakes and also in consider-

---

[1] *langesehen* in transcript.

A.D. 1503. unng] das Er von unns furderungs brief ge[hebt hat, bewillight ein hilff, neuchli]chen[1] mit Drew Tausent guldin Reinisch [zu thun]. Und darrauf mit Cunraten Neuman [unnsern] Burger zu Antdorff sovil gehanndlt, das er [Inen] an sollicher Irer schuld yetzo unverzogenlichen Tausent gulden Reinisch bezalen werde. Darzu so Schickhen Wir Inen hirmit ain Verweisung und Descharge auf den Renntmaister in Brabant, lauttend, der werde Inen von der steur so unns durch unnser Nider-Burgundisshen Lannde auf, zu kunst unnsers Suns und Fursten Ertzhertzogen Philipsen zu Osterreich, &c., bewillight und zugesagt ist, so bald solich Steur gefallen wurdet, zway Tausent gulden Reinish auch antwurten und geben.

Und so der gemelt unser Jegermaister in Gheldren, Jheronimus Lay, dise Werbung muntlich an die von der Stat Ach gethan und geworben hat, soll er Inen

ation of his having had letters of recommendation from us, consented to give some assistance, namely with three thousand Rhenish florins; and in consequence have so far arranged with our citizen at Andorff, Conrad Neuman, that he shall pay them on this their debt, now without any delay, 1000 Rhenish florins. Moreover, we at present hereby forward to them an assignment and discharge upon the chamberlain in Brabant, which is to the effect that he shall also deliver over and give to them 2000 Rhenish florins, from the taxes which are promised and allowed to us through our Nether Burgundian lands, in favor of our son and prince the archduke Philip of Austria, &c, as soon as such taxes fall due.

And as soon as this our said master of the hunt at Gueldres, Jerome Lay, shall have done and performed this business orally with those of the town of Aix, he shall

[1] Sic, for *nälmlichen*.

darauf und daneben solich Werbung, nach laut der A.D. 1503.
artickhl diser instruction nacht der leng in geschrift
uberant wurten und dar Innen nichts auslassen.[1]

thereupon, in addition to this affair, according to the tenor of the articles, deliver to them this instruction at length in writing, and not omit anything therein.

## XXII.

### NEGOTIATIONS OF THE ENGLISH AMBASSADORS[2] WITH MAXIMILIAN.[3]

[MS. Cott., Galba B. II. f. 110.]

. . . . . . . . . that on Tuesday [which was the] A.D. 1503. 31 Jan.
last day [of January the king o]f Romaynes then lyeng
. . . . two myles . . . . [th]e monastery . .
of Saynt . . sent unto us the . . . . . . .
Lang fore . . of August and . . . m . . . .
maistre to thentent to advertise . . . . . . . .
same daye at nyght the said king wold be . . . .
And . . . at thabbaye of Saint Mighel . . . .
Wednesday then next ensueng he wold . . . . us
co[me] unto his presence and give us benygn audience.

[1] The original contains an additional paragraph relating to a different subject, and is dated at the end, but the date is mutilated. So far as visible, it is "18th day of the "month of [. . . . fifteen hun- "dred] and three, 18th year of "Maximilian's reign."

[2] Their names were Sir Thomas Brandon and Nicholas West (afterwards bishop of Ely). Rymer XIII. 35.

[3] This document is unfortunately so mutilated by the fire that the order of the pages depends only on internal evidence. The modern foliation of the MS. is given in the margin.

A.D. 1503. 31 Jan. S[aying] that the king wold not have com so som[1] . . . . had . . . . . . for oure sonar expedicion.

Sayeng fu[rther] . . . . . . the said king was right sorye that we ha . . . . to com unto hym.

According to the same advertisement the sa[id king of] Romaynes come downe by water and arrive [at Antwerp] the said Tuesdaye at evenyng. And . . . . . .

1 Feb. [W]eddnesdaye which was the [eve of the Fea]st of the Purification of oure Lady . . . . . the bisshop of Laufenburgh, doctor H[aydon, one of] his counseil and the marshall of his . . . . . . . the whiche come and shewe[d us that] the kinges pleasire was that we shold com[me] . . . at afternoon towardes us long tyme . . . . . . ambassadors . . . . . . . . send unt[o] . . . . . . . he wold . . . . . . . . . . . . . . . . ve had . . . . . . . that th . . . . . . . . . called hym . . . . . . . prin . . . . . . . loked to have . . . . . . . yng as standing. An[d] . . . . . . the same [*f. 110 b.] opinion . . . . . . . [2] * ma . . . . . . g to the churche and beyng there . . . . d please . . majeste to assign and comma . . . . places according . . youre oratours or els . . . . . pleas hym to resp . . . . . . oure comyng unto hys majeste till the tyme and place where we shold have audience.

Question of precedence between Spain and England.

Of . tymes the said bisshop, doctor, and marshall come . . and went betwixt us. And first alleged divers causes un[to] us for the whiche the Spaynyeshe oratour shold have preemyne[nce] before youre oratours, seyeng that they so had in the courte of Rome, but we proved the contrary; and that the kin[g] of Spayn had doon meny grete and notable acts in subduen[g o]f Granada and other wise. And som

---

[1] Qu. *sone?*

[2] Possibly an entire line is lost here at the beginning of f. 110 b.

said apart that the [said kin]g wold have the said orator of Spayne wele entret[ed until] his son tharcheduke were saufly com home . . . . t notwithstanding any motion we had allwaies a . . . . . . e duetie singuler respecte unto your honour. And . . . . . . eire reasones wold not agre to com toguyder in p . . . [t]he said Spaynyard giving preemynence of place . . . . . . therfor finally it was shewed unto us yn good w . . . . . . king for theviting of thinges whiche mowg[ht] . . . . . parte to the derogation of your honour whiche h[e hath in like c]onsideration as his owne. He had devised . . . . . . ld be brought into the quere of the churche [of Seint Mi]ghels where he wold hier evensong before h . . . . . . thuder, and directly before the place apoyn . . . . . ing to abide his commyng. And . . . . . . d the delivery of youre lettres unto hym . . . . . ng his sa . . . . . . for hym in chur[ch upon the ri]ght side of . . . . next towardes the hi . . . . . . brought incontynently and sett in the st. . . . . e quere directly . . . nst the king. And th . . . . . . to sitt on the . . . . . of the king *same side . . . . . . was appoyncted. [*f. 111.

A.D. 1508. 1 Feb.

The whi . . . . . . . [to] us was thought most honorable . . . . . . And therf . . . went unto the chu[rch] . . . d according to the same devising every thing ens[u]engly on that behalve w . . doon. And in deliveryng of youre saide letters we . . wordes of youre recommendations unto the king. And h[e] said that it was evensongtyme and therfor he wol[d] hier evensong and after that give us audience.

In commyng into the quere all thambassators . . . bey . . come before the king except the Spanyard, whiche f . . . . on the lefft hande.

The place appoyncted for the king was han[ged

A.D. 1503. 1 Feb. with] clothe of gold in the length of iiij stalles of . . . . open without any travars. And next the . . . . . of blakke velvett, where the Spanyard . . . . . . Saxon, the marques of Brandeburgh . . . . . . bisshop of Laufenburgh were sett.

Maximilian gives audience to the ambassadors. Evensong nygh ended, the king comaund[ed the said] bisshop, the doctor, and the marshall to [come into] his chambre, and he wold sone after comme t[o them] Wherupon we went unto his chambre . . . . . king come sone after. The whiche sta[nding beneath] his clothe of estate red your saide lettres; an[d when he had] herd oure proposicion before hym made th . . . the said provost Lang after the king had . . . . . of his counseil in communication gave auns . . . . name that his majeste full acceptably . . . . . . every thyng as well in your saide lettres . . . . . us preposed. And . . . thamyte be[twixt him] and your grace concluded and confermed [it was unto] hym right joyous and syngulerly accep[table] . . .
[*f. 111 b. . . . . . . . . . . . * . . . . . . . . wold observe and fulfill every . . . . . . comprehended. And dothe take and repu[te] . . . . . during his lif your grace as his dier brother . . . . Whiche thinges shold at all tymes herafter appere by dede as largely as they beth nowe spoken and promysed by worde. And as to any thing that we had to comyn aparte with his majeste, he wold assign an other daye for the same.

Thes things in effecte spoken, the king taking us aparte, asked right hertily of your prosperous estate and of the tranqui[lite] of your reames. The whiche when he by oure relation h[ad] undrestande he gretly rejoyced therof. And furthermor[e s]hewed unto us that he was right sorye that we had labo . . . . long tyme before he gave us audience. Howesobeit h[e said] that his busynes was suche in every

place that he cow . . . . . . no convenient layser A.D. 1503.
to hier us till his commyng hu . . . . . herfor 1 Feb.
he wold give us nowe the better audience and sh . .
. . . cion. And because it was then within ny . .
. . . . was about vij of the clokke, therfor he
wold app . . . . . . er tyme to comen with us
and then to send fo[r] . . . . . so deliverd us
for that tyme.

. . . . were present at the said proposing the duke of Sax[ony, the m]arques of Brandenburgh, thoratours of Spayne . . . . . the said bisshop of Laufenburgh, the said b . . . d Cambremaistre, Sir Cornelius de Bargges, th . . . . . . of Anwarpe, Sir Joys Prant, and meny other [ . . . . . c]hambre full.

*On Thurs[day which was the day of the fea]ste of the [*f. 112.
Purification o[f Our Lady about . .] of the clok before 2 Feb.
noon the said bisshop, [doctor, and] marshall come to fett us unto the churche o[f Sainte Ma]rye, whiche is the principal churche of the said towne, sayeng that the king [wold] be there at high masse and there offerre his cand[le] and all thambassadors in like wise to doo. Howe sobei[t we] supposyng that in goyng to thofferyng the Spanyard [should] be preferred, for the same cause we desired to be had ex[cused] of oure thuder commyng. Wherupon the king efts[ones] sent unto us the said bisshop and others, sheweng [that] he wold commen with us after masse in the said . . . .
and that nother we nor the Spanyard shold off . . .
our stalles in thoffering tyme. And so w . . . .
candeles by thaym prepaired, beyng holden be . . .
masse tyme brennyng with skochions of . . . . .
thaym. And the Spanyardes in like wise and . . .
sators with tharmes of theire princes th . . . .
after the masse ended werre taken by the d . . .
with oure offeringes.

The king when mas was fynesshed and . . . .

A.D. 1503. 2 Feb. downe from oure stalles towards hy . . . . unto us, seyeng that about ij of the clo . . . . he wold have secrete comynycation w . . . . of us whiche and howe meny of his . . . . have present at that communication. Th . . . . unto his pleasire. And so we depart . . . . . quere by his commaundement there 1 . .

[*f. 112 b.] *At tw . . . . . . . . . . [t]he king sent for us by the bisshop, doct[or, and marshal abo]ve said. And yn the same place where . . . . . we recited every thing acording to oure instr[ucti]ons for the first day, of oure communication. Wherupon the said lord provost Lang, after communication had by the king aparte with hym and others of his counseil, shewed openly that the king was contented to observe thorughly everything comprised yn the said amyte for his parte and toke it right acceptably that your grace bare so good mynde towards hym, promyttyng that he wold yn like wise do towards you [w]hile he lived.

[An]d as to the othe, his majeste was pleased to give it [in the] churche on Sonday then next commyng. [And] for the maner and circumstance of the givyng of it [he would] send certain of his counseil unto us the next day, [the which]e shold be Friday, or upon Satreday, to comyne . . . . de with us upon the same. Being pres[ent at this] communication the said lordes, provost Lang, the . . . . . the said bisshop of Laufenburgh, Sir Joys P[rant, the doctor H]aydon, and the said marshall, and at thend [of our communica]tion come yn Sir Cornelius de Bargges . . . . aunswere given with oure congratulation . . . dly disposicion in that behalve in the best w . . . . The said king toke us aparte and said . . . had long tyme been in communication and now . . . . con[c]luded, whereof he was right glad. . . . . . . shold be wole observed and good off . . . . . . e therof.

. . . . [s]aid that he was mouche bounden unto your [grace for tharc]heduke his son, to whom in all his neds ye [had been a p]atron and fadre and succurred hym me[ny] *tymes wh[en] . . . . . not succour nor helpe hy[m]. A.D. 1503. 2 Feb. [*f. 113.

Wherupon we s[aid that your] grace before ye had seen the said archeduke b[are goo]d mynde towardes hym, as appered by your grete actes doon for hym; but aft[er] ye had seen hym and comyned with him as ye d[id] ye had mouche better, and as good mynde towards h[ym] as ye cowd have to your naturall son.

For the whiche he entierly thanked you.

On Satreday while the king rode on . . . . . . come unto us the said lordes provost and . . . . . . whiche beth chief of counseil and may . . . . . . . theire maistre of any men as we can per- . . . . . . . . man saythe and also doctour Haydon wh . . . . . . . . bothe lawes and knight. 4 Feb.

They shewed unto us that for the . . . . othe the king was resolved into th . . . . . . . forme followenge. First whe . . . . . . . beyng with him he appoyncted so . . . . . . for the tyme of givyng of the said . . . . . . . differre it till Mondaye next commyng . . . . . . . been accustumed at all tymes to make . . . . . . . werkendaye and never upon an holy d[aye] . . . . . . *custume he . . . . . . . . hen to give it yn the grete churche of . . . . . . f Saint Mighell aforsaid. And undre this ma[ner.] Form in which the Emperor proposed to take the oath. [*f. 113 b.

When the masse b. . . . . . hym were almost at sacryng, then we to com unto hym and require hym to suere acco[r]ding to the contentes of tharticle, we redyng to hym the same contentes. And therupon he layeng his right hande upon the Holy Evangelistes and at thelevation of the sacrament openly lokyng upon the same wold saye, *Juramus.*

Ayenst the whiche daye, the tyme of the masse and

A.D. 1503. 4 Feb. Objections of the ambassadors.

t[he] forme, we persuaded. First ayenst the daye, bec[ause t]hacte was solempne and to be doon to the laude of Allmyg[hty God] and to the strengthe and encreace of Christen feyth, it sho[ld be done] on a solempne daye. And also every other prince giv . . . the accustumed the same. And therfor we . . . . his majeste beyng above all other princes wold doo s . . . . te nor with lesse but rather with more solempn . . . . . se persever in his first aunsuere to give it on Sonda[ye].

[And as to] the said tyme of the masse, we said it was mome . . . . . . the reding of the forme of thothe by us with th . . . . . g of thothe by hym cowd not folowe according . . . . le of thamyte. And also that the sacryng tyme . . . tyme convenient therfor, but suche a tyme as . . . . ld applye thaym self to devotion and to no such . . . . .

[And as to] the forme and maner we seid that thothe was . . . and of mere motion assented and promysed . . . . . n. And therfor the giving of it shold procede . . . . . re facte of the giver. And over that we were . . . . . . . to putt any othe unto hym but assigned . . . . ym to give thothe and to be present at the gi[ving] *of it accordin[g] . . [*f. 114. . . . . behalve.

Furthermore as [. . . . sa]ide churche of Saint Mighel we thought it [a con]venient place for the giving of the said othe because it is a solempne churche of a grete indowed monastery. Howe be it we asked yn what place of the churche and howe the king shold stande at the giving of the said othe.

They said yn his travers to be made nygh to the high auter. Wherunto we persuaded that it was not [well] according so solempn an acte to be doon so prively b[ut] openly. And so we disired to have it doo[ne] upon a festefull daye, in the saide churche . . .

before the high auter, before Agnus Dei t. . . . . A.D. 1503. 4 Feb.
. . then torning about with the sacrament. A. . . king to rede thothe hym self according to th[e form] to thaim delivered. And the same to subscribe [with his own] hande. And to require the notaries that th . . . . to make an instrument upon the same. [And that] doon to have tharticles of thamyte to be red . . . . . to be blowen, *Te Deum* to be song with [ringing of] belles and making of fyres thorugh the . . . . . .

With meny reasones and persuasions we jus . . . . . . of the premisses to thaccomplisshing of . . . . . on every parte insuchewise as they t . . . . . considering the same as they wold she[w] . . . . . condescend to every poyncte of oure des . . . . . the notaries which they said he w . . . . doon, for he thought that the testifieng . . . . whiche shold be present shold suffise . . . . . accordyng.

*. . . . . . . . . . . . [Tu]esday the vij[th] day 7 Feb. of February [we were with th]aim ayen in[1] communi- [*f. 114 b. cation. In the whiche d . . . . . . . with thaym two sondry times. First in . . . onyng at oure lodgyng, where they shewed that the king upon oure motions and persuasions was agreable to make this othe at the said churche of Saint Migheles on Sonday then next ensueng, because we desired it to be doon in a solempn daye and openly without his travers, and that the notary shold inacte the same.

Howe so be it he wold have the masse first doon Discussion as to the time. and then to go to the high auter, and an hoste to be taken out of the pix over the high auter, and before . . . . same to give his othe to be redd by hym self. Albe . . re more brief forme then we shewed. [Nev]erthelesse we insisted as we dud first specialy . . . he congruence of the tyme after the Pater-

[1] *in*, repeated in MS.

A.D. 1503. 7 Feb. noster [ . . . m]asse. So after thothe made then the preste tha . . . . the masse shold folowengly syng *Pax D[omini]* . . .

. . . nd tyme of oure communication with thaim the sa . . . . . . . . at the lodgyng of the marques of Branden[burgh . . . . . . . ]s to a grete sowpar and to a goodly bankett [where he shewed u]nto us that the king wold not be agreabl[e . . . . . ]tyme before Agnus, but after the masse. .

. . . . reste that shall syng the masse to consecra[t . . . . . . ] And thothe to be given before the hoste th . . . . . . . ayne. Albeit [*f. 115. we persisted as we dud . . . *before all . . . . . . ng of that thing whiche myght . . . . . or suspicion or doubt layeng unto thaym th . . . rd and suspicious myndes of the people.

9 Feb. On Thursdaye the ix. day of February, the . . . unto us in the mornyng to prepaire us ayenst . . on hawking with hym. And in likewise dud . . . and Wednesdaye next before, but the wedre [was not] convenient. And at noone there come . . . . . . of Thorne and Vertenberg and brought [us unto . . . ] the monastery gate where the kinges lodg[ing was, we] abiding his commyng. And sone after he c . . . . . . horsebakke with meny noble men about . . . . toke us on his lefft hande and bothe on . . . . . . . homwardes comyned with us all the w[ay . . . . . . . .] passe thorugh the towne and suburbes w . . . . . . . . . . litle waye.

He asked what newes we had, and we s[aid that we had] none. Then said he that he wold shewe [us some,] seyeng that he had certain knowlege [how that [*f. 115 b. the] *Frenshemen [had suffered] a grete fall and discomfite by th[. . . , an]d that on the Frenshe partie were slayne . . . de of Besynyan an Italian and other grete capitanes with x.m<sup>l</sup>. men. And over that the lord Daubeney[1] with iij$^{c}$. speres furnesshed and thre thousand fotemen was also discomfited. A.D. 1503. 9 Feb.

The whiche newes the king reherced with grete rejoycing of the fall of the Frenshe parte.

As we founde tyme convenient so we made instance unto hym for oure expedicion. And he said that on the next daye his counseil shold conclude with us upon thothe to be made on Sondaye next commyng.

[T]he next day, whiche was Friday, the counseil com . . . . us, of whom we obteyned thothe to be doon and . . . . at suche tyme and with suche solennyteis and [other circum]stances as wele contented us. Nothing restin[g to be con]cluded but only the forme of thothe, the which [in no] wise we cowd obteyne to be according to the forme [by us r]eceived of your counseil, for it was aunsuerd u[nto us *Non*] *decet tantum principem præstare juramentum* . . . *sticorum*, but that fewar wordes shold suffise . . . nce. And that therfor the king hymself . . . med thothe out of tharticle in suche a forme [as they had] shewed unto us herafter foloweng the sa . . . sayeng unto us that for the service he owet[h . .] *and[2] wold doo [ . . . . . . . . ca]used us to be contented with that forme . . . . or styking at the matier we mowght be fur[ther from our]e purpose. The whiche forme here foloweth.

10 Feb.

The Emperor's Council think there should be fewer words in the oath.

[* f. 116.

" Ego Maximilianus promitto in verbo regio per Sancta De[i] Evangelia corporaliter tacta ac per sacrosanctum Corpus Domini nostri Jesu Christi corporaliter visum, quod bona fide, et sine fraude a[ut] dolo aut sinistra interpretatione quacunque, bene, fideliter ac inviolabiliter omnia et singula capitula tractatus

[1] Robert Stuart Sieur D'Aubigny.

[2] *and*] Perhaps a line is lost before this word at the beginning of f. 116, in addition to a short space at the bottom of the preceding page.

A.D. 1503. 10 Feb. inter me e[t] serenissimum principem dominum Henricum regem Angliæ fratrem [meum] charissimum nuper facti, ac omnia in eodem contenta tenebo, obser[vabo] et adimplebo, ac a meis teneri. adimpleri et observ[ari faciam] ac mandabo, nec aliquid contra aliquam partem ali[cujus] articuli tractatus prædicti, publice vel occulte fier[i vel] attemptari permittam, sed expresse [et in] effectu contradicam et impediam."

And notwithstanding the counseil of the s[aid commissioners] we after that have so endevoired us as we ob[tained such] additions unto the above written othe, as apperi[the in a boke] given by the king, howe beit it was ix. [of the clokke] on the same Sonday in the whiche thothe w[as given or] we cowd it so obteyne.

The circumstances and solemnyteis of givin[g the same] othe herafter appereth.

12 Feb. On Sonday the xij day of February in t . . . . the monastery of Saint Mighel in Anwar . . . . x. of the clokke before noone, we beyn[g . . . .] before the place prepaired for the king w . . . . stalles on the right hande towardes the . . . . .

*[f. 116 b. *the whiche [. . . . . cl]oth of gold iiij. stalles long and th. . . . . . with cloth of gold of like length all op [ . . . . t]ravers, and from thens towardes the quere [and] certaine stalles and the deskes hanged and covered with blakke velvett and other blakke silkes; and in likewise the other side of the quere ayenst the same. The king come into the said quere in a gowne of clothe of gold; and we humblyng oure self unto hym, he gave us very good chier and countenaunce, seying, "Nowe shall we performe all thinges."

Then he ascended into his said place. And in the stalles next unto his clothe stode the marques of Brandenburg[he,] the dukes of Mechelburghe and of Theek.

And he commaunded us to be in the stalles directly befor[e hy]m, being next unto us in the same side the deane [of the] churche of Colone, whiche is one of the dukes of Bo . . . . . . . orator from the archebisshop of Colone,[1] Thora . . ice and the bisshop of Luke.[2] And the row[me betw]ixt the quere and the highe auter was full of no[ble men and] gentilmen. A.D. 1503. 12 Feb.

[And the] bisshop of Beryten *in pontificalibus* song the h[yghe mass]e, which was full solempnly doon, which the b . . . . ell organs, trumpettes and other instrumen[ts].

[When] the Pater Noster was songen of the high masse [and the bi]sshop had given the benedictions, then the [ . . . k]ing from his said place called us unto hym . . . . us on his lefft hande went unto the highe [. . . . . be]fore the high auter, the said marques, d[uke, an]d bisshoppes folow eng.

The ceremony of ratification.

[The sai]d bisshop whiche sang the masse torned from [the au]ter and stode before the king very nygh and . . . tly unto hym, having the patene of the ch[alice]* in his lefft h[and] . . . . . of the Hoste broken yn his right h[and] . . . . . patene. And the deane of the chap[ell . . . . h]eld open the masseboke, upon thewhiche the king leyd his right hande. And in his lefft hande he had a parchement wherin thothe w[as] writen; whiche he, loking first upon the sacramen[t], dud rede, word by word, we kneling at his lefft side w[ithout] any voide space betuixt hym and us. And the said marq[ues,] dukes, and other estates standing nygh on every side. [*f. 117.

The whiche othe when the king had distinctly red [and] subscribed it with his owne hande, and delivered it u[nto the] notarie Thomas Laurence, requyryng hym at [our] instaunt petition to make an instrument upon t . . . . and the noble men standing about to be

[1] Herman, son of Lewis I., landgrave of Hesse.

[2] *i. e.* of Liege, Jean de Horn.

A.D. 1503. 12 Feb. witnes[ses, as] we made like requisition. And incontyne[ntly after] the said bisshop as he stode before the kin[g] . . . . . . . . towardes the quere with the saide parte of th . . . . . . . . his hande, openly before and in the sight of . . . . blissyng with it, sang *Et pax Domini sit se[mpiterna]*. And then torned unto the auter.

This doon the king repaired into his said . . . also the said lordes orators and we to oure fo . . . . After that the said bisshop of Luke broug[ht . . .] unto the king. And when the king had ta . . . . and the said bisshop had delivered the pat[ene unto the] deane of the chapell, then the king com[manded the] same deane to bryng the Pax unto us . . . . . he and to none other.

When the masse was endend[1] the said . . . . . standyng about the myddes of the quere . . . . . the highe auter, full eloquently declared . . . . . [* f. 117 b. * voice and g . . . . . . . . . ande of God and strengthe of Christen feyth [ . . . . bet]uixt the said king and youre grace concl[uded and c]onfermed and at that day by the said king his maister sworn. The whiche he by his said maistirs commaundement there declared to the dukes, erles, lordes, and to all people, to thentent to give congratulation therof; sheweng that because it shold not be doubtfull to any man what that peace and amyte was, the same worde by worde as it was concluded, shold be forthewith redd open[ly], prayeng every man to give good hiryng therunto.

And therupon incontynently one of the secretaries standing by the same doctor having the same boke of thamyte whiche was by your commissionars sealed with [a]udible voice red it word by word.

[A]nd that doon the trumpettes were blowen in the rode [ . . . An]d after that the said bisshop

[1] Sic.

standing still at the hy[ghe au]ter *in pontificalibus* A.D. 1503.
beganne Te Deum, the cha . . ting the same with 12 Feb.
solempne song and organes [ . . . T]hewhiche ended the said bisshop sang this versic . . . . *e fiat pax in virtute tua, etc.*, and red the collect [*Deu*]*s a quo, etc.* And also the belles were rongen [in all t]he churches of the towne.

[When] this solempnyte was thus doon, the king commy[ng down] from his said place, toke one of us on his right [hand and the] other on his left hande. And so goyng thor[ugh the qu]ere and churche seyd unto us, "Nowe blissed be Go[d, we hav]e made an end of this matier." And we shew[ed our sel]f right joyous therof, with as good wordes as . . . . . And when he entred into the cloistre w . . . . . e weye to his lodging on the right hande, a . . . . . . the lefft hande, he wold not suffre us furt[her . . .] *further [*f. 118.
to go . . . . . . . . . ng that we offered unto hym and . . . . . . . we myght give attendance upon hym.

At nyght there were fyres made rownde about all the markett place and other principal places thorugh the towne, with brennyng cressentes out at the wyndowes the most parte of the nyght and grete sembleis and tryumphes made in meny places.

After the said Sonday the xij. day of Februar[y it was] Wednesdaye then next ensueng, the xv. da[y of 15 Feb.
the] same moneth er we cowde upon oure daily . . unto the kinges presence. On the whiche d[ay about] iij. of the clok at after noone in the same . . . . place where he allwaies gave us audience v . . . . . of estate, beyng present the bisshop of Via . . . . . . . provost Lang and Cambremaister, and doct[or Haydon] we proposed the matier for the receiving of [thorder of] the Gartier. In the whiche matier s . . . . . . . . was had before betwixt his counseil and [us . . . .] on theire partie by

Interview as to the Emperor's receiving the Garter.

A.D. 1503. 15 Feb.

occasion of s . . . . . . . . . commission wherin is specified bothe th . . . . and of the Gartier.

Provost Lang says he had received it before;

Wherupon, after the king had comyned [with his] counseil, the said provost Lang aunsuerd [that the king] had received the said ordre yeres passe[d . . . . . ] Gartier, mantell, and statutes, and swor[n . . . . . . . .] *And therf[ore . . . . . . . . i]f nowe eftsones he shold receive [. . . . . . . . t]hothe ayenne, he shold do thing contrary . . . .

[* f. 118 b.]

to which the ambassadors reply that he had not been installed within the necessary time.

Whereupon we shewed that because his proctor come not to be enstalled for hym, and to present his helmet, &c. by the tyme lymyted by the said statutes, therfore aswel the receiving of the said ordre as the givyng of thothe were voide and of none effecte, likewise as if they had never be doon. Wherfor, inasmouche as it is an article comprised in thamyte that after the conclusion and confermation of the same amyte, he shold accepte the said ordre upon hym, we instanced hym eftsones that he wold so doo.

Wherunto the said provost, after the king had comyned with hym and others aparte, aunsuered that his majes[te wo]ld send unto us the next day some of his counseil to [she]we unto us his further mynde upon the same.

[Then] at the same tyme we shewed of the proclamations [and] banneshementes made by your commaundement yn pl[aces und]re your obeisaunce, according to thamyte, [as] appered by a copie of the same proclamations wh[ich we] said we had to shewe; Beseching his majeste [to com]maunde semblable proclamations and banneshemen[ts to be] made in cities and townes undre his obeisaunce; [with t]he whiche, after brief communication with his said . . . al, the said provost Lang aunsuerd that his ma[jeste was co]ntented to do make proclamations and banneshe[ments in iii]j. of the principal cities of thempire, and

[. . . o]f the succession. But in whiche cities, an[d undre] what forme those proclamations shold be made [we sho]ld knowe by his said counseil the next day; [we in]stancyng that the towne of Acon myght be [oon of] thaym. And the king lawgheng at th[at] *desire saide . . . . . . . . . have it there then yn all thother . . . . . . . . . ye nor nay to oure said desire. A.D. 1503. 15 Feb. [* f. 119.

And immediately therupon the said provost Lang asked of us whether we had any auctorite or noo to comyne [of] any matier concernyng Edmund de la Poel, whom h[e] called the duke of Suffolk; for the king entend[ed] to purchesse his pardone and grace of your highnes, or [to] helpe that some composition myght be had for hym; wherin he wold comyne with us if we had any s[uche] auctorite. Maximilian desired to obtain a pardon for Edmund De la Pole.

To the whiche we aunsuerd that we had no suc[h auctorite], but reherced the menyfold offenses and lightn[esses of the] said Edmund, with thabomination he is h . . . . . . humble petition of your counseil, the resolu . . . . . . . . grace upon the same with every other thin[g . . . . . ] according to oure saide instructions in the . . . . . . . . we cowd to putt hym out of allmaner of t . . . . . . suche thing to be obteyned. And so req[uired him] to make no suche petition, for the thing w[as such as cowd] not stande with your honor to graunte, bu[t . . . . . . .] incontynently to banneshe hym accordin[g . . . . . . . . .] by hym confermed and sworn.

Wherupon the king, having communication . . . . . . . . . said counseil, there was a grete lawghyn[g] . . . . . . . . . . at the first worde that the king spak . . . . . . . . . . . what it was we knowe not. And . . . . . . . . . . . . comynycation the said lord Lang, sta[nding . . . . . . . .] king as he allwayes dud when he g . . . . . . . . . . shewed unto us, that though his ma[. . . . . . . . . . to comyne

A.D. 1503. 15 Feb. [*f. 119 b. for some composition to be ha[d for the said] *Edmund . . . . . . . . . . . nor entente to give unto hym suc[cor, aid, nor comfort he]nsforthe, but to observe every poynt of th[amity . . . .]gin, and all others like as he is.

And then incontinently the king toke us aparte, saieng that he wold have broken with us in meny matiers touching the Frenshe king, yn the presence of thorator of Spayne, because it touched the king of Spayne; but the said orator is so full of ire because of this contention and variaunce betuixt us and hym, that he wull yn no wise be present toguydre with us. And therfor he wold commytte those matiers unto his ambassators to shewe the same unto your grace yn the presence of thorator of Spayne that ys with your [h]ighnes yn England.

The ambassadors charge him with giving assistance to English rebels.

[W]e seying this tyme convenient to breke with the [kin]g yn thother matiers comprised in oure instructio[ns, she]wed unto hym at large of the reporte made unto [your] grace of the aid, comforte, and relief by hym giv[en unto] your rebelles beyng in Acon according to oure [said]e instructions; addyng therunto that we [had] spoken with Robynet Ruffyn, whiche confesse[d to b]eryng of money and writing from the said [king] to the comforte of the said rebelles, and th[at we h]ad seen his lettre late sent unto the bisshop [of Liege[1]] for like entente; all contrary to thamyte concl[uded and con]fermed.

[Th]e whiche said thinges rehereed of oure instr[uctions, with yo]ure saide additions he confessed to have b[een done b]y his commaundement, and of his knowleg[e, sayin]g that he thought he mowght with his . . . . so doo notwithstanding the saide amyte [so conclu]ded and also confermed, as long as [*f. 120. there . . . . . . *any thing . . . . . . . . . . . . . . as there dud all . . . . . . . .

[1] See page 148.

The whiche othe . . . . . . . . . . n he may not nother wull from hensforthe g[eve u]nto your said rebelles, any aide, comforte, or relief in any wise, but fulfill and kepe e[very]thing according to the said amyte. A.D. 1503. 15 Feb.

To the whiche aunsuere where as we replied, all . . . his confirmation, subscription, and sealyng of the [said] amyte, the whiche dothe bynde hym to observe the s[ame], though the said othe were never given nor requy[red] to be given. He said as he dud before, s[aying] further that he knewe not whether that amyte [would] stande or noo, because it was shewed unto h[ym that] your grace was not in mynde to kepe thamyte . . . . . And over that unto the tyme he had spoken . . . . . . and herd us as he hath doon, it was suppos[ed] . . . . wold have desired some other thinges of hym . . . . . concluded in the saide amyte, or els contra . . . . . . amyte to the breche therof. And therfor . . . . . . . he thought not hymself before the caus . . . . . . . . comyng knowen, and thothe given to be . . . . . . . amyte.

None other aunsuere nor excuse he gave [save that he] promysed never herafter to give any maner [aid, succour,] or relief to the said nor other rebelles [and likewise] to observe every poynte of the saide amyte.

Item, we shewed unto the said king of [the treaty] and alliaunce that nowe beth betuixt [your grace and] the king of Scottes. And of the m[arriage which shall be] solennysed this next somer, according to [the same]. The whiche thinges the said king sei . . . . . . . . and smylyng seid, "It is meny yeres p. . . . . . . * of England . . . . . . . . . . The whiche thing, he [* f. 120 b. said, is as gr[ . . . . . . . ki]ng of Hungary to wedd a lady out of Fra[nce.]" Howe be it he said that he undrestode she was an Englishe woman, called the lord Kendales doughter, whose landes he supposed to lye in England.

A.D. 1503. 15 Feb.

And we aunsuerd that she was none Englishe woman, nor yet that her fadre had any landes within England, but that, as we supposed, his auntecetry come out of England at the tyme of the subdueng of Fraunce.

Item, we asked of hym whether there were peace betuixt hym and the said king of Hungary or noo.

The Emperor's relations with Hungary and France.

He said yee, but not very good peace, for there was a litle grouge betuixt thaim. Howebeit, he said, that [th]e king of Hungary dud nothing to hym, nor he to [th]e king of Hungary.

. . . we desired to knowe what peace was betuixt hym [and] the Frenshe king. He aunsuerd undre this form[e, follo]weng, "We have peace, but I shall shewe you ho[w th]e last somer the Frenshe king laye at Millain, and . . . . . . . at Trent, within iiij. daies jorney to Millain. [And I ha]d assembled myne hoste ij. tymes to have fough[t with] hym, having meny Souchyvers in my said host. [And i]n like wise the Frenshe king had goten meny of [them] into his parte. The Souchyvars whiche [were] appoyncted to kepe my vanguarde avaunced tha[ym for]wardes without my knowlege, not stoppyng . . . . . . . . come to Millain, supposing that I had folow[ed. And the Fren]she king supposing in like wise that I had . . . . . . . . departed from Millain to Pavia, where he . . . . . . . . grete ryver betuixt hym and me that it w[old not b]e possible for me to come to annoye hym.

"[The Fr]enshemen remaynyng in Millain with th[e] [* f. 121.] * Lumbardes, if . . . . . . . . . . ars, and discomfited thaim. T . . . . . . . . n I undrestode I was myscontented w[ith them that] they had approched so nygh to Millain, without my [com]mandement, and they in like wise were not contented that I folowed not to their su[ccour, as] they supposed I wold have doon. And in the mean [time] the Frenshe king sent his ambassators unto me to tre[at for] peace, whiche was at that tyme concluded betwixt u[s,] writen only in a papir. And before it was conferm[ed] the Frenshe king had begonne warre ayenst the king [of] Spayne in Napules. Wherfor, when the Frenshe k[ing] come eftsones unto me with a confirmation of th[e same] undre his sign and seale, I wold not receive, nor . . . . . but said that I wold have an universal peace, or els . . . . . . Howsobeit I trust that my son tharcheduke [coming] homwardes shall take som good conclusion . . . . . . . The which so doon we shall have good pea[ce] . . . . . . shall have warre."

A.D. 1503. 15 Feb.

Item, we desired to knowe what he entend[ed against] Millain. He said, "Nothing;" for the Frensh . . . . . and agreid to hold it of hym as his vasall . . . . . . . Seyeng further "that thentrates and rem . . . . . . . beth vj hundred thousand ducates yerly . . . . . king hath appoynoted iiij hundred thous[and . . . . . ] and defence of the countrey and ij^c t[housand . . . . .] he take the to his owne profite, whiche . . . . . . . And thus the Frenshe king, what by . . . . . . . Napules and his owne countreys recei . . . . . . . somouche money yerly that he know . . . . . . . therwith but to oppresse his own ne . . . . . . . daily dothe and wull doo. Wher[fore . . . . .] king of England and I wull have oure . . . . [1] and reig . . . . . . for us to take hede u[nto . . . . . . . w]hiche matier I praye you to commende . . . . th the matier of Turkes, ayenst whom I en[tend]e to make warre after my warre be doon ayenst the Geldres. And at this next somer to kepe a diete for the saide matier of the Turkes; to the whiche I wull praye the king of England to send his orators, like wise as every other prince shall doo."

His intentions regarding Milan.

[*f. 121 b.

[1] Besides a word or two at the bottom of f. 121, it is not unlikely that a whole line is lost at the beginning of page 121 b.

A.D. 1503. 15 Feb. After we had given laude to his noble purpose ayenst the said Turkes, he said that the Grete Turke feared not the pope, the Frenshe king, nor the king of Spayne, nor yet any other prince, but only hym; and therfor the Turke hath often tymes sent unto hym for peace, the whiche he hath [a]llwaies denyed to take with hym. And the said Turke [se]yng that he cannot obteyne to have peace with hym [the]rfor he hath defied the king of Romaynes and acer[tained him] that he wull destroye his countreys. And thus . . . . . . that he must nedes make warre ayenst the Turke.

[Wh]erupon we shewed unto hym the same tyme, and [like]wise at other tymes to other lordes at divers communicati[ons, accor]ding to our instructions howe we herd y[our highness diver]s tymes in comynyng of that holy viage wissh [that] ye wer in his companigh in the said viage, [and t]hat so undoubtedly ye wold be if ye were as ny[gh unto] hym as the king of Hungary.

[To th]e whiche he said with herty maner, "I thanke h[is grace of his] good mynde, for I had lever have his perso[n in my comp]anigh then any other thing."

[* f. 122. 16 Feb. * On Thurs[day after, which was t]he xvj. day of Februa[ry] there come u[nto us the bishop of] Laufenburgh, the prov[ost] Lang and Cambr[emaister and doc]tor Haydon. And the provost recited the substaunce of [the] saide petitions made unto th[em] for the Gartier, proclamations and banneshements, giving [unto] us like aunsuere upon the matier of the Gartier as was [doon] the day before in the presence of the king; sayeng th[at the] king was determyned in his mynde not to accepte of ne[w the] said ordre, nor to give thothe, but to stand to that he had . . . . and by his proctor, whom he wold send with his orators per . . . the residue.

The Emperor still declines to receive the Garter a second time.

Wherupon we alleged tharticle of thamyte byndyn[g him to] the contrary, and persuaded unto thaim by meny r[easons in] the best wise we cowde, and so playnely as th[at they were] somwhat meoved and myscontented with us [therein but] fynally they were pacified and convinced by . . . . . . so as they were contented and thought it . . . . . . . eftsones to meove the king to accepte this ord[re . . . . . . ] we rehereed that he dud not were the Ga[rtier as he was] bounde to doo by thothe that he made when h[e accepted] thordre. They aunswerd that they doubt[ed not but he] wold were it, and the Cambremaistre had . . . . . . had the Gartier there, for he had it carried al . . . . . . . Then we shewed unto thaim of a George w[hich the knights] of that ordre shold were, and also a colar . . . . . . . we shewed unto thaim according to oure in[structions . . . ]. And they said that [the king had undrest[ood . . . . . . .] George, the whiche he wold be contented to [were . . .] . that every thing performed according to thor . . . . A.D. 1503. 16 Feb.

And as to the proclamations and banneshe[ments they gave] unto us the names of the cities of themp[ire where they should] be made, that is to saye, Colone, Osbroke,[1] . . . . Norimberg and Lubek.

*And as to th[e proclamations and ba]neshementes to be made in Acon [they said that the kin]g was determyned to differre the procl[amations and] baneshementes there till the commyng of h[is am]bassators unto your grace, and in the meane tyme to monyshe Edmund de la Pool to prepaire hymself to departe out of all lordeshippes undre hym and thempire, and also give warnyng unto his creditors of his said monition, to thentent they shold see for theire contentation of suche summes as he owed unto thaim. And if after the communication of the kinges said ambassators with your grace no compo- [*f. 122 b. He wishes to defer the banishments.

[1] Augsburg.

A.D. 1503. 16 Feb. sicion cowd be had for the said Edmund, then he incontynently therupon to do make the said proclamations and banneshementes yn Acon. [W]herunto we replieng said that suche delaye was contra[ry to t]hamyte, and over that the cause of suche delaye, [the h]ope to obteyne suche composicion of your grace for the [said] Edmund, whiche is also ayenst thamyte, is but vay[n . . . . ]es, rehercyng at large according to oure instruc[cions, lik]ewise as we dud before to the king, sayeng b[oth to the] king and to thaim that it was aparte of oure cr[edence to she]we the same. And so we persuaded those proclam[ations and b]anneshementes to be made in Acon incontynently. [They] aunsuerd that the king denyed not to do it, a[lbeit in consi]deration aswele of his owne honor as of the h[onor a]nd wele of your grace he was determyned to diff[erre it as is] abovesaid; sheweng furthermore howe [at the fi]rst commyng of the said Edmund unto the king [he had promi]sed unto hym favor and succor for the lady Mar[garet's sake and] at her instaunce, aunte unto the said Edmund . . . . . . e unto hym his salveconduct. And also w . . . . . . for hym to be had in suche [* f. 123.] favor, trust, and c[redit] *as he hath . . . . . . . . [t]he singuler trust of h . . . . comforte and su . . . . . . . his promys. And therfore if nowe he shold sodenly . . e and bannesshe hym, tho[rough] the whiche percaas his creditors, whiche have trusted hy[m . . ] upon the said kinges writing wold destroye hym, it [shold] redounde to his grete dishonor, and tiranny shold [be] ascribed unto hym for the same.

In consideration wherof, and also for the restfulnes an[d] profite of your grace in evityng of the daunger and trou[ble] that might ensue, as have doon in like caas hertofore . . . . if this matier were thus at large and rawly lefft [he] wold be glad to putt his handes to have suche a co[ncord] as mowght ap-

peace all parties if it cowd be had, [whereby] he A.D. 1503.
wull leve his handes of hym in suche hon[or as] 16 Feb.
is according for a grete prince to departe fr[om one]
that hath putt trust in hym.

Seyeng furthermore upon oure replieng . . . . considerations that it sholdbe a soden bann[eshment, that] sithens thamyte was no rather perfeite till . . . . . . were given by bothe princes, as it was not y[et done.]

We aunsuerd that thamyte was full perfite . . . . . . therof, though there were never othe given to then . . . . . . . . and banneshements sholdbe therupon inco[ntinently made] as appereth by an article of the same . . . . . . . desired the saide proclamations and bann[eshments to be] made in Acon without delay accordi[ng . . . . . ] and not to deferre it one mynute of . . . . . . discomodite or dammage that was feare[d might come to your] grace or to your reame by this light man . . . . For no suche thing can ensue sithens h[e is held in] no regarde but had in despecte and ab[horrence of all]* people with [*f. 123. b.
. . . . . . . . nes and menyfold offenses and trato- . . . . . . . . . specialy after the singuler grace, pardone, and bo . . . . usnes he founde in your highnes.

Upon the whiche and meny other aunsuers and replications they were contented to meove the said king according to oure desires, and to acertain us the next day of his mynde i[n] the same and in the matier of the Gartier; and also to bring the forme of the proclamation and banneshement to be made incontynently in the saide cities, for the king wold not folowe the forme brought with us.

[On] Satreday then next ensueng, the xviij day of
[Febru]ary come unto us the said provost Lang, the [18 Feb.
Cambre[maister and] doctor Haydon. They shewed unto us that acco[rding to thei]re promysses they had

A.D. 1503. 18 Feb. shewed unto the king suc[h reason]es and persuasions as we had made for the takyng [of the o]rdre of the Gartier, and for the banneshementes [to be inconty]nently made in Acon and other places. Howebe[it they sa]ide that the king was thorughly determyned [to send] his ambassators unto your grace to comyne with y[ou on thie]s matiers, and also a proctor sufficiently auctor[ised to be inst]alled for hym, and before their commyng un[to you he w]old no thing doo further in that matier. [And further, t]ouching the wering of the Gartier they sa[id that the] king supposed the Gartier to have be there b. . . . . . . . . . And then we said we wold provide for

[* f. 124. on . . . * They said it . . . . . . . . . king wold differre every thing in that [matier till the com]yng of his said ambassat[or] and proctor unto your grace. They brought ayenne the s . . . . patron of the colar, seying that the king wold be [content] to were a colar according to the same upon Saint G[eorges] daye.

And as to the forme of the proclamations the shewed [us a] mynute therof, the whiche with certain additions th[at] we desired to be made therunto, and they condescended [to] the same, we thought to be good and according to tha[myte,] and trusted the same to be putt in execution. A[nd they] promysed to make up the same forme perfectly accord[ing as] it was then agreid amongst us and to send it . . . . . And over that we eftsones so convinced tha[im touching the] matiers of the Gartier and banneshements [which should be] made in Acon that they said they wold a[dvise . . . ] the king to do according to oure desires th[erein].

20 Feb. The Monday then next ensueng they c[ame again unto] us after the king was riden on huntyng [and told us that] the king persisted allwaies in like mynde

[touching the] banneshements in Acon as is above A.D. 1503. 20 Feb.
rehe[rced, and would not] for any reasonyng chaunge his said m[ynde].

And as touching the forme of the proc[lamations they said] that they had made it according to o[ur desire . . . ] and delivered it unto the king, whiche . . . .] And at his retornyng home ayenne w[hich would be]next daye they wold send it unto us.

* . . . . . . . . . . . . . . . . . . . . [* f. 124 b.

. by all oure p . . . . meanes to have it and that it ow[ . . . inco]ntynently in Acon. Wherupon they a[nswered] that, the wordes of thamyte of thempire wele pondred and considered, themperor was not bounde to make any banneshements nor yet proclamations within thempire.

From the whiche theire opinions we by our persuasions remeoved thaim; and so they remayned.

On Tuesday, late in the evenyng, the king come 21, 22 Feb. home, and on Wednesdaye then next ensueng, the xxij day [of] February, they sent unto us by doctor Petre, secretary . . . . tyn, the forme of a proclamation, acerteynyng us [that i]t was conceived by the mynde of the king.

[The w]hiche forme and none other he wold to be publis[hed; and whe]n we had seen it, it pleased nothing, for it w[as but o]nly a notifieng undre fewe wordes howe that [peace] is concluded betuixt your grace and hym, nothing . . . . yng what is the tenor or effecte of that amyte [nor of] any article therof nor yet sownyng to any ma[nner ban]eshements, as appereth by a copie therof write[n by the sa]id secretary. And therfor we wold not . . . t, but made contynuel sute to have it mad[e in the f]orme made by your grace, whiche was according . . . . . And we sent owerly unto the conseil for . . . .

A.D. 1508. 22 Feb. [They an]suerd that the king hath been accustum[ed . . . . ]nes in semblable cases to make his proclama[tions in tha]t generall forme, the whiche he [* f. 125. wold not ch[aunge. * . . . . . . . [1] exp . . . . . . . . . . . . . hym confermed . . . sworn wh . . . . . . . . . y besought hym . . . . And as to his ambass[ador a]nd proctor we offerred our . . . and in like wise at all tymes before desired to go in . . . . with thaym.

Wherunto the said provost Lang, after the king had c[omyned] with hym and his counseil, seid that for suche re[asons and] considerations as were shewed unto us divers tym[es before] by his counseil we shold be contented with suche au[nsueres] as the same counseil had given unto us and tak[e this for] a fynal aunsuere.

The Emperor insists on delay till his ambassadors have spoken with Henry.

Albe it we made replications therunto in su[ch wise that] the king, leving his counseil and all the l[ordes took us] aparte and praied us to recommaunde hym [unto your] highnes as to his lovyng and dier broth[er and promise] unto you that he wull performe and fulfill [the ,amity in] every poynt. Howsobeit he differ[red the] tyme till his ambassators had spoken with [your grace]. And we said that it was contrary to tha[myte to make] any suche delaye, and that therfor y[our highness] wold not belive us that we had doon o[ur duty] yn pursute of the same. Wherfor we be . . . . to have that aunsuere to be putt undre w[riting which] he graunted and commaunded the said . . . . . . . doon, and so he dud. Albe it the . . . . . . . . shold not have in writing all his my . . . . . . . . . reserve those matiers with others to . . . . . . . his said ambassators.

Wherupon we shewed unto hym th[at] . . . . .

[1] Most probably a line has been lost before this fragmentary word at the top of page 124.

his proctor must be a knight, as none . . . . A.D. 1503.
appoincted to be his ambassators. 22 Feb.

*And he said [ . . . . . . . . . . s]heweng [*f. 125 b.
[us] that his said a[mbassator . . . . ] with hym and sholdbe depecched . . . hens. And the knight whiche shold be his proctor was at Saint Omers in their waye. Then we desired that his commission myght extende not only to thenstalling and presenting of the helmett and other thinges, but also to do every other thing in that ordre as he shold do if he were there in persone. Wherunto he aunsuerd, "Doubt ye not it shalbe wele inough, for he shall have power to doo every thing that shalbe agreid betuixt the king and myne ambassator[s]."

[Fu]rthermore, upon his promys made unto us for his [proclama]tions to be made incontinently in Acon [we be]sought hym for that thing to be doon according [to the] same.

[Wheru]nto he saide it shold be doon incontynently [How]beit he marvailed that we were so importun[ate in tha]t behalve, sithens the said Edmund is upon . . . . ging. We besought hym to knowe whidr[e] . . . . . he knewe not, but to seke his fortune.

[And] where as we at oure last communication withe th . . . . desired theim to meove the king to have th . . . . present when we shold be with his majes[te] . . . . . t as wele to perceive what the matier shold . . . . . the Frenshe king as is above reherced. As . . . . . . our commaundement touching the demeany[ng of the sai]d Spanyard for your said rebell.

The king shewed that he had doon accordi[ng . . . .] *our . . . . . . . . snes they myg[ht] [* f. 126.
not give unt . . . . . . . to take aunsuere . . . . the king hymself.

Wherupon we made su[te to] come unto the kinges pre[sence;] and so we dud on the Thursday then next 23 Feb.

A.D. 1503. 23 Feb. ensueng . . . . On the whiche daye when the king had dyned . . . . was commyng unto a place about the myddes of th . . . to se newe clothes of Arasse, he sent noble men [unto] us to come unto hym. And so we dud. And taking . . . . on his leffte hande riding thorugh the towne unt[o his] lodgyng, fell in communication of the duke of Geldre, seyeng that he was the unkyndest man in the [world,] for he had norisshed hym and brought hym up of a [boy in] his hous and afterwardes suffred hym to occu[py the said] dukedom of Geldre, not withstanding th . . . . . . . . of the same made by his fadre.

Upon the whiche his sayeng we inconty[nently asked] hym to considre the like and grettar thin[ges of your] rebell at Acon, whom your grace besides [bringing] up of hym, had, after his rebellion and [many other] offenses, given ayenne unto hym his land . . . . . with meny other gracious favors and be[nefits.]

To the whiche the said king aunsuerd ". . . . of trouthe, and therfor I wull not couns[el his grace] to take hym into his reame ayenne." A[nd this will] he saye unto the said rebell if ever it [fortune him] to speke with hym, for he said he t[hought him] but a lyght persone.

And with that we lighted downe of . . . with the king come into the chambr[e . . . . . seasons he gave us audience. And t . . . . . . provost standing next unto the ki[ng . . . . ] and meny noble men standing abou[t . . . . .
[*f. 126 b.] . .[1] *shewe . . . . . . . . . . . . . . . us and given . . . our commyng unto hym benygn audie[nce and touchi]ng thamyte hath fulfilled every

[1] Possibly some entire lines lost here, besides the dotted space.

thing h[ide]rto. And so desired us to shewe and reporte unto your highnes. Howbeit he thought there was difference betuixt his majestie and us in certain thynges, the whiche he supposed we wold shewe unto your grace. And he had commytted unto his ambassators to comyne and conclude with youre highnes upon the same, whom he wold spede in all goodly haste, praieng us take oure jornay before thaim unto Calis, to thentent that at theire commyng thuder they myght have spedy [p]assage to come without delaye unto the presence of your [high]nes, to whom he desired us to make entire recommen[dation]s as to his dier and lovyng brother. A.D. 1508. 23 Feb.

[Wher]upon we, marvailing of this soden depecching . . . . al aunsuere seyng divers matiers as undeterm[yned . . . . . ]erd that for the favorable accepting and benign[e receivin]g of us we humilly thanked his majeste, . . . . s to thexpedicion of the matiers of thamyte fo[r the whi]che we were sent unto hym, we said that as [touchin]g thothe we cowd make reporte howe he had [taken i]t, but as to thexpedicion of the matiers of . . . . proclamations and banneshements we besoug[ht him . . ]e to pardone us, for we cowd make no relatio[n of our] expedicion on that behalve; reherceyng . . . . that audience to thaunsuers given unto us by . . . . the whiche we expresly there shewed to b[e contrary t]o thamyte; and therfor whatsoever aunsu[er . . .] his counseil, we doubt not that his maj[este being so ex]cellent a prince, wold give us aunsuer . . . .

## XXIII.

[MS. Cott., Galba B II. 59, burnt in the margin.]

A.D. 1503.

Memoire [a Wilshere[1]] dentendre de Messire Charles comme il se devra conduyre pardela es affaires du Roy nostre Seigneur.

Wiltshire is to inform the king of the motions of the rebels.

PREMIEREMENT remonstrera audict Messire Charles comme la mageste du roy la ordonne en son absence de se tenir et resider pardela pour une espace de temps, affin de temps a aultre luy faire savoir de telles nouvelles quil pourra entendre et savoir du fait et gouvernement de ses rebelles, et ou ilz deliberent daller, et quilz entendent de faire.

Et que pour plusfacillement en estre adverty, que ledict Messire Char[les] luy face avoir congnoissance

---

TRANSLATION.

Memorandum [to Wiltshire] to learn from Messire Charles how he is to conduct himself there in the affairs of the king our master.

FIRST, he shall show to the said Messire Charles how the king's majesty has appointed him in his absence to remain and reside there for a space of time, to inform him from time to time of such news as he can learn and know of the actions and conduct of his rebels, and where they purpose to go, and what they intend to do.

And to be the more readily informed thereof, let the said Messire Charles put him in communication with such spies as

---

[1] Probably Sir John Wiltshire, who was appointed Controller of Calais in 1503. French roll, 18 Henry VII m. (2).

avecques telles espyes quil a en main. [Et] ledict Wilshere en pourra praticquer daultres affin den estre acerte[int] a la verite de tous costez, pour veritablement en advertir la Majeste d[u Roy]. A.D. 1503.

Item, ledict Wilshere solicitera tellement envers ledict Messire Charl[es quil] le accointe et face avoir congnoissance avecques les entrep[renneurs] et aultres quil a praticquez dempuis sa demeure et residence p[ardela . . ] Et se mectra ledict Wilshere en son effectuel devoir, tant avec[ques lesdicts] entreprenneurs que aultres quil pourra pratiquer, que . . . . . entreprinse puisse sortir a bon effect et conclusion sy po[ssible est] dele faire en quelque maniere que ce soit, a celle fin que [sil vient] aucun bien en ladicte entreprinse que le roy en puisse part[ticulierement etre] adverty, a intencion de les remunerer selon quilz le deserv[ent. Et] pour laccomplissement dicelle ledict Wilshere mectra tou[sjours lesdicts] entreprenneurs en bon espoir et confort,

En les advertissans que silz peuent parvenir alexe-

---

he has in his employ. And the said Wilshere may use others, in order to ascertain the truth from all sides, and to inform the king's majesty of it truly.

Also, the said Wilshere shall so solicit the said Messire Charles that he shall make him known to and cause him to have intelligence with the enterprisers and others whom he has engaged since his residence in those parts. And the said Wilshere shall use his utmost efforts, both with the said enterprisers and others whom he can engage, that [the said] enterprise may lead to good effect and conclusion, if [it be possible] to do it in any manner, to the end that . . . . . . . any good in the said enterprise that the king may [be particularly] informed thereof, in order to remunerate them as they deserve. And for the accomplishment of the same, the said Wilshire shall always put the said enterprisers in good hope and comfort,

Informing them that if they can achieve the execution of

A.D. 1503. cucio[n deladicte] entreprinse que le roy le recongnoistra tellement enver[s eulx que] par raison ilz auront cause deulx tenir pour bien cont[ent. Et a ce] que leur a este offert parcidevant par ledict Messire C[harles pour] parvenir a ladicte execucion delentreprinse que le roy ser[a prest a] parfourmer et accomplir ausdicts offres precedentes [sans faire] aucune difficulte, ja soit ce que les endentures so . . . .

Whenever the league with Maximilian is confirmed, Wiltshire shall go through Germany with Norroy, and see it proclaimed;

Item, quant ledict [Wilshere] aura congnoissance que largent que le r[oy doit] payer au roy des Romains soit paye en la cite de Londres et les lect[res] patentes delivrez de lentreeschange delamytie conclute et accor[dee] entre le roy et le dict roy des Romains, solicitera envers les commissai[res] dicelluy roy qui pource auront charge de incontinent ordonne[r un] officier darmes dudict roy des Romains pour et[1] en la compaig[nie] de Norrey[2] aller es Allemaignes affin de faire publier par

---

the said enterprise the king will acknowledge it to them in such wise that in reason they shall have cause to hold themselves well satisfied. [And as to] what was formerly offered them by the said Messire Charles for the accomplishment of the said enterprise, the king will be ready to fulfil the said former offers [without making] any difficulty, even if the indentures be . . . . . .

Also, when the said [Wilshere] shall have intelligence that the money which the king is to pay to the king of the Romans is paid in the city of London, and the letters patent delivered of the amity concluded and granted between the king and the said king of the Romans, he shall solicit the commissioners of the said king, who shall have charge to that effect immediately to appoint an officer of arms of the said king of the Romans to go in the company of Norroy[2] into Germany in order to

---

[1] *et*] Sic in MS.

[2] Christopher Carhill. *See* Appendix A.

les gr[andes] villes, citez, et aultres villes et places de lempire et des lieux d[u] patrymoyne dudict roy des Romains ladicte amytie. A.D. 1503.

Semblablement la bagnyssement des rebelles du roy nostredict sire hors d[e tous] les lieux et places de sondict patrymoyne et succession; et que [ladicte] proclamacion soit faicte aux prouchaines bonnes villes du [pays] ou se tiendront lesdicts rebelles du roy, tout ainsi en la four[me et] maniere quil est contenu en la proclamacion qui a este dev[isee en] francois et en latin par le conseil du roy laquelle est b[aillee] audict Wilshere pour la delivrer audict Norrey quant le c[as le] requerra. Et fera ledict Wilshere icelle translater en all[emain] affin de la monstrer aux commissaires dudict roy des Rom[ains. Et] que ledict Norrey soit tousjours present a veoir faire ladicte pr[oclamation.]

with the banishment of the rebels.

Item, ledict Wilshere baillera par escript audict Norrey les no[ms et] surnoms des rebelles du roy

---

proclaim the said amity through the towns, cities, and other towns and places of the empire and of the lands of the patrimony of the said king of the Romans.

Likewise the banishment of the rebels of the king our said lord out of [all] places of his said patrimony and succession; and that the said proclamation be made at the neighbouring good towns [of the country] where the king's said rebels shall be, exactly according to the form and manner that it is contained in the proclamation which has been devised in French and in Latin by the king's council, which has been given to the said Wilshere to deliver to the said Norroy when the case shall require it. And the said Wilshere shall cause it to be translated into German, in order to show it to the commissioners of the king of the Romans. And let the said Norroy be always present to see the said proclamation made.

Also, the said Wilshere shall give in writing to the said Norroy the names and surnames of the king's rebels that they

A.D. 1503. pour les faire bagnyr, nomm[ant] chacun par soy, come il appartient, par lesdictes bonnes villes [et citez] des Allemaignes, assavoir du patrymoyne et succession dudict roy [des] Romains.

He is to get Sir George Neville banished from Maestricht, Item, se ledict Wilshere entend que Messire George Neville nest [pas] encoires bagny hor de Mastryc, quil le face faire ; et sy ap[res] ledict bagnyssement il reside et se tient en ladicte ville ou aultr[e] dela subgection et obeissance delarcheduc ou delevesque dul[. . .] quil pourchasse a en faire faire lexecution, et de tous les ault[res re]belles quil entendra estre es lieux dont ilz auront este bagn[ys.]

and to promise the king's pardon to any servants of Edmund De la Pole, who will give information. Item, trouvera moien au mieulx [quil pou]rra de pratiquer aucuns des serviteurs de Edmond de la Polle pour luy faire savoir tousjours des nouvelles, en luy promectant delapart du roy son pardon par ainsi que il declairera ceulx quil congnoist et entend estre de laffinite dudict Edmond, et ce a sa venue et arryvee devers le roy nostredict sire.

Item, sil ya aucuns aultres des gens et serviteurs

---

may be banished, naming each one separately in due form through the said good towns and cities of Germany, to wit, of the patrimony and succession of the said king of the Romans.

Also, if the said Wilshere hear that Sir George Neville is not yet banished from Maestricht, that he cause it to be done ; and if after the said banishment he reside in the said town, or any other under the rule of the archduke or of the bishop of . . . that he procure his execution and that of all the other rebels whom he shall learn to be in the places from which they shall have been banished.

Also, he shall find means, to the best of his power, to engage some of the servants of Edmund de la Pole always to give him intelligence, promising him [them], on the king's part, his pardon, on condition that he will declare those whom he knows and understands to be of the affinity of the said Edmund, and this on his coming to the king our said lord.

Also, if there are any other of the gentlemen and servants

dudict Edmond De la Polle qui desirent a avoir leur pardon et abolucion.[1] le roy est conten de leur pardonner leurs vies moiennant quilz feront declaira[cion] de tout ce quilz scayvent et congnoissent. A.D. 1503.

Le bon plaisir du roy est que ledict Wilshere revisite souvent s[es] instructions, affin quil ne puisse riens mectre en oubly [dans le] contenu en icelles, sans les monstrer a personne quel[conque] fors seulement a Messire Charles.

H. R.

---

of the said Edmund De la Pole who desire to have their pardon and absolution, the king is content to pardon them their lives, provided they make declaration of all that they know.

The good pleasure of the king is that the said Wilshere revise frequently his instructions, in order that he may not forget anything in their contents, without showing them to any person whatever, except only to Messire Charles.

H. R.

## XXIV.

### Depositions touching Edmund De la Pole.

[MS. in Record Office.]

Byfor my departing out of England, shewing my mynd to W[. Huse] in what wise I shuld departe, I asked hym his advise. A[nd his] conseil was that I shuld not refuse the jorney, and that I . . . . incontinent commyng by yond the see applye me to the A.D. 1503.

[1] Sic in MS.

A.D. 1503. true and feithful service of Ed. De la Pole. And I said to doo hym true service shuld be my mynd; howbeit, I wold not incontinent appr . . . therunto to such tyme as I myght undrestond of astronomyers what shuld be his liklye *fortune*. And if so be that ye her say that be with him in his service and compaignye, trust than verely tha . the judgement of astronomyers hee shal come to his desires.

Astrologers to be consulted as to the chances of De la Pole's success.

Item, W. Huse said he wold to no service, if he might know that . . . . fortunate, and that he wold shortlye com. And I said the uttremes . . . knowleg that I cowde gete he shuld have hit shortly after. And . . delivred he me his tokens.

Item, he shewde me in the Towre that he was acerteyned how that E[dmund] within v. or vj. nyghts of his departing bankketid prively in a place in London with lord marques,[1] lord Essex, lord William of Devonshire, and leffed them ther and departid, and with hym Sir Thomas Grene. And tha[t] this was commyn to the kinges knowleg, he bad me shew hym. And so [I] ded; and his answer was, "it happed soo often tymes that we wer in such compaignye to geder, but to say they knew of my departing that I p . . . you they ded not, and Sir Tho. Grene was in no such compaignyon."

Suspicions created by his departure.

Item, Ed. de la Poul shewde me that he said to my lord marques and lo[rd William] when he was apointed to ther unwitting to departe, "Sirs, I have geven to either of you an horse. I wil advise you take them by . . . . and send to my stable." And who had them I woot not.

Item, I showd to Ed. that I understode by the said Huse that to litil afor his departing he shuld have dynyd in Warwik Lane witherl of Devonshir, and

[1] Thomas Grey, first marquis of Dorset.

that therle cam unto his uttre jayet to receif hym A.D. 1503. with gret reverence, for[1] the which it is thought in many mens myndes that your jornee was not unknown to hym, but he was therunto agreable, and also that ye shuld apoint you to land in his countree, or nygh to him. Hee ansuerd no mor but this, "I see weill ther ys many praty castinges of eyes made to eny cowntenanse that was shewde me; but no force . . . . . . let them judge by utward cowntenanse what they wil."

Item, forasmoch as I cowde gete noo counseil of the astronomyers, bicause they had not his nativite like as I promysed, I kept me from his compaignye, and by rapports of such newes as I hard, gate the most favor I cowde of hym and his; and thes newes, specialy such as wer eny thing thankful and secrete, John Chambrelen shewde me them to the entent I shuld send them to hym.

Item, he bad me shew hym that Hourts was a bought to do hym a grotter displaisir than was the deliverance of the prisonner, and how Hourts servant and John Brit had ben in England with the kinges grace.

Item, hee gave Gelikin warning in Lent last passed that Will'm Cowper was a bought to get away the shipp maister, and at that tyme Ed. wold not byleve hit. Afterwards fro tyme to tyme, as the said Cowper cam to sollicite the same purpose, he shewde hit sum tym to Gelikyn, and sum tyme to me; so that Ed., wenyng that all thies advertysements had comen fro me, gave me grete thanks.

Item, he shewde Gelikin that Wilshire[2] had fro the king pardones for Edward Awnsham and Derick. And Gelkin desired me that I wold write hit to Acon, by-

---

[1] *for*] This word struck out with the pen.

[2] Sir John Wiltshire. See p. 224.

A.D.1503? cause his messager lay seck of thapes. And Ed. wrot a gain to Gilkin and me, and bad us speke no mor of Edward nor Derick, for he knew all that matier.

Item, Ed. sent to me that I wold purvey hym a crosbow of Bruxells or of Andewarp, making to the weight of iiij.li. And by cause I had noo money I shewde this to John Chambrelen, and he spake to Richard Symonds bedell of the English nation to espye hym a gode bow for asmoch as he cowde skill of a bow. And so he ded, and John Chambrelen paied therfor xij.s. flemmysh; and I sent hit to hym and shewde hym a welwiller of his had paied therfor which at that tyme wold be nameles.

Item, at the retornyng of my messager which of Sir Ro. Cursun byhalf shewde me that in breve tyme they wold depart fro thens, I, to the entent I myght know wheder they wold departe, went to Acon, and ther likewise as I shewde to the kinges grace Ed. shewde me. And at that tyme cowde I gete noo knowleg of his aied, ner of the countre ther he loked for his ayed, ner of than shipping ner of his conforte at his landing, but hee desired me labor to the astronomyer to know what day wer most expedient and surest for hym to make a privey jorney, and bringing that day I shuld know mor of his jorney. And at that tyme I advised hym as thus; "For eny povertie or nedynes make noon hasty passage without ye be assured to passe strongely or ellys to fynde them byfor you in England that ye be assured of shall ayed and strength you sufficiently a gaynst all that shal make resistence; and cast not a way your self for hastynes and without favor of astats. Trust not the comyns, for in them without theyr hedys never was ner shalbe stedfastnes." And he said, "Goo a bought that, I desire you, and herafter ye shal know that shal content you."

Item, he bad me at my commyng to Malyns speke with Gilkyn . . . . . of hym he said, "I shuld know tidings fro the countres he had . . . . . . ben yn." And I ded speke with hym, and he shewd me . . . that seith the tyme of the lege he had ben with king of [Romans] and that the king gave hym answers to such as he cam froo th . . . . nether for lege nor seal they shuld mystrust hym, for his cos[in] of Suffolch ayed shuld not be dymynyshed, ner his jorney by on howr for that bond. A.D. 1503.

Item, Ed. shewd me that it was rapported to hym how th . . . . knyghts of the North shuld be prisonners in the Towre. He desir[ed me] to make all the diligens I cowde to send hym ther names and . . . .; yet I sent hym no word therof, for asmoch as I have ben a . . . . . . and Barough ever sith All Halowmasse.

---

## XXV.

### Warrant of Maximilian.

[MS. in Record Office.]

A.D. 1503 3 July. For a payment to be made in behalf of Edmund De la Pole.

Wir, Maximilian, von Gotes genaden Romischer Kuning, zuallentzeiten merer des Reichs, zu Hungern, Dalmacien, Croacien, Eertzheztog zu Osterreich, Hertzog zu Burgundi, zu Brabant, und Phaltzgrave, &c., Einbieten unnserm getreuwen lieben Martan Aichorn unnserm Camermaister zu Innsprugg unser gnad, und alles gut. Als unnser und des Reichs lieber getreuwer-

---

#### Translation.

We, Maximilian, by the grace of God king of the Romans, perpetual augmenter of the kingdom, of Hungary, Dalmatia, and Croatia, archduke of Austria, duke of Burgundy, of Brabant, and Palsgrave, &c., send to our faithful and beloved Martin Aichorn, our chamberlain at

A.D. 1503. 3 July. * * *[1] burger zu Ach den Hertzogn van Suffocq, dasebst zu Ach von unnsern wegen ab gesprochen hat, nemlich umb zwaytausend gulden Reinisch; Demnach Emphelhen wir dir mit ernnst daz dw dem bemelten * * *[1] solich zwaytausend gulden Reinich von unnsern Reuntu, und gulten deines Empfangs, von Weichenechtn schierest kunftig uber ain Jaer, gegen seiner quittung ausrichtest und bezallest. So zollen dir dieselben zway tausendt gulden auf dits unnser geschefft, und die berurt quittung in deiner Rayttung gelegt und ab gezogen werdn; und tu duest daran unnser Ernstlicher maynung segen.

Zu Fuessen am drittn tag des monats Julij, anno Domini funffzechnhundert und in drittn, unnserer Reiche des Romschen im achzechendn, und des Hungrischn im vierzechnden Jaren.

---

Innspruck, our grace, &c. Whereas our and the kingdom's beloved and faithful * *[1], burgess of Aix, has asked the duke of Suffolk there at Aix for 2,000 Rhenish florins on our account; therefore we earnestly request you that you settle and pay such 2,000 Rhenish florins within a year from Christmas, next ensuing, for his acquittance. And the same 2,000 florins for this our business; and the aforesaid acquittance shall be placed to your discharge and taken off. And therein you shall give us singular satisfaction.

At Fuessen, on the 3d day of the month of July, 1503, the 18th year of our reign of the Romans, and the 14th of Hungary.

---

[1] Blank in MS.

## XXVI.

### Flamank's Information.

[MS. in Record Office.]

To the Kynges Most Noble Grace. A.D. 1503?

About the last day of Septembre last past, beyng in a secrett counter within your deputie[1] is place at Calis, he, Sir Hughe Conway, your treserer ther, and Sir Sampson Norton, master porter of that your sayd toune, cald to them my brodre William Nanfan and me. Then said my master your depute to us, "Sirs, we must comyn here now of many great matres touchyng the kyngis grace and the surtie of this hys toune of Calis. Therfore by cause ye be next unto me, I must somtyme put you in tryst more then other. Ye shall hyre here thees matrys that we intend to comyn of; but first ye shall be boythe sworen upon a boke that ye shall never utter nothyng that is now here spoken, without it be to the kyngis grace yf nede shall require, or els to non lyvyng creature." Then after many matris spoken by my master your depute and resonned to the same by your treserer and porter, wiche matres and wherof they were I ame and shalbe [ready][2] to shew to your hygnes at suche tyme or tymes that best shall plese your grace that I so do.

Then seid Sir Hughe Conwaye, "Master depute, yf ye knew as moche as I do, ye wolde saye that ye hade asgrett cause to take kepe to your sylfe as ony lyvyng creature; and therto ye be asmuche bownden to thank God for that ye have askaped hetherto as ye have, for I know thoos persons that have be sett to murdre you, and by whoos cause and menys they so dyde." Mi master askyd hym what they were he wold then shew hym, but seid that he wold shew hym more of that mater at a nodre tyme when we shall have more

Sir Hugh Conway cautions the deputy of Calais against conspiracies.

[1] Sir Richard Nanfan.

[2] Om. in MS.

A.D. 1503? layser. So for what he said now ame I and master porter asfyr into the daunce as ye be, for I promyse you of my faythe that all thoos that be and were profferred hydre into ther romes by my Lord Chamberlayn[1] shall never love non of us, and specially thoos that were his houssold servauntis tofore. The cause whij they soo do I cannot tell, but for that we folow the kyngis plesure and so wildo. Therfor good yt is that we see to our owne surtie, aswell as fore the surtie of this the kyngis toune, that yt may be sure to hym and his, wat world so ever shall hapen to fall here after, to have in remembrans that the gretter and more partie of thoos that be in the kyngis retenu here be of[2] my lordis prefferment. Also loke hoo stronge he is in the kyngis courte of his houshold servauntis for the more partie of his garde be of thoos that were my Lord Chamberlayn servauntis tofore. and hard hyt is to know mennys myndis yf God should send a soden change, as he hayth here tofore.

Then said my master, your depute, that "I darst reseve the sacrament that my lord is as true to the kyngis grace as ony man lyvyng;" and in lyke wyse seid master porter.

Item, my master your depute, said, "My lord Chamberlayn was very shlake in oone jorny, wherwith I knowell that the kingis grace was discontent; for and he had done his parte welle, the Cornyshe men hade never made the kynge feld at Blake hethe, but had all ben distroyed longe before ther comyng thedre, that I knowell the kyngis grace hade lever hade be done then. xx$^{ml}$. li for his honour.

Item, after many wordes spoken, Sir Hughe Conwey seid, "Mastres, I hanot spoken theys wordis for no untrothe that I do thynk be now in my lord Cham-

[1] Giles lord Daubeney, formerly deputy of Calais.

[2] *of* repeated in MS.

berlayn. for I dar say now as ye do that he lovyth the kynge aswell as any man cando lyvyng; but yt haith be sene in tymys past that chaynge of worldis hayth caused chaynge of mynd." A.D.1503?

Item, the same Sir Hughe said, that "we be here now togedres the kyngis true servauntis to lyve and dy, and also to spend all that we have in the world to do his grace servis. Therfore watt so ever we speke or comyn for his surtie, and for the surtie of this his toune, canbe no tresone; so good yt is that we loke and speke of thyngis to come as well as thoos present. I do speke this for a cause that is good that we loke sadly to, for the kyngis grace is but a weke man and syklow, not lykly to be no longe lyvis man. Yt ys not longe sithens his hygnes was syke and lay then in his maner of Wangsted. Hyt hapned the same tyme me to be emonges many grett personages, the whiche fele in communicacion of the kyngis grace and of the world that shouldbe after hym yf hys grace hapned to depart." Then he said that some of them spake of my lorde of Buckyngham, sayng that he was a noble man and woldbe a ryall ruler. Other ther were that spake, he said, in lykwyse of your troytor Edmond De la Pole, but none of them, he said, that spake of my lord prynce. Then said master porter to hym, "Have ye never broken to the kyngis grace of this mater?" Then said Sir Hughe Conway to hym agayn, "I pray you souffer me to tell forthe my talle, for I amnot yet athe ynd. Ye have in mynde wat that I have shewed you touchyng this matris. Of my fayth, in lyke wyse sythens my comyng I have shewed the same to Sir Nycholas Voux, lieutenant of Gysnes, and to Sir Antony Broune, lieutenant of the castell here, and they answeryd me both this, that they had to good holdes to resorte unto, the wiche thay seid sholdbe sure to make their paxce, ho so ever the worlde tourne." Then my master youre depute, and master porter,

The king's health being bad, men in England spoke differently as to who should succeed him.

A.D. 1503? boyth said to hym that he could no lase doo but shew thes matres unto youre hyghnes. He said that, "Hyt ware good that the kyngis grace knew thees sayyngis, but asyet I have not shewed hym no part theroff, nother never I wildo." Then said master porter to hym angrely, and sware by Godis precious soule he be the more to blame to kepe suche matris from his hygnes; and in lyke wyse said my master your depute, and all we beyyng there.

But it is dangerous to disclose such matters.

Item, after many wordis spoken touchyng the same, Sir Hughe Conway said, "Yf ye knew kynge Harry oure master as I doo, ye woldbe ware how that ye brake to hym in ony suche matres, for he wold take yt to be said but of envy, yll wille and malis. Then should anion have blame and no thanke for his trouth and good mynd; and that have I welle proved here to fore in lyke causes, for that tyme that the lord Lovell lay in Colchester a trysty frend of myn came to me and shewed me in councell the day and tyme of hys departyng, and of alle hys purpos. I was sworen to hym that I should never utter thys to man lyvyng to hys hurte; butt yet forthwith after wardis, by cause of myn alegens, I came to Sir Raynold Bray and shewed hym all as is abowe, and forthwith he said that Master Bray shewed the same unto the kyngis.[1] Wheruppon I was brought byfore hys hygnes and I affirmed all to be true as my seid frend hade shewed; and the kynge said that hyt could not be so, and resoned with me alwayes to the contrary of my said sayynges. At last he asked what he was that told me thus tale of hys departyng. I prayed hys hygnes to pardon me, for I said that I was sworen to hym that I should never utter hym, to be drawen with wyld horsses; wherewith the kynge was angry and displesed

When Conway gave information of lord Lovel's intrigues, the king was displeased with him for refusing to name his informant.

[1] Sic.

with me for my good wille. I shall no more tempt hym wile I lyve in suche causes." Then said master porter, "I thynk that ye drast never speke thees wordes to the kyngis grace as ye have rehersed them now here," and he sware many grett othes that he dyde. A.D. 1503?

Item, my master youre deputie said that "I knowell that the kyngis hyghnes is harde of credens in suche matres; and that knowe ye," he said, "master porter, aswell as I, for how longe was yt er hys grace and hys councell wold belyve ony thyng of untrothe to be in Sir Jame[1] Tyrell; and some said I dyd seke to do hym hurte for malis. It was long before he doubted Sir James Tyrell's fidelity.

"Item, a nodre tyme I dyd wryt unto his hygnes that oone hade shewed me that Sir Robert Clyfford should say here in this toune to a lady that Perken Warbeke was kynge Edwardes sone. Never wordes went coldre to my hart then they dyd. Hys hygnes sent me sharpe wrytyng agay that he wold have the prouffe of this matier. I hade no wittnes then but my sylfe; but as hyt hapned afterwardes I caused hym by good crafte to confesse the same he had said to me be fore hym that was marshell here at that tyme, and els I hade lykly to be putt to a grett plonge for my trothe. At the last al thought that hit was not to shewe this to youre grace without better proffe; yet master porter said yt was grett pitty that the kinge dyd not tryst hys true knyghtes better, and to geve them credens in suche thynges as they should shew for hys surtie, for grett hurt may come by that mene." Sir Robert Clifford had declared Perkin Warbeck to be the son of Edward IV.

Item, after this the treserer said, "Master depute and master porter, what daunger be we in now, remembryng all thynges welle, for we have no suche holdes to resort unto as thees other men have, consydryng also oure many enymies that we have in this toune and

[1] Sic.

A.D. 1503? els where that wilbe glade to distroy and murdre us all yf other should come to the kyngis grace then wele. And for trothe I knowell that he cannot longe contynu for hyt is wryten of hym that he shall no longer raygne then dyd kynge Edward, wiche," he said, "was but xxij^te yere and lytle more." Then said my master youre depute. "I by sherwe hys hart that so dyde wryte, and also I pray God send all them that thynk the same tobe true a shorte shamfull dethe." The treserer said agayn, "We may not be angry in this matris when we shall comyn for the surtie of oure sylfes aswell as of this the kyngis toune, for I thynk not veryly thus to be all true that I have said, but I knowell that every manys mortall and must dij, and that that I have said I shall shew you my boke that shall declare you the same playnly to be as I have said and spoken." Master porter said, "Then I pray you, master tresere, brene that boke, and a vayngens take the first wryter."

A book of prophecy declares that Henry VII will not reign longer than Edward IV. did.

Item, then said my master youre depute to master Convaye, "I pray you leve thys profyciyng of the kynge, for ye speke of thynges that I never kepe never hire nor see, and that my prayer is that I never leve day nother oure longer then the kyngis grace and hys chyldre shall have and inyoye the realme of Inglond." And likevise spake master porter and we all beyng there.

There is danger to the town of Calais as long as Lady Lucy is in the castle.

Item, then said master Conway, "All this that I have spoken is to thentent to have all thynges to be made sure for the kynge and hys chyldre, and specially this hys toune of Calis; and that cane never be done without good and wyse comunycacion had of the same byfore; for I tell you for surtie that that shall never be aslonge as the lady Luse shalbe in the castell, that we cane sure the kynge of thys hys toune, for the castell is the kay of this toune; he that is therin beyng of a contray mynd may lett men inow in

A.D. 1503?

oone nyght to distrij us alle wyle we shalbe in oure beddes sleepyng. I know, masters," he said, "wat longeth to suche matres better then ye do; therfore I pray you seuffer me for to speke. Lett not us thynk the contrarij but and the kyngis were ons departyd, she beyng in the castell here and Edmond De la Pole hire cosen at hys lyberte. but that she wolde helpe hym in hys causes with all hire poure and to lett hym come into this toune by the postren of the castell to the distruccion of us alle. Remenbre welle how ny that Kent is hydre, wat a lyans thay be of there." He spake of Sir Edward Poynynges, Sir Rychard Gylforth, Sir Thomas Bouchir. Wat he said of ther demener, master porter, yf youre grace exammen hym cane shew youre hygnes better then I can do. Also he said, "Remenbre all the company of this the kynges retenu here, wat ille mynde they bere unto us that wilbe all redy then to folow hyre mynd as they doo now, and to doo us the most myschyffe thay cando." and named Rychard Wodhouse and John Clynton speris. Item, Raynold of the Chambre, a constable of the retenu, with other. "Thees men," he said, "never lovyd the kyngis grace, nor never woldo, with many mo of the same mynd within this toune. Now I have shewed all the wyrst. This be a sherwde company sett in yll mynde. Dout ye not but this will falle in dede but good provysion be made for the remedy in tyme."

If the king were to die she would help her cousin Edmund De la Pole.

Item, then said my master your depute, "Yf suche thyng shall happen, as I pray God that I never leve to se, the kyngis grace to departe byfore me, but and yt please God that he shall so do, to be for the surte and use of my lorde prynce and for all my mastris childre to have this toune alle tymes at ther owne wille and rule; and rather then yt shouldbe otherwyse I hade lever souffer dethe. And we do wysly, I doutnot but by good counsell we shalbe able

A.D. 1503? by good polici to distrii alle the captayns and ryngledres that be of yll and contrarij mynde; that done, tho other wilbe good to rule. So I tryst that we shall alwayes kepe the toune and marches to the kyngis use and hys." More of this touchyng this last artycle was spoken, wiche is not now perfetly in my remenbrans; but well I remenbre that everyman named oone to ryde the wrold of, yf suche daunger should come to pase, as I tryst never to se by Godis grace, whoo ever preserve youre hygnes.

Item, by the fayth that I bere unto my Savyour Cryst Jhesu and to youre hygnes, this byfore rehersed was the sayyng of every of them as nyghe as I kan call now to my remenbrans.

Recapitulation of the charge.

Thees folwyng be the wordys that Sir Hughe Conway dyd speke in the hyryng of Sir Rychard Nanfan, knyght, youre depute of Calis, Sir Sampson Norton, your porter there, Welyam Nanfan and John Flamank.

First, he seid that the kynge is but a weke man and syklow, and not lykly longe to contynue; therfore good yt is that we see for oure owne surties aswell asfor the surtie of this hys toune of Calis.

Item, he said that my lorde chamberlayn was a stronge and mighti man of men in the kyngis courte aswell as within this the kyngis toune of Calis and els were, and said, "Put yt that he be true as ony man lyvyng to the kyngis grace now, yet chaynge of worldes haith caused change of men myndes, and that haith be sene many tymes.

Item, he said that the firthermust that he could ever se or rede of the kyngis grace was that he should raygne but as longe as kynge Edward dyde, whiche he said was but xxij^ti yere or lytle more.

Item, he said that when my master youre depute, and master porter wolde have hym, he wolde brynge hys boke of profici to Welyam Nanfan, and he should rede yt, wiche should playnly declare the same. A.D. 1503?

Item, he seid that the kyngis grace lay seke aboute a iiij. yeres past in hys maner of Wangsted;[1] "At wiche tyme," he seid, "fortuned me to be in the company of many dyvers and grett personages, the wiche as at that tyme hapned to commune of the kynge oure master, and wat world shouldbe yf hys grace deperted, and hoo should have the rule in Inglond then. Some, he said, spoke of my lorde of Buckyngham, that said that he woldbe a ryall ruler, and so gave hym grett prees; and other of them in lykwyse spake of the traytour Edmond De la Pole, but non of them, he said, spake of my lorde prynce."

Item, he said that he hade shewed all this mater to Sir Nychulas Voux, lieutenant of Gysnes, and to Sir Antony Browne, lieutenant of the castell in Calis, and said that ther answere to hym was saying that they had too good sure holdes to resort unto, the wiche should make ther peaxce hoo ever the worlde tourne.

Item, he said that the lady Luce was a proude hij myndyd woman, and lovyth not the kyngis grace, and that Edmond De la Pole was hyr kynnysman, to whom, he said, she wildo all the plesure and helpe she cando in the wrold, and that yf any thyng should come to youre grace other then wele he doutednot but she wolde lett hym by the postren of the castell to the distruccion of us all.

The cause and ground whij and to what intent he spake all thees wordes by me here wryten my master, youre depute, and Sir Sampson Norton, whoo herd all the same, and soo dyde Weliam Nanfan in lykwyse,

[1] It appears from the Privy Purse expenses of Henry VII. (Excerpta Historica, 123) that the king was at Wanstead in December 1499, which was probably the time referred to.

A.D.1503? that cane shew and declare alle unto youre hygnes moche better then I cando. Butt by the faythe that I owe and bere unto my Savyoure Cryst Jhesu, and to your most noble grace, I herde hym speke all thees wordes in ther presens, with more then my poure mynd cane serve me to declare unto [your][1] hygnes.

Item, I have herd master porter and Welyam Nanfan saij dyvers tymes, that they have herd Sir Hughe Conway say that ther shouldbe never more popys in Rome after hym that is now, nother kynges in Inglond after youre grace.

Item, upon a tyme I brought a letter to Sir Hughe Conway, that Sir Nycholas Voux had sent to my master. After that he had rede the same letter to theend, he toke me by the arme and said to me, "Brodre Flamank, thij master and master porter benot aswyse as I wold that they were; for now may ye see that other men cane have knowlyche dayly of every thyng or grett mater that is done in Inglond and we cane have no knowlych of nothyng but by them. This is not good, nother no sure waye for us. I have often tymes spoken to them to have a sure and a wyse man to lij a boute the court styll at oure coste and charges; he may all tymes send us how the world goyth. I pray you tell them that I wille bere halfe yf that hyt should cost me $x^{li}$ a yere, rather then to leve this to be done, for God knoweth how sodenly a change may fall;" with many more wordes touchyng grett peryll that my fall yf this be not don.

Youre most lauly sugett & servaunt,

JOHN FLAMANK.

[1] Om. in MS.

## XXVII.

### Ferdinand II. to Henry VII.

[Orig. in Record Office.]

A.D. 1504. 24 Nov.

Serenissimo principi Henrico, Dei gratia Angliæ regi, fratri nostro dilectissimo, Ferdinandus eadem gratia Rex Castellæ, Legionis, Aragonum, et utriusque Siciliæ, Granatæ, etc., salutem et prosperorum successuum incrementa. Accepimus litteras vestras quas Ferdinandus Dux orator noster ad nos attulit, qui ea omnia fideliter nobis retulit quæ secum ac cum doctore De la Puebla, oratore nostro, super materias spectantes ad augmentum affinitatis et amicitiæ nostræ et ad reliqua negotia contulistis. Mirum itaque in modum in primis delectati sumus cum certiores facti sumus de salute et prosperitate vestra. Propter nimium enim amorem quem erga vos gerimus non minus vitam et prosperitatem vestram quam propriam nostram exoptamus. Oblectati præterea sumus de salute principum, communium filiorum nostrorum; nam quamvis de illorum ac vestra incolumitate et secundis rebus sæpe per litteras istic factas certiores reddamur, cum id ipsum per personas quæ oculata fide omnia nobis particulariter enarrant, uti nunc Fernandus Dux fecit, ingenti afficimur gaudio. Quamobrem obnixe vos rogamus ut semper de salute et incolumitate vestra nos certiores reddere velitis. Quantum vero ad dictas materias quæ ad augmentum affinitatis et amicitiæ nostræ attinent, consideratis ingenti inter nos amore arctissimo affinitatis et amicitiæ nostræ vinculo, cognita præterea magna virtute vestra, lætabimur mirum in modum, cum affinitas et amicitia nostra modis omnibus quibus poterunt augeantur, atque id quamcitius fieri poterit ut fiat et concludatur curandum est. Et quoniam ad ea quæ circa hoc per eundem Ferdinan-

A.D. 1504. 24 Nov.

Ferdinand sends to De Puebla the bull of dispensation for the marriage of Henry and Catherine.

dum Ducem oratorem nostrum nobis referre fecistis, præfato doctori De la Puebla, oratori nostro copiose respondimus, obnixe vos rogamus ut illi plenam et indubiam fidem exhibeatis. Cæterum eidem doctori De la Puebla oratori nostro dispensationis bullam mittimus, quam sanctissimus papa noster concessit ad matrimonium celebrandum dictorum principum communium filiorum nostrorum, eidemque super ea re scribimus quæ ipse vobis referet, cui iterum ut fidem adhibere velitis oramus. Demum, priusquam Ferdinandus Dux huc appulisset, redditæ nobis fuerunt litteræ vestræ quas Anglico harum latori ad nos deferendas dederatis. In quibus mentio fit litterarum quas a nobis petitis circa vestrorum subditorum oneranda navigia in regnis et dominiis nostris. Primum igitur ut vobis morem geramus, tum ob ingentem amorem et indissolubile affinitatis et amicitiæ vinculum quæ inter nos sunt, tum quia volumus quod subditi vestri ita in regnis[1] et dominiis nostris tractentur acsi nostri essent subditi, tum etiam quia pro certo habemus quod absque ullo discrimine nostri subditi tamquam vestri in regno et dominiis vestris tractabuntur, litteras nostras super id ut petitis in pelle et Latina lingua scriptas et nostris manibus signatas, sigilloque nostro plumbeo munitas vobis mittimus, quarum vigore subditi vestri navigia sua et subditorum nostrorum libere onerare poterunt in omnibus regnis et dominiis nostris; quas quidem litteras per omnes portus regnorum et dominiorum nostrorum publicari jussimus, ut omnibus notæ sint et per omnes serventur. Serenissime rex, frater noster dilectissime, Omnipotens Deus regiam personam et statum vestrum diutissime et felicissime custodiat ad vota. Datum in oppido

[1] Indistinct.

Metinæ Del Campo, vicesima quarta die mensis Novembris, anno millesimo quingentesimo quarto. A.D. 1504. 24 Nov.

Yo el Rey,
Almaçan Secretarius.

*Addressed:* Serenissimo principi Henrico, Dei gratia Angliæ Regi, fratri nostro dilectissimo.

Endorsed in the hand of Sir Thomas Wriothesley, "Ferdinandus king of Castelle to the kinges Maᵗᵉ." This endorsement was doubtless made about the time of Henry VIII.'s divorce from Catherine of Arragon.

---

## XXVIII.

### The Bishop of Worcester to Henry VII.

[Orig. in Record Office.]

A.D. 1505. 17 March.

The Pope desires him to go to England with the dispensation for the marriage; a copy of which had been sent to Spain for the consolation of Queen Isabella on her death bed.

Sacra Regia Majestas, post humillimam commendationem, &c. Jam arbitror intellexisse potuit majestas vestra per breve apostolicum, et per instructiones ad Johannem Paulum fratrem meum una cum ultimis litteris missis, placuisse summo pontifici ut ad majestatem vestram venirem, et bullas originales dispensationis matrimonialis afferrem, legitimasque causas dilationis earundem, et animi dolorem ac molestiam quam Sanctitas sua contraxit ex transmissione ab Hispaniis in Angliam copiæ dictarum bullarum, quam ad ultimam consolationem serenissimæ ac Catholicissimæ dominæ Helisabeth Hispaniarum reginæ morientis oratori istic suo concessisset sub fide et sacramento silentii ac taciturnitatis, coram majestati vestræ exponerem, cum nonnullis aliis privatis negotiis, quæ mihi in mandatis datura erat; et insuper sacrum ensem, quo potissimum majestatem vestram ex omnibus principibus Christianis hoc anno insignire voluit eidem præsentarem. Sane si quid unquam votis optare, vel

A.D. 1505. 17 March. non immerito forsitan expectare potui ex hoc pontificatu Sanctissimi Domini nostri, cui me Altissimus affinitatis vinculo astringere dignatus est, satisfactum est amplissime desiderio et expectationi meæ, assequutus sum cumulate, et supra votum quod continue expectavi ex eo tempore ex quo aliquid esse incepi sola gratia et benignitate majestatis vestræ. Tandem concessum est creaturæ vestræ ad auctorem factoremque suum redire, et eum coram intueri revisere et venerari, cui non solum fortunas et facultates debeo, sed quod vivo, quod spiro, quod omnino aliquid sum eidem acceptum refero. Quam profectionem meam ad majestatem vestram, quoniam præ cæteris omnibus mihi gratissimam habeo, brevi accelerabo, et intra paucos dies ex Urbe me expediam. Non dubito quin adventum meum clementia vestra pro sua erga me benignitate et humanitate lætanter suscipere dignetur, et humilem creaturam suam eo vultu aspicere quo me ab humo tollere dignata est, et tot immortalibus beneficiis, honoribus ac dignitatibus honestare. Quibus cum nullæ gratiæ meæ pares esse possint, silebo potius quam infinita ejus erga me merita inepte recensendo minora faciam; sed me ipsum personamque meam eidem coram reverenter tradam; suum est quicquid ago, quicquid cogito, quicquid cupio. Rogo non verba, quæ debitum meum exprimere non possunt, sed corpus, spiritum et animum qui totus ex illa pendet, benigne accipiat, et ita de me sentiat, meipsum mihi ipsi tum demum placere posse, si cum ad illam venero inveniam aliquid a me factum quod majestati vestræ placere intelligam. Quam opto ut Altissimus diutissime conservet felicem, et cui interim me quam humillime commendo.

Novitatum nihil in præsenti est quod auribus majestatis vestræ dignum putem, præterquam quod superioribus diebus Sanctissimus Dominus noster in ægrotatiunculam levem incidit, quam, acceptis quibusdam pilulis, statim rejecit, atque in pristinam salutem continuo Sanctitas sua restituta est. In rebus autem quæ Sanctæ Romanæ Ecclesiæ statum concernunt Sanctitas sua die noctuque vigilantia quadam mira repetitura creditur quicquid occupatum superioribus annis fuerat, et nunc cum Venetis egit ut magna terrarum pars quas sibi ab ecclesia verterant, eidem Sanctæ Romanæ Ecclesiæ restituatur. Reliquum est ut me iterum clementissimæ majestati vestræ quam humillime commendem. Romæ die xvij. Martii I.D.V. A.D. 1505. 17 March.

Excellentissimæ Majestatis Vestræ

Factura et humillimus subditus,

SIL. EPISCOPUS WIGORNIENSIS.

Post scripta venit in mentem meam dignum esse ut majestatem vestram certiorem facerem de legatis sive oratoribus regis Poloniæ, qui superioribus diebus de consuetudine in Urbem suscepti, primam eorum audientiam a Beatissimo Patre nostro in publico auditorio die x. Martii superioris habuerunt, atque ipsi Sanctissimo Domino nostro obtulerunt varia munera, et quæ summam duorum millium ducatorum caperent.

*Addressed*, Sacræ Regiæ Majestati.

Endorsed in a 16th century hand, apparently Brian Tuke's, "the xvijth of March 1515."

## XXIX.

### Cardinal Hadrian de Corneto to Henry VII.

[Holograph in Record Office.]

A.D. 1505. 23 Oct.

Had urged the Pope to punish the forgery of the bull of the bishop of St. David's;

Sacra Regia Majestas, humillimas commendationes Quoniam his mensibus R. dominus episcopus Wintoniensis[1] scripsit Sanctissimo Domino nostro et mihi de illa falsitate comperta istic in bullo episcopi Menevensis,[2] rogans quod sua Sanctitas pro justitia et honore suo et Sedis Apostolicæ provideret ut illi falsarii punirentur et non transirent sine debita animadversione, et hoc ipsum episcopus Lincolniensis[3] etiam suæ Sanctitati et mihi per proprios cursores eorum sumptibus scripsit; et hoc fecerunt tanquam boni episcopi et pro fervore justitiæ et pro juramento quo astringuntur papæ et Ecclesiæ. Ego etiam ab illis et eadem ratione præstiti juramenti, et quia Polidorus scripserat mihi per plures suas, quarum copiam mitto majestati vestræ, quod tentaverat mentem vestram et eratis contentus, et ita volebatis quod justitia fieret; et quia etiam Sanctissimus Dominus noster, his omnibus lectis et visis, sic voluit et mandavit; propterea scripsi majestati vestræ et diligentiam adhibui ut omnis hæc falsitas in lucem prodiret, et veritas claresceret, non credens neque credere debens quod vestræ majestati in aliquo quod placuit displicuisset. Et hæc est mera et pura veritas. Quare vestra majestas dignetur neque ipsis dominis episcopis neque mihi, servitoribus vestris fidelibus, aliquid imputare.

but, as he now understands.

Postea enim intellexi per literas meorum vestram majestatem mutasse propositum, et ubi prius rogabat

[1] Richard Fox.

[2] Robert Sherborne, afterwards bp. of Chichester, was made bp. of St. David's on the 12 April 1505.

[3] William Smith.

ut fieret justitia, nunc . . . . . .[1] nia feci et faciam pro viribus, et quantum in me erit, ut vestra majestas cognoscat non stare per me quo minus sibi satisfiat. Et jam fui cum pontifice et usque ad reprehensionem oravi ut illis parceret, nec de cætero quoad potero desistam ut, si possibile sit, pontificis hactenus immutabile propositum flectatur. Et in hoc et in omnibus conabor obsequi voluntati et mandatis vestræ majestatis, cui me humillime commendo. Romæ, xxj Octobris, 1505.

A.D. 1505. 23 Oct. the king wishes them mercifully dealt with, has interceded for them.

Vestræ Majestatis
Servitor humilis,
HADRIANUS CARDINALIS S. CHRYSOGONI.

Nova nulla hic sunt, nisi de matrimonio Hispaniæ, et multi multa loquuntur de vestra majestate, sed quid sit verum adhuc nos latet. Veneti continuant occupare illas duas Ecclesiæ civitates, tamen sunt valde territi de pace ista quæ dicitur inter hos duos reges, et etiam acceperunt magnam jacturam in aromatibus quæ passim veniant de illis insulis per Portugallenses repertis. Florentini quiescunt sine civitate Pisarum. P[a]pa, intellecta compositione hujus pacis quæ dicitur facta inter istos duos reges, dixit mihi et multis aliis cardinalibus dum essemus in civitate Corneti, in qua ego natus sum, "Isti duo reges diviserunt sibi vestimenta mea, sed illis significari fecimus aliqua super his. Videbimus quæ sequentur." Postea dixit mihi soli post cœnam quod offerebant Ecclesiæ suum annuum censum, et quod habebat literas a Gallia quod vestra majestas dabat illustrissimo principi suo nato illam puellam Danguleme[2] in uxorem. Dixi non posse me hoc credere cum jam essent contracta sponsalia per verba

[1] Paper gone.

[2] Margaret, daughter of Charles duke of Angoulême, sister of Francis I. See State Papers of Henry VIII., vol. viii. p. 663.

A.D. 1505. 23 Oct. de præsenti cum filia Hispaniæ, media dispensatione suæ Sanctitatis, et quod hoc . . . . . . . [1] regi Hispaniæ. Respondit quod scribitur sibi quod in hoc consentit ipse rex Hispaniæ. Nunc vestra majestas habet quæ nova audivi a sua metuendissima Sanctitate. Die xxiij Octobris, Romæ

Vestræ Majestatis humilis Servitor,
HADRIANUS CAR[lis]. S. CHRYSOGONI.

*Ex literis Polidori ad Cardinalem S[ti]. Chrysogoni datis xxv. Junii 1505.*

Tentavi primum voluntatem regis ut casu quo Sanctissimus Dominus noster provideri vellet, sicut certo opus est, recte sciret quod regia majestas pro justitia favebit. Die xxij. præsentis . . . . .[1] tem suam et rem ab ovo narrare cœpi, quæ benigne mihi respondit, dixitque quod parata semper erit favere Sedi Apostolicæ ejusque honorem fovere, et ut nunc Sanctitas sua possit crimen persequi dominus Wintoniensis scripsit Sanctitati suæ rem omnem.

*Ex literis ejusdem, iij. Septembris.*

Comes Nuntius cum literis et brevibus Sanctissimi Domini nostri datis x. Augusti venit huc, quibus lectis statim ivi ad regem et suas reddidi ejus majestati, cui narravi quo studio et juris rigore, ut decet, Sanctissimus Dominus noster persequitur hos falsarios, eamque oravi ut in præsenti idem faceret, quandoquidem majestas sua jam habet negotium in manu sua, sicut illa his diebus prope Gilfort mihi dixit, se desiderare, videlicet, ut pontifex sibi scriberet. Tunc majestas sua multum sane commendavit Sanctissimi Domini nostri justitiam et severitatem in istis

[1] Paper gone

rebus, nam aliter omne decus curiæ Romanæ periret; et dixit se lecturum literas et breve pontificis, mox mihi responsurum. Posthæc sua majestas vocavit me, dicens, "Polidore, ego vidi breve Sanctissimi Domini [nostri et][1] literas cardinalis, et cognovi desiderium pontificis, videlicet ut isti falsarii puniantur sicut merentur; quod dignum et justum est quod pro rei magnitudine egomet unacum consilio meo volo hoc negotium bene examinare, et dum ero Londoni omnia adimplebo, et quod provisum est satis quod isti qui sunt suspecti non fugient. Et ita scribatis cardinali ut nomine meo referat pontifici." Et quia, ut videmus singulis diebus, magna vis est pecuniæ ubique gentium, cavendum est quod Sanctissimus Dominus noster non flectatur literis alicujus hominis quominus hi falsarii puniantur, cum præsertim tota patria hæc rem hanc cognoscat, ut de illa senex, fœmina, puerque loquantur, et certe non possem verbis explicare quibus laudibus domini hujus regni et alii omnes efferant Sanctitatem Domini nostri ejusque [justitiam][1] admirentur, utpote quæ ita præter spem istorum curialium curaverit tueri honorem Sedis Apostolicæ, de qua nonnulli sunt qui adeo male sentiunt, qui omnino credebant quod minima pecunia isti omnes impune evaderent. A.D. 1505. 23 Oct.

*Ex literis ejusdem, xx. Septembris.*

Mater regia, mulier sanctissima, promisit se locuturam cum serenissimo rege ut nullo pacto faveat falsariis, sicut ipsamet scribit in suis literis ad dominationem vestram.

---

[1] Paper gone.

A.D. 1505. 23 Oct.

*Ex literis ejusdem, xxj. Septembris.*

Regia majestas perstat in sententiam in isto negotio falsariorum, et dicit quod non vult impedire justitiam sed ipsamet dabit operam ut examinentur et debita animadversione puniantur.

*Ex literis Johannis Hans alterius ministri mei in Anglia, xvij. Septembris.*

Majestas regia replicavit sæpius quod non oblivis-cerer scribere ad dominationem vestram quod volebat omnino fieri justitiam. "Absit," inquit, "quod velim eam impedire; sed," inquit, "ad Sanctissimum Dominum nostrum scripsi in commendatione Wigorniensis sic . . . .[1] pietate motus, tamen volo expectare responsum a sua Sanctitate priusquam aliud scribam."

*Ex literis ejusdem, xxv. Septembris.*

Die xxij. hujus allocutus sum regiam majestatem, quæ mihi dixit quod isti episcopi dederant cautionem de comparendo esse repræsentando omnes quatuor suæ majestati ad suum beneplacitum sub pœna iiij$^{or}$ milium librarum; item, quod scripserat ad archiepiscopum Cantuariensem et Londoniensem ut exequentur commissionem Sanctissimi Domini nostri, et suam celsitudinem esse dispositissimam omnia agere secundum quod proxime Sanctissimus Dominus noster suis literis jusserit, adeo quod omnis res consistit in responso quod dabit sua Sanctitas.

*Ex literis ejusdem, ultima Septembris.*

Majestas regia iterum atque iterum dixit mihi quod isti non sunt ita culpabiles aut criminosi ut dicitur;

[1] Paper gone.

"quod si ego," inquit sua majestas, "scirem ipsos esse reos talis delicti sibi impositi, ego sum is qui primo animadverterem in eos." Hoc certe sæpius *mihi dixit*, et quod non videbat neque audiebat aliquid fieri in Urbe; in quo certe etiam concordat dominus Wintoniensis qui dixit quod nihil factum est in Urbe de illis incarceratis. "Et quare," inquit, "non fecerunt processum et miserunt huc?" A.D. 1505. 23 Oct.

Sacra regia majestas, omnia ex literis originalibus legi sæpius Sanctissimo Domino nostro qui dici non posset quantum laudaverit vestram majestatem quæ sit ita bene disposita erga justitiam et pro honore Sanctitatis suæ et hujus Sanctæ Sedis, dixitque et jurejurando affirmavit se non posse aut velle aliquo pacto parcere illis falsariis, etiamsi essent sui nepotes; quod etiam scribit per suum breve vestræ majestati, et addidit quod non potest sibi unquam persuadere quod vestra majestas, quæ supradicta omnia dixit et affirmavit, velit favere potius falsariis in tali ac tanto [facinore quam][1] Sedi Apostolicæ in justitia, et quod est et erit semper hujus firmi et immutabilis propositi, et sic mandavit etiam mihi ut scriberem vestræ majestati; et mittit processum authenticum contra eos hic formatum, qui non potuit ob absentiam ipsorum falsariorum plenius formari, scribitque illis archiepiscopo Cantuariensi et Londonensi ac Norwicensi episcopis, expectatque cum summo desiderio et firma opinione quod vestra majestas satisfaciat justitiæ juxta tot promissa vestræ majestatis quæ supradictis literarum clausulis continentur, neque vult audire quenquam pro illis loquentem, et sæpe increpuit diversos qui eos[2] misericordia aut amicitia moti eos[2] commendabant. Et his diebus dum Corneti esset s[ua Sancti]tas et quidam Bartholomæus Dorsini, Lucensis, affinis episcopi Wigorniensis, literas episcopi et majestatis vestræ Sanctitati

[1] Paper gone.

[2] Sic.

A.D. 1505. 23 Oct. suæ reddere vellet, pontifex ei dixit ut si amplius ante conspectum suum accederet cum talibus literis projici eum faceret de fenestris, noluitque literas episcopi accipere; solum illas legit quæ vestra majestas ei mittebat. Postea, die Mercurii, cum accepissem a Johanne Hans literas de ultima Septembris per proprium cursorem mira celeritate allatas, ivi ad Ostiam ubi erat sua Sanctitas, narravique qualiter vestra majestas etiam tertias literas commendatitias scribere pro eis decreverat ad suam Sanctitatem, sua Sanctitas severo vultu et turbato fronte admodum hæc audivit, dixitque eadem, videlicet, quod non posset sibi persuadere quod vestra majestas sit aliud factura quam totiens et ultro dixerit, et quod novit integritatem et constantiam vestræ majestatis, jussitque illi breve ut supra dixi scribi et processum et alia mitti per proprium ac celerrimum cursorem, quem voluit omnia deferre et brevia ad vestram majestatem manibus propriis consignare, aliquidque . . . . . . ministris murmurando suspicari visa est. Credat majestas vestra quod in similibus sua Sanctitas est rigorosa et ut dixi immutabilis, nec est homo vivens qui possit suam Sanctitatem ita deliberatam aliter flectere. Volui omnia vere et seriose scribere vestræ majestati, quæ pro sua sapientia et justitia omnia recte disponet, cui me humillime commendo. Romæ xxiij. Octobris, 1505.

Vestræ Regiæ Majestatis
Humilis Servitor
HADRIANUS CARLIS. STI. CHRYSOGONI.

Sacræ Regiæ Majestati Angliæ.

XXX. A.D. 1505.

EDMUND DE LA POLE TO THOMAS KILLINGWORTH.

[Addit. MS. 18,738. Brit. Mus., f. 8. Holograph.]

TOMAS KELLENGWORT, I prae yov goe yn to Breury-rissceles to the king,[1] and speke yov with my lord Wele, and with ys broder, and recomand me to them, de serreng them to be my govd frendes as my spesale treust ys yn them. And that yt veld ples them to remenber me to the K. And that yt vold ples the K. that ys gras vold be so god lord to me that I met be hovt of thest manse hand, for as I her that ale the land saeys planle he vele nat com to the K. And ef yt be so the K. mae se a lekleode wedder the dewke vele com at hem or nat; stresting my lord my cosons, bovthe my lord Vele and my lord Fennes ys broder the vele[2] have me yn rembererans, as the bovt[3] promes me. I ame her by the kinges comand ment, and ys as glad to do the K. pleser and sarves as onne mane. And sae thest vordes them "Ef I vare yn the fardes yend of the vord, I veld be at ys comand ment to fovelfele ys plessor and comand ment as hone sarvant of ys ys hovs." Marke vele thest and do yt vesle,[4] and planle, with govd and lovle as yov kane.

Also go to yenker Flovrens, and sae I recommand me to hem; and sae to hem that I send yov spesale to hem for my heelepe be chescheng[5] hem to speke to the K. for me, as ys vrytvn be fore; bovt yov mae nat let my lord Vele chake[6] that yov come

[1] Philip, king of Castile.
[2] "they will."
[3] "they both."
[4] "wisely."
[5] "beseeching."
[6] *chake cheke*, i.e. know. The word occurs frequently in Suffolk's letters, but nowhere else so far as the Editor is aware.

A.D. 1505. to yenker Flovrens, for hon of them lovef nat a nodder. Yov mae sae I ame her, and that the dewke of Gelder send me no vord vat I sale do, nor heelpes me nat with notheng, as Petter sale chove yov. bovt vane yov com therechove the Baster ale your masches[1] and fale nat the of.

Vat letters vat that the Baster sent you to Anssterdane vryt me yt yn Ingles.

Also I prae the Baster to send the menes I mae have som remede to have mone,[2] for ther vele none of my frendes vele heelpe me with a pene, as yov ma chowe hem as yov have haneser fro Pole[3] welyes[4] I be her with the dewke of Gelder. Also, ef yov se the K. of the Romes mak me recommand dase anurs[5] to hem, and as yov yov[6] cheke[7] hove the mater stovd be teven the K. of Romes and me, chev yt. And sae "the favt vas nat yn my lord, for my lord provfferd ef yovr gras veld en terten my lord for to monnet[8] with xij hores, my lord vas vel contend to beed yovr plsser, and vane my lord vas gone I bod be bend xx days to cheke[7] your plesser," with ferder as yov thenk best.

EDMUND SUFFOLK.

---

[1] "show the Bastard all your "message."

[2] "money."

[3] Qu. *Paul*, i.e. Paul Zachtlevent ?

[4] "whilst."

[5] "my recommendations"

[6] Sic.

[7] See page 253, note 6.

[8] "for two months"

## XXXI.

A.D.1503?

### EDMUND DE LA POLE TO [ ].

[MS. holograph in Record Office.]

* * * * *

wyt a letter to my lord Fennis and alletter to yes broder of recommand daseoun as lovwele as yov kane.

To my lord Chevers cosene yn my harteles wes[1] I kane I recommand me to, deserreng yov to be my govd frend. And, coson, yt has plessed the k. gras[2] that I hame yn yovre hand to bed[3] ys gras plesser, wches I have ben and voled be glad to hes gras plesser and sarves ef yt be yn my poovre. I deser yov, cosen, to beches the k. to be my govd lord as I have gevef ys gras kas and vold do wele I leuf.[4] Cosen, I prae yov that yt vold ples yov to gevf credens to thest berre.[5]

Prae . . . vele as yov kane for mony for . . . . for nonodder manner chov my lord Chevers yt ples the k. to send me ger,[6] bovt I have nodder doblet nor crest nor hoos, and I vas fane to be fover[7] for my goun for la . . d. And ef yov have mone send me a bonenit of reed and with aggelevttes as that I vare vane yov vare her bovt lett yt be govd.

Speke to my lord Vele and to my lovrd Fenes, I strest the k. vele lett me have some vatte to spend; and chove them that I vas fane to be fovre[7] for my gounes that the k. sent me and dobbeletes, as I have sade be fore.

---

[1] "heartiest wise"

[2] "the king's grace," Philip king of Castile.

[3] "bide."

[4] "as I have given his grace "cause, and would do while I "live."

[5] "this bearer"

[6] "my gear."

[7] "to buy fur"

A.D.1505?

## XXXII.

### EDMUND DE LA POLE TO THOMAS KILLINGWORTH.

[MS. holograph in Record Office.]

TOMAS KELENGVORT, I have reseved yovr letter, and also my schertes, and to cheerges, and a bonete, I thanke Clakes[1] Bakker. I marvele yov sond me nat my naggeletes,[2] and my haste[3] and bedes. I toked yov mone for yt, and thenke yov met velo send me that that I thake yov mone for; bovt I se vele of I thake yov no mone yov vold make bovt letaile cheeufe for me. Ther restes in yovr handes more thane xij. geldranes of the mone that Petter thoke yov to be my ger,[4] and also the mone vas as gevd mone as coode be. Yov have done viesle to send Parrelebene to my cousene Nevele to povt me to more coostes Yt vas nat my commandment that yov chovld do so. Me thenke yov do nat viesle nor honestele. I have notheng bovt bovt[5] yov have yt, and yov povt me to ale the coste, nat so meches as gakee (?) bovt I vas fane to geevf heme mone for ys retrovre, and yeet yov send nat me my ger, that I thoke yov mone to be[6] yt. And ale that I marvele nat so mes[7] as of yov, and of John Grevfovn, that yov send nat me vord with yn viij daes. A vas yovr a pontement with me. I vas yn that kas that I vest nat[8] vat vas best to do; for I had vent[9] yov and John boovt[10] had been trovbovld; and ef yt had ben so, parraventer

---

[1] *Clakes.* This word doubtful. There was a Nicholas or Claus Baker in the succeeding reign, who is mentioned in connexion with Richard De la Pole.

[2] "mine aiglets."

[3] "hat."

[4] "buy my gear."

[5] Sic, apparently a word repeated.

[6] "buy."

[7] "much."

[8] "in that case that I wist not."

[9] "weened," *i.e.* thought.

[10] "both."

I vold a found some remedie for my cheelvf, bovt be yovr bout folles thor met a theng a happenid veches ve ale met a repentte. Loke vat dae yov a pont me to have vord frome yov. Fale nat the dae. Ve sal her the K. ys nove cerstond . . . Also the capetene has vord that the K. of Romes has send for me my naggetels iiij. pore, a nodder rede bonet. Thest ys to lettele a gret dele, my beddes my chekves for ale thest yov have mone, for the reng I her no vord of yov. A.D.1505?

Let me have vord for yov with ale hast, as yov have vord form the marchand, and also as yov her vord of the K. Cheis vele with the herres for mone for me as veille as yov kane; yov mae sae I ame vele, and ef I hade mone. Ef you se the Bastard Oskereke, sae I vort to you that I marled I hard no vord of hem. He chekes[1] bettst hove I stand her; and ef he be the mane I thenke he be, me thenke he met best speke that I met have some honestle en tertanement with mone. And tele hem, thove he has for me, I have nat fore geet hem. And I strest hones for ale thest to make heme govd cher with govd maner, and pavt hem to the speches for yt; bovt be yov nat bee vane he spekes.[2] Also chove hem of my xx geldrens for the months of xx stevers for the geldrens, and yet I most bed tele the monthe be hovt[3] or I kane have my gret and honorerabovle entertanement.

Yov hade x geldrens for my chertes, and the cherggs veches I hade, and a geldrans for my caskeet; ver be comes ale the todder mone? Provf vele for my reng.

EDMUND SUFFOLK.

---

[1] See page 253, note[4].
[2] "but be you not by when he speaks."
[3] "bide till the month be out."

A.D. 1505?

## XXXIII.

### Richard De la Pole to his brother Edmund.

[Addit. MS. 18,738. Brit. Mus., f. 12. Holograph.]

Sir, I ombully recomaund me on to your grace. Sir, I beseche your grace gyf credens to Stase towchyng soche mater as ys brokyn to me of, and of the sayd mater that I may shortly have answare how ye wyll stonde in thys cawse.

Sir, I beseche your grace send me som what to helpe me with all.

Be your lovyng broder,
Richard Suffolk.

A.D. 1505.
6 July.

## XXXIV.

### Passport for Thomas Killingworth.

[From the Original in the Record Office.]

Lieve gheminde. Alzo Thomacs Killingwort, Engels man, mijn goede vriend, my te kennen ghegeven heeft hoe dat hij zeker saken te doene ende volgen heeft in den landen hier ontrent, ende besonder op ende over

Translation.

Dear and well-beloved,—Whereas Thomas Killingworth, Englishman, my good friend, has given me to understand that he has certain things to do and execute in the lands hereabouts, and especially upon and beyond the Zuyder Zee, we

der Zuyder Zee, Begeeven daer omme an u lied ende an elcken van u besondre, dat ghij den selven Thomaes veylick wilt laten passeeren, gaen, ende keeren, doende zijne vornaemde affairen ende saken, Behonden dat de selve syne zaken in geender manieren hindedic[1] scadelic noch lettelic wesen en sullen der K. M., zijnen landen, noch onder saten voors. In Kennessen mijns handteckens hier onder ghestelt, den zesten in Julio, anno xv$^{c}$. vive. A.D. 1505. 6 July.

Uwe goedwillende, Schout van Amsterdamme, overste ende superintendent der Wapeninge, opter Zuyderzee, geordonneert bij der K. M.

JO. BANNICKER.[2]

---

notify therefore to you and every one of you that you will let the same Thomas freely pass, go and come, doing his aforesaid business; provided that the same his business in no manner interfere with the interests of his royal majesty, nor his countries. In witness whereof I have subscribed my signature hereto, the 1st July 1505.

Your well-willer, the "schout" of Amsterdam, chief and superintendent of the "Wapeninge," appointed by the King's Majesty.

JO. BANNICKER.[2]

---

[1] Sic MS.

[2] Signature doubtful. Initial letter B or V. The last syllable expressed by a k. with an abbreviation mark, k̃.

A.D. 1505. 28 July.

## XXXV.

### [EDMUND DE LA POLE] TO PAUL ZACHTLEVENT AND OTHERS.

[From copies in Record Office.]

Desiring his presence at Hattem.

FIDELISSIME mi amice, ego me vobis affectuosissime recommendo, maximas vobis agendo gratias propter vestras benevolentias et amicitias mihi et meis semper gratissime approbatas; quæ omnia, Deo favente, ita adeo considerabo quod spero in paucis diebus ad magnum vestrum honorem erit. Et qua in causa modo extitero non est vobis ignotum credo. Propterea, si vobis placuerit huc in civitatem de Hattem mihi venire, ego ad hoc vos instantissime desidero et quæso pro certis causis meam utilitatem concernentibus, cujus rei fiduciam in vobis præ cæteris omnibus ad vestri adventum propalabo. Et rogo quod credentiam super hoc velitis adhibere domino Waltero mei capellano, hujus literæ latori. Valeatis in bono. Raptim in civitate de Hattam xxviij die Julii anno xv. C. v.

Et vos exoro, mi amice, ut ibi in vestris partibus intimos mei singulos amicos ex meis verbis salutetis. Iterum vale, hominum constantissime.

To my frend Paulus Zachtlevent
in Amsterdammiis.

To the "schout" of Amsterdam.

Salutes plurimas. Vestræ maximæ benevolentiæ et amicitiæ, amice mi præstantissime, quas non solum in nos, verum etiam in nostris gratissime habuistis, nonnullas dominationi vestræ gratias nos semper referre cogunt. Qua ut in re perseverare amicabiliter velitis, dominationem vestram instantissime quæso causa ob quam præcipue vobis modo literas dederim; hæc est, credo quod dominationi vestræ non latet, quod Dei providentia et metuendissimi regis Catholici subventione et tuitione, nos ex castro, et si verius dicam, ex carcere deliberari, et in civitate modo de Hattam per paucos dies moram trahere, ubi id quod nostri commodo fieri[1] possit nobis providere necesse est. Quamobrem nostro amico fidelissimo Paulo Zachtlevent jamjam literis nostris significavimus ut nostri desiderio sibi placuerit sic nos cum omni diligentia visitare. Nam et vestri et sui et aliorum nostrorum amicorum auxilium admodum nobis implorandum est. Dominationem vestram proinde affectuosissime exoramus quatenus ad hoc vestri consilium sibi adhibere dignemini. Et hoc unum pro firmo sciatis, si Superi id faveant ut res ad vota prosperius succedant, nos semper ad vestri optata et desideria paratissimi fore, et hæc pro vobis in brevi facere confidimus, quod imperpetuum et vestri et posteriobus[2] vestris in maximum erit honorem. Valeatis.

A.D. 1505. 28 July.

Scultketo in Amsterdammis.

Plurimas salutes et dilectionis affectum. Honorabiles et approbatissimi domini, viri consultissimi. Vestræ omnes humanitates et amplissimæ amicitiæ quas nobis, et post nostri a civitate vestra decessum carissimo nostro fratri habuistis, nonnullas dominationibus vestris gratias nos semper referre cogunt. Quæ omnia, Deo favente, si vixerimus, erga vestri dominationes considerare plenarie speramus. Et quamquam sinistra fama diu retulit nos hic ad placitum proprium et voluntatem exstitisse, prudentias vestras non latet existimo, et vos et creditores diversimode alias per nos certificari contrarium. Et si plures fortassis ad id credentiam minime adhibuere, verumtamen jamjam omnibus cujusque generis rei veritas experta est. Superis quoque attestamur quod singularis causa hujus nostri periculi et incarcerationis et ita nos posuisse in manus ducis Geldriæ sub sui salvo conducto, nullo certe alio affectu fuit nisi ut libere sui patriam præterire potuis-

To the burgomaster and Council of Aix.

Had placed himself in the power of the duke of Gueldres in his endeavour to

[1] *fere*, MS.

[2] Sic in MS.

A.D. 1505. 28 July. satisfy his creditors; and is now delivered into the hands of the king of Castile.

semus, et quosdam nostri amicos pro debitis creditorum solvendis approbasse. Difficultate hujus adversitatis non obstante, nunc Dei provisione civitas de Hattem et nos cum castro in manibus regiæ majestatis Castellæ sumus deliberati. Et si res adeo prospere successit ut speramus, et maximas vestri benevolentias et gratissimas vestri amicitias, ut decet, ac etiam creditorum debita quam citius nobis possibile erit totis nisibus promereri conabimur. Et super hoc nobis profecto gratissimum semper acciderit quicquid pro dominationibus vestris nos licite reddere possimus. Et ut mentibus creditorum de his satisfacere velitis, prudentias vestras instantissime quæsumus. Valete, hominum constantissimi. Raptim de civitate de [Hattem.][1]

Vestri Amator perseverandissimus.

Venerabilibus dominis, burgi magistris
et consiliariis civitatis Aquisgrani,
viris prudentissimis, suis amicis
constantissimis.

To his brother.

Charissime et mi dilectissime frater. Ego me tota mentis affectione vobis recommendo, fraternitatem vestram certificando civitatem, me et castrum de Hattem in manus regiæ Castellæ majestatis jam fore redditos. Et non est vobis ignotum, charissime mi frater, credo, quod super salvum conductum ducis Geldriæ me sui patriam præteriisse proposui versus ducem Saxoniæ et comitem de Guidon pro quibusdam promissis inter nos factis, et præcipue pro debitis creditorum obtinendis; pro qua singulari causa in his periculis diu steterim; et quamvis pluribus incredituni fuit, tamen rei veritas omnibus modo nota est. Et quam cito Deo placuerit me illam potestatem habere (quod in brevi confido), ego et vos ad libertatem reducam et creditorum debitis satisfaciam. Ad quam quidem rem totis viribus, ut

Hopes soon to set him at liberty and

[1] Blank in MS.

convenit, me penitus applicabo. Interim fraternitatem vestram exoro quatenus hoc in omnibus faciatis quod est in mei et vestri honorem semper fore possit. Valeat fraternitas vestra in prosperitate. Ex civitate de Hattem.

A.D. 1505. 28 July. satisfy his creditors.

## XXXVI.

### [KILLINGWORTH (?) TO EDMUND DE LA POLE].

[MS. in Record Office.]

A.D. 1505?

SIR, and if your frend[1] here had not been, I had sent to you or this tyme. He taried soo lang or he sent to you to thentent he wold have certified you of som newes oute of England; but as yet he hath herde noon. And he bad me write to you, that touching you he hereth noo thing but good; and also he bad me write to you of tharresting of the shippes in the kinges[2] landis; whiche men saye secretly shuld bee for you. And, sir, upon the caas he sigh you in him sylf, he sendeth you iiij elles of the best saten he can bye here, and lynyng therunto, and clothe for ij paire hosen and lynyng. And with this gere he sendeth a servant of his own for fere it mighte bee taken from Sir Water[3] [and also, as me seemeth, to thentent his servant maye see howe ye stande; for I perceived by the sculken[4] he mistrusteth your caas.][5]

For your gown he axked me howe many elles velvet wold serve you. I told hym xiiij. Englishe yerdis; and then he saied, "What lynyng thereunto?" I answerde "Sarcenet," by cause of the lest coste to helpe it forward. And he saide to me, "Wel, I shal see what I can doo therin." Soo, sir, if it please you to write to him in Duche, and thank him, and geve but oon worde therein

[1] Probably Paul Zachtlevent mentioned in the preceding document.

[2] Probably Philip king of Castile.

[3] De la Pole's chaplain mentioned at page 260.

[4] The "schout."

[5] This passage struck out with the pen.

A.D.1505? towching your gown, I doubte not ye shal have hyt. And as to the helpe of my lord Nevyll[1] and your servauntis, and for the hooste in Zwolle, I meved him therin after your mynd, and thus muche I perceive that [seing the povertie ye bee in][2] that my lord Nevyll, I think he wol helpe of a gown and a bonet, but further he speketh not, neither for the payment of the hoost nor yet for the helpe of your servauntis. And also he sayeth ye spake not to hym of noo suche thinges. And, sir, and ye had therin spoken playnely to hym, it had been otherwise. For he is a kynde and a frendely man, and oon worde of your own mowthe had been worth an c. of an other mannys. [And, sir, for your servantes some remedie must bee founden. Ther shulbe elles werke ynough to doo]. And, sir, . . . [3]ere you to write[4] the cause of my lord Nevill and your servauntis and the . . . ment of the hoost in your said lettre. I trust some good shal comme therof whiche shalbe for your honour, for oon remedy or other must bee founden, or elles ther shalbe . . . the . . . and your servauntis, and . . . . to know your plaisire therin also . . . shewed.

Nowe, sir, this day on Lady d . . . Mr. Paul shewed me[5] certain specialites and writinges under the signe and seal of the duc of Yorke[6] concernyng money as was due to hym by my lord of Yorke; and, sir, under this maner he brak to me. He wolde fayne helpe you and bee also hable to doo you good service at the point, and this is his meanyng. Howe bee it, therin noo thing wol he doo, but after your own mynd and plaisure. Yf it pleased you to bee content, he wold send by a bode of this towne to king Herry the copyes of suche writingis and dueties as the duc of York oweth hym under notaries signes, desiring hym

[1] Doubtless Sir George Nevill.

[2] These passages struck out with the pen.

[3] Faded.

[4] *joyne*, corr.

[5] *brake to me*, corr.

[6] Perkin Warbeck.

where as he hath lent his goodes unto the duc of York [which was the right king of England, and that][1] seing that he is dede without payeng, that it wolde please king H. to paye to hym the same money; and if king H. wol not soo doo, as he is sure he wol not, then he wold shewe king H. playnely that he wol leane to you and ayde you with his body and goodes to his power. This is oon waye whereby he wold perceive king H. answer. Item, sir, another waye is this. Paulus was borne in the Estland in the duc of Pombernes landes joynyng upon the king of Denmarke landes, whider dailly resorte merchantes of England, where the princes of the landes ar his frendes; and therfor, if it pleased your grace, this is his desire for that purpose. Ye knowe wel thabusion king H. hath made against the duc of Yorke that he was a counterfeyt. He desireth therfor to have your certificat that hit is untrue, and your auctorite, and if it please you to sette your signe manuel[2] to this parchement that this bringer shall,[3] and upon that the same writing salbe made here, if it bee your plaisure.[4] And theruppon he trusteth by the helpe of the king of Denmark and the duc of Pombernes to have recoverey shortely[5] of this good upon some Englisshe merchauntis, and that in short tyme [if your cause goo not wel] and helpe yoo therwith; and to thentent your grace shal perceve it is his owne desire he hath subscribed it with his owne hand, and also he sendeth your grace therwith the secret token bytwix your grace and hym; which secret token he beseecheth your grace to sende hym again by this bringer. A.D. 1505?

*Endorsed*:—Van der Visser Rosen.

[1] Struck out with the pen.
[2] *and seal* struck out.
[3] Sic.
[4] *if — plaisure*] corr. from "or "elles if your grace wol cause it to "bee made there, at your plaisure "he referreth it."
[5] Interlined.

A.D. 1505. 4 Aug.

## XXXVII.

### The Bastard of Oyskerk to [Killingworth ?]

[MS. in Record Office.]

Their master is in the hands of the duke of Gueldres; but does not wish his servants

Monseigneur le maistre, je me recommande bien a vous, vous layssant a savoir que monseigneur nostre maistre est mene en la ville de Wagenynghe en la mayn de duc de Gheldres par le commandement du roy; et sus este avecques, et monseigneur mon maistre ma comande que me laissiez savoir se maistre Pouwel est venu, que au cas quil soit venu que il vuellie venir, et vous avecque ly, jusques a Waghenynghe, car la paix est, et quil peult bien venir seurement pour parler a monsieur nostre maistre. Se au cas est quil fait defeculte pour venir en la ditte ville de Waghenynghe envoye missier Wauter ou aultre quelcunq. Monseigneur nostre maistre leur envoyra ung saufconduyt de par le duc de Gelres pour venir ou quelque eure quil vouldront et seurement. Et monseigneur le maistre, monsieur,

---

Translation.

Monseigneur le maistre, I recommend myself to you, letting you know that my lord our master is brought into the town of Wagenynghe into the hands of the duke of Gueldres, by command of the king. And I have been with him, and my lord my master has commanded that you let me know if master Paul (?) is come, that in case he be come he would go, and you with him, to Wagenynghe, for it is peace, and he may come in security to speak with my lord our master. If he make any difficulty to come into the said town of Wageninghe send Sir Walter or any other. My lord our master will send them a safe conduct from the duke of Gueldres to come in safety at whatever hour they please. And my lord

vous commande que vous tenez bonne maniere et que vous ne parlez point trop, et tous ses gens et serviteurs ; et leurs dites aynsy, car monsiegneur nostre maistre le veult et est bien content de estre la quil est, et je men voye pour cersier tout son cas enver le roy. Et vous savez bien comment les seigneurs ont parle a ly, et il vent tout sur ung pourpos ; et tenez pourtant bonne contenance, car tout est pour bien par la grace de Dieu, la quelle vous garde en bonne et longue vie. Escript a Arnhnem, le iiij^e jour de August lan xv.c. et cinq. A.D. 1505. 4 Aug. to complain of it.

Le tout vostre amy,
GRIFFON B. DE OYSKERK.

Monseigneur nostre maistre se commande bien amyablement a monseigneur Nevell et a tous aultres ses bons serviteurs, et leur prie quil soint bien content, car leur maistre est bien content.

---

the master, monsieur, commands you to keep a good manner, and not to speak too much, and all his people and servants; and you shall tell them so, for my lord our master wishes it, and is quite satisfied to be where he is; I am going to sound all his case with the king. You know well how the lords have spoken to him, it is all with one purpose; keep, nevertheless, a good countenance, for everything is for good by the grace of God, which I pray to preserve you in good and long life. Written at Arnhem the 4th of August, 1505.

Your entire friend,
GRIFFON BASTARD DE OYSKERK.

My lord our master commends himself in most loving wise to my lord Nevill and all his other good servants, and prays them to be satisfied, for their master is satisfied.

A.D. 1505. 4 Aug. Monseigneur le maistre, sachiez que Sir Water a este ycy mais est retourne sans parler a moy ou quelque aultre serviteur de nostre maistre, par quoy je ne say que response il a apporte, et pour tant pour ceste foiz rien plus vous ne say escripre. Et sachiez que je fuisse desja departi envers le roy ou fait de nostre maistre, se ne fuisse que je attens pour savoir la response que Sir Water a apporte, et ay pourtant envoye ung messagier apres ly pour savoir la response de ly. Et me laissiez aussy savoir response de vous, et se ledit marchant est avecque vous le confortes et ly dites hardiment quil ne sochie de riens, et je escry aussy une lettres a ly, et envoyez moy la causse de monseigneur.

A monseigneur le maistre
serviteur des monseigneur de Suffolk.

---

Monseigneur le Maistre, understand that Sir Walter has been here, but has returned without speaking to me, or any other servant of our master; wherefore I know not what answer he has brought, and accordingly at present I know nothing more to write to you. And know that I would already have departed towards the king on the business of our master, were it not that I am waiting to know the answer that Sir Walter has brought, and have accordingly sent a messenger after him to know the answer from him. And let me also have an answer from you; and if the said merchant is with you, comfort him and tell him boldly he need not be anxious about anything. I am writing a letter to him also; and send me my lord's cause.

To my lord le maître [d'hôtel ?]
servant of my lord of Suffolk.

## XXXVIII.

A.D. 1505. 24 Sept.

### STIPULATION FOR THE RANSOM OF EDMUND DE LA POLE.

[MS. in Record Office, corrected draft.]

PRÆSENS scriptum testatur quod ego dominus Carolus dux Geldriæ,[1] etc., tractavi, concordavi, et promisi Griffoni Bastardo Doysekerke, famulo domini Edmundi ducis Suffolchiæ de Anglia,[2] quod prædictus dominus dux Suffolchiæ solvat aut solvi faciat præfato domino Carolo de Gheldres m$^{l}$. m$^{l}$. millia[3] [florenorum][4] pro expensis ejusdem ducis Suffolchiæ et famulorum suorum in terra Geldrensi sub forma sequenti;[5] videlicet, quingentos aureos infra octo dies datum præsentium immediate sequentes Et infra tres septimanas dictos octo dies immediate sequentes alios quingentos aureos. Et infra duos menses prædictas tres septimanas immediate sequentes, mille florenas, in plenam solutionem prædictorum m$^{l}$. m$^{l}$. aureorum. Et prædictus dux Geldriæ[6] est contentus et per præsentes tenetur seipsum esse contentum de prædictis m$^{l}$. m$^{l}$. mille aureis, sic quod Anthonius de la Vaale, mercator Ispaniæ, commorans in oppido Andewarpensi, vult eidem domino Carolo pro eisdem pecuniis esse respondens sub forma ut prædictum est.[7] Et immediate cum prædicti primi prænominati quingenti aurei sunt[8] soluti prædicto domino

---

[1] *dux Geldriæ, etc.*] Corr. from *de Gheldres.*

[2] *de Anglia*] Corr. from *consanguineo meo carissimo.*

[3] Sic, pro *duo millia.*

[4] Om. in MS.

[5] *prædictus dominus dux Suffolchiæ—sequenti.*] All this is an interlineation substituted for the following words which formerly stood in the text:—*pro duobus millibus florenis aureis solvendis idem dominus dux Suffolchiæ habebit suam libertatem.*

[6] *dux Geldriæ*] Substituted for *dominus Carolus de Gheldres.*

[7] *prædictum est*] The clause following, down to the word *dilatione*, has been added afterwards.

[8] *sunt*] The words *præ manibus ut supradictum est* here stood in the text but are struck out.

A.D. 1505. 24 Sept. Carolo duci Geldriæ, et promissio habita super obligatione prædicti Anthonii de la Vale pro solutione de residuo prædictorum duorum mille florenorum eidem domino Carolo sub forma prædicta,[1] idem dominus Carolus dux Geldriæ firmiter promisit et promittit per præsentes quod immediate super hoc faciat prædictum dominum Edmundum ducem Suffolchiæ habendum suam plenam libertatem, eundum de manibus et terris suis ad placitum et voluntatem ejusdem domini Edmundi sine ulteriori dilatione. In cujus rei testimonium hoc præsens scriptum ego prædictus dominus Carolus de Gheldres manu propria subscripsi,[2] vicesima iiij^ta die Septembris, anno Domini millesimo quingentesimo quinto.

---

A.D. 1505. 17 Nov.

## XXXIX.

### Edmund De la Pole to the Bastard D'Oysekirke.

[MS. in Record Office. Copy.]

Bastart, je me recommende a vous. Jay receu vostre[3] lettres par Hans, et je suys bien joyous de vostre retourne, car jay forte doubte du departement

---

#### Translation.

Bastard, I recommend myself to you. I have received your letter by Hans, and I am very glad of your return, for I had great fears of the departure of the king before

---

[1] *sub forma prædicta*] Corr. from *ut prædictum est.*

[2] *et sigillum meum apponi mandavi.* Struck out.

[3] vr̃e, MS.

du roy devand vostre venue, vieant le caas en lequel A.D. 1505. 17 Nov.
je suys; car, comme vous savez bien, cy le roy fuys departe que je ne savoye de nul luy entendre le plaisir du roy. Surquoy jay envoye le maistre dostel denver vous, au la entencien que vous et luy ensemble faisent tout le diligence que vous poves denver le roy et son counsail pour moy et pour mees causes, en telle manier que vous dire. Et touchant les lettres que monsieur de Shevers ay envoye ycy au le receivour pour lentreteynement de mees servitures, le receivour ay responde au Donpeter que il ay parle au monsieur de Sheviers depuis que le lettre este fait, et que nul choise fuyt escript dedens le lettre touchant moy et mees servitures. Et touchand mon frere et roy Henry, jay espoir que jay bottre le matier in telle suretie que mon frere doyt faire comme je vouldray quil faiste en tous choises, et que il [ne] laisseray point defaire pour nul daungier ne povertie du monde. Et pour le conduit de ceste chois jay ayde au mon frere avecq mon argent,

---

your arrival, seeing the case in which I am; for, as you know well, if the king were gone I should not be able to learn from anybody the pleasure of the king. Wherefore I have sent the steward to you to the intent that you and he together use all the diligence you can with the king and his council for me, and my causes in such manner as I will tell you. And touching the letters which my lord Chievres has sent hither to the receiver for the entertainment of my servants, the receiver has answered to Don Peter that he has spoken with my Lord Chievres since the letter was written, and that nothing was written in the letter touching me and my servants. And touching my brother and king Henry I hope that I have put the matter in such security that my brother shall do as I would have him in everything, and that he will not neglect to do so for any danger or poverty in the world. And for the management of this thing

A.D. 1505. 17 Nov.

Et ainsy[1] il fault que jay luy ayde plus bien brief comme jay luy promise par mon escript que ch . . . . je fa . . . au monde.[2] Et Dieu vous garde. Escript a Namur les xvij. jour de Novembre.

Ausy, cy il est possible, Bastard, trouveres vous le manie pour argeant pour moy ayder pour mon frere et envoyes moy incontinent. Et parles vous meisme au Ha[ns][3] Wittershaw pour argeant.

Au mon servitur le Bastart
Le Oysekirke.

---

I have helped my brother with my money. And also it is necessary that I help him very shortly as I have promised him by my writing that . . . . . . And God preserve you. Written at Namur the 17th day of Novembre.

Likewise, if it be possible, Bastard, find you the means for money for me to help me for my brother and send [it] me forthwith. And speak yourself to Ha[ns] Wittershaw for money.

To my servant the
Bastard of Oysekirke.

---

[1] *ainsy*]. Probably for *aussi*.

[2] *il fault . . . . monde*]. Interlined over the following words, which have been struck out:—"jay luy "ayde aveqq . florens par ung "aultre amye comme mon maistre "dostell vous dire."

[4] Paper worn. The final dash of the *s* faintly visible.

## XL.

A.D. 1505
24 Nov.

RICHARD DE LA POLE TO HIS BROTHER EDMUND.

[From a copy in the Record Office.]

SIRE,

JE me recommande humblement a votre grace. Vous plaise assavoir que les bourgoys dAix sont retourne du roy de Castelle. Quel response il ont eu je ne scay, mais dedens iiij jours apres leur revenue vint a moy Martyn hoste du Pot, et diverse aultres, en la rue recontrant, en demandant de moy leur argent. Je leur donne la milleur response que je sceus pour les contenter. Au derrein il me dirent "Votre frere est le pluis false homme que oncques fuyt de sa promesse, et nous voullons faire a luy comme il doit estre servye. Nous luy voullons mettre sus en ceste ville et tous aultres villes partinent a lempire, que tout le monde sarra quil este ung false homme parjure; et nous voullons avoir notre argent de vous. Et sy vous ne voullons[1] trouver remede pour nous, nous avons[1] trou-

Impatience of De la Pole's creditors.

TRANSLATION.

SIRE,

I RECOMMEND myself humbly to your grace. Please it you to know that the burgesses of Aix have returned from the king of Castile. What answer they have had from him I know not, but within four days after their return came to me Martin host of the Pot, and divers others, meeting me in the street, and demanding their money of me. I gave them the best answer I could to satisfy them. At last they said to me, "Your brother is the falsest man that ever was of his promise, and we will do to him as he ought to be served. We will accuse him in this town and all the other towns belonging to the empire, that all the world may know that he is a false perjured man; and we will have our money from you. And

[1] Sic.

A.D. 1505. 24 Nov. vere le remedie pour nous meismes, et pour tant en toute haste faictes nous votre response."

Sire, tant que je puis persevoir il ont quelque comforte pour ce faire que de mettre votre grace a telle deshonnor et moy ainsy au deshonnor et graunt danger de mon corps; car je suys advise de deux persones quy sont mees bones amyes, que le roy H. ay desire des bourgois dAix quil moy deliverent trois lieuwes hors de la ville dAix, et il les pairay. Et ainsy ung ma advise que je ne voye pluis sus la rue, car sy je suis tue sur la rue, le roy Herry leur pairey leur argent. Je pense bien verytablement que se soit fait a fin que je soye mieulx contente de faire le plaisir au roy H., lequel este de vous abandonner et de feire comme il me commandre de faire: lequel serroit a votre deshonneur et de moyen tout le temps de notre vie. Neantmeyns, sire, se vous voullons faire envers moy comme jay deservie et comme ung frere doit faire a son frere, lequel este ycy en ostage pour vous, et que je puis veoir que vous faictes le mieulx pour moy pledger

Henry VII has offered bribes to get Richard De la Pole into his power.

---

if you will not find a remedy for us, we will find one for ourselves; and therefore make your answer to us in all haste."

Sire, as far as I can perceive they have some encouragement to do this, putting your grace to such dishonor, and me also to dishonor and great personal danger; for I am apprised by two persons who are my good friends, that king H. has desired the burgesses of Aix to deliver me three leagues out of the town of Aix, and he will pay them. And so I am advised no longer to go into the street, for if I am killed in the street, king Henry will pay them their money. I think in very truth, it was done to the end that I might be the more willing to do king Henry's pleasure, which is to abandon you and do as he shall command me; which would be to your dishonor and mine all our lives long. Nevertheless, sire, if you will do towards me as I have deserved, and as a brother ought to do to his brother who is here in hostage for you, and I see that you do the best to

dhors accordant a votre promesse, vous moy trouvereys votre loyal frere viengne que en venir porray. A.D. 1505. 24 Nov.

Sire, que vous desire semblement, sy pour caas este que lees bourgoys vous mettent sus en ceste ville ou je suis, a votre grant deshonnor et le moyen, comme il diste quil veulte faire, faictes votre mieulx pour vous declairer ung homme loyall, comme ung bon et loyall homme doit faire, comme vous moy voulles trouvere votre bon et loyal frere, comme vous avez faict, et tous jours ferez en ce faisant. Vous plaise de donner credence au Ewstas, porteur de cestez. Sire, jay ouy nouvelles de Derik. Jay esperance quil nous apporteray sauns accune faulte bonnes nouvellez. Rien pluis, cy non que Dieu vous donne bonne et longue vie. Escript a Aix le xxiiij jour de Novembre lan xv$^{c}$ cincq,

par votre loyall frere,
RICHARD SUFFOLK.

A monsieur mon frere.

---

ransom me according to your promise, you will find me your loyal brother, come what may.

Sire, I request you likewise, if the case be that the burgesses accuse you in this town where I am, to your great dishonor and mine, as they say they intend to do, do your best to declare yourself an honorable man, as a good and honorable man ought to do, as you would find me your good and true brother, as you have done and always will do, in so doing. Please it you to give credence to Eustace, bearer of these. Sire, I have heard news of Derik. I have hope that he will bring us good news without fail. No more, except that God give you good and long life. Written at Aix, the 24th day of November 1505,

by your loyal brother,
RICHARD SUFFOLK.

To my lord my brother.

A.D. 1505. 27 Nov.

## XLI.

### Edmund De la Pole to Oyskerk and Killingworth.

[From a copy in the Record Office, subjoined to the preceding.]

I have sent you a lettre by this berer which I praye you shewe to my lords Ville and Feynes, that they maye shewe it to the king; for what it is I cannot saye, but sythens the burgoys of Acon were with the K. they bee more herder both of there dedes, and also of their wordes. Howe it comes or by whom I cannot saye, but me thinketh if the kinges conseill had been my frendes it had not been after this manier. Wherfor I can see noon other remedie but my bro.[1] and I both must loke wel upon this matier and wol doo. I have great mervaille I here noo words from you howe my matier goes, and that I know not the kinges plaisir in noo thing. I have been in his hands thise iiij. monethes and mor, and you ij were the messengiers that broughte me worde from the king that I shuld putte noo doubte in him. He was my good lord, and wolde doo for me many things, but I cannot perseyve it. I lye here to my paine and shame, and also spende what I canne gette of my frendes, and I have noo thing but feire wordes; wherby I am as a man undoon by your message, and also my broder like to be delivered to K. H.,[1] or elles to be dryven by force to forsake me, or elles to be slayne in the towne of Acon by the borgoys;[1] and alle by the reason of my being here in prison, where I maye not goo to my frends to fynde the remedie, neyther for my broder ner for my sylf. Wherfor me thinketh, and if the king were advetized of me and my broder howe we stande, and al by reson that I am here at the K.'s command, I

Notwithstanding Philip's promises, he can get no relief,

and his brother in in great danger.

---

[1] A mark occurs in the margin of the MS. opposite these passages.

put noo doubte his grace wol have som regard what danger my broder is in. For my sylf I desire not soo great haast, but after that manier as I sent the K. word by Roderik de la Lain, by the bastard, and by the stewerd, wherof I praye you to take good regard. And shewe my lord Ville and my lord Feyneys, as they bee noble mon, to remember their promes whiche they made me for the king. A.D. 1505. 27 Nov.

Written the xxvij. day of November.

E. SUFFOLK.[1]

## XLII.

A.D. 1505? 31 Dec.

SIR GEORGE NEVILL TO KILLINGWORTH

[MS. Holograph in Record Office.]

MAISTER Steward, I hertyly recommend me unto you, thankyng you for your tokyns ye sent to me by Sir Thomas Grenhyll; I wold I hadde to do yow so grete plesur, but I have nat. Mr. Steward, I pray send me word whedyr ye contynew in that partyes or nat. Yff ye do, I wold be glad to kepe you company; yff nat, and yff ye come to this parties I shall make you as sure as ony burghgar of the towne. And what ye thynke best me to do I shallc gladly folow your mynde. I am very loth to tarry hier with owte compeny. Commend me to Sir Water. And I pray you to remembre

Is anxious to join Killingworth, or to have him in his company at Aix.

[1] The original of this letter exists in the Record Office in Edmund De la Pole's own hand writing, and has been printed by Ellis (Third Series, i. 138), in its own extraordinary spelling. It is addressed to the Bastard Van Oyskerke and Thomas Killingworth.

A.D. 1505? 31 Dec. me as I wold remembre you, yff I were yn your case. And ytt lye yn my poure, I shall nat forgete your kyndnesse, by Goddes grace, who evyr preserve yow. Wryten at Haye, the last day of Decembre.

By your frend,
Sir G. NEVYLL.

To hys ryght welbelovyd and
especiall good frend,
Thomas Kyllyngworth.

---

A.D. 1506. 24 Jan.

## XLIII.

### EDMUND DE LA POLE'S COMMISSION TO TREAT WITH HENRY VII.

[Orig. in the Record Office.]

The dispute between the King and himself, being a cause of troubles in England.

BE hit knowen to alle princes, nobles, and true Cristen men, by this present writing, that we, Edmund duke of Suffolk, of England, on the xxvj day of December last passed had certain comynycacions and wordes towching the troubles that ar in the reame of England, by reason that it standeth by twixt the king of England and me as hyt doeth.

Wherupon my servant, Thomas Kyllyngworth, my steword, axked me wheder my mynd and entent was as I spake it. I answerde "Ye on my faith;" and soo I, the said duc, shewed to hym more largely my said entent and mynd concernyng the same playnely as it is.

The said Thomas therupon hath retorned to me the xxij day of this instant moneth of January, shewinge and acerteyning me that he hath openned and disclosed my said entent and mynd to the kinges servant, John Chamberlayn, and that the same John is goon to the

A.D. 1506. 24 Jan.

kyng to thentent to yeve the king undrestanding and knowleage of the same. Wherwith I am contented and pleased. Wherupon I have nowe eftsones of newe comyned in this matier, and shewed my full entent and playne mynd to the said Thomas Kyllyngworth, and also to my servant John Gryffyth. And for the trust I have in the trowthes to me of the said Thomas and John, I have openned at large to theym my hert in this behalve. And by vertue and auctoritie herof I have yeven to the said Thomas and John, and by thise presentez yeve to them jointely full power and auctoritie to have comynycacion with suche person or persones, honnest, God dreding, as shalbe by the said king of England sufficiently auctorized, ordenned, and assigned. And whatsomever they shal on my behalve promise by their worde or writing touching the premisses, I, the said Edmund duc of Suffolk, promise and bynde me by this my present writing upon myn honnor and faith to God of a true Cristen prince that I shal and wolle faithfully and truely kepe and observe the same in eche point and article, like as I have further auctorized theym in that behalve. In witnesse wherof I, the sayd duke, have sette my signemanuell and seall to thise presents, and also undrewritten the same with myn own hand, the xxiiij day of January, the yere of our Lord God a thowsand fyve hundreth and sex.

Suffolk authorises Killingworth and Griffith to treat for its adjustment.

I [1] seste my hand to thest yn tent that ale manner of mene sale chake[2] that I vele parforvme thest be fore vrytvn, and also vat that the prommes on my be havalf.

EDMUND SUFFOLK.

[1] This paragraph added in Suffolk's own hand.

[2] See page 253, note 6.

A.D. 1506.
28 Jan.

## XLIV.

### Edmund De la Pole's Instructions to treat with Henry VII.

[Orig. in Record Office.]

Instructions yeven by the right excellent prince my lord Edmund duc of Suffolk, the son and heire of my lord John sometyme duc of Suffolk, to his trusty and welbeloved servantes Thomas Kyllyngworth his stewerd and to John Griffith, howe and undre what maner the said ducis full mynd, entent, and plaisir ar, that the said Thomas and John shal demeane and handell theym selfes on the said ducis behalve with the kinges highnesse for the pacifieng and fynal determinacion of suche gruges, variances, and causes as ar depending at this tyme, and long saison have doon, bytwixt the kinges said highnesse and the said duc their maistre.

Edmund Suffolk.

To offer De la Pole's submission and desire the King's pardon.

Furst, and principally the said ducis mynd is that the said Thomas and John on his behalve shal humbly beseche the kinges highnes to bee his good and gracious souverain lord, and that it maye please his grace to withdrawe from the said duc his high displaisir, and to putte clerely oute of his hert suche grugge and malice as his grace hath had ayeinst the said duc. And that it also mayе like the kinges highnesse to accepte and admitte the said lord Edmund to his estate as my lords his grantfader and fader were accepted and taken in tyme passed: and the said duc is and shalbe redy to receive the kinges pardon and wolbecomme his true sobget and liegeman, and semblably after the king our souverain lordes decesse contynue to my lord prince the kinges son and to his heires, withoute erring or declynyng from the same, whyles he lyveth.

Edmund Suffolk.

Secondaryly, the said Thomas and John shal on the said ducis behalf humbly beseche and require the kinges grace that it may please his highnesse, as honour and noblesse and right require, to restore to the said duc and to his heires alle the honnours, castelles, maners, lordships and heriditamentes apperteynyng to the said duchie of Suffolk, holly and entierly as the same were lefte to the possession of the said nowe dukes fader, with suche offices as my lordes his grantfader and fader have had of the yefte of the kinges or princes aforetyme or by inheritance. And over this, that they shal beseche the kinges grace that it maye please his highnes, as right and conscience requiren, to restore to the said duc alle suche sommes of money as his grace or any persones by his auctoritie and commaundement have received, aswele touching thannuyties of creacions yeven by kinges for thestat of the said duchie, as of the revenues of thinheritances aforsaid. from the tyme of the deth of the said duc John to this day; and also to bee restored to such goodes and stuf of howsehold as the same duc had at his departing fro England. A.D. 1506. 28 Jan. To desire restitution of the dukedom of Suffolk,

EDMUND SUFFOLK.

Thirdly, as to the town of Leighton Buzard, which king Edward enforced the said ducis fader to relesse to the colleage of Windesor, the said duc besecheth humbly the kinges highnesse to bee good lord to him therin, and that he maye be restored therunto, and that al things therin doon by my lordes fader maye bee disannulled by the lawe and by the parliament, the said duc restoring to the said colleage suche money as can bee duely proved that my lord his fader received for the same of king Edward, or of the said colleage. Semblably for the towne and castell of Orford with thapportenances, whiche the lord Willoughby hath; the maner of Filberdes which Sir Richard Gyldeford hath; the maner of Hanwel whiche the Coferer hath; and al Of the town of Leighton Buzzard and other lands.

A.D. 1506. 28 Jan.

othre lands alienned by the said duc, or by his fader to Sir Water Herbert, or any othre. And also as to the maners of Bulcamp, Hynham, Sidesterne, and Newton, whiche were relessed to Sir Tirry Robsert son at the labour of Sir William Carewe, that the said duc maye bee also restored to eche of the same, restoring again the money of theim received.

EDMUND SUFFOLK.

To ask Henry's assistance to recover his liberty.

Fourthly, if it shulde soo happenne that the king of Castelle, or the gouvernors of his landes in his absence, after the tyme that the kinges grace and the said duc bee accorded, wil not bee aggreable ner suffre that the said duc shal departe oute of their hands, but kepe him by force, the said duc then beseecheth the king to helpe him to his libertie under the maner as his grace shal seme best. And wher no creatur is sure of his lif it mighte peradventure in the mean tyme happe the said duc to dye, as God forbydde; neverthalas whatsoever maye fortune in this behalf the said duc wol bee and contynue the kinges true subject to thend of his lif. Beseching therfor humbly the kinges highnes that incontinent upon the said aggrement hit maye please his grace to suffre my lady the said ducs wif tordre and make officers in his lands as he shuld doo him sylf and to receive the revenues of the same during the tyme he shalbe kept as prisoner by the king of Castelle or any othre.

EDMUND SUFFOLK.

That if he die in prison without male issue, his widow may be allowed her jointure and

Fyftely, if it soo shal fortune, as Almighty God forbydde, that the said duc decesse withoute issue male of his body lieufully begotten and commyng in the mean tyme and saison of his keping prisoner as afore is saied or afterward. That then ymmediatly after the said dukes decesse hit maye please the kinges highnesse to permitte and suffre my lady the said ducis wiff to have, holde, and enjoye, paicibly and frely her jointour in the said lands for the terme of her lyff, according to the lawe of the land and her right. And that also at the humble request, desir, and supplication of the said duc, hit maye like the kinges said highnesse to bee agreable and to accorde, and that at this present comynycacion and tract hit maye bee accorded and finally concluded, that my lady Elizabeth, the doughter of the said duc, shalbe reputed, accepted, and takenne as the doughter and heire of the said duc, and that the same lady Elizabeth and the heires of her body lieufully begotten and commyng for evermor maye holde, possede, and enjoye the hole enheritaunces of the said duchie of Suffolk, as above is saied.

A.D. 1506. 28 Jan. his daughter to inherit.

EDMUND SUFFOLK.

Sextly, that it maye plese the kinges grace, aswele for the part of his grace and my lord prince as for the part and suretie of the said duc and his heires, upon such pointz and causes as shalbe accorded and concluded herupon bytwix the king and the said duc, or bytwix the king and the said Thomas and John, in the said ducis name, wheder the said pointz and causes bee herin expressed or not, of whatsoever weight and substance they bee, that the same maye bee engrossed under the writing or seales of the king and my lord prince, and also enacted and confermed by auctoritie of parliament under suche maner as shalbe to the king thoughte moost expedient. And also such writinges and bondes as shalbe divised by the king, and made for the part of the said duc by the said Thomas and John in his name and under his seal. For whiche entent the said duc hath to theym delivered his seal and certain blanks signed with his hand, or ells that shalbe made by the said Thomas and John, for the part of the said duc in their owne names, as it shal please the king, the said duc promiseth and obligeth hym sylf truely to observe and performe the same in eche behalf at the

That the points agreed upon may be drawn up in writing under the seals of the king and prince, and confirmed by parliament.

A.D. 1506. 28 Jan.

kinges plaisir in his own person, yf God sende hyme his lif and libertie, or larger as it shalbe devised by the kings grace.

EDMUND SUFFOLK.

That William De la Pole and others be set at liberty.

Sevently, that it maye please the kinges highnesse at the humble request of the said duc that, incontinent upon this aggrement, his grace wil putte to libertie my lord William of Suffolk, and al suche gentylmen and othre persones, whatsoever personaiges they bee, whiche ar in prison for the said ducis sake or cause, or at the kinges commandement under suretie; and that he and they maye bee restored frely to their goods and[1] lands, or their sureties to bee dischargeth, as the caas requireth. And that al suche gentilmen or othre persones, whatsoever they bee, that been dede, and have loste their landes for the cause of the said duc that their heires maye bee restored to their enheritances. And over this, that it maye like the kinges said highnesse to have respect unto Sir George Nevyll, and that the same Sir George maye have and enjoye such landes as he hath right unto in his own title, or in my lady his wifes touching her jointour and dower in therl Ryvers lands.

EDMUND SUFFOLK.

Eightely, the said duc faithfully byndeth him by thise presentez, and promiseth on his faith of a true Cristen prince, or elles uttrely to bee reputed the contrary, that never whiles he lyveth he shal breke nor doo contrary to the said promesses and aggrements, ner defaulte in hym shalbe founden; yeving by thise presentz full power and auctoritie to the said Thomas and John to conclude thorougly with the kinges grace, or with his deputies, in this behalf having the kinges power, like wise as the said duc shulde doo if he were present him sylf, the suretie for the said ducis person

[1] *and*, repeated in MS.

except, and for his submission and the maner of his commyng to the kinges presence, which the said duc reserveth, to commone therin hym silf, as he shal see cause to require, with suche nobles and men of honnour of the kinges counsail as shalbe in this partie deputed, and as therin he hath somewhat opened his mynd to his said servantes. And to thentent that thissame maye bee groundely and playnely knowen to all kinges, princes, and nobles, aswele in England, as elleswher that it is the full mynd, dede, and commandement of me the said duc, I have caused the said Thomas Kyllyngworth, to write thise articles, to every of the which I have sette my hand for record. At the castel of Namure, the xxviijty day of January, the yere of our Lord God, a thousand v^c and sex. A.D. 1506 28 Jan.

(L.S.) EDMUND SUFFOLK.

---

## XLV.

A.D. 1506. 9 April.

HENRY PRINCE OF WALES TO PHILIP KING OF CASTILE.

[Addit. MS. 21,404. Brit. Mus.]

TRESHAULT, tresexcellent, et trespuissant prince, je me recommande a vous le plus affectueusement et de bon cueur que faire puis. Pource que le chambellan de ma treschere et tresamee compaigne la princesse ma femme sen va presentement pardevers vous pour aucunes matieres quil dit avoir affaire pardela, ma supplie et requis vous voulloir escripre en sa faveur.

In behalf of the princess Catherine's chamberlain now going to Spain.

---

(TRANSLATION.)

MOST high, most excellent, and mighty prince, I commend myself to you in the most affectionate and hearty manner that I can. Whereas the chamberlain of my most dear and well-beloved consort the princess my wife is going at present to you for certain matters which he says he has to transact in that quarter, he has requested me to write to you in his favor. I pray you very heartily, most high,

A.D. 1506. 9 April. Je vous prye trescordiallement, treshault, tresexcellent, et trespuissant prince, que le vueillez en sesdites affaires avoir pour recommande, et me vouloir de temps en aultre advertir et faire savoir de vostre bonne sante et prosperite, laquelle je desire singulierement et de tout mon cueur estre de longue continuacion et bonne duree comme je vouldroye la myenne propre. Et de ma part, quant je pourray recouvrer messagier propice je suis bien delibere de vous faire le semblable.

En me signiffiant, au surplus, sil y a quelque chose pardeca enquoy vous pourroye faire honneur et plaisir et je mectre payne de vous y complaire de tout mon cueur, par le bon aide de Nostre Seigneur, auquel je prye vous donner, treshault, tresexcellent, et trespuissant prince, bonne vie et longue. Escript au manoir de Grenewiche, le ix[e] jour davril.

Vostre humble cosyn,
HENRY PRYNCE DE GALLES.

A treshault, tresexcellent, et trespuissant Prince, le Roy de Castille, de Leon, et de Grenade, etc.

---

most excellent, and mighty prince, that you will hold him recommended in his said affairs, and that you will apprise me from time to time and let me know of your good health and prosperity, which I particularly and with all my heart desire to be of long continuance as I would my own. And for my part, whenever I can find a fitting messenger I am determined to do the like to you.

Moreover, on your intimating to me if there be anything here in which I can do you honor and pleasure, I will take pains to satisfy you in it with all my heart, by the good aid of Our Lord, whom I pray to give you, most high, most excellent and mighty prince, good life and long. Written at the manor of Greenwich, the 9th day of April.

Your humble cousin,
HENRY PRINCE OF WALES.

To the most high, most excellent, and mighty Prince, the king of Castile, Leon, and Granada, &c.

## XLVI.

A.D. 1506.
27 May.

### THE KNIGHTS OF RHODES TO HENRY VII.[1]

[Orig., Cott. Charter VI. 10.]

SERENISSIMO ac illustrissimo principi, potentissimoque domino, domino Henrico Dei gratia Angliæ, Franciæ, &c., regi. Nos frater Emericus Damboise Dei gratia Sacræ domus hospitalis Sancti Johannis Jherosolymi magister humilis, pauperumque Jesu Christi custos; Et nos conventus Rhodi domus ejusdem, tamquam humiles servitores et clientuli, salutem in Domino prosperosque ad vota successus ac nostram humillimam commendationem præmittimus. Noster ordo et nos hic in oriente continuam residentiam facientes ac bellum gerentes pro defensione Christiani nominis proventus nostros in partibus occiduis hinc inde sparsos habemus, quos cum difficultate recolligimus et huc conduci facimus. Præterea, quia proventus ipsi sunt tenues, et ad ipsos multi sinistris viis anhelant, consuevimus protectores habere qui nos et res nostras Christiano nomini dedicatos contra Turcos defendant ut professionem nostram ad honorem Christianæ fidei complere valeamus absque Christianorum impedimento. Quare supplicamus humiliter vestræ sacræ regiæ majestati, veræ catholicæ et honoris Christiani zelantissimæ, non dedignetur has nostras literas hilari vultu et læto animo suscipere qui de vestræ sacræ regiæ majestatis benignitate, clementia, ac mansuetudine confisi, de nostro deliberato consilio ac certa scientia serie præsentium omni meliori via, modo, et forma quibus melius, decentius et magis convenienter facere possumus et debemus, vestram sacram regiam

[1] A copy of this letter was found lately among the Chancery records formerly in the Rolls Chapel, on a parchment roll larger than the ordinary rolls of Chancery, and containing this single entry.

A.D. 1506. 27 May. Nominating him Protector of their Order.

majestatem facimus, creamus, constituimus et solemniter ordinamus nostrum nostræque religionis et militiæ per universum Christianum orbem et in suis inclytissimis regnis protectorem, fautorem, patronum et defensorem, obnixe et affectuose ipsam rogantes ut ordinem ipsum ejusque milites et negotia in sua benevolentia recipere et tenere velit tamquam suos deditissimos servitores, et ipsos defendere et protegere contra quoscumque molestatores, et per suas literas Sanctissimo Domino nostro, ac sacro reverendissimorum dominorum cardinalium collegio, cæterisque ecclesiasticis prælatis et dominis commendatos facere ad hoc, ut nos et dictum ordinem in nostris privilegiis et immunitatibus sine molestia conservare dignentur; ut magis quiete bello contra infideles inservire valeamus, et sub suo præsidio, prout nostra firma spes est, molestiis extraordinariis careamus; pro quo quicquid facultatis in nobis est eidem offerimus, et ipsam participem facimus de meritis et omnibus bonis operibus, quæ hæc religio et ejus milites tam in oriente quam per universum orbem complent. Sperantes quod hæc nostra parva oblatio vestræ sacræ regiæ majestati erit grata non minus quam denarius ab anicula in gazofilatio positus. Deus vestram sacram regiam majestatem felicem conservet. In cujus rei testimonium bulla nostra communis plumbea præsentibus est appensa. Datum in nostro conventu Rhodi die vigesima septima mensis Maii anno millesimo quingentesimo sexto.

BARTH. POLICIANUS,
Vicecancellarius.

Rotulata in Cancellaria.[1]

(L.S.)[2]

[1] In the hand of Policianus.

[2] The leaden seal of the order attached.

## XLVII.

### Lewis XII. to Henry VII.[1]

[MS. Addit. 21,382. Brit. Mus.]

A.D. 1506. 31 Aug.

Treshault et trespuissant Prince, nostre trescher et tresame frere et cousin, a vous tresaffectueusement et de bon cueur nous recommandons. Et vueillez savoir que nous avons receu les lettres que nouz avez escriptes, tant par messire Francois Marezen chevallier, vostre famillier serviteur, que par Mace de Villebresme nostre varlet de chambre. Et par eulx avons amplement et bien au long entendu toutes les choses que de vostre part ilz nous ont dictes et declairees, et mesmement le desir, vouloir et affection que vouz avez a lentretenement et continuacion de la bonne amytie, confederacion, et fraternelle intelligence qui est entre nous; de quoy

Translation.

Most high and mighty prince, our most dear and well-beloved brother and cousin, we commend ourselves to you affectionately and sincerely. And please it you to know that we have received the letters you have written to us, both by Sir Francis Marsin, knight, your familiar servant, and by Mace de Villebreame, our valet de chambre. And by them we have fully and at length understood everything that they have said and declared to us on your part, and likewise the desire, wish, and affection that you have for the maintenance and continuing of the good amity, confederation, and brotherly understanding which is between us; for which we thank you

[1] From a copy in the hand of Henry VII.'s French secretary Meautis, doubtless that which was sent with the letter immediately following.

A.D. 1506. 31 Aug.

tant et si cordiallement que faire povons nous vous mercions. Et vous advertissons que de ce navons jamais eu et navons aucun doubte, et nous en sommes tousjours tenuz et tenons aussi certains que de nostre propre fait, et jusques icy effectuellement en toutes choses avons bien congneu vostredit bon vouloir. Aussi de nostrepart soiez sceur, treshault et trespuissant prince, nostre trescher et tresame frere et cousin, que vous nous trouverez a jamais en telle et semblable voulente sans variacion quelconque; car nous avons desire et desirons lentretenement de vostredite amytie et alliance pardessus toute aultre, et icelle inviolablement garder; vous priant tant et de si bon cueur que faire povons croyre fermement que vous nous trouverez a jamais vostre bon, loyal, et entier frere.

Et pource que nous avons entendu, tant parce que nous a dit vostredit serviteur, comme aussi par les lettres que avez envoyees par ledit Villebresme, le desir et affection que avez a ce que le different qui est entre nostre trescher et tresame frere et cousin le roy de Castille et nostre cousin le duc de Gheldres se

---

as much and as heartily as we can, and assure you that of this we have not and never have had any doubt, but we have felt as assured of it as of our own act, and up to this time have effectually known your good will in everything. Be sure that on our part, also, most high and mighty prince, &c., you will find us always in the like will, without any variation; for we have desired and do desire the maintenance of your said amity and alliance above every other, and to keep it inviolably; praying you as earnestly as we can to believe firmly that you will find us always your good, true, and devoted brother.

And because we have understood, both by what your said servant has told us, and also by the letters that you have sent by the said Villebresme, the desire and concern you have that the difference which exists between our very dear and well-beloved brother and cousin the king of Castile and our cousin the duke of

puisse appaiser par voye et moyen amyable, en delaissant les voyes de fait et hostillitez, pour les causes et consideracions que vostredit serviteur nous a dictes, lesquelles trouvons tresbonnes et raisonnables, et en ensuyvant icelles sommes deliberez de ace nous employer de nostrepart. Et pour ace mieulx et plus tost parvenir avons envoye a toute extreme dilligence et en poste, ung de noz varletz de chambre pardevers nostre cousin de Gheldres, pour surce luy declairer nostre vouloir et intencion qui est semblable et conforme au vostre, assavoir de prendre quelque bon moyen et expedient pour parvenir a paix en ceste matiere. Et entre aultres nous semble que si nostredit frere et cousin le roy de Castille, et nostredit cousin de Gheldres vouloient entierement soubz mectre tous les differends qui sont entre eulx sur vous et nous (ce que croyons que nostredit cousin de Gheldres fera), seroit le bien et prouffit deulx. Car nous sommes sceurs que vous et nous leur garderions a chacun ce

A.D. 1506. 31 Aug.

Lewis thinks that France and England should arbitrate between Castile and Gueldres.

---

Gueldres should be settled by amicable means, acts of hostility being abandoned, for the causes and considerations that your said servant has mentioned to us, which we find very good and reasonable, we are determined to exert ourselves according to the same for our part. And in order the better and more speedily to effect this, we have despatched with extreme diligence and in post one of our valets de chambre to our cousin of Gueldres, to declare to him on this matter our will and intention, which is similar and conformable to yours, that is to say, to take some good mean and expedient to attain peace in this business. And among others, it appears to us that if our said brother and cousin the king of Castile and our said cousin of Gueldres would wholly submit the differences between them to you and us (which we think our said cousin of Gueldres will do) it would be for their good and advantage. For we are sure that you and we would keep to each of them that which belonged

A.D. 1506. 31 Aug.

He has, therefore, countermanded auxiliaries that he was sending to the latter.

qui leur appartiendroit par raison. Et pàrce moyen cesseroient les voyes de fait de hostillite. Et soubz cest espoir avons incontinent contremande et fait arrester la plus grosse bande, que envoyeons a nostredit cousin de Gheldres, laquelle estoit sur lextremite des marches et frontiere de nostre royaulme. Et se plustost eussions este advertiz de vostre desir surce, neussions laisse partir ceulx qui desja estoient passez. Esperant aussi que de vostre part ne laisserez point partir les vostres jusques ace que aurez certaines nouvelles dece que nostredit varlet de chambre aura besoingne devers nostredit cousin de Gheldres, ceque esperons avoir dedens dix ou douze jours au plus tard; pendant lequel temps avons este daviz que vostredit serviteur deust icy demourer, lequel despescherons incontinent que aurons responce de ce que dit est. Et avecque luy envoyerons quelquun de noz privez serviteurs pour de ce et aultres choses vous advertir plusamplement de nostrepart. Priant Dieu a

---

to them in reason. And by this means acts of hostility would cease. And in this hope we have countermanded and stopped the largest band, that we were sending to our said cousin of Gueldres, which was on the extreme frontier of our kingdom. And if we had been apprised sooner of your desire on this point, we would not have allowed those to leave who had already gone. Hoping also that on your part you will not allow yours to leave till you shall have certain news of what our said valet de chambre shall have negotiated with our said cousin of Gueldres, which we hope to have within ten or twelve days at the latest; during which time we have been of opinion that your said servant should remain here, whom we shall despatch whenever we shall have an answer to what we have mentioned. And along with him we shall send some one of our privy servants to inform you the more amply on our part of this and other matters. Praying God, meanwhile,

tant, treshault et trespuissant Prince, nostre trescher et tresame frere et cousin, quil vous vueille tenir en sa saincte et digne garde. Escript a Bloys, le derrenier jour daoust. A.D. 1506. 31 Aug.

*Ainsi signe*, Vostre bon et loyal frere,
LOYS.

*Et du Secretaire*, ROBERTET.

*Et au dessus de la lettre.*—A treshault et trespuissant prince, nostre trescher et tresame frere et cousin, Le Roy Dangleterre.

---

most high and mighty prince, our most dear and well-beloved brother and cousin, to have you in his holy and worthy keeping. Written at Blois, the last day of August.

*Signed*, Your good and faithful brother,
LEWIS.

*and by the Secretary* ROBERTET.

*Superscribed:* To the most high and mighty Prince, our most dear and well-beloved brother and cousin The King of England.

## XLVIII.

### Henry VII. to Philip King of Castile.

[MS. Addit. 21,404. Art. 6. Brit. Mus.]

A.D. 1506. 16 Sept.

Treshault et trespuissant prince, nostre trescher et tresame frere, cousin, et bon filz, a vous nous recommandons tant affectueusement et de bon cueur que faire povons. Depuis les derrenieres lectres que nous vous avons escriptes de nostre chasteau de Windesore, nostre trescher et tresame frere le roy Loys de France, apres le retour vers luy de son varlet de chambre, Mace de Villebresme et arrivee de nostre serviteur Messire Francois Marezen, et entendu la declairacion de la charge que luy avyons baillee par instruction pour la lui exposer, delaquelle vous avons envoye le double; il a, puis quatre jours encza, envoye vers nous ung des chevaucheurs de son escuierie qui nous a presente unes lectres de sa part, par lesquelles il fait recit dela reception de celles que lui avyons escriptes par les dessusnommez et demonstre quil a bon vouloir,

As Lewis XII. has offered to mediate between

#### Translation.

Most high and mighty prince, our most dear and well-beloved brother, cousin, and good son, we commend ourselves to you as affectionately and cordially as we can. Since the last letters we wrote to you from our castle of Windsor, our most dear and well-beloved brother, king Lewis of France, after the return towards him of his valet de chambre, Mace de Villebresme, and arrival of our servant, Sir Francis Marsin, and having understood the declaration of the charge which we had delivered to him by instruction to show to him, of which we have sent you a copy, has within the last four days sent to us one of the grooms of his stable, who has presented to us a letter on his behalf, wherein he makes mention of the receipt of those which we had written to him by the above named, and declares that he has good will, desire, and affec-

desir, et affection que a nostre requeste et persuasion, le A.D. 1506. différent qui est entre vous et messire Charles de Gueldres puisse estre appaise par voie et moien amyable, en delaissant toutes voies de fait et de hostillitez, pour les causes et consideracions que nostredit serviteur lui a dictes et declairees par nostre ordonnance et commandement; et que a cest intencion il a envoye devers ledict messire Charles ung sien varlet de chambre, en le exhortant de prendre quelque bon moien et expedient pour parvenir a paix, et a aussi fait retirer incontinent la plus grosse bende quil envoyoit devers ledit de Gueldres; et que sil eust este plustost adverty de nostre desir, il neust pas laisse passer ceulx qui desja sont passez; esperant que nous ne laisserons point partir ceulx quentendons envoyer devers vostre lieutenant general, aumoins jusques ace que aurons certaines nouvelles du besongne de sondit varlet de chambre, quil espoire estre dedens dix ou douze jours ensuyvans la date de ses lectres, comme de toutes les choses dessusdites et daultres lesdites lectres le portent plus a plain, le

16 Sept.
Philip and Charles of Gueldres.

---

tion that at our request and persuasion the difference which is between you and messire Charles of Gueldres may be composed in an amicable manner, leaving all acts of hostility, for the causes and considerations which our said servant has shown and declared to him by our order and command; and that with this intention he has sent towards the said messire Charles, a valet de chambre of his, exhorting him to take some good means and expedient to arrive at peace, and has also immediately withdrawn the largest band that he was sending towards the said De Gueldres; and that if he had been sooner apprised of our desire he would not have allowed those who have already gone to pass; hoping that we will not allow to depart those that we intend to send towards your lieutenant-general, at least till we have certain news of the negotiation of his said valet de chambre, which he hopes to be within ten or twelve days following the date of his letters, as with regard to all the affairs abovesaid and others the said letters

A.D. 1506. 16 Sept.

double desquelles vous envoyons cy dedens encloz affin que puissez le tout entendre.

Et pour responce sur le contenu en sadite lectre nous le mercions du bon vouloir et affection quil demonstre avoir a nostre desir a la pacifficacion des dits differends. Et que entant quil a contremande la dite grosse bende qui estoit sur la frontiere preste a passer; aussi sur lesperance et bonne confidence que nous avons en luy quil fera retirer ses aultres gens de guerre quil a envoiez oudit pais de Gueldres, et de non y envoyer nulz aultres cy en apres, et quil face aussi cesser ledit messire Charles de toutes voiez de fait et de hostillitez, et de ne permectre ou souffrir estre fait aucune invasion ou exploict de guerre sur voz pais et subgetz aussi bien dedens ledit pais de Gueldres que ailleurs en vostre obeissance:—en ce cas avons este et suysmes contens de differer et retarder lenvoy de nostre secours que avons promis bailler et envoier, (lesquelz sont tous prestz apartir) aumoins jusques ace que soions a la verite acer-

Henry has delayed the succours he was about to send,

---

contain more at length, the copy of which we send you herein enclosed, in order that you may understand the whole.

And for answer to the contents of his said letters, we thank him for the goodwill and affection which he professes to have to the appeasement of the said differences. And that inasmuch as he has countermanded the said great band which was upon the frontier ready to pass; also in the hope and good confidence that we have in him that he will withdraw his other men of war that he has sent into the said country of Gueldres, and not send thither any others thenceforward, and that he will by all means restrain the said messire Charles from acts of hostility and not permit or suffer any invasion or warlike exploit to be done upon your countries and subjects, either in the said country of Gueldres or elsewhere in your dominions:—in this case we have been and are content to defer and put off the sending of our succours which we promised to give and send (which are quite ready to leave), at least till we be

tennez par nostredit serviteur Francois Maresen de la responce que aura faicte ledit messire Charles a sondict varlet de chambre. A.D. 1506. 16 Sept.

En le advertissant, oultre, que si aloccasion du retardement et envoy de nostredit secours ce que faisons de present a sadite responce, il y eust quelque invasion on exploict de guerre faicte sur vosdits pais et subgetz que len mectroit le deffault et blasme sur nous. Dont, se aussi advenoit, entant que nous avons retarde lenvoy de nostredit secours, la chose redonderoit a nostre deshonneur et reprouche, dequoy auryons tresgrant regret et desplaisir. Et pourtant quil y vueille bien penser et pourveoir, en telle facon et maniere que nostre honneur puisse estre garde on cest endroit.

Et dabondant nous lui signiffions, que nous serons bien joyeulx et contens de avec luy nous emploier en tout ce que pourrons ala pacifficacion desdits differens; mais nous semple que pour mieulx parvenir ala-

---

truly ascertained by our said servant Francis Marsin of the answer which the said messire Charles shall have made to his said valet de chambre.

Informing him, moreover, that if, in consequence of the delay of the envoy and of our said succours which we make at present to his said answer, there should be any invasion or exploit of war done upon your said countries and subjects, the default and blame would be laid upon us; to whose dishonour and reproach, if it so happened, the thing would redound inasmuch as we have delayed the sending of our said succours; whereat we should have very great regret and dissatisfaction. And therefore that he would think well and provide in such fashion and manner that our honor may be preserved in this behalf.

And moreover we signified to him that we shall be very glad to cooperate with him in all that we can to the appeasement of the said differences; but it appears to us that, in order the better to arrive at the said peace and union, it is

A.D. 1506. 16 Sept.

and advises Philip to submit to the arbitration of England and France.

dite paix et union, estre expedient et tresneccessaire, que les choses dunepart et daultre soient remises en lestat enquoy elles estoient au jour de vostre departement et allee en Espaigne; et des aultres choses qui resteront en difficulte, se vous et ledit messire Charles les voullez mectre en la judicature de nous et de luy, nous en deciderons et les vuyderons ala raison, selon droit et bonne equite, sans faire tord ne a vous ne a luy. En le advertissant pour la conclusion de nostredite lectre de responce, que des choses dessusdites en advertirions vostredit lieutenant-general et conseil quavez laissez pardela, en les conseillant et exhortant que de leur couste il ny soit trouve aucun deffault, et que de leur part toutes voies de fait et de hostillitez puissent cesser, et deulx condescendre a tout bon et raisonnable appoinctement; ce que leur avons escript et conseille faire, aumoins pendant vostre absence, pour evicter les dangiers et tresgrans inconveniens qui en pourroient ensuyvir, et pour non vous mectre,

---

expedient and very necessary that things be restored on each side to the condition in which they were on the day of your departure and going into Spain; and as to the other things which shall remain in difficulty, if you and the said messire Charles will put them in the arbitration of us and him, we will decide thereon and despatch them reasonably, according to right and good equity, without doing injury either to you or him. Notifying to him, for the conclusion of our said letter of reply, that we would inform your said lieutenant general and council whom you have left there of the things above said, advising and exhorting them that on their side there be found no default, that all acts of hostility may cease on their part, and that they should agree to any good and reasonable appointment; which we have written to them and counselled them to do, at least during your absence, to avoid the dangers and very great inconveniences which might ensue, and not to put you, your

voz pais et subgetz en charge, si la necessite grandement ne le requiert. Et avons adverty oultre vostredit lieutenant-general et conseil que oucas que ledit messire Charles ne se veult renger a la raison, et se condescendre a tout bon et raisonnable appoinctement que nous leur envoyerons nostredit secours, qui est desja tout prest apartir, comme dit est, quant besoing sera, pour le desir et affection que nous avons de vous complaire et faire plaisir en voz affaires. Et aussi tost que nous aurons entendu la responce que aura eu ledict varlet de chambre dicellui messire Charles, et sceu en ce lintencion, vouloir, et disposicion de nostredit bon frere le roy Loys en advertirons en toute extreme dilligence vosdicts lieutenant et conseil. Et avons cest espoir que ledit roy Francois fera et tiendra ce quil nous a escript, et quil se deportera de bailler aucun aide, faveur, et assistence audit messire Charles, entant quil congnoit, que [jam]ais nous voullons mesler de vostredit affaire de Gueldres en vostredite A.D. 1506. 16 Sept.

---

countries and subjects to expense, if necessity do not greatly require it. And we have further informed your said lieutenant general and council that, in case the said messire Charles will not yield to reason and condescend to any good and reasonable appointment, we will send to them our said succours, which are now quite ready to depart, as already mentioned, whenever necessary, for the desire and affection we have to satisfy you and do you pleasure in your affairs. And as soon as we shall have heard the answer which the said valet de chambre shall have had from the same messire Charles, and known herein the intention, will, and pleasure of our good brother king Lewis we will inform your said lieutenant and council thereof in all extreme diligence. And we have hope that the said French king will do and keep that which he has promised us, and that he will forbear to give any aid, favor, and assistance to the said messire Charles, inasmuch as he knows that we would never interfere in your said business of Gueldres in your

A.D. 1506. 16 Sept. absence ; car nous navons jusque a ores trouve faulte en promesse quil nous a faicte. De toutes lesquelles choses vous avons bien voulu advertir, comme a nostre frere, cousin et bon filz, lhonneur, bien, et prosperite duquel nous desirons singulierement estre de bonne et longue contynuacion et perseverance autant que de prince qui vive. Ainsi que scait nostre Seigneur qui, treshault et trespuissant prince, nostre trescher et tresame frere, consin et bon filz, vouz vueille entretenir en sa tressaincte garde. Escript en nostre manoir de Guylford, le xvj$^{e}$ jour de Septembre lan xv$^{c}$. et six.

Vostre frere, cousin, et bon pere,

(L.S.) HENRY R.

MEAUTIS.

*Addressed:* A treshault et trespuissant prince, vostre trescher et tresame frere, cousin, et bon filz, le roy de Castille, &c.

---

said absence; for we have not to this time found him wanting in any promise that he has made to us. Of all which things we have desired to give you intelligence, as to our brother, cousin, and good son, whose honor, weal, and prosperity we especially wish to be of good and long continuance, as much as of any prince living, as knoweth Our Lord who, most high and mighty prince, &c., preserve you in his most holy keeping. Written in our manor of Guildford, the 16th day of September 1506.

Your brother, cousin, and good father,

HENRY R.

To the most high and mighty prince, our most dear and well beloved brother, cousin and good son, the king of Castile, &c.

## XLIX.

### Maximilian to Henry VII.

[From copy on a parchment roll in the Record Office, found among the Chancery Records formerly at the Rolls Chapel.]

Serenissimo principi domino Henrico Regi Angliæ, &c., fratri et consanguineo nostro charissimo.

Maximilianus, divina favente clementia, Romanorum Rex semper Augustus, ac Hungariæ, Dalmatiæ, Croatiæ, etc., Rex, Archidux Austriæ, Dux Burgundiæ, Brabantiæ, etc., Comes Palatinus, etc., serenissimo principi, domino Henrico Regi Angliæ, etc., fratri et consanguineo nostro charissimo, salutem, et fraterni amoris continuum incrementum. Serenissime princeps, frater et consanguinee charissime, significavimus nuper serenitati vestræ pacem et concordiam inter nos et subditos ac incolas regni Hungariæ cum satisfactione nostra initam atque conclusam. Et cum pro singulari vestra in nos benevolentia ac mutuo fraterno amore non minus existimemus serenitatem vestram ex sinistris nostris successibus accipere mœrorem, quam ex prosperis et felicibus lætitiam et oblectationem; idcirco voluimus eidem tanquam amantissimo et confidentissimo fratri nostro significare, quamvis Francorum rex alias filiam suam unicam Claudiam illustrissimo Carolo, archiduci Austriæ, etc., nepoti nostro charissimo matrimonio locare promiserit, et nedum nobis super hoc literas et sigilla sua in validissima forma dederit, sed etiam strictissimo juramento super corpus Domini nostri Jesu Christi et ejus sacram crucem et sancta Quatuor Evangelia manibus suis corporaliter tacta, bona fide et in verbo regio, etiam sub censuris apostolicis quibus se in casu contraventionis subjecit, necnon sub obligatione et hypotheca omnium bonorum suorum præsentium et futurorum ac pœna perjurii quam possit tali casu incurrere, illud inviolabiliter observare solemniter se obligaverit; nihilominus, his omnibus non attentis, præfatam filiam suam, relicto matrimonio prædicto, cum

A.D. 1506. 14 Sept.

Lewis XII, in violation of his oath, has given his daughter in marriage to Francis duke of Valois.

A.D. 1506. 14 Sept. voluntate et consilio regni sui contra fidem et jusjurandum præstitum de novo duci de Valloys,[1] delphino, et successori regni Franciæ desponsavit; idque per oratores suos nobis palam et publice significavit, non alia excusatione usus, nisi quod prius existimavit matrimonium cum filio nostro Carolo fore utile et proficuum regno Franciæ; nunc vero edoctus sit illud cedere in maximum præjudicium et damnum regni sui; conatique sunt præfati oratores in conspectu nostro et plurimorum principum et procerum imperii et curæ nostræ fucato et phalerato sermone tam apertum et impudens facinus honestare et ostendere tanquam pro commodo et utilitate sua. Nihil sit quod eis non liceat, neque fides servanda sit nisi quantum expedit eis; quod cum timeamus nihil boni portendere neque ullum bonum finem sortiri posse, et merito omnibus Christianis regibus et principibus, quibus cum Gallis tractandum occurret, exemplo esse debeat ut aperte cognoscant, quotiens eis libuerit, quod pro eorum arbitrio et libidine, quoscumque tractatus violare non verebuntur, asserentes non esse ex utilitate et commodo ipsorum. Idcirco voluimus hoc serenitati vestræ per litteras nostras significare ut de iniquis et malignis Gallorum machinationibus certior esse possit, et si forte tanquam vulpes fraudes suas etiam apud serenitatem vestram colorare conarentur, quamvis non dubitemus ipsam de veritate jamdudum edoctam esse; tamen illa iterato intelligat et nullam eis fidem adhibeat. Et cum necessarium sit pro securitate nostra et statuum nostrorum contrahere novam affinitatem per desponsationem dicti nepotis nostri Caroli, cuperemus supra omnia illam cum serenitate vestra fieri, ut quanto major inter nos indies amicitia et conjunctio orietur tanto formidolosiores reddamur omnibus inimicis et adversariis nostris; possimusque[2] nedum eorum conatus reprimere sed etiam aliquando ita eos coercere et compescere, ne inposterum contra nos pro libidine ipsorum

[1] Afterwards Francis I.

[2] *possumusque*, MS.

moliri audeant. Et quum per nonnullos bonos viros et amatores communis beneficii nostri fuerimus admoniti, postquam illud matrimonium Caroli cum Francia nullum sortietur effectum ut cum filia vestra concluderemus, habuimus in hoc bonam complacentiam et desideramus quod concludatur cum conditionibus, quemadmodum super hoc latius scripsimus filio nostro serenissimo et Catholico regi Castellæ,[1] adhortantes ut de illo cum serenitate vestra tractari, et concludere faciat; et habemus pro certo quod illud non recusabit. Scimus enim, tum ob naturalem animi sui affectionem, tum beneficia et paternas demonstrationes ei post naufragium in mari passum a serenitate vestra exhibitas, eum non minus cordialiter et ferventer serenitatem vestram colere et amare, quam nos, suum proprium et naturalem parentem; neque nos aliud desideramus nisi quod nos ambo et communis filius noster simus una persona in voluntate et domus nostræ sint una[2] in perpetuum, cum tota sinceritate, firmæ et immutabiles ad utramque fortunam contra quoscumque, in quo ex latere nostro non deficiemus, sed ita in omnibus nos adhibuimus ut quos cognoverimus de vobis male meritos non minus existimabimus quam si nos ipsos offendissent, et communem semper nobis omnem fortunam vobiscum esse reputabimus. Significamus præterea serenitati vestræ nos diligenter fecisse inquisitionem de oratoribus Gallicis qui ad Hungariam per Venetias profecti fuerunt, et habemus compertum eos ad regem Hungariæ pervenisse et cum magno luctu fuisse per eos ploratum propter obitum reginæ.[3] Non tamen potuimus percipere quod frater ducis de Suffolch apud illos fuerit, quamquam, mortua regina, nullum ulterius periculum sit quod Hungari nunc propter nimiam eorum barbariem, nec modernus rex aliquid pro eo faciet. Nos tamen continuo inquiremus et conabimur intelligere ubi sit.

A.D. 1506. 14 Sept.

Maximilian is therefore desirous that a marriage be arranged between Charles and Henry's daughter.

---

[1] Philip.
[2] *unsa*, MS.
[3] Anne, queen of Ladislaus VI. of Hungary.

A.D. 1506. 14 Sept. et de omnibus serenitatem vestram certiorem reddemus; quod serenitatem vestram latere minime voluimus, ita enim reipsa experietur; quam diu incolumem in felici regimine perseverare cupimus. Datum in oppido nostro Celeya, die Lunæ decima quarta mensis Septembris anno Domini M. quingentesimo sexto, regnorum nostrorum, Romani vicesimo primo, Hungariæ vero decimo septimo.

MAXIus,
Votre bon frere.[1]
Ad mandatum domini regis proprium.

---

## L.

### MAXIMILIAN TO HENRY VII.

[From the same roll as the preceding.]

19 Sept. MAXIMILIANUS, divina favente clementia Romanorum Rex semper Augustus ac Hungariæ, Dalmatiæ, Croatiæ, etc. Rex, Archidux Austriæ, Dux Burgundiæ, Brabantiæ, etc., Comes Palatinus, etc., Serenissimo principi domino HENRICO Regi Angliæ, etc., fratri et consanguineo nostro carissimo, salutem et fraterni amoris continuum incrementum. Serenissime princeps, frater et consanguinee carissime; post expeditas proximas litteras nostras recepimus vestras litteras datas ex manerio suo Grenwici die xiij. Augusti plenas fraterni amoris et benevolentiæ; quæ nobis gratissimæ et supra modum expectatæ fuerunt. Et quia ad easdem per unum oratorem nostrum ad serenitatem vestram pro hoc et aliis negotiis summæ importantiæ responsuri sumus, ideo impræsentiarum noluimus aliud serenitati vestræ significare nisi quod

Acknowledging letters from Henry of the 13th Aug.

---

[1] *Maxius, votre bon frere*] The handwriting of these words in this and the two following letters appears to be an imitation of Maximilian's signature.

in omnibus æque respondebimus omni fraterna mutua benevolentia, ut serenitas vestra aperte cognoscat nos nihil magis appetere, nihil magis a Deo exoptare nisi quod præstetur nobis occasio ostendendi serenitati vestræ quam sincere illius voluntati commodis et dignitatibus adesse et morem gerere cupiamus. Quam Deus Omnipotens diu felicem et incolumem in suo regimine conservare dignetur. Datum in oppido nostro Petovia die Sabbati xix. Septembris, anno Domini millesimo quingentesimo sexto, regnorum nostrorum Romani vicesimo primo, Hungariæ vero decimo septimo. A.D. 1506. 19 Sept.

Votre bone frere,

MAXI^us.[1]

Ad mandatum domini regis proprium.

---

## LI.

### MAXIMILIAN TO HENRY VII.

[From the same roll as the preceding.]

MAXIMILIANUS, Divina favente clementia Romanorum Rex semper Augustus, ac Hungariæ, Dalmatiæ, Croatiæ, etc. Rex, Archidux Austriæ, Dux Burgundiæ, Brabantiæ, etc., Comes Palatinus, etc. serenissimo principi, domino HENRICO, Regi Angliæ, etc., fratri et consanguineo nostro carissimo, salutem et fraterni amoris continuum incrementum. 24 Sept. Serenissime princeps, frater et consanguinee carissime, quamquam frequenter per litteras manu nostra propria scriptas et oratores nostros et filii nostri missos apud illustrissimam Margaretam, archiducissam Austriæ, ducissam Burgundiæ, Brabantiæ, etc., viduam relictam Sabaudiæ, institerimus et nihil prætermiserimus ut eam induceremus ad præstandum consensum suum in matrimonium inter vestram serenitatem et ipsam per nos conclusum, tamen nuper habuimus responsum a præfatis oratoribus nostris quo intelleximus eam adhuc perseverare in opinione non contrahendi matrimonium sed continuo rem differre, certumque

The Emperor has not yet been able to persuade his daughter to a match with Henry VII.

---

[1] See note in preceding page.

A.D. 1506. 24 Sept. habemus id opera et studio atque artibus Gallorum fieri, qui omnes consiliarios et familiares secretiores prædictæ filiæ nostræ subornarunt et muneribus corruperunt ut eam in hac opinione teneant et per hoc serenitatem vestram nobis minus devinctam reddant. Quocirca volumus hoc serenitati vestræ significare, hortantes omni quo possumus studio ne hujusmodi sinistris æmulorum nostrorum artibus et conatibus cedere et assentiri velit. Nos enim pollicemur adhuc serenitati vestræ non desistere donec a filia nostra hujusmodi consensum obtineamus; et pro hac re, sive ante adventum nostrum ad Urbem sive post, si tam cito ituri sumus, personaliter ad filiam nostram pro hac re proficisci et eam inducere ut omnino voluntati nostræ morem gerat et consensum suum præbeat, quemadmodum hoc brevi latius per oratores nostros vestræ serenitati significabimus. Quam diu felicem et incolumem in suo regimine perseverare cupimus. Datum in oppido nostro Gretl., die Jovis vicesima quarta Septembris, anno Domini millesimo quingentesimo sexto, regnorum nostrorum, Romani vicesimo primo, Hungariæ vero decimo septimo.

but he will visit her to urge it.

Votre bone frer,

MAXI^us^.[1]

Ad mandatum domini regis proprium.

## LII.

A.D. 1506. 15 Nov.

### PASSPORT OF THE BISHOP OF LIEGE TO THOMAS KILLINGWORTH.

[MS. Cott. Vespasian F. III. No. 172.]

ERARDE De la Mark, par la grace de Dieu Evesque de Liege, Duc de Buillon, conte de Loz, etc. Savoir

TRANSLATION.

ERARD De la Mark, by the grace of God bishop of Liege, duke of Bouillon, count de Loz, &c. We make known to all

[1] See note at p. 304.

faisons a tous que nous avons donne, et donnons par ces presentes, bon et leal suretie et saufconduit duran du jourduy, date de cestes, jusques a quinze mois entiers prochammment venans, et apres non vaillable, au Thomas Kyllyngworth, maistre dostell de Monseigneur Edmund duc de Suffolk, de Engliterre, pour venir en nostre citie de Liege et aultres bones villes part tout nous pais en generael, et y estre, demourer, et sejourner, se mestier est, acompaniez de quatre servitures au dessoubz, portan[s] dagues, espees, javellines, ou aultres bastons non deffenduz, pour la suretie de leurs personnes et deffenses de leurs corps; Et en iceulx nous pais et lieux dessudits aler, venir, hanter, frequenter, demourer, et sejourner, se mestier est, pour aucuns leurs negocies, besongnes, et affaires durant ledit temps. Mandons pour ce, et commandons a tous nous justiciers et officiers, gardez de pontz, passages, bonnes villes et destroiez, et autres nous hommes, subgets et servitures, prions et requerous tous quil appartiendra que audit Thomas Kyllyngworth, se gens et servitures, en sejour- A.D. 1506. 15 Nov.

---

men that we have given, and give by these presents good and faithful surety and safe conduct enduring from to day, the date of these, to 15 whole months next coming, and not available afterwards, to Thomas Killingworth, steward of my lord Edmund of Suffolk, of England, to come into our city of Liege and other good towns throughout our countries in general, and to be, remain, and sojourn there, if need be, accompanied by four servants or under, carrying daggers, swords, javelins, and other weapons not forbidden, for the security of their persons and defence of their bodies; and in the same our countries and places aforesaid to go, come, haunt, frequent, stay and sojourn, if need be, for any their affairs and business during the said time. We therefore order and command all our justices and officers, wardens of bridges, passages, good towns and liberties, and other our men, subjects and servants; we pray and request all to whom it shall appertain that to the said Thomas Killingworth, his men

A.D. 1506. 15 Nov. nant, venant, retournant, passant ou repassant, a cheval ou a pie ou sur aultre monture, portans dagues, especs, javellines, ou autres bastons non deffendus, pour la suretie de leurs corps et personnes, ainsy que dit est, durant le temps et espasse de quinze mois entiers ilz ne meffacent, mael dient, mettent ou donnent, ne facent mettre ou donner, par eulx ne par autres aucun destourbier ou empeschement, en corps ne en biens, et quelque facon et maniere que ce soit, mais les laissent paisiblement aler, venir, sejourner, demourer et retournier en nostredito citie, villes et autres lieux de nous dit pais se mestier est. Pourveu toutesfoys que durant ledit temps ledit Thomas Kyllyngworth, se gens et servitures, ou acun deux, ne feront, diront, ne pourchaisseront aucune choise en nostre prejudice, ne noz gens, pais, subgets et servitures, en corps ne en biens, en quelque facon ou maniere que ce soit. Donne en nostredit chateau de Huye le quinze jour de mois de Novembre, lan mil cincqcens et six.

ERARD.

---

and servants, in sojourning, coming, returning, passing or repassing, on horseback or on foot or otherwise mounted, carrying daggers, swords, javelins, or other weapons not, forbidden, for the security of their bodies or persons, as above, during the time and space of 15 whole months, they do not cause or give, by themselves or by others, any disturbance or impediment, in body or goods, in any manner or mode whatsoever; but permit them peaceably to go, come, sojourn, remain and return to our said city, towns and other places of our said countries, if need be. Provided always that during the said time, the said Thomas Killingworth, his men and servants, or any of them, shall not do, say, or procure anything to our prejudice nor to that of our men, countries, subjects and servants, in body or in goods, in any mode or manner whatsoever. Given in our "said" castle of Huye the 15th day of the month of November in the year 1506.

ERARD.

## LIII.

A.D. 1507. 14 April.

RICHARD DE LA POLE TO THE BISHOP OF LIEGE.

[Addit. MS. 19.398, Brit. Mus.]

REVERENDISSIME præsul, illustrissimeque princeps, post debitam commendationem, rogamus atque excellentissimam vestram dignitatem supplicamus quatenus vestra illustrissima dominatio tantum ob amorem nostri agere velit, ac placeat providere quendam dominum Nicholaum de Haghe, Aquensem, harum latorem, de quadam præbenda aut in ecclesia Sancti Dionisii, Sancti Pauli, aut Sancti Johannis in civitate vestra Leodiensi. Si id illustrissima dominatio vestra nostri ob amorem fecerit, in futuro Deo dante recompensabimus, atque itidem aut majus, si opportunitas occurrerit, facturi sumus. Valeat vestra reverendissima atque illustrissima dominatio atque optata nobilissimi cordis vestræ Optimus Deus adimpleat. Datum Budæ xiiij[a]. die Aprilis, anno Domini, 1507.

Requesting preferment for Nicholas de Haghe.

Per vestrum consanguineum,
RYCHARD SUFFOLK.

*Addressed:* Reverendissimo in Christo patri, illustrissimoque principi, domino Erardo Episcopo Leodiensi, Duci Bullon' ac comiti Lossen', domino meo colendissimo.

## LIV.

[MS. in Record Office.]

MEMORIALE Sacræ Cæsariæ Majestati pro servitore Domini Edmundi Ducis Suffolchiæ.

A.D. 1507? SACRATISSIME Cæsar, maximas gratias vestræ majestati humiliter refero pro favore vestro mihi diversimode dato; in quo humiliter supplico ut vestra majestas ex gratia vestra perseverare velit, quia mea fidelitas vestræ majestati non latet, et in qua conditione modo pro eadem existo vestra majestas melius scit quam egomet scio. In qua causa humiliter supplico, ut ex gratia vestra mihi esse velitis bonus et gratiosus dominus.

Reminding the Emperor of a promise to procure the liberation of De la Pole.

Invictissime Cæsar, cum post deliberationem dicti domini ducis in manus regis Henrici veniebam vestræ majestati, me benigne et gratiose accepistis, et mihi dicebatis quod causa et liberatio domini mei de carceribus erant firmatæ in manibus vestræ majestatis, et quod videbatis in me quod ego nolebam dimittere hanc rem quousque finalem conclusionem vestræ majestatis inter regem H. et eundem ducem vidissem, et quod vestra majestas in hac parte talem respectum mihi habere vellet et pro me sic tractaret per quod negotium haberem bonum et honestatem.

Quamvis, sacratissime Cæsar, cum eram in Bulsano, habebam de vestra majestate aliud responsum, quod omnibus consideratis nolo, nec alias quam bene accipere possum, sed quod erga me geretis bonam gratiam vestram, quamvis non vultis quod omnes hoc sciant. Et ad finem quod vestra majestas videbit facta mea, et quod non sum, nec volo in hoc magno et arduo negotio esse levis, vestræ majestati certifico, quod pro servitio dicti ducis pariter cum servitio vestræ majestatis veni in hanc civitatem Constantiæ propter hoc quod mihi aperuistis vestram bonam voluntatem versus dominum meum; et ea de causa quod bene scio quod vestra majestas pro honore vestro et serenissimi regis filii vestri defuncti et conscientiis utrorumque, dictum ducem et liberationem suam de carceribus in intimo corde recommendatum habetis. A.D. 1507?

Et quoad intentionem regis Henrici versus me, et practicas suas ad finem quod venirem in regnum Angliæ, latius tangere non indigeo; sed vestræ majestati dico et certifico, facietis de me quidcunque volueritis, quia pro muneribus regis H. nec pro aliqua re mundi non dimittam dictum ducem in sua maxima necessitate, et alias non faciam quam deceat bonum et fidelem servitorem. Et hoc vestra majestas vidit semper in me et videbitis. Et si sit placitum vestræ majestatis, me in hac parte cum adjutorio vestro sic teneam sub tuitione et defensione vestræ majestatis.[1]

Though King Henry endeavours to win him over, nothing shall induce the writer to desert his master in adversity.

Et, sacratissime Cæsar, si sit placitum et voluntas vestræ majestatis quod in his partibus expectabo, supplico ac peto humiliter quod vestra majestas oculis gratiæ me aspicere velit quod possum vivere et necessaria habere et una pensione[2] et loco conveniente ubi secure stare potuero[2] assignatis, taliter faciam quod vestra majestas de me erit contenta. Et in conclusione spero pro eodem adjutorio vestra majestas magnum habebit honorem. Et quicquid super his erit voluntas vestræ majestatis, humiliter supplico quod illam scire possum.

Et si placet vestræ majestati, humiliter peto quod possum intelligere quomodo prædictus dux et causa sua se habent.

Expecto responsum Domini Cæsaris.

---

[1] *Notandum* is here written in the margin in another hand.

[2] Sic.

A.D. 1507?

## LV.

[MS. in Record Office.]

MEMORIALE Sacræ Cæsariæ Majestati pro parte servitoris Domini[1] Edmundi Ducis Suffochiæ de Anglia.

SACRATISSIME Cæsar, humiliter supplico vestræ majestati quod vestra majestas ex gratia vestra velit mihi esse bonus et gratiosus dominus, et quod possum habere favorem et gratiam vestræ majestatis tanto citius pro meo fideli servitio prædicto domino duci.

The Emperor knows how his fidelity to Suffolk has been tried for six years.

Et quoad fidelitatem meam dicto domino duci, me remitto vestræ sacræ majestati, quia hoc bene probavi coram vestra sacra majestate per vj. annos integros, et modo sum in septimo anno; et sub correctione vestræ majestatis, est probatio sufficiens pro uno homine; et dictum dominum ducem servivi per xx. annos, quod non est parvum tempus.

Et pro servitio dicti domini ducis, dimisi uxorem, amicos et bona mea, quæ me minime, quamvis est res innaturalis, gravent; sed mala fortuna prædicti domini ducis me intime et maxime graviter. Humiliter supplicamus vestræ majestati quod velitis esse bonus dominus prædicto domino duci, et pro honore vestræ majestatis et serenissimi regis filii vestri[2] defuncti ponere manus vestras in suum adjutorium et libertatem.

Reminds him of his promises in behalf of Suffolk and his brother Richard.

Etiam, sacratissime Cæsar, supplico humiliter ut velitis vestræ memoriæ nobilissimæ reducere quod ego veni vestræ majestati ea de causa quod pro adjutorio prædicti domini ducis taliter tractaretis quod dominus Richardus frater suus, qui modo est in Hungaria, non veniret ad manus Francorum, sed quando tempus esset

[1] *Dominii*, MS.

[2] Philip archduke of Austria and king of Castile. Ob. 25 Sept. 1506.

conveniens potuit esse ad voluntatem vestræ majestatis. In quo negotio vestra majestas dedit mihi valde bonum responsum, et quod vestra majestas voluit facere diligentiam vestram pro adjutorio domini mei in manibus regis Angliæ existentis. A.D. 1507?

Et quoad iter meum in Hungariam, non recedissem ibidem nisi ad rogatum Roderici van Riet, etc. (vestræ majestati veraciter dico); et post reveni in Constanciam vestræ majestati per mandatum prædicti domini Richardi in Hungaria existentis.[1]

The writer would not have gone to Hungary but at the request of Roderick Van Riet.

Sacratissime Cæsar, maximas gratias vestræ majestati refero pro omnibus quæ vestra majestas ex gratia vestra pro me fecit; pro quibus, sicut teneor, sum, et vita durante ero, servitor vestræ sacræ majestatis, etc., ut latius patet in articulis vestræ majestati deliberatis per dominum cancellarium Sarentiner.

*De sequentibus humiliter peto responsum de Cæsaria Majestate.*

Primo, supplico domino Cæsari quod sua majestas ex gratia sua velit mihi plane dicere quomodo dominus meus se habet, et in qua conditione estis cum rege Henrico pro causa sua et libertate.

Secundo, quod possum scire responsum vestræ Cæsariæ majestatis de et super articulis pro me vestro cancellario deliberatis et quid placitum vestræ majestatis erit quod ego faciam.

Tertio, quod possum scire voluntatem vestræ sacræ majestatis tangentem hunc militem de Anglia qui tantum desiderat mihi alloqui.

Quarto, et pro finali conclusione, humiliter supplico vestræ majestati quod velitis ex gratia vestra esse mihi bonus et generosus dominus, et quod possum scire voluntatem vestræ majestatis in omnibus requestis meis. Et si placet vestræ majestati me inter-

[1] *existes*, MS.

A.D. 1507? tenere, libentissime et paratissime ero ad mandatum vestræ majestatis, et ero vester servitor.

*Copia Articulorum Domino Cæsari deliberatorum per dominum Cancellarium Sarentynor, ex parte servitoris domini Edmundi Ducis Suffolchiæ.*

Sacratissime Cæsar, maximas gratias vestræ majestati refero pro omnibus quæ vestra majestas ex gratia vestra pro me fecit; pro quibus, sicut teneor, sum et ero servitor vestræ majestatis, sperans, si dominus meus per adjutorium vestræ majestatis ad suam libertatem perveniet, ex parte mea pro eisdem tales reddat gratias vestræ majestati quod eadem vestra [majestas[1]] erit bene contenta.

Verum est, benignissime Cæsar, quod primo et principaliter patior de mea necessitate pro servitio dicti domini ducis jam in manibus regis Angliæ existentis. Quia, si vellem relinquere dominum meum et me submittere regi Henrico, libenter me acciperet in gratiam, et mihi redderet mea et amplius, ut non dubito ante hoc tempus vestra majestas bene intellexit.

Tertio, ubi vestra majestas petiit de me si vellem patientiam sustinere quousque vestra majestas potuerit cum rege Henrico finalem conclusionem pro dicto domino duce tractare, vestræ majestati responsum dedi quod ita. Quare humiliter supplico, si placet vestræ majestati, quod possum scire quomodo dominus meus et causa sua se habent.

Secundo, sacratissime Cæsar, cum servitio dicti domini ducis, de bona fide vestræ majestati veraciter dico quod, sicut teneor, patior etiam in præmissis pro honore et servitio vestræ sacræ majestatis; ad quod[2] supplico humiliter ut respectum habere velitis.

[1] Om. in MS. | [2] *quid*, MS.

Et ubi, sacratissime Cæsar, pro vestris magnis et arduis causis, pro præsenti, forsan, non potestis finire causam domini mei, sed oportet quod vestra majestas sequetur mentem regis Henrici, supplico humiliter quod interim ex gratia vestra velit mihi dare unam provisionem in Partibus Inferioribus quod possum me intertenere [1] et vivere, etc. A.D. 1507?

Et cum hoc, quod vestra Cæsaria majestas velit me debinc exonerare de expensis,[2] et etiam dare unam summam pecuniarum ad emendum pro me et servitorem meum vestes et necessaria, et pro meo recessu ad placitum vestræ majestatis, ad finem quod pro præsenti vestra majestas mecum latius nec ulterius perturbetur.[3] Quia sub ista forma non possum vivere.

Quare humiliter supplico quod in præmissis possum intelligere integram voluntatem vestræ majestatis et semper ero servitor eidem vestræ majestati.

Supplico humiliter Cæsariæ Majestati de responso.

---

## LVI.

[MS in Record Office.]

### MEMORIALE ad Cæsaream Majestatem.

PRIMO, Thomas Kyllyngworth, magister curiæ et servitor domini Edmundi ducis Suffolchiæ, ex una parte intelligens ea quæ fuerunt aperta et dicta ex parte magni concilii parliamenti Parisiensis, secrete in Aquisgrano et in Colonia per unum militem nuncupatum Argenteyn dicens [4] seipsum esse unus [4] consiliariorum et camerariorum regis Francorum, tangentia dominum Ricardum fratrem prædicti domini Edmundi ducis; et ex alia parte, intelligens ea quæ fuerunt solicitata cum prædicto domino Ricardo in Hungaria ex parte

---

[1] *intertenerem*, MS.

[2] *de expensis*] deppensis, MS.

[3] *proturbetur*, MS.

[4] Sic in MS.

A.D. 1507? ejusdem regis Francorum per oratores suos ibidem existentes circa mortem reginæ ibidem nuper defunctæ:[1] prædicto Thomæ videbatur quod nihil boni, nisi pericula, et de malo in pejus, potuit sequi, prædicto domino Edmundo existente in manibus regis Angliæ, si dominus Ricardus esset in Francia vel ad mandatum Francorum. Et sic, propter servitium et honorem Cæsaris in hoc negotio, sicut tenetur, videns quod materia ista tangit honorem suæ majestatis, et propter bonum et servitium prædictorum dominorum Edmundi et Ricardi, dictus Thomas veniebat ad præsentiam Cæsaris, et supplicavit Cæsari ut sua majestas vellet esse bonus et gratiosus dominus prædicto domino duci Edmundo. Et super hoc idem Thomas, intelligens honorabilem mentem Cæsariæ Majestatis versus dominum magistrum suum et suam causam, prædicta requesta regis et regni Franciæ idem Thomas[2] Cæsari plane aperuit, et etiam dixit Cæsari se iturum versus dominum Ricardum in Hungariam.

It would be dangerous for Edmund De la Pole, who is in the hands of the king of England, if his brother Richard were in France.

Super quo Cæsar tunc respondebat et dixit, "Unus servitor[3] domini Ricardi fuit mecum, et breve per eum intellexi de istis negotiis, et misi eum domino Ricardo, et expecto responsum," etc. Et sua majestas ordinavit dictum Thomam eundum versus Brabantiam ibidem standum quousque adventum Cæsaris; quia sua majestas tunc dixit se breviter ibidem venturum, ad finem quod idem Thomas esset ibidem paratus sollicitandum in causa domini Edmundi ducis tali modo sicut per Cæsarem esset ordinatus.

Tamen, propter duas causas Cæsari declaratas, idem Thomas proponebat tenere iter suum versus Hungariam. Et etiam sic contingebat (et si Cæsar hoc intellexit vel non, sibi latet) prope Olmes. Prædictus servitor Domini Ricardi veniens de Hungaria cum responso

[1] Anne, queen of Hungary.
[2] Sic. A repetition.
[3] Derick Van Riet.

Cæsari et dictus Thomas insimul habuerunt obviam, et steterunt in Olmes per duos dies, et ibidem uterque eorum aperuit alteri in hoc negotio intentionem suam. Et super hoc idem Thomas proposuit dimittere iter suum versus Hungariam et perimplere mandatum Cæsaris.[1] Sed prædictus servitor domini Ricardi tantum rogavit dictum Thomam quod omnino iret in Hungariam et quod staret ibidem quousque medium quadragesimæ, ad finem, si aliqui venirent de Francia domino Ricardo, quod dominus Ricardus cum eis non intromitteret, et quod per illum diem idem servitor vellet in Hungariam esse reversurus. Et super hoc idem Thomas recessit versus Hungariam et ibidem stetit a prima die Martii usque xviij. diem Aprilis jam ultimo præterito, per mandatum domini Ricardi, attendens quotidie adventum servitoris prædicti, ut plenius apparet in literis ejusdem domini Ricardi regiæ majestati missis. Qua de causa, et ad perimplendum dictum mandatum, et ordinationem solicitandam pro domino duce Edmundo, dominus Ricardus me misit Cæsari cum prædictis literis et etiam cum una credentia, et etiam ad intentionem quod Cæsar expediret plus citius dictum servitorem suum; qui quidem servitor fuit expeditus ante adventum prædicti Thomæ.

A.D. 1507? Killingworth's visit to Richard in Hungary.

Et cum Cæsaria majestas cogitavit super dictam credentiam, quod si rex Francorum practicaret cum rege Hungariæ pro domino Ricardo, quod bene conduceret dominum Ricardum per medium [aliquorum amicorum regis in Hungaria ad locum securum, &c. si necesse fuerit, quoad hoc dictus Thomas dixit suam opinionem domino doctori Heydon][2] domini Cardinalis de Stra-

An asylum proposed for Richard in Austria.

[1] *et . . . . Cæsaris*]. Corr. from "et ire versus partes Inferiores, "sicut ordinatio regiæ majestatis "erat."

[2] The words printed within brackets are interlined in the MS., apparently as a substitute for the rest of the paragraph, which, however, has been left uncancelled.

A.D. 1507? bugen. et per fratrem unius Boemen hic existentem, qui sunt secrete amici regis, de illis partibus usque ad unum castrum existens in Austria pertinens regiæ majestati et in gubernatione fratris prædicti Boemen; et ea intentione quod Cæsar vellet dictum Boemum breviter expedire cum litteris suis domino Cardinali et fratri suo, ac etiam scribere litteras credentiales domino Ricardo, et quod ego scriberem etiam domino Ricardo in hac causa, ad finem quod dominus Ricardus daret meliorem et firmam fidem prædicto Boemmo.

Objections to it.

Quo ad hoc, serenissime rex, scio veraciter quod hoc proponitis de bona mente; quamvis supplico humiliter ut vestra majestas velit mihi parcere, quod ego tam plane respondeo. Vestra majestas bene[1] vidit malam fortunam domini ducis Edmundi fratris sui, et bene scio quod super omnes principes hujus mundi, dominus Ricardus dat et dabit vestræ majestati fidem. Tamen[2] pro firmo audeo dicere, quod in castrum nullius viventis dominus Ricardus tamen[3] in tali forma personam suam, quousque dominus frater suus erit per medium vestræ majestatis ad libertatem suam. Et si dominus Ricardus ad hoc vellet consentire, scio quod servitores de consilio suo hoc non permitterent. et vestra majestas bene cognoscit istos Hungarios et Boemmos, non est fides adhibenda eis. Et sub correctione vestræ majestatis, mihi videtur quod si dominus Ricardus consentiret ad hoc propositum, si casus necessitatis hoc requiret, forsan vestra majestas et ipsi possunt esse decepti. Et ulterius, serenissime rex, si ego aperirem hanc materiam domino Ricardo, vel per scriptum meum, credo firmiter quod nec ipse nec sui consiliarii, essent de hoc mecum contenti, nec omnino consentirent, sed forsan tenerent me valde suspectum, et sine causa. Quare humiliter supplico vestræ majestati ut mihi parcere velitis, quia in hoc negotio me non intromittam.

---

[1] *benet*, MS.

[2] The word *vacat* here occurs in the margin.

[3] Sic.

Et si placet Cæsari tenere suum propositum pro adjutorio domini Edmundi ducis, non dubito quin hoc bene facietis ad honorem suæ majestatis, et ad tranquillitatem et bonum totius regni Angliæ. Sed mora trahit periculum, quia non latet Cæsari debilitas regis Angliæ; et si contingat eum breviter mori, credatis firmiter ex una parte dominus dux Edmundus erit in maximo periculo, et forsan multi alii nobiles; et ex alia parte sic casus potest evenire quod forsan filius regis Angliæ potest post mortem regis patris sui esse in consimili periculo; et ideo pro utraque parte finalis et honesta conclusio esset bona; et hoc tanto[1] citius tanto melius. Et si aliquid mali eveniret domino meo (quod absit), bene scio quod esset in maximum displacitum Cæsaris.

A.D. 1507? If the king of England were to die, Edmund and many other lords would be in danger; perhaps also the king's son.

Quare, pro servitio Cæsaris, et pro bono et securitate dominorum meorum Edmundi et Ricardi in hac causa, et ad finem quod dominus Ricardus potest esse ad mandatum Cæsaris pro honore Cæsaris, et pro adjutorio domini fratris sui, et nullo modo esse ad mandatum regis Francorum, si placet Cæsari, et sub correctione suæ majestatis, mihi videtur, hoc erit bonum et optimum medium; quod dominus Ricardus potest esse conductus extra patriam Hungariæ et ire in unum locum secretum infra obedientiam Sacri Imperii, ubi stabit secrete sub salvo conductu Cæsaris et principis illius patriæ; et, conclusione facta per Cæsarem inter regem Angliæ et prædictum dominum ducem, ipso duce Edmundo et etiam prædicto Ricardo[2] existente ad libertatem suam, dominus Ricardus erit immediate ad voluntatem Cæsaris conductus ad præsentiam suæ majestatis. Et si sit voluntas Cæsaris ponere manus suas ad hanc rem et debursare conve-

---

[1] Sic in MS.

[2] *et . . . . Ricardo.*] These words, preceded by the word *Edmundo* repeated, are inserted with a caret after the word *ducem*.

A.D. 1507? nientem summam pecuniarum secrete pro intertentione domini Ricardi et famulorum suorum, concordia facta, dicta summa pecuniarum et iterum erit satisfacta Cæsari. Et etiam dictus Thomas cum uno servitore domini regis hic existente qui vocatur le Bastard van Oysekerke, vadat, si placet Cæsari, in Hungariam pro hoc negotio. Et ad finem quod Cæsar semper erit securus, cum tempus veniet opportunum, de domino Ricardo, dictus Bastardus semper permanebit cum domino Ricardo; et servitor domini Ricardi qui nuper fuit cum Cæsare et dictus Thomas revenient insimul Cæsari, et, si placet suæ majestati, stabunt cum sua majestate pro parte domini Ricardi, quod sua dominatio perimpleat hanc rem ut prædictum est.

Et prædictus Thomas supplicat Cæsari quod sua majestas reducere velit suæ memoriæ quod idem Thomas dimisit parentes suos et bona et Anglia[1] pro servitio dominorum prædictorum et ea ratione nihil habet unde vivere possit. Cæsar est princeps cum quo idem Thomas stetit per longum tempus pro parte domini magistri sui, et satis vidit et intellexit de fidelitate ejusdem Thomæ in causa domini sui. Quare insimul supplicat Cæsari quod ex gratia sua pro prædicto suo fideli sermone sua majestas admirare velit in hac sua maxima necessitate; et etiam quod Cæsaria majestas intertenere velit prædictum Thomam cum suo servitore quousque per Cæsariam majestatem finalis concordia et conclusio fieri potest inter regem Angliæ et prædictos principes.

[1] Sic in MS.

## LVII.

### [KILLINGWORTH] TO MAXIMILIAN.

[MS. in Record Office.]

A.D. 1507?

SACRATISSIME Cæsar, humiliter supplico vestræ sacræ majestati quod vestræ memoriæ nobilissimæ redigere velitis, quod ego hic per xxx. septimanas steti ad mandatum, voluntatem, et placitum vestræ sacræ majestatis. Et ego rogavi Bastardum Doysekerke quod vellet ex parte mea[1] sollicitare vestræ majestati. Et ille stetit cum vestra majestate per novem septimanas et amplius; et de eo in hunc diem habui nulla nova, nec aliquod responsum. Etiam, sacratissime Cæsar, ego hic sum in debito hospitis mei lij. florenorum et aliis xij flor. et sum in infirmitate et in maxima necessitate et miseria, non habens aliquod, nec scio ubi habere relevamen, nisi de vestra sacra majestate; et quæ humiliter supplico ut habere velitis respectum.

Has been awaiting the Emperor's pleasure thirty weeks.

Is in debt to his host.

Sacratissime Cæsar, præmissis humiliter supplico vestræ sacræ majestati ut velitis mihi esse bonus et gratiosus dominus, et quod ex gratia vestra, vestra majestas literas vestras scribere velit dominis financiarum vestrarum ad exonerandum me de ista civitate, et mihi dare aliquam pecuniam pro recessu meo, ad placitum vestræ majestatis; et durante vita mea ego ero vester fidelis servitor, et orabo Deum pro conservatione vestræ sacræ majestatis.

Ulterius, sacratissime Rex, intelligo quod dominus Edwardus Wyngfeld ex Anglia miles est cum vestra sacra majestate pro præsente ex parte domini Regis Angliæ. Et si idem dominus Edwardus habet onus communicandi cum vestra sacra majestate pro causa domini magistri mei existente in Anglia, si placet

[1] *mea* repeated in MS.

A.D. 1507? vestræ majestati, esset bonum quod ego venirem[1] vestræ majestati, secrete vel alias, sicut videtur majestati, ad declarandum vestræ majestati aliquas magnas causas hoc negotium tangentes. Humiliter supplicans quod in eodem negotio vestra majestas velit mihi habere respectum, et me non ponere in oblivionem.

A.D. 1507?

## LVIII.

### [KILLINGWORTH] TO "DOMINUS DIONYSIUS."

[MS. in Record Office.]

ROGO declaretis tenorem [2] præsentium domino Cæsari de verbo in verbum, vel faciatis quod dominus Cæsar potest semel legere.

Domine Dyonise, rogo quod ex parte mea detis maximas gratias domino Cæsari pro omnibus quæ sua Cæsarea majestas ante hæc tempora, et specialiter ad præsens tempus, mihi fecit; pro quibus sum et ero, vita mea durante, in omnibus causis ad voluntatem suæ Cæsariæ majestatis.

The writer hopes the Emperor will provide for him, seeing that he suffers poverty only for his master's sake.

Et cum non est in me Cæsariæ majestati prædictæ deservire, non dubito, si per medium domini Cæsaris dominus dux Suffulchiæ veniet ad suam libertatem, ipse dabit pro his Cæsari tales gratias pro parte mea quod dominus Cæsar erit bene contentus. Et spero quod Cæsar bene cognoscit et accepit quod ea quæ sustinui in hac parte et quotidie sustineo sunt propter honorem et bonum domini mei, &c., sicut ad largum domino Cæsari declaravi. Quia si vellem hanc rem dimittere non indigeo præsentem paupertatem[3] nec necessitatem habere.

[1] *venirem*] interlined in place of the words *possem loqui*, struck out.

[2] *tenorum*, MS.

[3] *palpertatem*, MS.

Super quo, pro finali conclusione in hac re, humiliter supplico domino Cæsari quod sua majestas ex gratia sua nobilissima pro me providere velit, quod possum secrete de sua majestate habere in Partibus Inferioribus unam honestam intertentationem quousque sua majestas potest facere unam finalem conclusionem inter regem Angliæ et dominum meum, et dominum fratrem suum in Hungaria existentem. A.D. 1507?

Et interim, cum favore Domini Cæsaris, stabo, et expectabo in Aquis-grano, et qualiscumque solicitatio[1] mihi erit facta pro parte regis Angliæ, non dubitat Cæsarea majestas quin de tempore in tempus, si casus sic advenerit, certificabo domino Cæsari de omnibus. Meanwhile he will remain at Aix.

Et super præmissa humiliter peto responsum domini Cæsaris, et quod per votum, domine Dionesie, illud responsum potest mihi conduci per Bastardum de Oysekerke cum omni conveniente diligentia.

Supplico domino Cæsari quod potest super me taliter aspicere oculis gratiæ quod possum vivere et haberem[2] victum et[3] vestitum.

---

## LIX.

A.D. 1507?

[Addit. MS. 21,382. Brit. Mus. f. 17.]

Breve Summarium eorum quæ dicta sunt oratoribus Serenissimi Regis Angliæ ex parte Sacratissimæ Majestatis Cæsareæ.

Primo, qualiter Majestas Cæsarea citra quatuor aut quinque dies continue laboraverit cum illustrissima domina Domina Margareta Austriæ et Burgundiæ, suæ majestatis filia carissima, et singulis diebus intraverit The Emperor had personal conferences with Margaret for four or six

[1] *solutacio*, MS.
[2] *erem*, MS.
[3] *est*, MS.

A.D. 1507? cum ea personalem conferentiam super matrimonio jampridem concepto et concluso per quondam bonæ memoriæ Ph[ilippum] Regem Castellæ, inter serenissimum ac potentissimum Angliæ Regem et eandem illustrissimam dominam.

days on the proposed marriage between her and Henry VII.,

Ad quod sua Majestas Cæsarea mirum in modum fuit et est inclinata, tam propter singularem amorem quem habet ad serenissimum Regem Angliæ, tum quia *alias sua Majestas* in hoc matrimonium consensit et *desuper literas tradiderit*, tum etiam quia omnes suæ *Majestatis consiliarii* ipsum matrimonium maxime *suadent*, cupiunt et desiderant.

which he recommended by many arguments.

Et ut sua Majestas Cæsarea illustrissimam dominam ad hoc matrimonium facilius inclinaret, demonstravit multis rationibus et argumentis illud matrimonium non solum esse honorificum atque utile suæ Majestati, ipsi Dominæ illustrissimæ, atque domibus Austriæ et Burgundiæ, sed etiam non mediocriter necessarium.

Honestum seu honorificum, quia serenissimus Rex Angliæ rex est dignissimus, prudentissimus, potentissimus, atque omnium virtutum cumulatissimus, cui merito conjungi debeat uxor seu conthoralis omnium nobilissima ac prudentissima qualis ipsa est.

Utile, propter regnorum et patriarum vicinitatem, propter mercatorum et subditorum utriusque regni continuam frequentationem et mercium commutationem, propter harum provinciarum tranquillitatem.

Necessarium, propter pacis cum Gallis observationem, propter futuræ Hispanicæ successionis securitatem, propter pacis Gheldrensis conservationem, propter singulorum negotiorum Cæsareæ Majestatis, necnon hujus inclytæ domus Burgundiæ dilectionem.

Quod si forte hoc matrimonium, quod absit, non perficiatur, timendum est quod ipse serenissimus Angliæ Rex aliam ducet uxorem ex alia familia et gente, forte Cæsareæ Majestati et suæ domui non amica, unde plurima incommoda his patriis et provinciis possent imminere, adeo quod affinitas nuper facta inter illustrissimum dominum Archiducem et dominam Mariam parvæ erit utilitatis. A.D. 1507?

His rationibus et aliis quamplurimis sæpius prudentissime repetitis per Cæsaream Majestatem ore proprio, ac etiam aliquando per organum alterius in præsentia suæ Majestatis et nonnullorum suæ Majestatis consiliariorum ipsa illustrissima domina semper respondit in hunc qui sequitur modum.

Her reply.

"Quod ipsa illustrissima domina multum est devincta et multa debet serenissimo Regi Angliæ, qui, cum sit omnium regum ac principum hujus nostræ ætatis prudentissimus ac virtuosissimus, velit et cupiat eam habere in uxorem et conthoralem.

"Quod si aliquando ipsa illustrissima domina maritum superducere vellet ipsa non posset digniorem optare, sed illum serenissimum Regem Angliæ cæteris principibus et regibus orbis anteferet.

Having been divorced by her first husband, and having lost two others in their youth she is determined to remain a widow.

"Verum, cum jam trina vice jussu ac mandato sacratissimæ Cæsareæ Majestatis nupta fuerit et tres maritos habuerit, quorum primus eam repudiaverit, et alii duo in juvenili ætate et immature obierunt. Tantum infortunium passa et experta, timet in illud reincidere; quare decrevit apud se nunquam quartum maritum superducere, sed in sua viduitate permanere.

Fears she would have no children.

"Præterea, cum matrimonia communiter fiat ad prolem suscitandam, timet illustrissima domina ne ad hoc sit minus apta; quod si ita esset, serenissimo Regi Angliæ aliquando displicere posset.

Thinks the dowry too large,

"Item, dos præmissa per matrimonium supradictum est adeo immensa quod sine magna læsione illustrissimi Domini Archiducis, sororum et patriarum suarum non poterit persolvi.

and the terms too favourable to England.

"Item, facit illustrissima domina sibi aliquam conscientiam quod tanta bona extrahantur ex domo Burgundiæ et remaneant in Anglia, ex quibus suæ neptes poterunt maritari.

A.D. 1507? "Item, quantum ad necessitatem allegatam, dixit quod illa cessat cum jam sit pax facta et conclusa cum Gallis, et etiam in Gheldria, cum etiam serenissimus rex Arragonum cupiat et prosequatur amicitiam Cæsareæ majestatis, et quod non sit verisimile quod illustrissimo domino archiduci suo nepoti velit nocere aut juri suo in aliquo derogare, cum nemo umquam carnem suam odio habeat; quibus attentis non esset verisimile quod matrimonium quod poterit facere rex Angliæ debeat huic domui esse damnosum.

"Maxime cum jam affinitas facta sit et contracta inter ipsum illustrissimum dominum archiducem et filiam regis Angliæ, quare non solum ipse rex Angliæ sed etiam regnum ipsum est aliqualiter obligatum ad amicitiam cum iis patriis et provinciis."

Videns sacratissima Cæsarea majestas quod nihil posset apud præfatam illustrissimam dominam per se et consiliarios aliquos suæ majestatis proficere nec inducere eandem dominam ad consentiendum huic matrimonio, Cæsarea majestas fecit vocari illustrissimum dominum archiducem et totum consilium; in quorum et suæ majestatis præsentia iterato dicta sunt ad longum illustrissimæ dominæ ea quæ superius scripta sunt et multa alia ad hoc convenientia, ad finem ut eo facilius inclinaretur ad consentiendum. Quibus non obstantibus illustrissima domina firma permansit in suo proposito superius declarato, nec aliud responsum potuit Cæsarea majestas obtinere.

Ex quibus patet quantam operam, solicitudinem, ac diligentiam Cæsarea majestas sacratissima adhibuerit circa hoc matrimonium; verum cum illustrissima domina vidua sit nec jure possit aut debeat ulterius cogi aut premi, cupit sua Cæsarea majestas ut ea omnia bono modo et ordine regiæ celsitudini Angliæ referentur ad eum finem ut intelligat Cæsaream majestatem omnem diligentiam possibilem adhibuisse, neque aliquid prætermisisse quod ad inducendam filiam ad hoc matrimonium conferre visum est. Et si videatur dominis oratoribus quod Cæsarea majestas debeat aliquid amplius facere in hac causa pro contentatione strenuissimi regis Angliæ vellet sua majestas hoc intelligere et perficere. A.D. 1507?

*Endorsed:* Anglia.

## LX.

A.D 1507. May.

### Henry VII. to Margaret of Savoy.

[From a contemporary copy. MS. Cott., Caligula, D.VI. f. 72.]

Margaret requires that English merchants shall frequent the Low Countries in accordance with the treaty made with Philip of Castile.

Treshaulte et excellente princesse, nostre treschere et tresamee bonne cousine, a vous tresaffectueusement et de bon cueur nous recommandons. Receu avons les bonnes et cordialles lettres que vous nous avez derrenierement escriptes de Bruxelles, en date du viij[e] de ce present mois de May, responsives aux nostres derrenieres; par lesquelles entendons le vouloir, desir, et grant affection que vous avez que la communiquacion, hantize et frequentacion puisse estre entre noz subgetz marchans et ceulx depardela, sur lentrecours parcidevant fait et conclu par le feu sieur de Beures, Messire Paule de Baenst et aultres lors ad ce commis et ordonnez delapart de feu prince de bonne memoire

---

Translation.

Most high and excellent princess, our most dear and well beloved good cousin, we commend ourselves to you most affectionately. We have received the good and cordial letters which you last wrote to us from Brussels, dated the 8th of this present month of May in answer to our last; whereby we understand the will, desire, and great affection that you have that communication and intercourse should exist between merchants who are our subjects and those of your countries, according to the treaty formerly made and concluded by the late lord de Beures, Messire Paul de Baenst and others at that time commissioned and ordained thereto on the part of the late prince of good memory,

A.D 1507. May.

nostre cousin le roy de Castille vostre frere (a lame duquel Dieu par sa saincte grace face mercy) et ceulx par nous commis et depputez, nous requerant de en faveur de vous permectre ladite communiquacion et hantize selon ledit entrecours, lequel en ce cas ferez observer et entretenir par ceulx depardela, jusques a ce que par nostre bonfrere le roy vostre pere et nous en soit aultrement ordonne; offrant den faire despescher telles et semblables lectres que nous mesmes adviserons et que de nostre part en vouldrons donner.

Treshaulte et tresexcellente princesse, nostre treschere et tresamee bonne cousine, veritablement nous ne desirons pas seullement en ce vous complaire, mais en toutes aultres choses que bonnement faire pourrions; bien vous voullons advertir que neust este les nouveaulx tonnelieux, exactions, et imposicions que lon mist pardela sur nosdits subgetz et leurs marchandises apres avoir prins et conclu ledit entrecours, ilz ne se feussent point absentez hors des pais depardela, mais eust este ledit entrecours de duree jusques a present. Et com-

---

our cousin the king of Castile your brother (on whose soul God of His holy grace have mercy) and those commissioned and deputed by us, requesting us in your favour to allow the said communication and intercourse according to the said treaty, which you will in that case cause to be observed and kept by those on your side, until it shall be otherwise arranged by our good brother the king your father and us; offering to despatch such and like letters thereof, as we ourselves shall think proper and shall be willing to give on our part.

Most high, &c., truly we desire to please you not only in this, but in all other things that we reasonably can; nevertheless we wish to apprise you that had it not been for the new tolls, exactions, and impositions levied there upon our said subjects and their goods after the said treaty was taken and concluded, they would not have absented themselves from those countries, but the said treaty would have endured

bien que ou temps et du vivant du roy votredit feu frere nous luy en escripvismes par reiterees foiz le desirant, de on ensuyvant le traicte de lentrecours, quil voulsist faire abolir lesdites nouvelles imposicions et tonnelieux, en luy signiffiant quelles estoient directement contrevenir a icelluy traicte dentrecours, toutefoiz pour quelque rescripcion que nous luy en feismes, riens neu fut fait ny refourme. A ceste cause nosdits subgetz marchans nous supplierent et requirent en toute humilite que nous leur voulsissions permectre de tenir doresenavant lours foires et marchetz dedens nostre ville de Calais, ce que par bon advis et deliberacion de conseil, considere ce que dit est, ne leur povyons bonnement reffuser.

A.D. 1507. May.

It was to avoid new tolls, contrary to that treaty, that they obtained liberty to hold their market at Calais.

Neantmoins encoires dempuis ce, a este fait, conclu, et passe ung nouveau entrecours entre les commis et depputez du feu roy vostredit frere et les nostres, chacun en vertu de leurs commissions et povoirs, le jour et terme ordonne et appoincte pour lentreschange des lettres patentes de confirmac[ion] et ratifficacion dunc-

---

till now. And although in the time and during the life of the king your said late brother we repeatedly wrote to him desiring him, according to the treaty of intercourse, to abolish the said new impositions and tolls, intimating to him that they were in direct opposition to the treaty of intercourse; nevertheless for all the remonstrances that we wrote to him, nothing was done or reformed. For this reason our said subjects merchants have requested us in all humility to permit them to hold henceforward their fairs and markets in our town of Calais, which by good advice and deliberation of council, these things considered, we could not well refuse them.

Nevertheless, again there has since been made, concluded, and passed, a new treaty between the commissioners and deputies of the late king your said brother and our own, each by virtue of their commissions and powers, the day and term ordained and appointed for the exchange of the

A.D. 1507. May.

part et daultre; encoires de laparte de dela riens na este tenu, fourny, ne accomply, ja soit ceque dela nostre, nous avons este tousjours prestz de fournir ace que nous avyons promis et accorde, ainsi que le vous avons signiffie par aultres noz lettres.

Nevertheless, out of regard for Margaret, the King has recalled his licence and ordered them to repair to the Low Countries.

Et combien que nosdits marchans avoient fait desja publier leurs foires en nostredite ville de Calais et fait leurs preparatifs pour tenir aceste faicte dela penthecouste leurs foires en icelle; ce non obstant, pour le desir et affection que nous avons de vous complaire et satisfaire a vostredite requeste, et singulierement pour honneur et amour de vo[us], entant que sest la premiere requeste que vous nous avez faicte, suysmes contens [de] consentir et accorder que les subgetz dune part et daultre, voisent, hantent et co[mmuniquent] ensemble, en vertu dudit premier traicte prins avecque ledit feu Sieur de Beures; ce [que nosdits] marchans feroient bien enviz et a tresgrande difficulte, nestoit lordonnance [et] commandement que nous leur avons

---

letters patent of confirmation and ratification on either side; again, on your side nothing has been kept, done, nor accomplished; although on our side we have been always ready to do that which we have promised and granted as we have signified to you by other our letters.

And although our said merchants had already caused their fairs to be published in our said town of Calais and made their preparations to hold them therein this feast of Pentecost, this notwithstanding, for the desire and affection we have to please you and satisfy your said request, and especially for the honor and love of you, inasmuch as it is the first request you have made to us, we are content to agree and grant that the subjects on either side visit, frequent, and [communicate] together by virtue of the said first treaty taken with the said late lord de Beures, [which our said] merchants would do very unwillingly and with very great difficulty, but for the order and commandment we

donne pource faire. Et leur avons exp[ressement en-jo]incts de laisser leursdits preparatifz daller a Calais et deulx preparer . . . . . . desmaintenant es pais de nostredit cousin, vostre nepveu. A quoy congnoissan . . . . . . . . nostre plaisir et intencion, sont prestz a y obeir, et espoirent destre prestz a par[tir dedans] quinze jours. Et pour le bien et sceurte de nosdits marchans et de leursdites ma[rchandises] en ladvenir, nous avons, par ladvis de nostre conseil, conceu et devise en ensuy[vant leur] desir, une mynute, telle quil nous semble estre raisonnable pour la sceurte [deulxet] de leursdites marchandises, laquelle vous envoyons. Et si vostre plaisir est de ende[dens] quinze jours, les nous envoyer expediees et seellees ainsi quil appartient, vous . . . . . de tant plus meilleur vouloir et couraige a nosdits subgetz marchans daller p[our] y contynuer et resider. Et icelles par nous receues vous envoyerons les nostre[s au mesme] effect, ayans bon et ferme espoir que ferez doresenavant A.D. 1507. May.

---

have given them to do so. And we have [expressly ordered] them to leave off their said preparations for going to Calais, and to prepare themselves [to repair] from this time to the countries of our said cousin, your nephew. Whereto, knowing [that such is] our pleasure and intention, they are ready to obey, and hope to be ready to leave [within] 15 days. And for the good and surety of our said merchants and their said merchandises in future, we have, by the advice of our council, conceived and devised according to their desire a minute, such as appears to us to be reasonable for the security [of them and] of their said merchandises; which we send to you. And if it be your pleasure within fifteen days to send them (letters patent) despatched and sealed as it behoves, you [will cause] so much the better will and disposition in our merchants to go thither to remain and reside. And the same being by us received we will send our own [of like] effect, having good

A.D. 1507. May.

bien et favourable[ment] traicter nosdits subgetz, comme de nostrepart nous avons fait et avons intencion . . . . les subgetz depardela.

Touchant la priere et requeste que nous faictes davoir regart aux traictez, a[mities], et alliances faictes et conclutes pour nous et noz successeurs, et le roy vostredit fe[u frere] et les siens, et que en acquietant les promesses et obligacions esquelles nou[s sommes] tenuz et astrainct par icelles, de accorder aide et secours pour garder et def[fendre] nostre cousin, vostre nepveu, ses pais et subgetz, oucas quilz feussent par voie de . . . opprimez par nostre frere et cousin le Roy Loys de France ;—

Henry uses all efforts to protect the Low Countries from invasion.

Treshaulte et excellente princesse, nostre treschere et tresamee bonne cousine, . . . . faisons doubte que ne soiez bien advertie, et comme il est a ung chacun tout m . . . . et magnifeste que pour la bonne amour et affection que nous portons a [nostre] frere le roy, vostredit pere, et portions aussi au roy vostredit feu frere, nous nous s[ummes] effectuellement emploiez

---

and firm hope that you will cause henceforward our said subjects to be treated well and favourably, as on our part we have done and intend to do the subjects of those parts.

As to the prayer and request that you make to us to have regard to the treaties, [amities], and alliances made and concluded for us and our successors, and the king your said late brother and his, and in fulfilment of the promises and obligations, in which we are bound by the same, to grant aid and succour, to keep and defend our cousin, your nephew, his countries and subjects, in case they be oppressed by way of . . . . . . by our brother and cousin king Lewis of France :—

Most high, &c., we make [no] doubt but that you are well informed, and as it is quite . . . . and manifest to every one, that for the good love and affection which we bear to [our] brother the king, your said father, and bore also to the king your said late brother, we have effec-

a preserver, garder, et deffendre ses pais et subge[tz quand] ilz estoient en voie destre subjuguez par leurs ennemys et adverssaires, t[ant en] temps de sa mynorite que aultrement et aussi demptuis en lannee passee [au] fait de Gueldres. Et pour vous en parler plainement et alavraye verit[e, les] choses ont este aucunesfoiz pardela petitement recongnues et considerees . . . ce que nous avons pource faire eu le maulgre de nostredit frere et cousin, [le roy] Loys de France, et daultres princes noz confederez et alliez.

A.D. 1507. May.

Which caused him last year in the affair of Gueldres to incur the ill-will of France.

Et quant ace que nous requerez vouloir avoir regart aux traictez et a[mities] faitz entre nous et le roy vostredit feu frere; treshaulte et excellente [princesse,] nostre treschere et tresamee bonne cousine, nous vous voulons bien adve[rtir que] tous les traictez et amytiez que nous avons prins et faitz avecque ice[lluy vostre] feu frere, et avec quelzconques aultres princes que ce soient, nous [avons] jusques a ce jourdhuy bien entierement entretenuz et gardez, s[ans] jamais y avoir fait aucune faulte, ne les enfraindre, mais vr[ai est quil y eult]

---

tually laboured to preserve, keep, and defend his countries and subjects [when] they were in the way to be subdued by their enemies and adversaries, both in time of his minority and otherwise, and also last year [in the] affair of Gueldres. And to tell you plainly the very truth, things have been sometimes little acknowledged and considered on your side . . . . . that we have to do this incurred the illwill of our said brother and cousin king Lewis of France, and of other princes our confederates and allies.

And whereas you request us to have regard to the treaties and [amities] made between us and your said late brother; most high, &c., we desire to inform you that all the treaties and amities which we made with the same your late brother, and with any other princes whomsoever, we have this day fully kept without ever having made therein any fault or infringed them; but . . . . . . . .

A.D. 1507. May.

certains traictez faitez et concluz entre nous et le roy vostredit [feu frere, entre] lesquelz y eult ung traicte damytie qui fut fait en noz personnes, luy estant en nostre royaulme. Et oultre icelluy y avoit deux aultres traictez prins et concluz entre ses commis et les nostres. Et si sest cestuy traicte damytie par lequel vous nous voullez obliger et astraincter, le conseil depardela vous deussent avoir advertie, comme dedens lung desdits aultres deux traictez est expressement dit et declaire, que le roy vostredit feu frere ne feroit pas seullement innover ledit traicte damytie, mais aussi confermer lesdits aultres traictez, et le tout endedens certains jours et termes pource ordonnez et appoinctez les nous envoyer. Ce que na este fait ne accomply delapart de dela. Parquoy les choses a la verite bien et deuement considerees, nous ne suysmes, comme les gens de nostre conseil nous ont dit et remonstre, par ledit traicte damytie, aucunement chargez, astrainctz ne obligez, mais suysmes de nostrepart a nostre liberte; et ne sauroit ou

---

certain treaties made and concluded between us and the king your said [late brother, among] which there was a treaty of amity which was made in our persons when he was in our realm. And besides this there were two other treaties taken and concluded between his commissioners and ours. And if it be that treaty of amity by which you wish to bind us, the council there ought to have informed you, that in one of the said other two treaties it is expressly said and declared, that the king your said late brother would not only cause to be renewed the said treaty of amity, but also confirm the said other treaties, and all within certain days and terms ordained and appointed for the same to be sent to us, which has not been done or performed on that side. Wherefore, these things being a truth well and duly considered we are not, as the gentlemen of our council have shown to us, by the said treaty of amity in anywise burdened, bound, or tied, but are on our side at our liberty, and no one

pourroit lon par icelluy par voie dobligacion ou promesse aucune chose nous demander jusques ace que linnovacion deladicte amytie et confirmacion des aultres traictez soient faitz, delivrez, et entreschangez dunepart et daultre; lesquelz comme entendons sont entre vos mains, et de ceulx dudit conseil depardela. Et ce fait et accomply nous ne fauldrons point de fournir ace que nous estions tenuz; et obligez et plus singulierement en faveur, honneur, et amour de vous, et pour la bonne affection que nous portons a nostredit cousin vostre nepveu. A.D. 1507. May.

Et dabundant, veu et considere que le roy vostredit feu frere qui estoit lun des traictans, est alle de vie a trespas, et que nostredit cousin son filz est encoires en mynorite, il feust bien seant et convenable que tous lesdits traictez feussent confermez, tant par nostredit bon frere le roy vostre pere comme mainbournie de nostredit cousin vostre nepveu que par icelluy vostre nepveu. The treaties between Henry and Philip ought to be confirmed.

Pryant ausurplus Nostre Signeur quil vous ait, treshaulte et excellente princesse, nostre treschere et

---

can by it demand of us anything by way of obligation or promise until the renewal of the said amity and confirmation of the other treaties be made, delivered, and exchanged on both sides; which, as we understand, are in your hands, and those of the council there. And this done and accomplished we shall not fail to fulfil all that we are bound to do; and more especially in favour, honour, and love for you, and for the good affection that we bear to our said cousin your nephew.

And, moreover, considering that the king your said late brother, who was one of the contracting parties, is deceased, and that our said cousin his son is still in minority, it would be very meet and befitting that all the said treaties were confirmed, both by our said good brother the king your father as guardian of our said cousin your nephew, and by the same your nephew.

Praying, moreover, our Lord to have you, most high, &c.,

A.D. 1507. May. tresamee bonne cousine, en sa tressaincte et digne garde, et vous doint laccomplissement de voz bons desirs. Escript en nostre manoir de Grenewyche, le * * [1] jour dudit mois de May, lan xv° et sept.

---

## LXI.

### Henry VII. to the Lord Berghes.

[From the same MS. copy subjoined to the preceding.]

Has answered the duchess of Savoy's letter.

Trescher et tresame cousin, nous avons receu les lettres que nostre bonne cousine la duchesse douagiere de Savoye nous a escriptes, et les vostres pareillem[ent,] le contenu de toutes lesquelles nous avons bien au long entendu. E[t pour] la bonne amour et affection que luy portons, et pour satisfaire a s . . . . nous luy faisons de present telle responce que nous ne doubtons poi[nt sera a son] contentement. Et pource

---

in His most holy and worthy keeping, and to give you the accomplishment of your good desires.

Written at our manor of Greenwich, the * * [1] day of the said month of May, the year 1507.

---

Most dear and well beloved cousin, we have received the letters that our good cousin the duchess dowager of Savoy has written to us, and likewise yours; the contents of all which we have understood at length. And for the good love and affection which we bear her, and to satisfy . . . . . we now make to her such answer as we doubt not [shall be to her] contentment. And because we believe that the things

---

[1] Blank in MS.

que nous croyons que les choses viendront a [vostre] congnoissance, nous delaissons a ceste cause de vous en faire par cestes [aucun] recit. En vous advisant que des quelle nous aura envoye les lettres qu[elle] advise estre necessaires pour la sceurte de noz marchans et de leur[s dites] marchandises en ladvenir, expediees et seelees ainsi quil appartient, [nous] luy envoyerons les nostres de pareil effect; aiant bon et ferme espoir [que] nostredite bonne cousine, vous, et ceulx du conseil depardela, ferez doresena[vant] bien et favourablement traicter nosdits subgetz marchans, affin quilz a[uront] meilleur vouloir et courraige dy contynuer et resider ou temps adve[nir]. Et atant vous disons adieu qui, trescher et tresame cousin, vous [ait] en sa bonne garde. Escript en nostre manoir de Grenewiche, le * * [1] [jour] de May, lan xv^c. et sept.

A.D. 1507. May.

Hopes the English merchants will henceforth be favorably treated.

will come to your knowledge, we refrain on that account from making any recital of them to you by these. Informing you that as soon as she shall have sent us the letters which she considers necessary for the security of our merchants and of their said merchandizes in future, despatched and sealed as it behoves, we shall send her ours of like effect; having good and firm hope that our said good cousin, you and those of the council there will cause henceforward our said subjects merchants to be well and favorably treated, in order that they may have better will and disposition to remain and reside there in time to come. And so we commend you to God, who, most dear and well beloved cousin, have you in His good keeping. Written in our manor of Greenwich, the * * [1] day of May, 1507.

[1] Blank in MS.

A.D. 1507. 3 Sept.

## LXII.

### Henry VII. to Almaçan.

[MS. Egerton 616, No. 24.]

Was rejoiced to receive Ferdinand's letter on his return to Spain.

Henricus Dei gratia Rex Angliæ et Franciæ ac Dominus Hiberniæ, nobili atque egregio viro, domino Michaeli Almazano, serenissimi regis Aragonum et utriusque Siciliæ ac Hierusalem secretario, amico nostro carissimo, salutem. Accepimus nuper literas serenissimi fratris nostri, regis vestri, xx° die Julii ex Valentia ad nos datas, quibus cognovimus qualiter eo die illuc sospes et incolumis cum sua classe triremium applicuisset, qua quidem re cognita non facile diceremus quanto gaudio affecti sumus; quod, scilicet, omnes suos prosperos successus, proprios nostros reputemus; unde agimus in præsentiarum ingentes gratias suæ majestati literis nostris, quod de sua prospera navigatione, suoque adventu ad alia sua dominia nos certiores per suas literas facere voluerit Nec minus etiam laudamus plurimum et extollimus vestram diligentiam in ipsis literis scribendis et eo adventu nobis intimando adhibitam; ex qua re manifeste intelligimus optimum vestrum animum quem habetis ad nobis gratificandum et de nobis bene merendum. De quo, certe, plurimas habemus vobis gratias, et in posterum magis ac magis sumus habituri, vos rogantes quatenus in hoc vestro tam bono proposito erga nos velitis perseverare, et de his quæ occurrunt quandoque ad nobis scribere, quod sane nobis est futurum quam gratissimum. Cæterum habuimus et adhuc habemus oratores nostros paratos ad serenissimum fratrem nostrum mittendos, nil aliud expectantes nisi ut postquam filiam suam illustrissimam principem habuerit communicatam super causis prius pro majori vinculo inter nos contrahendo motis, suam prius mentem et animum super ea re clare intelligamus. Præterea scribimus eidem serenissimo fratri nostro, respondentes super nonnullis rebus quas per dominum Doctorem de Puebla suum oratorem fecerat nobis demonstrari. Et quia non dubitamus quin ipsæ nostræ literæ ad vestras manus sint venturæ, idcirco non erimus in præsentiarum longiores. Hoc tantum vobis dicimus, quod sua majestas in omnibus rebus quibus gratificari sibi poterimus, nos suum verum intimum et cordialem fratrem est semper habitura. Ex manerio nostro de Woodstoke, die tertio Septembris m.d.vij°. A.D. 1507. 3 Sept.

Scripseramus autem prius hasce literas, sed ob pericula quæ in longo itinere quandoque contingunt, jussimus illas reiterari.

HENRICUS R.

*Addressed:* Nobili atque egregio viro, domino Michaeli Almazano, serenissimi Regis Aragonum et utriusque Siciliæ ac Hierusalem secretario, amico nostro charissimo.

*Endorsed in two places.* Amj. Del Rey de Inglaterra de iij. de Setiembre de D.vij.

---

## LXIII.

A.D. 1507. 29 Sept.

### HENRY VII. TO FERDINAND II.

[MS. Egerton 616, No. 25.]

SERENISSIMO ac potentissimo principi, Domino FERDINANDO, Dei gratia Aragonum et utriusque Siciliæ ac Hierusalem Regi, fratri, consanguineo, et amico nostro charissimo, HENRICUS eadem gratia Rex Angliæ et Franciæ ac Dominus Hiberniæ, salutem et prosperorum successuum incrementa. Scripsimus paulo antea vestræ majestati cum ejus tabellario nonnulla tunc temporis Concerning an important commission made to him by De Puebla.

A.D. 1507. 29 Sept. occurrentia, quæ ob pericula et impedimenta sæpe in longo itinere contingentia per præsentium latorem reiteranda, et denuo scribenda duximus. Cæterum posteaquam ea scripsissemus, venit ad nos clarissimus orator vester Doctor de Puebla, qui licet non satis se bene ad sui corporis salutem habeat, nunquam tamen desistit in his quæ ad servitium vestræ majestatis pertinent, apud nos intercedere et instare, et officium boni oratoris ac servitoris facere; communicavitque nobiscum nonnulla non parvæ importantiæ, quæ audivimus perlibenter, et super quibus nostrum illi dedimus responsum, non dubitantes quin veram de ipsis rebus sic nobiscum per se communicatis sit vestræ majestati facturus relationem. Quæ postquam illi fuerint cognita putamus congruum fore ut quid super his sentiat quam primum nobis significet. Quam magnopere rogamus ut quanto citius fieri poterit, suam nobis superinde mentem aperiat. Non dubitamus autem quin, si ea negotia ad effectum deducantur, quamplurima exinde bona ad Omnipotentis Dei laudem, et totius Christianæ religionis nostrorumque utrinque statuum et regnorum augmentum, subditorumque hinc inde nostrorum commodum, sint secutura. Ex manerio nostro de Woodstoke, die xxviiij. Septembris, M.D.VII°.

Vostre bon frere,
HENRY R.

*Addressed;* Serenissimo ac potentissimo principi Domino Ferdinando Dei gratia Aragonum et utriusque Siciliæ ac Hierusalem regi, fratri, consanguineo et amico nostro charissimo.

*Endorsed.* A su al. Del Rey de Inglaterra xxviiij. de Setiembre de D.vij.

## LXIV.

A.D. 1508. March.

### James IV. to Henry VII.

[Orig. in Record Office.]

Richt excellent, right hie and michti prince, and our derrest fadre. We commend us unto ȝou in our mast h[erty wise], praying ȝou effectuisly to graunt at this oure request ȝour lettres of sauf conduct in dew form to ane Reveren[d fader in] God, and our richt trast counsalour Andreu bischop of Murray, commendatare of Pettinweme, &c.; and with him t[o the number] of fourty personis or within, his servauntis or utheris, saufly and seuerly to cum within ȝour realme of [Ingland by sey] or laund, on hors or on fute, with thare horssis, harnessis, bulgeis, males, money, conȝeit and unconȝeit l . . . . and all utheris thare lefull gudes; and to pas and repas throw ȝour saide realme for fulfilling of h . . . . doing of his uther lefull eraundes at the court of Rome and utheris partes beyond sey, without , . . . . port or passage of ȝour saide realm. And als with ane schip or schippis of the birth of ane hu[ndred . . . ] chargeit with ony lefull gudes with ane mastir, twa factours, ane skippar, ane sterisman, . . . . . . . . within. And for sic space as the peax requiris to endure. Richt excellent, right hie and michti [Prince and our] derrest fader, we pray God have you in his keping. Geven undre our signet at Edinburgh [the . . day of] March.

Requesting a safe conduct for the bishop of Murray.

ȝour Son,
James R.

*Addressed:* To the richt excellent, richt hie and michti Prince, and oure derrest fadre the King of Ingland, &c.

A.D. 1508.
14 June.

## LXV.

### The Provost of Cassel to Margaret of Savoy.

[Holograph, Addit. MS., Brit. Mus., 21,382. f. 23.]

Ma tresredoubtee dame. Je me recommande treshumblement a votre benigne grace. Madame, je voz ay escript nagheres, faisant responce a voz lettres du vij^e de ce mois. Et a voz en dire franchement la verite, javoye bien eu espoir de mieulx. Car a ce quil ma peu samble, je nay point trouve les courages si adonnez et enclins comme par si devant. Je ne say sylz se sont refroidez, ne pour quelle cause; mais je say bien de vray que en bien peu de tempz la pension de France se doit payer,[1] car les quitances sont signees. Il me samble que aulcquns pensent que noz les mesteryons volentiers en gheere alencontre des Francois, a quoy ilz ne sont enclins; car ung des grands me dit, en demandant, quil oiseroit conseillier au Roy soy bouter en telle mer, avec aultres choses, et que ce seroit

---

### Translation.

My most dread lady, I commend myself humbly to your benign grace. Madam, I have written to you lately in answer to your letters of the 7th of this month. And to tell you frankly the truth, I had hoped for better things: for, as it appears to me, I have not found men's minds so favourable and well disposed as hitherto. I know not if they be chilled, or for what reason; but I know well of a truth that in very short time the pension of France is to be paid, for the acquittances are signed. It strikes me that some think we want to get them into a war with the French, to which they are not disposed; for one of the grandees said on asking [me about it] that he dared [not] counsel the king to embark on such a sea, with other things, and that

---

[1] *se doit payer.*] Corr. from *est arivee.*

A.D. 1508. 14 June.

grand despens denvoyer les Angloix pardela. Toutesfois en tant quil touche a les $c^m$ escus, mais que les obligations soyent pardeca, me fut dit quil ny auroit point de difficulte.

Had reminded the Council they were bound to assist the Low Countries against the aggression of France.

Madame, voz me povez croire que je nay rien laisse a dire quil me sambloit servir a propos. Mesmement leur ay remante les bonnes lettres que le roy avoit escript, tant a voz, madame, comme a cheulx des estas, par les quelles yl promest toute assistence, etc. alencontre de cheulx qui vouldroyent envahir monseigneur ou ses pays, etc. A quoy me dirent que le roy de France nentendoit point envahir lesdits pays, mais seulement secourir le duc de Gheldres. Madame, soyez asseuree que sur ce point fust bien respondu. Et leur demanday par la meilleur doulceur que je povoy que chose estoit envahir, et se meurdre, occision, ardre, brusler, destruire, et desoler, tout nestoit point envahir? avec tant daultrechose. Mais, comme je vous ay dit ilz demourerent assez froitz reserve que pour

---

it would be a great expense to send the English thither. Nevertheless, as regards the 100,000 crowns, provided the obligations be here, I was told there would be no difficulty.

Madam, you may believe me that I have left nothing unsaid, which it seemed to me might be of service. I likewise reminded them of the good letters the king had written, both to you, madam, and to those of the estates, by which he promises every assistance, &c., against those who would invade my lord or his countries, &c. On which they said that the king of France did not mean to invade the said countries, but only to succour the duke of Gueldres. Madam, be assured they were well answered upon this point. And I asked them in the gentlest manner I could what was invading, and if murder, killing, burning, destroying, and wasting did not amount to invasion? with many other things. But, as I have said, they remained very cold except

A.D. 1508. 14 June.

tout resolution me dirent que le roy en escriroit volentiers au roy de France, et en froit parler a Dorisole. Et peu apres lung de eulx me dit a part que en vj. ou vij. jours je parleroy mesmes au roy.

Madame, je voz supplye que tout ce soit tenu secret, car yl y a tant de rapporteurs par le monde que lon noise aulcqune fois escriere le tout. Aussi voz supplye que ne me veulliez rien escriere que bien en voz lettres et laultre par billietz.

Au cas que les Francois et Messire Robert[1] viengnent, a votre tresnoble correction, je froy esmouvoir tout le pays par son de cloce et toute aultre maniere du monde, et froy prescher par toutes les villes et villages loultragieuse oppression desdits Francois. Quant a moy, se je y estoye joseroye bien par votre charge et commandement remonstrer au peuple de Gand ce que la conscience men juge et par avanture voz y froye aussi bon service que par deca.

---

that they gave me as all their answer that the king would willingly write about it to the king of France and would cause Dorisole to be spoken to. And shortly afterwards one of them told me apart that in six or seven days I should speak to the king himself.

Madam, I beg that all this may be kept secret, for there are so many talebearers in the world that one sometimes dare not write everything. Also I beg of you that you will write to me nothing but good in your letters, and anything else by private notes.

In case the French and Messire Robert[1] come, [subject] to your most noble correction, I would raise the whole country with alarm-bells and in every possible manner, and cause the outrageous oppression of the French to be preached through all the towns and villages. As for myself, if I were there I would venture by your command to show the people of Ghent what in my conscience I think of it, and perhaps I could do you there as good service as here.

---

[1] Robert De la Marck, duke of Bouillon, "the Boar of Ardennes."

Madame, je voz supplye tout jours me pardonner que jescris si privement. Il vault mieulx estre reprins de rudesse que daultre chose. Et pour finallement voz advertir de tout lextreme secret que je pouray jamais savoir, je ne say se chascun vouldroit que noz eussions tout le pays de Gheldres; et samble que noz serions trop couragieux et ne fryons point si grand estime de noz voisins, par quoy aulcquns peuvent estre bien contens se noz sommes bridez par ce bout, affin que soyons toutjours suppliantz. Et se quelque jour je me treuve devers voz, je voz en diray plus avant. A.D. 1508. 14 June.

Mais, madame, pour lhonneur de Dieu, tenez le secret, et soyez toute asseuree que quelque part que je soye, soit ycy ou par dela, je monstreray se je suis leal soubget ou non. Et de tant plus, puis quil voz plait estre contente et prendre en bonne part mon povre service, jamais temps sera que je ne penseray a desservir, syl mest possible, si grand honneur. Et affin, madame, que je ne voz celle rien, je croy que a la fin

---

Madam, I request you still to pardon me that I write so familiarly. It is better to be reproved for bluntness than for other things. And to tell you the upshot of the whole secret as far as I could learn it, I know not if every one would be satisfied that we should have the whole country of Gueldres. It seems that we should be too overbearing and not make so great account of our neighbours, so that some may be very well pleased if we are hemmed in on that side. in order that we may be always suppliants. If any day I find myself in your presence I will tell you of this more openly.

But, madam, for the honour of God keep it secret, and be fully assured that whatever part I take, either here or there, I will show if I be a loyal subject or no; and all the more because it pleases you to take in good part my poor services, there shall never be a time that I do not endeavour to deserve if possible so great an honour. And Madam, that I may conceal nothing from you, I think that

A.D. 1508. 14 June. ancoirez voz ourez parler du mariage de monseignieur le prince de Galles, et de madame Lyonoire,[1] quelque chose que je voz en ay escript parcidevant; toutesfois de cy a ung mois je voz en escriray plus certainement que je ne sauroye faire maintenant. Tant y a que pour maintenant je say de vray et le commandeur de Haro la dit publiquement, que le roy de France comme vray allie et ami du roy Darragon a puis nagheres escript au roy Dangleterre, le pryant bien acertes pour laccomplissement du mariage de madame Katherine Despangne, avec monseignieur le prince de Galles, etc. Et ma on dit que le roy Dangleterre na point este fort content que le roy de France sen mesle si avant. Et que plus est, lon dit que mondit sieur le prince ny est gheres enclin. Toutesfois, madame, en peu de temps lon en saura plus.

Ledit de Haro a bruyt destre fort Francois, et je le croy, car yl se declaire aulcqune fois trop quant

---

in the end you will yet hear of the marriage of my lord the Prince of Wales and madam Eleanor,[1] whatever I may have written to you of it heretofore; nevertheless, a month hence I will write to you with greater certainty than I can do at present. Thus much I know for truth, and the commander de Haro has said publicly, that the king of France as true ally and friend of the king of Arragon has lately written to the king of England urging him very earnestly for the accomplishment of the marriage of the lady Katherine of Spain with my lord the Prince of Wales, &c. And I have been told the king of England was not very well pleased at the king of France interfering in the matter so far. Moreover they say my said lord the Prince is hardly much inclined to it. Nevertheless, madam, in a short time we shall know more.

The said de Haro is reported to be very French, and I believe it, for it appears too evident sometimes when any news

---

[1] Eleanor, daughter of the late archduke Philip King of Castile, and sister of Charles, afterwards Charles V.

aulcqunes nouvelles viengnent. Mais il lui fait a pardonner; car son maistre est tel. Mais se Dieu donne sa grace touchant Gheldres, madame, voz cognoisterez grandz choses et toutz les amys de fortune demanderont votre ayde et assistence. Dieu voz en doint la grace, comme jespoire fermement quil fra; mais yl est mestier que chascun se mette maintenant en oeuvre plus que jamais a rebouter les Francois si viengnent. A.D. 1508. 14 June.

Ne pensez point, madame, que au cas que les affaires se portent bien en Gheldres, il ny aura roy de France ne Dangleterre quil ne voz estime plus que nulle aultre princesse, et le roy Darragon avecques. Mais principalement le roy Dangleterre; car jamais si dingne et profitable pour lui alliance ne pourra avoir en ce monde, comme quelque jour, quant yl voz plaira que je soy retourne, voz diray bien au long. Parquoy en bonne raison il pouroit avoir noz affaires pour recommandees; mesmement considere lestat ou quel cheulx de Gheldres sont maintenant, au fort yl noz fault ayder noz mesmes, dumoingz durant ses trois ou quatre mois. If things do well in Gueldres Lady Margaret will be highly esteemed; but they must help themselves.

arrive. But it may be pardoned in him, for his master is so. But if God grant us his grace touching Gueldres, madam, you will knew great things, and all the friends of fortune will seek your aid and assistance. God give you such grace, as I firmly trust he will; but it is needful every one now should bestir himself more than ever to repel the French if they come.

Doubt not, madam, but that if affairs go well in Gueldres, the kings, both of France and England, will esteem you more than any other princess, and the king of Arragon also; but chiefly the king of England, for never could he have in this world an alliance more worthy and profitable for him, as some day I will tell you more at length, if it please you that I be recalled. So that with good reason he may be interested in our affairs; especially considering the state in which those of Gueldres are at present, it is particularly necessary that we should help ourselves, at least during these three or four months.

A.D. 1508. 14 June. Madame, comme je voz ay escript pluseures fois que le delay de la venue de messieurs les ambassadeurs nest cy non pour entretempz veoir ou la Fortune favorisera, et selle est bonne pour lempereur et votre maison voz aurez des grandz offres de plaisirs et services.

Il y a ung astrologue par deca quil ma dit que des le xxii$^{e}$. ou xxiii$^{e}$. de ce mois la fortune de lempereur sera si grande et si bonne plus que jamais. Dieu le face ainsi. Je ny adjouste nulle foy; mais neantmoingz sy fault yl que chascun sy employe a son extreme possible a la conservatiou de la juste querele, mesurement de celle de Gheldres, ainsi que jay remonstre par deca si a plain que nul nen pouroit dire au contraire.

Madame, je voz pouroy tesner de voz escriere si longhe histoire, mais beauc[ou]p de chose ne se peult mestre en peu de langage. Voz pardonnerez a la simplesse.

Et a tant, ma tresredoubtee dame, yl voz plaira me

---

Madam, as I have written to you several times, the delay of the coming of the ambassadors is only to see which side fortune will favour, and if it be good for the Emperor and your house, you will have great offers of pleasures and services.

There is an astrologer here who has told me that from the 22nd or 23rd of this month the fortune of the emperor will be greater and better than ever. God make it so; I give no credit thereto; but nevertheless, it is necessary that every one set himself to do his utmost to maintain the just cause, especially that of Gueldres, as I have explained here so fully that no one had anything to say to the contrary.

Madam, I may weary you by writing you so long a story, but much matter will not go into few words. You will forgive plainness.

And, thus far, my most dread lady, it will please you to

commander voz tresnobles plaisirs pour selon iceulx me conduire. A layde de Nostre Seigneur au quel prye voz donner que plus desirez. A Londres, le xiiij$^{e}$. de Juing. A.D. 1508. 11 June.

Madame, se le roy Dangleterre se peult apercevoir que voz escris telles choses yl me tiendra pour ung espye, et par avanture me vouldroit nuyre. Dieu sait de quelle foy et lealte je y procede. Parquoy, Madame, voz prye de deschirer ses lettres quant voz aurez le tout [b]ien entendu.

Votre treshumble et tresobeissant serviteur,
G. DE THEIMSE[KE].

*Addressed:* [A ma] tresredoubtee Dame, &c.

---

instruct me of your most noble pleasure that I may conduct myself accordingly, by the help of our Lord, whom I pray to give you what you most desire. At London, the 14th of June.

Madam, if the king of England find out that I write such things to you he will hold me for a spy, and perhaps he would do me harm. God knows with what faith and honesty I act. Therefore, madam, I beg of you to tear up these letters when you shall have fully understood the whole.

Your most humble and obedient servant,
G. DE THEIMSEKE.

To my most dread lady, &c.

## LXVI.

A.D. 1508. 20 June.

### The Provost of Cassel to Margaret of Savoy.

[Holograph Addit. MS., Brit. Mus., 21,382. f. 25.]

Ma tresredoubtee dame, je me recommande treshumblement a votre bonne grace.

Reporting an interview with the King.

Madame, jespere que voz aurez receu mes lettres du xiiij$^{e}$ de ce mois par les quelles entre aultres choses voz ay escript que le roy vouloit parler a moy. Madame, je fuz hier mande vers lui, et eux audience bien trois heures, devisant seul avec lui en ung giardin ou yl estoit a cheval, et me ordonna prendre ma mule et deviser ainsi ensamble.

Madame, je vouldroy que jeusse la memoire si grande pour savoir bien raconter le tout, mais au mieulx que pourray voz escripray les principaulx pointz.

1. On the subject of Gueldres.

Le primier diceulx, apres avoir mande des nouvelles et samblables communes devises, estoit touchant Gheldres, comment, en ensuiant certaine ouverture ja pieca faicte par moy sur laffaire dudit Gheldres, il y avoit

---

Translation.

My most dread lady, I commend myself most humbly to your good grace.

Madam, I hope that you have received my letters of the 14th of this month, by which, among others, I wrote to you that the king desired to speak with me. Madam, I was yesterday sent for to him and had audience full three hours conversing alone with him in a garden, where he was on horseback, and ordered me to take my mule and converse thus together.

Madam, I would that I had a good enough memory to relate the whole, but to the best of my power I will write to you the principal points.

The first of them, after having talked of news and like ordinary conversation, was touching Gueldres; how according to a certain overture made long since by me on the matter of Gueldres, he had thought over it at great length, and

pense bien au long et par pluseures fois consulte envers soy mesmes, comment lon y pouroit mestre ugne bonne fin. Et pour sa finale resolution ne trouvoit moyen ne expedient plus convenable que de faire ungne treve pour certain tempz, chascun retenant ce quil a, pendant la quelle treve lon determineroit du principal par voye arbitrale ; assavoir que de nostre coste lon comprometera en lui comme arbitre ou arbitrateur, ou amiable compositeur. Et sait bien que du coste de Messire Charles Degmonde lon se compromettеroit au roy de France en pareille facon, et eux deux en certain tempz que a ce seroit ordonne wideroyent le different.

A.D. 1508. 20 June.

Henry recommends a truce.

Madame, sur ce point, devant tout oeuvre, je remerciay treshumblement le roy de ce quiluy avoit pleu avoir si bonne souvenance des affaires de Monseigneur, et mesmement touchant icelle affaire de Gheldres, la quelle estoit telle et de si grande importance que selle estoit bien wydee a son honneur toute la reste de ses aultres affaires se porteroit assez bien. Par quoy, voz,

---

several times deliberated with himself how a good end could be put to it. And for his final resolution he found no mean nor expedient more suitable than to make a truce for a certain time, each retaining what he has, during which truce a settlement should be made of the principal thing by arbitration ; to wit, that on our side it should be referred to him as judge or arbitrator or friendly composer of differences. And he knows well that on the side of Messire Charles D'Egmont, they will remit themselves to the king of France in like fashion ; and they two within a certain time, which should be appointed, would adjust the difference.

Madam, on this point, before proceeding to business, I thanked the king most humbly that he had been pleased to have such good remembrance of the affairs of my lord, and likewise touching that matter of Gueldres which was such and of so great importance that if it was well disposed of to his honour all the rest of his affairs would go on well enough. Wherefore you, madam, knowing truly

A.D. 1508. 20 June.

Madame, congnoissant de vray quil estoit le prince du monde qui mieulx, tant par sa tresgrande auctorite, reputation, et estime, que par le bon amour et affection paternelle quil avoit et portoit envers mondit seigneur, povoit regarir ceste playe, voz maviez charge et commande bien acertes de entendre son tresnoble plaisir touchant ledit Gheldres. Neant moingz, et a sa correction, je desiray bien lui remonstrer ung peu comment de prime face yl povoit sambler que pour le tempz present, consideree lextreme indigence en la quelle les Gheldrois sont maintenant, ceste treve ne seroit ne honorable ne proufitable, mais au contraire fort prejudiciable a mondit sieur. Car par le moyen dicelle les dits Gheldrois se renforcerient de rechief, ravitailleryent et se reserryent entierement ou maintenant ylz sont reduys si tresavant quil ne reste que ugne bonne adresche, secours et auyde pour en avoir la raison a toutjours; la quelle raison se noz povyons obtenir par son bon advis, conseil, et moyen, mondit sieur, voz, Madame, et tout les pays de pardela seroyent

Which the writer objected to, as the advantage would be all on the side of Gueldres.

---

that he was the prince of all the world, who, both by his very great authority, reputation and esteem, and by the good love and paternal affection which he had and bore towards my said lord, best could heal this wound, had very earnestly charged and commanded me to learn his most noble pleasure touching the said Gueldres. Nevertheless, and under his correction, I desired to shew him a little how it might appear *primâ facie* that for the present time, considering the extreme indigence in which the Gueldrians now are, this truce would neither be honorable nor profitable, but, on the contrary, very prejudicial to my said lord. Because, by means of it the said Gueldrians would reinforce themselves again, revictual, and draw together entirely where now they are so very much reduced that it needs but good address, succours, and aid to keep them in subjection for ever, which, if we could obtain by his good advice, counsel, and means, my said lord, you, madam,

a jamais de tant plus tenuz et obligez vers lui. En A.D. 1508. 20 June.
oultre lui dis que par icelle treve les dits Gheldrois seroyent relevez de toutz frais, missions et despens, et de nostre couste rien; car aussi bien fauldroit yl maintenir les garnisons a grandz despens comme selle nestoit point. Et qui est tout le pys, que ungne annee de telle treve seroit assez pour les Gheldrois pour apres noz faire de rechief plus forte gheere, ainsi que par lespace de si long tempz lexperience la monstre; avec pluseures aultres grandes devises, &c., lui suppliant que au lieu de telle treve yl noz voulsist plus to adrescher pour en avoir la fin finale du tout desmaintenant faire ungne bonne ferme paix, a lhonneur et utilite de mondit sieur ungne fois pour toute.

Madame, je ne say se jay bien dit ou non; car mes instructions ne se extendent point si avant. Toutesfois, a vostre correction, il me sambloit quil ny povoit avoir reprinse. Et le roy me donna si bonne audience quil me sambloit estre heure entendre de lui

---

and all those countries would always be under so much the greater obligations to him. Besides, I said to him that by this truce the said Gueldrians would be relieved of all costs and expenses, and on our side nothing; for it would be equally necessary to keep up the garrisons at great expenses as if it was not made. And what is still worse, a single year of such truce would be enough for the Gueldrians to make again more vigorous war, as experience has shown during such a long space of time; with a great deal of other conversation, &c., begging that in place of such a truce he would rather show us how to bring the thing to a conclusion by making, once for all, a good firm peace to the honour and utility of my said lord.

Madam, I know not if I have said well or not, for my instructions do not extend so far. Nevertheless, under your correction, it appeared to me that there could not have been any objection. And the king gave me such good audience that it seemed to me to be time to learn from him

A.D. 1508. 20 June. sa derniere volente, comme yl me samble qe jay entendu au mieulx que jay peu, ainsi que voz coingnoistrez.

The king's advice touching Gueldres. Ma dame, a ses devises le roy se tent pour quelque peu, et apres me dit en sourryant quil me savoit bon gre de parler ainsi francement, et quil vit bien que javoy grand desir de bien servir mon maistre. Aussi de son coste yl le vouloit adrescher le plus a bonne seurte que possible lui seroit, et me diroit aussi francement son avis et les raisons qui lesmovoyent. Et pour lentree me dit quil ne savoit croire que lesdits Gheldrois estoyent si bas et si pres prins comme lon dit; car yl sait de vray que le roy de France jamais ne les lauroit tumber en telle necessite et indigence, et que plus to yl y mesteroit toute sa coronne devant que cela adviengne, quelque chose que lon dye au contraire, dont, madame, yl voz asseure pour vray. Dit que icellui roy de France est riche, puissant de gens et de bien, et que davoir la ghere a lui il ne le con-

---

his latest will, which I think I have learned to the best of my power, even as you will understand.

Madam, after this conversation the king kept silence for some little time, and afterwards said to me, smiling, that he liked my talking in this frank fashion, and that he saw well that I was very anxious to serve my master well. He also on his side desired to induce him to the course which was the best possible for his security, and would tell me as frankly his opinion and the reasons which influenced him. And in the first place he said to me he could not believe that the said Gueldrians were so low and so nearly taken as was alleged, for he knows of a truth that the king of France would never have let them fall into such necessity and indigence, and that sooner than that should happen he would risk his crown, whatever is said to the contrary; which, madam, he assures you to be true. He says that the same king of France is rich, powerful in men and money, and that he would never counsel

seilleroit jamais. Dit aussi quil a entendu que les affaires de lempereur ne sont point si bien adreschees alencontre de ses ennemys que le roy de France aye grand peur de lui. Et mesmement quil a entendu puis na gheres que cheulx de lempire lui font bien petit secours, dont yl a grand regret. Aussi a bien entendu que les Venetians ont gagne sur lui grand pays, et journellement sefforcent de lui faire le plus grand grief quilz pouront; qui est bien mauvaise chose avoir a faire en tant de lieux si longtains sans prosperer; ce que lui a fait si grand mal quil lui a grandement retarde sa sainte. Car, quant sa fortune eust este meillieure seust este ugne grand joye pour lui et toutz ses alliez et eust on bien sceu mieulx conduire beaucop de chose que lon ne sauroit faire maintenant. Par quoy, ses choses considerees, yl se arreste a son advis; car, quant a lui, et au regard du secours quil pouroit de son coste envoyer en Gheldres, dit que en ce faisant yl se mestroit en ghere ouverte A.D. 1508. 20 June.

---

the making war on him. He said also, that he understood the affairs of the emperor are not so well disposed against his enemies that the king of France should have great fear of him; and likewise that he understood of late those of the empire give him very little aid, which he greatly regrets. And he has learned that the Venetians have gained much territory from him, and daily strive to do him the greatest injury they can. It is an ill thing to have to act in so many and so distant places without prospering, which has caused him so much annoyance that it has seriously retarded his health. For if his fortune had been better it would have been a great joy for him and all his allies, and one would have known better how to conduct many things than one can do now. Wherefore, these things considered, he remains in his opinion; for as to himself and the succours he might for his part send into Gueldres, he says that in so doing he should set him-

A.D. 1508. 20 June.

The king's advice touching Gueldres.

avec les Francois, ce que cheulx de son reaulme nelui conseillent point, ne yl nest point aussi de tel advis. Car puis quil peult vivre en bonne seure paix, jamais nentreprendra la ghere, mesmement ancoires pour chose que ne lui touche, du moingz si pres que il sen devroit mestre en telz dangiers et inconveniens. Dit oultre que lui donne grand merveillie que lempereur mesmes a qui la chose touche, trop plus ny mest ugne bonne fin au cas que la necessite y est si grande, avec tant daultres grandes raisons que certes, madame, il ne seroit point possible les toutz escriere, toutjours persistant en son premier advis.

A ce que par la treve les Gheldrois seroyent plus advantages que noz, et que ce seroit pour de rechief noz faire plus forte gheere, dit que ladvantage seroit tant pour lung que pour laultre ; car yl entent que durant la treve nul nentreprendra sur laultre, et au cas que aultrement se faisoit, yl se joindroit a lencontre de celui qui auroit encommence et auroit rompu ladite treve, et pareille-

---

self at open war with the French, which those of his realm do not counsel, nor is he himself in favour of such a policy. For since he can live in good sure peace he will never undertake war, at all events for a thing which by no means concerns him so nearly that he ought to put himself in such dangers and inconveniences on account of it. He said besides that he was much surprised that the emperor himself, whom it concerns far more nearly, does not put a good end to it, if the necessity be so great, with many other great reasons, which assuredly, madam, it would not be possible fully to recount, always persisting in his first opinion.

As to the Gueldrians being more benefited by the truce than ourselves, and that it would be an opportunity for making more vigorous war against us, he said the advantage would be equally great to the one as to the other; for he means that during the truce neither shall attempt anything against the other, and if it happened otherwise he would join against the party which had commenced and

ment froit le samblable quant la paix seroit faite. Car en ce, veu quil sen auroit mesle si avant pour le bien de paix, il pouroit abonne cause et juste querelle ayder et porter celle part qui auroit tenu et garde les dites treves et paix alencontre de laultre qui les auroit enfrainct. Ainsi que en foy et parolle de roy yl ma dit quil froit. A.D. 1508. 20 June.

Madame, comme je voz ay escrit derrenierement, les matieres me sont trop pesantes, mais je voz escris le tout au plus pres que je puis. Et mesmement pour ce que je persistay fort de plus to avoir ungne bonne, vraye, et ferme paix que telle treve, me dit que toutz les sages de France et de Flandres ne saroyent faire ungne paix, les choses estantz ainsi quelles sont, que preallablement lon cessa de faire la ghere, et treve precedente. Sur quoy, madame, apres avoir ung peu cesse de devises, et en se promesnant a cheval par ledit giardin il me dit quil me donnoit le plus seur conseil pour entretempz maintenir monseigneur en bonne paix

---

had broken the said truce, and he would likewise do the same if peace should be made. For in this, considering that he would have interfered so far for the good of peace, he might with good cause and just quarrel, aid and support that party which should have kept the said truce and peace against the other which should have violated them. Thus he declared to me that he would do, on the faith and word of a king.

Madam, as I last wrote to you, the matters are too weighty for me, but I write you the whole as nearly as I can. And likewise, because I insisted strongly on having a good, true, and firm peace, rather than such a truce, he told me that all the wise men of France and of Flanders could not make a peace, affairs being in such condition as they are, unless previously there were a truce and cessation of hostilities. Whereupon, madam, after a pause, taking a turn on horseback about the said garden, he told me he gave me the surest counsel to keep my lord meanwhile in good peace

A.D. 1508. 20 June. The king's advice touching Gueldres.

avec ses voisins et aussi avec ses propres soubgetz. Car yl est possible que sesdits soubgetz quelque jour se tenneront de contribuer et donner les aydes et aultres subsides. Avec ce me dit quil congnoit plus quil nest mestier de dire, et que paravanture tout le monde nest pas si enclin pardela et si resolu comme yl pouroit bien estre, et que de tant que yl y pense plus il sarreste de plus a son premier advis; me disant oultre quil avoit bien grand piete de voz, car, consideree la grandeur des affaires, yl estoit bien force que aulcqune fois voz estiez en grandz regretz et perplexitez, des quelles voz sortiriez par ce bout, &c.

Madame, en ses devises le roy vit bien de quel ceur je lui parlay, et en la plus grande reverence que faire savoye, lui regrestant toutesfois que ung prince de si grande extraction questoit monseigneur ne povoit consuir son droit et patrimoisne, ne par voye de justice ne aultrement; et mesmement considere que le roy de France par les traictez de Blaitz et de Trente avoit jure sur le Sainct Sacrament consacre par evesque, sur

with his neighbours, and also with his own subjects; for it is possible that his said subjects one day may weary of contributing aids and subsidies. In addition to this, he told me that he knew more than it was necessary to say, and that perhaps everybody is not so well disposed and resolute there as he might well be, and that the more he thinks of it the more he adheres to his first opinion; saying besides, that he had great pity for you, for considering the greatness of the affairs, it was impossible but that sometimes you must be in great troubles and perplexities, from which you might escape by this means, &c.

Madam, in these conversations the king saw well with what courage I spoke to him, and with the greatest reverence I could; regretting, nevertheless, that a prince of such great extraction as my lord could not pursue his right and patrimony either by way of justice or otherwise, especially considering that the king of France by the treaties of Blois and Trent had sworn upon the Holy Sacrament consecrated by a bishop,

le Saint Canon, sur les Sainctes Evangiles, de [ne] se point mesler des fiefz imperiaulx, tant hors des Ytales que dedans; en lui disant que Dieu quelque jour sen mesleroit pour conforter le bon droit, &c. A.D. 1508. 20 June.

En effect, madame, tout ce que jamais nay sceu penser je le remonstray a ma povre simplesse au mieulx que je puis. Car javoy si tresbonne audience que yl me samble que jamais nen auray meillieure. Mais, madame, chascun ne fait pas toutjours ce quil froit volentiers. Tant y a que envers Dieu et tout le monde je cuide avoit satisfait a mon serment. Et finablement je ne me sceus tenir de dire que qui auroit espoir dobtenir par ung moyen ou aultre les villes et fors qui povoyent le plus grever et nuyre au pays de monseigneur. Ancoires seroit ce bonne chose, mais je craindoy que jamais les Francois ny entendryent; car ylz ne veullient cy non noz grever et confundre se ylz povoyent, &c., avec tant daultres choses que il nest possible descriere.

---

upon the Holy Canon, upon the Holy Gospels, not to interfere with the imperial fiefs, either without or within Italy; saying to him that God would one day interfere to strengthen the just right, &c.

In short, madam, everything that I could ever think of I represented to him in my poor simplicity, to the best of my power; for I had such excellent audience that it appears to me I shall never have better. But, madam, every one does not always do what he would wish to do. At all events, towards God and everybody, I think I have fulfilled my oath. And, finally, I could not refrain from saying that whoever should have hope of obtaining by one means or another the towns and forts which could do most injury in the country of my lord, this, again, would be a good thing; but I feared the French would not listen to it, for they only wished to molest and confuse us if they could, &c., with many other things which it is impossible to relate.

A.D. 1508. 20 June.

Le roy veant que je persistoye fort changa propos; toutesfois sy me fist yl quelque responce ace dernier mot, disant que en toute chose yl y a ordre, et de maintenant parler de cela nestoit ancoires heure. Mais fauldroit premierement wyder ce quil avoit conseillie par avant, et apres lon se mestroit en devoir du remenant. Et atant commenca a parler dungne aultre matiere aussi pesante que ceste.

2. Of Spain.

A savoir, madame, des affaires Despangne et du roy Darragon. Et me demanda premierement se je nen sayoye aulcqunes nouvelles. A quoy lui respondis que non. Et lors me dit quil ny avoit homme a Parys plus Francois que ledict sieur roy Darragon, et savoit bien quil namoit point lempereur. Mais se lempereur lui vouloit croire il lui donroit tel advis, conduite, adresche, moyens, et advertissementz que ledict Darragon nauroit plus que faire en Castillie, et le tout se conduiroit de par lempereur, la royne, et monseigneur comme prince et heretier. Dit quil nest pas homme

Henry says he could tell the emperor how to obtain the entire administration of Castile.

---

The king perceiving that I insisted strongly on this, changed the subject, but nevertheless made me some answer on the last point, saying that there should be order in everything, and that it was not yet time to talk of that. But it would be necessary first to settle the matter which he had previously advised, and afterwards the rest would be taken into consideration. And then he began to talk of another matter as weighty as that.

That is to say, madam, of the affairs of Spain and of the king of Arragon. And he asked me in the first place if I knew of any news on the subject, to which I replied, No. He then said to me there was not a man in Paris more French than the king of Arragon, and he knew well that he did not love the emperor. But if the emperor would believe him he would give him such advice, guidance, means and intelligence that the said king of Arragon should no longer have anything to do in Castile, and everything should be conducted by the emperor, the queen, and my lord as prince and heir of the kingdom. He said he was not a man of two words, and

de deux parolles, et ce quil dit yl le tiendra. Dit oultre que le fait de Castillie est de si grande importance que se lempereur y avoit le main souveraine il froit trambler toutz ses ennemys. Disoit ancoires tant daultre chose a cell fin que en effect, madame, soyez toute asseuree quil y est enclin tout oultre. Et pource que jeusse volentiers entendu quelque chose plus avant, il medit que jamais ne me diroit les moyens; mais se jamais lempereur et lui se povoyent trouver ensamble il lui donroit a congnoistre le plus secret touchant ceste affaire qui est possible. Dit oultre que quant lempereur auroit le reaulme de Castillie que le fait de Gheldres se wideroit de soy mesmes, et, par consequent, toutes les pesantes matieres que lempereur pouroit avoir. Dit que il vouldroit que jamais lempereur ne fit entreprinses cy non celles qui seroyent bien deliberees par meur advis et conseil, des quelles yl pouroit avoir gloire et renon, comme seroit ceste syc. Non pas que pourtant yl y deut mesmes aller, cy non apres, quant toutes A.D. 1508. 20 June.

---

that which he says he will keep. He said besides that the affair of Castile is of such great importance, that if the emperor had sovereign authority there he would make all his enemies tremble. He said besides so many other things to the same effect that in short, madam, you may be fully assured he is thoroughly inclined that way. And because I would gladly have heard something further, he said he should never tell me the means, but if ever the emperor and he could meet he would give him the most secret knowledge possible touching this affair. He said besides, that when the emperor should have the kingdom of Castile, that the affair of Gueldres would settle itself, and consequently all the weighty matters that the emperor might have. He said he would the emperor never made expeditions except such as should be well weighed by mature advice and council, from which he might have glory and renown, as would be the case in this. Not, however, that he should go thither himself, except after-

A.D. 1508. 20 June. choses seroyent paraschevees, se son plaisir estoit tel. Dont yl na doubte nul que tout seroit a lui, et par ceste affaire yl seroit le plus grand qui fut en long tempz. Disoit aussi que il ne se deffye de rien de lempereur; aussi yl croit fermement que lempereur ne se deffye de lui, et le parlement de eulx deux ne greveroit ne a lung ne a laultre.

Madame, ce sy nest pas petite matiere et la fault tenir aussi secrete que la confession; aultrement, &c.

Madame, je lui demanday se son plaisir estoit bien que je voz en advertisse. Il y pensa ung peu et apres me dit quil en estoit bien content. Par quoy, madame, je men descharge. Neantmoingz syl voz plait que je lentretiengne en ce propos, ordonnes moy par voz premieres lettres que je le remerchye de cestui advertissement.

3. Of the coming of the Flemish ambassadors. Le tiers point du quel yl me parla estoit de la venue de messieurs les ambassadeurs, et en effect, combien quil est ancoires bien debile, toutesfois il est bien content

---

wards when everything had been accomplished, if such were his pleasure. He has no doubt that everything would turn out favorable to him, and by this affair he would be much greater than he has been for a long time. He said also that he in no wise distrusts the emperor; he also believes firmly that the emperor does not distrust him, and the interview between them would not be injurious to either.

Madam, this is no small matter, and it must be kept as secret as the confession, otherwise, &c.

Madam, I asked him if it was his pleasure that I should inform you of it. He considered for a short time and afterwards told me that he was content; wherefore, madam, I deliver myself of it. Nevertheless if you wish me to keep him to this intention, give me directions by your first letters to thank him for this information.

The third point on which he spoke to me was of the coming of the ambassadors, and in effect, although he is still very weak, yet he is content that they shall come at the end

quilz viengnent a la fin du moys de jullet prochain, et leur fra la meillieure chiere et expedition quil pou ra Par quoy, madame, voz frez merveilleusement bien de les despecher, affin quilz soyent y chy au tour du dernier jour de jullet. Yl ma aussi dit quil desire bien de savoir les personages quil viendront pour les faire logir et recevoir. Par quoy, madame, il ma ordonne den voz escriere; se vostre plaisir est voz men advertirez, car yl desire de le savoir. A.D. 1508. 20 June.

4. Of certain English rebels in the Low Countries.

Et finablement me dit comment passe vj. ou vij. jours yl avoit ordonne a messieurs de son conseil me parler daulcquns ses rebelles soubgetz et aultres qui journelement lui font blasme et deshonneur, dont me fut donne certain billiet, lequel voz ay envoye.

Madame, je ne voz sauroye point escriere comment yl a celle matiere a ceur et entend que lon envoye les contenuz audit billiet toutz prisoniers pardeca pour en faire la raison; aultrement yl ma dit quil non sera point content, du moingz de cheulx qui sont ses soub-

---

of the month of July next, and will give them the best cheer and expedition he can. So that, madam, you will do marvellously well to despatch them so that they may be here about the last day of July. He also told me he desires much to know the personages who shall come, in order to make arrangements for their lodging and reception. Wherefore, madam, he ordered me to write to you of it; if it be your pleasure you will apprise me, for he wishes to know.

And finally he told me how, six or seven days ago, he had ordered the lords of his council to speak to me of some of his rebel subjects and others who daily do him blame and dishonour, of whom a list was given me which I send you.

Madam, I could not write to you how he has this matter at heart and desires to have those contained in the said list all here as prisoners that justice may be done on them; otherwise, he said to me, he shall not be satisfied, at least as to those who are his subjects; and on the others he

A.D. 1508. 20 June. getz, et des aultres entend que lon en face pareillie raison par dela sans dissimulation ne advertissement pour eulx povoir saulver.

Madame, je neusse jamais cuide quil eut eu la chose tant a ceur. Dieu sait quelle honte que jen ay eu, et quelle chose il men a dit; et certes je vouldroye estre aillieur se je me devoye gheere mesler de telle chose. Car rien ne fut prys en gre de tout ce que je lui savoye dire. Il me doit souffire voz en avoir adverti par deux fois. Aussi de la part du roy, il peult bien penser que je suis homme desglise, &c.

Madame, jay le ceur trop pesant a voz en escriere ce que jay ouy, par quoy en fray fin.

Ma tresredoubtee dame, je prye a Nostre Seigneur voz donner que plus desirez. A Londres, le xx^e^. de Juing.

Vostre treshumble et tresobeissant serviteur,

G. DE THEIMSEKE.

*Addressed:* [A ma t]resredoubtee Dame, &c.

---

means that like justice should be done there without dissimulation, or warning by which they might save themselves.

Madam, I should never have imagined he had the matter so much at heart. God knows how much I was ashamed, and what things he said to me about it, and certainly, I should like to be elsewhere if ever I were to meddle much with such a thing; for nothing of all I could say to him was taken in good part. It ought to be enough for me to have given you notice of it twice. As for the king, he may well consider that I am a churchman, &c.

Madam, I have too heavy a heart to write to you what I have heard, so I shall make an end.

My most dread lady, I pray our Lord to give you what you most desire. At London, the 20th of June.

Your very humble and obedient servant,

G. DE THEIMSEKE.

To my most dread Lady, &c.

## LXVII.

A.D. 1508. 29 July.

### The Provost of Cassel to Lady Margaret.[1]

[Holograph, Addit. MS., Brit. Mus., 21,382. f. 29.]

Ma tresredoubtee dame, je me recommande treshumblement a votre beningne grace, Ma dame, pour ce que pas les deux derrenieres bougettes monsieur lambassadeur de Burgho ne moy avons receu aulcqunes lettres de voz, noz en sumes estez fort maris et perplex, et mesmement que entendons assez *le retardement des ambassadeurs.*

Ma dame, voz savez ce que ycellui seigneur de Burgho et moy voz en avons escript, et en effect je *crains que le roy Dengleterre se joindra avec le roy de France* entierement a notre *destruction.* Comme je voz ay escript par tant de fois, *le roy Dengleterre a*

Fears a combination between England and France.

---

TRANSLATION.

My most dread lady, I commend myself most humbly to your benign grace. Madam, as by the last two budgets neither my lord ambassador De Burgo nor I have received any letters from you, we have been much grieved and perplexed, especially because we are well aware of *the delay of the ambassadors.*

Madam, you know that this seigneur de Burgo and I have written to you of it, and in short I *fear that the king of England will join the king of France,* to our entire *destruction.* As I have written to you so many times, *the*

---

[1] The words in italics are written in cipher. A contemporary decipher is interlined.

A.D. 1508. 29 July. *toutjours espie la Fortune et ne vouldroit que eussions le pays de Gheldres.* A ceste fin yl fait les *difficultez* touchant *argent et le prest.*

Ma dame, au cas que *le roy Dengleterre soit* entierement *avec le roy de France* comme il fait *a craindre,* sans doubte *se les ambassadeurs ne viegnent,* tout se pouroit *perdre.* Voz en saurez bien user

Ma tresredoubtee dame, je prye a Notre Seigneur voz donner que plus desirez A Londres le xxix. jour de Jullet, apres soupe.

Votre treshumble et tres obeissant serviteur,

G. De Theimseke.

*Addressed:* [A ma] tresredoubtee Dame, &c.

---

*king of England has always favored the winning side and would not that we should have the country of Gueldres.* To this end he makes *difficulties* touching *money and the loan.*

Madam, in case *the king of England be* entirely *with the king of France,* as is *to be feared,* doubtless *if the ambassadors do not come* all might be *lost.* You will know how to act.

My most dread lady, I pray our Lord to give you what you most desire. At London, the 29th day of July, after supper.

Your most humble and obedient servant,

G. De Theimseke.

To my most dread Lady, &c.

## LXVIII.

A.D. 1508. 23 Aug.

### HENRY VII. TO THE BISHOP OF GURK.

[From the original Addit. MS. 19,398, Brit. Mus.]

HENRICUS Dei gratia Rex Angliæ et Franciæ ac dominus Hiberniæ, reverendo in Christo patri, domino Matthæo episcopo Gurcensi, archidiacono de Surrey, sacratissimæ Cæsariæ majestatis secretario et consiliario, amico nostro charissimo, salutem. Accepimus jamdudum ex relatu domini Andreæ de Burgo vestram reverendam dominationem cupidam esse ut unum ex nostris fidum ac circumspectum ad vos destinaremus, cui vestram erga nos singularem affectionem ac cordis arcana acsi coram essemus, sinceriter aperire pollicemini. Proinde votis vestris satisfacere cupientes, præsentium latorem ad vestram reverendam dominationem destinamus, eandem rogantes ut non modo eidem plenam ac indubiam fidem adhibere sicuti nobis ipsis velit, verum singula nobis significanda eidem aperire fidenter poterit, quod magnopere cupimus et ex corde rogamus. Datum apud Berwike die xxiij. mensis Augusti, anno Domini millesimo quingentesimo octavo et regni nostri vicesimo quarto.

Sending him a messenger to hear what he has to communicate.

HENRY R.

## LXIX.

A.D. 1508. 7 Dec.

### THE FLEMISH AMBASSADORS TO THE LADY MARGARET.

[Orig. Addit. MS., Brit. Mus., 21,382. f. 19.]

MADAME, tant et leplus humblement que povons nous nous recommandons a vostre bonne grace.

Madame, nous avons desavant hier v[eille] de Saint Nicolay aux Champs entre Dartford et ceste ville receu voz lettres de Cambray du second de ce mois; dont assez humblement ne vous saurions mercyer, car vous nous avez par icelles et par les bonnes et joyeuses nouvelles y contenues tant confortez et resjoys que ne le vous saurions escripre. Prians Dieu nostre Createur vous par . . ster jusques a lexecucion des matieres conceues, ainsi quil a fait jusques ores, et espero[ns] infailliblement quil fera enoultre jusques a la fin. Nous vous supplions aussi en toute humilite que en ensuyvant ce que de vostre grace vous a pleu nous escripre par vosdites lettres nous vouloir signifier de la con-

---

TRANSLATION.

MADAM, in as humble manner as we can we recommend ourselves to your good grace.

Madam, the day before yesterday, the eve of St. Nicholas, in the fields between Dartford and this town, we received your letters from Cambray, of the second of this month, for which we cannot sufficiently thank you; for you have by them and by the good news contained in them, given us such consolation and joy as we cannot describe to you. Praying God our Creator to . . . you until the execution of the matters projected, as he has done to this time, and we hope, without doubt, he will do henceforth, even to the end. We also request in all humility that according to what of your grace it has pleased you to write to us in your said letters, you will give us notice of the conclusion of the said matters when

clusion desdites matieres quant elle se fera pour icelle nostre joye confirmer et radoubler. A.D. 1508. 7 Dec.

Quant a noz nouvelles, madame, depuis que dernierement vous avons escript nostre arrivee a Douvres, sommes le lendemain[1] de la Saint Andrieu partiz dudit lieu de Douvres, accompaigniez du gra[n]t prieur de Canturbery, de messieurs Eduart de Pouninghe et Gilbert de Talbot d[e]pute de Calays, chevalier de lordre, et allez le[dit] jour augiste audit Canturberey en labbaye illec. A notre entree devant ladite abbaye furent audevant de nous [t]ous les officiers principaulx et gens de la ley de ladite ville en grant nombre, qui nous bienviengnerent et feirent tant bon recueil avec offre et presentacion de tout plaisir et service de si bonne sorte que riens plus. Et le soir nous vindrent faire presens de vin, cyre, espices, et pluiseurs autres choses, selon la coustume du pays, en grant quantite et bien h[o]norablement.

Relating their journey from Dover to London.

---

it shall take place, that our joy may be confirmed and doubled.

As for our news, madam, since we last wrote to you of our arrival at Dover, we left that place on the morrow[1] of St. Andrew, accompanied by the grand prior of Canterbury, Sir Edward Poynings and Sir Gilbert Talbot, deputy of Calais, knight of the order, and lodged that night at Canterbury, in the abbey. At our entry there were before us, in front of the said abbey, all the principal officers and men of the law in the said town in great numbers, who welcomed us and gave us such a good reception, with offers and presentation of every pleasure and service, that nothing could exceed it. And in the evening they came to make presents of wine, wax, spices, and several other things, according to the custom of the country, in great quantity and in very honourable fashion.

---

[1] 1 Dec.

A.D. 1508. 7 Dec. Le Samedy partismes, et venismes au giste a Setimborch, ung village a dix milles plusavant, dont aussi nous partismes le lendemain, qui fut Dimence, apres la messe, et venismes au giste a Rochestres. Dudit Rochestres feismes une autre journee, qui fut le Lundy, jusques a Dartfort, a douze miles pres de ceste cite. Et partout estions recueillez et tant bien venuz que merveilles. Jusques aupres dudit lieu de Dartfort nous convoyerent et conduirent tousjours le grant prieur de Canturbery et Messire Eduart de Pouninghe, qui furent a nous recevoir au descendre des navires audit Douvres, avec aussi le depute de Calays, et illec print congie de nous ledit sieur prieur et retourna en son eglise.

Lesdits depute et de Pouninghe nous ont tousjours accompaignie jus[qu]es icy. Et devant h[ie]r Mardy en deslogeant dudit Dartfort a demye lyeue pres dilleo, trouvasmes au devant de nous aux champs messieurs levesque de Woucestre,[1] le conte de Serosbery, grant

---

On Saturday we left, and came to rest at Sittingburn, a village ten miles further on, whence we again set out next day, which was Sunday, after mass, and lodged at Rochester. From Rochester we made another day's journey on Monday to Dartford, twelve miles from this city; and every where we were marvellously well received and welcomed. As far as to the neighbourhood of Dartford we were conducted by the grand prior of Canterbury and Sir Edward Poynings, who were at the receiving of us when we disembarked at Dover, along with the deputy of Calais; and there the said lord prior took leave of us and returned to his church.

The said deputy and Poynings have accompanied us all the way hither. And on Tuesday [the day] before yesterday, in our way from Dartford, at half a league from that place, we found before us in the fields my lord the bishop of Worcester,[1] the earl of Shrewsbury, grand master of England,

---

[1] Silvester de Giglis.

maistre Dengleterre, le commandeur de Saint Jehan, A.D. 1508. 7 Dec.
messire Eduart Brandon, chevalier de lordre, et le doctor West, avec grant multitude de gens de bien en nombre de cent et cinquante chevaulx ou plus; lesquelz avec aussi lesdits depute de Calays et le sieur Pouninghe nous conduirent jusques en notre logiz. A lentre de la ville trouvasmes nouvelle compaignie de gentilz hommes de lostel du roy et autres, bien accoustrez et montez. Le soir nous vint on semblablement faire des presens de par la ville, non moindres, ains plusgrans que jusques ores lon avoit fait, tousjours en accroissant.

Hier, le jour Saint Nicolay, entre une et deux heures apres midy vindrent devers nous en notredit logis messieurs larchevesque de Canturberey et le conte Doxenfort, ung des grans, et, comme lon nous dit, le principal personnaige de ce royaulme. Apres la congratulacion faicte de notre bien joyeuse et desiree venue, qui seroit trop longue a escripre, nous dirent que le roy estoit prest de nous recevoir et donner audience

---

the commander of St. John, Sir Edward Brandon, knight of the order, and Dr. West, with a great multitude of wealthy people, in number about 150 horse or more, who, with the said deputy of Calais and Sir Edward Poynings conducted us to our lodging. On entering the town we found a new company of gentlemen of the king's household, and others well accoutred and mounted. In the evening, likewise, people came to us to make presents on behalf of the town, not less but greater than ever, always increasing.

Yesterday, the day of St. Nicolas, between one and two o'clock after noon, came to us in our said lodging, my lord the archbishop of Canterbury and the earl of Oxford, one of the great, and, as we are told, the principal personage of this kingdom. After congratulations on our joyful and wished-for arrival, which would be too long to write, they told us that the king was ready to receive and give us audience when we would; and on our telling them we were

A.D. 1508. 7 Dec.

quant nous vouldrions, et en leur disant que nous estions prestz quant il plairoit a sa majeste, nous consignerent heure ce jourdhuy devers luy en sa court de Grunevuyse, hors de ceste ville, a unze heures devant midy. Et pour y aller nous envoya sa barge avec aussi les seigneurs et personnaiges dessus nommez.

Audience given to them at Greenwich.

Madame, nous y sommes allez a lheure assignee. Illec venuz avons trouve ledit sieur roy accompaignie de monseigneur le prince de Gales, son filz, de lambassadeur[1] du roy Darragon, de douze ou treize evesques, et de pluiseurs et la pluspart des princes et grans maistres de son royaulme. De vous escripre lonneur et le recueil quil nous feist et demonstra, ce seroit chose trop longue, et ne saurions. Il seroit impossible de meilleur.

Apres la presentacion et visitacion de noz lettres de credence, et lexposicion de notre charge, et responce de par luy surce faicte par la bouche de monseigneur de Canturbery,[2] son chancellier, nous dit et repeta a di-

---

ready when it should please his Majesty, they appointed us an hour this day [to be] before him in his court of Greenwich, out of this town at eleven o'clock before noon. And to go thither he sent his barge with the lords and personages above named.

Madam, we went thither at the hour appointed. Arrived there we found the said lord king accompanied by my lord the prince of Wales, his son, the ambassador[1] of the king of Arragon, twelve or thirteen bishops, and the greater part of the princes and leading men of the kingdom. To describe to you the honour and the reception which he gave us would be too long, and we could not do it. Nothing could have been better.

After the presentation and reading of our letters of credence, and the declaration of our charge, and answer thereupon made on his part by the mouth of my lord of Canterbury,[2]

---

[1] Gutiere Gomez de Fuensalida. | [2] William Warham.

verses fois et de tant bonne affection quil estoit possible, que nous luy estions les tresbien venuz. Il nous dit aussi que vray estoit quil avoit eu quelque regret et anvy a notre retardement et longue demeure; mais notredite venue, congnoissant par icelle la bonne et entiere affection le lempereur et de vous, madame, pour laccomplissement des choses faictes et traictees a Calays, luy fait oblier le tout. A.D. 1508. 7 Dec.

Apres, pour la presse qui estoit en la salle ou il nous avoit receu, nous mena en sa chambre, et illec se devisa longuement et priveement de sa grace avec moy, de Berghes, et me dit tout plain de bonnes choses. En effect, pour demonstrer quil a aussi grant desir a laccomplissement des choses traictees, et a nostre despesche comme nous meismes, nous dit que demain envoyera devers nous ses deputez pour veoir et visiter les lettres, tant dun coste que dautre, et apres adviser et conclure du jour de la solempnisacion des fianchailles et des choses qui en deppendent, tellement que esperons

---

his chancellor, he said and repeated to us divers times, with as much affection as possible, that we were exceedingly welcome. He told us also that it was true that he had felt some unpleasantness at our long delay; but our said coming, as he knew thereby the good and entire affection of the emperor and you, madam, for the accomplishment of the things done and treated at Calais, causes him to forget everything.

Afterwards, on account of the crowd in the room where he received us he took us into his chamber, and there of his grace, conferred long and privately with me, De Berghes, and said to me all sorts of fine things. Indeed to show that he has as great desire for the accomplishment of the things treated of, and for our despatch as ourselves, he said to us that to-morrow he will send to us his deputies to view and examine the letters on both sides, and afterwards advise and conclude touching the day for the solemnization of the betrothal and the things depending on it, so that we hope

A.D. 1508. 7 Dec. bien brief avoir bonne[1] expedicion du tout. Alayde du benoit Filz de Dieu, auquel prions, madame, vous donner bonne vie et longue, avec lentier accomplissement de voz tresnobles et tresvertueulx desirs. Escript a Londres le vij$^{e}$ de Decembre, xv$^{c}$ huyt.

Voz treshumbles et tresobeissans serviteurs,
J. DE BERGHEZ, DE GORREVOD,
SIGISMUNDE, J. LE SAUVAIGE,
ANDREA DA BORGO,
G. DE THEIMSEKE.

A Madame.

---

very shortly to have good despatch of everything by the aid of the Blessed Son of God, whom we pray, madam, to give you good life, and long, with the entire accomplishment of your most noble and virtuous desires. Written at London, the 7th of December, 1508.

Your most humble and obedient servants,
J. DE BERGHEZ, DE GORREVOD,
SIGISMUNDE, J. LE SAUVAIGE,
ANDREA DA BORGO,
G. DE THEIMSEKE.

To Madam.

---

[1] *bonne* repeated in MS.

# APPENDIX.

## I.—The Lords of Ireland to Henry VII.

[Orig. in Record Office.]

This letter is mentioned by Ware in his Annals of Ireland, and is attributed by him to the year 1486, to which date it appeared not unnatural to refer it. Taken, however, in connection with the two documents which follow, (and which have been erroneously attributed to the reign of Henry VIII.,) it appears that the date must be between 1489 and 1493.

### To the King our Soverayne liege lord.

Moost excellent Cristen kyng and our moost redoubted soverayne liege lord, in the humblest wise that eny subjettes kan or may, we recommaund us unto your moost noble grace. Please it the same that our right gode lord Gerald erle of Kyldare your depute lieutenaunt of this your land of Irland hath shewed unto us your gracieuse lettrez dated at your maner of Grenewich, the xxviij. day of July last passed, wherby we have well understaund your gracieuse mynd in the same that ye wold have our said gode lord to your noble presence, to thentent that he myght knowe therby your gracieuse mynde, and that your highnes myght have plenar communicacion with hym in all such thinges as myght concerne the wele of this your said land and for the reducyng therof and your subjettes of the same to a gode and lawefull ordre and obeisaunce, to the pleaser of God and the

The earl of Kildare is summoned by the King to England.

wele and profit of your said subjettes and land, as in your said lettre more amplier it dothe appere. Graciouse lord, and it like your highnes, we understand that he is bounden and sworne to be your trewe and feithfull subjet and liegeman as straitly and as sure as ever was eny subjet to his prince; the which othe and assuraunce our said gode lord hath wele and truly kept and observed contynuelly to this tyme, and undoubted will kepe during his lyve, and never will degresse from the said othe and assuraunce. And, graciouse lord, forasmoche as we understand the great daungiers and emynent periles that shold falle yif he shold depart owt of this your land, aswell by your Irishe enemys as otherwise; for when our said gode lord was seke, wherof we certified your highnes but late, it was playnl[y] and openly reported that our said gode lord was in grete joperdy of his lyve, by reason wherof diverse of the myghtiest of your Irish enemys confedered to gedir ymagyned and noysed a division t . . . . betwene them of your landes in this parties, yif God had don the will of our said gode lord. And in his said sekenes ther were diverse of your subjettes robbed, spoyled and taken prisoners and meny [othe]r grete hurtes done. And by the oothes that we have don to your highnes that is true withowte feynyng. Wherfor we in our moost humble and obeysant maner beseche your excellent grace to be his gode and graciouse lorde, and to have hym in your moost tendre favour, and that he may have your graciouse license at this tyme to abide at home for the defense and saufgard of us and others your feithfull subjettes, for diverse and meny urgent causes and greate daungiers, which we knowe rightwell shold fall in his absence yif he shold departe. And, graciouse lord, we beseche your highnes that what soever accusementes be made unto your grace on our said lord that therbe no credence takyn therto tyll his reason-

His presence in Ireland is essential to the safety of the country.

able excuses be had in the same. Moost excellent Cristen kyng and our moost redoubted soverayne liege lord, the Blessid Trinite graunte you meny prosperouse yeres to reigne upon us, with victory of your enemys. Yoven at your Cite of Divelyn in playne parlement undre the oone part of your grete seall of this your said land, the iiij. day of Juny.

Walterus Dublin.

Per Armacanum, manu propria.

Johannes Midensis.

Johannes Abbas Sancti Thomæ Martyris.

Valterius Abbas domus Sanctæ Mariæ Virginis.

Johannes Abbas Mellofontis.

Henricus Abbas domus Beatæ Mariæ de Vallesalutis

Nicholaus prior de Conall.

Rabart Preston Vicount of Gormanstoun.

James Flemyng Baron of Slane.

Richard Nugent Baron of Delvyn.

Edmund Plunket lord of Kyllene.

Nycolas de Sancto Lawrentio lord of Houthe.

Cristoforus Barnewelle Dominus de Trymletyston.

John Plunket lord of Dunsany.

By your true and feithfull subjectes the lordes spirituels and temporels and your Counseillours of your land of Irland in playne parlement ther assembled.

*Addressed*:—To the Kyng our Soverayne liege Lord.

## II.—Gerald Earl of Kildare to Henry VII.

[Orig. in Record Office.]

Has received the King's letter desiring his presence in England;

Moost excellent Christen kyng, and my moost redoubted soveraine liege lord, in as humble and obeysaunt maner as eny subject can or may doo to his soveraine, I recommaund me to your moost noble and benyng grace. Pleassed the same to be acerted that I have receyved your gracious lettres myssives dated at your manere of Grenewich the xxviij. day of Jullii[1] passed, wher by I have wele understand your gracious mynd that ye wold have me to your moste noble presennce that I mought ther by knowe your gracious mynd, and that ye mought have plenary communicacion with me in alle suche thynges as mought concerne the wele of this your said land, and that your subjectes of the same may be reduced to a good and lafull ordyr and obeisaunce to the pleayr of Godd, wele and profite of the same your land, as in your said lettres it doth appier more at large.

but has remained to adjust a difference between Desmond and the lord Bourk of Connaught.

Gracious lord, I, accordyng to your highe commaundement, was in full mynd and purpose to have accomplisshed and performed your moost noble plesyr in the same, settyng apart alle exscuses, till I was desyred by your true and feithfull subjectes of this your land, and my cousynes in especiall, therle of Dessemond and the lord Bourk of Connaght, that I shold not depart, but to abide for their defennce, and to apece such variennce as is dependyng betwix the said erle and lord Bourk, and that they wold take on them to write onto your highnes that your grace shold take noo displesyr with me herin, as it shall appier to your grace by their lettres and sealles more at large; the whiche I in my moost humble maner beseche your moost benyng grace to accepte and reputte for myn exscuse without eny displesyr to be had by your highnes herin with me, for I am and shalbe glade to see your highnes. And I beseche humbley your noble grace to be my gracious lord, for I am and shalbe duryng my lywe your true knyght, and never shalbe

[1] Sic, apparently written *Junii* at first and corrected by the addition of looped heads to the two minums of the *n*.

proved otheirwise. And what suerte or band other then I have made convenyently for the same may be had, I shall bynd me therto. And ower that, if it pleas your highnes to send a servaunt of yours, such as shall like you, into this your said land, I shall cause my said cousyn therle of Dessemond, and all the lordes spirituelles and temporelx of Mounester, the lord Bourk of Connaght, and all the lordes of the same contre, to be bonden as sure and as largely onto your grace as I am in presennce of your said servaunt, with diverse others whose ancesters was never bonden to noon of your progenytours kynges of England befor this tyme; soo that ye shall have noo cause of mystrust to be had ne understaund in me. And God knowethe whate laboure and peyn I have susteigned and daily doth susteigne to sett your said subjectes in easse, to my gret charge and coste. And by the othe that I have doo onto your highnes, ther shold nothyng be to me soo grett a plesyr, as oonly it mought be perfitly understaund to your grace what I have done for your honor and the wele of your subjectes of this your land.

Moost excellent Christen kyng and my moost redoubted soveraine liege lord, the Blessed Trinyte preserve your moost noble grace to reigne moost roially, and of your enymies and rebelles to have the victory. Written at your cite of Divelin the v$^{te}$ day of Junii,

By your true and feithfull subject,
GEROT ERLE OF KILDARE.

*Addressed:* To the Kyng, my soverayne liege Lord.

---

## III.—THE EARL OF DESMOND AND OTHERS TO HENRY VII.

[Orig. in Record Office.]

MOOSTE excellent Christen king, and oure mooste goode and gracious lord, in the mooste humble wise that we cane we recomaund us to your goode grace. Pleasid youre highnes that we ben enformyd that youre grace wold have our right goode lord therle of Kildare to your highness in to youre realme of Ingland for diverse causis considerid by your grace. Gracious lord, we know right well that his veray mynd and entent was to have performyd your noble plesire in that behalve; and we, undirstandyng that the mooste part of this lond, and in especiale For the protection of the

North against the Irish,

the North Parties and alle suche land as he have of late enhabit, the which was many ȝeris afor in the possession of your Irische enemice, schold have ben distruid in his absens, and also fering the grete danger and perelis that might fortune hyme by the se, as wel in his goyng as returnyng, and also for the grete trowbill, wariens, and discencion that dependith be thwene us

and for the pacification of feuds,

and the lord Bourke of Connaght and other lordis in that parties taking his parti, by reison wherof ther is like to be mortale werre and grete scheding of Cristyn blode by thwyxe us, which can in no wise be endid ne pesid with out our said goode lord be personaly with us, for we ben bound and sworn to abide his rule and jugement in this wariens aforsaid; for we the said erle of Desemond and the said lord Bourke, and the substance of us all, bene the nexte of oure said goode lorde blode in Irland, and ther is none can end our trowbill and wariens but onely hym silffe; and suche direccion and ordir as it shal like his lordischipe to take be thwene us we must and wil obey it, for we must be rulid by his consaile and he must be rulid by ouris.

they have persuaded Kildare to remain in Ireland.

Wherfor we have caused hyme to change his mynde and to abide at home for the causes forsaid, trusting in God that your highenes wold take no displesire with hym ne with us, the said causis by you gracinsly considerid. And, gracious lord, we undirstand that he is bound and sworn to be your trew feithfull subjet and ligisman as straitly as eny Cristin man may be; wich othe and band he haith kept and performyd truly to youre highenes syn the said othe and band unto this tyme. And thoght the said othe be a sufficient band for every Cristin man, ȝet we your subjectis for the contynuaunce and more largir assurans of the same, promit and bind us by this our writing and selis, that our said good lord shall truly kepe and observe the said othe during his live. Wherfor, gracious lord, we beseche your highenes to be his goode and gracious lord at this our louly peticionis, and that he may be pardonid to abide at home with owt youre displesire. And, mooste excellent Cristyn king, and our gode and gracious lord, the Holy Trinite preserve youe to reigne in prosperite on us youre subjectis, and of your enemice to have victori. Writtin at Lymrek the x day of Juyll.

Morice Erlle of Dessemond. Pers Buttbler therle of Ormond is depute.

Mor. lord Roche. Jamnes lord Cursy.

*With four seals pendent, in bad condition.*

## IV.—Octavian de Palatio, Archbishop of Armagh.

[See page 95.]

A letter of this prelate is mentioned in Harris' Ware, vol. I. p. 88, in which the writer not only disclaims complicity in Simnel's rebellion, but declares himself to have been the only one who opposed it. The following transcript has been kindly communicated to me by Mr. Hardinge of the Landed Estates Record Office, Dublin, from the MS. referred to, which is a seventeenth century copy in Marsh's library. The letter was probably addressed either to Cardinal Morton or to Fox, then bishop of Exeter.

Venerabilis in Christo pater, congrua commendatione præmissa, paternitatem vestram non celamus, quod profano coronationis pueri in Hibernia sceleri, me solo excepto, nullus obstitit manifeste; qua in re me maximis subjeci periculis vitæ, cum Lincolniensis comes, mihi tunc rabiosa invidia invidens, comitem Kildariensem inordinata adiens iracundia, potestatem quæsivit pariter et licentiam jura regalia in contradicentibus actui hujusmodi realiter exequendi. Attamen, quamquam dictus comes Kildariensis quod dictus Lincolniensis desideravit in ea parte eo instante abnuit, benevolentiam supradicti Kildariensis et aliorum procerum et primorum, cum eodem in actu hujusmodi profane participantium, cordialem me adipisci hactenus non sensi, imo in ambiguitatis amissionis bonorum et temporalium meorum perplexitate in dies permanere compellor. Et licet præfatus Kildar. et alii quidam magnates et primores Hiberniæ strenuo viro Richardo Eggecombe, militi, serenissimi domini nostri regis Henrici invictissimi in hac parte commissionario, nuper in Hiberniam destinato, nomine dicti domini regis homagium et fidelitatis juramentum præstaterint, nihilominus antiqui livoris fæcem in eis contra me remanere conspicio. Nam milite prædicto, ut opinor, nondum in Angliam applicato, nova contra me (sicut in literis quas præsentibus interclusas vobis transmitto latius continetur) incitamenta moverunt, instigante (ut æstimo) venerabili fratre meo, fratre Joanne Midensi episcopo, meo suffraganeo, qui in ambatiatorem dicti Kildar. atque magnatum ad regem mittendus est festinanter; materiem quippe hujusmodi novorum incitamentorum vestræ prædictæ paternitati me convenit explanare.

Post prædictam coronationem de facto celebratam, prænominatus comes Kildar. quoddam nomine dicti coronati magnum tenuit concilium, in quo Domini Spirituales in eodem concilio comparentes, me tamen absente, personaliter conscientiarum suarum morsibus vulnerati, quoddam subsidium ad sacrosanctam Sedem Apostolicam pro absolutione a sententiis et censuris quas forsan novos tumultus contra regem prædictum suscitantes incurrerunt, obtinenda, destinandum concesserunt super Hiberniæ clero. Et postquam serenissimus dominus noster rex ex sua benignitatis gratia generalem absolutionem expensis suis propriis obtinuit in ea parte petentibus, dictus comes Kildar., nitens subsidium hujusmodi contra formam concessionis ejusdem in proprios usus et utilitatem, pro suis apud regem expediendis hac vice negotiis, convertere, mihi reclamanti et alleganti quod cessante causa cessare debet et effectus, volentique clero meo defendere pro posse, noviter nocere demolitur, asserens me semper sibi et toti corpori terræ contrarium fore. Et scio pro certo quod si contingat dictum comitem Kildar. regimen Hiberniæ regia authoritate obtinere, ac cancellarium Hiberniæ ad nutum suum ordinare, spes non est mihi quietis in Hibernia. Et tunc infideles domino nostro gaudebunt, et ego pro fidelitatis meæ bravio opprobrium atque dispendium invidi rancoris reportabo. Si tamen prædictus serenissimus dominus noster rex me de cancellariatus officio Hiberniæ providere dignaretur, tanta columna suffultus partem dicti domini mei regis contra suos adversarios fortius possem sustentare, et dictum comitem et alios mihi et dicto domino meo contrarios minus ponderare. Quamobrem vestræ prædictæ paternitati precibus quibus possum supplico instantissimis, quatenus dicto domino regi præmissa suggerentes, meæ quieti in dicto cancellariatus officio mihi obtinendo adminiculum adhibeatis, et, si paternitas vestra me consulerit, ad Angliam personaliter accedam. Quicquid vero paternitas vestra viderit faciendum in præmissis me cum latore præsentium literatorie dignetur celeriter certificare, &c.

## V.—Agreement of Henry VII. with the Earl of Angus.[1]

[MS. in Record Office, among the Scottish documents formerly at the Chapter House.]

Memorandum. . . . this writing endented the xv[j] d[ay] of [November, in the year] of our Lord [God m.]cccclx[xxxj., the vij$^{th}$ of] the reigne of King Henry the vij$^{th}$, that it is agreed and con[co]rded [be]twixt [Sir John Cheyney and Sir Thomas Tiler knights on behalf of the king] their souverain lorde [on] that oon partie, and Archibald e[arl of] Anguyssh [on that other . . . . . . . . . . . . . . . . . ] forme that folowithe :— A.D. 1491. 16 Nov.

First, the said erle bindeth hym . . . . . . . . . . . . . . . . . . . . . . . . . . . to hym possible to moove t[he] king of Scottes . . . . . . . . . . . . . . . . . . . . . . . . . . . . . unto the sayd king of England, and to take and kepe ferm p . . . . . . . . . . . . . . . . . *isshed betwix both the roiulmes* . . . . . . *both* the sayd kinges. *And if* he may not atteigne his purpose . . . . *behalve bot that* [*wer*]*re be betwix the said kinges and roialmes, the said e*[*rle and his son*] shal [endeavour] theym to thuttermost *of* theire *powers to make* playn *werre* . . Scot . . . . that was contrary to their desire[2] *and purpose*, as touchyng the said am*ytie and peas*. *And if the case so fall*

---

[1] The document is very much mutilated and defaced. The words in italics are illegible, but are supplied from an original draft signed by Angus, which is also very badly mutilated, in the Cottonian MS. Calig. D. II. f. 14. The bracketed words are illegible in both MSS., and are supplied to suit the context.

[2] After the word *werre*, the Cottonian draft reads "upon all thoos "within [t]he roialme of Scotland "that wilbe contrary to ther de-"sire."

A.D. 1491. 16 Nov. *that the said erle* and his *son by* the might of their enemyes, *as God* defend, be put to that *extremytie that* they may not by the *eyde and supportacion of the* said kinges highnes of England broke or rejoyse theyr landes and revenues *within the roialme* of Scotland ne make their part*ie* good, that *they shall del[yv]er* unto the kinges highnes of Englond, or to such persones subjettes of the said *kinges*, as his highnes pleas to assigne, the *castell, callid* the Hermitage, with all the lordships and landes belonging to the same. And for the more suretie of *the* premisses the said erle is aggreed *to delyver* the said George, his eldest son, orells his own person to the said Sir John, to be *conveyd* unto the kinges highnes, *or wher his grace pleas* to assigne or appoynt him to be. And also in like wise Robert Elwolde, *son to Robert Elwold* of the Hermitage, *yonger*, whiche late deceassid, to be delivered *with the said* erles *son*, for the same or with hym self. And also to *bynde* hym self and his said son and heir to *the same by* their writinge under their seales. And over that to labour and requyre other of his frendes in Scotlond, as feere as he godly *may, to* be bounden for hym in like wise. For the which is also agreed that the kinges highnes of Englond, nor his commissioners nowe being upon the bordores, or any *other* commissioners hereafter shall conclude noe peas nor trieux with the Scottes comissioners, but *that the said erl* shalbe comprised . . . . and give his advice to the same. And if it come to that poynte, that the said erle delyvere the said castell of Thermytage *into the kinges* handes, as afore is said, than his highnes shall, according to his honor, helpe, soccor, and relief the said erle with landes and goodes within Englond, at the lest of as grete value and substance as the said castell, landes, *or lordships to* the same belonging be worth, *and of* yerely val*ue*. And also the said erle nor his said son shall in noo wise after this *day make poynteyment* for them self, nor f[or any] of their frendes with the said k[ing] of Scotland, nor of *him* receive pardone . . . . . . . . . . land or goodes within th[at realm without the] counsaill of the said king of Englond. And if the seid trieux be not had according to t[he] premisses, than [the s]aid Sir John a[nd Sir] William shall, for the wele of the said erle and his [said son], at their resonable request and desire, move prov . . . . . . . . . the borders . . . Englond to make sharpe warre upon the Scottes, and specially suche as be enemyes and adversaries to the said . . . . . . . . . . . . . to favor their frendes and lovers. And for the more suretie of the premisses the said Sir John and Sir Will[iam . . . . . . ] theyr writing on the king their soverain lordes behalve, that his highnes shall ratifie and conferme th . . . . . . writing . . . . . . . . . said erle undre his grete seale by the fest of Saint Hillary next comyng after the date of thies presentes. In witnesse wherof to the toon partie of this indentures remaynyng with [t]he said Sir John [and Sir Wi]lliam the said erle and George his son have set their seales. And to the other partie of the same indentures remayning [with] the said erle and George, the said Sr John and Sr William have set their seales. Yeven the day and yere above said.

A.D. 1491. 16 Nov.

(L.S.) (L.S.)

*Endorsed*:—"Articles agreed upon twixt Sr John Cheyney and Sr Thomas Tiler, Knightes, on the behalf of the king our soveraign lord on thone parte; and Archibalt Dowglas earle of Angwishe on thother parte."—*In a modern hand*, "Henr. 7. Dat. 1491, 16 Novembr. Scotia."

## VI.—THE CREATION OF HENRY DUKE OF YORK.

[MS. Cott., Julius, B. XII. f. 91.]

A.D. 1494.

IN the yere of oure Lord a m[l] cccc.iiij[xx], and xiiij[e], the tent[h] yer of the reigne of our souverain lord, kyng Henry the VII[the] beyng in his manoir of Wodestoke, determyned at Alhalowyn tide then folo[wing] to holde and to kepe roially and solemply, that fest in his palaice o[f] Westmynter, and at that fest to doube his ij[de] son knyght of the Bath, and after to creat hym duc of Yorc; and there apon directed his lettres missives, and allsoo writtes accordyng to the same to divers nobles of this his roiaulme to be of his sonnis bayne, and to receve thordre of knyghthod, of wiche att his commaundement came xxij., as schall folow after in this booke, and the remanent wer pardoned, or wer at their fynes. Knowlege wer of openly had in his court, iiij. noble men. and as men of great courage, and allsoo willyng and desiryng to honnour the said creacion and fest; and for the pleasir of our souverain lord, the quenes grace and the ladies, remenbringe theym selff that auncyent custume of thys his noble realme of Englond att suche roiall festes to be great a[nd] notable actis of armes, for the continuance of the wiche, and for the excersice of the same, and lest any oder schuld take that enterprinse beffore them, they besought the kyngis grace to licens and to permitte them at the said fest to hold and to kepe a justes roiall, and to aunswer all commers of what nacion so ever they bee, as well his subjectes as oder, accordyng to there articles, wiche they besought his grace, his licens ther apon graunted, to command his officiers of armes to puplishe the articles of there armes, as well in his noble court as in the cite of London. And thenne his grace thankkeffully graunted them, and asseigned their articles, and commanded Gartter principal kyng of armes, to assigne off hys compaignie, to proclame the said article[s] in places convenient for suche actis to be doon; wiche was furst proclamed in the kyngis great chambre of his maner of Wodestoke, after in the fair off the same towne, and after in London, in maner as folowithe.

Proclamation of tournament.

"Oyez, oyez, oyez. For asmoche as hit is comen to the notice and knowlege of iiij. gentillmen of the kyng our souverayne lord most roiall and honnourable court, that his highness endendith and purposithe by Goddis grace and sufferans in brief tyme to yeve creacion of duc on to the right high and excellent prince my lord Henry, ij[de] son to our souverayn lord kyng Henry the vij[the]; and att like tymes it hathe ben used alwey. and accustumed of auncyennyte with in this his most noble

realme of Englond, for the lawde and honnour of suche festes, to A.D. 1494.
have justis and turney accordyng to their articles: The kyng our
souverain lord, consideryng the noble and couragieuse desyres of
the said iiij. noble men, hathe thankkeffully graunted their
peticions in this behalve, and licenced thaym, and all oder gen-
tillmen of his said realme or oder nacions, to accumplishe the
articles folowyng, and hoo soo ever justithe best in the justys
roiall schall have a ryng of gold, with a ruby of the value of a
m[l] scuttes or under; and hoo soo ever torneythe best, and fairyst
accumplishit his strokkis schall have a ryng of gold, with a
diamant of like value."

And after the proclamacion of thes forsaid justys and turney
was proclaimed in the kyngis chambre as above and to scew
dyvers actis and exercises of armes, vj. oder gentillmen pre-
sented their articles to the kyngis grace, wiche his grace liberally
accordyd, and were proclaymed as the furst articles wer, and as
ensuyth. "Where it is soo that divers noble personnes hanne
enterprised and undertaked to hold a justis roiall and a turney
the iiij[the] and the ix. day of Novenbre, at Westmynster, as
playnley dothe apere by thair articles; and for as moche ys att
so noble fest divers and sundery excersices of armes is used; ther
for and to the entent, yf there bee any gentillmen or othre men of
armes that present nott theym selff at the said day of justes or
turney, there be vj. gentillmen that will make them disport
the xij. day of Novenbre, accordyng to thair articles, yf it schall
soo please the kyngis grace and highnes, for whoys pleasir. the
quenes grace, and all the ladies the under take the said enterprise,
and specially for the pleasir of thair redoubted lady and fairyste
yong princesse, the eldest doughter to our souverayn lord the
kyng."

And on Simon and Jude evyn, the kyng, the qwene, and my 27 Oct.
ladye the kyngis moder came from Schen to Westmynster to
dyner. And on the morne after Simon and Jude the kyng sent to
Eltam for to convoye the said lord Henry, wiche, with great
honnour, tryhumphe, and of great astates, was convoyed thorough
London, and receved with the maior, the aldermen, and all the
crafftys in their liveres, and soo honnorably brought to West-
mynster. And on the Thursday the xxx. day of Octobre the said 30 Oct.
lord Henry served the kyng of towell, and the lord Haryngton
toke to sey, and the lord Clyfford hild the bason, and the lord
Fitz-Waren bere the water, the lord Dacre of the Sowthe bere the
kyngis potage, Mr. Thomas Stanley and the remanent bere
dishes at the furst course or the ii[de]; and thenne thes lordes
servitors and the oder nobles, sum dyned in the chambre, and the
remanent satt in the hall, sum at my lord stewardis table, and

A.D. 1494. Ceremony of the Bath.

sum at master controller table, and after in like wise soo did they sope. And when it was nyght, and that their baynes were redy, furst, in the kyngis closett was the lord Henry bayne roially dressed, and a riche bed well empairelled; and therll of Oxinford red the advertisement, and then the kyng toke of the water, and putt on his schulder, and made a crosse, and kyst hit; and from thens went in to the qwenes closset, and like wyse advertised the lord Haryngton and the lord Clifford, and from thens went in to the parlement chambre, where wer xx. baynes, and beddes wiche hadden sparvers, and the best ordred that I have sien, and as folowyth:—Furst, in that chambre was the lord Fitz-Waren, the lord Dacre of the Sowthe, Sir Thomas Stanley, sonn and heir of the lord Strange, Sir John Arundell, Sir Water Gryffithe, Sir Gervoys of Cliffton, Sir Edmond Traford, Sir Robert Harrecourt, Sir Henry Marney, Sir Roger Neubourgh, Sir Rauff Rider, Sir Thomas Bawde, Sir John Speke, Sir Humfrey Fullford, Sir Robert Litton, Sir Piers Eggecombe, Sir Robt. Clere, Sir Thomas Fairfax, Sir Richard Knyghtley, Sir John Chooke. And after that the kyng of his grace and benevolens had viseted them alle in their baynes, he departed into his chambre: and thenne when they wer dry in their beddes they were revested in theyre heremites wede, and soo departed to the chappell, where they had spices, and their voidie, and the sergent of the confexcionary had of every knyght a noble.

31 Oct. And on the morne erley every man was shreven, and herde theyr messe, doyng all observance therto belongyng, retourned to thair beddys, and delivered thair russett gownes to the mynstrells; and it was so well ordred, and the howse soo well voided, and thenne kept that they toke good rest. And a non after, as it was day, and that they wer awaked, they well and liberally paid the fee of money to thofficiers of armes; that is to sey, the lord Haryngton, son and heyre of the lord marquis of Dorsett, l. s., and every baron above-named, xl. s., and everyche of the remanent xx. s. Item, they paid to the sergent of thwry every man xx. s. iiijd. Item, they rewarded the usere and the grome porter and there esquiers of honnour liberally, [an]d content the [se]rgent of the amedry all [hi]s fees, and yet they made a commune purse. When the tyme wos come that it was the kyngis pleasir that they schuld arise, therlle of Oxinford, therlle of Northumberlond, therlle of Essex, the lord Daubeney, with oder whent to the said lord Henry, and from hym to the lord Haryngton; and therll of Oxinford, great chamberlayn of Englond, gave hym hys shertt, and after hym the oder nobles did alsoo gyve them part of theyr abbelementes; and allsoo my lord of Oxinford with the forsaid lords hon-

nored them with his honde, gevyng them all their shertes, in ordre as above, and after as there beddes stode in ordre. And immediately after that they wer redey, they toke thair waye secretly by our ladie of Pieu thorough Saint Stephins Chappell on to the steyr foote of the Ster chambre end, where they toke their horsses, wiche in died wer simple and soo lytill of valeur, and nott to the worshipp of knyghthod. And that the olde ordonance was that thoos hors empairelled after the custume schuld be fee to the marishallis of England or a c. s., and in his abcense to the marishall of the kyngis hall, consyderyng that thoos hors for the most part wer so simple, and for an ensample that oder her after schuld come with better hors and more honnorably, for this oons my lord marishall, by thavys of his chiff counceill, toke of every man xl. s. for this time oenly, and pardoned the value of iij. li., and delivered there hors ageyn. And the lord William Courteney bere the said lord Henry swerde, and spores, the pomel upward; and wen he did a light of his hors Sir William Sanddis bere hym to the kyngis presens, and there therlle of Oxinford toke the swerde and spores, and presented the right spore to the kyng; and the kyng commanded the duc of Bokyngham to putt hit on the right hele of the said lord Henry, and in like wise the lifft spore to the lord marquis of Dorsett. And thenne the kyng gerd his swerde a bowt hym, and after doubbed him knyght in maner accustumed, and then sett hym apon the table. In tyme the kyng hade in like fourme doubed the lordis and Sir Thomas Stanley, &c., thenne Sir William Sanddys bere my lord Henry in to the chappell, and there at the highe aultre offred his swerd, and the lordis after in ordre; and after alle the knyghtes as they wer doubed. And when my lord was come out of the qwere dore, the kyngis maister cooke toke his spores for his fee, and in like wyse of every oder knyght and a noble. My said lord dined in his owne chambre, and the oder lords and new doubed knyghtes dined in the parlement chambre att a long table all on oon side, and their esquiers of honnour kerved byfore them, and the kyng licensed them to ett their mette (by cause hit was fastyng day), and after diner all thos new made knyghtes went in to a great chambre and did off their mantells, surcottes, gyrdils, and coyffes, and delivered them to thofficiers of armes, never better, and thenne clothed thaym in blew gownes with hodes. And immediatly after they went to counseill, and chase Sir Robert Litton to gyve the kyngis grace thankkynges.

A.D. 1494. 31 Oct.

Prince Henry dubbed knight, with 20 others.

And on the Saturday, Alhalowin day, after the kyng had herd matins and was retourned in to his chambre, and did on his robbes of astat roiall, and, crowned, came into the parlement

1 Nov.

A.D. 1494. 1 Nov.

chambre, and there stode under his clothe of astate, havyng many great astates by hym, as the cardinal of Canturbury and many oder prelatys, the duc of Bedford, the duc of Bokyngham, therll of Oxinford, therll of Essex, therll of Kent, therll of Willshir, and the substance of all the barons of this realme, all in there robbes; and in like wyse the juges, the master of the roullys,[1] the maior of London[2] with his bredren the aldremen, and great pres of knyghtes and esquiers and oder nobles; and out of the cloister a galary att the nether end of that chambre entred divers nobles and officiers of armes, and proceded towards the kynges presens; but Gartier, principal king of armes,[3] presented his patent, and after thre great astates in their robbes, that is to sey, therll of Suffolke, wiche bere a riche swerde, the pomell upward, therll of Northumberlond bere a rod of gold, and therll of Derby the cape of astate furred with ermyn thike poundred, of iiij. renges, and a riche coranall there apon; and therell of Shrewsbury bere the said yong prince. In tyme he entred the parlement chambre dore, and then the marquis of Dorsett and therll of Arundell lede hym to the kyngis presens, all being in theyre robbes of astates, and doyng their obbeissance as aparteynythe. And then the reverent fader in God the lord Oliver Kyng, bishopp of Excestre and the kyngis secretary, red the patent of his creacion presented by G[artier] as before, and soo there the kyng creatyd him duc of Yorc, with the gyfft of a thousand pond by yere; and after all the scremonys there to belongyng was doon, the kyng, being crowned, proceded in to the qwere of his chappell and stode in the denys stall, and taryeng there, ordred the procession: butt there were doubtes wethre therll of Suffolke or therll of Kent schuld goo before, and the kyng determined therll of Suffolke. A noder doubte was betwen the lord Grey and the lord Clyfford: the kyng by advys of his lordes ordeyned the lord Grey to goo before the said lord Clyfford. The qwne, my ladie the kyngis moder, was as yet in her clossett. The cardinal of Canturbury[4] did the devyn service *in pontificalibus*; alsoo the bishopp of Ely[5] was gospeler, the bishopp of Excestre[6] epistoler, the bishopp off Rochestre[7] croysyer, the bishoppis of Wynchestre,[8] Dirham,[9]

Created duke of York.

---

[1] William Warbam.
[2] Richard Chawry.
[3] Sir John Wrythe.
[4] Cardinal Morton.
[5] John Alcock.
[6] Oliver King.
[7] Thomas Savage.
[8] Thomas Langton
[9] Richard Fox.

London,[1] and Salisbury[2] and of Saynt Asse[3] [and] certain abbotes wer all *in pontificalibus*, and tharchebishopp of Yorc[4] was present but not *in pontificalibus*. This procession was the best ordred and moost preysed off all the processions that I have herd of in England, and this was the maner. Furst before the kyng therll of Arundell bere his swerde, and before hym on the right syde therll of Derby, constable of Englond, beryng the staff of his office, the duc of Yorc on his lifft hand borne by therll of Shrewysbury and his cape, with cornall on his hede, and his verge of gold in his hand. And Sir John Digby bere his staff of marchalse by fore hym, and Garter kyng of armes, and the maior of London, before them tharchebishopp of Yorke, and before hym maister Amoner,[5] the wiche accompened thambassateur of Naples, my lord Steward[6] and lord Tresorer[7] of Englond before them, and before them the trezorer Mr. Controller,[8] and before hym the kerver in his robbes, and next before them, on eyther syde the procession, thofficiers of armes, savyng Norrey kyng of armes, wiche accompened Marchemont herault of Scottland, wiche went be fore my lord Stewart. And after the kyng folowed his uncle, the duc of Bedford, and the duc of Bokyngham, and therll of Northumberlond, and all oder lordes, wiche had robbes, in ordre. After them juges, then the qwene crowned, my ladie the kyngis moder with a rich cournall; and after folowed ducesses, contessos, baronesses, and oder ladies and gentillwemen. After them folowed all oder lordes and knyghtes that had noo robbes, wiche richely by syen wer that day. After them Sir Charles Somersett with the garde. A.D. 1494. 1 Nov.

The kyng after masse did of his robbes of astate and came in to the great chambre, and there creat an herauld for the marquis of Dorsett, and named hym Dorsett the herauld. That doon, weshed and sett to diner, and the cardinal of Canturbury on his right hand, and non oder bodye at the borde that day. After the ij$^{de}$ cours, Garter kynge of armes and the oder officiers of armes gave the kyngis grace thankkynges for hys great largesse, and allsoo besought his grace to owe thankkynges to the high and myghty prince, his soon, the duc of Yorc, for the great and habundant largesse that he had geven them for his sake and for thonnour of his court. Where for after the kyngis largesse was cryed in bothe stilis accustumed,

---

[1] Richard Hill.
[2] John Blyth.
[3] Richard Redman.
[4] Thomas Scot, alias Rotherham.
[5] Christopher Urswick
[6] Lord Willoughby de Broke, steward of the Household.
[7] John lord Dynham.
[8] Sir Richard Guildford, controller of the Household.

A.D. 1494. 9 Nov.

he was cryed as folowyth:—"Largesse, &c., de treshault, puissant, et excellent prince, secound filz du roi nostre seigneur, duc de Yorc, lieutenant-general Dirlond, counte marishall, marishall Dengleterre, et gardien de Cinq Portz, Largesse par troys fois."

Tournament at Westminster.

And on the ix. day of the said monethe were the justys roiaulx in the kyngis palaice of Westmester; and as hit was prepared and fournyshed it was the most tryhumphant place that ever I sayw. Furst, to see the kyngis grace and the qwenys soo richely empairelled, his house and stage couvered with riche cloth of Aras blew, enramplished with fleurs de lis of gold, and with in fourthe hangid with riche clothe of Arras of oder ystorys, and ij. clothes of astate, oon for the kyng, a noder for the qwene, and riche coshyns of clothe of gold, accumpened with the substance of the great astatys of this realme, as the duc of Yorc, the duc of Bedford, the duc of Bokynham, and many oder, ellres (*sic*), barons, baneretes, and knyghtes, and as her after their names in ordre schall apere, &c. And owt of Westmynster hall came in to the felde the chalengers on helmed, and their hors richely trapped of the kyngis coulours, enramplised with sonnettes of silver, and summe whit and summe grene, with oder great gilt belles over the mane and alsoo the croper, with journates of the kyngis coulours. That is to say, therll of Suffolke, therll of Essex, Sir Robert Curson, John Peche, richely accompened with many lordes, knyghtes, and esquiers, merveleusly well by seen and with soo great richesses, in cheynys of gold, dyvers maners of way borne, bothe in goldsmythis werke and clothe of gold, both in journates, hoquetons, and hors harneys, and sum hors harneis of goldsmythis werke furred with ermyn. There schuld you have syen the good riders, the well doyng horsses, whatt gambadys, the changelyng of bellis, the glisteryng of spangils, and especialle among oder the lord Bourgavenny had a small blake hors wiche in montyng soo high a bove grounde did merveilles, and soo oftyn tyme. And when this noble and tryhumphant compeney had accompened the challengers a bowt the tilt, then and in the yest end thereof, they helmed thaym sellff.

And then out of the Kyngis strete entred the aunswerers, allsoo richely accompened, but they were helmed. There was therll of Shrewysbury and Sir John Cheney, so well horssed and soo richely by seen, that it was a tryhumphant sight to see them, and many oder, and soo in like wise rod a bowt the felde. And thenne therll of Suffolke and Sir Edward A Borough ran the vi. furst courses; and then therll of Essex and Sir Edward Dorell ran vi. the next courses; thenne Sir Robert Curson and Thomas Brandon vj. courses; then John Peche and

A.D. 1494. 9 Nov.

Matew Baker six oder courses. That doon, therll of Suffolke ran vj. courses with Guillam De la Rivere, and in like wyse therll of Essex with Rouland De Veilleville, and Sir Robert Curson with Henry Wynslow, and then John Peche and William Craythorn; butt the said erll of Essex and Rouland ran at the furst butt v. courses, by cause Rouland hors wold nott cope. Those courses accomplished, therll of Suffolke and Sir Edward A. Borough ran oder vj. courses, and in all that day brake apon Sir Edward ij. speres well brokyn, the iij$^{de}$ better; and the said Sir Edward brake a spere, well brokyn, and gave ij. good atteyintes. Then therll of Essex ran with Sir Edward Darell, and on his helme] brake a spere, by syde a great atteynt; and the said Sir Edward Darell brake ij speres well broken, the iij$^{de}$ better, and ij great atteyntes. Then in like wyse Sir Robert Curson and Thomas Brandon, and bothe conoyted soo moche the hede that they broke few stavys; butt Sir Robert gave good atteyntes, and Thomas Brandon brake ij. speres and gave ij. atteyntes. After them John Peche and Matew Baker. And John Peche in all that day brake apon the said Matew Baker v. speres well brokyn; and the said Matew Baker broke thre speres and a great atteynt. And then ran efftsonnes therll of Suffolke and Guillam de la Rivere; and therll brake on the said Guillam oon spere well brokyn, and Guillam brake on the said erll that day ij. speres well brokyn and oon under. Then therll of Essex and Rouland ran oder vj. courses, butt Rouland hors wold nott cope. After them Sir Robert Curson and Henry Wynslow, on whom the said Sir Robert brake a spere well brokyn, and gave a good atteynt. And the said Henry brake ij. sperers well brokyn. After them ran John Peche with William Craithorn, wiche John Peche brake that day on Craythorn vj. speres well brokyn, the vij. better, and over that gave a good ateynt; and the said Craythorn brake on the same Peche ij. speres well brokyn. And thenne was cryed *a lotell*, &c.

The prize given to John Peche.

And after the souper began the daunces: wiche doon, ij. right noble ladies maidyns, that is to say, the ladie Anne Persie and the ladie Anne Nevyll, presented John Peche to the right high and excellente princesse the ladie Margerete, the kyngis oldeste doughter; wiche by thavys of the kyng, the qwene, my ladie the kyngis moder, and of all the ladies, gave hym the price, that is to sey, a ryng of gold with a ruby, as be the proclamacion shall appere. And for asmoche as the wordes in the proclamacion wer generalle, "Who soo ever justethe best" and named nother the partie with in nor with owt, where for the price was geven to the partie with in. How be it, hithe hathe nott ben comenly sien, or elles

A.D. 1494. 9 Nov.

Sir Edward Darell schuld have had it for the partie with owt on that day, for he brake ij. speres well, the iij[de] better, and soo was alowed iiij. speres well brokyn, and gave ij. great atteyntes in rynnyng of xij. courses; and the said John Peche in rennyng of xxiiij. courses brac xij. stavys, wiche wer alowed xiij. speres well brokyn. And thes armes were accomplished the ix. day of Novembre, wiche[1] in maner above said, wiche schuld have ben doon the iiij. day, and wer defered by cause on the forsaid iiij[the] day was kept thobitt of the full noble memor the kyngis fader, and thos armes of turney that schuld have ben on the ix. were defferred to the xj. day of the said monethe. And thos armes of the oder vj. gentillmen wiche schuld have ben doon on the xij. day wer well and notably accomplished the xiij[e] day, as here after schall apere.

The obit of Henry VII's father kept on the 4 Nov.

11 Nov. Second day's tournament.

How the right noble lords therlles of Suffolke and of Essex, Sir Robert Curson, and John Peche, came in to the feld the ii[de] day at the tourney in this maner, every man under his pavilion, and a crest upon hit, with roundelettes of cramoisyn velvet with goldsmythys werke comyng under their chynnys and a bowt their helmes; thier journates of the couleurs of the duc of Yorc, that is to sey, blew and tawny. Allsoo their hors harneys was of blake velvet, bordred and losenged of goldsmythis werke, and on every corner of the said losenges a rounde silver bell, and in the myddys rosses, oon red, a nothre whit, and oon every roos a waffir gilt. And in this fourme came owt of Westmynstre hall. Therll of Suffolkes pavylion was of red double sarcenet and his worde writtyn there apon, "For to accumplisshe;" and his crest above was a lion of gold, the taille fourched, sett in maner of a curnalles with plumasses whit and grene, and ramplyshed with spangils. After hym entred therll of Essex under his pavylion, the wiche was of a darke tawny sarcenet, and his worde was, "Owr promesse made;" his crest a fawcon fleyng silver with a brused wyng, sett in like maner as therll of Suffolkis. Then entred Sir Robert Curson in his pavylion of blake sarcenett, and his crest a red dragons hede sett as above, and his worde was, "There to we be redy." And after hym entred John Peche in his pavylion of a light tawny sarcenet, and his worde embrowdered was, "In every thing," and his crest a lions hed of ermyn crowned with gold, sett in like plumasses as a bove said, and went a bowt the tilt. And when they yssewd owt of their pavylions besien as a bove, and thofficiers of armes toke them for their fee, then entred owt of the towne Sir Edward A Borough with a demy trapper of grene velvet, &c. enramplished with * * .[2]

---

[1] Sic in MS. | [2] Blank space in original.

A.D. 1494. 11 Nov.

And Sir Edward Darellis hors was empairelled with a demy trapper of grey velvet emramplished with * * .[1] Thomas Brandon hors was trapped with a demy trapper of gren velvet, as the oder a bove, enramplished with lions heddys rasyd and crowned gold. And then entred Rouland de Veilleville, wiche was trapped with russet sarcenett.

And then tourned furst therll of Suffolke with Sir Edward A Borough, and therll of Suffolke brake his swerde, and bothe they nobly and couragieusly accumplished their xxiij$^{o}$ strokkis. Then tourned therll of Essex and Sir Edward Darell, and therll of Essex brake his swerde, and bothe they furyeusly and natably accomplished their strokkis; butt the said erll ran soo firsly ayenst the schulder and the sadell of the said Sir Edward that Sir Edwardis hors was in doubte to have fallen. Then Sir Robert Curson and Thomas Brandon furieusly and couragiously ran to gedres, and after certain strokkis, there swerdes wer enterclosed with the gauntellet of the said Sir Robert, that Thomas Brandon with the ploke of Sir Robert was sum what meved of his sadell, butt soo well recouverd that the gauntellet with the swerde of Sir Robert felde to the ground, or ells hit was thought the said Thomas had ben in juberte to have ben on sadeled; but the kyng licenced the said Sir Robert to have his gauntellet a geyn, and thenne they bothe turned a geyn like ij. champions, and Sir Robert brake his swerde, and Thomas swerde brake in the hilt, and eyther of them had new swerdes and full valiantly accumplished thair armes. Then entred John Peche and Rouland de Veilleville, butt Rouland gave good strypis, and the said John Peche dyd full well, and courageusly accumplished their armes. And after that this tourney was soo well and notably accumplished, entred in to the felde to the justes roiaulx Sir Edward A Borough, his hors trapped with clothe of gold, bordred with blake velvet embrawdered with lettres of gold, couvered with sarcenet whit and grene voided. And then John Cheney came in to the feld, and his hors trapped with gren velvet and whit dasmaske paly enramplished with red rosses. And owt of Westmester hall came John Nevyll armed and helmed, his hors trapped with lawnd. And after them entred Rouland de Veilleville, and then they ran round. Sir Edward A Borough that day ran well and couragieusly, and brake a spere well brokyn, the ij$^{de}$ better, with a teynt. John Cheney brake ij. speres well, the iij$^{de}$ better, and gave a good atteynt. John Nevyll brake ij. speres well brokyn, and gave a good atteynt. Rouland brake ij. speres well, the iij$^{de}$. better, with a great atteynt, and fournyshed that justys honnorably, &c.

---

[1] Blank space in original.

A.D. 1494. 11 Nov. And after souper the ladies whent to the daunces, wiche doon the prices wer geven in maner as folowyth. Furst ij. fair and noble ladies, maidyns, that is to sey, the ladie Elizabethe Stafford, suster to the duc of Bokyngham, and the ladie Anne Nevyll, doughter to therll of Westmerlond presented the noble and couragiense knyght therll of Suffolke to the high and excellente princesses the ladie Margarete the kyngis oldeste doughter, wiche by thavys of the kyng, the qwene, and my ladie the kyngis moder, and of all the ladies, the said princes hathe awarded and geven the price for the partie with in to the forsaid erll of Suffolke, as be the proclamacion schall appere. "Oyez. The kyng our souverain lord and the qwenys grace and in especiall the noble and myghty prince the ij^de soon of the kyng our souverain lord the duc of Yorc, in the honnour of whoos creacion this noble justys and tournay hathe ben holden, gevythe thair especiall thankkes to all those noble and honnorable gentillmen that hathe at this tyme indevered thaym selff to the honnoryng of the said fest of creacion, and in accumplishyng of suche chalenges as the right noble lorddes, therlls of Suffolke and Essex, Sir Robert Curson, John Peche chalengers hathe honnorably accumplished. And where as in tymes past the price hathe ben commenly geven ocenly to the partie with owt, neverthelesse now it is thought that they that hathe ben chief causers and chalengers of this noble entrepris and actis of armes in thoos justys and tourney hathe deserved especiall thankkes and honnour, where for the right high and excellente princesse above said, by thavys of the kyng, the qwene, my ladie the kyngis moder, and of all the ladies, hathe awarded and gyven the price for the partie within to the right noble lord therll of Suffolke, that is to sey, a ryng of gold with a diamant." And in like fourme the right noble ladies the countesse of Northumberlond and the ladie Elizabethe Herbert presented the right valiant esquire Thomas Brandon to the excellente princesse afore said, to wom she gave the price for the partie with owt, as schall appere by the crie, "Oyez. And for the partie with owt that hathe soo honnorably and valiantly acquite them in answering the said tourney, that is to sey, Sir Edward A Borough, Sir Edward Darell, Thomas Brandon, and Rouland de Veilleville, the kyngis grace, the qwenes, my ladie the kyngis moder, and the said noble and excellente prince the duc of Yorke, geves them their especiall thankkes, and the right high and excellente princes the ladie Margarete the kyngis oldeste doughter, and by thavys of the kyng, the qwene, my ladie the kyngis moder, and of all the ladies, hathe yeven the price for the partie with owt to the valiant esquier Thomas Brandon, that is to say, a ryng of gold with a rubee."

Prize given to the earl of Suffolk, and to Thomas Brandon.

13 Nov. And on the xiij. day of Novembre, after that the kyng, the

qwene, &c. wer entred the felde to their house a fore said, and a long space of tyme loked that Thomas Rider and William Treury schuld have entred, wiche Treury was deseved of his hed piece for that tyme. then the kyng commanded William Craythorn and Henry Wynslow to entre the felde and to ren a cours openly with the spere, and thenne to the swerdes in tyme xviij$^{e}$ strokkis wer accumplished. And the said Craythorn hors was empairelled in paper in maner of a barde, whitt and red losenged, and soo openly torne in the feld, and sporned with the fett of his owne servantes, butt they wyst full lityll what they dyd their master that wrong. And Henry Wynslow hors was empairelled in like wyse in paper in maner of a demy trapper, ther apon peynted ij. men pleyng at dyse and certain othes writtyn nott wrothey her to be rehearsed. That was doon, as hym selff told me, to cause the kyng to laugh, and they bothe ran very ner the closer of the feld, but they coped nott with there speres, and Wynslow caused Craythorn to leese his swerde, butt yet the said Craythorn after his swerde was restored to hym, gave the said Wynslow great strokkis, &c., and with the pomell of his swerde smot hym on his helme, and hurt sore his honnd, wiche that nott with standyng lett nott to accumplishe his strokkys. That doon, the kyng commanded them bothe to onhelme them selff, and eyther of thaym to take a longe trunchun for to depart them that sculd turnay afterward. Then entered William Treury owt of Westmynster hall, helmed, his hors trappet with a trapper of whitt and grene damaske parted *par pale*, a bordre cheveronne of blake satin enramplished with pynne tres of fyne silver in plate and with spangils bramlyng among. And Thomas Ryder came owt of the towne, and to hym was presented ij. speres with moornes, where of he toke the choise and Treury toke the toder; and then they ran to gedres, and Thomas Rider gave William Treury a great atteynt, butt he brake nott his spere. Then every of thaym had a swerde and tourned to gedre, butt Thomas Rider caused the said Treury to lese his swerde, wiche was restored to hym a geyn, and after that, they strakke dyvers strokkys to gedres, butt then Thomas Rider sumwhat meved or declyned from the strokkis; wether hit was for the fault of his sight, or to voide the strokkis I can nott say, butt he was nott preysed for the voidyng. And after that they wer departed ther came owt of Westmynster hall in to the felde, helmed, and their horsses richely trappet, and also rood a bowt the felde, Syr Edward A Borough, Syr Edward Darell, Thomas Brandon, Matew Baker, Rouland de Veilleville; and Guillam de la Rivere came in afterward, by cause he had lent his hedpiece to William Treury. Then owt of the towne came

A.D. 1494. 13 Nov. Third day's tournament.

A.D. 1494. 13 Nov.

iij. gentill, fair and noble ladies, maidyns, ledyng iij. knyghtes and allsoo a noble maide ledyng an esquier, all iiij. in a seute, that is to say, the iiij. forsaid noble ladies. maidyns, and gentill-women[1] in oon a seute, and the iiij. gentillmen in a noder. The ladies wer abillide in this maner, everyche of thaym in a gowne of whitt damaske, their slevys of cramoisyn velvet sett to the bodies, and like wyse at thelbous with chenys of gold, and in there her, with riche serkellettes of gold and precieuse stonnys a bowt their heddys, with great chenys of gold about their myddlys, and mervyleuse riche bees a bowt their nekkes, a pon iiij. whit palfereys. The furst was the ladie Elizabethe Stafford, suster to the duc of Bokyngham, and she lade by a riche fause reigne the hors of therll of Suffolke. The ij^de^ was the ladie Anne Nevyll, doughter of therll of Westmerland, and she lade therll of Essex. The iij^de^ was the ladie Anne Percy, suster to therll of Northumberlond, and she lade Syr Robert Curson. The iiij^the^ was maistres Saint Liger, doughter of the ducess of Excestre, and she lade John Peche. And after them folowed John Nevyll, broder to the lord Bourgavenny, and John Williams, well horssed. And in especial the foure forsaid gentillmen apon foure balde horsses, well barded and like crestes on theyr heddys as wer on theire tentes stondyng be twen ij. great and high plumashis of whit, the toppis blake spangils, the thirde hangyng doon be hynd.

Then furst by the kyngis commandement and ordonans ran to gederes therlls of Suffolke and of Essex atoons ayenst Sir Edward A Borough and Syr Edward Darell. And Sir Edward A Borough at that cours brac his spere well apon therll of Suffolke; and the said erll glissed on the helme of the said Sir Edward, the wiche ran with speres with moornes; after them therll of Essex and Sir Edward Darell, butt they brake noo spere. That doon, Thomas Brandon and Matew Baker a yenst Syr Robert Curson and John Peche, but the said Thomas and the said Sir Robert brake noo spere, but John Peche brake his spere apon Mathew Baker. Then ran Gulllam de la Rivere and Rouland de Veilleville a yenst John Nevyll and John Williams, but they encountred nott. Then Sir Edward A Borough and Sir Edward Darell turneyed ayenst therll of Suffolke and therll of Essex, but therll of Suffolke at the ix. stroke gave suche a stroke to Sir Edward A Borough that is swerde was almost owt of his honde and brused his gauntellett. And as the said Sir Edward wolde have holpen hym selff and

[1] *And gentillwomen*] Crossed in original.

A.D. 1494.
13 Nov.
Third day's tournament.

amended hit with his bridyll hand, his hors tourned from therll and Sir Edwardes bake towardes him, supposyng to moche peple that the hand of the said Sir Edward had ben stonyed; butt when he had sumwhat amended his swerde, he tourned his hors and gave a light strokke over the helme of the said erll. Then therll wold furyeusly goon a yenst hym, and soo wer they departed. And Sir Edward Darell and therll of Essex bothe furyeusly accomplished their xij. strokkis largely. Then tourned Thomas Brandon and Mathew Baker a yenst Sir Robert Curson and John Peche. and there wer great strokkis geven, yett everyche of thaym had nott his felow that he supposed to have had. After them Guillam de la Rivere and Rouland de Veilleville a yenst John Nevyll and John Williams, wiche well and couragieusly accomplished their strokkis. After that they ran all xij. to gederes and strakke firyeusly and great strokkis be twen them. In tyme vj. strokkys wer accumplished, and soo with great honnour wer they departed. And at that stoure John Peche accumplished his strokkis a yenst ij., for asmoche as ij. sundry men strakke at hym, butt nott atoons; and thus with honnour every man departed the feld that day, God be thanked and Saint George! And after souper began the daunces, wiche doon ij. right noble ladies, the ladie of Northumberland and the ladie Herbert presented the right noble knyght Syr Edward A Borough to the right high and excellente princesse the ladie Margerete, oldest doughter to the kyng our souverain lord, to whom sche gave the price for the partie with in in maner as her after schall folow. And in like fourme ij. oder noble ladies, the ladie Anne Percy and the ladie Anne Nevyll, presented to the forsaid excellente princesse therll of Essex, to whom she gave the price for the partie with owt, as her after schall appere. That doon, Garter kyng of armes, accumpened with oder kynges of armez, harauldes, and pursuyvantes stondyng on high on a fourme, there declared the prices in maner as folowythe.

Prizes given to Sir Edward A Borough and the earl of Essex.

"The kyng our souverayn lord. the qwenys grace, and the right high and excellente princesse the ladie Margarete, their oldest doughter, for whoos sake and honneur the justes and turney hathe ben thys day entreprised and valiantly and couragieusly doon and accumplished, gyve their entiere and especiall thankkes, un to Syr Edward A Borough, Syr Edward Darell, Thomas Brandon, Matew Baker, Guillam de la Rivere, Rouland de Veilleville, entreprengneurs of the same justes and turney. And where as in tymes passed the price hathe be commenly geven oenly to the partie with owt, nevertheless now it is thought that they that hathe ben chief causers and chalengers of this noble enterprise and actis of armes in these justes and

A.D. 1494. tourney hathe deserved special rewarde and honnour. Wherfor the right high and excellente princesse the ladie Margarete the kyngis oldest doughter, wiche by thavys of the kyng, the qwene, my ladye the kyngis moder, and of all the ladies, hathe awarded and geven the price and laude for the partie with in to the right honnourable knyght Syr Edward A Borough, wiche as thus day hathe well and honnorably brokyn his spere, and alsoo hathe well behaven hym selff at the tourney, that is to sey, a ryng of gold with a dyamant. And where as the partie with owt, that is to wete the right honnourable and noble lordes therlls of Suffolke and of Essex, Sir Robert Curson, John Peche, John Nevyll, John Williams, answerers to those said justes and turney hathe soo honnorably and valyantly acquited them in the same, our said souverayn lord, the qwenys grace, and their oldest doughter the ladie Margerete byfore named, yeven to theym their right enteer thankes; and morover the right high and excellente princesse the same ladie Margarete, by thavys of the kyng, the qwene, my ladie the kyngis moder, and all the ladyes, hathe awarded and geven the price and laude for the partie with owt to the right noble lord therll of Essex, wiche as this day hathe geven great strokkis in this tourney and long contynued in the same, that is to sey, a ryng of gold with an emerauld."

The names of thastates, lordes, banerettes, and knyghtes beyng at thys fest:—

Furst the Kyng
The Qwene
My ladie the King's moder
The Duc of Yorc
Thambassateur of Naples
The Duc of Bedford
The Duc of Bokyngham
The Marquis of Dorsett
Therll of Arundell
Therll of Oxinford, great chamberlayn of Englond
Therll of Northumberland
Therll of Derby, constable of Englond and juge ordred all thynges doon in the feld thos iijd ys.
Therll of Shreuesbury
Therll of Suffolke
Therll of Essex
Therll of Kent
Therll of Wilshir
Therll of Urmond
The Lord Haryngton
The Lord William Courteney
Therll of Kyldare son and heyre
The Lord of Saint Johns
The Lord Grey
The Lord Clyfford
The Lord Bourganny
The Lord la War
The Lord Scropp
The Lord Grey of Wilton
The Lord Fitz Waren
The Lord Zouche
The Lord Dacre of the Sowthe
The Lord Dacre of the Northe
The Lord Dodeley
The Lord Bauchamp
The Lord Hastynges
The Lord Dynham
The Lord Dawbeney
The Lord Broke

The Lord Wylougby
The Lord Hosey
The Lord Bryan
The Lord Hodye
The Lord Borhwell
The Baron of Slane

*All the Ladies of the Court in great numbre.*

The Ducesse of Bedford
The Marquisse of Dorsett
The Countesse of Kent
The Ladie Burgavenny
The Ladie Dodeley
The Ladie Dynham,
and soo many mor in numbre, and allsoo I have nott halff their names.

*The names of the Prelatys.*

The most Reverent Fader in God, the cardinal of Cantorbury
Tharchebishopp of Yorc
The Bishopp of Ely
The Bishopp of Wynchester
The Bishopp of Duresme
The Bishopp of London
The Bishopp of Salesbury
The Bishopp of Excestre
The Bisshopp of Saint Asse
The Bishopp of Rochester,
and many oder abbottes, priours, docteurs, and oder clerkes.

*Banerettys and Knyghtes.*

Sir John Cheney, baneret and knyght of the garter
Sir Thomas Mongomere, knyght of the garter
Sir John Arundell, baneret, broder to therll of Arundell
Sir Gilbert Talbot, baneret
Sir Edward Stanley, baneret
Sir John Fortescu, baneret
Sir Humfrey Stanley, baneret
Sir Edmond Bedynfeld, baneret
Sir John Sayvell, baneret
Sir Richard de Labere, baneret A.D. 14[illegible]
Sir James Tyrell, baneret
Sir Christoffor Ward, baneret
Sir Piers A Ligh, baneret
Sir Thomas Stanley
Sir Charles Somersett
Sir Richard Gilford, controller of the kyngis house
Sir Davy Owen
Sir Thomas Bourser of Barnes
Sir Walter Hungerford
Sir Henry Vernon
Sir Thomas Butteler
Sir Reignold Bray
Sir Thomas Lovell
Sir Thomas Darcy
Sir John Arundell of the West contre
Sir John Riseley
Sir Nycholas Vaux
Sir Edward A Borough
Sir Edward Barkeley
Sir John Wyngfeld
Sir Edward Darell
Sir Robert Curson
Sir Roger Neubourgh
Sir William Knevett
Sir William Bolen
Sir Matew Browne
Sir Henry Wiloughby
Sir John Gyse
Sir John Hastynges
Sir William Scott
Sir John Sabacottes
Sir Walter Gryffithe
Sir Gervoys Clifton
Sir Edmond Traford
Sir Rauff Rider
Sir Robert Harcourt
Sir Henry Marney
Sir John Speke
Sir John Turberville
Sir Henry Roos
Sir William Uvydall
Sir Piers Eggecombe
Sir Robert Litton

A.D. 1494. Sir Robert Clere
Sir Thomas Tirell
Sir Humfrey Fullford
Sir Richard Lews
Sir Thomas Fairfax
Sir Richard Knyghtley
Sir John Chooke
Sir Olyver Mannyngham
Sir John Mannyngham
Sir John Halwell
Sir Robert Pointz
Sir John Norbery
Sir Henry Heydon
Sir Robert Ratcliff
Sir John Pikeryng
Sir Edward Wyngfeld
Sir Robert Brandon
Sir Thomas Bawde
Sir Thomas Tempest
Sir William Litillton
Sir Edward Pykeryng
Sir Robert Markam
Sir Gwy Fairfax
Sir John Digby
Sir William Vanpaige
Sir William Sanddis
Sir Nicholas Lisle
Sir Thomas Fitz William of York shir
Sir Thomas Hungerford wiche ther decesed
Sir Sampson Norton
Sir Roger Cotton
Sir Thomas Leighton
Sir Thomas Markenfelde
Sir William Caru
Sir William Wilougby
Sir Adam Fumeys
Sir John Lovesque
Sir John Browne of London
Sir Hugh Brise
Sir Thomas Fitz William of Lyncolnshir
Sir William Martin
Sir Rauff Ostrishe, obiit
Sir William Horn
Sir John Persevall
Sir William Capell
Sir John Fenkyll
Sir Simon Monfort.

Finis.

---

## VII.—Arrangements for the Reception of Catherine of Arragon.

[One scheme of these arrangements has been printed in the Hardwicke State Papers from a modern MS. in the Harleian Collection. The present differs from it considerably, and is from an original draft by Henry VII.'s Council in the Cottonian volume, Vespasian C. xiv. f. 81. An account of her actual reception will be found in Leland's Collectanea (2nd Edition) vol. V. 352.]

A.D. 1501. Oct. * * * * * * * * * * * *

barges and great bootes to the said Westminster. And as for the princesse, it is thought that she shuld be with the quenes grace in her barge.

[1]The charge of warning of all the lordes bothe for the prepayring and arredieng of thaym self, and warnyng of the tyme of theyr attendaunce in thayr barges is comitted to my lord chambrelayn.[2] A.D. 1501. Oct.

And besides this provision that the kinges great and litell bootes be purposely prepaired and kept, nott onlie for suche estraungiers as shall come with the said princesse, wherof my lord chambrelain hath taken the charge, butt also for her and the said ambassadours servauntes.

Item, when alle thies barges and bootes of the lordes spirituel and temporall shalbe thus appoynted and redy upon the Thamys to sette forthwardes towardes Westminster, then the said lordes spirituel and temporall hover and attende every man in his barge or bote in the ryver upon the kinges barge. And when the king in his said barge shall sette forth from the said Baynardes Castell, then alle thoder barges and bootes to rowe by the king and about the king as the space of the river with thebbe or flode, and good ordre shall lede theim till the tyme his grace shalbe landed at the great bruge of Westminster, and that the quenes grace and alle the ladies, and certain lordes to be appoynted by the kinges grace to attend upon her, folowe in the company of the king, and when she shall come to the great bruge at Westminster, that then she, her ladies and lordes attending upon her pause and rest in their barges till suche tyme that the king with his company be landed and entred into the palois.

[Memorandum, to appoynt two faire and large barges, thoon for thambassadours of Spayne, and thother for the ambassadours of Scotland, besides the kynges two bootes for thayr servauntes. The Archebishoppe of Cauntreberys barge and the abbott of Westmynsters barge been th[e most] mete and convenient for the said ambassadours.][3]

And esfor justes, torneys and suche other cerymonyes thei be remytted to the said Mr. comptroller sergeant of the kinges armoury.

Item, it is thought wele fitting and honorable that every lord spirituel and temporall, that shall gief their attendaunce at this tyme, kepe his house during the said fest, and till the king departe from Westminster.

Item, that my lord chambrelain send certain of the huisshers of the kinges chambre to take up Herons house within the saintwary, and to serche alle the loginges that be within thabbey

---

[1] This sentence is inserted in the handwriting of Ruthal.

[2] Giles lord Daubeney.

[3] This paragraph is inserted in Ruthal's hand but scored out.

A.D. 1501. and Chanen Rowe, and cause the owners of theim to dresse and
Oct. fornysshe theim with convenient stuf, and to make their reaporte of every of the same by writing.

Item, my lord stieward[1] and the comptroller shall cause vj. of th[e] best fornysshed loginges, and the towne of Westminster to be reserved and kept for estraungiers.

Item, that Robert Suthwell and Sir William Vampage shall have eithr[e] of theim a hool copy of this boke to thentent thei may often oversee and perfitely peruse the same, and not oonly to advertise every man that hath eny charge to hym to be redy to doo their offices, but also to calle upon theim for thexecucion of the same.

Item, that certain officiers at armes, that is to saie Richemount king of [arms], Somerset, Rugedragon heraldes, and Mountorgell pursuyvaunt, Conyers, John Craford, John Molle, Cholmeley, sergeantes-at-arms, goo with my said lord steward, and gief their attendaunce, and serve the said princesse as the shalbe commaunded by my said lord steward.

Item, that xij. palfraies and a litter upon Friday the viij. day of Octobre, departe and drawe streight to Honyngton, in Devonshir, and ther tary and abide the commyng of my said lord stieward, and at his commyng thider go streigh[t] with hym to Excestre, to thentent to serve the said princesse and her ladies, wherof my lord stieward shall gief her knowelege, and cause theim to be ordred and disposed after her pleasure.

17 Oct. And that my said lord steward, with suche as shall attende upon hym be at Excestre the Sonday, which shalbe the xvijth day of this moneth of Octobr at the ferrest.

Item, that the Tuesday next ensuyng, that is to saie the xixth day of the said moneth, the said princesse accompanyed with alle the nobles of Devon and Cornwall that brought her to Excestre, departe thens and the night folowing loge at Honyington.

Item, the Wednesday then next ensuying, which shalbe the xxth day of the said moneth the said princesse accompanyed with the said nobles of Devon and Cornewall shall departe from Honyngton, and goo to Crokehorne, and ther loge in the parsonage the night ensuyng.

And ij. or iij. myles befor the come to Crokehorne she shalbe met with Sir Amys Paulet, Sir Hugh Lutterrell, Sir John Speke, Sir William Willoughby, Sir John Wodham, John Sydenham, of Brympton, and John Horsey. And soo fourthe attende upon her, and bring her to Shirbourne, and there departe.

---

[1] Lord Willoughby de Broke, steward of the king's household. See Leland, Coll. v. 353.

Item, the Wendisday the xxvijth day of this moneth, the said princesse, accompanyed with the said Sir Amys Paulet, and thoder, shall disloge fro Crokehorne, and drawe towardes Shirborne. and there loge in thabbey that night and the Friday folowing alle day. A.D. 1501. Oct.

Item, ij. or iij. myles befor the come to Shirborne, to be mette by Sir Thomas Lynde, William Martyne, Sir John Turbrevile, Sir Rogier Newburgh, Richard Willoughby, William Basket, Henry Stanguysshe, and so forth attend upon her, and convey her to Shaftesbury, and there departe.

Item, the Saterday next ensuyng, which shalbe the xxxth day of Octobre, the [said] princesse, accompanyed with the said Sir Thomas Lynde and thoder, shal dis . . from Shirborne, and drawe towardes Shaftesbury, in there loge in thabbey that night and the next day folowing, which shalbe the Sonday, and Monday all day, which shalbe all Alon day.

Item, ij or iij myles befor she come to Shaftesbury to be mette with Sir Morys Barowe, John Monpesson, Thomas Long, John York, yong Baynard, Waltier Servington, John Gawen, Richard Clifford, William Lamberd, John Ludlowe, Waltier Bonham, James Lowder, Waltier Torney, John Burley, William * [1] Robert Unwyn, and soo forth, to convey her to Ambresbury, and ther departe.

Item, the Tewsday next ensuyng, whiche shalbe the ij$^{d}$. day of the said moneth, the said princesse, accompanyed with the said Sir Maurice Barowe and thoder, shall disloge from Shaftesbury, and drawe towardes Ambresbury, and ther loge the next night in thabbey. 2 Nov.

Item, it is appoynted that my lady of Norffolk, with certain ladies awaiting upon her at the namyng of the quene and my lord tresourer, be at Ambresbury, upon Monday the xxvth day of Octobre, ther and then to mete and receyve the said princesse after the maner folowing, that is to saie, my lord tresourer, accompanyed with the Bisshops of Bathe and Hereford, thabbots of Abandon and Reding, my lord Dacre of the South, my lord Zouche, Sir Robert Poyntz, Sir William Sandes, Sir John Seymor, Sir Christofer Wroughton, Sir John Brereton, and Sir John Chok, to mete her iij. or iiij. myles befor she come to Ambresbury. And the said duchesse of Norfolk, to receyve her after her offring in som convenient place betwix that and her loging, at which tyme William Hollybrand, which shall awaite upon her, shall in the Spanysshe tong, in the name of the said duchesse welcome the said princesse with suche wordes

---

[1] Blank in MS.

A.D. 1501. 2 Nov. as be delyvered to hym in writing. And that the said duchesse have warnyng hereof by * * and the said Hollybrand by my lord chambrelain.

Item, that there be a chare redy at Ambresbury the same tyme, for the said princesse to put her in the next day, or at eny other tyme when it shall please her, wherof the charge apperteigneth to[1] * *

3 Nov. Item, the Wensday next folowing, which shalbe the iij$^{d}$. day of the said moneth, the said princesse, accompanyed with the said duchesse and tresourer, and the nobles that attended upon theim, and in the said chare, if it shal soo please her, shall disloge from Ambresbury, and drawe towardes Andovor, and ther loge the night ensuyng in the inne of Thaungell.

4 Nov. Item, the Thursday next ensuyng, which shalbe the iiij$^{th}$ day of the said moneth, the said princesse, accompanyed as above, shall disloge fro Andovor, and drawe towardes Basingstoke, and ther the next night loge in Kingesmelles hous.

5 Nov. Item, the Friday next ensuyng, which shalbe the v$^{th}$. day of the same moneth, the said princesse, accompanyed as afor shall disloge fro Basing Stoke, and drawe towardes Dogmersfeld, and ther loge in my lord of Bathes place that night, and the next day folowing, which shalbe the Saturday the vj$^{th}$ day[2] of the said moneth.

6 Nov. Item, the Saterday next ensuyng, which shalbe the vj$^{th}$. day of the said moneth, the said princesse, accompanyed as afor, shall disloge from Dogmersfeld, and drawe towardes Chertesey, and ther in thabbey loge the night folowing, and the Sonday and Monday next ensuyng.

8 Nov. Item, the Monday next ensuyng, which shalbe viij. day of November, the said princesse shall disloge from Chertesey, and drawe towardes Croydon, and ther in tharchebisshops place loge the next night ensuyng, and the Tuesday next day folowing

And betwix Chertesey and Croydon, at the fote of Banstede Downe the said princesse shall be met with the personages folowing, that is to say, my lord of Buk, therle of Kent, my lord Fitzwarren, my lord Saintmond, the lord Stourton, my lord Dudley, thabbotes of Bury and * *,[1] Sir Waltier Hungerford, Sir Edward Darell, Sir Robert Harecourt, Sir Rogier Lewkenor, Sir Giles Bruges, Sir John Guys, Sir John Longford, Sir John Huddelstone, Sir Alexandre Bayneham, Sir John Rodney, and Sir Edmond Gorge, wherof thei shall have warnyng by my lord chambrelain.

---

[1] Blank in MS.

[2] *Saturday the vjth*] *Friday the xxixth* in the text, corrected as above in a modern hand to agree with contemporary alterations in the dates throughout.

Item, the Tewsday, which shalbe the x$^{th}$.[1] day of Novembre, and it be a fayer day, and elles upon the Friday v$^{th}$.[2] day of the same moneth, the said princesse shall departe fro Croydon towardes London, and ther make her entre, and loge in the Bisshops palois. A.D. 1501. 10 Nov.

Item, it is to be remembred that the lordes and other nobles that shal mete and receyve the said princesse at eny tyme, be alwaies redy with their attendaunce at every disloging, and departe not till she be logied, and in good and honorable maner and ordre, contynuelly kepe her company betwix loging and loging till she come to London. And that no persone commyng with theim in their companyes, except he be a necessary officier, ride befor out of the company of the said princesse, but alwaies in journeyng the gentilmen to ride befor her and the yeomen behynde, for the better ordre and the more honour. And that the said lordes and nobles be advertised hereof by my lord stieward and officers of armes. And the same officiers and som of the servauntes of my lord stieward to be by hym commaunded to see that this ordenaunce be duly kept and observed. And that noon of the said lordes ner noon othre persone attending upon the said princesse, take their loginges at their owne handes, or be their owne herbegers, but alwaies resorte unto the kinges herbegers, to take their loginges by their assignement.

Item, after her departing fro Croydon, she shalbe conveied to my lord of Rochestre is place besides Lambithe, and ther loge that nyght, and hir ladyes; tharchebisshop, the bisshop, therle, and the remenaunt of her compaignye to loge in the towne of Lamhythe. And the Thursday, if it be a fayre daye, or ellys the Fridaye, by x. of the clok byfor none, to be receyved into a[3] richer litter then thoder, and in the same to make her entre into London; and that the same lytter be at the said place of my lord of Rochestre over even, or at good hour in the mornyng.

Item, that iij. henshmen, in side sadeles and hernes alle of oon sute, be arredied by the maister of the quenes horses, to folowe next unto the said princesse lytter, and that thei be at the said place over even, or erly in the mornyng.

Item, that a palfray with a pylion richely arraied, and led in hand, be then at the said place for the said princesse, and doo folowe next unto the said hensmen.

---

[1] The words *Tewsday* and *xth* are a correction from *Thursday* and *iiijth*; but the corrector has forgot to make corresponding alterations.

[2] See preceding note.

[3] *into a*]. After the words "my "lord of Rochestre," this passage is an interlineation in the hand of bishop Fox, in place of two lines scored out.

A.D. 1501. Nov. Item, that xix. palfraies, alle of oon sute, be then in the said place, redy ordeyned for suche ladies as shall folowe next unto the said pylyon.

Item, that v chares diversely apparaled be then redy in the said place, wherof oon of the chief most be richely apparaled and garnysshed for the said princesse, and thoder iiij. to serve suche ladies as shalbe appoynted by the quenes chambrelain. And that the same folowe in suche ordre as the same chambrelain shall appoynte.

Item, that betwix every of the said chares ther be v. or vj. palfraies with suche ladies and gentilwomen as shall come to the fest for attendaunce gyving upon the quenes grace.

Item, the same chambrelain hath also the ordering of the said palfraies, as well as the chares. And if there fortune eny more chares to come then is above assigned, then the same to be ordered by the said chambrelain.

Item, the said princesse shall in saynt George is felde be mette with my lord of York, the kinges second son, attended upon with the lordes folowing, that is to saie, tharchebisshop of York, the bisshop of Winton, therle of Essex, the lord Harrington, the lord Straunge, the lord of Bergevenny, the lord Willoughby, the lord William of Devon, the lord William of Suffolk, thabbotes of Westminster and Saint Albane, Sir Gilbert Talbot, Sir Edward Ponynges, Sir Edward Stanley, Sir John Risley, Sir Nicholas Vaux, Sir Thomas Cheyne, Sir Mathewe Broune, Sir Thomas Grene, Sir William Tyrwit, Sir John Longvile, Sir Marmaduc Connestable, Sir John Sayvile, Sir William Gascoigne, Sir John Huse, Sir Henry Heydon, Sir William Bolloigne, Sir Robert Broughton, Sir William Scot. Sir Hugh Conwey, Sir John Raynesford, Sir Henry Merney, Sir Richard Lewes, Sir Thomas Tyrell, Sir John Pastone, Sir Philip Calthorp, Sir Robert Brandon, Sir Thomas Wortley, Sir George Maners, Sir George Veere, Sir Robert Tyrell, Sir Rogier Wentworth, Sir John Ferrys, Sir Thomas Rotheram, Sir John Audeley of Suffolk, Sir Edward Raughlegh, Sir John Verney, Sir John Digby, Sir Robert Clere, Sir Henry Willoughby, Sir Edward Stanhop, Sir John Wynfeld, and Sir Robert Peyton. And to calle alle thies to guyders, and to gief theim warnyng herof, the Bisshop of Winton, and Sir John Risley, have the charge.

Item,[1] itt is appoynted thatt att entring into the citie the archebischoppe of Yorke shall kepe cumpenie with the archebischoppe of Spayne,[2] and the duke of Bukkyngham with the erle of Cabra,

[1] The whole of this paragraph is inserted in the margin in Ruthal's handwriting.

[2] Alonso de Fonseca, Archbishop of Sant Jago.

the bischopp of Winchestre with the bischoppe of Mayorke, and with thoder lordes and nobles of Spayne certayn lordes and nobles to be appoyntid after the discresions of the lord tresourer, and the said bischoppe of Winchestre. A.D. 1501. Oct.

Item, that the maire, citesens, and craftes of London attende upon the said princesse, at the crosse in the Chepe, ayenst her commyng to the citie, in suche maner and such solempnitie, and with suche pagentes and cerymonye as thei have devised for thonor of the citie, and of the fest, wherof they shalbe advertised by the lord Bergevenny.

Item, that the said princesse be conveied thorough Southwerk, streight ove[r] London Bruge, and soo thorough the Bruge strete to Greschurch strete, streight to Leden Halle corner, and then into Cornell, and fromthens through Chepe, and then entre into Paules Churche yerd by the gate that is against Saint Michell Churche, and then out at thoder gate, streight south against that gate, and soo into the brode strete to the west dore of the churche, where she shalbe receyved with procession by tharchebisshop of Canterbury *in pontificalibus*, accompanyed with suche bisshops and abbotes as be commaunded to come to the feste and not appoynted to be at eny of the said metinges, and suche other wherof the names folowe; that is to saie, the bisshops of Ely, Lincoln, Rouchestre, Landaff, and Bangore; thabottes of Stratford, Barmondesey, and Towre Hill, all and every of theim being *in pontificalibus*, and fro the said churche dore with the quere of the churche processionally, to bring her to the high aultier, and there to do suche cerymonyes as in suche case is accustumed. And after her offring to be conveied to the litell dore ayenst the consistory that ledeth into the palas, and soo forth brought to her chambre within the said palois; and for her long travaill and labour it is thought that she shall tary within the said palois oon day at the leest before the day of her mariage, and more as the case shall require, and as it shall please the king, and to lede and convey the said company thorough the stretes above named to the said west door of Paules, and to see good ordre kept in riding. And that there be nouther to great hast ner tomoche tarying by the way my lord Bergevenny hath the charge, wherof my said lord stieward shall gief to hym advertisement.[1]

[1] Added in Fox's hand, but afterwards scored out :—"and that "tharchiebisshop of York kepe "compaignye, with tharchiebisshop "of Spaigne, my lord of Buk with "therle and therle (*sic*) of Wynchestre with the bisshop; and with "other lords and nobles of Spaigne, "lords and nobles after the discrecion of my lord tresorer and my "lord previscale."

A.D. 1501. Nov.

Item, that tharchebisshop, the bisshop, therle, and the ladies and gentilwomen that come out of Spayne, be logied in the dean and chanons loginges and other honest houses adjoynyng [1]to the said palois by Whiting [and Trefrye][1] gentilmen huissher[s][1] by the oversight and ordering of my lord chambrelain, and that a consideracion be had that thei be logied after their honour and degrees.

Item, it is appoynted that at the after noon of the day next ensuing the day that the said princesse shall come to the palois, the same princesse in her lytter, accompanyed with the duchesse of Norfolk in her litter, and certain ladies, som of the quenes, and some of the said princesse at the quenes nominacion, and suche lordes and nobles as be appoynted for thattendaunce gyving upon the lordes of Spayne, shalbe conveied by Paules Chene, downe Lamberdes Hill to the quene being at Baynardes Castell. And that the quenes chambrelain receyve her at the fote of the greee that goth up to the quenes chambre, and goo before her to the quenes great chambre. And after she hath seen the quene, and made a certain pause, she shall retourne to the palois.

Item, that Lamberdes Hille be sanded by the maire of London by the same tyme; and that the sergeant porter be warned that no maner persone en[tre] the gate but oonly the said princesse, and her lords and ladys, and such as accompaigne them.

Item, as for the day of mariage. It is thought that, for the more solempnitie of the fest, it shuld be upon the Sonday or som holy day, and that the said princesse be going out of her chambre towardes the church, somwhat before ix. of the clok.

Item, it is ordeyned that the bisshops of Excestre, Herford, Bath, Lincoln, Sarum, Chestre, Rouchestre, and Norwich, and thabbotes of Westminster, Bury, Saint Albane, Glastonbury, Abendon, and Reding, alle *in pontificalibus* gief theire attendaunce, the day of the said mariage, upon tharchebisshop Cauntirbery, executor of the said mariage.

And asfor the princes commyng to the citie, it is thought that he shuld be there a day or ij. before the commyng of the said princesse to the palais, and that he shuld loge in the Warderobe,[2] and the day of mariage to make his dutie into the churche somwhat before the princesse commyng thither, which entre is

[1] Crossed out.

[2] *Warderobe.*] This word is interlined by Ruthal in place of "bis-"shop of Sarum place," which originally stood in the text, with these words added: "till the night "next before the day of the ma-"riage, and that night for his more "redynesse for the busynesse of the "next day, to loge in the Warde-"robe."

devised to be at the south doore, next westward to our Lady of A.D. 1501.
Grace in the body of the churche, and the princes houshold ser- Nov.
vauntes to gief their attendaunce, and convey hym to the haulte place to be made before the consistory in the said body of the churche somwhat before her commyng thider.

Item, the said princesse, accompanyed with the grettest estates of the lordes and ladie[s to] goo out of the palois at the great gate and entre by the west dore of said church, and soo to goo to the same mantle place, led by my lord of York.

Item, for the more easy commyng of the said princesse it is devised that barres shalbe made from the said palois gate unto the said great west doore of the church, and soo from thens to the fote of the galory.

And as for the haulte place, it is devised to be set in the navy and body of the churche, even anempst the consistory, to thentent that the king and quene may secretly goo out of the bisshop's palois into the same consistory, and ther to here and see the cerymonyes of the mariage at their pleasure. And for this cause a bak doore most be made in the same consistory, wherof maister comptroller and Sir Charles Somerset have the charge.

Item, the faction of this haulte place is devised to be made like unto the haulte place at the cristernyng of the kinges childern, with brode and large greces and steppes, and with a good large space, alle on high on loft to thentent that executor of thoffice of the mariage, and the ministres of the church necessary for to doo that acte, and the prince and the princesse, may be toguyder, and no moo above in the said space, alle on high then be necessary. And the bisshops, abbotes, and other prelates and other officers may stande lower upon the said steppes and the haulte place, soo as therby growe noon impedyment to the sight of the people. And that fro the said haulte place to the quere dore there be a stage of v. fote high, with a raile upon either side; and Sir Charles Somerset and the comptroller of the kinges house have take upon theim that the said work shalbe made sure and sustanciall.

Item, that the church of Paules be hanged with aras soo high that the lowes[t] parte therof be vij. or viij. fote from the ground, and my lord chambrelain hath taken the charge of this matier upon hym.

Item, that the trompettes stande alofte over the same west door, and blowe contynuelly after the furst commyng out of the said princesse of the great gate of the said palois, till the tyme she be in the churche upon the haulte place; and then furthwith when she shalbe there the trompettes to ceasse, and thordering, and guyding of the said trompettes and ministrelles for the tyme

A.D. 1501. Nov.

of the fest is committed to Thomas Lovell, yeoman huissher of the kinges chambre.

[And when the said prince and princesse shalbe on the said haulte place on loft, and the banes asked, than that Mr. Secretary objecte openly in Laten ayenst the said mariage, allegging that the same mariage cannot be laufull for suche reasons as he shall exhibite there, supposed to be grounded in the lawes of Cristes Churche; whereunto Mr. Doctor Bernes[1] shal replie and declare solemply in like wise in Laten the said mariage to be good and effectuell in the lawe of Cristes Churche by vertu of a dispensacion which he shall have there redy openly to be redde, and therupon furthwith to delyver to thexecutor officii, and the same executor to commaunde his chauncellor to rede it, the same objections made or eny other to be made ayenst the same notwithstanding.][2]

And when the said princesse schalbe on the sayd haulte place on lofte, than schall the kynges secretarie purpose the proposition for the lawde and prayse of the matrimonie, whiche he hath for that intent devised; whiche thinge doone the banys shalbe solempnelie askyd, and thexecutor oficii schall farther procede to the solempnizing of the same matrimonie.

Item,[3] itt is requisite that the count, according to the custume and maner of Ingland, geve and deliver the said princesse to the executour of the office.

Item, when alle shalbe fynysshed that is to be doon, the said haulte place for the matrymony, then shall the prince and princesse goo toguyder upon the said levye hand in hand all along the body of the said churche, streight aforehed up to the quere, and thorough the quere towardes the high aultier, to theire places appoynted there.

Item, assone as the prince and princesse shall begynne to departe from the said haulte place, then shall alle the ministrelles, every man after his facultie, oon after another, being alle on high in the vawtes of the churche, doo theire partes in musik contynuelly, as shall come to their course, till the prince and princesse shalbe before the high aulter, and then alle the ministrelles to ceasse.

And to thentent that the prince and princesse may have som place secretly to resorte unto for suche casualties as may falle

[1] William Barons, afterwards master of the rolls and bishop of London.

[2] This paragraph is cancelled and that which follows substituted for it in the margin in Ruthal's hand.

[3] This paragraph is interlined by Ruthal in place of one struck out.

during the high masse. It is to be forseen that the prince shall have a traverse seled, made, and sette on the north side the quere nere the high aultier, in place convenient, with a rennyng curteyn to serve, when nede shalbe, soo as the ministres about the high aultier ner those in the vawtes shall not mowe see what shalbe doon in the said traverse. And semblably an other traverse to be made in likewise, and to be set on the south side of the quere, also in place convenient for the said princesse to resorte unto, if eny occasion soo demaunde; and my lord chambrelain hath take upon hym the provision and making of thies traverses. A.D. 1501. Nov.

Item, asfor the careclothes, it shalbe of white bawdekyn, and provided by my lord chambrelain, and by hym delyvered to the princes chambrelain, and the spices and wynes to be provided by my lord stieward, and delyvered to the princes chambrelain and his officers, thei to have the ordering of the same; and that and that the carecloth be holden by two barons, to be assigned by my lord chambrelain.

Item, after this solempnitie of matrymony shalbe fully doon the prince shall furst, and before the princesse, departe with his company down alle along the hawt place, and goo thorowt the consistorie in to his chambre, to thentent he may be redie in the same palois to receyve the said princesse at her chambre dore at her cummyng.

Item, the said princesse, soone after the departing of the said prince, ledde by my lord of York, shall retourne the same way she went; that is to saie, thorough the qwere down upon the said levye alle along the body of the church, out at the great west doore of the same, and in at the great gate of the bisshops palois; and soo to her great chambre, where at the dore therof, the prince shall receyve her as the custume of England is.

Item, that furst the ministrelles, and after the trompettes, every man after his course and facultie, dou their partes when the princesse shall retourne towardes the palois of the bisshop, as thei did at her commyng from the same.

Item, it is thought good that somwhat besides the great west dore of the churche, on the south side therof, there shalbe a solempne conduyte vele and pompousely divised for to renne diverse sortes of good wynes, and the said conduyte to begynne to renne assone as the princesse shall be entred into the said palois, and soo contynuelly to renne alle that day, and parte to renne alle that night folowing.

Item, it is thought convenient that suche hede officers as shal have charge of the fest day of the said mariage, doo provide among other thinges, that the halle of the bisshop of London palois, aswele in enhawnsing of the boordes, tables, and fourmes

A.D. 1501. Oct. therof, and in hanginges of the house, as in making of cupbordes, as wele in the chambre where the said princesse shall dyne as also in the halle, and otherwise thought necessary, but weale and honorably garnysshed and dressed, soo as it shalbe best divised for thonour of the said fest. The charge of the hanging of the said paloys is committed to my lord chambreleign.

Item, asto the fest, that matier is remytted unto the stieward, comptroller, and hede officers of the kinges most honorable houshold.

Item, that the iij$^{de}$ day next after the day of the mariage the said prince and princesse shall departe fro the said palois towardes Baynardes castell to goo to Westminster with the kinges grace, and that the said princesse soo departing shall ride in her lytter, or upon her spare horse, with the pylion behynde, a lord to be named by the king, and xj. ladies upon palfraies after her. And that a certain convenient nombre of the said lordes and nobles be named, and warned by my lord chambrelain, then also awaite upon her on horsbak, with the same nombre of their servauntes with theim upon fote, that thei had betwix the Towre and the church of Paules, keping company with the lordes of Spayne, as thei did before, taccompany the said princesse to Baynardes castell, where the king and the quene shalbe, and soo forth to goo to Westminster with the king by watier. And for this to be weale doon, two thinges be behovefull. Thoon is that the stretes from Paules chene, down Lamberdes Hille, betwene therle of Derbys Place on thonside and the undertreasoures loging, to the said Baynardes castell be weale gravaled and substancially cast with sand, by the maire of London, for the horses, more surely to kepe theim silf uprigh in the great discent of the hille forsaid. Thoder is that the said princesse disloge the said iij$^{de}$ day from the said bisshops palois, at suche good houre as she may come to the king and quene to departe, if the king soo be pleased, the same day at tyme convenient from the said Baynardes castell to the kinges palois of Westminster.

If that the great bruge at Westminster be amended by the tresourer of England, and the kinges beestes and armes be renued and newe peynted.

Item, that the florth of Westminster Halle be new dressed, and the wyndowes of the same glased, whereof Mr. comptroller, and Worley have taken charge.

Item, that the Wollebruge at the said Westminster be also new repaired at the king[es] cost.

And for the more roialtie of the going of the king and the quene, of the prince and of the princesse, unto Westminster by water, it is according that the king and quene, and the prince have their barges apart, weale and pompously rigged and addressed. A.D. 1501. Oct.

Item, that in likewise alle the lordes spirituall and temporall, that have yeven their attendaunce at this fest, accompany the king in theire [1] * * *

Item, that the barges of tharchebisshoppe of Cauntirbery, and thabat of Westmynstyr be appoyntyd, prepaired, and arredied for the ambassatoures of Spayne and Scotland.

---

## VIII.—Norroy's Instructions. See page 222.

[From a modern copy in Anstis' MS. Collections relating to the Officers of Arms, Heralds' College.]

A Remembrance given by the King's highness unto Norroy King at Arms, shewing how he shall order himself with the King of Romans in such matters as be committed unto him by the King's said highness. A.D. 1503.

First, he shall address himself to the Cambremaister of the said king of Romans, and follow his advice, direction and counsel, as well in the time and manner of presentation of the king's letters, the delivery of the George, mantle, collar, garter, and other things concerning the Order of the Garter to be by him presented and delivered unto the said king, as also in soliciting for the proclamations and banishments to be made by the commandment of the said king of Romans in those parts after the form hereafter ensuing. To communicate with Maximilian's chamberlain as to the time and manner of delivering the Garter.

Also the said Norroy, at such convenient time as shall be limited and assigned unto him by the said Cambremaister, shall resort unto the presence of the said king of Romans, to whom he shall on the king's behalf make due recommendations and reverently deliver his letters as it appertaineth, desiring at his good pleasure and leisure to have answer upon the same.

And at a convenient time after the presentation of the king's said letters, when the said Norroy shall have perfect knowledge by the said Cambremaister or otherwise, that the king of Romans woll be contented and agreeable to accept and receive the ornaments of the foresaid Order of the Garter, then he, using the advice of the said Cambremaister, shall, in good, discreet and honest manner deliver the same ornaments to the said king, using such kind, loving, and substantial words at the deliverance of the same as the said king thereby may well perceive the

---

[1] Here the original text of the fragment ends, the item below being one of Ruthal's insertions at the bottom of the page.

A.D. 1508. inward love, zeal, and affection that the king's highness perseverantly beareth unto him. And the said Norroy shall well note the manner and words that the said king shall use and speak at the acceptation thereof, with every circumstance of the same, as near as he shall mowe, and advertise the king's highness thereof at length by his writings.

To note well the manner in which it is received,

Item, the said Norroy shall, during his abode in the said king's court, daily note and well regard, whether the king of Romans at any time wear and use the said ornaments of the Garter, or any of them, and how often, and advertise the king's highness in the specialty thereof by his writing.

and whether Maximilian wears it.

Item, at time convenient by the advice and counsel of the said Cambremaister, he shall shew that the king's highness hath sent him thither to be present with some other officer at arms, to be deputed and assigned by the said king of Romans in such cities and places where the proclamations of the peace and amity, the proscriptions and banishments of the king's rebels, shall be made, desiring the said king to cause his said writings and mandements to be made in due and effectual form for the same proclamations and banishments, in such form and manner, and within the cities and towns specified in the copies of the said proclamations delivered unto the said Norroy, which forms have been devised and communed betwixt the king's highness and the ambassadors of the said king of Romans, as it appeareth by the letters of recesse resting in the hands of the said ambassadors.

To be present along with an officer of Maximilian at the proclamation of the peace and banishment of the rebels.

And for the obtaining of the said proclamations to be made in the best and most effectual form and manner as they be now devised, the said Norroy shall, by the advice of the said Cambremaister, insist and endeavour himself in his best manner.

And if any difficulty be made therein because of the additions now made and set to the said proclamations, he shall in cold and sober manner, shew that forasmuch as the other form of proclamation was in so general manner devised and made that by the same no specialty was expressed whereby the said king's subjects mought have notice or knowledge of the conclusions or articles contained in the said peace and amity, by reason whereof they might pretend ignorance therein, and so not observe the same; to the intent therefore that some particular knowledge and specialty of the said treaty might be declared and shewed unto the said king's subjects, it was thought right, convenable, and expedient that those small additions, which in substance compriseth no more but the effect of one article of the said peace and amity, should of congruence be put thereunto. And inasmuch as the king's highness hath caused the said peace and amity and every article of the same, wholly, entirely, and

How he shall answer, if the additions made to the proclamations be objected to.

particularly to be proclaimed and published in the principal cities and towns of his realm, it is thought to his grace and his council that no difficulty should be made in this form of proclamation with the small additions, which neither containeth the tenor of all the articles, nor yet wholly the effect of one of the same, but shortly and summarily toucheth part thereof. A.D. 1506.

And in case the said Norroy may perceive that the said king and his council will in nowise be agreeable to have the proclamations made in any other form than in the general manner by them first devised, the copy whereof the said Norroy hath also now with him, then he shall, without further difficulty making therein, be agreeable thereunto, and desire the king's writings, mandements and his officer at arms, for the same to be made as well within the town of Achon, as in all the other cities mentioned in the form of the said proclamation, and with the same officer personally to be present and see the said proclamations effectually to be done in all the places therefor appointed and assigned, as solemnly as he may obtain it to be done, and to endeavour himself to cause the officers of all the cities and towns, when the said proclamations shall be made, to be present at the making of the same. If insisted on, these additions shall be abandoned.

Item, the said Norroy shall take with him the king's poursuivant Rougedragon, to the intent that he may not only convey unto the king's grace such writings as the said Norroy shall send unto his highness concerning his expedition in all the premises, but also advertise the Cambremaister thereof to the intent that if the said king of Romans or the Cambremaister woll write any thing unto his said grace, the said Rougedragon shall be redy to bring the same with all speedy diligence.

H. R.

---

## IX.—Letter to Killingworth.

[From a copy in Killingworth's hand, in the Record Office.]

Maister Steward, to write our povertie hyt nedeth not, for alle the worlde knoweth hyt wel ynough. But where hit is soo that ye desire to knowe my mynd, hit is soo that I spake not with my lord our maister sythen the xvij. day of October, and al by the meanes of that false errant traytor, the mynyster of Hownsloo, that utterly hath conspired the destruction of my lord oure maister and me. Yet neverthalas, I shall doo to you as a true man aughte to doo with A.D. 1505. Jan.

A.D. 1505. Jan. his maister, and with suche as have been to hym as ye have been. This it is. The man that ye knowe of, spake with our maister on Sonday last past, at xj$^{th}$ of the clok in the nighte, and was with him iij. howres and more; and I truste of suretie, and also I perceive by certain signes bytwix our maister and me, that good direction is taken bytwixt theym for his synglier welthe and owres, and shortely I truste it shal comme to passe of this secret practise; alle the world knoweth it not but they ij. and oon more whiche under *jugo confessionis* hath shewed it to me. This kepe to your sylf as your lyf, and utter hit not to noo creature as ye love your maister. *Pauca sapienti*. Provyd for your silf a litle while, and lette me knowe where ye bee, and as I am true servant to God and to our maister, as the matier werketh soo shal ye knowe hyt, in that I can or maye. I hope to God he shalbe shortely hable to have you with hym and al his true servantes, and I doubte not the matier is concluded. Nowe, maister stewerd, I committe this secretnesse to your wisdam; and concernyng the cause, write not nor do no maner thing that shal discontent the parties; and advise other men to suffre, and to bee ware of great wordes, for a lytle thing maye hurte where muche cannot helpe. Geve your good counsaill to theym soo to doo, and bee wel ware of any comfort that ye have. Hyde this in your hert and brenne this letter. There is noo man lyving knoweth this. Departe secretly and sende me worde by this bringer where I shal fynde yowe, and noo more a doo. Within xiiij. daies I truste ye shal here other thinges.

[1] Recepi hanc literam v$^{ta}$ die Januarii, die Dominica, vigilia Epiphaniæ. In claustro prope Zwolle appunctuavi obviam cum Thoma.[2]

[1] Added by Killingworth.

[2] *Tho'*., MS.

## APPENDIX B.—MUTILATED PAPERS AND ABSTRACTS.

---

### I.

### ORATION TO THE POPE AFTER HENRY VII.'S MARRIAGE.

IN the Cottonian MS., Cleopatra E. III. f. 123, is the rough draft of an oration intended to be delivered to the Pope and Cardinals by an ambassador of Henry VII., shortly after his marriage with Elizabeth of York. This speech is alluded to in Bacon's History of Henry VII. It is quite an unfinished composition. The substance is as follows:—

At the commencement the pope is complimented as one who had led a celestial life from his earliest years on earth, who had endured great labours in the cause of religion, in many journeys through many countries, and whose breast might be called the home of all liberal arts and sciences. The king of England, who had been tossed on the waves and exposed to innumerable dangers, like another Æneas, having been nearly fifteen years an exile, acknowledged that it was by divine aid and beyond all human expectation that he had recovered in so brief a space the throne of his ancestors. To put an end to civil war, he had, at the request of all the lords of the kingdom, consented to marry Elizabeth, daughter of Edward IV., though he was free to have made a profitable foreign alliance. Of her it is said, "Hujus plane forma pudicitiaque tanta est, "ut neque Lucretia neque Diana ipsa vel speciosior vel casta "magis fuerat unquam. Tanta deinde est ei virtus ac morum "elegantia, ut certe nutu quodam divino ab ipsa sua nativi-"tate ad hæc usque tempora sibi consors et regina reservata "esse videatur."

The pope, it is added, had opportunely sent a legate to celebrate the nuptials, at a time when the kingdom again appeared to be in the greatest danger from the fraudulent machinations of certain persons. Following the example of Theodosius and Constantine, Henry desired to acknowledge his subjection to the Church, &c.

## II.

### BLYTH'S ORATION AT CAMBRIDGE.

IN the Bodleian Library, MS. 13, formerly 2,357, is an elegantly written copy of an oration delivered in the presence of Henry VII., his mother the Countess of Richmond, and Prince Arthur, at Cambridge. It bears internal evidence of having been composed by John Blyth, bishop of Salisbury, who was chancellor of the University between the years 1493 and 1495. The following is a brief outline of its substance, which is in many respects remarkable :—

After comparing the king to Moses, on account of the dangers escaped in infancy from the hands of his persecutors.—" Sed
" quorsum ista? Nimirum, ut intelligamus quanta sit mag-
" nitudo tua, rex illustrissime, qui tam mirabiliter natus es,
" atque in lucem editus a nobilissima principe genitrice tua
" nunc præsenti, quæ tum annum non implevit quartum-
" decimum, rarus profecto partus et insolitus, ipsaque (ut
" cernimus) non magnæ staturæ fœmina est; et multo tunc
" (ut asseritur) minoris fuit, adeo ut miraculum cunctis vide-
" batur in illis annis, et in illa corporis parvitate gnatum
" aliquem, maxime tam procerum, tam elegantem edidisse.
" . . . . . . . . . Nam et dum in utero por-
" taret te mater, vix discrimen pestis evasisti quæ teneriores
" fœtus facile consuevit interimere, de qua et pater tuus
" princeps illustris interiit. Mater deinde viro orbata te
" peperit orphanum,[1] a cujus uberibus mox abstrac tus,
" illorum custodiæ traditus fueras qui bellis assiduis im-
" plicabantur. Castellum in quo tenebaris obsessum in manus
" inimicorum tuorum venit; qui tamen, Deo ita providente,
" te (ut præclarum sanguine deceret) educaverunt egregie.
" Inde quæsitus ad necem, patriam deserens, ubi ad cognatum
" tuum regem Francorum ire destinaveras, in Minoris Britan-
" niæ ducem utilius incidisti, quamquam ab eo rursum tan-
" quam captivus detinebare. Sed, pace cum eo facta, quum in

[1] When the editor called attention to this fact in *Memorials of Henry VII.* (see note at page xxiv of the Preface), he was not aware that there was any other evidence of it than the Inquisitions *post mortem*.

"patriam redire statuisti, tanto ventorum impetu classis tua jac-"tabatur ut vi compulsus retro retulisti pedem. Deo rem ita dis-"ponente, ne forte in manus inimicorum tuorum venisses qui "tunc insidias pararant tibi. Post hæc Britanni te venalem "offerebant capitalibus inimicis tuis, nihil majus quam tuum "sanguinem sitientibus. Quid multis? Convenit inter eos de "pecunia; sed tu interea, Deo mirabiliter subveniente, cum "tuis omnibus effugisti salvus in Galliam. Unde quum "denuo temptares venire in patriam, dirigente tunc tuum iter "et prosperante Deo, parva manu ingressus hoc tuum regnum, "regem qui tunc fuit cum universo ipsius exercitu fudisti "quamprimum. In solio demum confirmatus (me Jesu) quot "adversæ fortunæ machinatas insidias? quot proditiones clan-"culum excogitatas? quot murmura et rebelliones nefariorum? "quot formidanda ob eventum maxime ancipitem prœlia (quæ "nos omnes recenti adhuc memoria tenemus) tu ad tuam in-"gentem gloriam, non nisi divinitus, superasti semper." The orator went on to say, that he need not recount Henry's descent from so many most holy ("sanctissimis") kings, nor his many personal and mental qualities (which, however, are fully enumerated). He begged him to take compassion on that ancient university, which had been in existence *certainly* long before Honorius I., who was 160 years before Charlemagne, the founder of the university of Paris. Doubtless the latter university took its origin from theirs, viz., from Alcuin, Joannes and Rabanus, whom even Gaguin admitted to have been alumni of Cambridge.

They had been endowed by various kings.—"Henricus tertius "has ipsas ædes in quibus nunc sumus a fundamentis "erexit." Henry VII had already shown a disposition to encourage learning, as no one could better witness than the orator: "Me ipsum (inquam) quem incredibile cunctis fuit ad "episcopatum tam repente promoveri; quippe qui paucos "annos habuerim. qui nunquam in curia obsequium præstiterim, qui nullis ante dotatus beneficiis. Et quamobrem ego "ad episcopatum assumerer? Quid tuam ad hoc admirabilem "sapientiam movebat? Nihil profecto aliud nisi ut studiosis "omnibus liquido constaret illorum causa id factum esse." The king had done it quite unsolicited by man or woman, to encourage virtue and learning. To show his regard for scholars—"Anno superiori cum ad nos venisti, dignatus es disceptationi-"bus interesse, atque id per omnium Facultatum scholas. . . "Postridie cum hæc audieris ingentem auri summam cum "magno ferarum numero in publicam compotationem uni-"versis scholasticis maxima tua liberalitate contulisti," &c.

## III.

### NORROY'S MISSION TO JAMES IV.

ABOUT the beginning of the year 1498, Norroy King of Arms was sent by Henry VII. to James IV. His instructions signed by the king are contained in MS. Cott., Vespasian, C. xvi. f. 115, and are to the following effect:—

1. To thank James for his kind and loving letters sent by Lyon King at Arms, expressing his desire to observe the amity. The king had received the letters patent confirming the treaty made by the English and Scotch commissioners. (See Rymer xii. 673.) The declaration made by James in the 4th article appeared unsatisfactory, as it only ratified by an *inspeximus in hæc verba* the conventions made by the commissioners of both princes.

2. To explain that the words *ad nocendum alteri* are omitted in the new letters patent sent by Henry to "his said cousin," because each prince was bound to refuse aid or succour to the rebels of the other, and these words might afford a pretext for evasion. Either prince might refuse to give up rebels, saying he would keep them so strictly that they should have no power *ad nocendum alteri.*

3. That the words *salvis conductibus, etc.* are also omitted, because James's chief reason for inserting them was the safe conduct he had given to Perkin, who was now in the king's keeping, and would never again be in a position to benefit thereby.

4. The king thinks that James, out of his desire for the due punishment of murders and robberies, will be satisfied with these alterations and deliver letters patent of like effect.

5. But if he cannot be induced to consent, Norroy is to deliver Henry's ratification under the Great Seal, of the same tenor as that of James.

## IV.

### Commerce with the Low Countries.

Some very mutilated dispatches of the bishop of Rochester (Fitzjames), Warham and Sir Richard Hatton, written from Calais in March 1499, exist in the Cottonian MS., Galba B. II. 46. They relate to the negociations with the commissioners of the archduke Philip, for a commercial treaty having special relation to the export of wool. A letter sent to them by the king in answer dated Greenwich, the . . . April, follows at f. 49 b. The contents of the papers are of no great value.

## V.

### Instructions to Richmond, King of Arms.

In the same very mutilated volume, Galba B. II., ff. 108, 109, is contained a copy of instructions to [Richmond, king of] arms, of Clarencieux, [sent to the king of the Romans and his] son the archduke of Austria. They commence on the reverse of f. 109, and appear to have reference to the proposed marriage of Henry duke of York with Philip's daughter, referred to at p. 167, *ante*.

## VI.

### Wolsey's Negociations in Flanders.

These interesting papers relating to the services in which Wolsey was engaged in the year 1508, with reference to the two projected marriages; first, between Henry VII. and Margaret of Savoy; and, second, between Charles prince of Castile and the princess Mary, have unfortunately suffered most severely in the Cottonian fire. Those which are in Wolsey's own handwriting, being rough drafts very much corrected, are from this cause peculiarly difficult to decipher.

### I.—The King's Instructions to Wolsey.

[MS. Cott. Galba B. II., f. 184.]

H, R. [Instructiones da]tæ p[er re]giam maje[statem] fideli [et dilecto] capellano suo domino Thomæ Wolseye, &c.

Inprimis, post commendationes regias idem capellanus dicet quod post reditum suum in Angliam, cum sacræ regiæ majestati ea omnia p[er] ordinem retulisset quæ A. sibi declaravit regiæ majestati aperienda, admodum grata atque accepta suæ celsitudini singula fuerunt. Ex his denique sua celsitudo plane intellexit, quod sibi semper antea persuasum habebat, illum, scilicet, intimum amorem, sinceram mentem, et cordialem affectionem, quæ idem A. erga eum hacten[us] gessit et indies magis ac magis gerit atque ostendit.

Et quamvis celsitudo sua hæc omnia antehac evidentissimis atque apert[issimis] argumentis, demonstrationibus et experimentis penes se te . . . . . atque ob id singularem et præcipuam suam confidenciam in eode[m posuerit] et locaverit, sicuti tam ex literis suis antehac eidem sæpius [ostensis] quam etiam ex his quæ sibi referenda domino Edwardo Wy[ngfeld] oratori suo istic commisit, intelligere potuit, tamen . . . . quæ inter dictum A., et eundem capellanum communi[cata fuerunt], et quæ serenitati suæ per ordinem fideliter accurate at[que] . . . . recitavit, oculata quodammodo fide et luce clariu[s innotescere] re ipsa comprobavit dictum A. eum virum esse qui , . . . . exaltationem suæ majestatis felices atque prosperos success[us omnium] negotiorum suorum summopere cupit atque exoptat; quibus [ . . . . . . . . s]ua serenitas jam vehementius accenditur atque excitatur [ . . . . . i]mpellitur ut non modo eundem A. amore ma[ . . . . . . . sed] etiam ut de eodem A. tanquam de præcipuo suo [apud Cæsaream] majestatem amico confidat et tanquam de sua majestate op . . . . . . . . . erbis se memorem reddat.

The king desires the continuance of A.'s. good offices,

[A] git igitur imprimis sua sacra majestas eidem A. . . . . [gratias] illas quas potest maximas pro hac sua præcipua erga e[um] dilectione, gratitudine et observantia, proque maximis labori[bus] curis et solicitudinibus circa causarum et negotiorum suorum felicem expeditionem habitis et impensis; rogatque et ex corde prec[atur] ut quemadmodum idem A. hactenus humanissime cœpit, ita posthac velit pergere et perseverare, sibique persuadeat celsitudinem regiam se tam gratum tamque munificum principem erga eundem exhibiturum, officiorumque et meritorum suorum e[am] condignam rationem habiturum ut in gratum atque munificen[tem] principem obsequium collatum sentiet et experietur, et ita tractabit eundem A. quod liquido constabit Cæsari, dominæ ducissæ ac omnibus aliis, eum esse in præcipua gratia et auctori[tate] ac multum valere apud majestatem suam.

Et, ut reipsa potius quam verbis id comprobetur, id[em] capellanus dicet, quod sacra regia majestas sibi injun[xerit. quod] eundem A. certiorem reddat, quod pro memoriale[1] . . . . suorum meritorum in suam majestatem aliquale (licet non co[gatur pro] retributione et pro futura sua in causis et negoti[is agendis] fide, solicitudine, observantia, gratitudine atque di[ligentia], et ut majestas sua plene de eo tanquam de præcipuo [et] fidissimo suo amico confidere, et suis operibus sicut . . . . consiliarii sui uti poterit, si mediis, prudentia . . . . dexteritate sua hæ affinitates inter Cæsarea[m majestatem e]t celsitudinem regiam tractatæ et inceptæ . . . . . . . . s duobus contractubus matrimonialibus inter [ regem et] ducissam Sabaudiæ, principem Castellæ [et] clarissimam filiam suam dominam Mariam, [cum omnibus et] singulis conditionibus et dependentiis super eisdem, ad honorem, contentationem et complacentiam suæ celsitudinis perficiantur et ad optatum finem deducantur; ac quod in hac conventione sive dieta inter ducissam Sabaudiæ et legatum Franciæ in tractatu pac[is] inter Cæsaream majestatem et regem Lodwicum Franciæ habenda et fienda, nihil fiat aut concludatur quod in dispendium regii honor[is] aut in damnum sive præjudicium dictarum duarum affinitatum quovismod[o] cedere possit, sua serenitas providebit eidem A. infra regnum suum in spiritualibus promotionibus ad bonum valorem.

and hopes by his means the two marriages may take effect, viz., 1, between Henry VII. and Margaret of Savoy, and, 2, between Charles of Castile and the princess Mary.

Et quamvis majestas regia speret et firmiter confidat quod infr[a breve] tempus eidem A. providebitur in hujusmodi promotionibus . . . . interim, et quoadusque idem A. per suam majestatem si[c . . . ] promotus fuerit, celsitudo sua singulis annis eidem A. . . . . . . solvet mille nobilia Anglicana, *angelettes* vulga[riter dicta], præter et ultra exitus, redditus et proventus beneficiorum [quæ] jam habet in regno Angliæ, ad duos anni terminos, [quorum primus] terminus incipiet in festo Paschæ proximo futuro et se[cundus in festo Sancti] Michaelis Archangeli tunc proximo et immediate sequente, et sic [de anno in] annum quousque de dictis promotionibus ecclesiasticis per r[egiam majestatem] sibi provideatur, dummodo præmissa per eundem A. con[ficiendatur e]t ad optatum finem deducantur, de quibus sua majestas . . . . . . partes suas effectualiter interponere voluerit.

The king will give him a pension and new benefices in England,

[1] Sic.

and if the marriage take effect, will give him the chief rule in the Low Countries.

[E]t præter ac ultra præmissa, si, matrimonio inter s[uam majestatem re]giam et ducissam Sabaudiæ contracto, aliqua [ . . . au]ctoritas in regimine sive administratione ipsarum [patriarum] suæ majestati et prædictæ ducissæ committatur, regia majestas ob illum præcipuum amorem et singularem fiduciam quam erga prædictum A. habet, non modo procurabit et faciet regi[men] ipsarum patriarum eidem A. sub se committi, postpositis aliis omnibus et penitus semotis, sed etiam, si promotio aliqua honorifica in partibus illis pro tempore quo auctoritas prædicta erit penes suam majestatem et dictam ducissam vacare contigerit, illam pro viribus suis sibi concedi curabit, et [pro] posse suo eundem A., auctoritatemque et potestatem sibi in ea parte concedendam manutenebit et plenam fide[m] et confidenciam in eo tanquam in amico suo præcipuo et carissimo locabit.

Quæ omnia et singula regia majestas cum effectu fa[ciet] si præmissa per eundem A. debite impleantur, prout s[ua] majestas non diffidit quin perficientur si partes suas . . efficaciter interponere voluerit.

Præterea significavit idem capellanus regiæ m[ajestati quod] prædictus A. retulit sibi de domino Bergensi v . . . . . . in omni tractatu et communicatione quos m[utuo sunt] habituri de matrimonio suo cum domino Bergensi f . . . . . . regia ad contentationem dicti Bergensis.

Et quoniam hæc verba adeo generalia atque . . . . . ut regia majestas aperte nequit perpe . . . . . . . super his eidem domino Bergensi ad animi s . . . . . respondere possit; idcirco sua celsitudo eundem A. rogatum habet ut clare et specifice velit eidem capellano suo declarare mentem et intentionem suam in ea re, et consilium suum super eadem significare.

The king desires to know from him wherein the Emperor's difficulties consist.

Et quia non dubitat regia majestas quin omnes difficultates tractatus matrimonialis inter suam majestatem et ducissam Sabaudiæ (si quæ fuerint) eidem A. bene cognitas esse; idcirco precatur regia majestas ut d[e his] et aliis in quibus Cæsarea majestas judicat regiam majestatem t[am] duriter et modo mercatorio potius quam regio incede[re], necnon quo tendant illa verba, "Venient oratores [Cæsaris] principaliter ad exsequendum "ea quæ erant conclus[a, etc.] cum moderamine domini Andreæ "de Burgo," idem A. [regiam] celsitudinem per capellanum suum prædictum certio[rem faciat].

Cumque idem A. dixerit unam difficultatem esse . . . . . tractatu matrimoniali eo quod domina non revertetur [ad partes] illas, dignetur etiam idem significare utrum men[s et intentio] Cæsaris et dominæ sit quod expresse per articulum in tra[ctatu] matrimoniali caveatur ut domina ducissa Sabaudiæ [post] matrimonium solemnisatum vivente rege poss[it ad] votum suum, quandocumque ei libuerit et placuerit, revert[i ad partes i]llas; quæ res si ita procederet, tenderet in [dispendium re]gii honoris et maxime dictæ dominæ ducissæ et no[n decet] quod illud petant aut petere velint; idcirco arbitratur regia majestas quod dictus capellanus eundem A. in ea re clare non intellexerit.

His difficultatibus intellectis, et consilio dicti A. super eisdem cognitis, majestas sua eidem domino Burgensi respons[a] congrua aptare poterit, et certe persuadeat sibi dictum A. regiam majestatem ob illas præclaras et egregias virtutes qu[ibus] ipsam dominam ducissam Sabaudiæ abunde refertam [esse] audivit, obque illas maximas gratitudines signaque et . . . . amoris suæ majestati ampliter et continue ostensa ita affi[ci] eidem dominæ ut ad contrahendum cum ea matrimonium [præ] cæteris aliis principibus optime disponatur, adeo ut [melius] disponi non possit; omniaque majestas regia pro part[e sua] faciet quæ honorifica et rationabilia videbuntur, [et quæ] commode fieri poterint, nec per eum stabit quomi[nus illud] matrimonium debitum sortietur effectum; quæ o[mnia] bona opportunitate regia majestas cupit ut id[em A.] significet eidem dominæ ducissæ

Præterea, cum idem A. promiserit dicto capella[no se] missurum exemplar instructionum oratorum Cæ[saris a]d celsitudinem regiam, dignabitur igitur e[asdem i]nstructiones jam mittere, et, si commode fieri [poterit, co]pias etiam instructionum quas domina ducis[sa se]cum habebit in hac conventione cum legat[o Franciæ]; in quo rem supra quam dici potest gratam suæ majestati faciet.

Cupit præterea atque exoptat majestas regia de his omnibus quæ, vel in hac conventione inter dominam ducissam Sabaudiæ et legatum Franciæ vel alibi, suam celsitudinem aut honore[m] suum quomodolibet tangentibus, tractabuntur, per prædictum A. certio[rem] fieri nunc et posthac de tempore in tempus, per se vel alium, sicuti dicto capellano promisit; et propterea majestas regia [eundem] A. rogatum habet ut non modo super præmissis omnibus et si[ngulis] mentem, consilium, et intentionem suam eidem capella[no] quantocius commode poterit aperiat et declaret, sed etia[m si] aliqua alia nova istic contigerint ex quo dictus C[æsar] hinc discessit, vel si aliquid a domino Andrea de Bu[rgo audierit] ex Hispania, aut quidquam actum vel dictum fuerit ci[rca mutuum] Cæsaris et regis conventum, et utrum aliquid Cæsar[iæ majestatis] oratoribus superinde committetur, dignetur suam [majestatem superinde] per capellanum prædictum certiorem reddere. [Quæ] adeo secrete servabuntur ac si in armariolo pect[oris sui] recondita essent, et non minus honorem suum [majestas r]egia commendatum habebit quam proprium.

[I]nsuper capellanus prædictus significabit eidem A. q[uod rex i]nstruxit et expedivit oratores suos ad Cæsarem et [sunt in itinere ve]rsus Cæsaream majestatem, atque eo citius sua majestas eosdem s[uos oratores] expedivit et destinavit quo istic esse possent cum Cæsare priusquam domina ducissa et dictus A. discedant et proficiscantur versus hanc conven[tionem] sive dietam cum legato Franciæ habendam, nonnulla Cæsariæ [majestati] significaturi quæ sibi grata et accepta erunt et quæ prædictæ con[ventioni] utilia esse possunt.

The rule of Ferdinand in Castile is considered a usurpation.

Significabit præterea dictus capellanus eidem A. quo[modo] res et negotia regni Castellæ consistunt, dicetque quod jamdud[um] recepit regia majestas literas recentissimas in zifris scriptas per q[uendam] servitorem suum[1] istuc moram trahentem, ex quibus plane perpend[it quod] tam dux de Nagera et marchio de Plego quametiam Gundisa[lvus] Fernandus magnus capitaneus, unacum omnibus aliis dom[inis et] nobilibus dicti regni ægre ferunt hanc usurpationem regimin[is regis] Aragonum in dicto regno Castellæ ac pessime contentantur cum [jurisdictione] sua in eodem, quærentes occasionem et modum quomodo ip[sum regem] a regno Castellæ expellere possint, qui plurima enorm[ia et] exorbitantia istic facit in præjudicium juris et tituli pri[ncipis], et pejora timenda sunt si non occurratur hujusmodi c[onvenienti] tempore Quod si prædicti domini haberent aliquam spem sub[sidii et] relevaminis a Cæsare, sive per oratores suos in regnum [Castellæ] mittendos seu aliquo alio modo, non sinerent dictum rege[m Aragonum] diutius regere in ipso regno. Nam ut publice ibidem asseritur, [conatur] exhæreditare principem Castellæ et præficere fratrem . . . . . . . Fernandum in regem, quod dicti domini nullo pacto pati . . . . . . . . quam ob alia exorbitantia et justitiæ atque rationi dissona a[ . . . . . . ] vellent eum expellere a regno si aliquam spem subsidii [haberent. Expedit] ergo ut Cæsarea majestas suos oratores in dictum regnum [mittat ad] confirmandum et animandum eosdem dominos in hoc propo[sito contra] regem Aragonum pro conservatione juris et tituli prædicti princip[is . . . ] timendum est ne deteriora succedant et sequantur. proind[e] . . . . occurrendum et subveniendum est hoc magno malo.

H. [R.][2]

---

[1] Doubtless John Stile.

[2] Only the beginning of the H of the king's signature is visible.

### II.—Articles to be communicated to A. on the part of Henry VII.

[Draft in Wolsey's hand.—MS. Galba B. II. 127.]

Quod mediis et dex[terita]te vestra hæ duæ affinitates inter Cæsaream [majestatem] et celsitudinem regiam cum omnibus et singulis conditionibus et dependentiis [super] eisdem, ad honorem, contentationem et complacentiam suæ celsitudinis p[erficientur], et quod in hac dieta inter ducissam Sabaudiæ et legatum Flandriæ nihil f[iat aut] concludatur quod in dispendium regii honoris aut in damnum sive [præjudicium] dictarum d[uarum] affinitatum quovismodo cedere possit.

Declaret vestra dominatio specifice intentionem et consilium suum quid . . . . . ad domini Bergensis animi satisfactionem regia majestas res[pondeat].

Quo tendant illa verba, "Venient oratores Cæsaris principaliter "ad [exsequendum ea] quæ erant conclusa Calisiis quo ad "solemnitatem matrimonii cum moderamine domini Andreæ "[de Burgo]"?

Quæ sunt illa in tractatu matrimoniali quæ majestas [Cæsarea vult] mitigari, et in quibus judicat regem tam duriter et m[odo mercatorio] potius quam regio incedere?

[Utrum] mens et intentio Cæsaris sit quod expresse per articulum [in tractatu matrimo]niali caveatur ut domina ducissa perfecto matrimonio [possit, vivente rege, ad] votum suum, quandocunque ei libuerit, reverti ad partes [Flandriæ]?

[Quid int]elligat Cæsar per illa verba "non revertetur ad "p[artes illas]?"

[Ro]gat regia majestas quatenus dignemini mittere co[pias instructionum orat]orum Cæsaris et etiam copias instructionum dominæ [ducissæ Sabaudiæ super] hac conventione cum legato Franciæ, etc.

[C]upit rex certior fieri de omnibus quæ tractabuntur, vel in hac [conventione inter dominam et lega]tum Franciæ, vel alibi suam celsitudinem [aut honorem suum tangentibus, nunc et post]hac de tempore in tempus.

*[Utrum a]liq[u]a nova [istic contigerint ex quo Cæsar hinc [*f. 12 discessit], vel si aliquid a domino A[ndrea] de Burgo audierit ex Hispania?

Utrum quicquam actum vel dictum fuerit circa mutuum Cæsaris et Regis conventum?

Utrum aliquid Cæsariæ majestatis oratoribus superinde committetur?

Et majestas regia vestram reverendam dominationem rog[atam] habet ut mentem, consilium et intentionem suam su[per] præmissis omnibus et singulis quantocius commode poterit aperi[et] et declaret; in quo rem supra quam dici potest gratam [suæ] majestati faciet.

*Ea quæ sunt dicenda dominæ ex parte Reg*[*is*].

[De adve]ntu oratorum suorum et quod jam sunt in itinere versus Cæsa[rem, quos eo citius] mittit, quod istic esse possint cum Cæsare priusquam domina d[ucissa et A. discedant versus hanc] conventionem, et quod sint nonnulla Cæsari significat[uri quæ prædictæ conventioni] utilia esse possint.

[In quo s]tatu res et negotia regni Castellæ consistunt, et quod d[omini istius regni ægre ferunt usurpationem] regiminis regis Aragonum in dicto regno, ac p[essime contentantur cum jurisdicti]one sua in dicto regno, quærentes modum quo . . . . . . . . . . . . modo idem rex exhæreditare conatur principem C[astellæ . . . . . . . . . . ]; quæ omnia domini ipsius regni multum ægre fer[unt . . . . . . . . . ] et rationi et justitiæ dissona vellent . . . . . . . . . . . subsidii haberent. Expedit ergo ut [Cæsarea majestas mittat] suos oratores in dictum regnum ad animandum [eosdem dominos in] hoc proposito contra prædictum regem ne deter[iora succedant].

[*f. 128. *Et quod dominatio [vestra] . . . . tate dicat do[minæ ducissæ] quod sua majestas ob præclaras et egregias virtutes quibus ipsam dominam a[bunde] refertam audivit, obque illas maximas gratitudines, si[gnaque] et officia amoris suæ majestati ampliter et continue ostensa, ita affici [eidem] dominæ ut ad contrahendum cum ea matrimonium præ cæteris aliis principibus . . . disponatur, adeo ut melius disponi non possit; omniaque sua majestas [pro parte] ejus faciet quæ honorifica et rationabilia videbuntur et quæ commod[e facere] poterint, nec per eum stabit quominus illud matrimonium debitum sort[iatur effectum].

## III.—Answer to the Preceding.

[Draft in Wolsey's hand.—MS. Galba B. II. 129.]

A. professes his devotion to England,

In primis A. ag. . . . . . . . . . . . . . . . . . . . . . . . . . . . Angliæ quod tantum dign[atus] est visitare ipsum A. non solum verbis suavissimis et humanissimis, sed etiam rebus amplissimis, et quod sincere et aperte [de] omnibus secum dignatur loqui, et de eo tamquam suo fideli servitori s . . . et confidere, pro quibus idem A. promittit se fideliter et diligenter i[nservire] suæ majestati, et satagat pro posse suo quod omnia sua negotia hic [perficiantur] ad honorem, exaltationem, et complacentiam suam, et quod post Cæsarem et dominam et . . . . . . . cum quibus a teneris fuit educatus, sibi inserviet ante omnes [principes] mundi; et istud firmiter credat et speret rex Angliæ, et quod iste A. . . . . . .non inservient A. pro promotionibus ecclesiasticis aut spe alicujus muneris, sed plus pro amore quem habet [erga] ipsum et quod in eo confidat et quanto magis amaverit . . . . . . . melius si fieri poterit illi inservire studebit prædictis . . . .

Et quantum ad istas duas affinitates inter regem [Angliæ et Cæsaream] majestatem, mediantibus his duobus contractibus matrimoni[alibus inter regem] Angliæ et ducissam Sabaudiæ, principem Castellæ et [dominam Mariam . . . . . ]s prædict., dicit A. istud esse fundamentum totius . . . . . . . . . semper intelligens quam conjunctæ sunt istæ duæ patr[iæ . . . . . . . . i]sta patria et quam utilis sit una alteri, semper [. . . . . . . . uti]litate istarum patriarum, studuit modum et viam quomodo istæ [duæ patriæ essent conjun]ctæ per unam strictam amicitiam et confœderationem [inter Cæsaream majesta]tem et regem Angliæ ad prædictam confœd[erationem . . . . . . . ]s dedit operam suam et post hac præst[abit] . . . . suo nec constabit cum omni effectu [ . . . . . . . . d]uæ affinitates inter Cæsarem et regem Ang[liæ cum singulis conditionibus et depe]ndentiis super eisdem ad honorem, contenta[tionem, et complacentiam regis] Angliæ perficiantur et optatam finem dedu[cantur]. and his desire to promote the two alliances.

*[Et dicit A. quod nihil fiat in hac dieta quod in damnum sive præjudicium] regis Angliæ ve[l] dictarum duarum affinitatum quovismodo c[edere possit, sed] sciet majestas regis Angliæ quod re et non verbis sibi fidelissime inserviet, et istud fideliter pro [se] promittit quantum in eo erit. [*f. 129 b.

Et quantum ad consilium ipsius A. super istis verbis, "Faciet "rex ad cont[entationem] domini Bergensis," consilium ipsius A. super hac re est quod rex Angliæ faciet bonum . . . . pro matrimonio dominæ cum domino Bergensi et gubernatore, quoniam non decet quod ips . . . iant hujusmodi communicandi, et ideo non habebunt auctoritatem incipiendi, sed [postquam] inceperit rex Angliæ tunc habebunt auctoritatem l[oquendi et . . ]sionandi cum dicto rege super eodem matrimonio et super articul[is ejusdem].

[ . . . . . a]rticulo dotis ubi est provisum quod rex haberet[1] tr[ . . . flore]norum et quod centum millia solvantur

[1] An Arabic numeral 3 is here struck out.

quando erit d . . . . quod animus Cæsaris erit quod minuatur ista dos vel s . . . . . . sed [ . . . . . . . Bu]rgundiam ex dono Cæsaris cujus annuus [valor est] . . . . florenorum vel plus: ideo dominus Bergensis et G[ubernator volunt disp]utare cum rege super ea re et quærere ac int . . . . . . . . . estri super ea rê quid et quantum velit habere . . . facient Cæsarem certiorem, in qua re et s . . . . imperator faciet quod videbitur consonum ratio[ni].

[*f. 130.

Objections of the Emperor.

*Sunt duo alii articuli qui videntur Cæsari valde duri; primus, vide[licet,] quod mortuo rege Angliæ domina relinqueret dotem et medietate[m] jocalium, et sic mortuo rege rediret ad patrias istas quasi ancilla regis . . . . et per eum esset depauperata. Non ita fuit actum cum illa, neq[ue de] Hispania neque Sabaudia, sed, mortuis principe Hispaniæ et d[ucissa] Sabaudiæ, rediit[1] ad patrias istas cum dote et jocalibus . . . contra dote; et si vivente rege Angliæ illa obiret diem summum quod . . . . nihil disponeret de jocalibus et bonis suis q . . . alibi perquisivit cederet in damnum domus Burgundiæ . . . . . . ista videntur minus dura et non . . . . . Cæsaris quod nihil horum fiet neque quod hæc totaliter abolentur sed ratione mitigant[ur], quia jam erit desponsata . . . . . . . et potenti principi. Igitur in omnibus istis erit tractatus . . . . gubernatorem et majestatem regis Angliæ ad rect . . . . . . . [ar]ticulos secundum rationem et honestatem pro utroque . . . .

[Articu]lus tractatus qui videtur durus quod . . . . [rex A]ngliæ, domina, Cæsar, et tota ista patria oblig . . . . [omne]s et singulas conventiones in prædicto tractatu . . . . . . . . censuris ecclesiasticis iste modus non videtur . . . . . . . . s sed minus servilis, sed domina et imperator . . . . . . . rex Angliæ haberet per perimpletionem omnium . . . . . . . . . mo omnem securitatem rationabilem et hon . . . . . . . . et rex Angliæ cum domino B[ergensi] . . . . . . . . rationabili et honesto q . . . . ipsi facient . . . . . . . i et super easdem imperator scribet eis . . . . . . . . . . tis oratoribus regis Angliæ dabit eis a[uctoritatem ad conc]ludendum super omnibus et singulis præmissis.

[*f. 130 b.

*. . . . . . . . . . . . . . . . . sua majestas . . . . toto isto tractatu ma[jestas . . . . . . . . . .] A. interponet part[es] suas pro toto suo posse quod id fiet ad beneplacitum suum.

Quantum ad articulum illum quod domina non revertatur ad patrias istas, et quod astringatur quod nullomodo vivente rege possit reverti ad patrias is[tas], est nimis[2] durum, et pro altera

---

[1] *rediis*, MS. | [2] *minus*, MS.

parte quod poterit libere reverti quando voluer[it], est inhonestum; sed mens Cæsaris est quod singulis annis aliqua parte . . . . . ri beneplacito regis Angliæ una cum rege si velit vel si[ne eo domin]a poterit descendere ad visitandum et attendendum gubernationem prædictarum pa[triarum. Nam] Cæsar est totaliter resolutus committere regimen istarum patri[arum prædictæ] dominæ et nulli de hac patria, et videtur A. quod iste . . . placebit regi Angliæ.

[Inten]tio istorum verborum "Venient Oratores ad exequen-"dum e[a . . . . . Ca]lisiis cum moderamine domini An-"dreæ de Burgo" . . . . . . . . . quendum ea quæ erant conclusa Calisiis sol . . . . . . . bi conclusum cum moderamine domini Andreæ de B[urgo . . . . .]lia ratione mutui impignorandi jocalia sicut . . . . . . . . .
de Burgo.

[Quantum] ad copias instructionum cogitavit A. quid facere
. . . . . . . videtur sibi quod cum honore suo non potest mittere
h . . . . . quod si mitteret quamvis rex Angliæ ill . . .
. . . . . geret illum et pro centum mille ducatis . . . .
. . . . . . . . . rex Angliæ quod non est aliquid . . .
. . . . . . [quam quod] prædictum est et quantum ad . . . .
. . . . . . non est aliquid in illis instructionibus quod . .
. . . . . . . . ere possit regi Angliæ vel cedere n . .
. . . . . nec fiet dummodo A.[1] impedire pote . . . . .
*Et . . . . . . . . . . . . . . . . . . . . . . [*f. 131.
vel alibi sua . . . . . . . . . . . . . . . . . . . .
tempus ego promitto . . . . . . . . . . . . . . . .

Et quantum ad dominum Andream de Burgo, nihil aliud audivi ab [eo quam] quod rex Aragonum est totus malus et non vult permittere eum intrare [regnum] Castellæ, et sic credit ipse quod redibit.

Et quantum ad adventum oratorum regis vestri, domina multum . . . de adventu eorum, et quod velit ad x. dies diffe[rre] profectionem ejus ad dietam expectando eorum adventum . . . desiderat audire ea quæ sunt dicturi ex parte regis v[estri].

[E]t quantum ad regem Aragonum et negotia regni [sui . . . . re]x Aragonum non comprehendatur in ista intelligent[ia . . . . pl]acent ea quæ dicuntur per regem et etiam orato[res] . . . . . videtur multum bene quod oratores regis vestri . . . . te regis vestri in ea re sic quod illi et no[bis] . . . . . ure unde bonum. . . . .

[Et o]blata bona opportunitate, ego dominæ dicam singula illa . . . t me dicere pro parte sua dominæ sicut semper dixi.

---

[1] *A.*] first writen *ego*, then corrected.

[Et q]uantum ad regimen istarum patriarum si videbitur . .
. . . . ego potero eis aliquid inservire in ea re et a . . .
. . . . . . ero ad aliquod tempus contentus hic St. . .
. . . . . . ter aut quater, quod post decessum s . . . .
. . . . . . re, quia nullus est præter me cui committ .
. . . . . am sub quodammodo officia ducatus . . . . . .
[qui]a non potest diu et pro semper abesse.

. . tria habeat sub eis regimen ne fort . . . . . .
. . . . [G]allorum ad quas modo sunt multum incl[inati].

[*f. 131 b. * . . . . . . . . . . . . . . . . . . .
. . . . . . . . . [dominus B]ergensis convalu[it] quia est pomposu[s] . . . . . . . . . . facere apud regem et vidit quod non sunt plura prædict . . . commissa, ideo redit jam se difficile et cupit exspectare adventum Cæsa[ris] quatenus possit habere majores commissiones, sed sciat pro vero [quod nullas] habebit alias commissiones; et ideo scripsi Cæsari quod imperaret il . . pergat de incontinenti et absque mora, et si moram fecerit inveniemus alium modum quo fiet nolens volens etsi ille imperator . . fiet; et igitur firmiter credat rex Angliæ quod de incontinenti ven[iet].

[Si aliq]uid actum vel dictum sit circa mutuum regum conventum et utrum . . . . eodem, oratoribus suis comittatur.

[*f. 132. *Quantum ad . . . . . . . . . . . . . . . . .
. . . . duæ patriæ et quod . . . . . . . alteri . . [pro ho]nore Cæsaris et utili[tate] . . . . studuit modum et viam quo istæ duæ patriæ essent similiter conjunctæ per unam [strictam] amicitiam et confœderationem et quinetiam ipse A. vidit Cæsarem et re[gem] meum optime etiam ad illam dispositos hactenus studuit et dede . . . et posthac præstabit et faciet pro toto posse suo quod hæ duæ affinitates in[ter] Cæsarem et regem Ang[liæ] ad honorem, contentationem, et complacentiam regis Angliæ perficiant[ur et ad] optatum finem deducantur cum singulis conditionibus et dependent[iis super] eisdem. Et promittit idem A. quod nihil fiet in hac dieta quod in da[mnum seu] præjudicium regis vel dictarum duarum affinitatum quovismodo [cedere possit,] sed sciet majestas regis Angliæ quod re et non verbis sibi [fidelissime] serviet; et hoc fideliter promittit quantum in eo erit.

Consilium A. quantum ad secundum articulum est quod rex Angliæ [faciet . . . . .] super matrimonio dominæ cum domino Bergensi et gubernatore . . . . . . . . . auctoritatem incipiendi, sed postquam rex inceperit [habebunt auctori-

---

[1] One entire line lost.

tatem lo]quendi et ratiocinandi cum dicto rege super eodem ma[ritagio].

. . . . . dote quæ extendit ad tria millia florenorum non cred[it A. . . ] quod minuatur dos sed quia domina habebit . . . . . . . . nos, ideo dominus Bergensis debet disputare . . . . . . . . gere animum regis quid et quantum amplius vel . . . . . . . . certiorem. In qua re et singulis aliis . . . . [responsum] detur consonum rationi.[1]

* . . . . . . . . . . . . . . . . . . . . . ietate [*f. 132 b.
. . . . . . . . . [in Hispani]a neque in Sabau[dia] . . . quod vivente rege . . . . . . eret de . . . omnibus istis erit tract . . . . . Bergensem et gubernatorem ad rectificandum istos articulos ad rationum et h[onorem] pro utraque parte.

Quod omnes tractatus istius matrimonii serventur sub pœnis et censuris ecclesiasticis videtur tollere libertatem et quodammodo facere dominam servam et quod iste . . . . . . videtur regius, sed domina et imperator erunt contenti quod habeat omnem securitate[m] rationabilem et honestam; in quibus omnibus disputet cum domino Berge[nsi et] gubernatore super rationabili et honesto quin ipsi facient creditum [. . . . . Cæ]sari et super eadem imperator scribet eis animum suum et forte . . . . bus vestris dabit eis auctoritatem ad tractandum et concludend[um . . . . . . . ] majestas sua A. quid velit rationabiliter fieri et ipse . . . . . . uas pro posse.

[Quod domina a]stringatur quod nullo modo possit reverti vivente rege [ . . . . . . . a]liqua parte anni cum beneplacito regis una cum rege . . . . . sola ad visitandum et attendendum[2] gubernatorem.

*. . . . . . . . . . . . . . . . quod . . . . . . [*f. 133.
. . . . . plementum . . . . . . . . . . . . . . comitatu Burg[undiæ] ad terminum vitæ suæ cujus annuus valor extendit, ut Cæsar prædicto A. sign[ificavit], circa xx. mille florenos . . . . . communiter vocatos *Renyche gylders* ad er- . . . . . . . quod cum centum mille coronis quas dictam sperat A. prædicta domina habe . . . . . supra Burgundiam et cum ipso annuo valore prædictæ Burgundiæ rex . . . . . . habere in effectu et æquivalentia prædictam integram dotem trecen[tarum] millium coronarum, et credit A. si Cæsar et rex Angliæ in aliis poterunt cont[entari] in articulo dotis non erit magna difficultas. Sed Cæsarea majestas [est cont]enta quod

---

[1] Underneath in the margin at the bottom of f. 132, some words are scrawled by Wolsey, apparently as mere memoranda. Among these may be read *De adventu Oratorum*.

[2] *attendendum*] attentendum, MS.

prædictus rex Angliæ habeat pro firma et secura solu[tione] . . . . . dictæ dotis omnem securitatem rationabilem et honestam, verùm . . . . . . . non est dum plene resolutus quo modo et sub qua forma et sp . . . . . . . . habebit prædictum comitatum, sed hoc fiet per disputationes cum o[ratoribus regis] Angliæ quia oratores Cæsaris, puta Bergensem et Gubern[atorem . . . . . . . ] habebunt auctoritatem tractandi et ratiocinand[i, tam super] dotem [quam super] alios articulos duros, sicut speravit et credidit A., sed totam hoc fie[t . . . . . . . ]estres.

*De Oratoribus Cæsaris.*

. . . . . . dicit A. quod oratores Cæsaris qui venient ad regem . . . . . . . de articulis, videlicet, dotis et aliis, nec h[abebunt auctoritat]em pro matrimonio dominæ nisi solus gubernator ad o[ . . . . . . . . r]egis, et quem animum et affectionem rex gerit erga præd[ict . . . . . . . .] faciet reditum dominæ . . . . . . et tantum ad solemnizandum matrimonium con . . . . . . . . . pecuniarum eo modo sicut prædictum est.

## IV.—Wolsey to Henry VII.

[From a corrected draft in Wolsey's own hand.—MS. Cott. Galba B. II. f. 138.]

Aftyr most humble comendacions. Pleasyt your nobyll grace to undyrstand [that the] iiij^th day of thys present moneth in the towne of Meclyne, I kam to the presen[ce of] A., wher aftyr your rygth herty comendacions and overture of myn inst[ruccions] at the leynth, wych the seyd A. was nat only dissyrous to know but [also] gave to them rygth good audyens and attent he—

The lorde Bergen covettyng to appere to yowr grace that he war in gre[at aucto]ryte and credens with the Emperor, and the lady, hath[1] solacky[d his] komyng[2] and desyryng to have a large commission, . . . as wel to komyn as to conclude the ladis maryage wych in [no] wyse sche wold he schuld have.

[The] lord Bergensis [is] nat contentyd that ys hys commissyon.

---

[1] *hath* repeated in MS

[2] *komyng* repeated in MS.

. . . . he by the slacknes and ontowardes of the lord Ber[gensis . . . . . con]tentyd with hys comissyon, bu dissyryng to have yt . . . . . . . . . . . auctoryte to . . . . . ferther then ys seyd in the lady . . . . . . . . . sche in no wyse contentyd he[1]—

[The lord] Bergensis somewhat purpose dissyryng to be sen . . . . . . that he war of gret auctoryte with the emp-[eror] . . . . . . . hys comyng forward dyssyryng . . . . . . afore hys departing, trustyng that yf he so dyd he shuld have . . . . . to intreate and conclude of the ladys maryage, wyche . . . . . . . ld he shuld have, and so . . . . . . . . at mydnygt he reparyd to the emperor . . . . . . . . havyng knowleg preventyd seme dyss . . . . . . . . vyse as yet he geve hym ferther commission . . . . . . . . . yn that owt any ferther delay he d . . . . . . . . . so that A. dowth nat that within vj. day . . . . . . . forth komyng for both the lady and . . . . . . . . . . content with for hys long delay.

## V.—Wolsey to Henry VII.

[From a corrected draft in Wolsey's own hand.—MS. Galba B. II. f. 139.]

Pleasyt your nobyl [grace to understand that since the writing of m]y laste letters sent [unto your grace] datyd the x[th] day of [this month I have l]ernyd n[o th]yng of importance to be [written] to your grace, but only that A. the xj[th] day of the seyd moneth, havyng word [that the] ambassadors wer kom to Andwerp, departyd from Meclyn to the emperor . . . . in Holand in distans from thens xviij. Duche mylys, wyllyng me to m[ake my] abood style at Mechlyn, promysyng within vj. days at the most . . . . Howbeyt as yet we have no suer knowleg of hys komyng thethe[r] nor [yet of] the emperors. Ther ys here so myche inconstance, mutabilte, and lytyl re[gard of] promysys and causes, that in ther appoyments ther ys lytyl [trust] or suerte; for thyngs suerly determyd to be downe on d[ay are] changyd and alteryd the next, and as fast as on set forward another,[2] wher with, as I undyrstand, the lady ys nat a lytyl dys[pleasyd] and abashyd, feryng that every thyng thyng shal folow and insue

---

[1] Sic, apparently an unfinished sentence

[2] *another*] Sic, the clause is interlined and left incomplete.

ac[cording to] suche wryityng as she have sent to yow, the forseyd xj[th] day . . . . . . . [d]epartyng shenyd how that the day before the lady had v[ery loving l]etters from your grace wryttyn with yowr awne hands, wych w[ere . . . . p]lesant and joyfull, but also she mervelyd to se how wys. . . . . . . . . . encyonsly they wer conceyvyd, and the wordes of . . . . . . . . . . . . ther, afferm- yng that by them yt apperyd how gret an . . . . . . . . . . . . . . . . grace had nat content with onys or twys redyng of them . . . . . . . . . . . . . . . de them, and the oftynner she so dyd the more she d . . . . . . . . . . . be hold the said A. was very glade nat . . . . . . . . . . . . yrly fyxyd hyr hert and mynd on yow and every th . . . . . . . . . . . . . grace wold re- sanably dyssyre. And in cas ye wold folow . . . . . . . . . . . . he shuld shen to yow mervelos conclusyons t . . . . . . . . . . . . . lower contreys.

[The x]ij. day of the seyd moneth the lord Bergens ka[me] . . . . . . . . . . . . . . at whos kommyng yt was suerly appoyntyd that . . . . . . . . . . . re set forward. Howbeyt that appoyntment ys chang[ed . . . . . . . . . . . instr]uccions and ratyfycacion ys in doctor Fluc hand . . . . . . . . . . . . . . . . . . . yse to the hands of the lord Bergens with . . . . . . . . . [l]eter from the emperor for hys dyscharge and th . . . . . . . . . . them wol in no wyse set forward, seying that . . . . . . . . . . . [com]mysyon.[1]

*f. 139 b. *[The] lord Bergensis . . . . . . . . . . . . . . . . . . . . . . . . . . . . . . . . . . . wardes on to suche tyme . . instru[ccions and ratifica]cion be in hys hand . . . . . . . . ythe doctor Flucke wyl nat delyv . . . . to hym without specyall [warrant a]nd dyschard from the em- peror, so that ther ys stryf betwen them tweyn w[hether o]f them shulde bryng the seyd wryttyng. The other cause ys the emperor [hath ha]d of the marchant Fokers l. thousand crownys, leyng to them in pleg for [the p]ayment ther of certayne juelles, wyche the seyd merchant Fokers be content to d[eliver at] Kales, ther to be leyd in gauge for suche money as the emperor [shall bor]row of your grace, so that they may [be repa]yd of the sume wych the . . . . . . ly promysyd to do. And for the assuryd performans ther of the seyd . . . . standyth bownd to the seyd mer-

[1] The latter part of this paragraph is scored through with the pen.

chant Fokers. Wher for on to su[ch time as the] emperor send to hym a letter to save hym harmeles . . . . . . [ind]-empnyte he wol nat set forwards. Thys letter ys every da[y expected, but a]s yet yt komyth nat; yt shalnat, they sey . . . . . . . . after they wyl set forwardes myche of the fawte why . . . . . . . . be so long taryd ys imputyd to the by . . . . . . . . . in trowth all ther prevy dryftes be to be sen to do . . . . . . and to get thanckes of your grace wych *your grace [shall better unde]rstand at ther komyng*[1] than I can wryt, perceyv[ing that there is none] here that regardyth or hedyth ther masters ho[nor, but only their own particu]ler profygt and avantage.

. . . . iij. of the seyd moneth master Wyngfyl and I dynyd with . . . . parte of the seyd dyner talkyd of your grace preysy[ng . . . . . ]ng these words: *Rex Angliæ vester et meus non . . . . . . [Cæ]sar neque potest tam sero et mane comedere sicut Cæ[sar] . . . . . . . . subtilem et clarum et quædam* . . . . . . . . emperor and this contrey seye *non* . . . . . . *ra nisi ista poma et dominam.*

. . . . . . of the seyd moneth in the after none I was . . . . . . . . . nd at my komyng into Ynglond to have h . . . . . . . mendyd to your grace sheuyng to the sa . . . . . . . . . . *[esp]ecyal love in . . . . . . . . . [*f. 140.
. . princes . . . . . . he world nat only . . . . . . . . wy . . . . . . . and other gret . . . . . . . . God hath induyd yow w[ith] but . . . . . . . there was no Chrynstyn prince wych was [more] met and convenyent for the exspedicon ageinst the Turke, for [that i]ncas the emperor, Frenche kyng or the kynges of Arragon, Portugal, Hongerey, or the Venyshyans shuld interpryse and take thys thyng op[on th]em yt shuld be thougth that they dyd it for ther singuler awan[tage ra]ther to recovyr suche thynges as they have lost or to atteyne to that [they] have no rygth on to or to be revengyd of them wych hath don them [injur]e in tyme past, wych thynges cowde nat be jugyd or fownde in your grace; wher[for, they] seyd, ye war *instrumentum Christi maxime idoneum ad debellando[s] Christianæ religionis hostes*, exortyng your grace that lycke wyse [as ye had well a]nd blessydly be gone so to contynue and go forward and helpe forwardes . . . . . se he seyd he had to love yow for my L[ady, the] wych was hys gret mustres dowthtyr

---

[1] The words in italics here are scored through with the pen.

and also hys . . . . . . . . . . d most specyaly for the yong prince of Castell, wych ys b . . . . . . . . re and lord, so that thes forseyd thynges movyd hym [to love you more than] other princes. Wherfor from tyme to tyme he wold put . . . . . . . aid and assystans to the furtherans of al su[ch matters and] causes as your grace had to be donne in the cour[t] . . . . . hys lyf to declare and specke your vertuys your nam[e . . . . . . . ot]her good wordes of semblale eff[ect].

Touchyng your ambassadors [to]wards the court of Rome, the xxv. day of thys mo[neth[1]] they ly as yet . . . . . . . yng wher or when they shal repare to the E[mperor . . . t]hys moneth the lady sent to them the kapteyn . . . . [willing th]em to make ther abode styl at Andwerp [till such time as s]he shal asserteyne them of the emperors ferth[er] my[nd] . . . . day of thys moneth the truge begenyth bet[wene . . . . . . . F]renche kyng. Other neuys [have I none.]

And thus Jesu preserve your grace your m . . . . . . . Wryttyn at Mechlyne, the xxiij. day of O[ctober by] yowr humble servant.

[*f. 140. *I undyrst[and] . . . . . . . . . . . . . . . . . . . . . . . . . . . . . . . and hyr ladys shal . . . . . . . . . . . . . . . . . . . apparell and be ch . . . . . in tawny satten and oth . . . . . . ers.

## VI.—Wolsey to Henry VII.

[MS. Galba B. II. f. 141.]

Pleasyt yowr grace . . . . . . . Octobyr . . . . . e towne of Andwerp at v [of] the clocke at nygth, I [ressay]vyd your most honorabyl letteres datyd at Gre[enwich], the xxij. day of the seyd moneth, with certayne instruccions in Lattyn to [have] disclosyd on to A., by the contynue whereof I perceyve that your hygnes a[nd your] most honorabyl consell juggyth on artycle wych I wrot to yowr grace [in the] Ynglyche tonge consernyng the dote shuld implie contradiccion, mervelyng t[hat there] was mad no mensyon in the artycle in

---

[1] *towards—moneth*] These words are an interlineation.

Latyn of suche words as war . . . . in Ynglyshe tong, neyther of rebuttyng any part of the seyd dote and appese wych shuld be betwyx your grace and the lordes Bergensis and Governer, nor yet that the assignacion . . . . counte of Burgon to the lady shuld be for terme of hyr lyf as . . . . nat presumyng to defend the contrary parte of yowr hy juggement, but to decl[are my poor] mynde and what I perceyve in that behalf, wych I beseche yowr [grace] humble to accept in god parte. Wher I seyd that the emperors m . . . . he dote of thre hunderyth thousan . . should nat be mynishyd or browt to any lower sume, I undyr . . . . . have the seyd integyr dote in effect and equyvalen . . . . . . . . . e Lady shuld have the county of Burgone t[he annual value wh]er of extendyth to xx^ti^ thousand florens and above to . . . . . . . . tayne other sums such as shuld be appeysyd and thowth r . . . . . . . e and the lordes Bergensis and Governer . . . . . . . he words as yt ys implyd in . . . . . . . . *mam habebit Burgundiam ex dono Cæsaris, cujus an[nuus valor extendit ad] xx^ti^ millia florenorum vel plus. Ideo dominus Bergensis* . . . . . . . . *t disputare cum rege super ea re et quærere ac intelligere* . . . . . . *[qu]antum velit habere supra illam summam* . . . . . *etc.* . . . . . . d bes sume what that obs . . . . . . . of the seyd A. overtures be for a suerte al . . . . . . . gth, nor as yet he, as I thynk, hath not groundly oversen . . . . . ymony concludyd betwyx kyng Phylyp an . . . . . . esolute mynde of the emperors in the seyd . . . . . . . rest opon, for I suppose the emperor as yet k . . . . . . . . apon he wyl rest.

*Wherfor in the se . . . . . . . . . . . . . . . . . [*f. 141 b. entent that suche articles as I have sent to your hygnes . . . . . . shuld nat be thougth . . . words, but the playne overture of A., I have sent to your grace with thes my letteres a boke of the seyd articlys by hys awne hand correctyd, with hys interliniacion in such places as he thowthe be of importance; prayng yowr [grace] that the same may be sent to me ageyne, for he hath oftyn tymys askyd the delyvery therof, howbeyt I have by as good [means] as I kan use pot of the deleverans of yt and shal do [ if it] may be without hys displesure or myscontentacion. Wher also I seyd the lady shuld have the seyd counte of Burgon dur[ing her] lyf, makyng no mencion ther of in the artycle of Lattyn, veryl[y the] seyd A. so seyd to me and the duches. And why that was nat commyttyd to . . . . yng as the residue yowr grace shal know at my commyng to the s[ame].

In that hys seyng I have musyd how yt mygth b . . . e . duches shuld have the seyd conte duryng hyr lyf, seyng that y[t is part of] the yong princes[1] inherytans. Wherfor I shal by a[ll manner m]eanys and wys that I kan use, accordyng [to your graces] commande to know for how long she shal have the . . . . . . . . . the very value ther of of hys and what and nat . . . . . . . other thynges, to the intent at my komyng I may . . . . . . . declare to yowr grace as fere as shalbe lern . . . every poynt.

. . . . . . . day of the forseyd mone at vj. of the cloke in the . . . . . . . d leysor sheuyd to him my instruccions with suche oth[er things] . . . the same thyngs as your grace wold I shuld d . . . . . . . causyd hym as of my owne hed with owt comande . . . . . . . . instruccions. Wher with he was wel contentyd . . . . . . . . . [su]bstancyally to be rememberyd in the seyd . . . . . . . or his departyng to the dyet pleynly to ass . . . . . . all thynges. *At that tyme he sheu[yd to me that Andreas de] Burgo was arreyvyd latly agen in to y . . . . . . yn letters he shuld be arryvyd un to yn . . . . . .*[2]

. . . . . . seyd A. sheuyd to me that the Lady shuld h[ave the county of Burgundy] wher of I have myche musyd, seyng that [it is part of the prince] of Castellys inherytans. The cause why yt was na[t . . . . . . . your grace shall kn]ow at my komyng, wych I tr[ust] . . . . . . .

* * * * * *

[*f. 142. *furryd with s . . . . . . . . . . . . . . . . . . . havyng on hys hed [a] cap of scarlet . . . . . . . . . . . . . . . whyt heres.

The last day of [October] in the towne of Andwerp betwen v. and vj. [of the] clocke at nygth yowr ambasadors accompanyd with the byshop of A. the emper . unky and A. B. and C. kam to the emperors presens, wych ware resseyvyd undyr [form] folowyng. The emperor with the yong prince of Castell on hys rygth h[and] with man[y] . . . . . . . stod at the upper part of the chambyr. Unto hom your ambassadors enteryng . . . . the same made thrys . . . convenyent genufleccions; and at ther komyng to hys presen[ce[3] his majesty] toke my lord Treserer[4] by

---

[1] "*Dukys*" corrected.
[2] These lines struck out.
[3] Psen . . ., MS., the latter part of the word burnt away.
[4] Thomas earl of Surrey.

the hand, and lycke wyse the master of the [rolls[1]], nat avalyng hys bonet to them. Mastyr Wyngfyld for as myche as he [thought] hym nat on aqueyntyd with the emperor pressyd nat hymsylf to tak . . . . . by the hand; wych the emperor perceyvyn[g] . . . . to hym with lauthyng cowntenans seyng "I wyl tak . . . . . by the hand." Thys done, my lord of Surrey with the residue on their k[nees, after] makyng yowr commendacions, delyvery[d your letter][2] to the emperor, wych as sone as my lord namyd . . . . . . hys bonet eftsonys my seyd lord tresorer on hys kneys mad[e your commen]dacions and delyveryd your letters . . . . . . . . . ygt boldly and quycly or that my lord tresurer had endyd . . . . . . . . Frenche tonge how that your grace faryd. Wher at the . . . . . . . . . . hertly. Thys done the emperors secretary red such letter[s] . . . . hyn and the yong prince of Castyl that he had herd . . . . . . . and glad was he to here what they had . . . . . . . . . the emperor set hym sylf doune undyr the clothe of . . . . . . [prin]ce of Castell on hys rygth syd and a lytyl lower on that syd ther . . . . . . . [Co]unt Palantyne the markes of Brandborow and other . . . . . . er sate the byshops of Turnocke and Gurcen with the . . . . . . . . . ayenst the emperror. Your orators wer . . . . . . . . [the master of t]he Rolls began hys oracion wych was uttered and p[ronounced very] wel and dystynctly with good spryt and bol[ness] . . . . . . . . . . to the contentacion of them that wer present, the sume wher of I wryt nat yowr grace for . . . . . . . . . . osse the same nat on knowyn . . . . . . . . . s mad by the byshop of Gurcen wych thow . . . . . . . . . . best pronowncyd, nor the Latyn ther of most . . . . . . . . . was very good and furnyshyd with many a . . . . . frendly . . . . . . . . . thys.

*The emperor and the yong prince of Castylle . . . . [*f. 142 b.
ornat oracion, gretly . . . . . . that yt had pleasyd the kyng of Ynglond hys . . . . . . and the seyd princes father to send to them so gret and honorabyl men of suche gravyte . . . . . hym wher in he sheuyd hys fraternall and fatherly love gret and . . . . . . . wher of the emperor and yong prince hath ben allweys desyros . . .

---

[1] Dr. Young. He was sent to the Emperor in July 1508. See Memorials of Henry VII. 125.

[2] These words appear on a previous line, crossed out with the pen.

. . . . . . suche gret effectes and comodytes as may aryse ther of to the gret honor . . . . . . . acion and suerete of yow both and gret prosperyte of yowr reamy[s] and subgettes, and to redounde to the singulare name and fa- . . . . . throwth a . . . . . . Wherfor the emperor nat only to geve consell on the yong prince of Castell . . . . . . . . that intent that suche amyte as had ben begon betwyx hym and your [grace shou]ld be knyt *perpetuo quodam fædere et nexu indissolubili* hath des . . . . . . . . . . . kom doune to thys contreys. In seconde parte of hys answer he sheuy[d . . . . . . . .]orys that allweys the hows of Borgon had ben allyd and . . . . . [ky]nges of Ynglond wych hath proceyd of very good reason for [that those count]rys be so nere and ther condicions so lycke . . . . . . . . . . . . . . . . the emperor had ap- poyntyd men of gret sadnes and honor . . . . . . . . . good brother to fynyshe the nygt affynyte wyche . . . . . . . . . . . . . And that ther shuld be no let but profygt indevo . . . . . . . . . . [a]myte confederaacion and shuld suerly be made betw . . . . . . . . . . . . . indure, ne nevyr to be brockyn to the gret he . . . . . . . . . . . . both your chyldern, yshu and succeccion, ream[is] . . . . . . . . . . . . . . . . subjects for evyr maye. And thus . . . . . . . . . . . don the emperor rosse up and yowr orators . . . . . . . . . . hyn secret co- mynycacion.

[*f. 143. *In the se . . . . . . . . . . . . . . . . . . . . . . . . . . . . . . . . . . that the . . . . . . . . . . . . . . meyne . . . . . singuler w . . . . the how[se] of Burgone hath . . . . . singuler . . . . to be allyed with kynges of Ynglond a fore other princes, wych ys very agreabyl to reason, seyng thes ij countreys so nygth and con- dicions of the inhabitantes in them so lycke; the wych thyn[g the] emperor substancyally consyderyng hathe begone and contractyd s[uch] a amyte with hys brother the kyng of Ynglond, [for the] acomplyshment wherof he hath appoyntyd men of gret honor to be sent in legacye [to his] seyd brother, and that ther shuld be in hym no stop [nor] let but perfygt indever that suche a amyte and confederacon s[hould be made] suerly betwyx them wych shal ever indure nevyr to be brokyn to the . . . honor, weil, and suerte of them, [their] chyldern, ishu a[nd successors], and the prosperite of your subjects, reamys, londes and . . . . . . and to yowr inestymabyl renown, glory, and s . . . . . . . all the world evyr to indure. And thus he mad a ende; a[nd this] downe, the emperror ros up, kalling yowr orators to hym .

. . . . . . . to them in Almayne tonge, afterward declaryd to them [by the bishop] of Gurce in Latyn hys excuse why they had b[een] . . . . . . . . hys presens praying them not to be myscontentyd ther . . . . . . . . . . . h[e] demandyd whetther they had commyssyon [or licence] to be at the commynycation of peax with the . . . . . . . [a]nswerd Nay. Than the emperor prayd them to wryt by p[ost to your grace for t]he seyd lycens, for he was very desyros that [they should be present a]t the seyd dyet and to have yowr ad[vice upon] all suche thyngs as shuld be concludyd ther. [Whereupon they an]swerd that they wold wryt to yowr grace sheu[ing]. . . . . the emperors request and desyre, nat dowttyng . . . . . . . . . grante and assent to the same. Thys done . . . . . . . . . . . . . . . . . . of the byshop of Grucen causyd all yowr . . . . . . . . . let in to the chamber, takyng every on of the . . . . . . . . . . . wer talmen and by lyclyud good . . . . . . . . . . . *ittare vobiscum.* Thys don the Emperor b . . . . . . . . . . . . . . r orators departyd to their loggyn, accompanyd . . . . . . . . . . . . . . ch browt them to hys presens.

*. . . . . . me day in the towne of Andwerp betw . . [*f. 144.
. . . . . . . . . . . . clocke at nygth yowr ambasadors accompany . . . . . . . . . . . . nd the lord Chevers and Mons . . kam to the . . . . . . . . .

*The fyrst day of . . . . . . . . . moneth . . . . . of [*f. 145.
the clocke in the mornyng sheuyd to me that y[our] grace had wryttyn to hym a mervelos god let . . . . wher by he was gretly movyd and provokyd and . . . . . to apply all hys wyt and power to se that all yowr c[auses] and matters shuld be browt to good effect yowr complacens a . . . . . . . . . . . purposse. I have also for my parte metly wel . . . . . . . . . . . . so that yf he performe hys seyng and promyse, by hys polytyce meany[s your] mynd shalbe in al thyngs fulfyllyd. Over thys he sheu[yd] me that the emperor thowth yt kam of a singuler god mynde towardes [him] and hys that ye had sent to hym so honorabyl ambasyat [being] men of suche gravyte and personages whom he was gretly desyrous t[o be] present at the commynycacion of peax be twyxt hym and the s . . . . . . . to the yntent he mygth have yowr consell and thers [in] what maner of wyse he shuld conclude with the seyd Frenche k[ing, whom] the emperor and A. in no wyse lovyd but accomptyd . . . . . . . . . . suttell, and fayne wold the emperror be to take suche weys as . . . . . . . the lessyng and mynishing of the seyd Frenche kyng . . . . . . . was so am-

byshyous that he nat content . . . . . . . . . desyryd to have all. To thys I answeryd seyng . . . . . . . . [F]renche kyng lowe and that hys power shuld be m[inished] substancyally constantly and fr . . . . . . . . . joyne hymsylf with the kyng my master . . . . . . . . . . . . . nat to be dowyt the Frenche kynges power shal nat . . . . . . To thys A. answerryd that the emperor was . . . . . . . thus to fast. And suerly to adyoyn hym self . . . grace. Wherfor he advysyd the same to be cont[ent . . . . . . . . . a]mbassadors shuld accompagne the b . . . . . . . . . . . . et for the causes above rehersyd. And that . . . . . . . . . no tyme shuld be sclackyd or lost . . . . . . . ys contenttyd to geve hym auctoryte to komyn with yowr [grace touching] all the artyclys of the seyd matrimony . . . . . . . . ys as he wyl use yowr grace shal have your ples[ure].

[*f. 145 b. *And to yntent that y . . . . . . . . . . . . . d thys auctoryte [for] yowr ambasadors thus to be present at [the said] dyet the emperor [hath] wryttyn to hys ambasador ther to move your grace in [that] behalf to assent to hys forseyd desyre and petycion. And the seyd . . . . wold I shuld writ to yowr *grace*[1] with al sped in the same. Wherfor [for] lacke of tyme I beseche yowr grace of pardon yf I wryt nat so p . . . . . in every thyng as I shuld do. Thys day A. sheuyd to me that . . . . . ambasadors aftyr dynner shuld be [with] the emperor agayn, and that they shuld be present with hym also [at] evyn songe. How he intreattyth them then I shal asserteyn yowr grace [in] my next letters.

[A]s for the komyng of the ambasadors towards your grace A. seyth [tha]t incontynently they shal kom without ferther delay, and that thy . . . . . . . . . . . d hath nat ben by the emperor but by the lord Bergensis . . . . . . . of pompe and serymonys, desyrous to have gret . . . . . . . . . . . . . . . . have the ratyficacion with other wryttyng in hys handes . . . . . . . . . . [t]he emperor ys very yl contentyd with hym, w . . . . . . . . . . . . have in commyssyon. Or yf the emperor . . . . . . . . . . . . . . d yowr orators wyl change or alter any thy[ng] . . . . . . . . . ch was to fore commyttyd to them, the seyd A. . . . . . . . . . . . . yowr grace by me ther.

---

[1] Scored out.

. . . . . . . . last nygt the emperor send by . . . . . . . to kom to Mecklyne, ther to here and speke [with him]. And thus Jesu preserve your grace. From Andw[erp], the fyrst day of [November by the han]des of your humble servant.

## VII.—Henry VII. to Wolsey.

[MS. Galba B. II. F. 146.]

H. R. By the king

Trusty and well-beloved, we grete you well, and have receyved [your] lettre dated at Mechlyne the xxij daye of Octobre, by the con[tinue] wherof amonges other thinges we perceyve what communycacion [A.] hath had with you for our mariage with the duchesse of Sav[oy,] not doubting but every thing shuld comme to passe as we [would] reasonably desire; and shewing furthermor that in ca[se we] wold sumwhat folowe his mynde and counsaill he [would shew] unto us mervelous conclusions touching the rule and [governance] of those Lowe parties.

As unto that matier, forasmoche as those wordes [be of great] substaunce waight and importaunce and tha[t knowledge] of his further entent therin is necessary . . . . [we] wol that ye eftsones entre communicacion . . . . . . And to thentent the said A. shuld clere[ly show and] declare his full entent and mynde unto y[ou therein] we have now directed to hym our lettres [desiring him to] yeve unto you ferme credence.

And therfor in thentring of this matier ye may [say that ye by] youre writing have made reapport unto us . . . . . . . . . concernyng the rule and gouvernance of th[ose countries], and that we bee not oonly greately desirous to [understand] his mynde and opinion therin, but also sha[ll conform] ourself to his advise and counsaill in th[e same. Ye may] further saye that a better acte or dede c[ould not be for] the honor, weale and suertie of the yong [prince of Castile, his] cuntreys and the conservacion of his. . . . . elles where, then to bring the governa[unce into our] handes during the minorite of the said y[oung prince. And the] mariage oones concluded betwixt us [and the said duchess] of Savoye, and the rule and governaunce being committed to us and the said duchesse, we cowde bee contented to make our abode in the said cuntreys by a good space and season every yere for the quiete and restfull ordre and governaunce of the same. And welle assured maye they bee that, the said rule resting in oure auctoritie, and we being in thoes parties, there is noon outward prince that wold attempt or doo any thing to their inquietacion or trowble, and suche as nowe attempteth against the yonge princes inheritaunce elleswhere wold soone forbere soo to doo, or elles by meanes and powair of themperor of us and of those cuntreys, they shuld bee [e]n-forced to desist, whether they wold or not. Soo that by [m]eanes therof aswell this and manye other notable effectes and [com]modities shuld and mought ensue to the suertie and weale of [the] said yonge prince, his reames, cuntreys and subgiettes. [And] if they wold not bee contented to committe the said auctorite [to us a]nd hir joynctely, we cowde not oonly bee contented [rather] than to fayle, that she shuld have the rule therof [her] self and aloon, but also that she shuld reasort [unto those co]untreys for the better ordre and governaunce of theym [as shall be con]venient and at her pleasure. Howe bee it more . . . . . . it were that the said auctorities were committed to us [and her j]oynctely; and therfor ye shall on our behalf make . . . . unto the said A. for the knowleage of his furth[er mind, ad]vise and counsaille in that matier, and to put th[e same in] writing, extending it at good length, to thente[nt we may] clerely and openly bee instructed upon the same. [And the same] knowen we shall declare unto hym our advi[se and give] unto hym suche aunswer as he shalbe right w[ell content]. For in caas the said A. by his wisedome . . . . . . . . in and wol reduce and bring the auctorite rul[e and governaunc]e of the said contrayes to us, and the said [duchess of] Savoye, or to the said duchesse oonly if it ma[y not otherwis]e be gotyn, than she being maried to us . . . . maye bee well assured that it is and shalbe our hole mynde and will that the said A. shall nat oonly have under us and her the hool rule and governaunce of the said cuntreys and noon other, but also we shall in suche thankful maner remembre his kindenesse, and geve unto hym a farre better remembraunce than we willed you to offre unto hym by our last instruccions, as he shalhave good cause to bee contented. And over [this,] seing the great honor, prouffit and promocion that he shall mowe have therby, we thinke that of his g[reat] wisedome he shuld bee gladde to bring the said a[uctorite] into our and the said duchesse hands, and und[er us] to take the same uppon hym.

And ye ma[y further] saye that these matiers brought into good e[ffect and] parfaite conclusion he shall assuredly trust [that we shall] always entende the furtheraunce of his . . . . suche thinges as for the tyme shall for[tune to be] voide in those parties, preferring hym . . . . . Willing you substancially to note and . . . [his] aunswer therin, to thentent ye maye . . . . . . . ascertaigne us therof. And in ca[se it shall] fortune you before the receipt of these o[ur letters to be] in your reatorne towardes us aud thou . . . . . in your journey towardes us as farre a[s] . . . . nevertheles we wol ye reatorne and r . . . . . . said A. for the declaracion of the [premises and for] knowleage of his perfitte mynde upon [the same; which] had, we can bee contented ye reatorne. [And for] youre costs and charges to be susteigned [in this behalf] we shall soo see unto you therin at yo[ur return that] ye shall have cause to be contented.

Over this, albe it that ye by your sundery lettres and instruccions hertofore sent unto us have declared and shewid on the behalf of A. that the lorde Barges shuld bee auctorised to treat and commune with us of and upon oure mariage with the duchesse of Savoye, exhorting and counsailling us therefor to take a speciall regarde unto the said lord Barges, who shuld fele our mynde upon suche difficulties as bee made there in the treate of our said mariage, and therupon make relacion unto themperor; yit nevertheles we have been nowe of late credibly enformed that the said lord Barges as yit hath not, nor as it is supposed shalhave, any maner of commission or auctorite geven to hym to treate with us of any thing concernyng [ou]re said mariage, wherof we greately mervaile [con]sidering the sundry writinges diverse tymes [heret]ofore by you sent unto us, wherin ye declared [exp]ressely that auctorite shuldbe yeven to the s[aid lord] Barges at his commyng unto us in that beh[alf. Exp]edient therfor it is that ye shewe the premisse[s unto t]he said A. desiring hym not oonly to shewe [unto] you the verraye certainte where any suche [comm]ission be geven to the said lord Barges for o[ur said] mariage, or in caas he have noon suche aucto[rite, what] is the occacion and cause therof, but also . . . . . the said A. to endevor hymself that comm[ission may] bee yeven to the said lord Bergos or [to some other] as it shall please themperor for the decla[ration of his] mynde therin. For remembring the l[ove and kindness] that have been used in the tracting of [our said m]ariage hitherto, if they have noo commiss[ion at] this tyme it is noo signe of any towardnes that they have to the spedy accomplisshement therof. For we entend nat to bee delayed or abused in this matier any further, but loke to have a fynall aunswere at thi[s] tyme without any further delayes.

Fynally. for your good devoir in ascertaignyng us aswe of the premisses as also of the ordre d maner of that . . court, of the causes of the retardacion of their ambassad[e,] and of such communyeacion as the legate there h[ad] with you, we can you right good thanke. Yeve[n under] our signet at our manoir of Grenewiche the v[ . day] of Novembre.

H.R.

*Addressed:* To our trusty and welbeloved clerc and chapelain Maister Thomas Wolcey.

---

LONDON:
Printed by GEORGE E. EYRE and WILLIAM SPOTTISWOODE,
Printers to the Queen's most Excellent Majesty.
For Her Majesty's Stationery Office.

# LIST OF WORKS

PUBLISHED

**By the late Record and State Paper Commissioners, or under the Direction of the Right Hon. the Master of the Rolls, which may be had of Messrs. Longman and Co.**

## PUBLIC RECORDS AND STATE PAPERS.

ROTULORUM ORIGINALIUM IN CURIA SCACCARII ABBREVIATIO. Henry III.—Edward III. *Edited by* HENRY PLAYFORD, Esq. 2 vols. folio (1805—1810). *Price*, boards, 12*s.* 6*d.* each, or 25*s.*

CALENDARIUM INQUISITIONUM POST MORTEM SIVE ESCAETARUM. Henry III.—Richard III. *Edited by* JOHN CALEY AND J. BAYLEY, Esqrs. 4 vols. folio (1806—1808; 1821—1828), boards: vols. 2 and 3, separately, *price*, boards, each 21*s.*; vol. 4, boards, 24*s.*

LIBRORUM MANUSCRIPTORUM BIBLIOTHECÆ HARLEIANÆ CATALOGUS. Vol. 4. *Edited by* The Rev. T. H. HORNE, (1812) folio, boards. *Price* 18*s.*

ABBREVIATIO PLACITORUM, Richard I.—Edward II. *Edited by* The Right Hon. GEORGE ROSE, AND W. ILLINGWORTH, Esq. 1 vol. folio (1811), boards. *Price* 18*s.*

LIBRI CENSUALIS vocati DOMESDAY-BOOK, INDICES. *Edited by* Sir HENRY ELLIS. Small folio (1816), boards (Domesday-Book, vol. 3). *Price* 21*s.*

LIBRI CENSUALIS vocati DOMESDAY, ADDITAMENTA EX CODIC. ANTIQUISS. *Edited by* Sir HENRY ELLIS. Small folio (1816), boards (Domesday-Book, vol. 4). *Price* 21*s.*

Statutes of the Realm, in very large folio. Vols. 1 to 11 (except vols. 5 and 6), including 2 vols. of Indices (1810—1828). *Edited by* Sir T. E. Tomlins, John Raithby, John Caley, and Wm. Elliott, Esqrs. *Price* 31*s.* 6*d.* each.

*** The Alphabetical and Chronological Indices may be had separately, *price* 30*s.* each.

Valor Ecclesiasticus, temp. Henry VIII., Auctoritate Regia institutus. *Edited by* John Caley, Esq., and the Rev. Joseph Hunter. Vols. 4 to 6, folio (1810, &c.), boards. *Price* 25*s.* each.

*** The Introduction is also published in 8vo., cloth. *Price* 2*s.* 6*d.*

Rotuli Scotiæ in Turri Londinensi et in Domo Capitulari Westmonasteriensi asservati. 19 Edward I.—Henry VIII. *Edited by* David Macpherson, John Caley, and W. Illingworth, Esqrs., and the Rev. T. H. Horne. 2 vols. folio (1814—1819), boards. *Price* 42*s.*

"Fœdera, Conventiones, Litteræ," &c.; or, Rymer's Fœdera, A.D. 1066—1391. New Edition, Vol. 2, Part 2, and Vol. 3, Parts 1 and 2, folio (1821—1830). *Edited by* John Caley and Fred. Holbrooke, Esqrs. *Price* 21*s.* each Part.

Ducatus Lancastriæ Calendarium Inquisitionum post Mortem, &c. Part 3, Ducatus Lancastriæ. Calendar to the Pleadings, &c. Henry VII.—Ph. and M.; and Calendar to Pleadings, 1—13 Elizabeth. Part 4, Calendar to Pleadings to end of Elizabeth. *Edited by* R. J. Harper, John Caley, and Wm. Minchin, Esqrs. Part 3 (or Vol. 2) (1827—1834), *price* 31*s.* 6*d.*; and Part 4 (or Vol. 3), boards, folio, *price* 21*s.*

Calendars of the Proceedings in Chancery in the Reign of Queen Elizabeth, to which are prefixed examples of earlier proceedings in that Court from Richard II. to Elizabeth, from the originals in the Tower. *Edited by* John Bayley, Esq. Vols. 2 and 3 (1830—1832), boards, each, folio, *price* 21*s.*

Parliamentary Writs and Writs of Military Summons, together with the Records and Muniments relating to the Suit and Service due and performed to the King's High Court of Parliament and the Councils of the Realm. Edward I., II. *Edited by* Sir Francis Palgrave. (1830—1834). Vol. 2, Division 1, Edward II., 21*s.*; Vol. 2, Division 2, 21*s.*; Vol. 2, Division 3, folio, boards, *price* 42*s.*

Rotuli Litterarum Clausarum in Turri Londinensi asservati. 2 vols. folio (1833—1844). The first volume commences A.D. 1204 to 1224. The second volume 1224—1227. *Edited by* Thomas Duffus Hardy, Esq. Together, *price* 81*s.* cloth; or the volumes may be had separately. Vol. 1, *price* 63*s.* cloth; Vol. 2, cloth, *price* 18*s.*

THE GREAT ROLLS OF THE PIPE FOR THE SECOND, THIRD, AND FOURTH YEARS OF THE REIGN OF KING HENRY THE SECOND, 1155—1158. *Edited by* the Rev. JOSEPH HUNTER. 1 vol. royal 8vo. (1844), cloth. *Price* 4*s*. 6*d*.

THE GREAT ROLL OF THE PIPE FOR THE FIRST YEAR OF THE REIGN OF KING RICHARD THE FIRST, 1189—1190. *Edited by* the Rev. JOSEPH HUNTER. 1 vol. royal 8vo. (1844), cloth. *Price* 6*s*.

PROCEEDINGS AND ORDINANCES OF THE PRIVY COUNCIL OF ENGLAND, commencing 10 Richard II.—33 Henry VIII. *Edited by* Sir N. HARRIS NICOLAS. 7 vols. royal 8vo. (1834—1837), cloth 98*s*.; or any of the volumes may be had separately, cloth. *Price* 14*s*. each.

ROTULI LITTERARUM PATENTIUM IN TURRI LONDINENSI ASSERVATI, A.D. 1201 to 1216. *Edited by* THOMAS DUFFUS HARDY, Esq. 1 vol. folio (1835), cloth. *Price* 31*s*. 6*d*.

*** The Introduction is also published in 8vo., cloth. *Price* 9*s*.

ROTULI CURIÆ REGIS. Rolls and Records of the Court held before the King's Justiciars or Justices. 6 Richard I.—1 John. *Edited by* Sir FRANCIS PALGRAVE. 2 vols. royal 8vo. (1835), cloth. *Price* 28*s*.

ROTULI NORMANNIÆ IN TURRI LONDINENSI ASSERVATI, A.D. 1200—1205. Also from 1417 to 1418. *Edited by* THOMAS DUFFUS HARDY, Esq. 1 vol. royal 8vo. (1835), cloth. *Price* 12*s*. 6*d*.

ROTULI DE OBLATIS ET FINIBUS IN TURRI LONDINENSI ASSERVATI, tempore Regis Johannis. *Edited by* THOMAS DUFFUS HARDY, Esq. 1 vol. royal 8vo. (1835), cloth. *Price* 18*s*.

EXCERPTA E ROTULIS FINIUM IN TURRI LONDINENSI ASSERVATIS. Henry III., 1216—1272. *Edited by* CHARLES ROBERTS, Esq. 2 vols. royal 8vo. (1835, 1836), cloth, *price* 32*s*.; or the volumes may be had separately, Vol. 1, *price* 14*s*.; Vol. 2, cloth, *price* 18*s*.

FINES SIVE PEDES FINIUM SIVE FINALES CONCORDIÆ IN CURIA DOMINI REGIS. 7 Richard I.—16 John (1195—1214). *Edited by* the Rev. JOSEPH HUNTER. In Counties. 2 vols. royal 8vo. (1835—1844), together, cloth, *price* 11*s*.; or the volumes may be had separately, Vol. 1, *price* 8*s*. 6*d*.; Vol. 2, cloth, *price* 2*s*. 6*d*.

ANCIENT KALENDARS AND INVENTORIES (THE) OF THE TREASURY OF HIS MAJESTY'S EXCHEQUER; together with Documents illustrating the History of that Repository. *Edited by* Sir FRANCIS PALGRAVE. 3 vols. royal 8vo. (1836), cloth. *Price* 42*s*.

DOCUMENTS AND RECORDS illustrating the History of Scotland, and the Transactions between the Crowns of Scotland and England; preserved in the Treasury of Her Majesty's Exchequer. *Edited by* Sir FRANCIS PALGRAVE. 1 vol. royal 8vo. (1837), cloth, *Price* 18*s*.

ROTULI CHARTARUM IN TURRI LONDINENSI ASSERVATI, A.D. 1199—1216. *Edited by* THOMAS DUFFUS HARDY, Esq. 1 vol. folio (1837), cloth. *Price* 30*s*.

REGISTRUM vulgariter nuncupatum "The Record of Caernarvon," e codice MS. Harleiano, 696, descriptum. *Edited by* Sir HENRY ELLIS. 1 vol. folio (1838), cloth. *Price* 31*s*. 6*d*.

ANCIENT LAWS AND INSTITUTES OF ENGLAND; comprising Laws enacted under the Anglo-Saxon Kings, from Æthelbirht to Cnut, with an English Translation of the Saxon; the Laws called Edward the Confessor's; the Laws of William the Conqueror, and those ascribed to Henry the First; also, Monumenta Ecclesiastica Anglicana, from the 7th to the 10th century; and the Ancient Latin Version of the Anglo-Saxon Laws; with a compendious Glossary, &c. *Edited by* BENJAMIN THORPE, Esq. 1 vol. folio (1840), cloth. *Price* 40*s*.

—— 2 vols. royal 8vo. cloth. *Price* 30*s*.

ANCIENT LAWS AND INSTITUTES OF WALES; comprising Laws supposed to be enacted by Howel the Good; modified by subsequent Regulations under the Native Princes, prior to the Conquest by Edward the First; and anomalous Laws, consisting principally of Institutions which, by the Statute of Ruddlan, were admitted to continue in force. With an English Translation of the Welsh Text. To which are added a few Latin Transcripts, containing Digests of the Welsh Laws, principally of the Dimetian Code. With Indices and Glossary. *Edited by* ANEURIN OWEN, Esq. 1 vol. folio (1841), cloth. *Price* 44*s*.

—— 2 vols. royal 8vo. cloth. *Price* 36*s*.

ROTULI DE LIBERATE AC DE MISIS ET PRÆSTITIS, Regnante Johanne. *Edited by* THOMAS DUFFUS HARDY, Esq. 1 vol. royal 8vo. (1844), cloth. *Price* 6*s*.

DOCUMENTS ILLUSTRATIVE OF ENGLISH HISTORY in the 13th and 14th centuries, selected from the Records in the Exchequer. *Edited by* HENRY COLE, Esq. 1 vol. fcp. folio (1844), cloth. *Price* 45*s*. 6*d*.

MODUS TENENDI PARLIAMENTUM. An Ancient Treatise on the Mode of holding the Parliament in England. *Edited by* THOMAS DUFFUS HARDY, Esq. 1 vol. 8vo. (1846), cloth. *Price* 2*s*. 6*d*.

REPORTS OF THE PROCEEDINGS OF THE RECORD COMMISSIONERS, 1800 to 1819, 2 vols., folio, boards. *Price* 5*l*. 5*s*. From 1819 to 1831 their proceedings have not been printed. A third volume of Reports of their Proceedings, 1831 to 1837, folio, boards, 8*s*. 3 vols. together, boards. *Price* 5*l*. 13*s*.

THE ACTS OF THE PARLIAMENTS OF SCOTLAND. 11 vols. folio (1814–1844). Vol. I. *Edited by* THOMAS THOMSON and COSMO INNES, Esqrs. *Price* 42*s*.

*** Also, Vols. 4, 7, 8, 9, 10, 11, 10*s*. 6*d*. each Vol.

THE ACTS OF THE LORDS OF COUNCIL IN CIVIL CAUSES. A.D. 1478—1495. *Edited by* THOMAS THOMSON, Esq. Folio (1839). *Price* 10*s*. 6*d*.

THE ACTS OF THE LORDS AUDITORS OF CAUSES AND COMPLAINTS. A.D. 1466—1494. *Edited by* THOMAS THOMSON, Esq. Folio (1839). *Price* 10*s*. 6*d*.

REGISTRUM MAGNI SIGILLI REGUM SCOTORUM in Archivis Publicis asservatum. A.D. 1306—1424. *Edited by* THOMAS THOMSON, Esq. Folio (1814). *Price* 15*s*.

ISSUE ROLL OF THOMAS DE BRANTINGHAM, Bishop of Exeter, Lord High Treasurer of England, containing Payments out of His Majesty's Revenue, 44 Edward III., 1370. *Edited by* FREDERICK DEVON, Esq. 1 vol. 4to. (1835), cloth. *Price* 35*s*.

—— Royal 8vo. cloth. *Price* 25*s*.

ISSUES OF THE EXCHEQUER, containing similar matter to the above, temp. Jac. I., extracted from the Pell Records. *Edited by* FREDERICK DEVON, Esq. 1 vol. 4to. (1836), cloth. *Price* 30*s*.

—— Royal 8vo. cloth. *Price* 21*s*.

ISSUES OF THE EXCHEQUER, containing like matter to the above, extracted from the Pell Records; Henry III. to Henry VI. inclusive. *Edited by* FREDERICK DEVON, Esq. 1 vol. 4to. (1837), cloth. *Price* 40*s*.

—— Royal 8vo. cloth. *Price* 30*s*.

LIBER MUNERUM PUBLICORUM HIBERNIÆ, ab an. 1152 usque ad 1827; or, The Establishments of Ireland from the 19th of King Stephen to the 7th of George IV., during a period of 675 years; being the Report of Rowley Lascelles, of the Middle Temple, Barrister-at-Law. Extracted from the Records and other authorities, by Special Command, pursuant to an Address, an. 1810, of the Commons of the United Kingdom. With Introductory Observations by F. S. THOMAS, Esq. (1852.) 2 vols. folio. *Price* 42*s*.

NOTES OF MATERIALS FOR THE HISTORY OF PUBLIC DEPARTMENTS. By F. S. THOMAS, Esq. Demy folio (1846). *Price* 10*s*.

HANDBOOK TO THE PUBLIC RECORDS. By F. S. THOMAS, Esq. Royal 8vo. (1853.) *Price* 12*s*.

STATE PAPERS DURING THE REIGN OF HENRY THE EIGHTH. 11 vols. 4to. (1830—1852) completing the work in its present form, with Indices of Persons and Places to the whole. *Price 5l. 15s. 6d.*

Vol. I. contains Domestic Correspondence.
Vols. II. & III.—Correspondence relating to Ireland.
Vols. IV. & V.—Correspondence relating to Scotland.
Vols. VI. to XI.—Correspondence between England and Foreign Courts.

*** Any Volume may be purchased separately, *price 10s. 6d.*

MONUMENTA HISTORICA BRITANNICA, or, Materials for the History of Britain from the earliest period. Vol. 1, extending to the Norman Conquest. Prepared, and illustrated with Notes, by the late HENRY PETRIE, Esq., F.S.A., Keeper of the Records in the Tower of London, assisted by the Rev. JOHN SHARPE, Rector of Castle Eaton, Wilts. Finally completed for publication, and with an Introduction, by THOMAS DUFFUS HARDY, Esq., Assistant Keeper of Records. (Printed by command of Her Majesty.) Folio (1848). *Price 42s.*

HISTORICAL NOTES RELATIVE TO THE HISTORY OF ENGLAND; embracing the Period from the Accession of King Henry VIII. to the Death of Queen Anne inclusive (1509 to 1714). Designed as a Book of instant Reference for the purpose of ascertaining the Dates of Events mentioned in History and in Manuscripts. The Name of every Person and Event mentioned in History within the above period is placed in Alphabetical and Chronological Order, and the Authority from whence taken is given in each case, whether from Printed History or from Manuscripts. By F. S. THOMAS, Esq., Secretary of the Public Record Office. 3 vols. 8vo. (1856.) *Price 40s.*

# CALENDARS OF STATE PAPERS.

[IMPERIAL 8vo. *Price* 15*s*. each Volume.]

CALENDAR OF STATE PAPERS, DOMESTIC SERIES, OF THE REIGNS OF EDWARD VI., MARY, ELIZABETH, 1547-1580, preserved in the State Paper Department of Her Majesty's Public Record Office. *Edited by* ROBERT LEMON, Esq., F.S.A. 1856.

CALENDAR OF STATE PAPERS, DOMESTIC SERIES, OF THE REIGN OF JAMES I., preserved in the State Paper Department of Her Majesty's Public Record Office. *Edited by* MARY ANNE EVERETT GREEN. 1857–1859.

Vol. I.—1603–1610.
Vol. II.—1611–1618.
Vol. III.—1619–1623.
Vol. IV.—1623–1625, with Addenda.

CALENDAR OF STATE PAPERS, DOMESTIC SERIES, OF THE REIGN OF CHARLES I., preserved in the State Paper Department of Her Majesty's Public Record Office. *Edited by* JOHN BRUCE, Esq., V.P.S.A. 1858–1859.

Vol. I.—1625–1626.
Vol. II.—1627–1628.
Vol. III.—1628–1629.
Vol. IV.—1629–1631.

CALENDAR OF STATE PAPERS, DOMESTIC SERIES, OF THE REIGN OF CHARLES II., preserved in the State Paper Department of Her Majesty's Public Record Office. *Edited by* MARY ANNE EVERETT GREEN. 1860-1861.

Vol. I.—1660–1661.
Vol. II.—1661–1662.

CALENDAR OF STATE PAPERS relating to SCOTLAND, preserved in the State Paper Department of Her Majesty's Public Record Office. *Edited by* MARKHAM JOHN THORPE, Esq., of St. Edmund Hall, Oxford. 1858.

Vol. I., the Scottish Series, of the Reigns of Henry VIII., Edward VI., Mary, Elizabeth, 1509–1589.

Vol. II., the Scottish Series, of the Reign of Queen Elizabeth, 1589–1603; an Appendix to the Scottish Series, 1543–1592; and the State Papers relating to Mary Queen of Scots during her Detention in England, 1568–1587.

CALENDAR OF STATE PAPERS relating to IRELAND, 1509–1573, preserved in the State Paper Department of Her Majesty's Public Record Office. *Edited by* H. C. HAMILTON, Esq. 1860. Vol. I.

CALENDAR OF STATE PAPERS, COLONIAL SERIES, preserved in the State Paper Department of Her Majesty's Public Record Office. *Edited by* W. NOËL SAINSBURY, Esq. 1860.
Vol. I.—1574–1660.

CALENDAR OF STATE PAPERS, FOREIGN SERIES, OF THE REIGN OF EDWARD VI. *Edited by* W. B. TURNBULL, Esq., of Lincoln's Inn, Barrister-at-Law, and Correspondant du Comité Impérial des Travaux Historiques et des Sociétés Savants de France. 1861.

CALENDAR OF STATE PAPERS, FOREIGN SERIES, OF THE REIGN OF MARY. *Edited by* W. B. TURNBULL, Esq., of Lincoln's Inn, Barrister-at-Law, and Correspondant du Comité Impérial des Travaux Historiques et des Sociétés Savants de France. 1861.

## *In the Press.*

CALENDAR OF STATE PAPERS RELATING TO IRELAND, preserved in the State Paper Department of Her Majesty's Public Record Office. *Edited by* H. C. HAMILTON, Esq. Vol. II.

CALENDAR OF STATE PAPERS OF THE REIGN OF HENRY VIII. *Edited by* the Rev. J. S. BREWER, M.A., Professor of English Literature, King's College, London, and Reader at the Rolls.

CALENDAR OF STATE PAPERS, COLONIAL SERIES, preserved in the State Paper Department of Her Majesty's Public Record Office. *Edited by* W. NOËL SAINSBURY, Esq. Vol. II.

CALENDAR OF STATE PAPERS, DOMESTIC SERIES, OF THE REIGN OF CHARLES I., preserved in the State Paper Department of Her Majesty's Public Record Office. *Edited by* JOHN BRUCE, Esq., V.P.S.A. Vol. V.

CALENDAR OF STATE PAPERS, DOMESTIC SERIES, OF THE REIGN OF CHARLES II., preserved in the State Paper Department of Her Majesty's Public Record Office. *Edited by* MARY ANNE EVERETT GREEN. Vol. III.

CALENDAR OF STATE PAPERS, DOMESTIC SERIES, OF THE REIGN OF ELIZABETH, preserved in the State Paper Department of Her Majesty's Public Record Office. *Edited by* ROBERT LEMON, Esq., F.S.A.

## THE CHRONICLES AND MEMORIALS OF GREAT BRITAIN AND IRELAND DURING THE MIDDLE AGES.

[ROYAL 8vo. *Price* 8s. 6d. each Volume.]

1. THE CHRONICLE OF ENGLAND, by JOHN CAPGRAVE. *Edited by* the Rev. F. C. HINGESTON, M.A., of Exeter College, Oxford.
2. CHRONICON MONASTERII DE ABINGDON. Vols. I. and II. *Edited by* the Rev. J. STEVENSON, M.A., of University College, Durham, and Vicar of Leighton Buzzard.
3. LIVES OF EDWARD THE CONFESSOR. I.—La Estoire de Seint Aedward le Rei. II.—Vita Beati Edvardi Regis et Confessoris. III.—Vita Æduuardi Regis qui apud Westmonasterium requiescit. *Edited by* H. R. LUARD, M.A., Fellow and Assistant Tutor of Trinity College, Cambridge.
4. MONUMENTA FRANCISCANA; scilicet, I.—Thomas de Eccleston de Adventu Fratrum Minorum in Angliam. II.—Adæ de Marisco Epistolæ. III.—Registrum Fratrum Minorum Londoniæ. *Edited by* the Rev. J. S. BREWER, M.A., Professor of English Literature, King's College, London, and Reader at the Rolls.
5. FASCICULI ZIZANIORUM MAGISTRI JOHANNIS WYCLIF CUM TRITICO. Ascribed to THOMAS NETTER, of WALDEN, Provincial of the Carmelite Order in England, and Confessor to King Henry the Fifth. *Edited by* the Rev. W. W. SHIRLEY, M.A., Tutor and late Fellow of Wadham College, Oxford.
6. THE BUIK OF THE CRONICLIS OF SCOTLAND; or, A Metrical Version of the History of Hector Boece; by WILLIAM STEWART. Vols. I., II., and III. *Edited by* W. B. TURNBULL, Esq., of Lincoln's Inn, Barrister-at-Law.
7. JOHANNIS CAPGRAVE LIBER DE ILLUSTRIBUS HENRICIS. *Edited by* the Rev. F. C. HINGESTON, M.A., of Exeter College, Oxford.
8. HISTORIA MONASTERII S. AUGUSTINI CANTUARIENSIS, by THOMAS OF ELMHAM, formerly Monk and Treasurer of that Foundation. *Edited by* C. HARDWICK, M.A., Fellow of St. Catharine's Hall, and Christian Advocate in the University of Cambridge.
9. EULOGIUM (HISTORIARUM SIVE TEMPORIS), Chronicon ab Orbe condito usque ad Annum Domini 1366; a Monacho quodam Malmesbiriensi exaratum. Vols. I. and II. *Edited by* F. S. HAYDON, Esq., B.A.

10. MEMORIALS OF KING HENRY THE SEVENTH: Bernardi Andreæ Tholosatis de Vita Regis Henrici Septimi Historia; necnon alia quædam ad eundem Regem spectantia. *Edited by* J. GAIRDNER, Esq.

11. MEMORIALS OF HENRY THE FIFTH. I.—Vita Henrici Quinti, Roberto Redmanno auctore. II.—Versus Rhythmici in laudem Regis Henrici Quinti. III.—Elmhami Liber Metricus de Henrico V. *Edited by* C. A. COLE, Esq.

12. MUNIMENTA GILDHALLÆ LONDONIENSIS; Liber Albus, Liber Custumarum, et Liber Horn, in archivis Gildhallæ asservati. Vol. I., Liber Albus. Vol. II. (in Two Parts), Liber Custumarum. *Edited by* H. T. RILEY, Esq., M.A., Barrister-at-Law.

13. CHRONICA JOHANNIS DE OXENEDES. *Edited by* Sir H. ELLIS, K.H.

14. A COLLECTION OF POLITICAL POEMS FROM THE ACCESSION OF EDWARD III. TO THE REIGN OF HENRY VIII. Vols. I. and II. *Edited by* T. WRIGHT, Esq., M.A.

15. The "OPUS TERTIUM" and "OPUS MINUS" of ROGER BACON. *Edited by* the Rev. J. S. BREWER, M.A., Professor of English Literature, King's College, London, and Reader at the Rolls.

16. BARTHOLOMÆI DE COTTON, MONACHI NORWICENSIS, HISTORIA ANGLICANA (A.D. 449—1298). *Edited by* H. R. LUARD, M.A., Fellow and Assistant Tutor of Trinity College, Cambridge.

17. The BRUT Y TYWYSOGION, or, The Chronicle of the Princes of Wales. *Edited by* the Rev. J. WILLIAMS AB ITHEL.

18. A COLLECTION OF ROYAL AND HISTORICAL LETTERS DURING THE REIGN OF HENRY IV. Vol. I. *Edited by* the Rev. F. C. HINGESTON, M.A., of Exeter College, Oxford.

19. THE REPRESSOR OF OVER MUCH BLAMING OF THE CLERGY. By REGINALD PECOCK, sometime Bishop of Chichester. Vols. I. and II. *Edited by* C. BABINGTON, B.D., Fellow of St. John's College, Cambridge.

20. THE ANNALES CAMBRIÆ. *Edited by* the Rev. J. WILLIAMS AB ITHEL.

21. THE WORKS OF GIRALDUS CAMBRENSIS. Vol. I. *Edited by* the Rev. J. S. BREWER, M.A., Professor of English Literature, King's College, London, and Reader at the Rolls.

22. LETTERS AND PAPERS ILLUSTRATIVE OF THE WARS OF THE ENGLISH IN FRANCE DURING THE REIGN OF HENRY THE SIXTH, KING OF ENGLAND. Vol. I. *Edited by* the Rev. J. STEVENSON, M.A., of University College, Durham, and Vicar of Leighton Buzzard.

www.ingramcontent.com/pod-product-compliance
Ingram Content Group UK Ltd.
Pitfield, Milton Keynes, MK11 3LW, UK
UKHW020653230426
12043UKWH00018B/128

9 781022 812994